KNOWLEDGE MANAGEMENT

Sara Miller McCune founded SAGE Publishing in 1965 to support the dissemination of usable knowledge and educate a global community. SAGE publishes more than 1000 journals and over 800 new books each year, spanning a wide range of subject areas. Our growing selection of library products includes archives, data, case studies and video. SAGE remains majority owned by our founder and after her lifetime will become owned by a charitable trust that secures the company's continued independence.

Los Angeles | London | New Delhi | Singapore | Washington DC | Melbourne

Peter Massingham

KNOWLEDGE MANAGEMENT
Theory in Practice

Los Angeles | London | New Delhi
Singapore | Washington DC | Melbourne

Los Angeles | London | New Delhi
Singapore | Washington DC | Melbourne

SAGE Publications Ltd
1 Oliver's Yard
55 City Road
London EC1Y 1SP

SAGE Publications Inc.
2455 Teller Road
Thousand Oaks, California 91320

SAGE Publications India Pvt Ltd
B 1/I 1 Mohan Cooperative Industrial Area
Mathura Road
New Delhi 110 044

SAGE Publications Asia-Pacific Pte Ltd
3 Church Street
#10-04 Samsung Hub
Singapore 049483

Editor: Kirsty Smy
Assistant editor: Martha Cunneen
Production editor: Sarah Cooke
Marketing manager: Lucia Sweet
Cover design: Francis Kenney
Typeset by: C&M Digitals (P) Ltd, Chennai, India
Printed in the UK

Library of Congress Control Number: 2018938206

British Library Cataloguing in Publication data

A catalogue record for this book is available from
the British Library

ISBN 978-1-4739-4819-8
ISBN 978-1-4739-4820-4 (pbk)

At SAGE we take sustainability seriously. Most of our products are printed in the UK using responsibly sourced papers and
boards. When we print overseas we ensure sustainable papers are used as measured by the PREPS grading system. We
undertake an annual audit to monitor our sustainability.

In memory of my father, Rex Robert Massingham, and my mother,
Marlene Elisabeth Massingham-Cooper.
Thank you.

This book is dedicated to my wife Rada and my daughter Jana.

You are my justified true belief.

You give me purpose, identity, and reality.

There would be no meaning to anything without you.

PRAISE FOR *KNOWLEDGE MANAGEMENT*

'Peter has written a contemporary book on knowledge management that can be used by managers and on professional development, undergraduate, and post-graduate courses. The book provides both theory and practical insights, using several important case studies from around the world.'

Professor James Guthrie AM, Macquarie Business School

'It is clear this is an outstanding textbook. A lively and engaging look at this dynamic discipline, it is a comprehensive guide to understanding and managing knowledge – one of the most important assets of an enterprise.'

Peter Fritz AM, Group Managing Director, TCG

'This book represents an insightful synthesis of academic research in the multidisciplinary field of knowledge management. In this exemplar, scholarly knowledge is presented in an easy-to-comprehend, efficient format suitable for academics, students, and professionals.'

Professor Alexander Serenko, Lakehead University, Canada

'Dr. Massingham has provided a thoughtful and thorough treatment of the heterogeneous, complex and cross-disciplinary literature related with the discipline of Knowledge Management. His work provides a clear yet comprehensive account of the key aspects of this emerging field of management science. The book provides a succinct overview of both Knowledge Management theory and practice, and is equally useful for scholars, students, and professionals.'

Aino Kianto, Professor of Knowledge Management, LUT University, Finland

BRIEF CONTENTS

CONTENTS

ACKNOWLEDGEMENTS

I would like to acknowledge the influence of Alan Mackay, Richard Grellman, Richard Lumley, and Colin Greig on my career and my thinking with this work: truly great men. I am also grateful to the Australian Research Council and the Royal Australian Navy (RAN) for supporting me with a research grant which allowed me to test and develop many of the ideas in this book. I appreciate the cooperation of staff from the RAN and Navy Engineering Division, particularly Pablo, Kurt, and John B. Thank you to Kirsty, Ruth, Sarah and Lyndsay from SAGE Publishing for their expert help and guidance.

ABOUT THE AUTHOR

 Dr Peter Massingham is an internationally recognized expert on knowledge management. He has published widely in leading journals and has won a number of awards for his writing. He has been awarded multiple competitive research grants, including from the Australian Research Council. Most recently, Peter has completed major research projects with the Australian Department of Defence (2008–2013), Saudi Arabian research institutes, and sharing retirees' knowledge. He is currently working with a not-for-profit organisation, a major consultancy firm, and the Australian Department of Defence on a range of new projects. His PhD is in management, and he works as an academic in a Faculty of Business. Peter teaches in the areas of strategic management, international business management, change management, and knowledge management. He was the Director of the Centre for Knowledge Management from 2002 to 2014. Peter is a member of the Australian Government Consultative Committee on Knowledge Capital. Before academia in 1998, Peter was a management consultant, most recently with KPMG. Peter lives in Sydney, Australia, with his wife Rada, daughter Jana, and dog Milly.

LIST OF CASE STUDIES

OPENING MINI CASE STUDIES

CLOSING CASE STUDIES

BOOK STRUCTURE

Figure 0.1 shows how the book is set out.

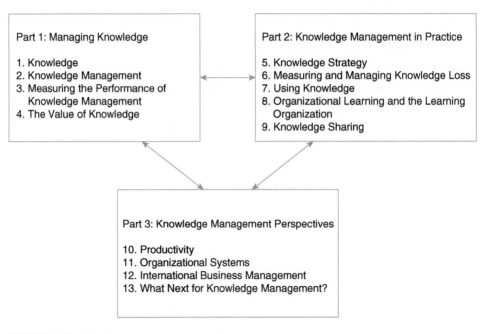

Part 1: Managing Knowledge

1. Knowledge
2. Knowledge Management
3. Measuring the Performance of
   Knowledge Management
4. The Value of Knowledge

Part 2: Knowledge Management in Practice

5. Knowledge Strategy
6. Measuring and Managing Knowledge Loss
7. Using Knowledge
8. Organizational Learning and the Learning
   Organization
9. Knowledge Sharing

Part 3: Knowledge Management Perspectives

10. Productivity
11. Organizational Systems
12. International Business Management
13. What Next for Knowledge Management?

FIGURE 0.1 *Book structure*

Welcome to *Knowledge Management: Theory in Practice*. Knowledge management is increasingly important for many employees, managers, and executives in the private and public sectors across domestic and international business environments. Therefore, an understanding of knowledge management is a central topic for professional development and for undergraduate and postgraduate courses in business to address. The book's focus is on connecting the theoretical basis for knowledge management with workplace realities. So the book combines an explanation of theory with practical insights. It aims to offer both breadth and depth, helping you navigate the landscape of knowledge management and, in doing so, look at the topic from multiple perspectives.

PART 1: MANAGING KNOWLEDGE

Part 1 examines knowledge and its management from multiple perspectives. It looks at knowledge as a resource (Chapter 1); knowledge management as a capability (Chapter 2); and how to measure change, growth, and performance in both resources and capability (Chapters 3 and 4). Part 1 establishes platforms for the study of knowledge management and poses important questions about your view of knowledge and its management, and how this creates value for organizations.

The purpose of *Chapter 1: Knowledge* is to explore what knowledge is. The multi-disciplinary interest in knowledge and its management has caused disagreement about definitions, language, and theoretical concepts. In tackling the issue, this chapter explores definitions from a multi-disciplinary perspective, discusses the epistemology of knowledge, contrasts the product and practice-based views of knowledge, and looks at the ownership of knowledge in terms of individual, group, and organization. The discussion examines what is meant by the phrase 'justified true belief', whether knowledge can be separated from the knower, and knowledge as skilful knowing. These themes will be important in the management of knowledge (see Chapter 2).

Chapter 2: Knowledge Management explains how knowledge management has evolved, why its definitions are fragmented, and its value and purpose. There are numerous perspectives on the practice of knowledge management. These are organized into architectures, systems, tools, and technologies. This provides a typology of layers of knowledge management from the broad to very specific. The chapter concludes with an alternative definition of knowledge management based on temporal dimensions.

Chapter 3: Measuring the Performance of Knowledge Management explains why knowledge and its management have attracted so much interest. Underlying assumptions about knowledge management are examined by criticism that knowledge management has failed to deliver on its hype. A framework for making investment decisions about knowledge management is presented. The chapter concludes with a model for evaluating the value of knowledge management: a focus on practical outcomes.

While there is widespread agreement that knowledge has value, there is also disagreement about what this value is and how to measure it. *Chapter 4: The Value of Knowledge* explores the measurement of the value from a multi-disciplinary perspective, evaluates popular methods, and looks at the future of the measurement, for instance integrated reporting. The discussion explores further whether knowledge can be separated from the knower, and knowledge as skilful knowing. These themes will be important in knowledge strategy (see Chapter 5).

HOW PART 1 IS INTEGRATED WITH PARTS 2 AND 3

Chapter 1 connects with Chapter 7 regarding creating value from knowledge, and with Chapter 9 in terms of what is being shared when we talk about knowledge sharing. Chapters 2, 3, and 4 connect with Chapter 5 in terms of how knowledge management may contribute to competitive advantage; Chapter 10 regarding how knowledge and its management can improve productivity; and with Chapter 11 regarding systems necessary to support knowledge management.

PART 2: KNOWLEDGE MANAGEMENT IN PRACTICE

Part 2 looks at the key activities associated with doing knowledge management, including: strategy (Chapter 5), knowledge retention (Chapter 6), usage (Chapter 7), learning (Chapter 8), and sharing (Chapter 9). Part 2 explores best-practice knowledge management from multiple perspectives and, in doing so, covers the main areas of research in the field.

An underlying assumption of this book is that knowledge is the most valuable resource. It follows that the management of this resource may lead to superior organization performance, profitability, and sustainability. *Chapter 5: Knowledge Strategy* examines effective knowledge strategy to achieve these goals. Guiding theories are the resource-based view of the firm and the knowledge-based view of the firm, which explain how knowledge is a source of sustainable competitive advantage. These theories also challenge underlying assumptions about organizations and their management. The main challenges are cooperation and coordination. These require innovative new business models, with fluid organizational boundaries, enabling knowledge to flow from external knowledge sources and for internal development. This chapter focuses on aggressive knowledge strategy. An aggressive strategy is required when the organization lags behind competition or is defending a knowledge position.

Organizational knowledge loss has emerged as one of the most important corporate risks today. The first part of *Chapter 6: Measuring and Managing Knowledge Loss* measures the impact of knowledge loss. The likelihood and consequences of knowledge loss are explored from multiple perspectives. This considers what happens after knowledge loss, at the individual level, i.e. the remaining employees, and at the organizational level in terms of performance. The second part of the chapter discusses how to manage knowledge loss. This is considered from both short-term and long-term perspectives.

Chapter 7: Using Knowledge has three main themes: awareness of the problem of knowledge usage, frameworks for learning from experience, and a method for evaluating the value created from using knowledge. A major focus in the chapter is how to learn from experience. Three tools are discussed: peer assists, after action reviews, and retrospects. These explain that knowledge usage involves learning from experience before, during, and after activities. This temporal perspective ensures that we learn from the past, improve the present, and plan for the future.

Chapter 8: Organizational Learning and the Learning Organization begins by defining organizational learning at the individual, group, and organizational levels. The process of organizational learning is then explored with a focus on the cognitive and behavioural aspects of learning. The way knowledge is combined to achieve skilful knowing is discussed through the theory of absorptive capacity. Action learning is used to differentiate between classroom learning, i.e. staff training, and learning on the job. The main learning frameworks are then introduced as models for managers to consider when choosing to take action about learning gaps. The second part of the chapter explores the learning organization. This describes an organization that learns from experience, responds to change, and grows its knowledge resources. The chapter examines previous research, including criticisms of learning organization and its measurement, and concludes with a new model.

Chapter 9: Knowledge Sharing begins with the three main approaches to knowledge sharing in the literature. The conduit model of knowledge sharing sees knowledge as an object which is passed from the knower (sender) to the learner (receiver). The process model of knowledge sharing describes it as a series of steps which must be moved through to achieve learning. The constructivist model of knowledge sharing focuses on the social interaction of people who find meaning via dialogue. The epistemological and ontological perspectives on knowledge sharing are discussed. The chapter uses systems thinking to explore the multiple social systems which influence knowledge sharing in any organization. The chapter develops a paradigm that views knowledge as a systemic, socially constructed, context-specific representation of reality. Knowledge-sharing barriers and solutions are discussed in terms of the individual, the organization, and the knowledge itself.

HOW PART 2 IS INTEGRATED WITH PARTS 1 AND 3

Chapter 5 connects with Chapter 4 on resource appraisal. Chapter 6 connects with Chapter 3 on the process of managing risk, and with Chapter 4 concerning identifying which knowledge resources to protect. Chapter 7 connects with Chapter 3 on getting value from knowledge management. Chapters 8 and 9 connect with Chapter 1 on the process of becoming a skilful knower.

PART 3: KNOWLEDGE MANAGEMENT PERSPECTIVES

Part 3 challenges the underlying assumptions of knowledge management in terms of whether it can improve productivity (Chapter 10), whether it is a separate or integrated organizational function (Chapter 11), its role in international business (Chapter 12), and whether it has a sustainable future in terms of practice and research (Chapter 13).

Chapter 10: Productivity looks at how knowledge management may improve performance within the context of change management. The main productivity models are examined. Productivity presents challenges for the dichotomy of the technology and personalization views of knowledge management presented in this book. The personalization view approaches productivity in terms of individual employees. This is about improving performance via work quality (better work) and work quantity (doing more). The motivation issues surrounding knowledge sharing (see Chapter 9) are an example of performance improvement at the individual level. The technology view looks at productivity from an organizational perspective. This is about codifying best practice, sharing this with employees, and ensuring compliance. A challenge for knowledge management surrounding this topic is that traditional productivity improvement methods are based on scientific management rather than on humanistic management. The chapter presents an alternative perspective that by focusing the individual employee on making them skilful knowers, within the context of improving the work processes they do, this will help them adopt a systems thinking perspective, and allow knowledge management to be embedded in problem routines.

Chapter 11: Organizational Systems looks at the role of information technology, accounting, human resources, and structure in enabling knowledge management. It adopts a systems thinking perspective. The chapter provides further perspective about the social reconstruction of the reality of knowledge management. Knowledge management faces challenges to demonstrate its value and to justify its return-on-investment. In organizational systems where competition for resources is often fierce, knowledge management needs to work with, rather than against, competing forces. The chapter discusses how this may be done.

Knowledge management is a source of competitive advantage for multinational enterprises (MNEs). *Chapter 12: International Business Management* examines how knowledge management is done by MNEs from three perspectives: (1) how knowledge management influences strategy and structure, with a particular focus on transnational management; (2) how knowledge flows in international business, with a specific focus on the role of expatriates; and (3) whether knowledge management should be standardized or adapted across the MNE's global operations.

The objective of *Chapter 13: What Next for Knowledge Management?* is to reflect on the lessons learned from this book and consider the future of knowledge management. First, the chapter explores the technology-versus-personalization view of management. As global business becomes increasingly digitized, what will this mean for knowledge management? Second, the issue of respect is examined from the perspective of the academic literature and practitioners. If knowledge management is to continue to grow, it must be recognized as a mainstream organizational activity by the top journals and by business leaders. Third, the chapter revisits the knowledge-based view of the firm (KBV) and asks whether it will still be relevant in the future. Finally, the chapter discusses the biggest threat to business globally – the ageing workforce demographic – and how knowledge management may help knowledge organizations survive this threat.

HOW PART 3 IS INTEGRATED WITH PARTS 1 AND 2

Chapter 10 connects with Chapter 2 on the technology view of knowledge management. Chapters 10 and 12 connect with Chapter 3 about creating value from knowledge management. Chapter 11 connects with Chapter 2 on knowledge management and systems thinking; with Chapter 5 regarding strategic alignment of the workforce; and with Chapter 8 on the role of human resource management in organizational learning. Chapter 12 connects with Chapter 5 on the role of knowledge and knowledge management in competitive advantage in international business.

THEORY, PRACTICE, AND YOU

Theory and practice should inform each other. Cousequently, this book aims to be as practical as possible while also establishing a strong theoretical platform to help you make sense of knowledge management. Theory may be used to make useful predictions about the future. The book may, therefore, help you understand that if X happens then Y will result. It has a forward-thinking perspective, for instance Chapter 5 on knowledge strategy. Its practical focus aims to help you make sense of complex organizational situations and how to use knowledge management to solve problems and create value, while theory may also open up new insights. The book aims to help you to 'reconsider' workplace situations and to look at the complexity of knowledge and its management from a new perspective.

HOW TO USE THIS BOOK

- **Introduction**: each chapter opens with an introduction and a list of key topics. This provides a map to navigate through the material and summarize the main topics covered.
- **Management issues**: key challenges for managers related to each chapter are listed. These help you to connect the theory with practice and consider what you need to do.
- **Core concepts**: summarize key theoretical issues for you.
- **Deep thinking**: presents challenging issues for you to consider as deep learning. They are useful for discussion and reflection.
- **Theory in practice**: these are longer examples of how the theory being discussed may be applied or illustrated in practical settings.
- **Integrative case study**: this is a long case study at the end of all but the last chapter, with questions, providing an opportunity to explore issues in greater depth after reflecting on reading the chapter. The integrative nature of the case means that a single case study is used to explore the theory in each chapter. This allows you to build an understanding of the case and how management may be used in a single organizational context.
- **Review and discussion questions**: these enable you to relate your learning to your own experiences and reflections on the chapter, and encourage you to consider further personal development.
- **Further reading**: an annotated list of suggested reading is provided at the end of each chapter to offer you ways to extend your learning.
- **Bibliography**: a chapter-specific list of references is supplied at the end of each chapter.

ONLINE RESOURCES

Visit **https://study.sagepub.com/massingham** for access to a wide range of online resources for students and lecturers.

FOR STUDENTS

- **Further Reading** – book and article recommendations, as well as a selection of free SAGE journal articles, to further develop and support your understanding.
- **Interactive flashcard glossary** – online flashcards to help you get to grips with the key terms introduced in the book. All the terms in the book's glossary can be found here.
- **Scorecards** – performance management tools and techniques to help you evaluate effectiveness and answer the case study questions at the end of each chapter.

FOR INSTRUCTORS

- **PowerPoint slides** – a suite of PowerPoint slides highlighting the main points in each chapter. Customisable to suit your lecture style and learning objectives.
- **Instructor's manual** – a summary of the key points in each chapter along with notes to support your teaching.
- **Case guides** – a guide to the case studies in the book, including assignment questions and teaching outlines and analysis.

PART 1
MANAGING KNOWLEDGE

1

KNOWLEDGE

LEARNING OUTCOMES

After completing this chapter, the reader should be able to:

1. Define knowledge
2. Discuss how philosophy influences the interpretation of knowledge
3. Contrast the views of knowledge as a product and as practice
4. Compare individual, group, and organizational knowledge

MANAGEMENT ISSUES

Knowledge requires managers to:

1. Understand what knowledge is
2. Decide on the firm's epistemology
3. Decide on the firm's approach to ownership of knowledge

Knowledge involves the following challenges for management:

1. Understanding what it is you know
2. Articulating knowledge so that it is tangible for stakeholders
3. Aligning the organization's view of knowledge with its knowledge management

LINKS TO OTHER CHAPTERS

Chapter 2: on the process of knowledge management
Chapter 4: concerning the value of knowledge resources
Chapter 7: regarding creating value from knowledge
Chapter 9: what is being shared when we talk about knowledge sharing?

OPENING MINI CASE STUDY

ROSIE'S FIRST WEEK AT OXFORD CONSULTING: ACCESSING ORGANIZATIONAL KNOWLEDGE

Rosie Cunningham sat on the train thinking about her day ahead. It was her first day at Oxford Consulting. Oxford Consulting was a leading management consulting firm in Melbourne, Australia.

Rosie had recently graduated from the University of Melbourne with a Bachelor of Commerce with first class honours. She was a bright, hardworking student, who topped her class. Getting a start at a prestigious company like Oxford Consulting was a great opportunity. She was excited about her first day and keen to showcase her talent.

As she entered the foyer of Oxford Consulting's head office, Rosie first heard the sound. A string quartet was playing in the corner. She then noticed the people – men and women in suits all walking quietly towards the elevators where they waited patiently in line. There was almost no talk, just an occasional quiet good morning. As she rode the elevator to the 25th floor where she was told she would be working, she looked around at others squeezed into the small space, but no one held her gaze. Most people looked at the elevator door.

As she stepped out of the elevator, she looked around for help. Someone asked her who she was looking for and then pointed her in the right direction. As she walked towards her partner-in-charge's office to report on her first day, she noticed that there were some offices but most staff were sitting in small cubicles in an open-plan setting. Her partner-in-charge was busy, so his secretary took Rosie to her desk. She explained that the desk was shared with another consultant who was working at a client's today. If both were in the office at the same time, one would have to find somewhere else to sit. The secretary gave Rosie her laptop computer and said the partner-in-charge would see her when he was finished with his meeting.

Rosie sat at her desk and looked around. Staff were busy working at their stations. They did not talk. They ignored her. She wondered why no one had bothered to say hello. Surely they could see she was new. She got up from her desk and walked over to the nearest person and introduced herself. The person looked up from his computer surprised that he was being interrupted by this new person. After a few polite sentences about what their practice area was (i.e. their area of expertise), Rosie left and moved on to the next person. She walked from person to person and introduced herself to everyone on the floor. Most people were like the first person: busy and happy to get back to their work. (Over the next 12 months, Rosie saw many new people start on the 25th floor. Not one of them got up from their desk to introduce themselves to the others on their first day.) Rosie returned to her desk and opened up her computer. She found folders on the intranet which explained the company and its products and services. She read these for the rest of the day. The partner-in-charge did not find time to greet her.

The next day, Rosie went straight to her desk and opened up her computer. She looked around and everyone was busy. No one looked at her, no one said hello. She opened up her laptop and found folders on the intranet about how to write proposals, how to manage clients, how to write good reports, and how to deliver excellent presentations. She watched video clips of consultants meeting with clients and giving best practice presentations. She found training videos on sales techniques, project management, and building relationships. She studied templates on proposals, reports, and sales brochures. She talked to no one on her second day.

On her third day, she began working through some of the information she had found on the intranet. The secretary told her the partner-in-charge was ready to see her. He apologized for

(Continued)

(Continued)

being too busy to see her, asked how she was settling in, and explained who she would be reporting to. He told her that she would be attending an induction course this morning and that he would catch up with her next week.

At 10.00am she caught the elevator to the 20th floor where human resources was located. In the elevator, she asked others if they too were going to the induction. Two of the staff in the elevator were and she tried to engage them in conversation. She was excited to meet new people who were like her – new. The new staff were met by a woman from human resources who ushered them into a training room. As the training progressed, Rosie found she was asking most of the questions. Everyone else was fairly quiet. The trainer seemed bored. The new staff induction was mainly about how to use their laptop and how to find information on the intranet.

On her fourth day, Rosie found information listing the company's main clients. She was excited. They were big companies and she was sure she could sell them her services. She had topped her honours class at the University of Melbourne. Surely they could use someone like her. She made a list of clients to target. She used the sales template to develop a brochure. She wrote an introductory letter she could email to her target clients with the brochure as an attachment. She then emailed the director who was her supervisor to arrange a meeting to discuss this. After their meeting, the director organized for her to meet with her partner-in-charge. At that meeting, the partner-in-charge explained that she needed approval before she could contact any clients. This approval could only be given by the partner who was the relationship manager for that client. He had a look at her list of target clients and said he would organize some meetings.

On her fifth day, Rosie attended her first 'sales' meeting where her partner-in-charge introduced her to another partner. The partner she was introduced to was in charge of the banking industry group. She listened politely to Rosie as she explained who she was and what capabilities she could offer the major banks. Rosie felt that it was like another job interview. Her partner-in-charge tried to add his support for Rosie, but the meeting ended disappointingly. The banking partner was non-committal. She said she would think about it and get back to them. But Rosie could sense that the partner was not really interested in her.

In the elevator back up to the 25th floor, her partner-in-charge tried to console her. He told her not to worry about it. He said the partners jealously guarded their clients and were reluctant to take risks with new consultants which might damage their relationship with their clients. He said he would try to organize some meetings with other partners regarding target clients on her list. As Rosie sat on the train on the way home on that Friday afternoon, she wondered what went wrong in her first week. She did not understand anything. She did not know why partners would not trust her to work for them. Surely she was one of them. She was one of their employees. They trusted her enough to employ her but not to let her meet clients. She did not know how she was going succeed at this company. She was not looking forward to her second week.

CASE STUDY QUESTIONS

1. Discuss the type of knowledge Rosie brought to her new job.
2. Discuss the type of knowledge Rosie discovered was owned by Oxford Consulting during her first week.
3. What is Oxford Consulting's justified true belief about knowledge (i.e. knowledge you can trust because you believe the evidence)?
4. What is your advice to Rosie for her second week?

INTRODUCTION

The purpose of this chapter is to explore what knowledge is. The knowledge-based view of the firm argues that knowledge is the most valuable resource (Grant, 1996). The knowledge economy explains how knowledge is the main driver of economic value (Drucker, 1988, 1999). As a result, knowledge and its management have attracted interest from researchers and practitioners across multiple disciplines. This has caused disagreement about definitions, language, and theoretical concepts. While there is widespread agreement that knowledge is important, there is also disagreement about what it is. In tackling the issue, this chapter explores definitions from a multi-disciplinary perspective, discusses the epistemology of knowledge, contrasts the product- and practice-based views of knowledge, and looks at the ownership of knowledge in terms of individual, group, and organization. The discussion examines what is meant by the phrase 'justified true belief', whether knowledge can be separated from the knower, and knowledge as skilful knowing. These themes will be important in the management of knowledge (see Chapter 2).

CORE CONCEPT: Skilful knowing (Tsoukas, 2003) is knowledge which emerges in the act of doing something.

DEFINITIONS OF KNOWLEDGE

Knowledge is an intangible resource and it combines with other firm resources, such as financial and physical, to create capabilities (Grant, 2013). Knowledge resources are often classified as either tacit (implicit) or codified (explicit). Tacit knowledge is the knowledge in an individual's head (Polanyi, 1967). Codified knowledge is knowledge that is transferable in formal, systematic language, such as via 'documentation', reports, and databases (Nonaka and Takeuchi, 1995: 69). Tacit and codified knowledge are two sides of the same coin in the sense that you need one to use the other (Tsoukas, 2003).

There are a range of disciplines interested in knowledge and its management, which provide different perspectives on the definition of knowledge. Table 1.1 provides a summary.

TABLE 1.1   Comparing discipline perspectives on the definition of knowledge

Discipline	Definition	Source
Knowledge management	Practitioners get better at deploying their technical knowledge because they figure out how to participate at work … the artful competence of handling complexity, instability, and value-conflict when engaging people and problematic situations	Schön, 1983: 328
	Know-what (cognitive or technical knowledge), know-how (professional or practical), know-why (cause and effect or problem solving), and care-why (self-motivated creativity or innovation)	Quinn et al., 1998: 183
	The capability to draw distinctions, within a domain of action, based on an appreciation of context or theory or both	Tsoukas and Vladimirou, 2001: 979
	Rather than talking of knowledge … it is more helpful to talk about the process of knowing … knowing is situated, distributed, and material	Blackler, 2002: 56
	… think of data as being located in the world and of knowledge as being located in agents, with information taking on a mediating role between them … knowledge is not a single 'thing' … it is like a set of complex activation patterns that can vary greatly from agent to agent … [it involves abstraction which] either invokes or creates the minimum number of cognitive categories through which an agent makes sense of events [and codification, which] refines the categories the agent invokes or creates so that it can use them efficiently and in discriminating ways	Boisot, 2002: 67–68
	Adding purpose to information transforms it into knowledge	Davidson and Voss, 2002: 53
	… has normative force, i.e. individuals are in various states of having or not having knowledge (possession)	Fuller, 2002: 61–62
	[This paper defines] knowledge as 'justified true belief' … [W]hile [traditional epistemology] emphasizes the absolute, static, and non-human nature of knowledge, [the theory of knowledge creation] sees knowledge as a dynamic human process of justifying personal beliefs as part of an aspiration for the 'truth'	Nonaka, 2002: 438

Discipline	Definition	Source
	… knowledge occurs in explicit form (documents and data), tacit form (human education, experience, and expertise) and also in implicit form (in cultures and communities)	Barth, 2005: 348
	… knowledge is seen to emerge as people interact recurrently in the context of established (and novel) routines and procedures … This implies a social constructivist view of knowledge, whereby all human knowledge is developed, transmitted and maintained in social situations	Newell et al., 2006: 116
	Reflective practice based on a language action perspective where communication modelling can help reflection	Aakhus, 2007: 4–5
	The capacity (potential and actual) to take effective action in varied and uncertain situations	Bennet, 2007: 513
	Knowledge in an organization is a construction of reality by means of managers' perceptions rather than true in any abstract or universal way … it is dynamic, relational, and based on human action: it depends on the situation and people involved rather than on absolute truth or facts	Ichijo, 2007: 85
	Knowledge is not just expressed in documents containing information. It can be embedded in tools and designed artefacts (chairs 'teach' us how to sit, hammers 'teach' us how to hit a nail) … It can also be embedded in designed environments (an auditorium 'teaches' us how to project our voice, a coffee shop 'encourages us' to have conversations). It is found in ways of doing things, processes, unwritten scripts, routines, well-worn paths and habits. Knowledge [is not] an abstract entity inside people heads … it is inextricably mingled with this embodied, social world	Lambe, 2007: 2
	… the tendency is to treat [knowledge] as a thing that can be possessed, measured, stored, processed, and readily distributed to people designated as 'users' … Tacit knowledge is personal knowledge rooted in individual experience and involving personal belief, perspective, and values	Thatchenkery and Chowdhry, 2007: 27
	… a valuable commodity that is embedded in products … and in the tacit knowledge of highly mobile employees … a company's knowledge base [is] populated with valid and valuable lessons learned and best practices … companies need to learn from past errors and not reinvent the wheel	Dalkir, 2011: 2

(Continued)

TABLE 1.1 (Continued)

Discipline	Definition	Source
	… the basis for good judgment and of good decision making … an asset for your business	Barnes and Milton, 2016: 17
	takes many forms. It includes the competencies and capabilities of employees, a company's knowledge about customers and suppliers, know-how to deliver specific processes, intellectual property in the form of patents, licenses and copyrights, [and] systems for leveraging the company's innovative strength. Knowledge is the product of individual and collective learning and is embodied in products, services, and systems. Knowledge is related to the experiences of people and in the society, but only a small part is made explicit. Tacit knowledge largely determines how people behave and act	North and Kumta, 2014: 31
	Knowledge is a fluid mix of framed experience, values, contextual information, expert insight, and grounded intuition that provides an environment and framework for evaluating and incorporating new experiences and information	Davenport and Prusak, 1998: 5
Accounting	… information combined with experience, context, interpretation, and reflection. It is a high-value form of information that is ready to apply to decisions and actions	Davenport and Prusak, 1998: 43
	Intangible assets – human capital, structural capital (sometimes called organizational capital) and customer capital (sometimes called relational capital)	Stewart, 1997
Economics	Knowledge is the relatively permanent record of the experience underlying learning (Anderson, 1995). It encompasses declarative (facts), procedural (know-how), and conditional knowledge (knowing under what circumstances the knowledge applies) in both its implicit and explicit dimensions … one person's knowledge is just too fluid, subjective, and context specific to be more than another's information	Huizing and Bouman, 2002: 186–187
Human resource management	[Human capital] is the collective knowledge, skills, abilities, and other characteristics (that is, all of the capabilities combined) … that create a capacity … for competitive advantage	Lengnick-Hall and Lengnick-Hall, 2003: 45

Discipline	Definition	Source
Information technology	… frequently pictured at the top of a hierarchy, with information below it, and data at the bottom … knowledge is more valuable [as a] temporal sequence (knowledge is based on information, which in turn is based on data) … is structured, contextualized and interpreted information [has a] potential for action. [Knowledge is primarily] held by people … Some knowledge has been documented; [it] is also embedded in software and equipment.	Rollett, 2003: 6–7; see also Ackoff, 1989
	[The three types of process knowledge are:] Process template knowledge: The process template plus analysis and simulation information derived from the template design phase. It also includes the history of evolution of the template. Process instance knowledge: A set of process instance information along with process performance measure according to evaluation criteria of a given enterprise. It also contains information about environment, resource, results, and so on. Process-related knowledge: A knowledge set created and used within a business process. General explicit knowledge of traditional knowledge management is summarized	Jung et al., 2007: 23
	Distinctions related to the degree to which knowledge is tacit or codified, and to whether it takes the form of knowledge about the state of the world ('know-what') or competence knowledge ('know-how')	Edmondson et al., 2003: 199
Operations management	Knowledge as subjective rather than objective. From the objective stance, knowledge is considered as an object, which is representative of the world, independent of human perception, and exists in a variety of forms and locations. We view knowledge as subjective. This perspective contends that knowledge does not exist independent of human experience; instead, it develops through the social creation of meanings and concepts, and therefore loses a universal, objective character. The subjective nature of knowledge is apparent in the view that knowledge resides in the individual, in Nonaka and Takeuchi's view of knowledge as 'a dynamic human process of justifying personal belief toward the "truth"' (1995: 58),) and organizational knowledge as embodied in individuals and groups. The subjective and context-sensitive nature of knowledge implies that its categories and meanings depend on individual perception	Sabherwal and Becerra-Fernandez, 2003: 226

(Continued)

TABLE 1.1   (Continued)

Discipline	Definition	Source
Operations management (cont.)	Procedural knowledge (routine or simple tasks), declarative knowledge (targeted), actionable knowledge (if-then propositions) and pragmatic knowledge (willingness to act)	Cavaleri et al., 2005: 203–204
	… there are at least four substantially different forms of knowledge – propositional [the object], experiential [source], performative [representation], and epistemological [truth]	Mingers, 2006: 7
Systems thinking	Justified beliefs about relationships among concepts relevant to that particular area	Becerra-Fernandez and Sabherwal, 2010: 19
	Information is not knowledge … Knowledge is the primary form of capital. All other forms are dependent and deprived, only secondary to knowledge … Knowledge gives life to all … knowledge is the ability to coordinate one's actions, alone and with others, effectively and purposefully, and is embedded within and activated by human, social, and cultural institutions	Zeleny, 2005: 2–7
Interdisciplinary	[Organizational knowledge is] interpreted organizational information which is processed from data (i.e. facts and events) that helps organizational members to take purposeful actions and make decisions in order to accomplish their assigned tasks	Jasimuddin, 2012: 7

Several themes emerge from Table 1.1. *Epistemology*: this examines knowledge as a desire for truth (Nonaka, 2002) or as a construction of reality (Ichijo, 2007). This perspective focuses on evidence which enables trust in the knowledge. Evidence is determined by whether you believe in rationalism (scientific fact) or empiricism (sensory experience). While experience plays an important role in the scientific method via observation of events, the contrast between rationalism and empiricism presented here emerges in the distinction between objectivity and subjectivity. Rationalism argues that the reality is repeatable, i.e. that the observer's experience would be the same for others, that is, objective. Empiricism argues that reality is individual, i.e. that the observer's experience may be different from others, that is, subjective.

Tacit and codified: tacit knowledge is located in people's heads (Polanyi, 1967), whereas codified knowledge is written down as reports, policies, procedures, and other work outputs (Barth, 2005). Tacit knowledge is regarded as the most valuable, largely because it determines how people behave and act (North and Kumta, 2014).

Cognitive: this looks at knowledge as a capability, such as the process of knowing (learning capacity) (Blackler, 2002), the capability to draw distinctions (sensemaking) (Tsoukas and Vladimirou, 2001), and relationships among concepts (cause and effect) (Becerra-Fernandez and Sabherwal, 2010).

Stages: this views knowledge as sequential as people move from a state of being unknowledgeable (or unknowing) to knowledgeable (or knowing). Schön (1983) describes this as achieving artful competence. This has normative force because individuals may be described as having or not having knowledge (Fuller, 2002). This perspective enables knowledge to be linked with organizational learning.

Hierarchy: knowledge is regarded as an outcome of using information to interpret data (Boisot, 2002). Tiwana (2002: 37) argues that knowledge in the business context is 'nothing but actionable information'. The DIKW hierarchy of knowledge is commonly used (Ackoff, 1989). This hierarchy transitions from data to information, knowledge, and wisdom through an increase of connectedness and understanding. It is helpful to view data, information, and knowledge as separate constructs that are linked sequentially (Jasimuddin, 2012: 11).

Types: researchers have produced a wide variety of typologies which attempt to classify differences in knowledge. These include:

- Know-what, know-how, know-why, and care-why (Quinn et al., 1998)
- Intangible assets or capital: human, structural, and customer (e.g. see Stewart, 1997)
- Procedural, declarative, actionable, and pragmatic (Cavaleri et al., 2005)
- Propositional, experiential, performative, and epistemological (Mingers, 2006).

These typologies are helpful in distinguishing knowledge in terms of its source (e.g. know-what is cognitive), and its application (e.g. procedural is routine or simple tasks). Therefore, they are useful in linking knowledge with knowledge management.

Action: this is the role of knowledge in organizations. It views knowledge as reflective practice (Aakhus, 2007), as practical (Jasimuddin, 2012), and as the ability to coordinate actions (Zeleny, 2005). It focuses on creating value from knowledge by taking effective action (Bennet, 2007) and is used as the basis for good judgement and for good decision making (Barnes and Milton, 2016). This is helpful for measuring the value of knowledge.

Subjective: knowledge is personal and context dependent (Huizing and Bouman, 2002). It involves experience, insight, and intuition (Tiwana, 2002). This perspective regards meaning as that interpreted by individual perception (Sabherwal and Becerra-Fernandez, 2003). It includes a social constructivist view of knowledge, where knowledge emerges from social situations.

Embedded: this sees knowledge as embedded in products and systems (Dalkir, 2011) and as embodied in the social world (Lambe, 2007). This perspective sees people as gathering knowledge from their interactions with their physical and social environments, as well as organizations being able to capture knowledge in these contexts. It contrasts with the concept of codified knowledge which captures knowledge in written form.

DEEP THINKING: In this book, knowledge is defined as the capacity of an individual to find interpretation and meaning, leading to action that creates value for the organization. This definition is grounded in the idea that knowledge is essentially related to human action (Nonaka and Takeuchi, 1995: 59) and that knowledge creates organizational value via its application (Grant, 1996). Knowledge management research tends to privilege the individual over the group based on the argument that organizational learning is really about the individual. The focus on the individual is often traced back to Polanyi and Prosch, who felt that all knowledge is personal (Polanyi and Prosch, 1975: 44). Polanyi and Prosch reject the idea that there is such a thing as 'objective' knowledge – self-contained, detached, and independent of human action. Polanyi and Prosch's article adopts an empiricist view based on the logic that the value of knowledge is influenced by the organizational context and is generated by individuals who have the capacity to take action, that is, to use their knowledge to create value for the organization (Massingham, 2016).

JUSTIFIED TRUE BELIEF

While the definition of knowledge is controversial, there are some principles that are relatively widely accepted which provide a useful platform. 'Western philosophers have generally agreed that knowledge is "justified true belief", a concept that was first introduced by Plato in Meno (1997), Phaedo, and Theaetetus' (Nonaka and Takeuchi, 1995: 21). The key word in this phrase is 'justified'. While truth is an objective condition, belief is a subjective condition. You can believe something is true but not know for certain it is true. Justified means there is evidence to trust the knowledge. The definition of evidence is explained by epistemology.

CORE CONCEPT: Justified true belief is knowledge you can trust because you believe the evidence.

EPISTEMOLOGY

Epistemology is the philosophy of knowledge. People have been interested in knowledge at least since the time of the ancient Greek philosophers Plato and Socrates (around 400 BC). This chapter focuses on the contrasting fields of rationalism and empiricism.

RATIONALISM

Rationalism argues that true knowledge is deduced by ideal mental process (Nonaka and Takeuchi, 1995) by using judgement to interpret evidence. The interpretation of evidence is the foundation of scientific thought and research and introduces the concept of proof. It is learning by discovery. Rationalism is, therefore, objective knowledge available to all and able to be proved. In organizational terms, it may be described as a single best practice.

The importance of evidence led philosophers to question reality. Descartes (1596–1650) was a rationalist in the sense that he felt knowledge was only attainable through reason (1996 [1641]). He was also a mathematician and he trusted science to find philosophical answers. He felt that what we can know from our senses is untrustworthy. Therefore, even though we can feel that we are alive, this does not prove we exist. He suggested that our lives may actually be a dream. He posed this possibility by asking us to consider whether we feel we are experiencing reality when we dream. If so, is there any difference between our dreaming feelings and our waking feelings? If not, perhaps we are always dreaming.

As a scientist, Descartes sought the answers to his questions of identity and reality by looking for facts and evidence. He went back to first principles and doubted everything. His doubts focused on our senses – what we can see, touch, feel, smell, and hear – because even they may be deceiving us. His breakthrough came when he deduced that the one thing he knew to be true was that he doubted. By questioning his own existence, it proved that he was thinking, and in doing so, that he was a thinking being. Descartes found truth in his pursuit of identity by questioning his own existence. If he did not doubt, he might simply be living in a dream.

The phrase *I think, therefore I am* also contributed to the development of philosophical and scientific enquiry. Descartes resolved the conflict between rational and sensory thought by arguing that as he realized he was a thinking being, he found he was more real than the material world around him, which he perceived with his senses. This established the mind and reason as more important than nature and the senses. It also distinguished between quantitative and qualitative enquiry. Things that are measurable, such as length, breadth, and depth, are more important than sensory perceptions, such as touch and smell.

Kant (1724–1804) developed transcendental idealism. He believed that knowledge emerges when both the logical thinking of rationalism and the sensory experience of empiricism work together (Nonaka and Takeuchi, 1995: 24). Kant appears to be an empiricist because he begins with the proposal that all knowledge is experience. However, he also argues that the mind provides the tools to make sense of this experience and allow understanding. So he is usually categorized as a rationalist.

Hegel (1770–1831) considered knowledge as the pursuit of intellectual freedom (Hegel, 1997). He argued that the advancement of knowledge, through the process of Socratic questioning, develops the mind and society. The synthesis of opposing views enables new knowledge to be created. These ideas would later become a foundation for creativity and were conceptualized as creative abrasion, which involved a process of divergence (encouraging different ideas) and convergence (finding agreement) (Leonard and Sensiper, 2002).

Husserl (1859–1938) established a movement called phenomenology, which built on Kant's attempts to link rationalism and empiricism. It still accepted the power of the mind in determining knowledge but privileged the individual's influence in this process. According to Nonaka and Takeuchi (1995: 26), it aims for 'pure consciousness', achieved through 'phenomenological reduction', where all previous knowledge, such as facts and assumptions about an object or topic, are set aside so that pure intuition is used. This movement extended Descartes' concept of the power of the mind. Phenomenology argued that consciousness – our perception of the world and what is happening to us – is not subject to the rules of causality. Evidence was found in the individual's perception. It also extends Hegel's ideas about intellectual freedom to allow the individual freedom to decide truth. However, this should not be confused with empiricism (see below). Phenomenology still argued that the mind is more important than the senses. It contributed to the two most important themes in modern epistemology: consciousness and reality. For the first theme, we will discuss the work of Michael Polanyi, and for the second theme that of Stephen Hawking.

TACIT KNOWLEDGE AND CONSCIOUSNESS

Polanyi's famous statement 'I shall reconsider human knowledge by starting from the fact that we can know more than we can tell' (Polanyi, 1966: 4) declared the importance of tacit knowledge or the knowledge inside people's heads. Polanyi felt that all knowledge was personal and that it was difficult to express and, therefore, share with others. Polanyi proposed that 'tacit knowledge forms a triangle, at the three corners of which are the subsidiary particulars, the focal target, and the knower who links the two' (Tsoukas, 2003: 112; see also Polanyi and Prosch, 1975). According to Tsoukas (2003), to understand these terms it is useful to begin with the focal target, using one of Polanyi's favourite examples: hammering a nail. Two kinds of awareness operate when exercising a skill: focal and subsidiary (Polanyi and Prosch, 1975). As you hammer the nail, your main focus of attention is the nail – that is your task – but you are also subsidiarily aware of the hammer through the feelings in your hand. Subsidiary awareness is the combination of subconscious knowledge which we apply to the focal task without even thinking about it. In this sense, it is a type of intuition which we draw on to complete the focal task. The importance of this construct in managing knowledge transfer is illustrated by its mutual exclusivity. When hammering the nail, if we switch our attention to the hammer, rather than the nail, and concentrate on how we hold the hammer and swing it, our movements would become clumsy and we will likely do a poor job of hitting the nail. In transferring knowledge, it is necessary to account for both the focal knowledge and the subsidiary knowledge associated with the focal task. The focal target and subsidiary awareness represent opposite ends of a tacit dimension, an approach consistent with Polanyi (1962).

According to Tsoukas (2003), the third part of Polanyi's (1962) tacit triangle is the knower, who links the focal target with the subsidiary particulars. The knower, the person with the knowledge, is the crucial part of the triangle. The other two dimensions of tacit knowledge (focal awareness and subsidiary awareness) lie dormant unless the knower decides to use them to complete a task. Thus, the link of focal awareness and subsidiary awareness is an act performed by the knower. This discussion forms the basis of Polanyi's (1962) points about knowledge being personal, and all knowing being action. Knowledge has a recursive form: given a certain context, we 'black-box' (assimilate, interiorize, instrumentalize) certain things in order to concentrate or focus on others (Tsoukas, 2003). The tacit knowledge we use depends on the nature of the task. For example, the knowledge I have as an academic does not help me understand what is wrong with my car. Tacit knowledge also depends heavily on the person. The knower draws on their personal experiences and knowledge to complete a task, thus the knower has a unique perspective.

REALITY

Rationalism argues that we can find justification for knowledge through scientific testing. Stephen Hawking, who died in 2018, and his co-author Leonard Mlodinow stated that the ideas of the ancient Greek philosophers 'would not pass muster as valid science in modern times' (Hawking and Mlodinow, 2010: 22). They made this claim because 'their theories were not developed with the goal of experimental verification' (2010: 22). This is a foundation of modern science's perception of reality. Ideas or beliefs cannot be accepted as knowledge, i.e. justified as truth, unless they can be observed and proven. In other words, they need to be able to be tested.

How then do Hawking and Mlodinow view reality? Science is based on 'the belief that there exists a real external world whose properties are definite and independent of the observer who perceives them' (Hawking and Mlodinow, 2010: 43). This thinking is based on rationalism and objective truth. In making sense of reality, measurements exist which allow us to define the world around us and its properties. In Hawking and Mlodinow's world, mathematics and most especially physics are all that is needed to perceive reality. If it can be measured and tested: it is real. Hawking's pursuit of the theory of everything, which will prove why the universe exists and the meaning of life, and which he called M-theory (2010: 181), was the ultimate demonstration of scientific realism. Hawking believed that physics can produce a model which tells us everything we need to know about life – reality summarized in a complex equation.

EMPIRICISM

Empiricism argues that knowledge can be attained inductively from sensory experiences (Nonaka and Takeuchi, 1995: 21). The founder of empiricism was Aristotle. Plato (384–322 BC) used metaphysics to question underlying assumptions. The word 'question' is the foundation of philosophy and introduces the concept of opinion. It is learning by doing. Empirical knowledge is, therefore, subjective knowledge created by the individual and dependent on context. In organizational terms, it may be described as multiple best practices.

Locke (1632–1604) argued the importance of sensory experience. He developed the concept of an idea, which was the mind's sensory image of an experience (Locke, 1998). These ideas are mental models, based not on what others have discovered or tell us is true, but rather on what we have experienced to be true. Berkeley (1685–1753) famously claimed that nothing exists except the mind and its ideas. When told that Berkeley's claim could not be refuted, Johnson (1709–1784) equally famously walked over to a large rock and kicked it, exclaiming 'I refute it thus' (Hawking and Mlodinow, 2010: 45). Johnson was a practical man and he was demonstrating that there was more to reality than his mind and that he could prove the rock existed by the pain he experienced in his foot after kicking it.

Dewey (1859–1952) developed our awareness of knowledge in practice, by arguing that knowledge is closely bound with activity (Jashapara, 2004). Dewey (1929: 138) explained that 'ideas are worthless except as they pass into actions which rearrange and reconstruct in some way, be it little or large, the world in which we live.' In this way, Dewey introduced the relationship between learning and doing, and laid the foundations for our current ideas about creating value from knowledge. Dewey's main focus was on the nature of ideas (something tangible needs to come out of them), rather than the contemporary focus on value (worthless unless they create an improvement). In this way, Dewey presented the basis of the practical perspective that knowledge lies idle unless it is used to create value for organizations, i.e. by individuals doing work. This was a precursor to action research (e.g. see Neuman, 2006).

Wittgenstein (1889–1951) examined the role of language as a theory of meaning (Wittgenstein, 1953). He regarded words and sentences as the way the mind determines facts and meaning. These combine to form our mental models of the world. The importance of Wittgenstein's work is that it introduces us to the idea of cognition and how the mind works. It suggests that when we think, we talk to ourselves, and in doing so the language we use has meaning – and this contributes to how we see the world. It pushes the boundaries of sensory experience by suggesting that we can have private conversations with ourselves, which are entirely unique because we develop our own private language with variations on the meaning of words and their combination as sentences. In this way, language contributes to individual knowledge through different uses of words and their meaning when making sense of experiences.

KNOWLEDGE AS A PRODUCT

The idea of knowledge as a product emerged from the resource-based view of the firm (RBV) (e.g. Wernerfelt, 1984) and the knowledge-based view of the firm (KBV) (Grant, 1996). These theories of strategic management gained widespread popularity in the 1990s amongst researchers and practitioners. They promoted the notion that knowledge was a valuable resource which could be managed like other organizational resources. Intellectual capital measurement (e.g. Bontis, 1998) built on the principles of the KBV by trying to find a way to objectively measure, in accounting terms, the contribution that the intellectual assets of the workforce can make to organizational value and performance.

This perspective is called 'knowledge as a product' because it is seen as something that can be produced. Researchers exploring this perspective have called knowledge 'structural' (Newell et al., 2002), an 'asset' (Empson, 2001), and an 'object' (Hislop, 2011). The epistemological assumption is that knowledge is an objectively definable commodity (Jasimuddin, 2012: 15). In seeing knowledge as a thing, this perspective enables knowledge management to look for ways to separate knowledge from the knower via codification (Hislop, 2011: 17). Cook and Brown (1999) describe this perspective as follows:

> We call this understanding the 'epistemology of possession' since it treats knowledge as something people possess. Yet, this epistemology cannot account for the knowing found in individual and group practice. Knowing as action calls for an 'epistemology of practice'. (1999: 381)

Here, Cook and Brown are explaining the need for dual epistemologies which capture both a body of knowledge (possession) and individual knowing (practice). For instance, an individual may possess knowledge of a discipline, such as nursing, but develop their own unique way of knowing how to practise nursing. Cook and Brown further explain their ideas within the context of the 'Cartesian tradition' of distinguishing between tacit and codified knowledge (1999: 384) to help us understand the difference between knowledge and knowing:

> We believe Cartesian epistemology needs to be broadened into an 'epistemology of possession' that can incorporate a conceptually sound and useful understanding of knowledge possessed tacitly and knowledge possessed by groups. We mark this distinction by referring to it as 'knowing' rather than 'knowledge'. Furthermore, we believe that knowing does not belong to an epistemology of possession, but rather that it calls for an epistemology of practice. (1999: 386)

Cook and Brown provide bridging epistemologies that enable distinction between the ownership of knowledge (possession) and the use of knowledge (practice).

The product perspective is based on rationalism and this means knowledge is deduced by the individual. It is not owned by the individual; it is discovered by the individual and is owned by all, i.e. it is objective knowledge. The objectivist perspective proposes that knowledge is owned by the organization, not the individual.

KNOWLEDGE AS PRACTICE

The idea of knowledge as practice is grounded in Polanyi's concept of 'skilful action' (Polanyi, 1962). This perspective emphasizes that knowledge is 'embedded within and inseparable from work activities or practices' (Hislop, 2011: 31). Researchers exploring this perspective have described knowledge as 'know-how', i.e. it may require practice or discussion (Edmondson et al., 2003), as a 'process' (Empson, 2001), 'socially constructed' (Newell et al., 2006), 'context-sensitive' (Sabherwal and Becerra-Fernandez, 2003), and 'embedded' (Lambe, 2007).

This view holds that knowledge cannot be separated from the knower (e.g. see Tsoukas, 2003). In seeing knowledge as personal (Polanyi, 1962), this perspective enables knowledge management to develop skilful knowing in the act of doing (Tsoukas, 2003). Skilful action means that knowledge emerges in the act of doing something. It is only in the act of doing that the individual becomes fully aware of the knowledge necessary to complete the activity. It is at this point that conscious learning occurs.

This theory of skilful knowing sees work as an adaptive process where the individual tries to turn given situations into preferred situations (Aakhus, 2007). Rather than following bureaucratic guidelines, professional practice involves a process of problem framing and problem solving based on the individual's theory of practice (Schön, 1983). The individual uses their experience to make sense of the work situation. In this way, knowledge involves technical knowledge but also judgement, i.e. the competence of handling complexity, instability, and value-conflict when engaging people and problem situations at work (Schön, 1983). This view focuses on individual knowledge because it allows the individual to learn from their experience, i.e. reflect-in-practice, and to apply this to a new work situation. It recognizes that knowledge may be created within a group; it may produce collective know-how (e.g. Edmondson et al., 2003), even across and between organizations, and it may produce organizational know-how (e.g. see Reagans and McEvily, 2003).

CORE CONCEPT: This book tends to privilege tacit knowledge as the most valuable knowledge (Massingham, 2016). Its higher value is due to its interpretative capacity. Tacit knowledge involves using judgement, intuition, and experience to interpret a body of knowledge and apply it to an organizational context. This process generates value for the individual and their organization via skilful knowing. Therefore, it adopts an activity- or practice-based view of knowledge (Aakhus, 2007). This means that knowledge emerges in the act of doing something. It is only in the act of doing that the individual becomes fully aware of the knowledge necessary to complete the activity.

INDIVIDUAL KNOWLEDGE

The most common way of defining individual knowledge is to describe it as tacit or as the knowledge in people's heads. As outlined in the previous section, Polanyi felt that all knowledge occurs in the act of knowing. All knowing involves 'skilful action' (cited by Tsoukas, 2005: 109). This means that knowledge emerges in the act of doing something. It is only in the act of doing that the individual becomes fully aware of the knowledge necessary to complete the activity. If the individual stops doing it, they cannot fully recall what it is they did. They may recall particulars, which Polanyi calls focal awareness, but there will be plenty that they cannot recall or express. This latter knowledge Polanyi calls subsidiary awareness. Polanyi was an empiricist. For him, the idea that knowledge could exist objectively and independently of human action, i.e. be represented as an object or a thing, is wrong. All knowing is personal knowing (Polanyi and Prosch, 1975).

At the individual level, this raises important questions about how people work, and learn how to do their work better. Traditional views of knowledge as an informational product present a technocratic conceptualization of work (Aakhus, 2007). This conceptualization sees work as information-seeking behaviour. Professional decision making involves a bureaucratic process of resolving choices – i.e. should I do it this way or that way? – by searching for an appropriate rule, policy, or procedure, and then applying that to the situation (Aakhus, 2007). This view privileges organizational knowledge because it asks the individual to follow the organization's guidelines rather than think for themselves.

An alternative view of knowledge is as an organizational system driven by the individual. This conceptualization sees work as an adaptive process where the individual tries to turn given situations into preferred situations (Aakhus, 2007). Rather than follow bureaucratic guidelines, professional practice involves a process of problem framing and problem solving based on the individual's theory of practice (Schön, 1983, cited in Aakhus, 2007). This individual uses their experience to make sense of the work situation. In this way, professional knowledge involves technical knowledge but also judgement, that is, the competence of handling complexity, instability, and value-conflict when engaging people and problem situations at work (Schön, 1983, cited in Aakhus, 2007). This view privileges individual knowledge because it allows the individual to learn from their experience, i.e. reflect-in-practice, and to apply this to a new work situation.

TECHNICAL KNOWLEDGE

Knowledge is commonly represented in the literature as technical knowledge, which is the knowledge the individual needs to do their job. It involves discipline-related knowledge, such as qualifications and training, as well as knowledge gained from on-the-job learning, i.e. experience related to technical aspects of work. The activity- or practice-based view of knowledge is grounded in the issue of how individuals learn and use their knowledge to benefit the organization they work for. How do doctors, mechanics, lawyers, engineers, nurses, teachers, plumbers, and others learn how to do what they do and then become good at what they do (Aakhus, 2007)? This point of view suggests a career continuum from novice to expert practitioner. How do people move along this continuum? What do they know at the start and what do they learn along the way? What job-related knowledge makes them different from us?

COGNITIVE KNOWLEDGE

Knowledge is also represented in the literature as cognitive knowledge. This is the individual's process of making sense of the world and may include judgement, intuition, and perception. Cognitive knowledge may include other non-technical knowledge unique to the individual's work context such as behaviours, attitudes, and social capital. Researchers have examined these processes using a socio-cognitive approach, suggesting that meaning is mediated by private and cultural models generated by the individual's own cognitive dispositions, including memory and emotions, as well as socio-cultural interaction (Ringberg and Reihlen, 2008). This socio-cognitive approach to knowledge explains that the individual's environment, concep-tualized as organizational systems, helps define the individual's knowledge. As the individual performs their work, cognitive processes exchange within the broader strategy, structure, and culture of their organization to help them find meaning. This thinking has developed a paradigm that views knowledge as a systemic, socially constructed, context-specific representation of reality. Recent research has found that the individual's psychology is part of their knowledge because it influences their cognitive processes and the application of their knowledge at work (Massingham and Tam, 2015).

DEEP LEARNING: Critics of knowledge management's treatment of tacitness argue that it is misunderstood (e.g. see Tsoukas, 2003), based largely on the proposition that tacit knowledge cannot be separated from the knower. Critics believe that this proposition is the justification for the misunderstanding; that is, people believe tacit knowledge may be separated from the knower when critics believe it cannot. This proposition is based on the importance of the unconscious when we perform tasks or activities. Polanyi felt that 'tacitness enabled every thought and action' (Ray, 2005: 4). It allows us to do things without thinking about them. We may know how to do something in practice but find it difficult, perhaps impossible, to explain how we do it. Polanyi's famous (1966: 4) statement 'We can know more than we can tell' suggests why tacit knowledge cannot be expressed. The 'more' part of our knowledge is the subconscious, or what Polanyi (1962) describes as subsidiary awareness. Our subconscious knows more than we can explain because we cannot recall it, or certainly not all at the same time. Ray (2005: 5) cites Tor Nørretranders who suggested that 'human sense perceptions deliver more than 11 million bits of information per second (at least 10 billion bits of which come from the eyes) but consciousness can only process 40 bits of information per second – at best.' It is not that we do not want to share; it is that we simply are not capable. This presents the problem that tacit knowledge is hidden from us in the sense that we are not aware of it. If it does not emerge in our consciousness, we cannot explain it.

GROUP KNOWLEDGE

Knowledge may be created by groups. The group may be as small as two people or much larger. Humanistic management (e.g. see Mayo, 1933) sees workers as social beings who enjoy working in groups. This has encouraged thinking about knowledge as social practice. When people work together in groups, they have the opportunity to share knowledge and to create new knowledge as a group. This knowledge may be shared work practices and routines (Hecker, 2012) and shared assumptions, perspectives, and mental models (e.g. see Senge, 1990).

There are three schools of thought about group knowledge. The first school of thought sees social practice knowledge as the codified outcomes of the group's work, such as reports, presentations, and meeting minutes. The group produces outcomes which represent the new knowledge created by individuals within the group sharing their knowledge. Hislop (2011) proposes that the group's knowledge is more than their work outputs; they may produce a set of structural capital, which he calls objectified group knowledge. This is a 'documented system of rules, operating procedures, or formalized organizational routines' (Hislop, 2011: 23). It is unlikely that this type of knowledge would be created by informal or short-term work groups. However, regular committees, or larger groups such as departments or divisions, are likely to produce this type of codified knowledge.

The second school of thought sees social practice knowledge as a set of shared mental models. It is an informal way of doing business that the group develops over time and that works for them. Spender (1996) calls this collective tacit knowledge. It is the value systems, norms, and attitudes which the group shares. It provides them with mutual understanding about how the group works, but also the (1) knowledge that the individual possesses which they can contribute to the group, which Hecker (2012) calls shared knowledge; (2) awareness of the knowledge of others in the group, which Hecker calls complementary knowledge; and (3) the capacity to explain the group's work outputs or products, which Hecker calls artefact-embedded knowledge.

The third school of thought sees social practice knowledge as social capital. From this perspective, knowledge emerges as people interact recurrently in the context of established and novel routines and procedures, i.e. in the act of doing work (Newell et al., 2006). The social constructivist view of knowledge argues that knowledge is developed, shared, and maintained in social situations (Tsoukas and Vladimirou, 2001). There is increasing interest in knowledge as a tacit contextualization process within the context of social interaction (Massingham, 2015). This involves the knowledge in one person's head (the sender) being transferred to the head of another person (the receiver) (Easterby-Smith and Prieto, 2008).

ORGANIZATIONAL KNOWLEDGE

Organizational knowledge is knowledge owned by the organization. It may best be understood by starting with an overview of management theory as it relates to knowledge. The history of economic and management theories in the 20th and 21st centuries has centred on 'repeated challenges of the "scientific" view of knowledge from the "humanistic" view' (Nonaka and Takeuchi, 1995: 32). This book holds that scientific management is an outdated and ineffective way of management which is no longer relevant in the 21st century knowledge economy; however, both views are presented to allow you to form your own opinion.

Scientific management was founded by Taylor (see Nonaka and Takeuchi, 1995: 35) who was obsessed with increasing worker efficiency. Taylor (1911: 36) saw 'workers' knowledge as an opportunity to capture experience and skills and convert them into objective knowledge, that is, rules and formulae'. The idea was that management could capture this knowledge by analysing what workers do and finding more efficient ways of doing it. It emphasized control, rules, and formal structures. It was the basis of a rationalist, positivist view of management which led to bureaucratic control as a form of organizing. It placed power with management and emphasized the importance of eliminating wasteful activity, specialization, and doing things right. It introduced behaviours and attitudes which were the antithesis of the type of flexible, agile, adaptable work environment desired by the 21st century's knowledge workers.

Human relations theory developed in the 1920s and 1930s in opposition to scientific management. Led by Mayo (1933), this field showed that social factors such as 'morale, a sense of belonging, and interpersonal skills improved productivity' (cited in Nonaka and Takeuchi, 1995: 36). It contrasted the view of scientific management of workers as machines with a new view of workers as social beings. It led to a humanistic view of management which argued that knowledge emerges from social practice, and that by understanding the social needs of workers, knowledge could be increased. This encouraged attitudes and behaviours, such as cooperation, collaboration, and teamwork, which develop a work environment desired by the 21st century's knowledge workers.

Attempts to integrate scientific management and humanistic management led to a focus on problem solving and decision making, which in turn led to the importance of information processing as an organizational capability (e.g. see discussion of Barnard and Simon in Nonaka and Takeuchi, 1995: 36–38). This view suggests that knowledge is something that can be separated from the knower and managed more effectively by the organization. It aims for increased productivity through efficiency gains in information processing, i.e. reducing time spent.

The integrated approach was challenged by the 'garbage can' model of organizations first proposed by Cohen et al. (1972). This model argued that organizational reality is 'problem solving, and decision making is irrational and ambiguous' (Nonaka and Takeuchi, 1995: 39). It presented organizations as disordered chaos where individuals tend to react to crises. Organizational learning, therefore, involved individuals finding new ideas 'more or less randomly' (1995: 39). This led to Weick's theory of organizational sensemaking (Weick, 1993) where he argued that the only way to make sense of this organizational chaos is to anchor meaning to the specific context, i.e. the routines and behaviours. It provided a modern view of organizational empiricism by relying on our natural need to make sense of the world around us – in this case, the place we work.

The late 1980s saw the emergence of the resource-based view of the firm (RBV) and, soon after, the knowledge-based view of the firm (KBV). While the science of business strategy had begun in the 1960s with the Boston Consulting Group's experience curve concept (Nonaka and Takeuchi, 1995: 40), the RBV and KBV thrust knowledge into mainstream management from both an academic and practitioner perspective. These theories explained that knowledge was a firm resource and that it could be combined with other resources, such as technology, capital, and materials, to create value for the firm via organizational capabilities. The KBV made knowledge matter. It was argued that knowledge was the most valuable firm resource and the key to its competitive advantage and success (Grant, 1996). The RBV and KBV were based on a rationalism epistemology and they viewed knowledge as an object which could be separated from the knower. The key to their success as theories was the reusability of knowledge as a resource. It was unlike any other resource: it did not deplete when used. If it was the most valuable resource, and it could only ever increase (e.g. via organizational learning), it had magical qualities – all one needed to do was manage it effectively and business success was assured. As we will see, it is not that simple but we can thank the RBV and KBV for making knowledge something worth managing. Related concepts, like the knowledge economy and intangible assets, emerged in response to the interest created by these pioneering theories on knowledge management.

This led to two views of organizational knowledge – (a) structural capital and (b) tacit social practice. Structural capital is part of intellectual capital (IC) theory (e.g. see Dumay, 2014). IC is a popular example of trying to break knowledge down into manageable chunks. IC's key attributes are its three types of capital: human capital, structural capital, and customer capital. Structural capital is codified knowledge owned by the organization, such as policies, procedures, systems, and products.

Individuals can only access this knowledge through social interaction with those in the know, i.e. other organizational members who know the corpus of generalizations. Further, individuals will vary in their capacity to access this knowledge. Each individual has only a partial view of knowledge about a particular organizational routine or practice (Newell et al., 2006). Therefore, organizational knowledge is integrated across groups and communities.

THEORY IN PRACTICE

STRUCTURAL CAPITAL

Management consulting firms rely heavily upon structural capital. They normally have two main types of portals in their intranets: practice and customers. The practice portal contains information to help staff be better consultants. It includes policies and procedures such as guidelines on project management; templates for proposals, reports, and presentations; work outputs such as client reports; and operational issues such as human resource management, finance, and information technology. It also contains information about the firm's products and services. The customer portal contains information to help staff develop knowledge that will help them sell the firm's services. This is usually organized by industry, such as financial services, manufacturing, and retail. The aim is to develop deep knowledge about the customer's industry so that staff can adapt their subject matter expertise to apply it to the customer's problems. This portal also contains industry benchmarks and other information about best practice in that industry.

TACIT SOCIAL PRACTICE

Tacit social practice is organizational knowledge found within unique organizational contexts and work situations. Tsoukas and Vladimirou (2001) call this a corpus of generalizations. It is 'how we do business around here.' But it is much more than the norms and values of organizational culture. It is a secret recipe of business success within this unique organizational context. It is secret because only organizational members can access it and it is usually not written down in any codified form such as policies or procedures; otherwise it would be structural capital.

Since the 1960s, the Japanese automotive manufacturers had a competitive advantage over their US rivals. The US firms were keen to know why the Japanese firms were able to manufacture at low cost and high quality. First, they studied some of the Japanese management systems such as kaizen (total quality management). Second, they asked the Japanese firms to share their knowledge. The Japanese firms were very cooperative and even allowed the US firms to visit their factories and observe their work practices. Despite this, the US firms were still unable to discover the secret of the Japanese firms' success. In desperation, they began to headhunt some of the leaders of the Japanese firms with lucrative contracts to come to the USA and run their firms. But the Japanese leaders could not make the US firms like the Japanese firms. They could not transfer the secrets of their business success to the USA. Perhaps differences in national culture or the lower labour costs of the Japanese were the reasons for this. However, the real problem for the US firms was that they lacked the tacit social practice of the Japanese firms. The Japanese staff knew something that could not be captured and transferred. It was the subtle nuance of day-to-day work routines developed over many years. The US firms would have to transplant the entire Japanese workforce to the USA if they wanted to copy this knowledge. It was not isolated in the head of one individual; therefore recruiting the Japanese leader was ineffective.

DEEP THINKING: Polanyi explained that 'the aim of a skilful performance is achieved by the observance of a set of rules which are not known as such to the person following them' (1962: 49). This statement is explained by Polanyi's tacit triangle concept. It is useful to see the distinction between focal and subsidiary awareness in terms of learning steps. An individual needs to know certain things in order to know how to do other things. It is like prerequisite or background knowledge. But once the individual knows these things, they are stored away in the subconscious, and only recalled and used when necessary, i.e. in the act of doing. The medical student who learns how to read an x-ray produces radiology knowledge, which becomes subsidiary awareness to help understand the information on the image (focal awareness), which then tells them what they are observing (Tsoukas, 2005: 114). In this way, the individual has learned what is wrong with the patient by assimilating the three parts of the tacit triangle – the knower's perspective, and focal and subsidiary awareness.

Tacit knowledge is the sort of knowledge that exists only in use and cannot be translated into a set of rules or guidelines (Tsoukas, 2005: 118). This seems like subsidiary awareness but it is really the combination of all three parts of the tacit triangle. This combination contains an ineffable element; it is based on an act of personal insight that is essentially inarticulable (2005: 121). This does not mean that tacit knowledge can never be shared with others. Through language such as 'Look at this', 'Have you thought about this?', 'Try this', or 'Imagine this' (2005: 121), it is possible to engage the knower and others in a social practice which reviews the situation and allows those involved to see connections between the focal and subsidiary particulars. To surface subsidiary awareness, we need to trigger cognitive switches. We need to remind ourselves about what we know.

Tacit knowledge, therefore, is subsidiary particulars which we only become aware of as we focus on something else. These particulars cannot be separated from the knower, because they will lose their meaning. While an individual can switch their focus to these particulars (making them the object of focal awareness) and try to explain them, they cannot do this in the context of the action in which they become subsidiarily aware of them (Tsoukas, 2005: 122). It needs a combination of the three – the knower, the focal, and the subsidiary in the act of doing. Only during the act of doing can others learn tacit knowledge from an individual.

CONCLUSION

Knowledge is a complex concept. In an organizational context, it is the individual who creates value for their organization through the work they do. By applying what they know, individuals use their knowledge and, in doing so, they create value. Otherwise, knowledge is an idle resource. Knowledge therefore begins with the individual. Knowledge may be created and owned by groups and organizations but the outcomes are the work of the individuals within that social practice. The group or the organization is made up of individuals. Knowledge is information until individuals can make sense of it and make it their own knowledge. Finally, individuals develop levels of knowledge: there is the basic knowledge necessary to become competent in a job, and then there is the more advanced knowledge which enables subject matter expertise. In managing knowledge in organizations, the practical questions are how to enable someone to first gain competence and second gain expertise. The first is about learning and the second about experience. These are explored in Chapter 2.

CLOSING CASE STUDY: KNOWLEDGE AT THE CASE STUDY ORGANIZATION

The research study which forms the basis of the integrated case studies at the end of each chapter in this book aimed to measure and manage the impact of lost organizational knowledge. The case study organization (CSO) was a knowledge-intensive organization employing approximately 150 professional engineering and technical workers. It was responsible for managing engineering risk for the Australian Federal Government. Its customers were responsible for designing, building, maintaining, operating, and disposing of significant government assets. The service provided by the CSO was to regulate engineering risk associated with these assets and provide engineering technical advice to customers. The CSO staff were subject matter experts. Their role was to ensure customers followed their technical specifications of material through the life cycle of these assets. If customers follow these specifications, the technical risk will be managed.

The need for the research study was created by the loss of key staff. Their exit created knowledge loss because their experience was no longer available, and remaining staff could no longer ask them for help. New replacement staff did not have the same level of knowledge. The CSO also felt this risk was increasing as its workforce was ageing and a high proportion of staff were due to retire.

The CSO had a large set of knowledge repositories which we will call the Operational Requirement Set (ORS). The ORS represented the CSO's collective wisdom: it was organizational memory, and defined the material requirements for the assets. The ORS comprised a total of 128 documents. Each of the documents was owned by a subject matter expert (SME). The document represented the SME's lifetime experience and knowledge of the topic area. Their job was to write and then maintain their ORS.

An example of this type of knowledge is provided by Stuart McDonald. Stuart was an expert in lifeboats. He had a lifelong passion for lifeboats and had read widely about their history and about current products and their capabilities. He was constantly researching the latest developments in lifeboat technology. His passion was important to the CSO. Lifeboats are an essential safety item on ships – they save lives. Therefore, his knowledge added value to the CSO because he knew about the technical specifications necessary to ensure safety, including how to incorporate lifeboat storage into new ship design. The CSO trusted him to know which manufacturers best meet their needs for lifeboats. Over time, Stuart broadened his range of expertise into other safety areas such as fire-fighting systems.

The CSO managed customer relationships. SMEs had to respond to customer requests for information or advice. They also needed to monitor customer activities to ensure they were following their technical specifications. In this way, the relationships were advisory and regulatory. However, customers could be very difficult: some were reluctant to follow the advice. And the SMEs preferred to make their own decisions – they trusted their own judgement. The customer relationship was influenced by CSO staff experience.

CASE STUDY QUESTIONS

1. Discuss the nature of the CSO's knowledge.
2. What is justified true belief at the CSO?
3. What type of knowledge is being lost at the CSO?

REVIEW AND DISCUSSION QUESTIONS

1. How does epistemology change your perspective about knowledge?
2. Critically evaluate the concept of skilful knowing.
3. Discuss the ownership of knowledge.

FURTHER READING

Edmondson, A.C., Winslow, A.B., Bohmer, R.M.J. and Pisano, G.P. (2003) Learning How and Learning What: Effects of tacit and codified knowledge on performance improvement following technology adoption. *Decision Sciences*, 34 (2): 197–223. An alternative perspective from operations management.

Tsoukas, H. (2003) Do We Really Understand Tacit Knowledge? Chapter 21 in Easterby-Smith, M. and Lyles, M.A. (eds) *Handbook of Organizational Learning and Knowledge Management*, Hong Kong, Blackwell, pp. 410–427. This chapter provides insight into tacit knowledge and also the product versus practice debate.

BIBLIOGRAPHY

Aakhus, M. (2007) Conversations for Reflection: Augmenting transitions and transformations in expertise. Chapter 1 in McInerney, C.R. and Day, R.E. (eds) *Rethinking Knowledge Management: From knowledge objects to knowledge processes*, New York, Springer, pp. 1–20.

Ackoff, R.L. (1989) From Data to Wisdom. *Journal of Applied Systems Analysis*, *16*: 3–9.

Anderson, J.R., (1995) *Learning and Memory: An Integrated Approach*, Chichester, Wiley.

Barnes, S. and Milton, N. (2016) *Designing a Successful KM Strategy: A guide for the knowledge management professional*, Medford, NJ, Information Today.

Barth, S. (2005) Self-organization: Taking a personal approach to knowledge management. Chapter 28 in Rao, M. (ed.) *Knowledge Management Tools and Techniques: Practitioners and experts evaluate KM solutions*, Oxford, Elsevier, pp. 347–364.

Becerra-Fernandez, I. and Sabherwal, R. (2010) *Knowledge Management: Systems and processes*, Armonk, NY, M.E. Sharpe.

Bennet, D.H. (2007) Learning and the Knowledge Worker. Chapter 31 in Koenig, M.E.D. and Srikantaiah, T.K. (eds) *Knowledge Management Lessons Learned: What works and what doesn't*, Medford, NJ, Information Today, pp. 511–525.

Blackler, F. (2002) Knowledge, Knowledge Work, and Organizations: An overview and interpretation. Chapter 3 in Choo, C.W. and Bontis, N. (eds) *The Strategic Management of Intellectual Capital and Organizational Knowledge*, New York, Oxford University Press, pp. 47–64.

Boisot, M. (2002) The Creation and Sharing of Knowledge. Chapter 4 in Choo, C.W. and Bontis, N. (eds) *The Strategic Management of Intellectual Capital and Organizational Knowledge*, New York, Oxford University Press, pp. 65–78.

Bontis, N. (1998) Intellectual Capital: An exploratory study that develops measures and models. *Management Decision, 36* (2): 63–76.

Cavaleri, S., Seivert, S. and Lee, L.W. (2005) *Knowledge Leadership: The art and science of the knowledge-based organization*, Burlington, MA, Elsevier Butterworth-Heinemann, KMCI Press.

Cohen, M.D., March, J.G. and Olsen, J.P. (1972) A Garbage Can Model of Organizational Choice. *Administrative Science Quarterly, 17* (1): 1–25.

Cook, S.D.N. and Brown, J.S. (1999) Bridging Epistemologies: The generative dance between organizational knowledge and organizational knowing. *Organization Science, 10* (4): 381–400.

Dalkir, K. (2011) *Knowledge Management in Theory and Practice*, Cambridge, MA, MIT Press.

Davenport, T.H. and Prusak, L. (1998) *Working Knowledge: How organizations manage what they know*, Boston, MA, Harvard Business School Press.

Davidson, C. and Voss, P. (2002) *Knowledge Management: An introduction to creating competitive advantage from intellectual capital*, Auckland, NZ, Tandem Press.

Descartes, R. (1996) *Meditations on First Philosophy* (J. Cottingham, ed. and trans.), Cambridge, Cambridge University Press.

Dewey, J. (1929) *The Quest for Certainty: A study of the relation of knowledge and action. Gifford Lectures, 1929, London*. London: Allen & Unwin.

Drucker, P.F. (1988) The Coming of the New Organization. Chapter 1 in *Harvard Business Review on Knowledge Management*, Boston, MA, Harvard Business School Press, pp. 1–19.

Drucker, P. (1999) Knowledge-worker Productivity: The biggest challenge. *California Management Review, 41* (2): 79–94.

Dumay, J. (2014) 15 Years of the Journal of Intellectual Capital and Counting: A manifesto for transformational IC research. *Journal of Intellectual Capital, 15* (1): 2–37.

Easterby-Smith, M. and Prieto, I. (2008) Dynamic Capabilities and Knowledge Management: An integrative role for learning? *British Journal of Management, 19* (3): 235–249.

Edmondson, A.C., Winslow, A.B., Bohmer, R.M.J. and Pisano, G.P. (2003) Learning How and Learning What: Effects of tacit and codified knowledge on performance improvement following technology adoption. *Decision Sciences, 34* (2): 197–223.

Empson, L. (2001) Introduction: Knowledge management in professional service firms. *Human Relations, 54* (7): 811–817.

Fuller, S. (2002) *Knowledge Management Foundations*, Burlington, MA, Butterworth-Heinemann.

Grant, R.M. (1996) Towards a Knowledge-based Theory of the Firm. *Strategic Management Journal, 17*: 109–122.

Grant, R.M. (2013) *Contemporary Strategy Analysis*, 8th edition, Chichester, Wiley.

Guthrie, J. and Petty, R. (2000) Intellectual Capital: Australian annual reporting practices. *Journal of Intellectual Capital, 1* (3): 241–251.

Hawking, S. and Mlodinow, L. (2010) *The Grand Design: New answers to the ultimate questions of life*, London, Bantam Press.

Hecker, A. (2012) Knowledge beyond the Individual? Making sense of a notion of collective knowledge in organization theory. *Organization Studies, 33* (3): 423–445.

Hegel, G.W.F. (1997) *On Art, Religion, and the History of Philosophy* (J.G. Gray, ed.), Cambridge, MA, Hackett Publishing.

Hislop, D. (2011) *Knowledge Management in Organizations: A critical introduction*, 3rd edition, Oxford, Oxford University Press.

Huizing, A. and Bouman, W. (2002) Knowledge and Learning, Markets and Organizations. Chapter 11 in Choo, C.W. and Bontis, N. (eds) *The Strategic Management of Intellectual Capital and Organizational Knowledge*, New York, Oxford University Press, pp. 185–206.

Ichijo, K. (2007) Enabling Knowledge-based Competence of a Corporation. Chapter 6 in Ichijo, K. and Nonaka, I. (eds) *Knowledge Creation and Management: New challenges for managers*, New York, Oxford University Press, pp. 83–96.

Jashapara, A. (2004) *Knowledge Management: An integrated approach*, Harlow, Pearson Education.

Jasimuddin, S.M. (2012) *Knowledge Management: An interdisciplinary perspective*, Singapore, World Scientific.

Jung, J., Choi, I. and Song, M. (2007) An Integration Architecture for Knowledge Management Systems and Business Process Management Systems. *Computers in Industry, 58*: 21–34.

Lambe, P. (2007) *Organising Knowledge: Taxonomies, knowledge and organizational effectiveness*, Oxford, Chandos Publishing.

Lengnick-Hall, M.L. and Lengnick-Hall, C.A. (2003) *Human Resource Management in the Knowledge Economy*, San Francisco, Berrett-Koehler.

Leonard, D.A. and Sensiper, S. (2002) The Role of Tacit Knowledge in Group Innovation. *California Management Review, 40* (3): 112–132. Reprinted with new introduction in Choo, C.W. and Bontis, N. (eds) *Strategic Management of Intellectual Capital and Organizational Knowledge*, New York, Oxford University Press.

Locke, J. (1998) *An Essay Concerning Human Understanding* (A.S. Pringle-Pattison and D. Collinson, eds), Ware, Herts, Wordsworth Editions.

Massingham, P. (2015) Knowledge Sharing: What works, what doesn't and why? A critical systems thinking perspective. *Systemic Practice and Action Research*, *28* (3): 197–228.

Massingham, P. (2016) Knowledge Accounts. *Long Range Planning*, *49* (3): 409–425.

Massingham, P. and Diment, K. (2009) Organizational Commitment, Knowledge Management Interventions, and Learning Organization Capacity? *The Learning Organization*, *16* (2): 122–142.

Massingham, P. and Tam, L. (2015) The Relationship between Human Capital, Value Creation, and Employee Reward. *Journal of Intellectual Capital* (Special Issue), *16* (2): 390–418.

Mayo, E. (1933) *The Human Problems of an Industrial Civilization*, New York, Macmillan.

Mingers, J. (2006) *Realising System Thinking: Knowledge and action in management science*, New York, Springer Science.

Nelson, R. (1991) Why Do Firms Differ, and How Does it Matter? *Strategic Management Journal*, *12*: 61–74.

Nelson, R.R. and Winter, S.G. (1977) In Search of a Useful Theory of Innovation. *Research Policy*, *6* (1): 36–77.

Nelson, R.R. and Winter, S.G. (1982) *An Evolutionary Theory of Economic Change*, Cambridge, MA, Harvard University Press.

Neuman, W. (2006) *Social Research Methods: Qualitative and quantitative*, Boston, Pearson International.

Newell, S., Robertson, M., Scarborough, H. and Swan, J. (2002) *Managing Knowledge Work*, Basingstoke, Palgrave Macmillan.

Newell, S., Robertson, M. and Swan, J. (2006) Interactive Innovation Processes and the Problems of Managing Knowledge. Chapter 6 in Renzl, B., Matzler, K. and Hinterhuber, H. (eds) *The Future of Knowledge Management*, New York, Palgrave Macmilan, pp. 115–136.

Nonaka, I. (2002) A Dynamic Theory of Organizational Knowledge Creation. Chapter 24 in Choo, C.W. and Bontis, N. (eds) *The Strategic Management of Intellectual Capital and Organizational Knowledge*, New York, Oxford University Press, pp. 437–462.

Nonaka, I. and Takeuchi, H. (1995) *The Knowledge-Creating Company: How Japanese companies create the dynamics of innovation*, New York, Oxford University Press.

North, K. and Kumta, G. (2014) *Knowledge Management: Value creation through organizational learning*, Cham, Switzerland, Springer International.

Plato (1997) Meno. In Cooper, J.M. (ed.) *Plato: Complete works*, New York, Hackett Publishing.

Polanyi, M. (1962) *Personal Knowledge*, Chicago, IL, University of Chicago Press.

Polanyi, M. (1966) *The Tacit Dimension*, London, Routledge and Kegan Paul.

Polanyi, M. and Prosch, H. (1975) *Meaning*, Chicago, IL, University of Chicago Press.

Quinn, J.B., Anderson, P. and Finkelstein, S. (1998) Managing Professional Intellect: Making the most of the best. Chapter 8 in *Harvard Business Review on Knowledge Management*, Cambridge, MA, Harvard Business School Publishing, pp. 181–206.

Ray, T. (2005) Making Sense of Managing Knowledge. Chapter 1 in Little, S. and Ray, T. (eds) *Managing Knowledge: An essential reader*, London, Sage, pp. 1–20.

Reagans, R. and McEvily, B. (2003) Network Structure and Knowledge Transfer: The effects of cohesion and range. *Administrative Science Quarterly*, *48* (2): 240–267.

Ringberg, T. and Reihlen, M. (2008) Towards a Socio-Cognitive Approach to Knowledge Transfer. *Journal of Management Studies*, *45* (5): 912–935.

Rollett, H. (2003) *Knowledge Management: Processes and technologies*, Norwell, MA, Kluwer Academic Publishers.

Sabherwal, R. and Becerra-Fernandez, I. (2003) An Empirical Study of the Effect of Knowledge Management Processes at Individual, Group, and Organizational Levels. *Decision Sciences, 34* (2): 225–260.

Schön, D. (1983) *The Reflective Practitioner*, New York, Basic Books.

Senge, P.M. (1990) *The Fifth Discipline: The art and practice of the learning organization*, London, Random House.

Spender, J.-C. (1996) Making Knowledge the Basis of a Dynamic Theory of the Firm. *Strategic Management Journal, 17*, Winter Special Issue: 45–62.

Stewart, T.A. (1997) *Intellectual Capital: The new wealth of organizations*, New York, Doubleday.

Taylor, F.W. (1911) *The Principles of Scientific Management*, New York, Harper and Brothers.

Thatchenkery, T. and Chowdhry, D. (2007) *Appreciative Inquiry and Knowledge Management: A social constructivist perspective*, Northampton, MA, Edward Elgar.

Tiwana, A. (2002) *The Knowledge Management Toolkit: Orchestrating IT, strategy, and knowledge platforms*, 2nd edition, Upper Saddle River, NJ, Prentice-Hall.

Tsoukas, H. (1996) The Firm as a Distributed Knowledge System: A constructionist approach. *Strategic Management Journal, 17*: 11–25.

Tsoukas, H. (2003) Do We Really Understand Tacit Knowledge? Chapter 21 in Easterby-Smith, M. and Lyles, M.A. (eds) *Handbook of Organizational Learning and Knowledge Management*, Hong Kong, Blackwell, pp. 410–427.

Tsoukas, H. (2005) Do We Really Understand Tacit Knowledge? Chapter 5 in Little, S. and Ray, T. (eds) *Managing Knowledge: An Essential Reader*, 2nd edition. London: The Open University in association with Sage Publications, pp. 107–125.

Tsoukas, H. and Vladimirou, E. (2001) What is Organizational Knowledge? *Journal of Management Studies, 38* (7): 973–993.

Weick, K.E. (1993) The Collapse of Sense Making in Organizations: The Mann-Gulch disaster. *Administrative Science Quarterly, 38*: 628–652.

Wernerfelt, B. (1984) A Resource-based View of the Firm. *Strategic Management Journal, 9*: 443–454.

Winter, S.G. (1987) Knowledge and Competence as Strategic Assets, in D.J. Teece (ed.) *The Competitive Challenge: Strategy for industrial innovation and renewal*, New York, Harper & Row, pp. 159–184.

Wittgenstein, L. (1953) *Philosophical Investigations* (G.E.M. Anscombe, trans.), Oxford, Blackwell.

Zeleny, M. (2005) *Human Systems Management: Integrating knowledge, management, and systems*, Hackensack, NJ, World Scientific Publishing.

2

KNOWLEDGE MANAGEMENT

CHAPTER OUTLINE

Learning outcomes

Management issues

Links to other chapters

Opening mini case study: Accenture

Introduction

The nature of management

The history of knowledge management

Discipline perspectives on knowledge management

The influence of philosophy: The product and process views of knowledge management

The purpose of knowledge management

Implementing knowledge management

A temporal definition of knowledge management

Conclusion

Closing case study: Knowledge management

LEARNING OUTCOMES

After completing this chapter, the reader should be able to:

1. Define knowledge management and its history
2. Discuss the purpose of knowledge management
3. Contrast the product and process views of knowledge management
4. Discuss the practice of knowledge management and its implementation
5. Discuss different discipline perspectives to knowledge management

MANAGEMENT ISSUES

Knowledge management requires managers to:

1. Understand what knowledge management is
2. Decide on the firm's approach to knowledge management
3. Decide whether the firm's approach to management is scientific or humanist and how this fits with its knowledge management

Knowledge involves these challenges for management:

1. Understanding why you do knowledge management
2. Articulating the value of knowledge management so that it is tangible for stakeholders
3. Considering a temporal perspective about knowledge management – the past, present, and future

LINKS TO OTHER CHAPTERS

Chapter 1: on the definition of knowledge
Chapter 3: concerning the performance of knowledge management
Chapter 5: how knowledge management may contribute to competitive advantage
Chapter 10: how knowledge management can improve productivity
Chapter 11: how knowledge management is supported by organizational systems

OPENING MINI CASE STUDY

ACCENTURE'S BEST PRACTICE KNOWLEDGE MANAGEMENT SYSTEM: IS INFORMATION TECHNOLOGY UNDERMINING HOW CONSULTING FIRMS MANAGE KNOWLEDGE?

Accenture began as the business and technology consulting division of accounting firm Arthur Andersen. It is one the world's leading management consulting and technology services companies. It works with its clients across nearly every major industry to help them 'realize their visions and create tangible value' (Accenture website). It delivers the following services:

- Identifies critical areas with potential for maximum business impact
- Innovates and transforms the processes in these areas
- Delivers performance improvements and lowers operating costs by assuming responsibility for certain business functions or areas (i.e. outsourcing)
- Holds itself accountable for results. (Falk, 2005)

Accenture and Microsoft are the only organizations which have been recognized as Global MAKE Winners every year since the MAKE research studies began in 1998. The Most Admired Knowledge Enterprises (MAKE) study is part of Teleos's MAKE research programme. The MAKE study was established in 2002 to recognize organizations for their ability to create shareholder value (or, in the case of public and non-profit organizations, to increase stakeholder value) by transforming new as well as existing enterprise knowledge into superior products/services/solutions.

Accenture was recognized in the 2014 Global MAKE study for delivering value based on stakeholder knowledge. Accenture is a 17-time Global MAKE winner. Accenture is in the knowledge business: it sells its knowledge to clients. It is an award-winning knowledge factory. How then does it manage its knowledge?

Accenture began its knowledge management journey in 1992 with a Lotus – Notes-based infrastructure put in place to enable consultants to contribute to and find knowledge capital across the firm's global network (Falk, 2005). From these modest beginnings, Accenture's knowledge management system evolved through four phases: (1) early enabling infrastructure – build it and they will come, such as Lotus Notes, discussion databases – the result was global communications; (2) knowledge as a by-product – document libraries, contributions – the result was organizational memory captured; (3) actively managed knowledge – structured, portals, organization-wide KM – the result was quality content delivered when needed; and (4) knowledge-enabled enterprise – enterprise content, continuous learning, enablers, tools – the result was people guided by knowledge (Falk, 2005). Accenture moved towards a knowledge repository approach with an intranet called Knowledge Exchange (KX). By the mid-2000s, the Knowledge Exchange was hosting 400,000 orders for knowledge capital and over 2,000 contributions each month (Falk, 2005).

Accenture began with the aim of connecting people globally. The idea that you could learn from someone collaboratively in another country was very appealing. A culture of knowledge sharing via information technology platforms emerged. Accenture aimed to become a learning organization. Knowledge sharing became intrinsic to the execution of Accenture's business strategy (Falk, 2005).

What did Accenture actually do with its knowledge management? Like most top consulting companies, Accenture divided its business into two structures: industries and service lines. Industries at Accenture included communications, high tech, financial services, products, resources, and government. Service lines included strategy, consulting, digital, technology, and operations. The intranet (Knowledge Exchange) provides access to a wide range of information in these two business structures, including: proposals, client deliverables (e.g. reports), methodologies, White Papers/thought leadership, links to external information (e.g. government reports), project plans, and links to experts (Falk, 2005).

There are two key elements to the success of Accenture's knowledge management system: (1) clear benefits and (2) learning to share. Accenture aims for a 'win–win' situation where all participants benefit from knowledge management. From the organization's perspective, there are benefits in terms of (a) an increased rate of innovation, (b) a decreased time to competency, and (c) increased productivity. From the individual's perspective, there is the opportunity to learn from others' solutions, avoid the same mistakes, reduce duplication, and avoid reinventing the wheel. In terms of learning to share, Accenture employees are trained how to navigate the Knowledge Exchange system, to find what they are looking for, and make contributions.

In reflecting on the way the world's best knowledge factories (i.e. the leading consulting firms) manage knowledge, it is interesting to consider some concerns raised by McKinsey partners about the future of the firm. There was a feeling that technology may erode personal networks. One partner felt that 'there is a dark side to technology … it can drive out communication and people start believing that e-mailing someone is the same thing as talking to them'; another felt that the more time spent searching for information or an expert on an intranet, the less time spent thinking creatively about the problem, adding: 'I worry that as we increase the science, we might lose the craft of what we do' (Mintzberg et al., 2002) (see www.accenture.com/au-en/careers/accenture-way; www.kwork.org/Whitepapers/KMAT_BOK_DOC.pdf).

CASE STUDY QUESTIONS

1. What are Accenture's knowledge resources? (see Chapter 1)
2. Does Accenture's knowledge management try to separate knowledge from the knower? Discuss.
3. What is the most appropriate way to manage knowledge in global consulting firms?
4. Discuss the McKinsey quote about the future of global consulting firms at the end of the case.

INTRODUCTION

Now that we understand what knowledge is, how do we manage it? This is not an easy question to answer. There are many definitions of knowledge management, which reflects its history, its multi-disciplinary nature, its underlying assumptions, and its implementation. The result is fragmented. There is no consensus amongst researchers or practitioners about what knowledge management is. This makes it difficult to know what to do when asked to do knowledge management. Returning to Chapter 1, what may cause us to have justified true belief about knowledge management? There are so many views on this, who should we trust? Who is telling the truth?

CORE CONCEPT: Knowledge management has many definitions influenced by its evolution, its multi-disciplinary nature, and its practice.

Your view on epistemology might influence your opinion. If you are a rationalist, you may be searching for the one best definition. If you are an empiricist, you may be happy to accept that there are multiple good definitions, and which one you use will depend on the organization and its context.

Knowledge management is defined by several contexts:

1. What is management?
2. The history of knowledge management
3. The multi-disciplinary nature of knowledge management
4. The influence of the definition of knowledge
5. The purpose of knowledge management

Together, these contexts provide an important starting point for any organization on its knowledge management journey. They establish a philosophy, a vision, and a sense of meaning and purpose. Together, they form shared mental models about knowledge management which are necessary before the organization takes its next steps on the journey.

CORE CONCEPT: The definition of knowledge management depends on whether you feel knowledge may be separated from the knower. If so, then the product view (codification) may suit you. If not, you may prefer the process view (personalization). Definitions of knowledge management should include its purpose because this focuses on what knowledge management hopes to achieve, and its value for the organization. There are numerous perspectives on the practice of knowledge management. These are organized into architectures, systems, tools, and technologies. This provides a typology of layers of knowledge management from the broad to the very specific, and helps guide implementation. My definition of knowledge management is provided in a Deep Thinking box in the section on a temporal definition of knowledge management later in this chapter. Figure 2.2 also provides a broad context.

The chapter begins by explaining the context of knowledge management. This examines the history of management and knowledge management, its multi-disciplinary nature, and its underlying assumptions. It explains how knowledge management has evolved, why its definitions are fragmented, and its value and purpose. The next section looks at the implementation of knowledge management. This examines how to do knowledge management. The chapter concludes with an alternative definition of knowledge management based on temporal dimensions.

THE NATURE OF MANAGEMENT

Management describes both a type of employee and an organizational function. However, the two aspects are related. Management is about planning, organizing, and controlling, which involves dealing with financial and material resources, as well as people (Hooper and Potter, 2001: 59). It is about making sure people are doing things right. Leadership, on the other hand, is about setting direction, aligning people, and motivating and inspiring them; it is purely about people (Hooper and Potter, 2001: 59). It is about making sure people are doing the right thing.

Chapter 1 described how the history of management has involved two dominant themes: scientific management and humanistic management. Scientific management is the traditional view of management, focusing on control and bringing order and predictability. Humanistic management is about empowering people to bring positive social and organizational change. Knowledge management should be about leadership rather than management (in the scientific management perspective). It should develop positive work attitudes and behaviours such as cooperation, collaboration, teamwork, trust, and respect. Drucker (1988) first explained why scientific management would not work for knowledge management. He proposed that there would be a shift in command and control organizations (scientific management) to information-based organizations: the organization of knowledge specialists (1988). At the time, he said that we do not know what this knowledge organization would look like, but it was the managerial challenge of the future (1988). More than 30 years later, we can now draw a picture of this organization and how it manages knowledge.

THE HISTORY OF KNOWLEDGE MANAGEMENT

Chapter 1 introduced the origins of Western philosophy and the views of Plato and Aristotle. The management of knowledge has been around for a long time. From an organizational perspective, Chapter 1 outlined how scientific management sought to control workers, and how humanistic management emerged to protect them. Penrose (1959) was the first to look at knowledge at an individual firm level, and she suggested two very important ideas: (1) the firm is a repository of knowledge, and (2) the firm's collective experience allows it to develop differential capacity to evaluate its competitive environment and position. Drucker coined the term knowledge worker in the 1960s (Drucker, 1964). In 1969, the launch of the ARPANET allowed scientists and researchers to communicate and share data across computer networks (Dalkir, 2011: 18): the internet was born. The field of strategic management gave theoretical legitimacy in the 1980s and 1990s with the resource-based view (Wernerfelt, 1984) and the knowledge-based view of the firm (Grant, 1996). Senge (1990) popularized organizational learning. Nonaka and Takeuchi (1995) popularized knowledge management with their knowledge-creating company text. The booming information technology industry created widespread interest in knowledge technology and information science. Interest from multiple disciplines exploded. Accounting led the charge with intellectual capital theory. The 1990s had numerous popular books on knowledge measurement – for example, Kaplan and Norton (1996), Edvinsson and Malone (1997), and Sveiby (1997). The past decade has seen the emergence of work on how to do knowledge management, i.e. practice-based research, and most recently, whether it is worth it in the first place. The field is currently focusing on the value created from knowledge management and how to measure its return on investment (e.g. see Massingham and Massingham, 2014).

There have been several attempts to synthesize the chronology of knowledge management. Two examples are discussed. Koenig and Srikantaiah (2007) divide it into three stages:

Stage 1: the internet/intellectual capital phase, consisting of information technology, intellectual capital, and the internet (including intranets). This had a best practices or lessons learned focus.

Stage 2: the human and cultural dimensions, known as the human relations stage, consisting of communities of practice, organizational culture, the learning organization, and the tacit-to-codified knowledge conversion. This had a social practice focus.

Stage 3: the content and retrievability stage, including structuring and descriptors. The focus is on content management and taxonomies.

This interpretation of knowledge management's evolution has a product view of knowledge management, starting with IT and sharing organizational knowledge, switching to the people side to persuade them to cooperate, and ending with a repository perspective and making knowledge accessible. It assumes that knowledge can be represented as a thing, to be separated from the knower (notwithstanding stage 2). Ponzi (2007) provides further support for the argument that knowledge management's birth was due to technology and computers in particular. An analysis of the early publications in knowledge management by discipline showed that computer science dominated, hitting a peak of 43% of publications in KM in 1997 (still 36% in 2001) (Ponzi, 2007). The journals supporting KM in these early days were all about information or computers; for example, the main outlet between 1995 and 2001 was *Information Week* (5.6% of total KM-based articles) followed by *Computer World* (4.5%) (Ponzi, 2007). The first business journal on the list was the *Journal of Intellectual Capital* (ranked 14th with 1.3%) (Ponzi, 2007). This illustrates the IT focus for early knowledge management.

North and Kumta (2014) provide an interesting alternative perspective on knowledge management using a maturity model:

First degree of maturity: IT solutions, looking at knowledge as symbols and data

Second degree of maturity: specific individual solutions, looking at knowledge as information and finding meaning

Third degree of maturity: professional knowledge organization, looking at knowledge and know-how, and introducing a process view of KM initiatives such as networking, as well as a product view of KM initiatives such as technologies

Fourth degree of maturity: knowledge-based management of company, linking actions (motivation) and competence (strategy) with competitiveness (uniqueness). (After North and Kumta, 2014: 37–39)

DEEP THINKING: North and Kumta (2014)'s model provides the sensible perspective that organizations go through a learning cycle in terms of their knowledge management activities, and that organizations that have been doing it for some time, i.e. mature KM organizations, are likely to be doing much more than those at the start of their KM journey. It is also aspirational in the sense that organizations may seek to attain the fourth degree of maturity to capture true value from knowledge management.

The chronology of knowledge management's evolution may be summarized in terms of a timeline in Figure 2.1.

The two fundamental influences on our current view of knowledge management are (a) the resource-based view of the firm (RBV) and (b) humanistic management theory. Nelson and Winter (1977, 1982) developed the first ideas about how knowledge contributes to technological change and also organizational knowledge (routines). It was the precursor to the RBV. The humanistic view of management (Mayo to Weick) argued that human factors play a big role in productivity (e.g. motivation). From our perspective, humanistic theory morphed into several important themes:

1. Shared experience, group dynamics, social capital, social network analysis (see Chapter 9)
2. Organizational culture, learning organization (see Chapter 8)
3. Psychological contract, cognitive knowledge (see Chapter 4).

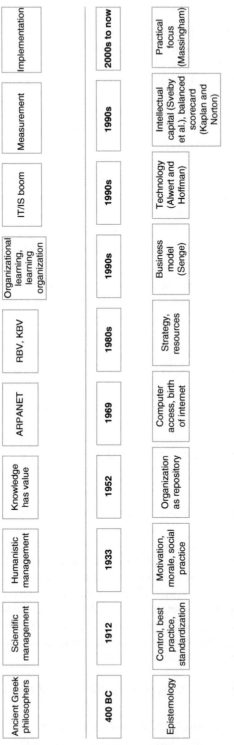

FIGURE 2.1 *A summary timeline of knowledge management*

Drucker (1999) introduced the concept of the knowledge society (or economy). In this society, the basic economic resource is no longer capital or natural resources, or labour, but it is and will be knowledge, and it will create the new role of 'knowledge workers'. The management of knowledge in organizations is primarily about managing these knowledge workers. Organizational learning emerged. Theories such as double-loop learning (e.g. Argyris and Schön, 1996) focused on improving organizational performance by challenging the underlying assumptions of how work is done. This thinking introduced learning into performance, taking staff training out of the classroom and into the workplace. The outcome was continual business process improvement. This led to the current phase of knowledge management which focuses on generating practical value for organizations (e.g. Massingham and Massingham, 2014).

DISCIPLINE PERSPECTIVES ON KNOWLEDGE MANAGEMENT

There are multiple disciplines interested in knowledge management. These include anthropology, economics, sociology, strategic management, humanresource management, library and information science, philosophy, management science, computer science, psychology, accounting, cognitive science, and journalism. They employ technologies like helpdesk systems, database technologies, collaborative technologies, electronic performance and support systems, document and information management, decision support systems, web technologies, artificial intelligence, and technical writing.

This is a large list of diverse fields with an interest in KM. The latter field, journalism for example, shows how accessible KM is for researchers and practitioners. A journalist interested in oral histories might use their skills to capture knowledge and codify it for others. People with technical skills can get involved in multiple areas associated with knowledge repositories and their accessibility. KM is a fascinating discipline because it is so accessible, and as a result it is indeed multi-disciplinary. However, this presents challenges in finding a satisfactory definition of KM because these disciplines see KM differently.

Cognitive science, for example, looks at how KM contributes to intelligence. This field tends to look at knowledge as enabling intelligence, i.e. being smart, and KM as producing smart behaviour. A typical definition is:

> Knowledge – the insights, understandings, and practical know-how that we all possess – is the fundamental resource that allows us to function intelligently ... Knowledge is ... the principal factor that makes personal, organizational, and societal intelligent behaviour possible. (Wiig, 1993: 38–39)

Library and information science sees KM as information management. A typical definition is as follows:

> KM is predominantly seen as information management by another name. (Davenport and Cronin, 2000: 294)

The view of library and information science focuses on codified knowledge, such as texts and documents, and ignores the fact that KM also involves a far more complex domain: individual knowledge and the management of tacit knowledge.

Information science (IS) focuses on how information is turned into knowledge and made accessible for those who need it. A typical definition is as follows:

> Knowledge management is the concept under which information is turned into actionable knowledge. (Angus et al., 1998: 59)

Information science researchers argue that technology has created the need for knowledge management and is the reason for its growing popularity. Pearlson and Saunders (2006), for example, argue that managing knowledge is not new – ancient civilizations did it but that it has suddenly gained interest due to new collaborative technologies and the emergence of the internet and intranets. The authors are also dismissive of the people side of knowledge management, arguing that while knowledge has always been important to the success of organizations, the natural informal flow of knowledge between people meant there was no need to actually manage it (see Pearlson and Saunders, 2006). They propose that the changing nature of work has made knowledge management necessary; and that as work has become more complex and chaotic, a sharing of best practices has become increasingly important (2006).

THE INFLUENCE OF PHILOSOPHY: THE PRODUCT AND PROCESS VIEWS OF KNOWLEDGE MANAGEMENT

Chapter 1 illustrated the many definitions of knowledge. Your view of knowledge will influence your definition of knowledge management. Your view of epistemology will determine whether you see knowledge as tacit or codified, and as owned by individuals, groups, or organizations.

Your views will determine the fundamental question in knowledge management: can knowledge be separated from the knower? This question divides the knowledge management discipline. Some feel that knowledge may be captured, codified, and shared with others who may then reuse it. This view is common to many definitions of KM. Others feel that knowledge is personal and its management must be done through social practice.

Easterby-Smith and Lyles (2005) argue that the idea of knowledge management is based on simple logic. If we accept the 'neo-economic view' of the strategic value of knowledge, then we use familiar IT software such as databases and electronic conferencing, i.e. virtual collaboration, to facilitate the acquisition, sharing, storage, retrieval, and utilization of knowledge (Easterby-Smith and Lyles, 2005: 12). This assumes that knowledge is valuable and, therefore, we need to use technology to manage it. It is a view that KM can separate knowledge from the knower. Easterby-Smith and Lyles (2005) acknowledge this by stating that this definition ignores the social architecture of knowledge exchange within organizations, thereby at least alluding to the importance of the social practice view of KM.

A good way to examine these two perspectives on knowledge management is the product versus process view of KM.

CORE CONCEPT: The product view implies that knowledge is a thing that can be located and manipulated as an independent object. This view of KM tries to separate the knowledge from the knower.

The product view is based on managing structural capital: document-management systems, databases, and lessons learned. It is about sharing best practices, standard operating procedures, and storage and retrieval (i.e. structuring repositories) (after Mentzas et al., 2003: 4). The product view has these characteristics:

- Focus: capturing and storing knowledge
- Strategy: exploitation of reusable knowledge, linking people through technology
- Human resources: recruitment focus on reusing knowledge, passive training (courses) rewarded for using and contributing
- Information technology: heavy investment in IT retrieval tools
- IT here focuses on multiplatform storage and retrieval, internet, intranet, and file servers
- Search engine tools and artificial intelligence are the big movers in terms of theoretical development on this view of KM. (Mentzas et al., 2003: 5)

THEORY IN PRACTICE

Mature knowledge companies tend to adopt a product view. They do this because they have invested in enabling systems, including information technology which supports the capture, sharing, and use of knowledge (see Chapter 11). The product view also tends to be adopted by large organizations, particularly global companies, due to their scope of operations. Organizations like Kraft, for example, adopt a product view of KM due to their business complexity. Kraft is the world's second-largest processed foods company and has more than 80 brands that generate annual revenues of more than $100 million each. The company is organized by geographic region and product sector. The main opportunity to create synergy across these multiple businesses globally is via its value chain. Synergy may be created in its downstream value chain, i.e. distribution channels. This tends to

(Continued)

> (Continued)
>
> emerge in cross-selling and joint promotional activities, where opportunities for skills transfer and sharing of best practices exist – for example, for Kraft Foods in biscuits, cheese, and beverages. Mature products or services, like Kraft's established brands, also require less innovation and less haste in decision making. This means that there is more time to capture, store, and share best practices.

The process view is also known as the personalization approach. It emphasizes ways to promote, motivate, encourage, nurture, or guide the process of knowing, and abolishes the idea of trying to capture and distribute knowledge (Mentzas et al., 2003: 4). Knowledge is closely tied to the person who created it and is shared through person-to-person contact. The process view has these characteristics:

- Focus: human contact and relationships
- Strategy: build social capital/networks, facilitate discussion
- Human resources: recruitment creativity, on-the-job training (learning by doing), rewarded for group work
- Information technology: heavy investment in IT retrieval tools
- IT here focuses on virtual workspaces encouraging interaction (e.g. groupware)
- Workflow and document management software are helpful if people can use them to share experiences
- Communities of practice (CoP) is the biggest tool and there is growing interest in virtual CoP (e.g. online collaboration). (Mentzas et al., 2003: 5)

DEEP THINKING: The product view and the process view present two contrasting opinions of knowledge management. Which one is best? The answer is defined by the product or service. Mature or standardized products should use the product view. Customized or very innovative products should use the process view. An integrated view, i.e. using both the product and the process views, requires facilitating tacit flow combined with management of best practice.

KNOWLEDGE COMES FROM INTERACTION AND DEBATE

CORE CONCEPT: The process view sees KM as a social communication process, facilitated by collaboration and cooperation support tools. This view of KM does not try to separate the knowledge from the knower.

These two views were contrasted in recent articles on managing knowledge resources and knowledge flows (Massingham, 2014a, 2014b). The KM toolkits examined in the knowledge resources article most closely fit with the product view in the sense that knowledge is represented as an object that can be separated from the knower and grown, retained, and measured. That article defined the management of knowledge resources as identifying the firm's competitive position in terms of what it knows (strategy), protecting this position (retention), growing this position (creativity), and benchmarking (measurement) (Massingham, 2014a).

THEORY IN PRACTICE

Immature knowledge companies (i.e. those new to KM) tend to adopt a process view. They do this because they do not have the enabling systems necessary to separate knowledge from knowers and share this with others. The process view also tends to be adopted by small to medium-sized organizations because they generally have simpler organizations and cannot afford to invest in KM enablers.

The KM toolkits examined in the knowledge flows article (Massingham, 2014b) most closely fit with the process view of KM (see Mentzas et al., 2003) in the sense that knowledge movement is best done by creating organizational systems that enable socialization (sharing), targeted learning (acquisition), and mentoring (usage). The toolkits do include some aspects of the product view, i.e. knowledge preservation, but there is still a strong focus on using individuals with relevant tacit knowledge to provide accessibility to the captured knowledge (e.g. metadata). In summary, the article defined the management of knowledge flows and enablers as connecting those who know (senders) with those who need to know (receivers) (sharing); sharing experience (usage); using external experts to fill competency gaps (acquisition); and capturing collective wisdom and making this accessible (preservation) (Massingham, 2014b).

THE PURPOSE OF KNOWLEDGE MANAGEMENT

Some definitions of knowledge management focus on its purpose. These definitions are helpful because they focus on what knowledge management hopes to achieve, and its value for the organization. The main themes in these definitions are:

1. To create competitive advantage
2. To improve performance
3. To become a learning organization
4. To improve knowledge sharing
5. To increase knowledge resources.

TO CREATE COMPETITIVE ADVANTAGE

The first purpose of knowledge management is to achieve sustainable competitive advantage. This thinking emerged from strategic management theory – more specifically, the resource-based view of the firm (RBV) and the knowledge-based view of the firm (KBV). While some argue that Nonaka and Takeuchi's (1995) book was the cause of the KM boom (see Easterby-Smith and Lyles, 2005), the RBV and KBV gave it legitimacy and academic credibility. The RBV emerged in the early 1980s (Wernerfelt, 1984). It represented a theory of the firm designed to explain inter-firm performance differences outside of the market (Conner and Prahalad, 2002). It aimed to identify sources of competitive advantage which the firm could control. The RBV is based on the idea that the firm is essentially a pool of resources and capabilities, and that these resources and capabilities are the primary determinants of success (Grant, 2002a). In this theory, competitive advantage was attained through the development and deployment of resources and capabilities. Inter-firm differences would emerge either by superior access to these resources or better implementation. The challenge was to identify what resources and capabilities created competitive advantage. There was no silver bullet: the answer is contextual and varies by industry and firm. However, RBV researchers did develop two practical guidelines. First, they identified a typology of resources: tangible – financial and physical; intangible – technology, reputation, and culture; and human – skills/know-how, capacity for communication and collaboration, and motivation (Grant, 2002a). These resources combine to provide capacity to undertake a particular productive activity, which is called capabilities (Grant, 2013). The second practical guideline was a set of criteria to identify the value of resources and capabilities, called the profit or rent-earning potential (Grant, 2013). These included scarcity, relevance, replicability, and so on. The importance of the RBV for knowledge management was that it highlighted the importance of knowledge as a resource and its value in combining with other resources to create important capabilities. It was the closest thing to a silver bullet explaining sustainable competitive advantage.

The KBV emerged out of the RBV in response to a growing recognition of knowledge as a productive resource (Grant, 2002b). It replicated the logic of the RBV, differing only in that it saw the firm as a set of knowledge assets and focused on the role of the firm in generating and deploying these assets to create value (Grant, 2002a). In terms of knowledge management, the KBV was helpful in identifying two systems – (1) knowledge generation (exploration) and (2) knowledge application (exploitation) along with a set of knowledge tools (which the KBV called knowledge processes) which included:

1. Knowledge generation:
   a. knowledge creation – research
   b. knowledge acquisition – training, recruitment, intellectual property licensing, benchmarking.

2. Knowledge application:

   a. knowledge integration – new product development, operations
   b. knowledge sharing – strategic planning, communities of practice
   c. knowledge replication – best practices transfer, on-the-job training
   d. knowledge storage and organization – databases, standard operating procedures
   e. knowledge measurement – intellectual capital accounting, competency modelling
   f. knowledge identification – project reviews, competency modelling. (After Grant, 2002a: 179)

This is a helpful list as it includes many of the KM processes commonly associated with effective knowledge management.

CORE CONCEPT: The KBV's real value lies in how it can extend existing theories and techniques about management and organizations.

The KBV challenges us to think of these things in different ways. It does so through its underlying assumptions, which help us to recognize the importance of knowledge and its role in 21st century organizations:

1. Knowledge is the most valuable resource.
2. Knowledge varies in its transferability.
3. Knowledge is subject to economies of scale and scope – it is expensive to create but relatively cheap to replicate.
4. Knowledge is created by human beings – specialization is good (i.e. subject matter expertise).
5. Producing anything of value, such as a product or service, usually requires application of knowledge. (Grant, 2002a: 136)

The KBV, therefore, uses these assumptions to provide a sense of purpose about KM. If these assumptions are accepted, it is easier to persuade managers and staff that KM is worthwhile, and to begin to discuss how to do it.

Massingham (2004) developed an early framework for linking business strategy and knowledge management activities, in a stage model connecting KM with strategy-making processes. Table 2.1 summarizes Massingham's (2004) model of knowledge-based strategy making.

TABLE 2.1   Massingham's (2004) model of knowledge-based strategy-making processes

Stage no.	Stage title	Actions
1	Clarify strategy	Decide on the generic strategy to be used and get buy-in to it from senior management
2	Identify strategic themes	Determine the activities that are key to achieving the strategy
3	Identify knowledge resources	Identify the role of knowledge resources which are key to the agreed strategy
4	Evaluate knowledge resources	Evaluate whether the firm's existing knowledge resources are adequate to allow the effective execution of the firm's strategic activities
5	Make knowledge decision	Decide what actions are necessary to develop and/or sustain the firm's resources

TO IMPROVE PERFORMANCE

The second purpose of knowledge management is to achieve change in performance. Research in this area has a pragmatic approach, with two themes: (1) business process improvement and (2) capability development.

The business process improvement theme looks at knowledge management as a way to solve problems. The key aspects of this definition are access and action. Becerra-Fernandez and Sabherwal (2010) define knowledge management as introducing systems and processes which allow knowledge to be used to benefit the organization. The main focus is to make knowledge available for use. Similarly, Gorelick et al. (2004: 3) provide this definition: 'knowledge management is fundamentally a systematic approach for optimizing the access, for individuals and teams within an organization, to relevant actionable advice, knowledge and experience from elsewhere.' Knowledge management from this perspective is about getting people sharing knowledge and then using it. A further example is provided by Probst et al. (2002) who suggest that knowledge management should translate the organization's problems into knowledge problems, help understand these problems, focus on action and solutions, and fit within existing systems. Heisig (2003) proposed business-process-oriented knowledge management as the most effective way to integrate knowledge management with business process improvement (BPI). There are two main reasons behind this approach to KM:

1. The business process provides the context for knowledge, leading to a user-focused assessment of the knowledge used and produced in business tasks.
2. It enables a greater involvement of employees, which helps achieve their commitment and motivation from improvements to the way knowledge is handled. (After Heisig, 2003: 15–16)

These are very sound principles which allow for the practical reality of how knowledge may be used to create value via work (i.e. processes) and the humanistic management necessary to persuade people to use knowledge (i.e. involvement). Heisig's (2003: 15) model has the interesting perspective of supply and demand. Based on the design of four dimensions – (1) apply, (2) distribute, (3) store, and (4) generate – the demand side manages what happens for those who seek knowledge (i.e. those who need to know), while the supply side manages how those who have knowledge (i.e. the knower) can provide this to seekers. It is an interesting framework for addressing the epistemological (tacit versus codified) and ontological (individual, group, and organization) issues, and maps various KM tools over these dimensions.

Recent research has found that practitioners realize that knowledge management (KM) requires an investment of scarce resources, and that they are, therefore, interested in 'managing knowledge not for the sake of knowledge management, but because ... it can support business performance improvements' (Schiuma, 2012: 516). Research on KM and business process improvement has focused on a diverse range of KM systems including: knowledge capture (Gavrilova and Andreeva, 2012), knowledge usage (Canonico et al., 2012), knowledge creation (Iacono et al., 2012), knowledge strategy (Bettiol et al., 2012), knowledge measurement (Andreeva and Kianto, 2012; Lerro et al., 2012), learning (Di Vincenzo et al., 2012), and knowledge sharing (Franssila et al., 2012; Vuori and Okkonen, 2012). Of these articles, only two – Andreeva and Kianto (2012) and Iacono et al. (2012) – really look at how KM improves business performance: the former because it distinguishes between knowledge processes and knowledge management (KM) practices; the latter because it looks at the relationships between the processes of knowledge creation and transfer, and business performance improvements. The other articles mainly look at the KM system itself, and not how the system is connected to other business capabilities. Edmondson et al. (2003) found that improvement rates are higher for dimensions of performance that rely on tacit knowledge rather than codified knowledge. This finding illustrates the importance of knowledge sharing as a social practice. It supports a conceptualization of BPI via removing waste points in knowledge flows, which is covered in Chapter 10.

The second theme is capability development. This approach looks at knowledge management as a capability which improves firm performance, defined by processes and infrastructure (Gold et al., 2001). This model distinguishes between KM activities (referred to as knowledge process capability) and enablers (referred to as knowledge infrastructure capability) (Gold et al., 2001).

The KM process elements are:

- Acquisition:
  - Seek and acquire new knowledge
  - Create new knowledge out of existing knowledge

- Conversion:
  - o Organize and structure knowledge
  - o Transform tacit knowledge to explicit
- Application:
  - o Store and retrieve
  - o Security:
  - o Protect against inappropriate use and theft (e.g. punishments).
    (After Gold et al., 2001)

Recent research in this area seems to focus on innovation as the 'engine for competitiveness and sustainability' (Schiuma, 2012: 516). KM creates value via innovation in broad capabilities such as customer and stakeholder management, product development, researching of new market opportunities, development and engagement of human resources, reorganization of the supply chain, and development of new business models (2012: 516). This research highlights how KM creates value by improving the way capabilities are performed.

TO BECOME A LEARNING ORGANIZATION

The third purpose of knowledge management is to achieve a business model called the learning organization (see Chapter 8). This is an aspirational organizational design which captures a way of doing business which enables the behaviours, attitudes, and processes that support knowledge management and the management of knowledge workers. A breakthrough in the development of the learning organization model came in the early 1960s with the idea that an organization could learn in ways that were independent of the individuals within it – this was key in the development of the theory (Cyert and March, 1963). The model was grounded in a general theory of organizational learning as part of a model of decision making within the firm. Argyris and Schön (1978) pointed out that human behaviour within organizations frequently does not follow economic rationality. Both individuals and organizations seek to protect themselves from the unpleasant experience of learning by establishing defensive routines.

The concept of a learning organization emerged in the late 1980s but was popularized by Senge (1990). The learning organization is one that learns from experience, responds to change, and grows its capability. Senge's (1990) book defines four attributes of a learning organization: personal mastery, mental models, shared vision, and team learning. Easterby-Smith and Lyles (2005) distinguish knowledge management as a separate field from three interrelated fields: organizational learning, the learning organization, and organizational knowledge. The learning organization is examined in detail in Chapter 8.

TO IMPROVE KNOWLEDGE SHARING

The fourth purpose of knowledge management is to increase connectivity between those who have knowledge (knowers) and those who need knowledge (seekers) (see Chapter 9). Dalkir (2011) calls this the business perspective of KM. The following definition suggests that the aim is to capture knowledge from individuals and share it with others:

> Knowledge management is the process by which we manage human centred assets ... the function of knowledge management is to guard and grow knowledge owned by individuals, and where possible, transfer the asset into a form where it can be more readily shared by other employees in the company. (Brooking, 1999: 154)

This leads to discussion of how knowledge sharing can be managed. The power of connectivity lies in the idea of knowledge reuse. If I tell five people what I know, and they each tell five different people, all of a sudden 125 people will know what I know. I have not lost my knowledge, and it can all happen in the blink of an eye or a click of a mouse. The question is, how should I share my knowledge? There are two schools of thought. First, the technology view or product view of knowledge management looks at information systems and information technology as the way to increase connectivity between knowers and seekers, and also provides seekers with access to organizational knowledge, such as policy, procedures, reports, and data. This is about knowledge capture and codification (e.g. see Alavi and Tiwana, 2005). Second, the people view or process view of knowledge management looks at social practice as the best way to share knowledge. This is about providing opportunities for people to socialize for real, such as in meetings or in virtual environments, for example online (e.g. see von Krogh, 2005).

The technology view dominated the early evolution of knowledge management; but more recent research has found technology to be a support function rather than the main driver of connectivity. It raises important questions about the relationship between knowledge, technology, and social interaction. The technology view tends to see knowledge management as information-seeking behaviour. If an individual does not know something, they use technology to help find the answers. However, researchers have argued that meaning comes from engagement practices with other people, rather than a computer. The implication is that learning comes from a cultivation of judgement rather than the acquisition of information (Aakhus, 2007).

DEEP THINKING: Knowledge comes from interaction and debate where people work out the truths, commitments, perspectives, and identities central to their work (Aakhus, 2007: 2). People find justified true belief via interaction with other people,

(Continued)

(Continued)

not via interaction with technology. What then is the role of technology? It plays an important role as a pragmatic web, enabling human meaning negotiation – it facilitates individuals and groups to interact, negotiate, and find meaning (Aakhus, 2007). Therefore, technology is an important enabler but is an idle resource unless people use it to connect with other people and their knowledge.

Recent developments in systems thinking and social construction have improved the understanding of knowledge sharing. This has developed a knowledge-sharing paradigm that views knowledge as a systemic, socially constructed, context-specific representation of reality. In this conceptualization, knowledge dissemination describes the internal transfer of knowledge within an organization. The disseminative capacity builds on social capital networks and explains 'knowledge flow' as the rotation between the sender and receiver to enable dissemination. In this way, useful knowledge *spreads* and remains embedded within multiple social structures (Swan and Scarbrough, 2005). The management of knowledge, therefore, should focus primarily on building social structures that can diffuse and embed tacit knowledge, which provides support for the people view of knowledge management.

TO INCREASE KNOWLEDGE RESOURCES

The fifth purpose of knowledge management is to increase the organizational knowledge base (OKB) (see Chapter 5). Dalkir (2011) calls this the knowledge assets perspective of knowledge management. There are two themes from this perspective of KM: (a) measuring the OKB (i.e. what does the organization know?) and (b) workforce planning (i.e. enterprise management).

The first theme involves the theory of intellectual capital which emerged in the early 1990s in response to growing interest in intangible assets. Intellectual capital research examines the measurement and reporting of intangible assets, such as knowledge resources. Chapter 4 provides further details.

The second theme is enterprise resource planning, which includes competency mapping, strategic human resource management, and workforce planning. Massingham (2016) has recently developed a method to measure the value of individual knowledge called the Knowledge Accounts, which is discussed in Chapter 4.

Figure 2.2 provides a summary of this section and a checklist to use when assessing an organization's context. The context helps find answers to the questions about knowledge management:

1. What are we doing? (Strategic)
2. Why are we doing it? (Tactical)

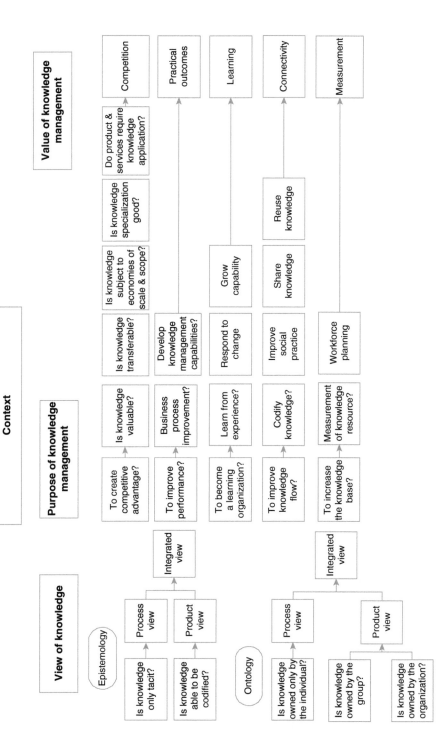

FIGURE 2.2 *The context of choosing a knowledge management system*

On the left-hand side of the figure, the questions will help you identify whether the product or the process view best fits the organization or whether both fit, i.e. the integrated view. In the middle of the figure, the questions will help you determine the purpose of doing knowledge management. As you move along each row in the figure, you will be able to reflect on the real purpose, leading towards the final boxes at the right-hand side of the figure. These clarify the organization's objectives with knowledge management.

IMPLEMENTING KNOWLEDGE MANAGEMENT

Many definitions of knowledge management focus on its implementation or how to do it. These approaches define knowledge management implementation at various levels, involving different layers of detail. They may be summarized in terms of the following:

1. *Architectures*: these are a blueprint which provides a common understanding of what the organization is trying to do with its knowledge management. They represent a set of *capabilities* which the organization hopes to develop from its knowledge management. They are most useful if translated into managerial terms rather than knowledge management jargon, as this makes them more accessible for managers.

2. *Systems: these are frameworks* that design the set of activities necessary to achieve the organization's knowledge management objectives. They represent a delivery mechanism for providing knowledge management to the organization. It is helpful if they are linked to the organization's architecture, so managers can see the relationships in a cascading effect. Their descriptors are usually knowledge management language.

3. *Tools*: these are steps that organizations take to perform knowledge management activities. They represent specific knowledge management *initiatives* or *actions*. It is helpful if they are linked to the architecture and systems. They are sometimes called knowledge processes or practices.

4. *Technologies*: these include hardware, software, and services that enable organizations to *facilitate* knowledge management. They represent the information technology and information systems part of knowledge management. Their main focus is on the capture and codification of knowledge but they are also important in providing access for knowledge seekers both to people, i.e. knowers, and to organizational knowledge.

These layers of knowledge management implementation combine to represent a complete picture of how to do KM. Few definitions of knowledge management from researchers or practitioners cover all four layers. They may be used to identify the type of knowledge management at any organization and also gaps in the implementation strategy.

KNOWLEDGE ARCHITECTURES

Knowledge architectures are described in various ways, including as models, schools, cycles, and dimensions. In the literature, there are two types of models proposed as architectures. The first are theoretical models which have had significant influence on the practice of knowledge management. Nonaka and Takeuchi's (1995) knowledge-creating spiral is an example. Dalkir (2011) includes a chapter on knowledge management models, including the Choo sensemaking model, the Boisot I-Space KM model, and the EFQM KM model. He argues that knowledge management needs 'conceptual frameworks', i.e. these models, 'to operate within', because 'otherwise, the activities will not be coordinated and the expected benefits will not result' (Dalkir, 2011: 59). He is proposing that these models help management and staff make sense of knowledge management, and develop shared mental models about what KM is and how to do it. If so, these models represent an initial step in the KM architecture. However, in my experience, starting with conceptual models is a recipe for disaster. Practitioners see this as too theoretical, too abstract, and largely irrelevant to the practical reality of their working environment.

The second type of model is the typology. Three typologies are discussed here. The first is from Hansen et al. (1999) who developed a codification versus personalization framework. The codification strategy creates the 'possibility of achieving scale in knowledge reuse and thus of growing the business' (Hansen et al., 1999: 108). It aims to codify knowledge 'using a "people-to-documents" approach: it is extracted from the person who developed it, made independent of that person, and reused for various purposes' (1999: 108). The main KM activity is to transfer knowledge from people to documents; the human resource management implications are to 'motivate people to codify their knowledge, provide training in relevant information technology, and reward people for codifying' (1999: 109). The personalization strategy aims to improve the socialization of knowledge sharing, i.e. 'face-to-face' contact between knowledge workers (1999: 115). The model is helpful as the forerunner of the product (codification) versus process (socialization) view of KM.

The second typology comes from Earl (2001) who summarized the different approaches to knowledge management at the time by identifying seven schools classified into three broad approaches. The first approach is technocratic, which is IT driven, and includes three schools: systems (codification into databases), cartographic (expert registers connecting experts with others, for instance social network mapping), and engineering (sharing codified knowledge about operational tasks and processes) (Earl, 2001: 218). The second approach is economic, which is profit driven, and has one school: commercial ('explicitly concerned with both protecting and exploiting a firm's knowledge or intellectual assets to produce revenue streams'; 2001: 222). The third approach is behavioural, which enables people to share knowledge with one another, and includes three schools: organizational (communities of practice supported by organizational culture and IT-mediated interaction tools), spatial (creation of spaces, both physical and virtual, enabling people to interact), and strategic (culture, shaping attitudes and behaviours, raising awareness of KM and encouraging communication, teamwork, and so on) (Earl, 2001: 223–229). Even though this framework was developed some time ago now, it is still very helpful in classifying the different KM approaches. It is particularly useful in organizing the multi-disciplinary nature of KM, and the three broad approaches – technocratic, commercial, and behavioural – cover a lot of ground. As an architecture, it also allows for the possibility that a single organization may have multiple ways of managing KM: some parts of the business could benefit from a technocratic approach, others from a behavioural approach, and so on. The product and process views of KM are not necessarily mutually exclusive.

The third typology of knowledge management presented here is Alvesson and Karreman's (2001) knowledge management approaches. It combines four management philosophies as the basis for developing four approaches to knowledge management. The management approaches have two dimensions: 'mode of managerial intervention and mode of interaction' (2001: 1004). The former refers to degree of control and has two concepts: coordination (weak management) and control (strong management). The latter refers to degree of social connection and has two concepts: attitude-centred (encouraging positive attitudes like cooperation) and technostructural (encouraging positive behaviours like teamwork). By combining these four approaches in a 2 × 2 matrix, Alvesson and Karreman (2001: 1005) identified four KM approaches. *Coordination and social* lead to a community approach, with a focus on the sharing of ideas. It is manifested in the idea of communities of practice as a voluntary activity: you cannot force it; you can only encourage it, and hope it works out. *Coordination and technostructural* lead to an extended library, with a focus on information exchange. It is manifested in the idea of intranets, and bureaucratic repositories of how we do business – full of policies and procedures. *Control and social* lead to a normative control approach, with a focus on prescribed interpretations. It is manifested in terms of cultural control, such as the learning organization, where employees are encouraged to 'buy into' KM and adopt the necessary cultural norms and values. *Control and technostructural* lead to enacted blueprints, with a focus on templates for action. It is manifested in the sharing of lessons learned and best practice.

A common approach in the literature is to view knowledge management as a series of cycles. An example is Dalkir's (2011: 53) integrated KM cycle based on three broad systems:

1. Knowledge capture and creation, which are assessed to ...
2. Knowledge sharing and dissemination, which are contextualized to ...
3. Knowledge acquisition and application, which are then updated to begin the cycle again.

This architecture captures some of the main elements of knowledge management: essentially separating the knowledge from the knower, making it accessible for others, and then using it to create value. The notion of knowledge management being a circular and continuous cycle, rather than a linear movement from the knower to user, is useful and fits with the concept of organizational learning and knowledge growth.

Stankosky (2005) was one of the pioneers of knowledge management in the sense that he moved from being a practitioner to an academic in 1998 and set about designing a curriculum to teach students KM. His approach has four pillars of knowledge management:

1. *Leadership/management*: covers knowledge strategy and the decisions associated with effective KM, with a focus on using knowledge resources to create value

2. *Organization*: addresses the operational issues of KM, i.e. implementation, with a focus on metrics and business process improvement

3. *Learning*: looks at the behavioural aspects or the people side of KM, with a focus on sharing and learning organization attributes

4. *Technology*: the tools necessary to support KM, with a focus on codification, i.e. separating knowledge from the knower. (After Stankosky, 2005)

This is a practical and sensible definition of KM. It includes strategy and both the people and technology side of KM. Therefore, it covers both the product and process view of KM, and ensures these activities are linked to value creation.

Davenport and Prusak (1998) made two important contributions: (1) the way they discuss knowledge management systems and (2) their discussion of KM in practice. Davenport and Prusak's (1998) KM system had these elements: (a) generation (i.e. creation), (b) codification (i.e. making it accessible), (c) transfer (i.e. sharing), (d) roles and skills, and (e) technologies. This is a typical list and it includes elements common to many knowledge systems. The only different area is the concept of roles and skills. This is something rarely covered by definitions of KM. Davenport and Prusak address the important issue of not making KM a separate, additional, and often isolated function, while also recognizing that some knowledge management activities require specialists and, therefore, people with new skills. This topic is covered in Chapter 11 under the heading of Organizational Structure. In terms of knowledge management practice, Davenport and Prusak (1998) found these tools were common: (a) expert networks (i.e. communities of practice), (b) document repositories (i.e. codification), (c) new knowledge (i.e. creation), (d) a lessons learned database (i.e. use), and (e) evaluation and compensation (i.e. learning organization – behaviour). It is helpful as it includes aspects of both the product view (e.g. repositories) and the process view (e.g. expert teams).

KNOWLEDGE SYSTEMS

The difference between knowledge architecture and systems lies in the level of detail. Whereas architectures are broad capabilities which enable knowledge management to take place in organisations, systems are specific activities required to implement knowledge management.

The theory of systems thinking provides an understanding of knowledge systems. Systems thinking places knowledge management within the situational context of the organization's environment, particularly social practice. In this way, it extends the humanistic view of management by arguing that organizations are living organisms not machines. This perspective has been studied by the field of human systems management, which is about living beings, their learning and action, their networks, orders and systems, and interaction and communication (Zeleny, 2005). Zeleny argues that knowledge management has suffered from a lack of process orientation. Therefore, definitions of knowledge systems included here have a focus on processes, i.e. the day-to-day routines that involve knowledge management.

Dalkir (2011: 31) cites four main approaches to KM systems (he calls them cycles), namely those designed by Meyer and Zack (1996), Bukowitz and Williams (2000), McElroy (2003), and Wiig (1993). The Meyer and Zack approach focuses on capturing, storing, and sharing knowledge. It is very much a product view of KM and it aims to separate knowledge from the knower via acquisition, validating this knowledge (refining), storing it, distributing it (online), and presenting it (access) (Dalkir, 2011: 33). The Bukowitz and Williams cycle has two paths: the individual and the organization. For the individual, it covers getting knowledge, using it, learning, and contributing. At the organizational level, there is assessing (validation) and building/sustaining or divesting (strategy) (2011: 38). It is limited in scope of activities and tends to privilege the individual, i.e. a process view, but this is not made clear. However, it does include some strategic decisions, which is helpful. McElroy's cycle focuses on organizational learning. It includes knowledge production (creation) then organizational knowledge (structural capital) followed by knowledge integration (validation, then use), distributed knowledge assets (organizational assets/resources), and business process improvement (BPI) (double-loop learning) (2011: 43). This has a helpful feedback loop component and a link to value/outcomes via the BPI step. However, its three early steps covering the knowledge process environment are quite broad and it is unclear how they occur. The Wiig KM cycle has four phases: build knowledge, hold knowledge, pool knowledge, and use knowledge. It is helpful as it includes a situational perspective, i.e. it places knowledge within the social practice of work. It begins with learning (build), tries to separate knowledge from the knower (hold), manages both codified (databases) and tacit knowledge (groups) (pool), and places it into a work context (use) (2011: 51). The Wiig cycle led to the systems approaches (e.g. Probst et al., 2002).

Probst et al.'s (2002) system is typical of an integrated system in the sense that it combines the people and IT perspectives. The system is presented as a set of building blocks for knowledge management which Probst et al. call the core processes:

1. *Identification*: how can we achieve internal and external transparency of existing knowledge?
2. *Acquisition*: what form of expertise should we buy from outside?
3. *Development*: how can we build new expertise?
4. *Sharing*: how can we get the knowledge to the right place?

5. *Utilization*: how can we ensure knowledge is applied?

6. *Retention*: how can we ensure that we do not lose knowledge?

7. *Objectives*: how can we give direction to learning?

8. *Assessment*: how can we measure the success of learning processes? (After Probst et al., 2002)

This is useful because it is comprehensive and covers much of good practice knowledge management. It also divides knowledge management into discrete processes which are relatively easy to define and implement. A similar synthesis by Dalkir (2011) is an updated version of the earlier systems. It includes the core activities of capture, creation, sharing, and use, as well as activities which emerged as important in the implementation of knowledge management such as validation (filtering and selection), access, and evaluation.

A typical information technology definition of knowledge management systems is provided by Becerra-Fernandez and Sabherwal (2010) as follows:

1. *Knowledge application systems*: systems that utilize knowledge including technologies such as artificial intelligence and case-based reasoning. This is an information technology driven system.

2. *Knowledge capture systems*: systems that preserve and formalize knowledge including capturing tacit knowledge via storytelling, concept maps, and context-based reasoning. This is a product view of knowledge management, i.e. separating knowledge from the knower.

3. *Knowledge sharing systems*: systems that organize and distribute knowledge, viewing the organization as a knowledge market and using computers as the access point via best practice databases, lessons learned systems, and expert locator systems. This views the organization as a knowledge repository, where use of taxonomies to facilitate access and searchability of online resources is the key.

4. *Knowledge discovery systems*: systems that create knowledge involve the use of technologies such as data mining to help business understanding. This is an information-systems-driven system. (After Becerra-Fernandez and Sabherwal, 2010: 62–65)

This is a useful framework because it illustrates an information systems view of knowledge management. While it appears restricted by its dependence on technology, it does highlight some of the more powerful tools used in managing codified knowledge.

KNOWLEDGE MANAGEMENT TOOLS

Knowledge techniques enable knowledge systems to be implemented. Rao (2005) defines knowledge management as a systematic discipline and a set of approaches to enable information and knowledge to grow, flow, and create value in an organization. This involves people, information, workflows, enabling tools, best practices, alliances, and communities of practice (Rao, 2005). In interpreting this view of knowledge management, it is useful to look at how practitioners do knowledge management. Table 2.2 summarizes Rao's (2005) survey of leading organizations in terms of their knowledge management tools.

TABLE 2.2 Summary of practitioner knowledge management tools

Tool	Organizations	Examples
Repository	Accenture	Knowledge Exchange hosts reports, proposals, experts
	KPMG	Virtual library
Real-time collaboration	ABB	
	Ericsson Research Canada	Knowledge networking (Xpertise)
	Ernst & Young	Knowledge web
	Fuji Xerox	Virtual space for knowledge workers
Content management	APQC	
Intranet	APQC	
Taxonomies	Cable & Wireless	Knowledge index
Incentives	Cable & Wireless	Knowledge dollars
Lessons learned database	DaimlerChrysler	Engineering book of knowledge
	Rolls-Royce	Lessons learned log
Structuring	Easyjet	Knowledge fracture augments intranet
Expert registers	Ernst & Young	Centre for Business Knowledge
	Rolls-Royce	People Pages
Best practice capture and sharing	Ford	Knowledge-based engineering
Communities of practice	Hewlett-Packard	CoP handbook
Innovation	Unilever	Mindjet's MindManager helps manage product innovation
Empowerment	World Bank	YourNet

Source: Rao (2005)

This list of tools has several themes: enterprise portals for storage, content management for accessibility, collaboration to build teamwork and sharing, expertise maps to help searchability, and idea management to help creativity.

It is also useful to look at how best practice knowledge management organizations are judged. The criteria used helps define knowledge management, particularly in terms of what the world's best KM organizations are doing. The highest award in KM is Most Admired Knowledge Enterprises (MAKE), administered by Teleos, an independent KM research company based in the UK (Buckman, 2004). Global winners of the MAKE award are judged on best practice exemplars in the following:

1. Creating a knowledge-driven culture
2. Developing knowledge workers
3. Delivering knowledge-based products and services
4. Maximizing intellectual capital
5. Collaborative knowledge sharing
6. Creating a learning organization
7. Delivering value for customer knowledge
8. Transforming knowledge into shareholder value. (Buckman, 2004: ix)

This list may be translated into knowledge management systems as follows: KM involves (numbers in brackets match the exemplars above): (a) learning organization *1, 6*; (b) organizational learning *2*; (c) knowledge value *3, 7, 8*; (d) resource growth *4*; and (e) knowledge sharing *5*. There is a strong focus on learning and creating value or practical outcomes of KM. These exemplars are covered in this book in terms of (a) Chapter 8, (b) Chapter 8, (c) Chapter 3, (d) Chapters 4 and 5, and (e) Chapter 9.

KNOWLEDGE MANAGEMENT TECHNOLOGIES

Knowledge management technologies are those which automate and support the handling of electronically available knowledge resources (Alwert and Hoffmann, 2003). A broad definition of a knowledge management technology might include email and intranets. Their main purpose is to help structure knowledge and make it more accessible for users. Structuring is the transition between content and a technical solution (2003). It uses words to visualize interaction between the system and the user. Structuring allows for procedures of knowledge retrieval, data and text mining, content analysis, automatic clustering, and so on (2003). The aim is to use technology to bring order to the vast amounts of codified knowledge available and to help people find what they want quicker. Alwert and Hoffmann (2003) provide the following list of popular KM technologies:

1. Completed KM suites
2. Learn and teach
3. Ontologies

4. Portals

5. Process-oriented KM

6. Search engines/categorization tools/intelligent agents

7. Skill management

8. Toolkits for developing individual solutions

9. Virtual teams/collaboration

10. Visualizing tools.

A TEMPORAL DEFINITION OF KNOWLEDGE MANAGEMENT

PERSONAL REFLECTION

Knowledge management is complex and finding a definition that suits you will be a challenge. This chapter will provide you with multiple perspectives to allow you to draw your own conclusions. The definition of knowledge management presented in this book is the result of my learning journey in KM. When I began my project with the Australian Department of Defence in 2006, I saw KM from two perspectives: (a) people and (b) systems. I dismissed information technology (IT) as simply the tools people use to do KM. On the people side, I felt it was about understanding why people with significant knowledge were unwilling to share it, and then finding ways to persuade them to share. On the systems side, I embraced the building blocks model (e.g. see Probst et al., 2002) and defined KM as a set of eight activities (e.g. knowledge creation, knowledge use) supported by the techniques necessary to perform these activities (e.g. communities of practice). However, as the project evolved, I learned that IT was important and that it represented both problems and solutions for KM. IT is particularly important in large organizations. In small organizations, there is a tendency to feel KM is unnecessary because people talk to one another. In environments where people can walk 100 metres and talk to anyone they want to, or easily pick up the phone or email and communicate very effectively, KM may be seen as a naturally occurring phenomenon and something that does not need managing (e.g. see Pearlson and Saunders, 2006). But KM is much more than people talking. The most obvious issue is ontology. Two people talking might benefit from some knowledge sharing, but it is restricted only to them. What if the rest of the organization needs to know what they know? I also learned that some people will not cooperate, no matter how hard you try to encourage them to. Therefore, rather than focus on eliciting knowledge from difficult people, I focused on providing the requisite systems and tools for those who wanted to cooperate. KM requires an organization-wide perspective.

My definition of knowledge management is built on the ideas in the Deep Thinking box below.

DEEP THINKING: We must first establish a purpose and the value of knowledge management, otherwise it will not happen. We must establish a baseline to understand what we know; and then grow, protect, and create value from this resource at the individual, group, and organizational levels. Following this, we must ensure that this resource is available to people who need it, when they need it, and ensure that it is used, and that learning and productivity increases occur at the individual, group, and organizational levels. Finally, KM needs to fit within existing organizational systems, and be supported by functions which are essential to its successful implementation, including leadership, organizational culture, accounting, human resource management, and technology. I also include a temporal perspective of knowledge management. I believe that knowledge management tries to capture the past, improve on the present, and plan for the future.

In this sense, knowledge management is a theory for all organizations and every manager. Good organizations and managers should be interested in learning from experience, improving performance, and developing sustainable competitive advantage. I propose a set of knowledge management tools that may be used to achieve these objectives. This makes knowledge management accessible for everyone.

A TEMPORAL PERSPECTIVE

My definition of knowledge management includes a temporal view. Knowledge is a dynamic and changing concept. The only temporal perspective on KM I have found in the literature is North and Kumta's (2014) KM maturity model. This is very useful in providing the context in which organizations progress through phases of commitment and a range of activity as they take their KM journey. My definition of KM introduces a different temporal perspective:

1. *Past*: capture the past, learn from it, and apply it in useful ways
2. *Present*: manage the present by sharing knowledge efficiently and improving the way work is performed
3. *Future*: plan for the future to ensure knowledge and its management create sustainable competitive advantage.

These temporal dimensions capture the reality of KM theory in practice. Figure 2.3 summarizes this definition.

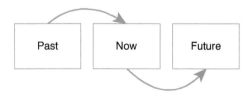

FIGURE 2.3 *Temporal perspective*

The temporal dimensions are overlaid by the systems in Figure 2.4.

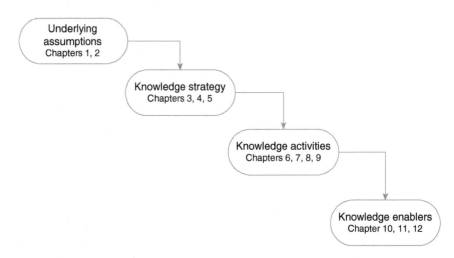

FIGURE 2.4   *Theory in practice knowledge management systems*

The systems are supported by tools. These are the KM techniques used to implement the four systems. They are presented within the context of the knowledge architecture to show how they address the past (Figure 2.5), present (Figure 2.6), and future (Figure 2.7).

Finally, knowledge management must become part of the way of doing business within organizations, rather than something extra to do. The definition of knowledge management presented does look like a new function (systems) and a set of activities (tools) that must be performed by someone else, i.e. new employees or KM specialists. It suggests that knowledge management is an isolated function separate from the rest of the organization. This will not work. To be successful, knowledge management must become integrated with the rest of the organization. Ideally, it should drive the entire business, as described by North and Kumta's (2014) fourth degree of KM maturity – the knowledge-based management of a company. The way to do this is to translate knowledge management into a business model which makes sense to managers and staff. It requires a change in mindset, flipping KM on its head, and embedding it in the type of business drivers which matter to practitioners. Figure 2.8 illustrates how I did this at the Australian Department of Defence. The figure shows how KM may be represented as a strategic management framework. In this way, practitioners can see how KM may improve business performance, and the causal relationships between KM activities and performance measures. Summarizing KM in a business model helps practitioners see its value. The theme of KM value is explored further in Chapter 3.

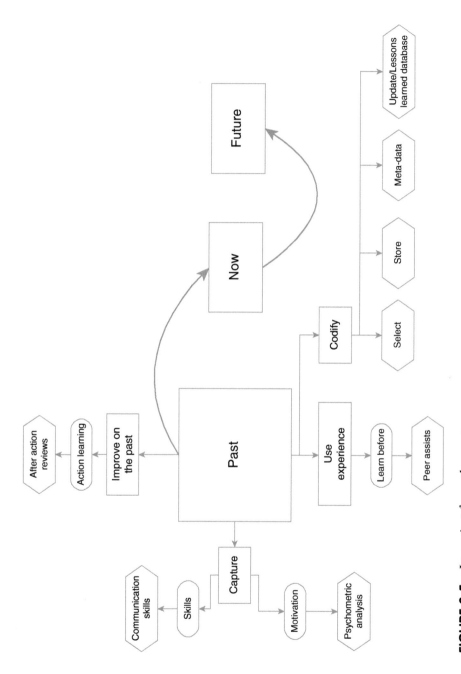

FIGURE 2.5 *Learning from the past*

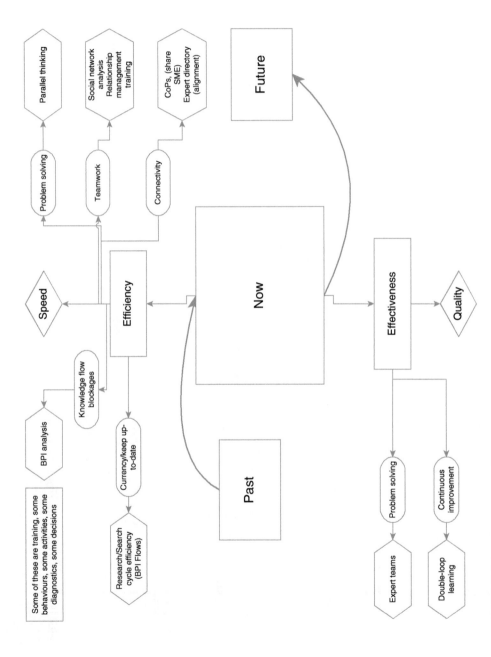

FIGURE 2.6 *Improving the present*

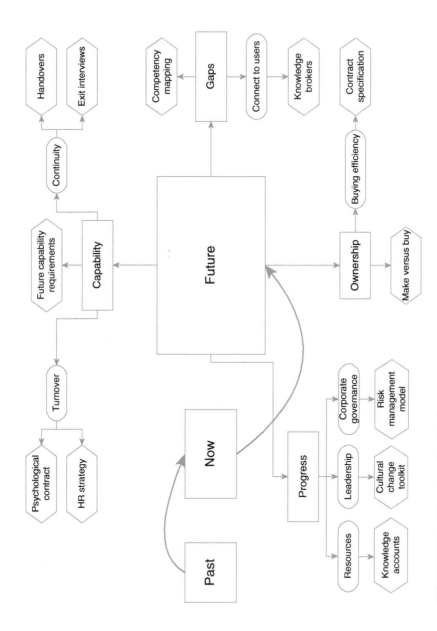

FIGURE 2.7 *Planning for the future*

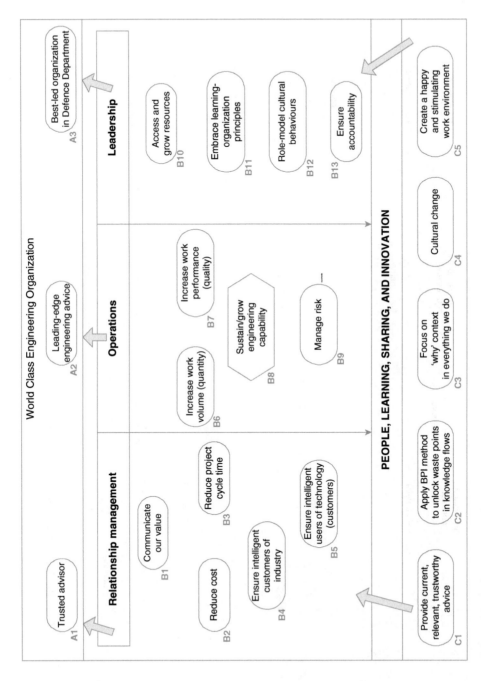

FIGURE 2.8 *Knowledge management business model*

TABLE 2.3 A checklist for developing a knowledge management approach

Underlying assumptions	Tick	Knowledge strategy	Tick	Knowledge activities	Tick	Knowledge enablers	Tick
Management philosophy:		Purpose:		Main competitive driving force		Tools:	
Scientific management		Competitive advantage				Repository	
Humanistic management		Improve performance		Typology 1:		Lessons learned database	
				Codification		Intranet	
Knowledge management maturity:		Become a learning organization		Personalization		Communities of practice, etc.	
1st degree: IT solutions		Improve knowledge sharing		Typology 2:		Technologies:	
2nd degree: individual solutions		Increase knowledge resources		Technocratic		Search engines	
				Economic		Skills management	
3rd degree: integrating product and process view		Goal:		Behavioural		Virtual communities, etc.	
		Manage knowledge resources		Typology 3:			
4th degree: knowledge-based company		Manage knowledge flows and enablers		Coordination and social			
				Coordination and technostructural			
Epistemology:				Control and social			
Tacit				Control and technostructural			
Codified							

(Continued)

TABLE 2.3 (Continued)

Underlying assumptions	Tick	Knowledge strategy	Tick	Knowledge activities	Tick	Knowledge enablers	Tick
Ontology:				Dimensions:			
Product view				Leadership/ management			
Process view				Organization			
Integrated view				Learning			
				Technology			
				Systems:			
				Identification			
				Acquisition			
				Development			
				Sharing			
				Utilization			
				Retention			
				Objectives			
				Assessment			

CONCLUSION

The chapter has explored the definition of knowledge management from multiple perspectives: its underlying assumptions, its strategy or purpose, its activities and its enablers. A broad range of theories and models were presented from a multi-disciplinary perspective. Table 2.3 provides summary guidelines which allow managers to decide on the most appropriate type of knowledge management for their organization.

KM is challenging because it is multi-disciplinary, and academics and practitioners from these disciplines have different perspectives. Table 2.3 provides a useful summary of these views by enabling you to find a context that best suits your organization. It also applies to organizations at different levels and for different purposes. Perhaps the easiest way to navigate through Table 2.3 is to identify your level of KM maturity. One of my biggest mistakes with my case study organization (see chapter closing case study) was assuming I could take the organization from having very little awareness of KM to becoming a knowledge-based organization. The organization simply was not ready to do that. KM is highly multi-faceted and complex; it is perhaps better to start off with bite-sized chunks, and progress steadily as the organization begins to accept and see value from the changes KM brings about. Ideally, the organization will manage its knowledge resources, and its knowledge flows and enablers – learning from the past, improving the present, and planning for the future. However, this requires the organization to see value in KM, which is discussed next in Chapter 3.

CLOSING CASE STUDY: KNOWLEDGE MANAGEMENT AT THE CSO

The case study organization (CSO) strategy was grounded in sustaining a capability to meet its customer's operational requirements. This requirement was to build and maintain significant public assets designed for national security. The CSO provided technical advice associated with the risk management of these public assets. The CSO's structure was a bureaucratic hierarchy. It involved a head (the senior industry partner on the project), three directorates (led by executive directors who were members of the project executive committee), and ten sections doing different technical work. The CSO's organizational culture was based on three drivers – people, performance, and professionalism – defined by a series of signature behaviours such as 'Respect the contribution of each individual', 'Fix problems and take action', and 'Strengthen relationships across the organization and beyond'. The signature behaviour most related to knowledge management was 'Communicate well and regularly'. These cultural statements were officially endorsed by the CSO's most senior executive and widely disseminated to all staff.

The project, which is presented in this book's closing integrated case studies as an organizational change strategy, was to make the CSO a learning organization. The project aimed to introduce a series of research interventions, followed by periods of implementation and reflection, over a

(Continued)

(Continued)

three-and-a-half-year period, in order to achieve its objective of learning organization capacity. The research interventions were knowledge management tools and techniques introduced by six training workshops. Each workshop covered a different aspect of knowledge management – knowledge creation, knowledge sharing, knowledge usage, knowledge acquisition, knowledge preservation, and knowledge retention – and each workshop was conducted over two days every three months, for 18 months. Respondents were invited to attend a different workshop every three months, and the hope was that after 18 months all respondents would have been trained in six KM systems.

The CSO was new to knowledge management. While the CSO was part of a very large government department (the second-largest in Australia) where pockets of knowledge management operated, largely in isolation, it had no formal knowledge management prior to the project. One of the work sections included a technical library; however, the CSO's efforts at KM were limited to information technology and a knowledge repository approach, i.e. intranets and document management.

A staff presentation was held at the CSO premises on 11 July 2008, where the chief investigator (CI) explained what the project was about, its significance, the methodology, and what staff were supposed to do, i.e. their role. The following extract shows how the research interventions were explained to staff:

> We want to ensure that the CSO has a critical mass necessary to be an intelligent customer of industry. It is perhaps easiest to think about the project in terms of short-term, medium-term, and long-term goals. In the short term, the project will directly focus on knowledge retention. In the medium term, the project will aim to change the organizational culture to help people work smarter. In the long term, the project will grow the knowledge base and increase the organization's capability.

> We will do this by introducing research interventions based on current best practice ideas. These exist but will be tailored to address the problems identified by an audit of the CSO's learning organization capacity. They will be discussed with the CSO management team prior to implementation. The research team will design a training package and documentation (e.g. a training manual) for each of the research interventions prior to launch. The research team will conduct training workshops for each research intervention. We will be available as a support for the CSO team during implementation but once we hand over at the end of the training workshops, the CSO will be responsible for managing the implementation of the interventions.

The selection of knowledge management tools for testing were chosen based on: (a) their use by organizations found in KM case studies (i.e. practical examples); (b) their coverage in the literature discussing practical solutions to the KM barriers found in the pilot study; and (c) their potential to address these barriers. The generalizability of this approach was that others may make choices at the strategy phase by situating KM tools as solutions to problems and referring to the tools found to work.

The knowledge management system introduced at the CSO was based on two systems of managing knowledge resources and then managing knowledge flows and enablers. Table 2.4 provides further details.

TABLE 2.4 Knowledge management system summary

System	Technique	What is it?	Description	What problem does it solve?	KM strategy	Performance change
1. Strategy	1.1 Future capability requirements	Tool – decision making	Introduce objectivity into workforce planning	What do we need to know?	Product	Rebuild engineering
	1.2 Competency mapping	Tool – gap analysis	Identify capability gaps	Where are we weak?	Product	Rebuild engineering
	1.3 Make versus buy	Tool – sourcing	Present business case for knowledge location decision (inside versus outside)	Who owns the resource?	Product	Rebuild engineering
2. Creativity	2.1 Parallel thinking	Training – efficiency	Manage creativity process	Reduce meeting time	Process	Cultural change
	2.2 Expert teams	Activity – teamwork	Create synergy amongst SMEs	Improved results focus	Process	Cultural change
	2.3 Information flow (BPI)	Activity – Research	Identify and remove blockages in knowledge flows	Improved efficiency in staff research knowledge seeking	Product	Rebuild engineering
	2.4 Double-loop learning	Training – productivity	Challenge underlying assumptions	Continuous improvement	Process	Cultural change
3. Sharing	3.1 Communities of practice	Activity – teamwork	Establish and maintain virtual technology support networks (VTSNs)	Closer working relationships	Process	Cultural change
	3.2 Social network analysis (SNA)	Diagnostic – solutions	Map formal and informal contacts	Closer working relationships	Product	Cultural change
	3.3 Relationship management training	Training – productivity	Provide awareness via SNA mapping and skills to build relationships	Closer working relationships	Process	Cultural change

(Continued)

TABLE 2.4 (Continued)

System	Technique	What is it?	Description	What problem does it solve?	KM strategy	Performance change
	3.4 Communication skills	Training – productivity	Provide skills to better share knowledge including ways to share, e.g. presentations, mentoring, writing	Separate knowledge from the knower (i.e. SME)	Product	Rebuild engineering
	3.5 Psychometric analysis	Diagnostic – metrics	Track cultural change	Measures sharing behaviours and attitudes	Product	Cultural change
4. Usage	4.1 Expert directory	Diagnostic – solutions	Map SMEs by level and in multiple contexts: technical, job-related, organizational knowledge	Improved efficiency in knowledge sharing and staff research (i.e. will save time)	Process	Cultural change
	4.2 After action reviews	Activity – lessons learned	Capture lessons learned	Separate experience from the knower, store experience and organizational memory	Product	Rebuild engineering
	4.3 Peer assists	Activity – lessons learned	Share lessons learned	Share experience beyond the local level	Process	Rebuild engineering
5. Acquisition	5.1 Business process improvement (BPI)	Diagnostic – problem	Map key business processes and identifies blockages and waste points in knowledge flows	Closer working relationships	Product	Cultural change
	5.2 Knowledge brokers	Activity – job redesign	Define role for knowledge flow specialist	Closer working relationships	Process	Cultural change

System	Technique	What is it?	Description	What problem does it solve?	KM strategy	Performance change
	5.3 Contract specification	Activity – intellectual capital transfer	Specify the asset to be captured from external experts	Reduced dependence on external experts and building internal capability	Product	Cultural change
6. Preservation	6.1 SELECT model	Diagnostic – solutions	Identify *what* knowledge should be captured and stored	Focus on the most valuable knowledge and ignore the rest (Pareto principle)	Product	Rebuild engineering
	6.2 Storage	Activity – information technology upgrade	Improve current IT systems via better file structure (i.e. warehousing)	Improves accessibility of knowledge stored (e.g. intranet)	Product	Rebuild engineering
	6.3 Meta-data	Activity – 'why' context	Provide explanation fields to help users understand why the knowledge is useful and in what context	Improvess searchability and usability of knowledge stored (e.g. intranet)	Product	Rebuild engineering
	6.4 Lessons learned database	Activity – lessons learned	Capture experience	Avoids mistakes and shares success	Product	Rebuild engineering
7. Retention	7.1 Handovers	Activity – Lessons Learned	Establish a handover file as an ongoing lessons – learned record and conduct handover at exit	Improved productivity in posting cycle (up to 25% salary savings p.a.)	Product	Rebuild engineering
	7.2 Exit interviews	Activity – employee exit	Interview to capture tacit knowledge before exit; package and share the outcomes with successor	Lost corporate knowledge is reduced	Product	Rebuild engineering

(Continued)

TABLE 2.4 (Continued)

System	Technique	What is it?	Description	What problem does it solve?	KM strategy	Performance change
	7.3 Psychological contract	Diagnostic – metrics	Track staff emotional relationship with the organization	Measures risk associated with key individuals in terms of knowledge loss and knowledge sharing	Product	Cultural change
	7.4 HR strategy	Activity – prevention	Reward and recognition, psychological contract, job redesign, career management	Addresses factors leading to employee turnover	Process	Cultural change
8. Measurement	8.1 Knowledge sccounts software	Diagnostic – metrics	Disaggregate quantified value of staff knowledge at multiple levels	Measures capability completely to enable better-informed decisions on workforce planning and organizational development	Product	Rebuild engineering
	8.2 Cultural change toolkit	Diagnostic – metrics	Track cultural change using best practice organizational models	Measures changes in attitudes and behaviours against strategic goals, which may be disaggregated at multiple levels	Product	Rebuild engineering
	8.3 Risk management model	Diagnostic – metrics	Track change in terms of technical and organizational risk	Measures risk in terms of traditional decision tree methods combined with new thinking on vulnerability caused by knowledge loss (e.g. single points of failure)	Product	Rebuild engineering

It was clear that many CSO staff did not feel there was a problem of knowledge sharing and therefore disagreed with their executive on the need for a project. The following was a critical interaction between the research team and a staff member at the staff presentation:

Staff: We don't need this project.

CI: Why not?

Staff: We already manage our knowledge well. We have the (organization intranet).

CI: Well, we are not talking about computers and databases here. Knowledge management is about people. It is about getting you to share the knowledge in your head with others.

Staff: We have already shared it. It is there on the (organization intranet). All you have to do is look.

CI: I'm sorry; I think you are missing the point.

This interaction highlights very important misunderstandings about the project on both sides. It illustrates confusion about knowledge as an object versus a process. The respondent here saw knowledge as an object, something that can be captured, stored, and shared with others via a computer. The CI saw knowledge as a process, something that can best be shared through human interaction. The critical mistake was that the CI did not ask staff at this presentation about their underlying assumptions. He did not ask them whether they felt knowledge sharing (KS) was a problem and, if so, how it could be fixed. He did not ask them how they felt about the training workshops, and how they should be conducted. He knew a contract had been signed and he and the case study executive had agreed on a research method. He assumed that the staff accepted this because a contract had been signed stating that KS was a problem and they would help him to fix it. Therefore, the learning flows could not move along the tactical level to help participants look at why the project was useful – i.e. personal and organizational gain – because the CI dismissed existing methods as irrelevant.

At a barbecue held following the staff presentation, several things happened which bothered the research team. First, the barbeque was not well attended. Of the 150 staff in the study, only about 30 attended. When the apparent lack of interest in meeting the research team was questioned, excuses such as staff being busy or working elsewhere were offered. Second, in discussions with staff, many seemed to have almost no idea what the project was about or why they were involved. Third, when the CI raised his concern that staff needed to be persuaded to engage with the study, senior management told him not to get involved.

The success of the KM system introduced at the CSO three years later was summarized in Table 2.5.

(Continued)

TABLE 2.5 Summary of overall results of knowledge management interventions

| KM toolkit | Learning organization capacity | | | | | Practical outcomes | | | Toolkit ratings |
| | Performance goals | | | | | | | | |
	Objective	LOC drivers	Indicators	Systems thinking barriers	Driver	Measure	Organizational changes	Organizational gain	Mean score (out of 20)
				Managing knowledge resources					
1. Knowledge strategy	Objective future workforce capability decisions	Better able to respond to change	Organizational direction, mission and values, role clarity	Operational learning: how do we make this work? Getting people to participate because it is not part of their job or they do not trust it. Organizational system problem	Strategic alignment	Whether it decreases the capability gap	Strategic purpose; competency gap; future capability requirement	Capacity utilization; productivity increase	13.75
2. Knowledge creation	Double-loop learning	Better respond to change	Change and innovation, motivation and initiative	Tactical learning: why is this useful? Explain why this is better than existing methods and benefits the individual. Tool problem	Value management	Whether it improves stakeholder perception of the value of the organization	Problem solving; creativity processes	Continuous improvement; customer satisfaction; discretionary services increase	6.20
3. Knowledge retention	Tacit knowledge capture	Learn from experience	Processes	Operational learning: how do we make this work? Persuading people to engage in artificial knowledge-sharing activities. Tool problem	Psychological contract	Whether it increases staff morale and productivity	Reduced employee turnover; improved psychological contract	Productivity increase; reduced employee turnover costs; positive cultural behaviours	7.80
4. Knowledge measurement	Auditable knowledge value metrics	Better grow staff	Resources, career management	Strategic learning: what are we doing and why? Management need to be willing to act. Organizational system problem	Value management	Whether it improves stakeholder perception of the value of the organization	Monitor work activity; monitor progress; cultural change	Resource acquisition	11.25

	Learning organization capacity					Practical outcomes			Toolkit ratings
	Performance goals								
KM toolkit	Objective	LOC drivers	Indicators	Systems thinking barriers	Driver	Measure	Organizational changes	Organizational gain	Mean score (out of 20)
Managing knowledge flows and enablers									
5. Knowledge sharing	Increased connectivity (more people know)	Better respond to change; better grow our staff	Cross-unit cooperation, teamwork, job satisfaction, organizational culture	Tactical learning: why is this useful? Explain to people why they need to do something better they feel they already do well. Tool problem	Connectivity	Whether it increases search cycle efficiency, i.e. the time taken to find the knowledge necessary to perform a new task	Increase social capital; reduce task completion time	Capacity utilization; productivity increase	4.65
6. Knowledge usage	Make knowledge/ experience accessible	Learn from experience	Processes, involvement	Action learning: how do we improve the process? Need to persuade people that organizational gain here is more important than personal gain, otherwise individuals will put themselves first (too busy to do it). Organizational system problem	Experience	Whether it increases sharing of experience	Value-creating work performance; experience diffusion	Work quality; work quantity	11.38
7. Knowledge acquisition	Targeted learning	Better grow our staff	Talent, customer satisfaction	Tactical learning: why is this useful? Limited relevance (only involves boundary spanners) and management are reluctant to empower these staff using appropriate job redesign. Organizational system problem	Learning	Whether it accelerates time to competence	Capability growth; career management	Performance improvement; increase customer retention; cost reduction	9.30
8. Knowledge preservation	Capturing and storing knowledge	Learn from experience	Processes, technology	Action learning: how do we improve the process? Need to persuade management to invest significant time and resources. Organizational system problem	Risk management	Whether it increases confidence in work outputs	External recognition; decrease inconsistent risk interpretations; minimise the impact of the risk event occurring	Corporate governance	12.38

(Continued)

(Continued)

CASE STUDY QUESTIONS

1. Use the framework provided in Table 2.5 to explain the type of knowledge management introduced at the CSO.
2. What type of knowledge management should have been introduced at the CSO? Why?
3. Evaluate the implementation of knowledge management at the CSO. Why did it work? Or why didn't it work?

REVIEW AND DISCUSSION QUESTIONS

1. Do you prefer the product view or the process view of knowledge management? Why?
2. What is the most compelling purpose of knowledge management? Why?
3. Which of the following do you feel has the most impact on the implementation of knowledge management: architecture, systems, technologies, or tools?
4. Critically evaluate the temporal model of knowledge management.

FURTHER READING

Becerra-Fernandez, I. and Sabherwal, R. (2010) *Knowledge Management: Systems and processes*, Armonk, NY, M.E. Sharpe. This book provides an alternative and contemporary perspective.

Easterby-Smith, M. and Lyles, M.A. (2005) Introduction: Watersheds of organizational learning and knowledge management. Chapter 1 in Easterby-Smith, M. and Lyles, M.A. (eds) *Handbook of Organizational Learning and Knowledge Management*, Hong Kong, Blackwell, pp. 1–15. This chapter provides an overview of the field.

Gold, A.H., Malhotra, A. and Segars, A.H. (2001) Knowledge Management: An organizational capabilities perspective. *Journal of Management Information Systems*, 18 (1): 185–214. This is a widely cited source which looks at knowledge management as a capability.

BIBLIOGRAPHY

Aakhus, M. (2007) Conversations for Reflection: Augmenting transitions and transformations in expertise. Chapter 1 in McInerney,C.J. and Day, R.E. (eds) *Rethinking Knowledge Management: From knowledge objects to knowledge processes*, Berlin, Springer.

Abeysekera, I. (2013) A Template for Integrated Reporting. *Journal of Intellectual Capital*, *14* (2): 227–245.

Alavi, M. and Tiwana, A. (2005) Knowledge Management: The information technology dimension. Chapter 6 in Easterby-Smith, M. and Lyles, M.A. (eds) *Handbook of Organizational Learning and Knowledge Management*, Hong Kong, Blackwell, pp. 104–121.

Alvesson, M. and Karreman, D. (2001) Odd Couple: Making sense of the curious concept of knowledge management. *Journal of Management Studies*, *38* (7): 995–1018.

Alwert, K. and Hoffmann, I. (2003) Knowledge Management Tools. Chapter 6 in Mertins, K., Heisig, P. and Vorbeck, J. (eds) *Knowledge Management: Concepts and practices*, New York, Springer, pp. 114–150.

Andreeva, T. and Kianto, A. (2012) Does Knowledge Management Really Matter? Linking knowledge management practices, competitiveness, and economic performance. *Journal of Knowledge Management*, *16* (4): 617–636.

Angus, J., Patel, J. and Harty, J. (1998) Knowledge Management: Great concept ... but what is it? *InformationWeek*, *673*: 58–70.

Argyris, C. and Schön, D. (1978) *Organizational Learning: A theory of action approach*. Reading, MA, Addison-Wesley.

Argyris, C. and Schön, D. (1996) *Organizational Learning II: Theory, method and practice*, Reading, MA, Addison-Wesley.

Becerra-Fernandez, I. and Sabherwal, R. (2010) *Knowledge Management: Systems and processes*, Armonk, NY, M.E. Sharpe.

Bettiol, M., Di Maria, E. and Grandinetti, R. (2012) Codification and Creativity: Knowledge management strategies in KIBS. *Journal of Knowledge Management*, *16* (4): 550–562.

Brooking, A. (1999) *Corporate Memory: Strategies for knowledge management*, London, International Thomson Business Press.

Buckman, R.H. (2004) *Building a Knowledge-driven Organization*, New York, McGraw-Hill.

Bukowitz, W. and Williams, R. (2000) *The Knowledge Management Fieldbook*, London, Prentice-Hall.

Conner, K.R. and Prahalad, C.K. (2002) A Resource-based Theory of the Firm. Chapter 7 in Choo, C.W. and Bontis, N. (eds) *The Strategic Management of Intellectual Capital and Organizational Knowledge*, New York, Oxford University Press, pp. 103–132.

Canonico, P., De Nito, E. and Mangia, G. (2012) Control Mechanisms and Knowledge Integration in Exploitative Project Teams: A case study from the coal-fired power plant industry. *Journal of Knowledge Management*, *16* (4): 538–549.

Cyert, R.M. and March, J.G. (1963) *A Behavioral Theory of the Firm*, Englewood Cliffs, NJ, Prentice-Hall.

Dalkir, K. (2011) *Knowledge Management in Theory and Practice*, 2nd edition, Cambridge, MA, MIT Press.

Davenport, E. and Cronin, B. (2000) Knowledge Management: Semantic drift or conceptual shift? *Journal of Education for Library and Information Science*, *41* (4): 294–306.

Davenport, T.H. and Prusak, L. (1998) *Working Knowledge: How organizations manage what they know*, Boston, MA, Harvard Business School Press.

Di Vincenzo, F., Hemphälä, J., Magnusson, M. and Mascia, D. (2012) Exploring the Role of Structural Holes in Learning: An empirical study of Swedish pharmacies. *Journal of Knowledge Management*, *16* (4): 576–591.

Drucker, P.F. (1954) *The Practice of Management*, New York, HarperCollins.

Drucker, P. (1964) *Managing for Results*, Oxford, Butterworth-Heineman.

Drucker, P.F. (1988) The Coming of the New Organization. Chapter 1 in (1998) *Harvard Business Review on Knowledge Management*, Boston, MA, Harvard Business School Press, pp. 1–19.

Drucker, P. (1999) Knowledge-worker Productivity: The biggest challenge. *California Management Review, 41* (2): 79–94.

Dumay, J. (2014) 15 Years of the Journal of Intellectual Capital and Counting: A manifesto for transformational IC research. *Journal of Intellectual Capital, 15* (1): 2–37.

Dumay, J. and Tull, J.A. (2011) Intellectual Capital Disclosure and Price-sensitive Australian Stock Exchange Announcements. *Journal of Intellectual Capital, 8* (2): 236–255.

Earl, M. (2001) Knowledge Management Strategies: Towards a taxonomy. *Journal of Management Information Systems, 18* (1): 215–233.

Easterby-Smith, M. and Lyles, M.A. (2005) Introduction: Watersheds of organizational learning and knowledge management. Chapter 1 in Easterby-Smith, M. and Lyles, M.A. (eds) *Handbook of Organizational Learning and Knowledge Management*, Hong Kong, Blackwell, pp. 1–15.

Edmondson, A.C., Winslow, A.B., Bohmer, R.M.J. and Pisano, G.P. (2003) Learning How and Learning What: Effects of tacit and codified knowledge on performance improvement following technology adoption. *Decision Sciences, 34* (2): 197–223.

Edvinsson, L. and Malone, M.S. (1997) *Intellectual Capital: Realizing your company's true value by finding its hidden roots*, New York, Harper Business.

Falk, S. (2005) Knowledge Management at Accenture. Chapter 2 in Rao, M. (ed.) *Knowledge Management Tools and Techniques: Practitioners and experts evaluate KM solutions*, Burlington, MA, Elsevier Butterworth-Heinemann.

Franssila, H., Okkonen, J., Savolainen, R. and Talja, S. (2012) The Formation of Coordinative Knowledge Practices in Distributed Work: Towards an explanatory model. *Journal of Knowledge Management, 16* (4): 650–665.

Gavrilova, T. and Andreeva, T. (2012) Knowledge Elicitation Techniques in a Knowledge Management Context. *Journal of Knowledge Management, 16* (4): 523–537.

Gold, A.H., Malhotra, A. and Segars, A.H. (2001) Knowledge Management: An organizational capabilities perspective. *Journal of Management Information Systems, 18* (1): 185–214.

Gorelick, C., Milton, N.J. and April, K. (2004) The Knowledge Management Mandate: Performance through learning. Chapter 1 in *Performance through Learning: Knowledge management in practice*, Amsterdam, Elsevier Butterworth-Heinemann, pp. 1–23.

Grant, R.M. (1996) Toward a Knowledge-based Theory of the Firm. *Strategic Management Journal, 17*: 109–122.

Grant, R.M. (2002a) *Contemporary Strategy Analysis: Concepts, techniques and applications*, 4th edition, Malden, MA, Blackwell Business.

Grant, R.M. (2002b) The Knowledge-based View of the Firm. Chapter 8 in Choo, C.W. and Bontis, N. (eds) *The Strategic Management of Intellectual Capital and Organizational Knowledge*, New York, Oxford University Press, pp. 133–148.

Grant, R.M. (2013) *Contemporary Strategy Analysis*, 8th edition, Chichester, Wiley.

Guthrie, J. and Petty, R. (2000) Intellectual Capital: Australian annual reporting practices. *Journal of Intellectual Capital, 1* (3): 241–251.

Guthrie, J., Petty, R. and Ricceri, F. (2006) The Voluntary Reporting of Intellectual Capital: Comparing evidence from Hong Kong and Australia. *Journal of Intellectual Capital, 7* (2): 254–271.

Hansen, M., Nohria, N. and Tierney, T. (1999) What's Your Strategy for Managing Knowledge? *Harvard Business Review, 77* (2): 106–116.

Heisig, P. (2003) Business Process Oriented Knowledge Management. Chapter 2 in Mertins, K., Heisig, P. and Vorbeck, J. (eds) *Knowledge Management: Concepts and practices*, New York, Springer, pp. 15–44.

Hobohm, H.-C. (ed.) 2004) Knowledge Management: Libraries and librarians taking up the challenge. *IFLA Publication Series 108*, Berlin, de Gruyter.

Hooper, A. and Potter, J. (2001) *Intelligent Leadership: Creating a passion for change*, London, Random House.

Iacono, M.P., Martinez, M., Mangia, G. and Galdiero, C. (2012) Knowledge Creation and Inter-organizational Relationships: The development of innovation in the railway industry. *Journal of Knowledge Management, 16* (4): 604–616.

Jashapara, A. (2011) *Knowledge Management: An integrated approach*, Harlow, Pearson Education/Prentice Hall.

Kaplan, R.S. and Norton, D.P. (1996) *The Balanced Scorecard*, Boston, MA, Harvard Business School Press.

Koenig, M.E.D. and Srikantaiah, T.K. (2007) Three Stages of Knowledge Management. Chapter 1 in Koenig, M.E.D. and Srikantaiah, T.K. (eds) *Knowledge Management Lessons Learned: What works and what doesn't*, Medford, NJ, Information Today, pp. 3–8.

Lerro, A., Iacobone, F.A. and Schiuma, G. (2012) Knowledge Assets Assessment Strategies: Organizational value, processes, approaches and evaluation architectures. *Journal of Knowledge Management, 16* (4): 563–575.

McElroy, M.W. (2003) *The New Knowledge Management: Complexity, learning, and sustainable innovation*, Burlington, MA, KMCI Press/Butterworth-Heinemann.

Massingham, P. (2004) Linking Business Level Strategy with Activities and Knowledge Resources. *Journal of Knowledge Management, 8* (6): 50–62.

Massingham, P. (2014a) An Evaluation of Knowledge Management Tools, Part 1: Managing knowledge resources. *Journal of Knowledge Management, 18* (6): 1075–1100.

Massingham, P. (2014b) An Evaluation of Knowledge Management Tools, Part 2: Managing knowledge flows and enablers. *Journal of Knowledge Management, 18* (6): 1101–1126.

Massingham, P. (2016) Knowledge Accounts. *Long Range Planning, 49* (3): 409–425.

Massingham, P. and Massingham, R. (2014) Does Knowledge Management Produce Practical Outcomes? *Journal of Knowledge Management, 18* (2): 221–254.

Massingham, P. and Tam, L. (2015) The Relationship between Human Capital, Value Creation, and Employee Reward. *Journal of Intellectual Capital* (Special Issue), *16* (2): 390–418.

Mentzas, G., Apostolou, D., Abecker, A. and Young, R. (2003) *Knowledge Asset Management: Beyond the process-centred and product-centred approaches*, London, Springer.

Meyer, M. and Zack, M. (1996) The Design and Implementation of Information Products. *Sloan Management Review, 37* (3): 43–59.

Mintzberg, H., Lampel, J., Quinn, J.B. and Ghoshal, S. (2002) McKinsey & Company: Managing knowledge and learning. Case 30 in *The Strategy Process: Concepts, contexts, and cases*, Upper Saddle River, NJ, Prentice Hall, pp. 319–332.

Nelson, R.R. and Winter, S.G. (1977) In Search of a Useful Theory of Innovation. *Research Policy, 6* (1): 36–77.

Nelson, R.R. and Winter, S.G. (1982) *An Evolutionary Theory of Economic Change*, Cambridge, MA, Harvard University Press.

Nonaka, I. and Takeuchi, H. (1995) *The Knowledge-creating Company: How Japanese companies create the dynamics of innovation*, New York, Oxford University Press.

North, K. and Kumta, G. (2014) *Knowledge Management: Value creation through organizational learning*, Cham, Switzerland, Springer International.

Pearlson, K.E. and Saunders, C.S. (2006) *Managing and Using Information Systems: A strategic approach*, 3rd edition, Danvers, MA, Wiley.

Penrose, E.T. (1959) *The Theory of the Growth of the Firm*, New York, Wiley.

Ponzi, L.J. (2007) Knowledge Management: Birth of a discipline. Chapter 2 in Koenig, M.E.D. and Srikantaiah, T.K. (eds) *Knowledge Management Lessons Learned: What works and what doesn't*, Medford, NJ, Information Today, pp. 9–26.

Probst, G., Raub, S. and Romhardt, K. (2002) *Managing Knowledge: Building blocks for success*, Chichester, Wiley.

Rao, M. (2005) Overview: The social life of KM tools. Chapter 1 in Rao, M. (ed.) *Knowledge Management Tools and Techniques: Practitioners and experts evaluate KM solutions*, Oxford, Elsevier, pp. 1–76.

Schiuma, G. (2012) Managing Knowledge for Business Performance Improvement. *Journal of Knowledge Management*, *16* (4): 515–522.

Senge, P.M. (1990) *The Fifth Discipline: The art and practice of the learning organization*, London, Random House.

Stankosky, M. (2005) Advances in Knowledge Management: University research towards an academic discipline. Chapter 1 in Stankosky, M. (ed.) *Creating the Discipline of Knowledge Management: The latest in university research*, Burlington, MA, Elsevier Butterworth-Heinemann, pp. 1–14.

Stewart, T.A. (1997) *Intellectual Capital: The new wealth of organizations*, New York, Doubleday.

Sveiby, K.E. (1997) *The New Organizational Wealth: Managing and measuring knowledge-based assets*, San Francisco, Berrett-Koehler.

Swan, J. and Scarbrough, H. (2005) The Politics of Networked Innovation. *Human Relations*, *58* (7): 913–943.

von Krogh, G. (2005) Knowledge Sharing and the Communal Resource. Chapter 19 in Easterby-Smith, M. and Lyles, M.A. (eds) *Handbook of Organizational Learning and Knowledge Management*, Hong Kong, Blackwell, pp. 372–392.

Vuori, V. and Okkonen, J. (2012) Knowledge Sharing Motivational Factors of Using an Intra-organizational Social Media Platform. *Journal of Knowledge Management*, *16* (4): 592–603.

Wernerfelt, B. (1984) A Resource-based View of the Firm. *Strategic Management Journal*, *9*: 443–454.

Whyte, M. and Zyngier, S. (2014) Applied Intellectual Capital Management: Experiences from an Australian public sector trial of the Danish Intellectual Capital Statement. *Journal of Intellectual Capital*, *15* (2): 227–248.

Wiig, K. (1993) *Knowledge Management Foundations*, Arlington, TX, Schema Press.

Zeleny, M. (2005) *Human Systems Management: Integrating knowledge, management, and systems*, Hackensack, NJ, World Scientific Publishing.

3

MEASURING THE PERFORMANCE OF KNOWLEDGE MANAGEMENT

CHAPTER OUTLINE

LEARNING OUTCOMES

After completing this chapter, the reader should be able to:

1. Discuss knowledge management's value proposition
2. Consider criticisms of knowledge management
3. Understand performance measurement criteria
4. Comprehend how knowledge management's value may be measured in financial and non-financial terms
5. Evaluate the practical outcomes of knowledge management

MANAGEMENT ISSUES

Measuring the performance of knowledge management requires managers to:

1. Understand how knowledge management can create value
2. Apply traditional performance metrics to knowledge management
3. Make investment decisions on knowledge management based on objective and auditable information

Knowledge involves these challenges for management:

1. Interpreting the direct and indirect impact of knowledge management in terms of cause and effect
2. Considering what you want knowledge management to achieve

LINKS TO OTHER CHAPTERS

Chapter 2: on the definition of knowledge management

Chapter 4: concerning the value of knowledge as a resource

Chapter 5: regarding how knowledge management may be a dynamic capability

Chapter 10: how knowledge management can improve productivity

Chapter 11: how knowledge management is supported by organizational systems

OPENING MINI CASE STUDY

THE UNITED STATES DEPARTMENT OF THE NAVY: THE IMPORTANCE OF MEASURING KNOWLEDGE MANAGEMENT PERFORMANCE

The United States Department of the Navy (USDN) was established during the American War of Independence (1775) and is the largest navy in the world; its battle fleet tonnage is greater than that of the next 13 largest navies combined.

The USDN is a five-time North American MAKE finalist and three-time North American MAKE winner (2002, 2003, 2010). The Americas Most Admired Knowledge Enterprises (MAKE) study is part of Teleos's MAKE research programme. The Americas MAKE study was established in 2002 to recognize organizations (founded and headquartered in North, Central, and South America) for their ability to create shareholder value (or, in the case of public and non-profit organizations, to increase stakeholder value) by transforming new as well as existing enterprise knowledge into superior products, services, and solutions (see www.knowledgebusiness.com/knowledgebusiness/templates/TextAndLinksList.aspx?siteId=1&menuItemId=133; www.navy.mil/navydata/nav_legacy.asp?id=146).

The USDN's award-winning knowledge management is recognition of its knowledge-driven organizational culture. The case examines how it has developed this culture based on designing an effective set of performance metrics.

The USDN's knowledge management journey began in 2002 when then president, George W. Bush, included knowledge management in his presidential management agenda by stating: 'the Administration will adopt information technology systems to capture some of the knowledge and skills of retiring employees. KM systems are just one part of an effective strategy … relevant to the organization's mission' (Ross and Schulte, 2005: 158).

The USDN felt that 'shared understanding provides a decisive edge in war fighting' (Ross and Schulte, 2005: 159). It aimed to build a knowledge-centric organization that 'connects people to the right information at the right time for decision and action; and learns, collaborates, and innovates continuously' (2005: 159). In designing a knowledge management system to achieve these goals, the US Department of the Navy developed five dimensions: technology, process, content, culture, and learning.

The USDN implemented this knowledge management system by focusing on a set of performance metrics. It began with two guiding benefits: (1) improved performance via increased effectiveness, productivity, quality, and innovation; and (2) increased financial value of the organization by managing human capital or knowledge as an asset (Ross and Schulte, 2005: 162). This created a sense of meaning and purpose about knowledge management for the organization. It tried to address the 'What's in it for me?' driver at the individual level

(Continued)

(Continued)

by arguing that knowledge management could help people make more efficient and agile decisions. The USDN applies three specific constructs to measure performance from a knowledge management perspective: outcomes, outputs, and system metrics (2005: 162). Outcome metrics measure overall organizational characteristics, including increased productivity and revenue; examples include time, money, or personnel saved (i.e. less staff required to do the same quality and quantity of work) as a result of a KM initiative (2005: 162). Output metrics measure project traits, including the effectiveness of lessons learned; examples include usefulness surveys on whether initiatives have helped, and usage anecdotes (2005: 162). System metrics measure the effectiveness, usefulness, functionality, and responsiveness of KM initiatives; examples include number of downloads, dwell time per page or section, frequency of use, and percentage of total employees using the tool (2005: 162).

The advantage of this approach is that it has clear measures which are linked to the organization's knowledge management goals and strategy. If the principle of 'what is measured gets done' is accepted, and employees are adequately recognized and rewarded for complying with these KM initiatives, then it is possible to see how the USDN could build a knowledge-centric culture with this approach. The disadvantage is that it seems to have a heavy emphasis on tools and technologies. It also has a focus on knowledge sharing through best practice directories, lessons learned databases, and expert registers. Therefore, it highlights the emphasis on the product view of knowledge management at the USDN. However, performance metrics for communities of practice (CoPs) show how the people side of knowledge management may be addressed with this approach. CoPs could be measured in terms of system measures like number of members, frequency of interaction, and number of contributions. Output measures for CoPs could be number of junior colleagues mentored by senior colleagues and number of problems solved. Outcome measures for CoPs could be captured organizational memory (knowledge asset change) and attrition rate of CoP members versus non-members (employee retention).

In their pilot study of a US Navy directorate, Ross and Schulte (2005) found that organizational culture was the most important factor in implementing knowledge management – more important than metrics, processes, or technology (the latter was considered the least important). Developing an effective culture included increasing awareness of knowledge management, identifying KM champions, the creation of CoPs, commitment from leaders, and story-telling to generate support (Ross and Schulte, 2005: 170).

CASE STUDY QUESTIONS

1. What are the US Department of the Navy's knowledge resources? (See Chapter 1)
2. Why does the US DN feel it is important to manage its knowledge? (See Chapter 2)
3. Evaluate how the US DN measures its knowledge management performance.
4. How well do you feel the US DN is managing knowledge?

INTRODUCTION

The purpose of this chapter is to examine how to measure the performance of knowledge management. The growing interest in knowledge management is based on three themes: (1) the transition from an industrial economy, where value was created by things or tangible assets, to a knowledge economy, where value is created by what you know, or intangible assets; (2) the information age being driven by the internet and a generation raised on smart technology; and (3) that knowledge management might be a source of sustainable competitive advantage.

The chapter begins by looking at the broader context of society and why knowledge and its management have attracted so much interest. Next, criticism of knowledge management is provided as an alternative perspective. There are some that argue knowledge management has failed to deliver on its hype. This allows us to challenge the underlying assumptions about knowledge management. The chapter continues with a framework for making investment decisions about knowledge management.

CORE CONCEPT: Managers tend to ask 'So what do I get in return?' when asked to invest in any project, including knowledge management.

The chapter will focus on answering this question and, in doing so, will provide a checklist for making sound investment decisions about knowledge management. The chapter concludes with a model for evaluating the value of knowledge management: a focus on practical outcomes.

KNOWLEDGE MANAGEMENT'S VALUE PROPOSITION

The growing interest in the value of knowledge management has been driven by the knowledge economy, the information technology boom, and the knowledge marketplace.

The knowledge economy is a concept, developed by Bell (1973) and popularized by Drucker (1988, 1999), which explained how knowledge is the main driver of economic value. The knowledge economy or society had replaced the industrial age and, therefore, the management of knowledge became the main focus of organizations striving to be successful in this new era.

The knowledge economy concept has three themes. First, there is the idea that knowledge is valuable and, indeed, is the most valuable resource. The knowledge-based view of the firm (KBV) promoted this idea (e.g. see Grant, 1996). This promises competitive advantage from differential access to knowledge and its management. Second, there has been a transition from manufacturing industries to information/knowledge-intensive industries as the key generators of wealth (e.g. Bell, 1973). This is a macro-environmental perspective which proposes that the nature of business, i.e. economics and competition, is changing and we need to keep up with the times. Third, there has been a fundamental change in the nature of work characterized by the emergence of knowledge workers (e.g. see Drucker, 1988, 1999). This has encouraged the notion that these workers need a new and different organization and way of being managed. Some researchers argue that the changing nature of business has made knowledge management essential for growth and survival (e.g. see Neef, 1999). Growth emerges from the ability to exploit existing and acquired knowledge assets, and survival is achieved by adapting to existing and emerging changes to the firm's competitive environment (e.g. see Quintas et al., 1997).

Knowledge management owes information technology, computers, and the internet a great deal. Knowledge management emerged in response to demand from practitioners, largely based on the need to manage the growing complexity of information generated by computers in the workplace. As shown in the timeline of the history of knowledge management in Chapter 2, information technology's influence may be traced back to 1969 with the invention of the first networked computers, i.e. the ARPANET. It may be argued that computers introduced the need to manage information-seeking behaviour. However, the most important influence of information technology is connectivity.

Connectivity is the capacity to link two or more people together in a virtual work space, so they can share knowledge. The real power in the concept of connectivity lies in its economic value. People can share knowledge at relatively low cost and the resource is reusable. The fact that knowledge does not diminish with use and that the opposite actually occurs – it gains value the more it is used – provides it with powerful potential value. Tapscott and Williams (2006) called this wikinomics. Their book *Wikinomics* describes how mass collaboration has changed everything about work. They call the 21st century the age of participation and explain how information technology has provided the opportunity to participate at the fingertips of everyone. Using wikis, blogs, and other online forums, more people are becoming involved in mass collaboration (Tapscott and Williams, 2006). This has changed the way goods and services are invented, produced, marketed, and distributed on a global scale. An example is Goldcorp, a gold-mining company that risked its secretive mining exploration to seek ideas from the global virtual community by offering financial incentives for good ideas (Tapscott and Williams, 2006); Goldcorp became a billion-dollar 'juggernaut' based on its willingness to share knowledge about its mining exploration activities, and use information technology to collect ideas.

Information technology has also responded to problems associated with the implementation of its tools and techniques. Traditionally, information technology focused on the capture and codification of knowledge and on making it accessible for others to use. It has moved towards the application of advanced information technologies, such as intranets, web browsers, data warehouses, data mining, and artificial intelligence, to systemize, facilitate, and expedite organization-wide knowledge management (Alavi and Tiwana, 2005). In this way, information technology has evolved to help knowledge management combine its technological and behavioural elements.

The knowledge marketplace has demonstrated how knowledge has commercial value. Davenport and Grover (2001) argued that knowledge management emerged first in organizations that sell knowledge, i.e. consulting firms and those in research and development. The concept of knowledge as a product which may be packaged and sold required a system to manage it. For instance, Pfeffer and Sutton (2000) explain that organizations spend billions of dollars annually around the globe on management consulting.

CORE CONCEPT: The knowledge marketplace requires firms to develop the capability to sell their knowledge, and customers to recognize the value of the knowledge they are paying for.

Huizing and Bouman (2002: 185) see knowledge management as a discipline 'bridging information demand and supply in support of learning processes within organizations'. This perspective considers the knowledge market as the transaction space for filling knowledge gaps (see Chapter 5).

While these factors have attracted interest in knowledge management, its value proposition lies in several claims it makes. First, knowledge – KM's resource – is a source of competitive advantage. This is grounded in the knowledge-based view (KBV) of the firm's proposition that knowledge is the firm's most valuable resource (e.g. see Grant, 1996). The KBV argues that knowledge is now more important than the traditional sources of economic power (Storey and Barnett, 2000), mainly because knowledge is embedded in products and services and this makes it difficult for competitors to copy.

CORE CONCEPT: Knowledge meets the criteria for competitive advantage found by the resource-based view (RBV) of the firm, such as being valuable, rare, or difficult to imitate (e.g. see Grant, 2013).

Second, knowledge management is the cause of inter-firm differences in performance. This is grounded in research into the difference between book and market value of the firm (e.g. see Mouritsen et al., 2001). Increasingly, leading firms, such as Microsoft, have a market capitalization much greater than their tangible assets. This has occurred because the market placed a value on their intangible assets above the firm's book value. Firms are being rewarded by the market for what they know, which concludes that economic value is increasingly being driven by intangible assets, i.e. knowledge (Boisot, 2002). Researchers have argued that KM produces a capability which improves firm performance, defined by processes and infrastructure (Gold et al., 2001).

Third, KM improves growth prospects (e.g. see Grant, 1996). This is grounded in organizational learning theory where KM can be considered a change initiative designed to increase the organizational knowledge base (see Massingham and Diment, 2009). If people are learning, their knowledge is increasing (see Chapter 8). The organizational knowledge base is the stock of knowledge, i.e. its intangible assets, and increases should be reflected in higher market capitalization.

Fourth, KM enables best practice business models. The knowledge economy's aspirational model is learning organization capacity (LOC). LOC is considered ideal for 21st century organizations where knowledge is considered a valuable resource (see Chapter 8). LOC is characterized by effectively managing knowledge resources (Grant, 1996), responding to forces for change (Senge, 1990), and learning from experiences (Coulson-Thomas, 1996). Attaining LOC status is seen as demonstrating the capacity to manage knowledge effectively, and the outcomes of improved organizational learning and increased organizational knowledge base are assumed and reflected in improved financial and non-financial performance.

CRITICISM OF KNOWLEDGE MANAGEMENT

If knowledge management is to survive and grow, it must demonstrate value to those who make investment decisions and those who will do knowledge management as part of their work. There must be clear evidence of organizational and personal gain. The 'What's in it for me?' syndrome is never stronger than with knowledge management. At a broad level, knowledge management suffers from the fact that it is intangible. Knowledge management is intangible in the sense that it is difficult to identify its impact on organization performance, growth, and profitability. This causes uncertainty and increased risk, particularly in terms of investment decisions. However, knowledge management has also been criticized regarding confusion over its theoretical assumptions and their interpretation.

Theoretical criticisms may be summarized by Tsoukas's view (2003). Tsoukas's criticisms of the field lie in strong intellectual debate about the nature of knowledge. Based on his reading of Polanyi's work on tacit knowledge (see Polanyi, 1962; Polanyi and Prosch, 1975), Tsoukas (2003) argues that proponents of knowledge management misunderstand and misapply tacit knowledge. His attack focuses on the notion of professional or theoretical knowledge. While he agrees that the nature of work has changed and that it has become more complex, the problem lies in the relationship between knowledge and work. He argues that knowledge economies, knowledge-intensive organizations, and knowledge workers use codified knowledge rather than tacit knowledge. The objective theoretical knowledge learned at university must be applied to unique organizational contexts. Even the most theoretical of knowledge, such as pure mathematics, requires the skills of the mathematician to use it in practice

(Tsoukas, 2003). This means that professional theoretical knowledge is used in a non-codifiable and non-theoretical manner (2003). Tsoukas's criticism is that the notion of the knowledge economy, and its underlying premise that knowledge-intensive organizations are differentiated from others by a higher level or theoretical knowledge, are flawed because this knowledge cannot be managed by organizations.

DEEP THINKING: The value of knowledge is created by the individual who uses it to do work which is important to the organization. It is the individual's skill in applying this knowledge to the work context which creates value, rather than a knowledge management system.

This seems to focus attention on learning – within the unique context of each individual and their work in their organization – as the value-creating activity, rather than knowledge management.

Criticism regarding the interpretation of knowledge management (what it is and how it may be implemented) may be summarized by Ray and Clegg's (2005) view. Ray and Clegg's (2005) concern is that knowledge management promises to do two things which are contradictory and, therefore, it makes false claims. The first claim is that knowledge management allows people to discover and share universal truth – theoretical knowledge or what may be described as best practice in an organizational setting. The second claim is that knowledge management requires the individual to internalize and apply knowledge based on their human experience. These two claims appear contradictory to Ray and Clegg because personal belief must be part of the objective universal knowledge sought. This appears impossible because human experience is so diverse. How can everyone agree that one business practice is the best in all situations and at all times? Ray and Clegg (2005) argue that knowledge management is an illusion because it tries to solve this dilemma by using the noun 'knowledge' as an adjective, which suggests that knowledge can be moved around, through knowledge sharing and knowledge flows. Ray and Clegg (2005: 340) ask: 'what exactly is shared and what flows?' If someone shares what they know with you, you may learn something, but you have not taken their knowledge from them. They still have that knowledge. You now have something else, which is your knowledge.

DEEP THINKING: Ray and Clegg (2005) blame knowledge management's illusion on Nonaka and Takeuchi's (1995) famous knowledge-creating spiral, where knowledge is converted from tacit to explicit (codified) and back again. The flaws in this model will be examined in Chapter 5. The knowledge-creating spiral is, after all, just a learning loop. But the promise of discovering the secrets of Japanese business success led

(Continued)

(Continued)

to its success. Ray and Clegg's main concern with it is the fourth step – internalization – which they feel contradicts the objective best practice sharing idea of the model. These issues may be resolved by revisiting the phrase 'justified true belief'. Objective theoretical knowledge needs all three criteria to be met. The key word is 'true'. How does the knower trust that it is true? This requires validation and collective agreement. Nonaka and Takeuchi tackle this with a subtle sleight of hand; they say justified belief is enough. If the individual or the small group believe it is true, and it works for them, they can claim it as knowledge. In this way, the knowledge is internalized and the fourth step in the knowledge-creating spiral is achieved.

Knowledge management, therefore, has attracted much interest, as well as criticism. We now turn to look at how to decide whether to invest in knowledge management.

PERFORMANCE MEASUREMENT

OVERVIEW

The measurement of knowledge management (KM) performance is necessary to convince management and stakeholders that, first, it is worth investing in and, second, that it is adding value to the organization. There are a variety of methods used to assess how well KM is succeeding, including milestones and formative evaluation, and how well KM is helping attain organizational goals, i.e. outcomes and summative evaluation (Dalkir, 2011). The decision whether to invest in knowledge management begins with methods used to evaluate any organizational project. Managers must determine first whether the necessary funds are available, and then whether the project is worthwhile (Langfield-Smith et al., 2012: 996). In order to make sensible decisions about the evaluation, approval, and monitoring of investments in knowledge management, managers require an understanding of its value proposition (Zyngier, 2006).

CORE CONCEPT: The value proposition explains to stakeholders the benefits of knowledge management and how the risks of implementation will be managed (Zyngier, 2006).

Empirical evidence of the benefits of knowledge management has been inconclusive (Zack et al., 2009). Researchers have argued that KM produces a capability which improves firm performance, defined by processes and infrastructure

(Gold et al., 2001). This model distinguishes between KM activities (referred to as knowledge process capability) and enablers (referred to as knowledge infrastructure capability) (2001).

DEEP THINKING: Attempts to prove KM's capability, by decomposing Gold et al.'s (2001) model, have produced mixed results. Researchers argue that KM outcomes can only affect 'intermediate' firm performance and, therefore, can only be indirectly linked to firm financial performance (Lee and Choi, 2003). Zack et al. (2009) found a direct relationship with intermediate measures of organizational performance. These intermediate measures were based on three value disciplines: customer intimacy, product leadership, and operations excellence (Treacy and Wiersema, 1995). However, Zack et al. (2009) found that there was no significant relationship between KM practices and financial performance. Further research has found that KM capability can have an indirect impact on firm performance, but not a direct impact, i.e. financial performance. Mills and Smith (2011) showed that organizational structure, knowledge acquisition, knowledge application, and knowledge protection were significantly related to organizational performance; however, technology, organizational culture, and knowledge conversion did not have a significant impact. If Gold et al.'s (2001) model is disaggregated, this suggests that some processes and some infrastructure may help the firm, while others do not. Those that do help provide only intermediate impact.

Source: Massingham and Massingham (2014: 222)

MEASUREMENT CRITERIA

A KM measurement strategy should answer the following five questions:

1. Why are we measuring?
2. What are we measuring?
3. For whom are we measuring?
4. When are we measuring?
5. How are we measuring? (After Dalkir, 2011: 340)

This would establish how well KM is done.

DEEP THINKING: A KM measurement method should address two contexts: measurement theory and the measurement purpose. From a measurement theory perspective, Pike et al. (2002: 660) suggest that suitable criteria to assess measurement methods

(Continued)

(Continued)

are that: (1) it is auditable and reliable (2); it does not impose a large measurement overhead; (3) it facilitates strategic and tactical management; and (4) it generates the information needed by shareholders and investors. This list highlights the need for objectivity and usefulness. From a measurement purpose perspective, Andriessen (2004) explained that measurement methods should produce information that is useful (desirable) based on a non-monetary criterion which can be translated into observable criteria (objective, testable, and provable).

Source: Massingham (2016: 410–411)

DEEP THINKING: Investment criteria are usually divided into hard (financial) and soft (non-financial) indicators (Tiwana, 2001). Research has found that managers do not always demand solid business cases for KM investments but they do have trouble making decisions based on 'soft' gains or benefits alone (Tiwana, 2001). Therefore, a range of financial and non-financial criteria are proposed to assess the knowledge management investment decision. Firm performance measures are often classified as lead and lag indicators (Eckerson, 2006). Results focus on reporting performance (lag indicators). Drivers focus on improving performance (lead indicators). Results can be short term or long term; long-term results tend to have trend analysis which can track performance changes, while short-term results tend to focus on the present. Drivers can also be short term or long term. Short-term drivers may be described as operational in that they focus on improving today's results. Long-term drivers are strategic and focus on building capabilities for the future (Eckerson, 2006). Designing lead and lag indicators for KM is very useful, as it helps translate the abstract notion of KM into practical terms. Managers can begin to visualise what needs to be done (lead indicators) and what will happen (lag indicators) if they invest in KM.

Source: Massingham and Massingham (2014: 224)

In terms of a measurement method that produces information which is useful, i.e. facilitates strategic and tactical management, and generates the information needed by shareholders and investors, integrated reporting (IR) may be the way forward. IR represents an opportunity for the management of intangible assets, such as knowledge management, to be captured as useful information (Cuozzo et al., 2017). IR is a single umbrella report that pulls together the key elements of all other reports, to produce information on which assurance conclusions may be drawn, and which follows high quality international assurance standards (IFAC, 2017: 1). IR has a six capitals framework (Abeysekera, 2013) including three which allow for the measurement of intangible assets: intellectual (structural), relational, and human capital. Therefore, it is familiar with intangible assets. The value of the management of these assets, i.e. KM, could be added to the IR framework.

PERFORMANCE MANAGEMENT SYSTEMS

There are numerous performance management systems. They include:

1. Benchmarking
2. Balanced scorecard
3. 'House of quality'
4. Result-based assessment. (Dalkir, 2011)

Benchmarking 'entails comparing how different companies (both inside and outside the industry) perform various value chain activities ... and then making cross-company comparisons of the costs and effectiveness of these activities' (Thompson et al., 2018: 104). Benchmarking aims to identify the best way to perform an activity and how to copy these best practices. From a knowledge management perspective, it is about capturing, storing, and using best practice, i.e. a codification strategy.

The *balanced scorecard* (*BSC*) emerged as a measurement framework that drives performance (Kaplan and Norton, 1996). The BSC approach uses the term balanced to reflect the balance of financial and non-financial measures, of short- and long-term goals, and of reflective (lag) and predictive (lead) indicators. It asks questions of the organization from four key perspectives:

1. *Financial*: To succeed financially, how should we appear to our shareholders? Profitable? Prudent?
2. *Customer/Stakeholder*: To achieve our vision, what should characterize how we appear to our customers? Purpose? Service? Quality?
3. *Internal*: To satisfy our stakeholders, what business processes must we excel at? Productivity? Efficiency? Streamlining?
4. *Learning and growth*: To accomplish our mission, and support internal processes, what kind of staff and information systems do we need? Innovation? Continuous learning? Intellectual assets? (Kaplan and Norton, 1996)

It is from the last perspective – learning and growth – that knowledge management can make the most direct impact (see Massingham et al., 2019).

The *'house of quality'* method is an example of performance assessment from the fields of quality management and business process improvement. It was developed to show the connections between 'true quality, quality characteristics, and process characteristics' (Dalkir, 2011: 354). The key elements of this method include desired outcomes, priorities attached to those outcomes, and appropriate metrics for each outcome (after 2011: 354–356).

The *results-based assessment* framework is a results chain which includes activities, immediate outcomes (outputs), intermediate outcomes, and final outcomes (impact) (Dalkir, 2011: 357). It places emphasis on realistic results, monitoring of expected results, reporting, and describing measurable change (2011: 356–358). It is useful because it measures progress over time and it is grounded in the value creation of work activity. There are no specific examples of how to apply knowledge management to this framework. However, it would not be difficult to do so as, for example, any knowledge management activity could be translated into outputs, outcomes, and impacts, such as via lead and lag indicators.

Despite this list of existing methods, Dalkir (2011: 358) admits that 'metrics in general and KM metrics in particular are still a long way from being an exact science' and 'causality still eludes us'. It is this latter point which most concerns me. If knowledge management is to demonstrate value, it must provide objective evidence of causality. Managers must know that if they do X, i.e. invest \$Y in KM, then Z will happen. We now turn to look at how this may be done.

THE FINANCIAL IMPACT OF KNOWLEDGE MANAGEMENT

There is a wide range of financial metrics that may be used to evaluate the value proposition for KM investment.

THEORY IN PRACTICE: FINANCIAL METRICS

Financial metrics include return on investment, cost–benefit analysis, and value appropriation. These measures are commonly used in financial reports which assess performance as well as investment. They are particularly useful for evaluating the use of capital from a forward-thinking perspective (Langfield-Smith et al., 2012).

The standard method for evaluating any organizational project's worth is *return on investment (ROI)* (Langfield-Smith et al., 2012: 127). Knowledge management (KM) faces several challenges in persuading managers it has worthwhile ROI. Primarily, it is difficult to define and understand: knowledge is an intangible resource which, by its nature, is difficult to measure. Therefore, KM is problematic from an ROI perspective because managers ask what it is they are investing in (Massingham and Massingham, 2014: 224–225).

ROI can be disaggregated into three types:

1. Time to payback: the lead indicator is the KM investment; the lag indicator is the time required to recover the capital invested in the solution. At the CSO

(see closing case study at the end of this chapter), KM investment to accelerate experience curve effects (e.g. a lessons learned database) was offset by reduced salary costs which were estimated at $3.9 million p.a. The payback period was six months.

2. Raw ROI: the lead indicator is the KM investment; the lag indicator is the ratio of expected cash benefits (decreased costs and increased revenue) to the costs associated with the investment. At the CSO, KM investment to improve connectivity (e.g. businesss process improvement) was offset by productivity gains which were estimated at a 10% decrease in salary costs per work output. The raw ROI was 20:1.

3. Time to value: the lead indicator is the KM investment; the lag indicator is the period between the system's acquisition and value delivery. The lag indicator is typically estimated based on business performance improvement, often increased customer satisfaction (i.e. quality). At the CSO, KM investment to improve external socialization (e.g. social network analysis) was offset by increased resource acquisition (budget). The value period was 12 months.

Source: Adapted from Massingham and Massingham (2014: 224–225)

DEEP THINKING: Boudreau (2003: 365) suggests a framework for measuring KM based on stocks, flows, and enablers. Stocks may be defined as the existing level of knowledge at a point in time (2003: 365). If knowledge is the firm's most valuable strategic resource (Grant, 2013) then increased knowledge stock must create value. Indicators include capability measures such as performance improvement (e.g. productivity gains). Flows may be defined as the movement of knowledge between entities, which includes individuals, organizational units, and organizations (Boudreau, 2003: 365). This is also called knowledge transfer, organizational learning, and social capital (Easterby-Smith and Lyles, 2003). If organizational learning is a source of competitive advantage (DeNisi et al., 2003) then increased knowledge flow must create value. Indicators include innovation measures such as new product sales (revenue increase) or process improvement (cost reduction). Enablers are defined as investments, structures, and activities established by organizations to increase stocks or flows (Boudreau, 2003: 365). Gold et al.'s model of KM capability (2001) defined enablers as knowledge infrastructure comprising technology, organizational culture, and organizational structure. If KM is a source of inter-firm performance difference (Boisot, 2002) then increased performance in KM enablers must create value. Indicators include growth prospect measures such as profitability.

Source: Massingham and Massingham (2014: 225)

DEEP THINKING: Cost–benefit analysis: KM's second challenge in persuading managers that it has worthwhile ROI is that it is difficult to measure in cost terms. This makes it difficult for managers to assess its ROI because the ROI model uses cash flow as its basic unit of measurement. Cash flow is literally the amount of cash that comes in or goes out – without any accounting adjustment. ROI is different from investment in a piece of capital equipment, where the latter can be depreciated over time, and the cost diffused. In ROI, the entire initial cost is treated as a single initial cash outlay. This method is supported by contemporary management accounting, which is increasingly using non-financial and qualitative information to help managers make decisions such as ROI (Langfield-Smith et al., 2012: 45). Indicators include the financial return from KM investment measured by net cash flow.

Source: Massingham and Massingham (2014: 225)

DEEP THINKING: Value appropriation: KM's third challenge in persuading managers it has worthwhile ROI is that it is causally ambiguous. This may be explained by value appropriation theory (Grant, 2013). The purpose of any organization is to create value. Value represents the money a customer is willing to pay a firm for its product or service, or the money investors are willing to pay to purchase shares in the firm is the monetary worth of a product or an asset (Grant, 2013). The more value customers or investors perceive the firm to offer, the higher the price the firm can charge for its product or service or shares. Firm strategy, therefore, should seek to create value for customers (Grant, 2013). This is applicable to both private and public sector organizations. In the private sector, indicators include superior performance measured by profitability that is higher than industry average (Porter, 1985). In the public sector, indicators include superior performance measured by work output measures, resulting in budget increases (i.e. funding).

Financial benefits can impact on the top line or the bottom line. Top-line impact is increased sales that would not have occurred without the KM investment. An example is a new product created by a KM investment. Bottom-line impact is cost reductions, typically reduced outlays eliminated by the KM project.

Source: Massingham and Massingham (2014: 226)

THE NON-FINANCIAL IMPACT OF KNOWLEDGE MANAGEMENT

There is a wide range of non-financial metrics that may be used to evaluate the value proposition for KM investment. These include market share, employee turnover, and customer satisfaction (e.g. see Tiwana, 2001).

DEEP THINKING: Corporate governance: KM's first non-financial value proposition is how it helps demonstrate good corporate governance. Corporate governance uses evidence, usually firm performance measures, to provide stakeholders with confidence that the firm is being managed appropriately. Firm performance measures have three functions. First, measures are needed to comply with a regulatory obligation; a typical example is an annual report to shareholders (Neely, 1998). The lead indicator is strategic alignment. The lag indicator is compliance with stakeholder expectations manifested in the societal contract (e.g. Deegan, 2009).

Second, measures are often used to check the financial and non-financial health of a firm on a regular basis; examples include monthly financial and operating reports (Neely, 1998). The lead indicator is resource management. The lag indicator is financial reporting ratios. Third, measures are used to challenge the assumptions that underpin strategy; strategy is essentially a set of hypotheses that link intended actions to expected results, and measurement assists in testing the validity of these hypotheses (Neely, 1998). The lead indicator is strategic management. The lag indicator is change management indicators.

Source: Massingham and Massingham (2014: 226)

Researchers argue that soft measures make managers uncertain about the ROI from intangible services such as KM (Tiwana, 2001). To address this, Tiwana suggests *benchmarking*.

DEEP THINKING: Benchmarking enables context by comparing against best practice. There are several ways to benchmark: (a) internally by comparing business units against one another; (b) using competition, by comparing against closest competitors; (c) as a comparison against overall industry standards; and (d) by cross-industry providing insight against non-competing firms (Tiwana, 2001). The lead indicator is knowledge strategy; the lag indicator is change management indicators. The best way to benchmark KM is against a traditional list of hard and soft performance indicators (see Tiwana, 2001). These are proxies for effective change management and include hard measures (e.g. cost savings, cost of sales/expense reduction, and profit margins) and soft measures, (e.g. customer satisfaction, employee loyalty, and cultural change).

The final way KM's value proposition is examined is by problem solving. Managers asked to invest in KM will ask: what will happen if I invest in KM? A persuasive argument may be produced by looking at problem solving. Practitioners may see KM's value if this is translated into how it may help them fix complex ongoing organizational problems. Massingham and Massingham (2014) identified

THEORY IN PRACTICE: PERFORMANCE DRIVERS

Performance drivers help translate performance measures into practical terms by focusing the firm on improvement. There are several ways to define performance drivers. Eckerson (2006) defines four levels: (1) day-to-day regular activities, (2) day-to-day resource consumption, (3) business process improvement, and (4) learning and growth. KM may create value, in practical terms, by demonstrating how it can improve firm performance in each of these areas.

At the CSO, knowledge management activities addressed these performance drivers in the following ways:

1. *Day-to-day regular activities*: learning economies result in reduced learning time; strategic alignment – less reworking; connectivity – less search cycle time; risk management – less firefighting; psychological contract – greater motivation and initiative.
2. *Day-to-day resource consumption*: experience economies increase capacity utilization (use experience); connectivity – work time rather than search time; risk management – customers use work outputs; psychological contract – cross-unit cooperation.
3. *Business process improvement*: connectivity – reduces the number of waste points; risk management – less duplication; psychological contract – better relational behaviours and attitudes.
4. *Learning and growth: experience economies* – accelerate younger staff; learning economies – accelerate new staff; value management – decrease capability gap; psychological contract – increase social capital.

These performance drivers are explained further in section 6 of Table 3.2.

seven practical problems which many organizations are likely to face. Their idea is that if KM can demonstrate how it can fix these problems, practitioners will see its value and will be more likely to invest in KM.

THEORY IN PRACTICE: PROBLEM SOLVING

There are three methods used to assess the benefits created by problem solving at the CSO:

1. *Activity* measures how busy staff are: experience economies – more staff working on important tasks; learning economies – more staff working on

continuous improvement; connectivity – more informed decisions; psychological contract – greater knowledge use.

2. *Efficiency* measures how productively staff perform their activities (this is doing things well): experience economies – more outputs from younger staff; learning economies – more task completion from new staff; connectivity – faster task completion; risk management – increased motivation; psychological contract – greater commitment.

3. *Effectiveness* measures what results the staff achieve in performing their activities (this is doing the right things): strategic alignment – less mistakes; psychological contract – more creativity.

These performance drivers are explained further in section 7 of Table 3.2.

CORE CONCEPT: If knowledge management can demonstrate that it can solve significant and ongoing organizational problems, and the benefits are provided in at least one of these three areas – activity, efficiency, effectiveness – then people will see both organizational and personal gain.

EVALUATING THE SEVEN PRACTICAL OUTCOMES OF KNOWLEDGE MANAGEMENT

Seven methods were identified by Massingham and Massingham (2014) for measuring the practical outcomes of knowledge management against the criteria developed to assess KM's value proposition presented in this chapter. Table 3.2 summarizes the results based on empirical evidence over the five-year study conducted with the case study organization. The first column is the criterion used to assess KM value, for instance financial indicators. The second column is the measure used to determine the value. The remaining seven columns are the seven practical outcomes that may be addressed by KM. The arrow symbols in the table refer to decreases or increases. The table provides a comprehensive checklist to make KM investment decisions. Practitioners may use the checklist to evaluate KM proposals and whether the investment should be approved, and stakeholders may use the checklist to later evaluate KM investments and whether management made the correct decision.

TABLE 3.1 Practical outcomes of knowledge management

Measure	Definition	Problem	Solution	Benefits	Summary
Learning curve (LC)	Productivity increases resulting from learning (Schenkel and Teigland, 2008). As people do tasks at work, they learn, and this learning accumulates over time. It quantifies the value of learning to the organization in terms of reduced cost and time.	Large proportions of new staff due to high employee turnover rates or an ageing workforce (e.g. retirements). New staff take time to become fully competent. During this period, their work will be slower and they will cost more per work output.	Better organizational learning. The KM tools are: exit interviews and handovers (knowledge continuity), expert teams (opportunities to learn), parallel thinking and double-loop learning (better learning capabilities), and contract specification with external experts (targeted learning).	Reduced staff salary costs and decreased waste and mistakes. Learning reduces the unit cost of direct labour and thus the overall product unit cost (Nieto and Perez-Cano, 2004). Competent staff can produce more than incompetent staff, and thus accumulated learning means lower-per-unit costs in terms of staff salaries. The main source of cost reduction created by the LC is decreased mistakes (Li and Rajagopalan, 1997). LC cost reduction may be measured in terms of salary costs per work output and salary costs to redo or fix defective work.	KM accelerates time to competence.
Experience curve (EC)	Value-added costs, net of inflation, decline systematically with increases in cumulative volume (Day and Montgomery, 1983). This means that the total costs per work unit will decrease as experience increases (BCG, 1972: 12).	Large proportions of young staff due to exiting older staff. Young staff take time to gain experience. During this period, they will produce less work, which is of less quality than experienced staff, and they will cost the organization more per work output.	Better sharing of experience. The KM tools are: psychometric analysis to address motivation of senders (those with experience), skills training (for both senders and receivers), action learning including after action reviews, peer assists, and lessons learned databases.	Increased innovation resulting from accumulated experience and reduced total cost of the workforce. LC effects are about gaining competence, while EC effects are about the value created by accumulated competence.	KM increases sharing of experience.

Measure	Definition	Problem	Solution	Benefits	Summary
	It quantifies the value of experience to the organization in terms of reduced total cost and increased innovation. As they do work, people gain experience, and this experience accumulates over time.			People who are experienced learn new tasks more quickly, contribute to business improvement, and produce more outputs per unit of time. These experience effects are the benefits accrued by knowing how to do a task well. Experience also has a direct impact on total cost. EC cost reduction may be measured in terms of replacement cost. While inexperienced staff cost less than experienced staff, they also produce less; therefore the organization must employ more of them to produce the same volume of work produced by the lost experienced staff.	
Strategic alignment (SA)	Whether staff capability matches job requirements. It ensures minimal waste, duplication, and also organizational learning benefits.	High proportions of incompetent staff caused by poor workforce planning. People in the wrong jobs produce poor quality work which causes customer dissatisfaction. These staff take supervisors or peers away from their work, decreasing overall productivity.	Objective decision models. The KM tools are: Knowledge Strategy, Knowledge Accounts, and Competency Mapping.	Improved workforce performance resulting from quicker task completion and reduced mistakes. SA effects are about reducing time spent on learning by doing, and need for supervision. There is also direct impact in terms of customer satisfaction from better quality work and faster task responsiveness.	KM ensures the right people are in the right job.

(Continued)

TABLE 3.1 (Continued)

Measure	Definition	Problem	Solution	Benefits	Summary
Connectivity	Productivity gains generated by social capital. The more search cycle efficiency, the more likely staff can find what they need to know when they need it.	High proportions of staff with weak social networks. They do not know who to ask for help or cannot get help from people if they need it. The cost is measured in terms of the time taken to find knowledge necessary to perform a new task by learning by doing rather than by getting help from others.	Improve social network structure. The KM tools are: Knowledge Topographies (e.g. expert directories) and opportunities to socialize via Communities of Practice. The KM tools used to address blockages in knowledge flow were based on business process improvement mapping and lean thinking principles.	Improved knowledge production function. This is the most efficient allocation of the resource inputs (human capital and ideas) to create maximum production outputs (innovation or knowledge) (Mishra, 2007). Connectivity effects are about increasing productivity by enabling people's access to tacit knowledge when they need it. Knowledge search involves: (1) learning by doing; (2) asking a work colleague for help; (3) using codified knowledge such as policies, procedures, reports, and intranet; and (4) if all else fails, going outside the organization for help (e.g. consultants). Connectivity improves efficiency in this search cycle by identifying where to best find necessary knowledge.	KM increases search cycle efficiency.
Risk management	The risk of knowledge loss associated with the organization's activities, and the nature of the risk. It provides a 'why' context by developing shared mental models about the risk of knowledge loss and what it means for the organization, as well as how to fix the problem.	Poor corporate governance caused by ineffective risk management. The monitoring cost of managing inter-personal conflict resulting from different goals and understanding about a risk.	Provide customers with better 'why' context The KM tools are: (a) knowledge risk management model to guide risk evaluation, (b) information technology improvements to capture 'why' context, and (c) information system improvements to improve searchability and accessibility.	Improved quality of work outputs (e.g. risk management) and reducing the costs of negotiation time over disputed risk factors. RM effects are about improving the ability to predict time, i.e. when failure will occur. The quality of risk advice is measured by its ability to quantify the risk likelihood against action. In other words, what is the likelihood of failure X, if action Y is done to try to prevent it?	KM increases confidence in work outputs.

Measure	Definition	Problem	Solution	Benefits	Summary
		There is also a negative impact on morale, productivity, and employee turnover due to inter- and intra-organizational conflict.		RM provides cognitive consensus too, i.e. agreement over the nature of the risk event and its consequences. Cognitive consensus creates objectivity in risk management and reduces cognitive bias. It also measures how well the organization is managing the risk.	
Value management	The value of the organization for stakeholders. This persuades stakeholders to invest the resources necessary for the organization's survival.	The organization is not able to explain how it creates value. This is caused by poor relationships or communication with stakeholders. Senior stakeholders cannot understand the value of the organization's services, and they reduce funding. Customers do not understand why they should follow the organization's advice, and do not use its work outputs. Customer reputation for dissatisfaction.	Improve stakeholder satisfaction with organization performance. KM tools include: Internally, morale can be addressed via cultural change; more specifically, improved reward and recognition. Externally, relationship management training; job redesign to incorporate boundary spanning roles; increased opportunity to socialize performance improvements.	Improved organization performance from focus on value-adding activities and increased customer satisfaction from quicker task responsiveness. VM effects are about allocating staff to activities which are complex and discretionary (i.e. not done when under-resourced) but customers perceive as valuable. Continuous improvement may also increase if staff have time to reflect on work practice and innovate. Organizational learning will increase. Customer satisfaction will increase because staff will have time to build relationships with customers and socialize improvements.	KM improves stakeholder perception of the value of the organization.

(Continued)

TABLE 3.1 (Continued)

Measure	Definition	Problem	Solution	Benefits	Summary
Psychological contract	Employees' emotional relationship with their organization. It develops strong organizational culture, job satisfaction, and morale.	The job is not meeting the expectations of its staff in terms of their emotional relationship with their organization. The cost combines three factors: (a) low productivity, (b) poor quality work, and (c) high employee turnover.	Improve human resource management. KM tools are: reciprocity is improved via career management planning; work meaning and purpose is addressed by job redesign, with a particular focus on cause and effect relationships between work outputs and customer use; insiderness is addressed by including the individual in intra-organizational discipline teams, i.e. a virtual technology support network, providing staff with a sense of societal contribution.	Increased positive cultural change behaviours such as cooperation, teamwork, and sharing; as well as organizational commitment, loyalty, and reduced employee turnover. PC effects drive organizational commitment (OC). OC is an exchange agreement between individuals and the organization (Coopey, 1995) and may be understood within the motivational processes of the norm of reciprocity (e.g. Homans, 1961). This creates two psychological states necessary for productivity: safety and commitment (see Lipshitz et al., 2002). If employees feel the organization is investing in them, they will then feel empowered and safe, and trust in management, leading to organizational commitment. Reciprocity involves not just the individual but also their place within the broader social system of their organization. A new form of PC is emerging that has a 'transpersonal perspective, an evaluation not only of "what's in it for me?" (transactional) and "what's in it for us?" (relational) but also of "what is the fit between me, us, and the rest of society?" (Burr and Thomson, 2002: 7). This level of reciprocity leads to reduced employee turnover.	KM reduces employee turnover and increases productivity and work quality.

Source: Adapted from Massingham and Massingham (2014)

TABLE 3.2 Knowledge management practical outcomes summary

Financial indicators	Measure	Learning curve	Experience curve	Strategic alignment	Connectivity	Risk management	Value management	Psychological contract
1. Return-on-investment	1.1 Time to payback	12 months	6 months	3 months	12 months	18 months	18 months	>Return on recruitment
	1.2 Raw ROI (cost/return)	1:10 ratio	1:4 ratio	1:5 ratio	1:15 ratio	<Customer salary costs per unit of work but n/a really		<Salary sunk costs
	1.3 Time to value	3 months	6 months	12 months	6 months	3 years	12 months	6 months
	1.4 Stocks	>Grow capability	>Learn from experience	>Grow capability	>Respond to change	>Respond to change	>Grow capability	>Learn from experience
	1.5 Flows	>Accelerate new staff	>Accelerate younger staff	>Accelerate incompetent staff	>Knowledge diffusion	>Diffuse risk manager knowledge	<Capability gap	>Teamwork
	1.6 Enablers	<Time to competence	<Time to subject matter expertise	>Accelerate employee competence	>Social capital	>Corporate governance	<Future requirements gap	>Positive work behaviours
2. Cost–benefit analysis		<Agency costs	<Coordination costs	<Agency costs	<Coordination costs	<Exchange costs		<Training costs
3. Value appropriation		<Cost of mistakes	>Work quality	<Cost of mistakes	>Volume of work output per staff member	<Inherent weakness in the risk event	>Increased resource allocation	>Creativity
4. Corporate governance	4.1 Compliance			>Jobs match capability		>Regulatory framework	>Performance metrics met	
	4.2 Resource health					>Future capability requirements	>Progress	
	Strategy check						>Performance metrics	

(Continued)

TABLE 3.2 (Continued)

Non-financial indicators	Measure	Learning curve	Experience curve	Strategic alignment	Connectivity	Risk management	Value management	Psychological contract
5. Benchmarking hard indicators	5.1 Cost savings	<Training costs	<Costs per unit of work	<Agency costs	<Exchange costs	<Reduced mistakes by customer		<Recruitment costs
	5.2 Customer retention	<Task completion time		>Customer confidence		>Customer confidence		
	5.3 Repeat purchases	<Task completion time		>Capacity utilization		>Capacity utilization		
	5.4 Market share							
	5.5 Customer acquisition rate					>Market reputation	<Time taken to develop trust in the organization	
	5.6 Cost of sales	<Agency costs						
	5.7 Bottom line affects							
	5.8 Profit margins							
5. Benchmarking soft indicators	5.9 Customer satisfaction	<Task completion time	>Work quality			>Accessible 'why' context	>Socialize performance improvement	>Relationships
	5.10 Customer loyalty	<Task completion time		>Customer confidence		>Customer confidence	>Customer confidence	
	5.11 Employee productivity	<Task completion time	>Outputs from younger staff	>Outputs from incompetent staff	>Outputs from all staff	>Outputs from anxious staff	>Purpose	
	5.12 Employee loyalty					>Trust in management		<Careerism

Non-financial indicators	Measure	Learning curve	Experience curve	Strategic alignment	Connectivity	Risk management	Value management	Psychological contract
	5.13 Employee empowerment	<Time to competence		>Locus of control	>Locus of control		>Role clarity	>Calculative reward, calculative approval
	5.14 Employee retention (turnover)	<Time to competence		>Personal outcome expectancy	>Accessibility (social capital)	>Affective attachment	>Organizational direction	<Employee turnover costs (recruitment, training)
	5.15 Market leadership							
	5.16 Organizational stability	<Time to competence				<Inconsistent risk interpretations (shared mental models)	>Results focus	
	5.17 Cultural change	<Agency costs						>Positive cultural behaviours
6. Performance drivers								
Short-term drivers	6.1 Day-to-day	<Task completion time		<Reworking	<Search cycle time	<Fire fighting	>Resources	>Motivation and initiative
	6.2 Capacity utilization (resource consumption)		>Use experience		>Work time rather than search time	>Customers use the organization's experience		>Cross-unit cooperation
Long-term drivers	6.3 Business process improvement				<Waste points	<Duplication	>Relationships	>Relationships
	6.4 Learning and growth	>Accelerate new staff	>Accelerate younger staff	>Accelerate incompetent staff	>Knowledge diffusion	>Diffuse risk manager knowledge	<Capability gap	>Teamwork

(Continued)

TABLE 3.2 (Continued)

Non-financial indicators	Measure	Learning curve	Experience curve	Strategic alignment	Connectivity	Risk management	Value management	Psychological contract
7. Problem solving								
Cycle times	7.1 Activity	<Task completion time	>Staff working on important tasks			>Staff working on risk factors	>Discretionary services (i.e. non-core)	
		<Task completion time			<Task completion time			<Task completion time
Work practices	7.2 Efficiency	<Task completion time	>Outputs from younger staff	>Outputs from incompetent staff	>Searchability (codified knowledge)	>Motivation	>Enablers	<Task completion time
	7.3 Effectiveness	<Cost of mistakes		<Cost of mistakes	>Volume of work output per staff	<Inherent weakness in the risk event		>Creativity
Performance improvement	KM improves performance	<Task completion time	<Task completion time	<Less mistakes	<Task completion time	<Risk		>Change management
	Challenge underlying assumptions		>Talent pool for double-loop learning			>Risk factor analysis	>Continuous improvement	
	Quality	<Cost of mistakes		>Customer confidence	>Informed decisions	<Impact of the risk event occurring (i.e. increase no. of risk managers)		>Knowledge use

CONCLUSION

The purpose of this chapter was to examine how to measure the performance of knowledge management. The increasing interest in knowledge management has been driven by the concept of the knowledge economy. The three themes of the knowledge economy were discussed: (a) the idea that knowledge is valuable and, indeed, is the most valuable resource; (b) the transition from manufacturing industries to information/knowledge-intensive industries as the key generators of wealth; and (c) a fundamental change in the nature of work characterized by the emergence of knowledge workers. The chapter also discussed knowledge management as a source of sustainable competitive advantage.

While knowledge management makes several important claims, empirical evidence of its impact on firm performance has been inconclusive. This causes uncertainty and increased risk, particularly in terms of investment decisions. Knowledge management has also been criticized regarding confusion over its theoretical assumptions and their interpretation. Tsoukas (2003) argues that proponents of knowledge management misunderstand and misapply tacit knowledge. His attack focuses on the notion of professional or theoretical knowledge. Ray and Clegg's (2005) concern is that knowledge management promises to do two things which are contradictory and, therefore, it makes false claims. The first claim is that knowledge management allows people to discover and share universal truth – theoretical knowledge or what may be described as best practice in an organizational setting. The second claim is that knowledge management requires the individual to internalize and apply knowledge based on their human experience. These two claims appear contradictory to Ray and Clegg because personal belief (the second claim) must be part of the objective universal knowledge sought (the first claim). This appears impossible because human experience is so diverse. This discussion helps us understand why it is necessary to explore the value of KM. Criticisms of KM encourage healthy debate about its claims, from both a theoretical and a practical perspective.

This chapter has argued that investment decisions regarding KM may benefit from focusing on significant and ongoing organizational problems, which will connect KM with firm performance and demonstrate financial and non-financial impact. Various measures were discussed. Tables 3.1 and 3.2 provide a checklist for measuring KM's impact. Seven problems were identified which were then linked to practical outcomes. In this way, problems such as having high proportions of new staff are connected to a practical outcome, in this case accelerating new staff down the learning curve, to produce a range of financial and non-financial outcomes. For practitioners, the tables in this chapter provide management with a checklist to make investment decisions regarding KM. The ideas summarized in this chapter from Massingham and Massingham (2014) present a framework for you to consider against the claims KM makes and also its criticisms. You might then decide whether it is worthwhile to invest in KM and, if so, why.

CLOSING CASE STUDY: EVALUATING KNOWLEDGE MANAGEMENT AT THE CSO

In early 2012, the Australian Research Council project was nearing completion after five years. The industry partner executives were struggling to find ways to transition it from project status to programme status. Programme status would enable the lessons learned from the project to be implemented as an ongoing programme of work, after the research team had completed their project and left the organization. To do this, the project needed a home and a sponsor. The chief investigator (CI) worked closely with the previous senior industry partner (PIP) to develop a transition strategy. The PIP had been replaced by a new senior industry partner (SIP) but was asked to work with the CI to complete the project. This involved regular meetings with senior management, most of whom had little awareness of the project.

At each meeting, the CI found himself frustrated by having to continually explain the project and how it might fit with review X. There seemed to be no commitment and often little interest. The CI was confused because he believed that the people he had been meeting with should have been told about the project and that they should be willing to cooperate. In other words, the strategic learning from meetings with the senior executive had not flowed down to the operational learning at these meetings, and nor had the tactical learning from meetings with the SIP, who was their boss. The CI felt that these meetings should be at the operational level, discussing value creation; however, each meeting began at the strategic level, trying to persuade people new to the project to participate, i.e. strategic participation.

There was a particularly important meeting in early 2012 with a manager who had responsibility for a large part of the activities which could use the project's recommendations. At the meeting, the CI incorrectly assumed that the strategic and tactical learning had flowed from the SIP to this manager. The CI focused specifically on the detail of knowledge-sharing tools, and the manager quickly lost interest. He later told the PIP that the project was 'just a survey' and he would not be using the CI's tools. It was a crushing blow. Five years of work had been dismissed by someone who had not been properly briefed. The impact of this unfortunate meeting was that the project was sidelined; the CI did not meet again with anyone from the CSO for five months. During this period, the CI worked on final project reports, and tried to organize meetings without success.

The CI finally met with the PIP who explained that 'there was no money' available to implement the project's recommendations and that the CSO was not going to do anything with the project's outcomes. It would not be carried forward as a programme of work once the project was completed. This was devastating to the CI as it signalled that the project had failed. The CI worked on the final reports and issued them to the PIP as each was finished.

A positive outcome of this activity was that the PIP found renewed interest in the project outcomes, when he saw that some of the findings were good news and could be used to promote positive cultural change to senior executives. There was a critical exchange at a meeting between the PIP and the CI in the final few months of the project, in which the PIP said:

> You need to focus on the practical outcomes. We don't need to know what you are going to do with KM for us, or how it works; we just need to know what it will do for us. How will it create value? The way you describe it is too abstract for us. You need to discuss it in practical terms.

This important exchange focused the CI on analysing the project outcomes in terms of practical outcomes in the final few months of the project. It also helped explain why the project had suddenly been dismissed after one brief meeting. The CI had to focus on operational action research – how to make this work – and concentrate on practical outcomes, i.e. how this could help the CSO solve important organizational problems.

This created a small window of opportunity for the CI. By giving the CSO some good news from his final project reports, he had been able to quickly move the project from the strategic level, where it was stuck for more than half a year, to the operational level. A change in senior executive created further momentum. The SIP had disengaged from the project and delegated involvement to his managers whom, as we have seen, had little interest in the project. However, the SIP was promoted and his replacement presented an opportunity for the project to engage with the sponsor group. The replacement SIP was an individual who had worked for the PIP at the beginning of the project, and he knew of the project, what it was trying to achieve, and most importantly he had worked closely with the CI on a workplace engagement project. The advantage for the CI was that this new SIP did not start at the strategic level. He was easily moved down to the operational level and the CI could work with him on practical outcomes. Despite these efforts, the new SIP eventually sent the CI an email stating that he would not be carrying the project forward due to government budget cuts. It ended with the submission of the final project report and a friendly lunch between the PIP and the CI, who had tried for four years to make the project work but both felt they had failed.

The final reports explained how knowledge management could produce practical outcomes for the CSO. There were three iterations of these final reports. The first focused on the 'winning' KM tools and how they could create value. This reporting tried to translate the tools in practical terms by: (a) describing them in managerial words; (b) defining the problem each solved; (c) positioning them as part of the overall KM system, such as whether they represent a product or process view of KM; (d) packaging the solution, i.e. summarising its value; and (e) how the tool fits with the sponsor group's goals, i.e. whether it aligns with their stated objectives. This reporting did not generate much interest from the practitioners because it focused on the KM tool and not enough on how this created practical outcomes.

The second iteration focused on the organizational problem, rather than the KM tool (see Table 3.1). For knowledge sharing, for example, the main problems were: (1) younger staff, (2) slow task completion, and (3) the inability to explain value to stakeholders. These problems were translated into practical outcomes by arguing the need for (a) accelerating experience (young staff), (b) increasing productivity via search cycle efficiency (slow task completion), and (c) increasing confidence in organization performance (stakeholder value). This iteration also explained the consequences of inaction, i.e. what would happen if the tool was not implemented and these problems remained unresolved. These consequences included: (a) staff work on less important activities, creating less value (young staff); (b) poor quality of work, delays (task responsiveness), and low staff morale (frustration); and (c) insufficient resources necessary to improve performance (stakeholder value). This type of reporting created more interest from the practitioners, but its value was still considered intermediate or as having an indirect impact on performance and, therefore, was still too vague to produce commitment from the senior executives.

The third and final iteration placed numbers around the KM toolkit by quantifying the impact, and the investment required in terms of budget and time. This iteration focused on seven organizational

(Continued)

(Continued)

problems which would create significant value, if resolved, and could be addressed by the KM system recommended by the project as an ongoing programme of work (see Tables 3.1 and 3.2). Knowledge sharing, for example, directly addressed three of the practical outcomes: (1) the experience curve, (2) connectivity, and (3) value management. It also indirectly addressed the learning curve (e.g. handovers). The quantification of impact and cost enabled senior executives to examine the return on investment (ROI) of the proposed KM toolkit. For example, accelerating staff down the experience curve would save the CSO $3.9 million p.a. in avoided sunk salary costs. The toolkit required to address the experience curve was budgeted at a one-off investment of $230,000, meaning an ROI ratio of 1:17 (i.e. for every $1 invested, the return would be $17). These figures were persuasive and senior executives were interested. However, despite this work, the KM toolkit was not formally adopted by the CSO due to government budget cuts.

CASE STUDY QUESTIONS

1. Why did the CI feel his project had failed?
2. Why do you feel the CSO needed the CI to demonstrate practical value?
3. Using Table 3.1, how would you persuade the CSO that KM provides practical outcomes?
4. Using the framework provided in Table 3.2, would you invest $1 million in knowledge management at the CSO? Why, or why not?

REVIEW AND DISCUSSION QUESTIONS

1. Do you feel knowledge management needs to demonstrate its value? Why or why not?

2. What is the most compelling measure for knowledge management – financial or non-financial? Why?

3. Critically evaluate the seven practical outcomes model. Which of the seven problem areas do you feel is the most persuasive for measuring the performance of knowledge management? Why?

FURTHER READING

Massingham, P. and Massingham, R. (2014) Does Knowledge Management Produce Practical Outcomes? *Journal of Knowledge Management*, 18 (2): 221–254. This article provides further explanation of the practical outcomes model.

Mills, A.M. and Smith, T.A. (2011) Knowledge Management and Organizational Performance: A decomposed view. *Journal of Knowledge Management*, 15 (1): 156–171. This article is a critical review of knowledge management as a capability.

Zack, M., McKeen, J. and Singh, S. (2009) Knowledge Management and Organizational Performance: An exploratory analysis. *Journal of Knowledge Management*, 13 (6): 392–409. This article provides an alternative perspective.

BIBLIOGRAPHY

Abeysekera, I. (2013) A Template for Integrated Reporting. *Journal of Intellectual Capital*, *14* (20): 227–245.

Adams, J. (1995) *Risk*, London, UCL Press.

Alavi, M. and Tiwana, A. (2005) Knowledge Management: The information technology dimension. Chapter 6 in Easterby-Smith, M. and Lyles, M.A. (eds) *Handbook of Organizational Learning and Knowledge Management*, Hong Kong, Blackwell, pp. 104–121.

Alvesson, M. (1995) *Management of Knowledge Intensive Firms*, London, de Gruyter.

Andriessen, D. (2004) *Making Sense of Intellectual Capital*, Burlington, MA, Elsevier Butterworth-Heinemann.

Bell, D. (1973) *The Coming of Post-Industrial Society*, Harmondsworth, Penguin.

Boisot, M. (2002) The Creation and Sharing of Knowledge. In Choo, C.W. and Bontis, N. (eds) *The Strategic Management of Intellectual Capital and Organizational Knowledge*, New York, Oxford University Press, pp. 65–78.

Boston Consulting Group (BCG) (1972) *Perspectives on Experience*, Boston, BCG.

Boudreau, J. (2003) Strategic Knowledge Measurement and Management. In Jackson, S.E., Hitt, M.A. and Denisi, A.S. (eds) *Managing Knowledge for Sustained Competitive Advantage: Designing strategies for effective human resource management*, San Francisco, CA, Jossey-Bass, pp. 360–398.

Burr, R. and Thomson, P. (2002) Expanding the Network: What About Including 'The All' in the Psychological Contract? In *Academy of Management Conference* (Denver, Colorado, USA ed.). Denver, Colorado, USA: Academy of Management.

Cavusgil, S.T., Knight, G., Reisenberger, J.R., Rammal, H.G. and Rose, E.L. (2014) *International Business: The new realities*, 2nd edition, Melbourne, VIC, Pearson Australia.

Coopey, J. (1995) Managerial Culture and the Stillbirth of Organizational Commitment. *Human Resource Management Journal*, *5* (3): 56–76.

Coulson-Thomas, C.J. (1996) BPR and the Learning Organization. *The Learning Organization*, *3* (1): 16–21.

Cuozzo, B., Dumay, J., Palmaccio, M. and Lombardi, R. (2017) Intellectual Capital Disclosure: A structured literature review. *Journal of Intellectual Capital*, *18* (1): 9–28.

Dalkir, K. (2011) *Knowledge Management in Theory and Practice*, 2nd edition, Cambridge, MA, MIT Press.

Davenport, T.H. and Grover, V. (2001) Introduction to Special Issue: Knowledge management. *Journal of Management Information Systems*, *18* (1): 3–4.

Day, G.S. and Montgomery, D.B. (1983) Diagnosing the Experience Curve. *Journal of Marketing*, *47* (2): 44–58.

Deegan, C. (2009) *Financial Accounting Theory*, 3rd edition, North Ryde, NSW, McGraw-Hill.

DeNisi, A.S., Hitt, M.A. and Jackson, S.E. (2003) The Knowledge-based Approach to Sustainable Competitive Advantage. Chapter 1 in Jackson, S.E., Hitt, M.A. and DeNisi, A.S. (eds) *Managing Knowledge for Sustained Competitive Advantage: Designing strategies for effective human resource management*, San Francisco, CA, Jossey-Bass, pp. 3–36.

De Zoysa, S. and Russell, A.D. (2003) Knowledge-based Risk Identification in Infrastructure Projects. *Canadian Journal of Civil Engineering, 30* (3): 511–522.

Drucker, P.F. (1988) The Coming of the New Organization. Chapter 1 in (1998) *Harvard Business Review on Knowledge Management*, Boston, MA, Harvard Business School Press, pp. 1–19.

Drucker, P. (1999) Knowledge-worker Productivity: The biggest challenge. *California Management Review, 41* (2): 79–94.

Easterby-Smith, M. and Lyles, M.A. (2003) Watersheds of Organizational Learning and Knowledge Management. Chapter 1 in Easterby-Smith, M. and Lyles, M.A. (eds) *Handbook of Organizational Learning and Knowledge Management*, Hong Kong, Blackwell.

Eckerson, W.W. (2006) *Performance Dashboards: Measuring, monitoring, and managing your business*, Hoboken, NJ, Wiley.

Gold, A.H., Malhotra, A. and Segars, A.H. (2001) Knowledge Management: An organizational capabilities perspective. *Journal of Management Information Systems, 18* (1): 185–214.

Grant, R.M. (1996) Towards a Knowledge-based Theory of the Firm. *Strategic Management Journal, 17*: 109–122.

Grant, R.M. (2013) *Contemporary Strategy Analysis: Text and cases*, 8th edition, Malden, MA, Blackwell.

Homans, G.C. (1961) *Social Behaviorism*, New York, Harcourt Brace and World.

Huizing, A. and Bouman, W. (2002) Knowledge and Learning, Markets and Organizations. In Choo, C.W. and Bontis, N. (eds) *The Strategic Management of Intellectual Capital and Organizational Knowledge*, New York, Oxford University Press, pp. 185–206.

International Federation of Accountants (IFAC) (2017) *Enhanced Organizational Reporting: Integrated reporting key*, Policy Position 8. New York, IFAC.

Kaplan, R.S. and Norton, D.P. (1996) *The Balanced Scorecard*, Boston, MA, Harvard Business School Press.

Kaplan, R.S. and Norton, D.P. (2001) *The Strategy-focused Organization*, Boston, MA, Harvard Business School Press.

Kaplan, R.S. and Norton, D.P. (2006) *Alignment*, Boston, MA, Harvard Business School Press.

Langfield-Smith, K., Thorne, H. and Hilton, R. (2012) *Management Accounting: Information for managing and creating value*, 6th edition, London, McGraw-Hill Education.

Lee, H. and Choi, B. (2003) Knowledge Management Enablers, Processes, and Organizational Performance: An integrative view and empirical examination. *Journal of Management Information Systems, 20* (1): 179–228.

Li, G. and Rajagopalan, S. (1997) A Learning Curve Model with Knowledge Depreciation. *European Journal of Operational Research, 105* (1): 143–154.

Lipshitz, R., Popper, M. and Friedman, V.J. (2002) A Multifacet Model of Organizational Learning. *Journal of Applied Behavioral Science, 38* (1): 78–98.

Looise, J.K. and Paauwe, J. (2001) HR Research in The Netherlands: Imitation and innovation. *International Journal of Human Resource Management, 12* (7): 1203–1217.

March, J.G. and Shapira, Z. (1987) Managerial Perspectives on Risk and Risk Taking. *Management Science, 22* (11): 1404–1418.

Martinus, K. (2010) Planning for Production Efficiency in Knowledge-based Development. *Journal of Knowledge Management, 14* (5): 726–743.

Massingham, P. (2010) Knowledge Risk Management: A framework. *Journal of Knowledge Management, 14* (3): 464–485.

Massingham, P. (2016) Knowledge Accounts. *Long Range Planning, 49* (3): 409–425.

Massingham, P. and Diment, K. (2009) Organizational Commitment, Knowledge Management Interventions, and Learning Organization Capacity. *The Learning Organization, 16* (2): 122–142.

Massingham, P. and Massingham, R. (2014) Does Knowledge Management Produce Practical Outcomes? *Journal of Knowledge Management, 18* (2): 221–254.

Massingham, R., Massingham, P. and Dumay, J. (2019) Improving Integrated Reporting: A new learning and growth perspective for the balanced scorecard. *Journal of Intellectual Capital: Special Edition, 20* (1): 60–82.

Mills, A.M. and Smith, T.A. (2011) Knowledge Management and Organizational Performance: A decomposed view. *Journal of Knowledge Management, 15* (1): 156–171.

Mishra, S.K. (2007) A Brief History of Production Functions. Available at: https://mpra.ub.uni-muenchen.de/5254 (accessed 7 November 2018).

Mouritsen, J., Larsen, H.T. and Bukh, P. (2001) Intellectual Capital and the 'Capable Firm': Narrating, visualising and numbering for managing knowledge. *Accounting, Organizations and Society, 26* (7): 735–762.

Neef, D. (1999) Making the Case for Knowledge Management: The bigger picture. *Management Decision, 37* (1): 72–78.

Neely, A. (1998) *Measuring Business Performance*, London, Economist Books.

Nieto, M. and Perez-Can, C. (2004) The Influence of Knowledge Attributes on Innovation Protection Mechanisms. *Knowledge and Process Management, 11* (2): 117–126.

Nishikawa, M. (2011) (Re)defining Care Workers as Knowledge Workers. *Gender, Work, and Organization, 18* (1): 113–136.

Nonaka, I. and Takeuchi, H. (1995) *The Knowledge-creating Company: How Japanese companies create the dynamics of innovation*, New York, Oxford University Press.

O'Donohue, W., Sheehan, C., Hecker, R. and Holland, P. (2007) The Psychological Contract of Knowledge Workers. *Journal of Knowledge Management, 11* (2): 73–82.

Paxton, L.J. (2006) Managing Innovative Space Missions: Lessons from NASA. *Journal of Knowledge Management, 10* (2): 8–21.

Pfeffer, J. and Sutton, R.I. (2000) *The Knowing–Doing Gap: How smart companies turn knowledge into action*, Boston, MA, Harvard Business School Press.

Pike, S., Rylander, A. and Roos, G. (2002) Intellectual Capital Management and Disclosure. Chapter 37 in Choo, C.W. and Bontis, N. (eds) *The Strategic Management of Intellectual Capital and Organizational Knowledge*, New York, Oxford University Press, pp. 657–672.

Polanyi, M. (1962) *Personal Knowledge*, Chicago, IL, University of Chicago Press.

Polanyi, M. and Prosch, H. (1975) *Meaning*, Chicago, IL, University of Chicago Press.

Porter, M.E. (1985) *Competitive Advantage: Creating and sustaining superior performance*, New York, Free Press.

Quintas, P., Lefrere, P. and Jones, G. (1997) Knowledge Management: A strategic agenda. *Long Range Planning, 30* (3): 385–391.

Ray, T. and Clegg, S. (2005) Tacit Knowing, Communication and Power: Lessons from Japan? In Little, S. and Ray, T. (eds) *Managing Knowledge: An essential reader*, 2nd edition, London, Sage, pp. 319–348.

Ross, M.V. and Schulte, W.D. (2005) Knowledge Management in a Military Enterprise: A pilot case study of the Space and Warfare Systems Command. Chapter 10 in Stankosky, M. (ed.) *Creating the Discipline of Knowledge Management: The latest in university research*, Burlington, MA, Elsevier Butterworth-Heinemann, pp. 157–170.

Rousseau, D.M. (1995) *Psychological Contracts in Organizations: Understanding written and unwritten agreement*, Newbury Park, CA, Sage.

Schenkel, A. and Teigland, R. (2008) Improved Organizational Performance through Communities of Practice. *Journal of Knowledge Management, 12* (1): 106–118.

Senge, P.M. (1990) *The Fifth Discipline: The art and practice of the learning organization*, London, Random House.

Storey, J. and Barnett, E. (2000) Knowledge Management Initiatives: Learning from failure. *Journal of Knowledge Management, 4* (2): 145–156.

Tapscott, D. and Williams, A.D. (2006) *Wikinomics: How mass collaboration changes everything*, London, Penguin Group.

Thompson, A.J., Jr., Peteraf, M.A., Gamble, J.E. and Strickland, A.J. (eds) (2018) *Crafting and Executing Strategy: The quest for competitive advantage – Concepts and cases*, 21st edition, New York, McGraw-Hill Irwin.

Thompson, P., Warhurst, C. and Callaghan, G. (2001) Ignorant Theory and Knowledgeable Workers: Interrogating the connections between knowledge, skills, and services. *Journal of Management Studies, 38* (7): 923–942.

Tiwana, A. (2001) *The Essential Guide to Knowledge Management: E-business and CRM applications*, Hoboken, NJ, Prentice-Hall.

Tovstiga, G. (1999) Profiling the Knowledge Worker in the Knowledge-intensive Organization: Emerging roles. *International Journal of Technology Management, 18*: 731–744.

Treacy, M. and Wiersema, F. (1995) *The Discipline of Market Leaders*, New York, HarperCollins.

Tsoukas, H. (2003) Do We Really Understand Tacit Knowledge? Chapter 21 in Easterby-Smith, M. and Lyles, M.A. (eds) *Handbook of Organizational Learning and Knowledge Management*, Hong Kong, Blackwell, pp. 410–427.

Von Nordenflycht, A. (2010) What is a Professional Service Firm? Towards a theory and a taxonomy of knowledge-intensive firms. *Academy of Management Review, 35* (1): 155–174.

Zack, M., McKeen, J. and Singh, S. (2009) Knowledge Management and Organizational Performance: An exploratory analysis. *Journal of Knowledge Management, 13* (6): 392–409.

Zyngier, S. (2006) Knowledge Management Governance. In Schwarz, D. (ed.) *The Encyclopaedia of Knowledge Management*, Hershey, PA, Idea Group Publishing, pp. 373–380.

4

THE VALUE OF KNOWLEDGE

CHAPTER OUTLINE

Learning outcomes
Management issues
Links to other chapters
Opening mini case study: The knowledge of academic staff at universities
Introduction
Knowledge's value proposition
Previous measurement methods
Knowledge Accounts
Future perspective: Integrated reporting
Conclusion
Closing case study: Knowledge Accounts at the CSO

LEARNING OUTCOMES

After completing this chapter, the reader should be able to:

1. Discuss why the value of knowledge is important
2. Consider existing methods for measuring the value of knowledge

3. Understand the Knowledge Accounts model
4. Reflect on the future of the measurement and reporting of intangible assets

MANAGEMENT ISSUES

Measuring the value of knowledge requires managers to:

1. Understand how knowledge can create value
2. Apply traditional measurement metrics to evaluate knowledge resources
3. Make enterprise resource planning decisions (e.g. workforce design) based on knowledge value measurement

Knowledge involves these challenges for management:

1. Interpreting the direct and indirect impact of knowledge resources on performance in terms of cause and effect
2. The capacity to quantify the value of knowledge in terms which stakeholders can understand

LINKS TO OTHER CHAPTERS

Chapter 1: on the definition of knowledge

Chapter 2: regarding the management of knowledge resources

Chapter 3: concerning the value of managing knowledge resources

Chapter 5: regarding how knowledge resources may represent a source of competitive advantage

OPENING MINI CASE STUDY

THE KNOWLEDGE OF ACADEMIC STAFF AT UNIVERSITIES: HOW TO MEASURE THE VALUE OF ACADEMIC KNOWLEDGE

Consider the lecturer standing before you teaching this subject (or any lecturer if you have already graduated). Do you value the knowledge of this academic? If so, how do you assess this value?

One way universities do this is through student surveys. At the end of the subject, you may be asked to complete a survey about your teacher. These surveys often have scales, for example 1 to 6, where students are asked to indicate whether they strongly agree (6) or strongly disagree (1) with a statement about their teacher, or anywhere in between 6 and 1. Statements tend to focus on the lecturer's style – for example, the teacher communicates clearly; process – for example, learning activities were effective and an efficient use of time; assessments – for example, feedback was helpful; and attitude towards students – for example, helpful in responding to questions or problems. The outcome is a mean score for each statement, indicating a sense of student satisfaction with the lecturer's teaching, as well as an overall mean score for all the statements. There are usually open-ended questions which also give students an opportunity to write comments.

This may tell us whether a lecturer is a good or bad teacher. But consider these statements and this process. Why would you rate your lecturer highly or lowly? Is it because you like them or not, or whether they give you good marks or not? Is it because their lectures are entertaining? Or is it because they really know their subject well? Do you feel these survey results accurately explain to the university the value of this person who is trying to teach you?

Academic staff do other things, much of which is not visible to students. They will do research, academic governance (administration), and sometimes community service or engagement. All of these activities have many facets. In simple terms, research may be considered in terms of inputs and outputs. Inputs are research activities which lead to outputs. Examples include designing a questionnaire, doing literature reviews, conducting fieldwork, analysing data, writing papers, writing research grant applications, and supervising higher degree research students. Outputs are completed research activities. Examples include journal articles published, successful research grants, commercial research income, and higher degree research student completions. However, there are problems with measuring the value of an academic's research in this way. First, inputs are not really recognized, and are very difficult to evaluate. An academic may be very research active in the areas outlined above, but this is only really valued when it becomes an output. For example, an academic may be writing five papers, but this is only recognized when the papers become published articles. Why does this occur? The papers may not be very good and might be rejected and never published in peer-reviewed journals. So, being busy is not enough. There must be an outcome.

Administration involves a range of activities, from being a subject coordinator to a course advisor to a head of school or other management position. It may also involve many routine but time-consuming activities, such as preparing and approving subject outlines, which take the academic away from the core business of teaching and research. Is administration more or less important than teaching and research? Should an academic who is good at administration be valued higher than those who are not?

There is much talk of universities having more impact in the 'real world' and being more relevant for business and local communities. Community service or working with industry and community is usually seen as a voluntary activity rather than a requirement for academics. However, given the trend towards greater community engagement, should academics who are good at external relationships be valued more than those who are not? Should community engagement be valued more than teaching and research?

How do you think universities value the knowledge of academics? You might say academics are classified in terms of their position. There are tutors (or associate lecturers), lecturers, senior

(Continued)

(Continued)

lecturers, associate professors, and professors. Is this an accurate way to measure the value of academic staff? Have you ever had a teacher who is at lecturer level who you felt was a fantastic teacher? Or an associate professor who does not seem to be as good a teacher as a lecturer? If so, how can this happen? How about academics at the same level? Do you see differences in teaching from academics at senior lecturer level within the same school, across disciplines or across the faculties? These people are paid the same, therefore their employer values them the same; why should there be differences in your perception of their value as teachers?

Consider research outcomes. How is one academic's research considered more valuable than another's? Is it quantity, i.e. the number of publications? Is it quality, i.e. the quality of publications? If quality, how do we measure that? There are journal rankings, but they vary significantly by discipline. Also consider differences in expectations across disciplines. A science article might be a couple of pages, whereas a qualitative social science or business article might be 40 pages long. The latter articles does not equate to 20 science articles; indeed, they equate to the same output: one journal article. There is increasing talk of measuring the impact of academic research. How can we know that articles are read and that their research makes a difference?

Finally, let us consider relationships. Have you ever come across an academic who seems very good at their job but they seem stuck at a certain level? Perhaps they are excellent teachers and have strong research outputs but have not been promoted. On the other hand, have you encountered academics who hold senior positions but do not seem to justify their salary? Perhaps they are younger than others below them or they have relatively few research outcomes. Have you ever wondered why this happens? Academics are recruited, selected, and promoted by their peers. Academic selection and promotion panels evaluate candidates against traditional criteria, much of which is set out above. Do you think the process is objective or subjective? Are academics valued on their merit or are there other factors involved? How important do you feel relationships are to answering many of the questions posed throughout this case?

CASE STUDY QUESTIONS

1. What knowledge do academic staff have? (See Chapter 1)
2. How do universities manage their knowledge? (See Chapter 2)
3. Do you feel that the knowledge of academic staff has value? Why, or why not?
4. Do you feel academic staff are evaluated on merit or are there other factors involved?

INTRODUCTION

The purpose of this chapter is to explore the value of knowledge. In Chapter 1, the importance of knowledge was introduced. There were two theoretical platforms. The knowledge economy explains how knowledge is the main driver of economic value (Drucker, 1988, 1999). The knowledge-based view of the firm (KBV) argues that knowledge is the most valuable resource (Grant, 1996). Chapter 5 explores this further within the context of knowledge strategy. In Chapter 2, these assumptions were used to provide a sense of purpose about knowledge management (KM). If these assumptions are accepted, it is easier to persuade managers and staff that KM is worthwhile. Two further theoretical platforms emerged: the role of knowledge in improving performance (Becerra-Fernandez and Sabherwal, 2010) and the importance of measuring knowledge as intellectual capital (Dumay, 2014). In Chapter 3, the value of the management of knowledge was discussed. The chapter explored financial and non-financial measures of KM and how these may be used to identify its value proposition. An alternative perspective was also presented. This suggested that it is the individual's skill in applying knowledge to the work context which creates value, rather than a knowledge management system. In either case, the value of the knowledge resource itself is important. What then is this value and how can we measure it?

CORE CONCEPT: Knowledge has value and this value may be measured.

The value of knowledge has attracted interest from researchers and practitioners across multiple disciplines. This has caused disagreement about definitions, language, and theoretical concepts. While there is widespread agreement that knowledge has value, there is also disagreement about what this value is and how to measure it. In tackling the issue, this chapter explores the measurement of value from a multi-disciplinary perspective, evaluates popular methods, presents a recent model called the Knowledge Accounts (Massingham, 2016), and looks at the future of the measurement of intangible assets, such as integrated reporting. The discussion explores further what is meant by the phrase 'most valuable resource', whether knowledge can be separated from the knower, and knowledge as skilful knowing. These themes will be important in knowledge strategy (see Chapter 5).

KNOWLEDGE'S VALUE PROPOSITION

A value proposition is the company's approach to satisfying buyer wants and needs at a price customers will consider good value (Thompson et al., 2016). Knowledge's value proposition, therefore, is to satisfy managers' (i.e. customers') expectations (needs) in ways that demonstrate value for money. Knowledge costs money. Whether knowledge is acquired (e.g. through recruitment of new staff or using consultants), developed internally (e.g. through staff training or innovation), or accessed through collaboration (e.g. external partnerships), it requires investment in terms of time and money. This investment is necessary to fill gaps between what the organization knows and what it needs to know (see Chapter 5). The exploration of knowledge's value has two main theoretical platforms: the knowledge-based view (KBV) of the firm and intellectual capital (IC). The KBV looks at the purpose of knowledge and IC enables evaluation of its use. The KBV, therefore, helps explain management's needs, while IC helps report on the cost of the investment.

STRATEGIC MANAGEMENT

The knowledge-based view (KBV) of the firm argues that knowledge is the most valuable resource (Grant, 1996). Strategy involves decisions managers take to improve the company's financial performance, strengthen its long-term competitive position, and gain a competitive edge over rivals (Thompson et al., 2016). The competitive edge is known as competitive advantage. A company achieves a competitive advantage when it provides buyers with superior value compared to rivals or offers the same value at a lower cost (Thompson et al., 2016). From a strategic management perspective, knowledge's value lies in how it can help the company create competitive advantage. A competitive advantage is called sustainable if it continues despite rivals' attempts to match or exceed this advantage.

THEORY IN PRACTICE: STARBUCKS' COMPETITIVE ADVANTAGE IN THE SPECIALTY COFFEE MARKET

Starbucks has developed a unique customer experience through its store ambiance, which is difficult and expensive for rivals to match. This experience, which includes the product, the environment it is served in, and the service itself, is intended to create an emotional attachment with the customers. Product offerings are broad and include not only coffee and specialty coffee drinks, but also teas, fresh pastries, and other merchandise. The global brand, the consistency of the customer experience, and the consistency of the store operations globally are difficult to copy.

The competitive power of a company's knowledge resources is measured by the ability to produce a sustainable competitive advantage. This ability is based on four tests of competitive power known as the VRIN test:

1. Is the resource or capability competitively *valuable*? Is it directly relevant to the company's strategy?
2. Is the resource or capability *rare*? Is it something rivals lack?
3. Is the resource or capability hard to copy, i.e. *inimitable*?

4. Is the resource invulnerable to the threat of substitution from different types of resources and capabilities, i.e. *non-substitutable*? (Thompson et al., 2016)

CORE CONCEPT: Knowledge's claim to being the most valuable resource lies in its capacity to meet the criteria of the VRIN test better than other resources.

Starbucks provides an illustration. At first glance, knowledge resources associated with Starbucks' competitive advantage are marketing skill (global brand), staff training (customer service), and business systems (operations). While these are important and do contribute to Starbucks' performance, they are not the real source of sustainable competitive advantage. Starbucks' advantage is the customer experience. It uses knowledge resources to create this experience by providing staff with knowledge about coffee – including memorizing recipes, learning procedures, and following rules in making coffee – and an organizational culture which empowers staff to be creative and continually look for new ideas, new products, and new experiences for customers. By investing in staff in this way, Starbucks generates value by employees enthusiastically communicating their knowledge about coffee to customers and exuding a passion about Starbucks. This is difficult for rivals to copy.

INTELLECTUAL CAPITAL

The theory of intellectual capital emerged in the early 1990s in response to a growing interest in intangible assets. According to Dumay (2012), intellectual capital theory has two foundations – the difference between market-to-book values (Mouritsen et al., 2001) and the disclosure of intellectual capital as a means to greater profitability through a lower cost of capital (Bismuth and Tojo, 2008).

DEEP THINKING: IC research has evolved over time. There have been three stages. The first stage was the development of a measurement framework (Guthrie and Petty, 2000). For example, Sveiby (1997) classified intellectual capital into three components: (1) internal structure, (2) external structure, and (3) employee competence. The most widely used classification is Stewart's (1997) model of (1) human capital, (2) structural capital (sometimes called organizational capital), and (3) customer capital (sometimes called relational capital). The second stage of intellectual capital research used these frameworks to empirically measure the value of intellectual capital and how this can be achieved in practice. This research included content analysis of company annual reports and the use

(Continued)

(Continued)

of various methodologies claiming to value intellectual capital; but this research has been criticised as 'over used, and lacking in new contributions and validity' (Dumay, 2014: 3). The third stage of intellectual capital research is more practice-focused, 'based on a critical and performative analysis of intellectual capital practices in action' (Guthrie et al., 2012: 69).

Source: Massingham and Tam (2015: 391–392)

CORE CONCEPT: An important challenge for intellectual capital research is the inability of the field to identify a set of measures which are widely accepted and adopted.

Intellectual capital risks being seen as an abstract idea that cannot be acted upon. Researchers have examined annual reports to identify whether companies are measuring and reporting on intellectual capital. An early study by Guthrie and Petty (2000) identified a lack of IC information found in annual reports, and a recent study by De Silva et al. (2014) revealed that the situation has not improved much since then. Dumay (2016: 176) details evidence that IC reporting, especially in stand-alone IC reports, has all but ground to a halt since 2013. IC research and IC reporting seem to have been limited to Australia, and parts of Europe. Cuozzo et al. (2017) found little interest in intellectual capital disclosure in the USA. This may be due to different terminologies. Cuozzo et al. (2017) suggested that IC research might gather more interest in the USA if it used the term intangible assets, which seems more widely understood and used in the USA. However, 'intangible assets' has no generally accepted meaning and is used interchangeably with the terms intellectual assets, intellectual capital, and intangibles (Eccles and Krzus, 2010). Cuozzo et al. (2017) suggest that US practitioners and researchers may be more interested in integrated reporting. Schaper et al. (2017) found that companies are abandoning dedicated IC reports for an integrated external reporting mechanism beyond the annual report.

This review suggests that the dominant field in measuring the value of knowledge – intellectual capital research – needs a shake-up. First, it should rename itself to intangible assets to reflect contemporary business models and needs. Second, it needs to explain how it creates value via sustainable competitive advantage. Third, its measurement and reporting must fit into contemporary models such as integrated reporting. Fourth, it must produce practical outcomes such as informing management action, helping stakeholder investment decisions, and meeting regulatory requirements. Previous methods for measuring knowledge value are discussed before looking at an alternative model which meets the criteria.

PREVIOUS MEASUREMENT METHODS

Interest in the value of knowledge is not new. The earliest attempts emerged from the field of human resources accounting (HRA) which aimed to measure employees as assets. In a review of this literature, Roslender (2000) explained that the field began in the mid-1960s with Hermanson's (1964) finance-oriented human asset accounting. This was followed in the late 1960s by Flamholtz (1973) who looked at human resource cost and revenue information for the management processes of control, planning, and decision. This was then followed by the sociology-oriented human worth accounting, which was based on a range of subjective employee worth assessments, and on softer measurement metrics such as retention rates. Finally, this led to the contemporary view which is referred to as human competence accounting.

Soon after Drucker's (1988) introduction of the concepts of knowledge economy and knowledge workers, there was a flurry of research; and many of the pioneering methods are still considered the best attempts (e.g. Stewart, 1997; and Sveiby, 1997). In a comprehensive early review, Andriessen (2003) identified 25 methods for measuring intellectual capital. I have found 42 different methods. Table 4.1 summarizes some of the most well-known.

These references are somewhat dated because those listed represent pioneering work in the field. There has been limited progress since these early efforts. A criticism of existing measurements of the value of knowledge is that they are subjective. An early review found that the extant methods do not actually measure value; rather they assess value (see Andriessen, 2003). The important distinction is that value measurement is objective, making results generalizable beyond the sample, while value assessment is subjective and limited in its broader applicability. Table 4.1 looks at this in column 3: type of method. Five of the ten methods are financial valuations, four are value assessments, and five are value measurements. A further criticism of existing methods is that they mix up their measures, i.e. they fail to distinguish between different classes of indicators. Indices of content (what does the knowledge base consist of today?) are mixed with indices of intervention (what knowledge interventions have been made, and what was their scope?), transfer (what effects did the interventions set in motion?), and classical financial indices (Probst et al., 2002: 255). As a result, contents, inputs, and outputs are mixed together and cannot be disentangled, and their inter-actions are difficult to interpret (2002: 255). Table 4.1 looks at this in column 6: type of indices. Seven of the ten methods outlined in Table 4.1 cover indice 1, four cover indice 2, five cover indice 3, and six cover indice 4. Therefore, the methods cover the four types of indices fairly evenly. It shows how the indices tend to be mixed. The ideal method is one which covers value measurement and includes indices of content (indice 1). Edvinsson and Malone's (1997) Skandia Navigator and Brooking's (1996) Intellectual Capital Audit are the best fit with these criteria.

TABLE 4.1 Summary of methods to measure knowledge value

Method	Author	Type of method	Type of IC	Metric	Indice type	Summary
1. Economic value added (EVA)	Weaver (2001)	Financial evaluation	All combined	EVA = Net operating post-tax profit – (Cost of capital Invested capital estimates share valuation premium)	Business results (Class 4) Cost of capital Invested capital	Class 4
2. Market-to-book (M:B) ratio	Stewart (1997)	Financial evaluation	All combined	Intangible Assets value = market value (share price)/ tangible asset value)	Business results (Class 4) Market value Tangible assets value	Class 4
3. Calculated intangible value (CIV)	Stewart (1997)	Financial Evaluation	All combined	Intangible Asset value = gap between market and book value (e.g. summarized by Tobin's Q or M:B ratio)	Business results (Class 4) Market value Tangible assets value	Class 4
4. Stages of knowledge growth	Bohn (1994)	Value assessment	Human and structural	Organizational knowledge is classified into a taxonomy – a hierarchy from ignorance to tacit knowledge to knowledge with increasing degrees of articulability	Organizational knowledge base (Class 1) Levels of subject matter expertise	Class 1
5. The Value Explorer	Augier and Teece (2005)	Value Assessment	All combined	Each asset type is evaluated according to predefined criteria in the following three categories: 1. Assessment of core competencies 2. Assessment of strengths 3. Measurement of values	Organizational knowledge base (Class 1) Skills and tacit knowledge Collective values and norms Interventions (Class 2) Technology and explicit knowledge Primary and management processes: leadership and communication Intermediate results and transfer effects (Class 3) Assets/endowments: brands and networks	Class 1, 2, and 3 mixed

Method	Author	Type of method	Type of IC	Metric	Indice type	Summary
6. Structural model of intellectual capital	Sullivan (1998)	Value measurement, value assessment, financial evaluation	All separated	Scorecard approach	Organizational knowledge base (Class 1) Employee attitude Intermediate results and transfer effects (Class 3) Knowledge worker turnover Proportion of new product sales Database replacement cost Customer satisfaction Brand equity Customer retention rate, Market-to-book ratio Business results (Class 4): Working capital turns Ratios of sales to sellers/admin costs	Mainly Class 3 but also Class 1 and Class 4
7. Skandia Navigator	Edvinsson and Malone (1997)	Value measurement	Human and structural	Humanist approach	Organizational knowledge base (Class 1) Empowerment Index: Motivation Awareness of quality demands Responsibility versus authority to act Competence Interventions (Class 2) Number of full-time equivalent (FTE) employees Number of managers Proportion of female managers Training costs Intermediate results and transfer effects (Class 3) Support within the organization	Mainly Class 1 and Class 2, also Class 3

(Continued)

TABLE 4.1 (Continued)

Method	Author	Type of method	Type of IC	Metric	Indice type	Summary
8. The IC index	Roos et al. (1997)	Value measurement	Structural, human, relational	Essentially based around the Skandia Navigator, but aggregates items into higher level areas combined into a single score	Organizational knowledge base (Class 1) Relationship Human Interventions (Class 2) Innovation Infrastructure	Class 1 and Class 2
9. Intangible assets monitor	Sveiby (1997)	Value measurement, value assessment, financial evaluation	All separated	Scorecard approach	Organizational knowledge base (Class 1) Measuring competence by: No. of years in the profession (exp.) Level of education (qual.) Stability measured by: Age of workforce Seniority (no. years in same organization) Relative pay position Interventions (Class 2) Competence-enhancing customers Intermediate results and transfer effects (Class 3) Training and education costs to organization Professional staff grading Employee turnover Measuring efficiency Proportion of professional staff Business results (Class 4): Financial capital	All four classes mixed

Method	Author	Type of method	Type of IC	Metric	Indice type	Summary
10. Intellectual capital audit	Brooking (1996)	Value measurement	Human and some social	This is a tool for planning rather than reporting	Leverage effect: Profit per professional = (profit) divided by (no. of employees). Further analysis done by (no. of employees divided by no. of professionals). Profit is divided then by the latter figure.	Mainly Class 1 but mixed with Class 3 and Class 4
					General efficiency indicator, Sales efficiency indicator, Personnel efficiency indicator	
					Value added per professional = (profit minus costs) divided by (market share)	
					Organizational knowledge base (Class 1)	
					Creative capability	
					Problem-solving capability	
					Psychometric data:	
					Ability to work in teams (personality)	
					Performance under stress	
					Education	
					Vocational qualifications	
					Work-related knowledge	
					Occupational potential	
					Personality	
					Work-related competencies	
					Collective expertise	
					Intermediate results and transfer effects (Class 3)	
					IP assets (trade secrets, copyright, patents, design rights, trademarks, etc.)	
					Business results (Class 4):	
					Market assets (intangibles)	
					Infrastructure assets (tangible and intangible)	

KNOWLEDGE ACCOUNTS

INTRODUCTION

Massingham (2016) recently developed an alternative model for measuring the value of knowledge called the Knowledge Accounts (KA).

CORE CONCEPT: The Knowledge Accounts measure the value of people for their organization. More specifically, they measure people's tacit knowledge. The method's focus on individual tacit knowledge is due to economies of effort.

To identify and evaluate every knowledge resource within an organization would create a management overhead so high that the costs would outweigh the benefits. Measuring codified knowledge, e.g. reports, policies, and other work outputs, would require individuals to evaluate a vast volume of material. The time required to do this would be enormous and pointless. Codified knowledge does not create value. A policy does not do work. People create value through their skilful action (see Chapter 1). By focusing on individual tacit knowledge, the method follows the principle that the real value in knowledge is in its application. By measuring tacit knowledge, the most value from the exercise is captured by focusing effort on that part of knowledge which is most important to the organization, such as the Pareto principle's 80/20 rule (80% of value is created by the 20% most important activities).

This approach is supported by IC theory. IC theory explains that human capital represents the human factor in the organization: the combined intelligence, skills, and expertise that give the organization its distinctive character (Bontis, 1998). Researchers argue that human capital is the firm's most important asset because it is the source of creativity and, therefore, innovation, change, and improvement (Carson et al., 2004). Research has found that increases in employee capabilities are seen to directly influence financial results, leading to a direct relationship between human capital and organization performance (Bozbura, 2004). Therefore, the focus on the individual is justified.

HOW IT WORKS

The Knowledge Accounts (KA score) allocates individuals a score out of 100. The score represents the value of their tacit knowledge to their organization. The score is calculated from responses to questions used to measure the individual's knowledge in terms of human capital, social capital, structural capital, and relational capital. For the majority of the questions, respondents are asked to indicate the extent of their agreement on a six-point Likert scale (1 = strongly disagree; 6 = strongly agree). Table 4.2 provides some example questions.

TABLE 4.2   Example questions

Human capital factors	
	HC1: Employee capability
Work skills	'I am an expert in my job'
	'There are some tasks required by my job that I cannot do well' (reversed)
	'I am able to deliver the quality of service expected by my customers' (6-point Likert scale)
	HC3: Employee satisfaction
Affective attachment	'I feel a strong sense of belonging to my organization'
	'I really feel that any problems faced by my organization are also my problems' (6-point Likert scale)
Social capital factors	
	SC1: Colleagues' attitude
Collective efficacy beliefs	'My immediate colleagues are expert in their jobs'
	'My immediate colleagues are able to develop new ideas' (6-point Likert scale)
Structural capital factors	
	StC3: Contribution
Motivation	'I really enjoy when people ask me to tell them how to do something'
	'Sharing my knowledge with others makes me feel worthwhile' (6-point Likert scale)
Relational capital factors	
	RC2: Informal ties
Social dependence	'How much do you depend on this external person at work?' Scale: 1 = not much at all, 2 = to some degree, 3 = it is good to have them around, 4 = they are my safety net, 5 = I couldn't really do my job without them

The response to each question is then converted into the 100 scale as follows: 6 = 100, 5 = 84, 4 = 68, 3 = 52, 2 = 36, 1 = 20. This makes it impossible for someone to have a score of zero; however, this recognizes that all people have some value and no one is completely ignorant. While this method is self-reporting, it has been proven to have good reliability and validity (Massingham et al., 2011).

The KA aggregates individual item scores (e.g. questions) into four further levels, as illustrated in Figure 4.1.

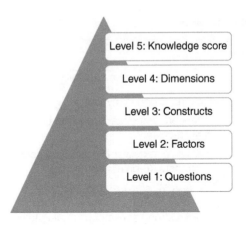

FIGURE 4.1   *The Knowledge Accounts levels*

In this way, each individual's answers to the KA questions are aggregated up into the following levels of analysis:

- *Knowledge score* (level 5): this is the overall KA score out of 100. It is the mean of the four level 4 scores.
- *Dimensions* (level 4): this is the four intellectual capital classifications:
  - *Human capital*: knowledge in people's heads
  - *Social capital*: knowledge gained from relationships at work
  - *Structural capital*: knowledge gained from using and contributing to the organization's codified knowledge, e.g. databases, reports, policies, procedures
  - *Relational capital*: knowledge gained from relationships outside the organization, e.g. customers, contractors, suppliers.
- *Constructs* (level 3): this is 11 classifications that help identify organizational issues such as employee capability and employee satisfaction.
- *Factors* (level 2): this is 46 classifications that guide managerial action, such as staff experience, density of social networks, expert status, and frequency of external contact.

Figure 4.2 illustrates the model. Further detail on the levels and their definitions is available from Massingham (2016).

The real power in the model lies in its levels and its ability to isolate problem areas, i.e. competency gaps, and to aggregate these at multiple levels. At an individual level, the model allows managers to identify why a staff member is not as productive as they would expect. At the group level, it may identify problems in the social network. At the organizational level, it might identify problems with staff morale. The score is contextual. Users of the KA will

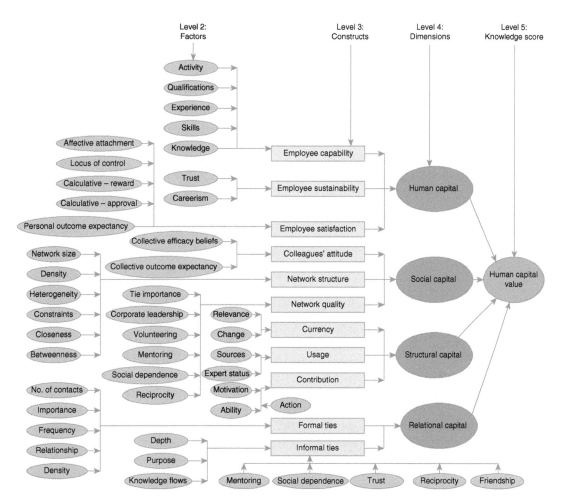

FIGURE 4.2 *Integrated model measuring the value of tacit knowledge*

need to follow these guidelines in order to interpret the scores at individual, group, or organizational level. First, set a baseline of management's expectations of knowledge scores by position. This provides important context as expectations will differ across firms and industries. Investors, in particular, are likely to focus more on the gap between actual and desired (baseline) scores than the actual scores. Second, remember that knowledge is dynamic and it is necessary to track changes in the stock of knowledge as well as revisit expectations by adjusting the baseline when necessary. Third, it will be necessary to weight the KA scores to reflect the specific context of the firm being measured. For example, relational capital and its constructs may be far more important to a marketing-focused firm than to a public sector organization. See Massingham (2016) for further details on the theory and measures underlying the KA method.

USING THE KNOWLEDGE ACCOUNTS

The Knowledge Accounts may be used by managers, stakeholders, and regulators.

MANAGEMENT

Managers can use the KA for workforce planning to assess the quantity and quality of their staff. The KA could be used as a budget of non-financial resources, i.e. staff, in the same way that managers are allocated a financial budget.

Tactical human resource management (HRM) identifies workforce gaps. It is used in workforce planning. This answers the question: do I have enough staff? Organizations typically answer this question in terms of staff numbers or budget. The KA may be used to measure the quantity of knowledge resources, i.e. staff, in terms of value rather than size (numbers) or cost (budget).

THEORY IN PRACTICE: TACTICAL HUMAN RESOURCE MANAGEMENT AT THE CSO

The KA identified that the CSO in the closing integrated case study had an organizational knowledge base (OKB) deficit of 23.1%. Its total knowledge score was less than the total baseline score, i.e. the knowledge expected by management. The deficit equated to having 18.5 fewer staff than it required. This was calculated by dividing the deficit score by the mean knowledge score. If the CSO recruited 18.5 new staff at the mean knowledge score, then they would bring the organization's OKB up to the required level. However, this is a short-term solution because it only makes the organization bigger, not better. The better solution is to increase the mean knowledge score, by addressing the competency gaps identified by the KA, which would increase the OKB and make the organization better.

Tactical human capital management (HCM) identifies job-related competencies. This answers the question: do I have the right staff? Organizations typically answer this question in terms of seniority levels or job types. The KA may be used to measure the quality of knowledge resources, i.e. staff. The KA compares the mean knowledge score with the mean baseline score, to measure the quality of its staff. If the mean KA is above the baseline, then knowledge is in surplus, and the organization may exploit this by leveraging this excess capacity. However, if the mean KA is below the baseline, then knowledge is in deficit, and the quality of its staff is less than required to meet the organization's capability. This analysis can be presented at organizational level (i.e. aggregating all individual scores), group level (e.g. work sections or other combinations of individual scores), and individual level, as well as at multiple system levels (e.g. job families, activities, subject matter expertise).

THEORY IN PRACTICE: TACTICAL HUMAN CAPITAL MANAGEMENT AT THE CSO

In 2009, the CSO's mean knowledge score was already in deficit by 25.6%. While the CSO knew that it had lost experience as high proportions of senior staff had retired in the years preceding the project (i.e. 2009), it did not know what the impact was, other than it had fewer senior staff members. It tried to fix the problem by promoting staff to fill the seniority gaps. However, it could not quantify whether its capability had been affected. The KA provided this information. It provided better information than traditional methods, i.e. job family analysis by seniority levels, by specifying capability gaps against management expectations (i.e. the baseline). Rather than saying 'We have only 200 lieutenants, and we need 250' – the latter figure based on abstract modelling – the KA provided hard data, stating that, for example, 'We have 200 lieutenants and they know 30% less than the job requires.' Even if they had promoted 50 staff to lieutenants to fill the gap from a seniority perspective, these new staff would not know what the baseline expected. The CSO would still be in deficit even though it had the required number of senior staff. The KA would reveal this capability gap, whereas the existing method, i.e. seniority analysis, would mask the problem.

Strategic human resource management can provide a broader perspective regarding job inputs and outputs. This answers the question: do I have the right staff in the right jobs? Managers can also use the KA for strategic alignment to assess the efficiency and effectiveness of their staff. Organizations typically answer this question in terms of performance appraisal. The KA is used here to measure strategic alignment (SA). SA measures the match between an individual and the job requirements. The KA provides a more accurate measure of SA by looking at technical and cognitive tacit knowledge (e.g. see Nonaka and Takeuchi, 1995). The primary technical knowledge is human capital (HC) as it measures traditional views on job competency, such as experience, skills, and qualifications. These may be seen as job inputs because they are required competencies. The cognitive knowledge may be called 'soft' capabilities in that they measure work attitudes and behaviours. In this sense, they may be seen as job outputs because they surface in the act of doing and in the use of technical knowledge.

THEORY IN PRACTICE: STRATEGIC HUMAN RESOURCE MANAGEMENT AT THE CSO

Social capital (SC) is a measure of cognitive knowledge. Between 2009 and 2011, the CSO's mean SC score decreased by 6.3%. The value generated from social networks (network quality) was the main cause of this decrease

(Continued)

(Continued)

(down by 8.2%) – how the individual is perceived within their social networks. It measures an individual's level of power (i.e. tie importance) as well as their level of 'giving' to others (e.g. mentoring, reciprocity). Individuals with power know the right people, are considered generous in their social interactions, and are likely to create high levels of respect, which they can use to access knowledge. In this way, it highlights the effectiveness of social networks in terms of goodwill and speed of access to important knowledge within the network. The decreased performance in this area means that staff are creating less value from their networks. From a strategic alignment perspective, this highlights how the CSO does not have the right staff in the right jobs, and that addressing social capital would help address this problem, particularly in terms of cognitive knowledge gaps.

Strategic human capital management identifies where and how to grow the organization's knowledge resources. This answers the question: what staff will I need in the future? Organizations typically answer this question in irregular strategic reviews often driven by external consultants. The KA is used here to measure future value-creating competencies from both a technical (hard) and cognitive (soft) perspective. The KA identifies future value by measuring system families in the four KA dimensions (e.g. HS, SC). By system, we mean classifying knowledge resources at multiple levels, i.e. job-related, activity-related, technical domains (i.e. subject matter expertise), and network-related. The mean knowledge scores of individuals are aggregated in these areas to allow for further analysis. The KA is then used to identify the future capability gap based on three trends: (1) mean knowledge scores (i.e. the 2009–11 survey results – what we know); (2) current versus future baseline (i.e. management's value rating of the knowledge resource – what we need to know); and (3) blue-sky thinking (i.e. entirely new future capabilities – what we do not currently know but will need to know). It is particularly applicable when we look at system families such as job-related (for new jobs), activity-related (new types of work), technical-related (new types of subject matter expertise), and network-related (new types of social interaction at work).

THEORY IN PRACTICE: STRATEGIC HUMAN CAPITAL MANAGEMENT AT THE CSO

We saw above that the value generated from the CSO's social networks (network quality, NQ) was the main cause of its social capital decline. Looking further into this problem we found that NQ's action factors had decreased significantly.

By action, we mean how individuals act within their social networks. Two factors in particular were significant: tie importance and reciprocity. Tie importance is about knowing the right people. It has a seniority dimension, i.e. whether contacts are superiors, peers, or staff. The result shows that the social networks at the case study organization became 'more horizontal' in the sense that there was less interaction with senior people. Reciprocity is about social exchange and being willing to share with others in order to receive. It is a measure of social intimacy. NQ action is a job output.

The KA may be used to inform the 'make versus buy decision' for future capability growth. This may be done by either promoting or developing existing staff to fill the KA scores required in the future. The KA could be used to identify which staff could help improve the network quality action scores. The 'buy' decision is to fill the gap externally. This may be done by recruitment to find new staff with the skills necessary to improve the network quality action scores. Increasingly, recruiters are using techniques such as psychological and personality profiles to assess work attitudes and behaviours difficult to surface at a job interview. The KA may be used to identify specific competencies at level 2 factors (see Figure 4.1).

STAKEHOLDERS

Stakeholders can use the KA to assess the firm's performance and its capability growth. Strategic HCM can improve external reporting on performance by explaining how well the organization is learning. This is important because it demonstrates how well the organization is managing its non-financial resources, i.e. its knowledge. Strong organizational learning performance indicates that the stock of knowledge resources (e.g. the OKB) will be increasing. Strategic HCM uses the KA to report learning and growth (L&G) information for balanced scorecard reporting. For example, Kaplan and Norton's (2006) five-step process for strategic alignment (SA) of HRM may be used to show how the KA can help external stakeholders assess strategic job families and their contribution to the organization's performance. Stakeholders can then assess the 'health' of each strategic job family in terms of strategic alignment, i.e. what the global and job-specific competencies are, whether these are in surplus or deficit, and whether things are getting better or worse. This then answers the question of whether the organization is learning in strategic capabilities.

Strategic HCM can improve external reporting on capability growth by explaining whether the organization is growing its strategic knowledge resources. Strategic HCM uses the level 2 results, that is, the factor scores to report L&G perspective information for balanced scorecard reporting. The main benefit in using the KA here is that it explains organizational performance in terms of: (a) Do we have the necessary capability? (b) If not, what is the size of the gap? And (c) what are we doing about it? The growth perspective is captured by trend analysis to determine whether things are improving.

The real value of the KA here is that it not only quantifies problems (i.e. strategic misalignment) but also tracks management action. External stakeholders should be happy if the KA shows that critical capabilities (e.g. value-creating job families) meet expectations – are not in deficit – and are growing. However, they may also be satisfied if gaps are being closed. The KA may be applied to system families, for example activity, job, technical discipline, staff categories, and seniority levels.

REGULATION

Regulators can use the KA to assess the societal contract. It answers questions about whether the firm is using its non-financial resources wisely. Government and industry bodies can assess the use of the factors of production (human resources) as well as outputs (work produced). The CSO is funded by the federal government. At this broad level, regulators may use the KA to examine the role of the organization and whether it is providing value for money for society. The accounting discipline's stakeholder theory (e.g. see Deegan, 2013) explains that organizations have a societal contract where society confers resources (e.g. staff, capital, land) in return for an expectation that the organization will use these resources wisely and create benefit for society (e.g. produce goods and services efficiently, and generate employment). The KA can measure how well the firm is meeting its societal contract by connecting inputs (people) with outputs (work produced) using various ratios.

EVALUATING THE KNOWLEDGE ACCOUNTS

The KA's key point of difference compared with existing methods is that it provides a value measurement, it is objective and auditable, and it has managerial application. It is not just a scorecard; it is a strategic management tool. It has two main advantages. First, it provides contextual data by allowing the KA score to be compared to a 'baseline' (the expectation of management regarding knowledge by job type) to calculate a knowledge gap, i.e. surplus or deficit. Second, it extends the traditional view of human capability, for example skills, experience, and qualifications, to include cognitive knowledge. Knowledge creates value for organizations through human action. The KA measures this value by combining technical knowledge (e.g. skills) with the individual's willingness to use their knowledge, share it with others, and create new knowledge. This introduces cognitive dimensions such as the individual's emotional relationship with the organization, as well as their relationships at work, as important factors in measuring their value to the organization.

Table 4.3 explains: (1) how the KA may be applied; (2) suggestions derived from the HRM and HCM literature; (3) the CSO's existing methods; (4) the KA findings; (5) the management response; and (6) why the KA method is better than existing methods.

TABLE 4.3 Summary of overall Knowledge Accounts model with results

Application	Literature	Existing methods	KA findings	Management response	Why KA is better
Internal management	*Tactical HRM:* Quantity of knowledge resources? Do I have enough staff?	Staff numbers and budget	The CSO's organizational knowledge base (OKB) decreased by 23.1% This equated to a deficit of 18.5 staff in terms of the mean knowledge score	The OKB deficit was used to argue for more staff	KA explains changes in ROI (staff budget) and productivity. For example, if ROI remains constant, but OKB declines, then productivity ratios such as ROI/work outputs will also decline
	Tactical HCM: Quality of knowledge resources? Do I have the right staff?	Seniority levels by job families	The CSO's mean knowledge score capability gap, i.e. difference between actual and baseline, was 25.6% deficit	Job family deficits are typically filled by recruitment or promotion, knowing a gap will exist.	KA quantifies the impact of workforce changes in terms of capability, i.e. what people know, rather than what they are paid (seniority) or what they are supposed to do (job families)
	Strategic HRM: job inputs and outputs Do I have the right staff in the right jobs?	Gaps filled by recruitment or internal transfer, with staff expected to 'grow into the job'	The primary driver: HC dimension; and secondary drivers: SC, StC, and RC all decreased at the CSO SC was used to illustrate a decrease in cognitive knowledge. Network quality decreased by 8.1% and showed that changes in social networks had created holes in SC	Embraced the 'soft' capabilities at an organizational level, i.e. need for cultural change, but not at individual level	KA identifies targeted learning on job inputs and outputs rather than traditional methods. The result is better workforce alignment, leading to learning cycle acceleration
	Strategic HCM: growing the organizational knowledge base (OKB) What staff will I need in the future?	Trend analysis by job family based largely on 'gut feel'; irregular strategic reviews driven by customer requirements which focused mainly on 'hard' (technical) capability	Future capability gap is specified by the difference between the actual current knowledge scores by capital type and the desired future levels, i.e. the baseline Relational capital: 171% deficit	Positive towards the underlying ideas, but struggled to grasp how to incorporate 'soft' capabilities such as SC, StC, and RC into job redesign	The KA builds objectivity into future capability requirements by specifying both hard and soft performance drivers, whereas existing methods focus on limited perspective about capability, i.e. hard only (technical knowledge)

(Continued)

TABLE 4.3 (Continued)

Application	Literature	Existing methods	KA findings	Management response	Why KA is better
External reporting	*Strategic HCM*: performance reporting How well is the organization learning?	Balanced scorecard (learning and growth dimension)	Strategic job family analysis StC construct – currency (level 3) – linked to job-related competency – demand input. Excellent relevance scores (86% and increasing) but unsatisfactory change scores (41% and decreasing) suggest need for management action to ensure knowledge is up to date	Problem is acknowledged; but there may be reluctance to report this to external stakeholders due to fear of consequences	Stakeholders can assess the 'health' of each strategic job family in terms of strategic alignment, i.e. what are the global and job-specific competencies, are these in surplus or deficit, and are things getting better or worse? This explains whether the organization is learning in strategic capabilities
	Strategic HCM: capability growth Are we growing our strategic knowledge resources?	Irregular response to strategic reviews' request for information, based on specifying what the organization does (activity) and number of staff by function	Relation capital factor scores (level 2) are used to illustrate Strategic misalignment caused mostly by lack of purpose (5%) and infrequent interaction (5%) with external stakeholders	Strong cultural resistance to the KA based on ownership problem; existing methods may be defended by staff who do not want strategic HCM	The KA quantifies problems (i.e. strategic misalignment) and also tracks management action. External stakeholders should be happy if the KA shows critical capabilities (e.g. value-creating job families) meet the management's expectations of KA scores against a baseline for benchmarking (i.e. not in deficit) and are growing. However, they may also be satisfied if gaps are being closed
Regulation	*Strategic HCM*: societal contract Are the organization's non-financial resources being managed wisely?	Focus is on the work produced by the organization and how this helps customers Evaluated against total workforce budget, i.e. cost–benefit analysis	HC was the main focus. Significant decrease in activity (41.7%) and experience (28.4%) indicate substantial decline in the value created by the organization	Problem is acknowledged. However, defensive reaction was that the situation would improve in coming years as new staff gathered experience. Ownership issues as well	The KA connects inputs (people) with the societal contract (outputs) via measuring the value of their HC, whereas existing methods focus on outputs only. The KA shows how well the workforce is being managed

Source: Massingham (2016). With permission from Elsevier

FUTURE PERSPECTIVE: INTEGRATED REPORTING

Measurement of the value of knowledge faces an uncertain future. As a field, it has been dominated by intellectual capital researchers. This field has clearly had an impact. Its most prolific author is Professor James Guthrie from Australia with 14 articles in the period 2000–2017 and 2,554 citations (Cuozzo et al., 2017). Guthrie and other leading IC scholars are being read and cited, which illustrates the topic's importance. However, the field seems to have hit a brick wall and risks becoming irrelevant (Dumay, 2016). In contrast, this book proposes that the measurement of knowledge value will become increasingly important. For this to happen, the field needs to move on to how firms may use intellectual capital theory to manage intangible assets. The Knowledge Accounts model provides examples of how to do that by focusing on:

- Tactical HRM
- Strategic HRM
- Tactical HCM
- Strategic HCM.

Integrated reporting (IR) provides an opportunity to make the measurement of knowledge value part of corporate governance. IR represents an umbrella approach which pulls together the key elements of all other reports, to produce information on which assurance conclusions may be drawn, and following high quality international assurance standards (IFAC, 2017: 1). IR has a six-capitals framework (Abeysekera, 2013), including three which allow for measurement of intangible assets: intellectual (structural), relational, and human capital. Therefore, it fits with intellectual capital theory.

Future research in this area might develop ideas on how intangible resources are combined with tangible resources to improve organizational performance. This addresses integrated reporting's need to include data that 'emanates from other management reports' to enable companies to include additional narrative information about intangible assets (Goebel, 2015: 688). Kaplan and Norton's (1996) balanced scorecard represents a good way to capture this narrative information. The balanced scorecard is a widely used strategy execution tool. Balanced scorecard reports could be consolidated into the integrated report. The balanced scorecard's learning and growth dimension presents an opportunity to provide a nuanced narrative about intangible assets which is interactive (learning) and forward-focused (growth) and has a systems thinking perspective (the balanced scorecard's cause and effect). Figure 4.3 provides an example of a strategy map using Knowledge Accounts as the basis for the balanced scorecard's learning and growth perspective. This may be aligned with the three other perspectives – financial, customer value, and internal – to achieve strategic alignment and execute the company's strategy (see also Massingham et al., 2019). The model's five learning and growth measurement constructs, such as learning from the past, identify how knowledge resources may create value and a

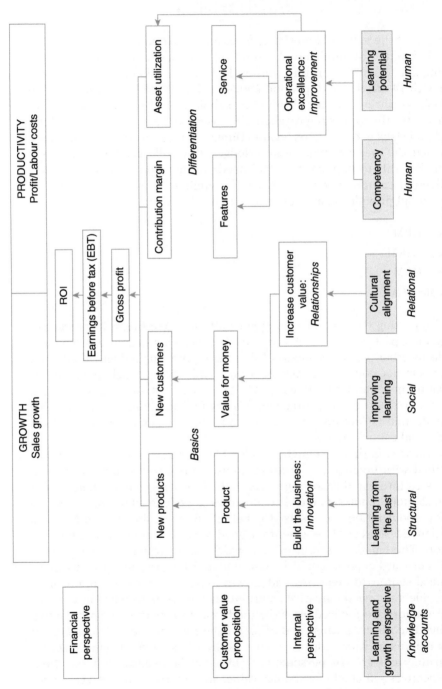

FIGURE 4.3 *Balanced scorecard learning and growth perspective adapted for Knowledge Accounts*

connection with the overall strategy. The Knowledge Accounts dimensions, such as structural, explain how measurement of the value of knowledge may be used to execute strategy.

CONCLUSION

As we transition from the industrial age to the knowledge economy, the current and future value and competitiveness of firms will increasingly be measured by intangible assets rather than tangible assets. The knowledge-based view of the firm explains that knowledge is the most valuable resource. Its value lies in its ability to combine other resources – both tangible and intangible – to create sustainable competitive advantage. The resource-based view of the firm's checklist, i.e. the VRIN model, provides a method to assess the contribution of knowledge resources, based on its uniqueness and difficulty for rivals to copy. However, this is a conceptual framework and its measurement is problematic. The field of intellectual capital research has developed a range of methods which have tried to measure and report on the value of knowledge. But no consensus has been reached.

The chapter introduced the Knowledge Accounts (KA) model (Massingham, 2016) as an alternative. The KA focuses on individual tacit knowledge as the key value-creating resource. The KA has five levels of data (see Figure 4.1) which provide it with considerable power to identify and isolate problem areas. The KA may be used to answer the following questions:

1. Do I have enough staff?
2. Do I have the right staff?
3. Do I have the right staff in the right jobs?
4. What staff will I need in the future?
5. How well is the organization learning?
6. Are we growing our strategic knowledge resources?
7. Are the organization's non-financial resources being managed wisely?

These are important questions for organizations seeking to maximize their workforce capability. The comparison of the KA against the existing methods used for tactical HRM, tactical HCM, strategic HRM, and strategic HCM provide evidence that the KA is a more powerful tool, leading to more informed internal management, external reporting, and regulation. Finally, the chapter considered the future for research on the topic of knowledge value and concluded that integrated reporting (IR) provides an opportunity to explain the measurement of management of intangible assets. The balanced scorecard was suggested as a good way to place knowledge value into IR. A model for using the KA to improve the balance scorecard's learning and growth perspective was suggested (see Figure 4.3).

CLOSING CASE STUDY: KNOWLEDGE ACCOUNTS AT THE CSO

This case provides detailed results of the Knowledge Accounts at the case study organization (CSO). The results are summarized for the CSO at each of the levels (see Figure 4.1). The case study shows what a set of Knowledge Accounts looks like and provides an opportunity to interpret them by using the guidelines for action presented in the chapter, for instance tactical HRM. In this way, the case study explores whether the KA may create value and how.

LEVEL 5: KNOWLEDGE ACCOUNTS SCORES

Figure 4.4 presents the mean KA score for the CSO over the three years of the project.

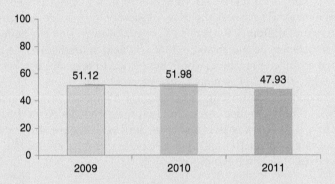

FIGURE 4.4 *Knowledge Account score (mean)*

The results reveal a decline in the CSO's knowledge resources. The average capability of its staff has decreased. This may inform tactical human resource management.

LEVEL 4: DIMENSION SCORES

The dimension scores (see Figure 4.1) are the first step in examining why the overall KA score has declined. Table 4.4 and Figure 4.5 present the dimension scores (mean) for the CSO.

TABLE 4.4 Knowledge Accounts Dimension scores

Year	Human capital	Social capital	Structural capital	Relational capital	KA
2009	61.7	65.1	50.6	27.2	51.1
2010	61.9	63.9	48.3	33.9	52.0
2011	56.3	61.0	50.3	24.2	47.9

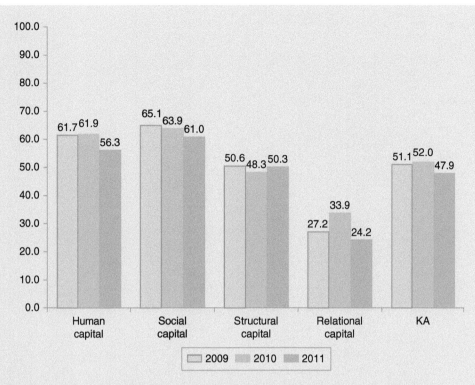

FIGURE 4.5 *Knowledge Accounts Dimension scores*

The results reveal a decline in the CSO's human capital, social capital, and relational capital. The impact might be explored by the strategic job family. This may inform tactical human capital management.

LEVEL 3: CONSTRUCT SCORES

The construct scores (see Figure 4.1) are the next step in examining why dimension scores have declined. In this case, the decline in social capital at the CSO is explored. Table 4.5 and Figure 4.6 present the results of the social capital scores (mean) for the CSO over the life of the project.

TABLE 4.5 Social capital constructs: KA scores (mean)

Year	Colleagues' attitude	Network structure	Network quality	SC
2009	88.1	52.7	54.5	65.1
2010	87.5	51.8	52.3	63.9
2011	83.9	48.9	50.1	61.0

(Continued)

(Continued)

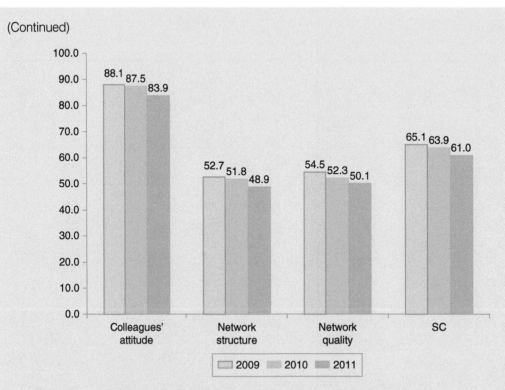

FIGURE 4.6 *Social capital constructs: Knowledge Accounts scores (mean)*

The three constructs measure an individual's motivation to interact with others at work (colleagues' attitude), the size of their social networks (network structure), and the value they can create from these networks (network quality). Therefore, social capital identifies people who are networkers at work. High social capital scores mean staff are socializing and, therefore, probably sharing knowledge and creating new knowledge together.

The results show that the main reason for the decline in social capital since 2009 is network quality (8.1%) closely followed by network structure (7.2%). This may inform strategic human resource management.

LEVEL 2: FACTOR SCORES

The factor scores (see Figure 4.1) are the next step in examining why construct scores have declined. In this case, the decline in network quality at the CSO is explored. Table 4.6 and Figure 4.7 present the results of the network quality scores (mean) for the CSO over the life of the project.

The results show that the main reason for the decline in network quality since 2009 is tie importance (39.9%), followed by reciprocity (23.0%). This may inform strategic human capital management.

TABLE 4.6 Network quality scores: KA scores (mean)

Year	Tie importance	Corp. leadership	volunteering	mentoring	Social dependence	Reciprocity	NQ
2009	49.4	46.9	63.0	75.5	24.1	68.2	54.5
2010	38.8	54.0	68.1	65.9	22.1	64.6	52.3
2011	29.7	48.8	65.7	71.5	32.5	52.5	50.1

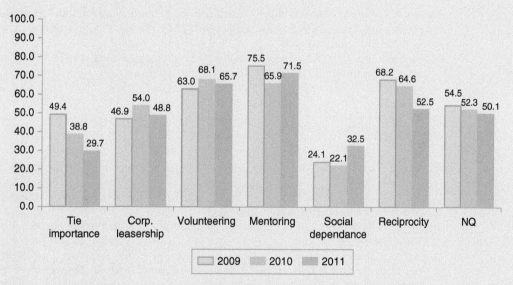

FIGURE 4.7 *Network quality scores: Knowledge Accounts scores (mean)*

CASE STUDY QUESTIONS

1. Examine the Knowledge Accounts at the CSO. What are the key findings for management?
2. What seems to be the main problem for the CSO, i.e. tactical HRM, strategic HRM, tactical HCM, or strategic HCM?
3. How should the CSO management respond to these results?
4. What are your recommendations for the CSO based on these results?

REVIEW AND DISCUSSION QUESTIONS

1. Do you feel the value of knowledge can be measured? Why, or why not?
2. Do you feel measuring the value of knowledge is useful? Why, or why not?
3. Critically discuss the Knowledge Accounts focus on tacit individual knowledge.
4. Examine the future of this topic. How can the measurement of knowledge value be relevant in the future?

FURTHER READING

Dumay, J. (2016) A Critical Reflection on the Future of Intellectual Capital: From reporting to disclosure. *Journal of Intellectual Capital*, 17 (1): 168–184. This article summarizes intellectual capital research.

Massingham, P. (2016) Knowledge Accounts. *Long Range Planning*, 49 (3): 409–425. This article provides insight about the Knowledge Accounts model.

BIBLIOGRAPHY

Abeysekera, I. (2013) A Template for Integrated Reporting. *Journal of Intellectual Capital*, 14 (2): 227–245.

Andriessen, J.H.E. (2003) *Working with Groupware: Understanding and evaluating collaboration technology*, London, Springer.

Andriessen, D. (2004) *Making Sense of Intellectual Capital*, Burlington, MA, Elsevier Butterworth-Heinemann.

Augier, M. and Teece, D. (2005) An Economic Perspective on Intellectual Capital. Chapter 1 in Marr, B. (ed.) *Perspectives on Intellectual Capital*, Oxford, Elsevier Butterworth-Heinemann, pp. 3–27.

Bailey, K.D. (1994) *Methods of Social Research*, New York, Free Press.

Becerra-Fernandez, I. and Sabherwal, R. (2010) *Knowledge Management: Systems and processes*, Armonk, NY, M.E. Sharpe.

Birdi, K., Allan, C. and Warr, P. (1997) Correlates and Perceived Outcomes of Four Types of Employee Development Activity. *Journal of Applied Psychology*, 82 (6): 845–857.

Bismuth, A. and Tojo, Y. (2008) Creating Value from Intellectual Assets. *Journal of Intellectual Capital*, 9 (2): 228–245.

Bohn, R.E. (1994) Measuring and Managing Technological Knowledge. *Sloan Management Review*, 36 (1): 61–73.

Boisot, M. (2002) The Creation and Sharing of Knowledge. In Choo, C.W. and Bontis, N. (eds) *The Strategic Management of Intellectual Capital and Organizational Knowledge*, New York, Oxford University Press, pp. 65–78.

Bontis, N. (1998) Intellectual Capital: An exploratory study that develops measures and models, *Management Decision*, 36 (2): 63–76.

Bontis, N. (2002) Managing Organisational Knowledge by Diagnosing Intellectual Capital: Framing and advancing the state of the field. In Choo, C.W. and Bontis, N. (eds) *The Strategic Management of Intellectual Capital and Organizational Knowledge*, New York, Oxford University Press, pp. 621–642.

Bozbura, F.T. (2004) Measurement and Application of Intellectual Capital in Turkey. *The Learning Organization*, *11* (4/5): 357–370.

Brooking, A. (1996) The Management of Intellectual Capital. *Journal of Long Range Planning*, *30* (3): 364–365.

Carson, E., Ranzijn, R., Winefiel, A. and Marsden, H. (2004) Intellectual Capital: Mapping employee and work group attributes. *Journal of Intellectual Capital*, *5* (3): 443–461.

Cleary, P. (2009) Exploring the Relationship between Management Accounting and Structural Capital in a Knowledge-intensive Sector. *Journal of Intellectual Capital*, *10* (1): 37–52.

Cuozzo, B., Dumay, J., Palmaccio, M. and Lombardi, R. (2017) Intellectual Capital Disclosure: A structured literature review. *Journal of Intellectual Capital*, *18* (1): 9–28.

Deegan, C. (2013) *Financial Accounting Theory*, 5th edition, North Ryde, NSW, McGraw-Hill.

De Silva, T.-A., Stratford, M. and Clark, M. (2014) Intellectual Capital Reporting: A longitudinal study of New Zealand companies. *Journal of Intellectual Capital*, *15* (1): 157–172.

Drucker, P.F. (1954) *The Practice of Management*, New York, HarperCollins.

Drucker, P.F. (1988) The Coming of the New Organization. Chapter 1 in (1998) *Harvard Business Review on Knowledge Management*, Boston, MA, Harvard Business School Press, pp. 1–19.

Drucker, P. (1999) Knowledge-worker Productivity: The biggest challenge. *California Management Review*, *41* (2): 79–94.

Dumay, J. (2012) Grand Theories as Barriers to Using IC Concepts. *Journal of Intellectual Capital*, *13* (1): 4–15.

Dumay, J. (2014) 15 Years of the Journal of Intellectual Capital and Counting: A manifesto for transformational IC research. *Journal of Intellectual Capital*, *15* (1): 2–37.

Dumay, J. (2016) A Critical Reflection on the Future of Intellectual Capital: From reporting to disclosure. *Journal of Intellectual Capital*, *17* (1): 168–184.

Dumay, J. and Rooney, J. (2011) Measuring for Managing? An IC practice research project. *Journal of Intellectual Capital*, *12* (3): 344–355.

Dumay, J. and Tull, J.A. (2011) Intellectual Capital Disclosure and Price-sensitive Australian Stock Exchange Announcements. *Journal of Intellectual Capital*, *8* (2): 236–255.

Eccles, R. and Krzus, M. (2010) *One Report: Integrated reporting for a sustainable strategy*, Hoboken, NJ, Wiley.

Edvinsson, L. (1997) Developing Intellectual Capital at Skandia. *Long Range Planning*, *30* (3): 366–373.

Edvinsson, L. and Malone, M.S. (1997) *Intellectual Capital: Realizing your company's true value by finding its hidden roots*, New York, Harper Business.

Eisenberger, R., Fasolo, P. and Davis-LaMastro, V. (1990) Perceived Organizational Support and Employee Diligence, Commitment, and Innovation. *Journal of Applied Psychology*, *75* (1): 51–59.

Flamholtz, E. (1973) Human Resource Accounting: Measuring positional replacement cost. *Human Resource Measurement*, *Spring*: 8–16.

Goebel, V. (2015) Is the Literature on Content Analysis of Intellectual Capital Reporting Heading towards a Dead End? *Journal of Intellectual Capital*, *16* (3): 681–699.

Grant, R.M. (1996) Towards a Knowledge-based Theory of the Firm. *Strategic Management Journal*, *17*: 109–122.

Grant, R.M. (1997) The Knowledge-based View of the Firm: Implications for management practice. *Long Range Planning*, *30* (3): 450–454.

Grant, R.M. (2002) The Knowledge-based View of the Firm. Chapter 8 in Choo, C.W. and Bontis, N. (eds) *The Strategic Management of Intellectual Capital and Organizational Knowledge*, New York, Oxford University Press, pp. 133–148.

Grant, R.M. (2013) Reflections on Knowledge-based Approaches to the Organization of Production. *Journal of Management and Governance*, *17* (3): 541–558.

Guthrie, J. and Petty, R. (2000) Intellectual Capital: Australian annual reporting practices. *Journal of Intellectual Capital*, *1* (3): 241–251.

Guthrie, J., Petty, R. and Ricceri, F. (2006) The Voluntary Reporting of Intellectual Capital: Comparing evidence from Hong Kong and Australia. *Journal of Intellectual Capital*, *7* (2): 254–271.

Guthrie, J., Ricceri, F. and Dumay, J. (2012) Reflections and Projections: A decade of intellectual capital accounting research. *British Accounting Review*, *44* (2): 68–92.

Hair, J.F., Anderson, R.E., Tatham, R.L. and Black, W.C. (1995) *Multivariate Data Analysis*, Hoboken, NJ, Prentice-Hall.

Han, J.K., Kim, N. and Srivastiva, R. (1998) Market Orientation and Organizational Performance: Is innovation a missing link? *Journal of Marketing*, *62* (4): 30–45.

Hermanson, R.H. (1964) *Accounting for Human Assets*. Occasional Paper No. 14. East Lansing, MI: Bureau of Business and Economic Research, Michigan State University. [Reprint Georgia State University, 1986.]

Housel, T. and Bell, A.H. (2001) *Measuring and Managing Knowledge*, New York, McGraw-Hill.

Huselid, M.A., Jackson, S.E. and Schuler, R.S. (1997) Technical and Strategic Human Resource Management Effectiveness as Determinants of Firm Performance. *Academy of Management Journal*, *40* (1): 171–188.

International Federation of Accountants (IFAC) (2017) *Enhanced Organizational Reporting: Integrated reporting key*, IFAC Policy Position 8. Available online: https://www.ifac.org/system/files/publications/files/PPP8-Enhancing-Organizational-Reporting-Jan-2017.pdf (accessed 10 September 2019).

Kaplan, R.S. and Norton, D.P. (1996) *Translating Strategy into Action: The balanced scorecard*, Boston, MA, Harvard Business School Press.

Kaplan, R.S. and Norton, D.P. (2001) *The Strategy-focused Organization*, Boston, MA, Harvard Business School Press.

Kaplan, R.S. and Norton, D.P. (2006) *Alignment: Using the balanced scorecard to create corporate strategies*, Boston, MA, Harvard Business School Press.

Leonardi, P. and Barley, S. (2010) What's Under Construction Here? Social action, materiality, and power in constructivist studies of technology and organizing. *Academy of Management Annals*, *4*: 1–51.

Marr, B. (2003) Why Do Firms Measure their Intellectual Capital? *Journal of Intellectual Capital*, *4* (4): 441–464.

Marshall, D.H., McCartney, J., Van Rhyn, D., McManus, W.W. and Viele, D.F. (2008) *Accounting: What the numbers mean*, 2nd edition, North Ryde, NSW, McGraw-Hill.

Marsick, V. and Watkins, K. (2003) Demonstrating the Value of an Organization's Learning. *Advances in Developing Human Resources*, *5* (2): 132–151.

Massingham, P. (2016) Knowledge Accounts. *Long Range Planning*, *49* (3): 409–425.

Massingham, P. and Massingham, R. (2014) Does Knowledge Management Produce Practical Outcomes? *Journal of Knowledge Management*, *18* (2): 221–254.

Massingham, P. and Tam, L. (2015) The Relationship between Human Capital, Value Creation, and Employee Reward. *Journal of Intellectual Capital* (Special Issue), *16* (2): 390–418.

Massingham, P., Nguyen, T.N.Q. and Massingham, R. (2011) Using 360 Degree Peer Review to Validate Self-reporting in Human Capital Measurement. *Journal of Intellectual Capital*, *12* (1): 43–74.

Massingham, R., Massingham, P. and Dumay, J. (2019) Improving Integrated Reporting: A new learning and growth perspective for the balanced scorecard. *Journal of Intellectual Capital: Special Edition*, *20*(1): 60–82.

Minbaeva, D., Pedersen, T., Bjorkman, W., Fey, C.F. and Park, H.J. (2003) MNC Knowledge Transfer, Subsidiary Absorptive Capacity, and HRM. *Journal of International Business Studies*, *34* (6): 586–613.

Mouritsen, J., Larsen, H.T. and Bukh, P. (2001) Intellectual Capital and the 'Capable Firm': Narrating, visualising and numbering for managing knowledge. *Accounting, Organizations and Society*, *26* (7): 735–762.

Nonaka, I. and Takeuchi, H. (1995) *The Knowledge-Creating Company: How Japanese companies create the dynamics of innovation*, New York, Oxford University Press.

Nunally, J.C. (1978) *Psychometric Theory*, 2nd edition, New York, McGraw-Hill.

Pike, S., Rylander, A. and Roos, G. (2002) Intellectual Capital Management and Disclosure. Chapter 37 in Choo, C.W. and Bontis, N. (eds) *The Strategic Management of Intellectual Capital and Organizational Knowledge*, New York, Oxford University Press, pp. 657–672.

Polanyi, M. (1962) *Personal Knowledge*, Chicago, IL, University of Chicago Press.

Porter, L., Steers, R. and Mowday, R. (1973) Organizational Commitment, Job Satisfaction, and Turnover among Psychiatric Technicians. *Journal of Applied Psychology*, *59* (5): 603–609.

Probst, G., Raub, S. and Romhardt, K. (2002) *Managing Knowledge: Building blocks for success*, Chichester, Wiley.

Rao, M. (2005) *Knowledge Management Tools and Techniques: Practitioners and experts evaluate KM solutions*, Oxford, Elsevier.

Reed, K.K., Lubatkin, M. and Srinivasan, N. (2006) Proposing and Testing an Intellectual Capital-based View of the Firm. *Journal of Management Studies*, *43* (4): 867–893.

Riggs, M.L., Warka, J. and Babasa, B. (1994) Development and Validation of Self-efficacy and Outcome Expectancy Scales for Job-related Applications. *Educational and Psychological Measurement*, *54* (3): 793–802.

Robinson, S.L. and Rousseau, D.M. (1994) Violating the Psychological Contract: Not the exception but the norm. *Journal of Organizational Behavior*, *15* (3): 245–259.

Roos, J., Roos, G., Dragonetti, N.C. and Edvinsson, L. (1997) *Intellectual Capital: Navigating the new business landscape*, London, Macmillan.

Roslender, R. (2000) Accounting for Intellectual Capital: A contemporary management accounting perspective. *Management Accounting*, *78* (3): 34–37.

Sackman, S.A., Flamholtz, E.G. and Bullen, M.L. (1989) Human Resource Accounting: A state of the art review. *Journal of Accounting Literature*, *8*: 235–264.

Schaper, S., Nielsen, C. and Roslender, R. (2017) Moving from Irrelevant Intellectual Capital (IC) Reporting to Value-relevant IC Disclosures: Key learning points from the Danish experience. *Journal of Intellectual Capital*, *18* (1): 82–101.

Sillanpää, V., Lönnqvist, A., Koskela, N., Koivula, U.-M., Koivuaho, M. and Laihonen, H. (2010) The Role of Intellectual Capital in Non-profit Elderly Care Organizations. *Journal of Intellectual Capital*, *11* (2): 107–122.

Stewart, T.A. (1997) *Intellectual Capital: The new wealth of organizations*, New York, Doubleday.

Stone, W. (2001) Measuring Social Capital: Towards a theoretically informed measurement framework for researching social capital in family and community life. Research Paper No. 24, February, Australian Institute of Family Studies.

Sullivan, P.H. (1998) *Profiting from Intellectual Capital: Extracting value from innovation*, Chichester, Wiley.

Sveiby, K.E. (1997) *The New Organizational Wealth: Managing and measuring knowledge-based assets*, San Francisco, CA, Berrett-Koehler.

Thompson, A.J., Jr., Peteraf, M.A., Gamble, J.E. and Strickland, A.J. (eds) (2016) *Crafting and Executing Strategy: The quest for competitive advantage – Concepts and cases*, 20th edition, New York, McGraw-Hill Irwin.

Weaver, S.C. (2001) Measuring Economic Value Added: A survey of the practices of EVA proponents. *Journal of Applied Finance, 11* (1): 50–60.

Whyte, M. and Zyngier, S. (2014) Applied Intellectual Capital Management: Experiences from an Australian public sector trial of the Danish Intellectual Capital Statement. *Journal of Intellectual Capital, 15* (2): 227–248.

Youndt, M.A., Subramaniam, M. and Snell, S. (2004) Intellectual Capital Profiles: An examination of investments and returns. *Journal of Management Studies, 41* (2): 335–361.

PART 2
KNOWLEDGE MANAGEMENT IN PRACTICE

5

KNOWLEDGE STRATEGY

CHAPTER OUTLINE

Doing knowledge strategy

Conclusion

Closing case study: Knowledge strategy at the CSO

LEARNING OUTCOMES

After completing this chapter, the reader should be able to:

1. Discuss strategy and its role in knowledge management
2. Understand the contribution of the resource-based view of the firm and the knowledge-based view of the firm to knowledge strategy
3. Define knowledge strategy and the key decisions involved
4. Examine how knowledge creation fills knowledge gaps internally
5. Examine how knowledge acquisition fills knowledge gaps externally

MANAGEMENT ISSUES

Knowledge strategy requires managers to:

1. Understand the value of knowledge resources and how they create sustainable competitive advantage
2. Determine how the firm wants to compete using knowledge resources
3. Decide on core competencies and dynamic capabilities
4. Understand the changing nature of organizational boundaries and the need for new business models

Effective knowledge strategy involves the following challenges for management:

1. What knowledge strategy will provide a sustainable competitive position now and in the future?
2. What are our knowledge gaps?
3. How should we fill those knowledge gaps?

LINKS TO OTHER CHAPTERS

Chapter 4: on resource appraisal

Chapter 8: concerning the capability gap and the make decision via learning

Chapter 9: concerning the capability gap and the make decision via sharing

OPENING MINI CASE STUDY

STARBUCKS' STRATEGY: IS STARBUCKS' KNOWLEDGE A SOURCE OF SUSTAINABLE COMPETITIVE ADVANTAGE?

Starbucks began in 1987 as a modest nine-store operation in Seattle, Washington state, selling what might be considered a commodity product – coffee – and grew quickly to become a successful global multinational. The global financial crisis in 2009 had a significant negative impact on Starbucks. In response, senior executives changed its strategy and introduced a series of transformation initiatives to improve the customer experience, including:

- Conducting a special retraining programme for all store employees aimed at reigniting their emotional attachment to customers and refocusing their attention on the details of delivering superior customer service and pleasing customers
- Sharing best practices across all stores worldwide
- Refreshing menu offerings at Starbucks stores
- Introducing improved and more environmentally friendly designs for future Starbucks stores
- Providing additional resources and tools for store employees, including laptops, an internet-based software for scheduling work hours for store employees, and a new point-of-sale system for all stores in the USA, Canada, and the UK
- Insisting that the entire Starbucks organization put renewed emphasis on product innovation and differentiation. (Thompson et al., 2013: 19ETNSect7Case24)

These initiatives worked and Starbucks had a strong recovery and accelerated its new store growth globally. Starbucks' business model aims to differentiate itself from other coffee retailers. Aspects of its business model include ownership, culture, and human capital. Its culture includes employees in decision making, requires management to be open and honest with employees, and seeks to build a company with soul. Its strategy is based on an innovative culture which gets employees to enthusiastically communicate their knowledge about coffee to customers, and to exude a passion about Starbucks. It does this by having employees memorize recipes, learn procedures, and follow rules in making coffee/espresso drinks. Employees are encouraged to constantly come up with new ideas, new products, and new experiences for customers to enhance the Starbucks experience. Starbucks sought to continually challenge the status quo, stressed innovation on an ongoing basis, and challenged store managers and employees to display passion and enthusiasm for delivering truly first-rate customer service, and devise with new ways to make visiting a Starbucks store appealing. Starbucks truly felt they had a 'mystique' which made them different to other coffee shops or cafés and which was the key to their success. (Adapted from Thompson et al., 2013)

CASE STUDY QUESTIONS

1. Describe Starbucks' knowledge resources (See Chapter 1)
2. What knowledge does Starbucks value? Why? (See Chapter 4)
3. What was Starbucks' 'mystique'? Why?
4. Describe how Starbucks uses its knowledge to develop competitive advantage.

INTRODUCTION

An underlying assumption of this book is that knowledge is the most valuable resource. It follows that the management of this resource may lead to superior organization performance, profitability, and sustainability. This chapter examines effective knowledge strategy to achieve these goals.

The chapter begins with the assumption that knowledge may be measured as a stock of organizational resources like any other resource. This is called the organizational knowledge base (OKB). The OKB is what the organization knows at any point in time. The Knowledge Accounts (see Chapter 4) provides the method to measure the OKB. The OKB establishes a baseline for the knowledge strategy. The organization may then identify whether it is below (deficit) or above (surplus) its requirements to deliver the capability necessary. This introduces the need to take action to ensure the organization has the necessary knowledge resources. The second assumption is that knowledge has a temporal dimension. The OKB is fluid, and knowledge strategy must consider current and future requirements. These two assumptions combine to establish capability gaps – the difference between what the organization knows and what it needs to know – which knowledge strategy must address. It also allows for the identification of excess knowledge which may be used to create value in other areas.

CORE CONCEPT: Knowledge strategy is the decisions made about an organization's knowledge resources and capabilities, including resource appraisal and deployment, and internal and external development, to address knowledge gaps now and in the future.

The firm must decide how it will compete based on its knowledge resources. Several frameworks are discussed which take into account the nature of the resource and the firm's competitive context. Guiding theories are the resource-based view of the firm and the knowledge-based view of the firm, which explain how knowledge is a source of sustainable competitive advantage. These theories also challenge any underlying assumptions about organizations and their management. The main challenges are cooperation and coordination. These require innovative new business models, with fluid organizational boundaries, enabling knowledge to flow from external knowledge sources and for internal development. Several theories are discussed which guide managers on the knowledge strategy decisions associated with internal and external development necessary to fill any knowledge gaps and ensure current and future capability.

An important framework is Zack's (2002) conservative versus aggressive dichotomy of knowledge strategy. A conservative strategy focuses on exploiting internal knowledge. Its value creation is restricted to what is already known, and there is limited investment in significant new knowledge growth. Conservative strategy is examined further in Chapters 8 and 9. An aggressive strategy is required when an organization lags behind the competition or is defending a knowledge position.

This chapter focuses on aggressive knowledge strategy. Figure 5.2 presents a framework for growing knowledge resources, which summarizes the conservative and aggressive strategies.

WHAT IS STRATEGY?

An organization's strategy is its action plan for outperforming its competitors and achieving superior profitability (Thompson et al., 2016). Strategy involves setting goals, understanding and responding to the business environment, resource appraisal, and implementation (Grant, 2013). Strategy is the overall plan for deploying resources to establish a favourable position. Strategic decisions are important, involve a significant commitment of resources, and are not easily reversible. Firms may build a competitive advantage by:

- striving to become the industry's low-cost provider (efficiency)
- outcompeting rivals on differentiating features (effectiveness)
- offering the lowest (best) prices for differentiated goods (best-cost provider)
- focusing on better serving a niche market's needs (efficiency and/or effectiveness). (Thompson et al., 2016)

A firm achieves a competitive advantage when it provides buyers with superior value compared to rival sellers or offers the same value at a lower cost to the firm. The firm achieves a sustainable competitive advantage if its advantage persists despite the best efforts of competitors to match or surpass its advantage. Strategy has both deliberate (proactive and emergent) (reactive) components. The firm's business model is the outcome of its strategy. It begins with the customer value proposition, which is how the firm satisfies buyer wants and needs at a price customers will consider good value. The greater the value provided (V) and the lower the price (P), the more attractive the value proposition is to customers (Thompson et al., 2016). Knowledge strategy should be able to describe the business model and how knowledge resources contribute to the successful implementation of this model.

RESOURCE-BASED VIEW OF THE FIRM

The resource-based view (RBV) of the firm argues that the firm's resources create competitive advantage (Wernerfelt, 1984; Barney, 1991; Grant, 1996). On the early resource-based view, researchers saw strategy as managing for uniqueness and developing a distinctive competence, but understood that being different was not enough; it was necessary to prevent rivals from imitating or even improving on what you can do. Barney (1991) explains that strategic management prior to the emergence of the RBV was based on two simplifying assumptions: (1) firms within an industry (or strategic group within an industry) are identical in the strategically important resources that they need and the strategies they pursue; and (2) any resource heterogeneity a firm may achieve (e.g. by new entry) will only be short term due to the availability of resources in factor markets (i.e. resources can easily be bought and sold). This means that resources are not really a source of competitive advantage because all competitors have equal access to them.

The RBV challenged these underlying assumptions about strategy. Barney (1991) specified the conditions under which firm conditions can be a source of sustained competitive advantage for a firm. He developed a list of criteria which made resources difficult for competitors to replicate, thereby providing a source of sustainable competitive advantage. These included: valuable (generate efficiency and effectiveness), rarity (not widely held), not imitable (difficult to copy), not substitutable (other resources cannot do the same function), not transferable (not easily bought from the external market), and unique (are firm specific) (Barney, 1991). Barney's list may be described as the resource-based view criteria. It represents a checklist for competitive advantage. It is still used today, although contemporary strategic management texts have narrowed it down to four key criteria, commonly referred to as the VRIN test. The VRIN test for sustainable competitive advantage asks if a resource is valuable, rare, inimitable, and non-substitutable (Thompson et al., 2016). The first and second criteria identify whether there is a competitive advantage, and the third and fourth criteria establish whether this advantage is sustainable (i.e. longlasting).

CORE CONCEPT: Knowledge strategy begins with the premise that knowledge is valuable. Interest in knowledge management (KM) has been driven by the proposal that knowledge – KM's resource is a source of competitive advantage.

While resources may pass the VRIN test, they are idle and create no value unless they are combined with other resources. Resources are typically classified as tangible and intangible. Tangible resources include: physical resources, financial resources, technology assets, and organizational resources. Intangible assets include: human assets and intellectual capital; brands, company image, and reputational assets; relationships, alliances, joint ventures, or partnerships; and the company culture and incentive system (Thompson et al., 2016). The resource-based view argues that the real sources of competitive advantage are to be found in management's ability to consolidate corporate-wide technologies and production skills into competencies that empower individual businesses to adapt quickly to changing opportunities (Prahalad and Hamel, 1990).

The knowledge resource, therefore, is not limited to human capital. It is an organizational capability which may be described as the 'intangible but observable capacity of a firm to perform a critical activity proficiently using a related combination (cross-functional bundle) of its resources' (Thompson et al., 2016: [*page no. for quote?]). It is knowledge-based, residing in people and in a firm's intellectual capital or in its organizational processes and functional systems, which embody tacit knowledge (2016). It is tacit organizational knowledge. Knowledge strategy includes the making of decisions about which capabilities to develop and also how to develop them.

The resource-based view, therefore, provides the following concepts for knowledge strategy: knowledge has value; it meets the criteria for sustainable competitive advantage; and it creates competitive advantage with the know-how to combine other resources into capabilities.

KNOWLEDGE-BASED VIEW OF THE FIRM

DEFINITIONS

The knowledge-based view (KBV) regards the organization as an institution for generating and applying knowledge (Grant, 1996). It argues that knowledge is now more important than the traditional sources of economic power (Storey and Barnett, 2000). It can make that claim because knowledge is embedded in products and services and this makes it difficult for competitors to copy. Knowledge meets the resource-based view of the firm criteria for competitive advantage, i.e. the VRIN test, better than other resources (Grant, 2013).

In Grant's view, the KBV is not a formal theory of the firm; rather, 'it is more a set of ideas about the existence and nature of the firm that emphasize the role of knowledge' (Grant, 2002: 135). This suggests that the KBV is a philosophy or way of thinking about the firm and its management, which transcends a single theory, with knowledge the driving force. Grant (2002) argues that it is not a theory for a new age, rather a theory for any age. He feels that the KBV recognizes 'aspects of the firm and its management that are valid in any era' (2002: 135). For Grant (2002: 134), the emergence of knowledge management and the KBV in the 1990s was not due to the 'digitally based, post-industrial economy'. The most 'powerful tools of knowledge management' are not concerned with the 'flows of information and codified knowledge' that have driven the information technology boom; instead, they address the 'oldest form of knowledge known to society: tacit knowledge' (2002: 134–135). Thus, the KBV explains that knowledge management is not about technology or its discipline, information science; rather, it is about people and their knowledge, and this has been and always will be a challenge.

CORE CONCEPT: The knowledge-based view of the firm challenges underlying assumptions about organizations and how they are managed.

Grant (1997: 454) holds that the KBV 'promises to have one of the most profound changes in management thinking since the scientific management revolution of the early decades of this century'. He feels this way because the emergence of the knowledge-based economy has created challenges in managing knowledge workers, which requires academics and practitioners to explore 'new perspectives on the theory of the firm implied by the characteristics of knowledge and its role in production' (1997: 454).

At the foundations of the knowledge-based view are a set of assumptions concerning the characteristics of knowledge and the circumstances of its creation and application:

- Knowledge is the most valuable resource. It is the most productive resource in terms of its contribution to value added and its strategic significance.
- Different types of knowledge vary in their transferability. The critical distinction is between 'explicit knowledge' which is capable of articulation (and hence transferable at low cost) and 'tacit knowledge' which is manifest only in its application and is not amenable to transfer. The ease with which knowledge can be transferred also depends on the capacity of the recipient to aggregate units of knowledge.
- Knowledge is subject to economies of scale and scope, particularly with explicit knowledge which, once created, can be deployed in additional applications at low marginal cost.
- Knowledge is created by human beings, and to be efficient it requires specialization. Individuals are the primary agents of knowledge creation and are the principal repositories of tacit knowledge. If individuals' learning capacity is bounded, knowledge creation requires specialization: an increased depth of knowledge normally requires sacrificing a breadth of knowledge.
- Producing an object of economic value, such as a product, requires the application of many types of knowledge. (After Grant, 1997: 451)

KNOWLEDGE-BASED VIEW OF IMPLICATIONS FOR THE FIRM

The KBV explained how managing knowledge workers would represent a significant challenge and this would change the way organizations were managed. Grant (1997: 452) introduced the importance of knowledge sharing when he summarized management challenges as 'establishing the mechanisms by which cooperating individuals can coordinate their activities in order to integrate their knowledge into productive activity'. For him, these coordinating mechanisms include the following characteristics.

First is the architecture of organizational capability: 'capability will require integration across a broad base of knowledge necessitating the establishment of a closely linked series of organizational routines' (Grant, 1997: 452). This suggests the need for a new set of capabilities necessary to share knowledge in the activity of doing work.

Second, competitive advantage is achieved via internal replication while avoiding external replication: 'the greater the span of knowledge being integrated and the more sophisticated the integration mechanisms, the more difficult is it for any potential rival to accomplish replication' (1997: 452).

DEEP LEARNING: Organizational knowledge meets the RBV criteria for sustainable competitive advantage better than the tacit knowledge of individual employees, because it is difficult for competitors to copy embedded knowledge, whereas tacit knowledge is lost to rivals if employers switch employees.

Grant also explains how the embeddedness of organizational knowledge represents challenges for transferring it within the organization. As organizations seek a 'better way of doing business', they also want to ensure this capability is applied throughout the business, which requires the 'systematization and replication of these business models' (Grant, 1997: 452). This introduces the importance of codifying knowledge as best practice and sharing this through information technology systems.

Third, coordinating mechanisms include vertical integration decisions: 'markets are usually inefficient in transferring knowledge except where knowledge is embodied within products' (Grant, 1997: 452). In this way, the KBV questions the optimal boundaries of the firm and whether knowledge is best developed internally or accessed externally. This introduced the need for knowledge strategy and vertical integration and outsourcing decisions, i.e. make versus buy.

Fourth is reformulation of some of the principles of organization design: 'displacement of scientific management by various forms of participative, employee-empowering management approaches partly reflects the motivational benefits of these systems, but is also a result of the greater efficiency of these systems in accessing and integrating the relevant knowledge' (Grant, 1997: 453). This explains that traditional hierarchies are deficient as an organizing device for knowledge-intensive organizations. It introduces new business models with flatter structures and fluid control systems to empower employees and enable the flow of knowledge vertically and horizontally.

Fifth is distribution of decision-making authority: the KBV emphasizes the 'importance of co-locating decision making and knowledge; whether this involves decentralization or centralization of decision-making depends very much upon the characteristics of the knowledge required' (Grant, 1997: 453). Tacit knowledge should be decentralized to the subject matter experts with decisions depending on local context, whereas codified knowledge may be centralized and managed as best practice. This introduces the importance of matrix structures.

Sixth is the role of strategic alliances: 'resorting to collaborative arrangements with other firms, a firm is able to both better utilize its internal knowledge resources and access the knowledge resources of outside firms' (Grant, 1997: 453). Differences between the knowledge associated with products and the firm's internal knowledge resources, combined with the need for firms to diversify product range, mean that firms need to look outside for knowledge. This introduces the need for new employment modes which redefine traditional organizational boundaries.

If individuals must specialize in knowledge acquisition (i.e. learning how to do this task) and if producing goods and services requires the application of many types of knowledge (people working together to combine other resources), the role of management is to organize production to combine these many types of knowledge while preserving the specialization of individuals (Grant, 1997). The firm is an institution which exists to resolve this dilemma: it permits individuals to specialize in developing specialized expertise, while establishing mechanisms through which individuals coordinate to use their different knowledge in the transformation of inputs into outputs, i.e. the production of goods and services (Grant, 1997). If we accept these assumptions, then it fundamentally changes our view of organizations and how to manage them. It focuses attention on the knowledge resource and, at its most pointed aspect, the tacit knowledge of employees and how best to manage that resource.

THE PROBLEMS OF COOPERATION AND COORDINATION

These problems of organizing create two types of issues for the firm and its management: cooperation and coordination. The cooperation problem results from the fact that different organizational members have different goals, while the coordination problem is the technical issue of how to integrate the separate efforts of multiple individuals (Grant, 2002: 136). Most organizational analysis has focused on the problem of cooperation, i.e. knowledge sharing; however, Grant considers coordination to be equally important. Grant addresses this issue with his concept of mechanisms for knowledge integration. He argues that collective knowledge is the 'result of aggregating and integrating individuals' knowledge' (Grant, 2002: 138). In this way, he accepts that knowledge is personal, but the firm can still manage it if it combined what individuals know. Grant's four integrating mechanisms outline how firms may 'achieve the integration of individuals' knowledge into the production of goods and services' (Grant, 2002: 138). They are summarized below:

- *Rules and directives*: these are 'standards that regulate the interactions among individuals'. They are policies and procedures about knowledge sharing.
- *Sequencing*: this is about organizing 'production activities in a time-patterned sequence such that each specialist's input occurs independently'. This is the forerunner of process management and business performance improvement views of knowledge management.
- *Routines*: these are the informal reality of everyday work, and for Grant: 'their interesting feature is their ability to support complex patterns of interactions between individuals in the absence of rules, directives, or

even significant verbal communication.' Routines vary in their complexity. Some have a 'high level of simultaneity', such as work at a fast food restaurant, which means that work can be defined in terms of single, or at least very few, ways of doing it efficiently and effectively. Others have 'highly varied sequences of interaction' which allow for individual judgement depending on the context. These are the shared mental models about how best to do work. It captures individuals' tacit knowledge via observation of their routines.

- *Group problem solving and decision making*: while the 'above mechanisms seek efficiency of integration through avoiding the costs of communication and learning, some tasks may require more personal and communication intensive forms of integration.' Grant discusses how to share knowledge within complex group situations, including having common knowledge, symbols, and communication of specialized knowledge. This is the ability of individuals within groups to engage in the constructive dialogue necessary to understand one another and to share and create new knowledge, i.e. absorptive capacity.

The KBV has had a strong influence on the field of knowledge management and on knowledge strategy. It focuses knowledge resources at the centre of strategy, competition, and sustainable competitive advantage. It also challenges underlying assumptions about organizations and their management.

DEFINING KNOWLEDGE STRATEGY

Knowledge-based strategy is 'competitive strategy built around an organization's intellectual resources and capabilities' (Zack, 2002: 270). Zack (2002: 255) suggests knowledge strategy is to 'ensure that the organization is making the best investment of its resources or that it is managing the right knowledge in the right way'. This defines knowledge strategy in terms of resource appraisal and deployment. It is supported by the KBV perspective about management focusing on production (Grant, 2013). The production function is the act of doing and ensuring that employees are skilful knowers at that moment. Knowledge strategy, therefore, is ensuring the workforce either has existing knowledge or access to knowledge at the moment of production, that is, when they are performing work.

RESOURCE APPRAISAL

Knowledge strategy begins with resource appraisal. Management must decide which knowledge resources are important on the Knowledge Accounts baseline (see Chapter 4). Knowledge strategy looks at this from a competitive context and identifies three types of knowledge resources:

- *Core knowledge*: 'the minimum scope and level of knowledge required' just to participate in the industry (Zack, 2002: 260). This type of knowledge is usually common to industry participants and, therefore, not a source of competitive advantage.

- *Advanced knowledge*: 'enables an organization to be competitively viable' (2002: 260). Specific knowledge content may allow an organization to differentiate itself from competitors, usually providing superior performance in a valuable capability.

- *Innovative knowledge*: 'knowledge that enables an organization to lead its industry and competitors and to significantly differentiate itself from its competitors' (2002: 260). This knowledge enables an organization to change the rules of the game, for instance via a significantly new product, process, or market, or even a completely new way of doing business.

This typology provides management with a framework for resource appraisal, which they can use to establish a baseline and classify the importance of their knowledge resources; they can then use the Knowledge Accounts to establish capability gaps. Organizations who match rivals in core knowledge are viable competitors; those who lead competitors in innovation knowledge are innovators; and those who lag behind rivals in innovation knowledge are at risk (after Zack, 2002: 261).

The resource appraisal may produce three outcomes: (1) surplus, (2) deficit, and (3) alignment (see Chapter 4). Knowledge strategy explains what to do in each scenario with two dichotomies: exploration and exploitation.

CORE CONCEPT: Knowledge resources in surplus may be exploited; resources in deficit require exploration; and those in alignment may be maintained.

EXPLORATION VERSUS EXPLOITATION

Exploration is about seeking new knowledge resources, mainly to remain competitive (Zack, 2002). Organizations with this strategy are simply trying to keep up, and seek the knowledge necessary to continue participating in an industry, perhaps where the knowledge in that industry is changing. Exploitation is about using existing knowledge resources for other purposes (Zack, 2002). Organizations with this knowledge strategy have excess knowledge and want to use it in other organizational contexts or markets, to create new value for the organization. This dichotomy explains that economic value creation requires two critical knowledge-based processes: knowledge generation and knowledge application in the production of goods and services (Grant, 2013). Knowledge application fits the surplus and alignment scenarios. When the resource appraisal reveals that the firm knows enough to perform activities well, management can then use this knowledge to create economic value. If there is a surplus, i.e. the firm knows more than it needs to know, management can use this excess knowledge for other purposes to create new economic value (see Chapter 7). Knowledge generation fits the deficit scenario. When the firm does not know enough, it needs to grow its knowledge resources. This is knowledge creation, which is covered in the second part of this chapter. Knowledge creation involves not only the search activities encompassed by exploration, but also all increases in an organization's stock of knowledge, including learning by doing, knowledge acquisition, and knowledge sharing (Grant, 2013). These represent choices about how to fill the capability gap and ensure the firm knows what it needs to know.

Knowledge resources in deficit may be addressed in several ways. These involve decisions about the resource itself and its importance. Managers must ask: Is the knowledge resource proprietary? Is it a source of competitive advantage, and is this advantage sustainable? The RBV and the VRIN tests are helpful here. The three types of knowledge resources (i.e. core, advanced, and innovative) also provide guidance, which enables managers to evaluate the relative importance of the resource in deficit.

The next decision is about the firm's knowledge strategy itself. Does the firm want to be a leader, challenger, or follower (Zack, 2002)? A leader focuses on innovation or advanced knowledge and has an advantage relative to competitors. A challenger focuses on core knowledge but has a similar capability to market leaders and is trying to grow innovation or advanced knowledge. A follower is focusing on core knowledge, while most competitors are growing their resources in innovation or advanced knowledge. This decision requires detailed knowledge about the firm's competitiveness in the resource.

DYNAMIC CAPABILITIES

The dynamic capabilities framework (Teece et al., 1997) emerged as the dominant RBV-based approach to knowledge strategy. Dynamic capabilities are the firm's ability to integrate, build, and reconfigure internal and external resources and competences to address and shape rapidly changing business environments (Teece, 2007). This definition explains that dynamic capabilities are what Grant (1997, 2013) described as organizational knowledge. Dynamic capabilities have three roles: 'sensing opportunities (building new knowledge), seizing these opportunities to capture value, and transforming the organization as needed to adapt to the requirements of new business models and the competitive environment' (Teece and Al-Aali, 2011: 507). They create value in the way they combine resources to 'determine the speed at, and degree to which, the firm's idiosyncratic resources and competences can be aligned and realigned to match the opportunities and requirements of the business environment' (2011: 509). The outcomes are the capacity to outperform competition. Specific examples of dynamic capabilities are change routines, such as product development, and strategic analysis of, for example, investment choices or market timing decisions. However, they are more commonly found in creative managerial and entrepreneurial acts (Teece and Al-Aali, 2011: 509), such as product, process, or market innovation.

Dynamic capabilities bring together the RBV, the KBV, and knowledge strategy to identify the knowledge resources which are truly important to the firm. They are the firm's core competencies. But they are not to be confused with the core knowledge described earlier. Core knowledge is the basic knowledge necessary to participate in an industry, i.e. perform the activities that must be done. Core competencies, on the other hand, are the firm's sources of competitive advantage – the organizational knowledge that differentiates the firm from its competitors. Core competencies are rare, valuable, inimitable, and non-transferable (Wernerfelt, 1984; Prahalad and Hamel, 1990; Barney, 1991). This enables managers to develop a further dichotomy: core and non-core competencies. Core competencies are assigned the highest value in resource appraisal.

ORGANIZATIONAL BOUNDARIES

The knowledge-based view of the firm (KBV) challenged the underlying assumptions about organizations and how to manage them. 'Hybrid orga-nizational forms that fall between markets and firm-based hierarchies' are emerging (Grant, 2013: 545). These include 'a variety of inter-firm collabora-tive arrangements, which are changing the traditional view of the organization, [and] include supplier–buyer partnerships, research consortia, outsourcing arrangements, patent pooling agreements, and other forms of resource-sharing arrangements' (2013: 545). As more industries embrace outsourcing, research-ers have questioned why hierarchically managed firms exist at all (Teece and Al-Aali, 2011: 506). Why not just organize the same activities using contracts (2011: 506)?. Why not outsource everything? These issues tackle the essence of the theory of the firm.

Research has attempted to answer these questions. Quinn (1992) argued that firms should focus on core capabilities while non-core capabilities should be brought in. Teece and Al-Aali (2011: 509) agree and state that 'the essence of … dynamic capabilities is that they cannot generally be bought; they must be built.' Such capabilities require time to develop into competitive advantage, however. Winter (1995) suggested that the dynamic aspects of capability are more involved with bringing in knowledge for long-term future positions, instead of short-run profits (Teece et al., 1997). Grant (2008) argued that internal capabilities provide greater security to long-term strategy in changing environments.

Almost 20 years after his seminal article, Grant (2013) reflected on the knowledge-based view. He begins by describing how organization theory has not kept up with the changing nature of developments in organizations. He suggests that the main change has been the emergence of new organizational forms. He then argues that the main relevance of the KBV, 20 years after its introduction, is to help understand these new business models, particularly coordination within them:

> Knowledge-based approaches to the theory of the firm offer new insights into the processes and institutions of economic organization. At the heart of this contribution is the insight that [the] knowledge-based view of the firm offers into the analysis of coordination in production. (Grant, 2013: 542)

Grant explains that the reason for his focus on new organizational forms is the two types of problems for the firm and its management: cooperation and coordination. In the 20 years since the emergence of the KBV, Grant argues that organizational theory has still not resolved the problem of coordination. The difficulty with coordination is to 'devise mechanisms through which the knowledge resources of many different individuals can be deployed in the production of a particular product' (Grant, 2013: 543). It is a challenge because it requires integrating mechanisms (see above discussion) while preserving the efficiencies of specialization. This means that the scale economies of being an expert must be traded off against the time it takes to engage with others. In organizational structure terms, specialization is vertical knowledge flows, and integration is horizontal knowledge flows (Massingham, 2010). Grant concludes that 'any system of production that requires that each individual learns what every other individual knows is inherently inefficient' (Grant, 2013: 543). This statement raises many questions about knowledge management. The most obvious is that codifying individual knowledge, storing it, sharing it, and making it accessible for others are inefficient. This argues against the technology view of knowledge management. It also tends to privilege individual knowledge, particularly tacit knowledge, and suggests that the individual creates most value working alone or with small groups of other, similar experts to increase their knowledge, rather than learning others' knowledge.

The RBV assumes that heterogeneity should be invested in to exploit differences, which suggests a need to limit importing capability when internal resources can be exploited (Prahalad and Hamel, 1990). The RBV encourages acquiring professional (market) knowledge from external sources but discourages it once firm-specific knowledge is developed (Tordoir, 1995). The decision whether to fill knowledge gaps internally or externally is an important part of knowledge strategy (Zack, 2002). The RBV and the KBV suggest that internally is the best decision, particularly for core competencies or dynamic capabilities, because it helps sustain competitive advantage. However, some firms prefer external knowledge because it provides new perspectives and benchmarking, such as best practice (Zack, 2002). Zack also describes an unbounded approach which means the organization accesses necessary knowledge from wherever it can get it, internally or externally, depending on the situation.

Zack combines the exploration versus exploitation dichotomy and the sourcing decision to describe an organization's attitude towards knowledge strategy. Figure 5.1 presents this typology.

The dichotomy of exploitation versus exploration is the horizontal axis. The sourcing decision internally developed versus externally acquired or unbounded is the vertical axis. The framework enables decisions to consider the speed of competition (vertical axis) and the importance of knowledge to competitive

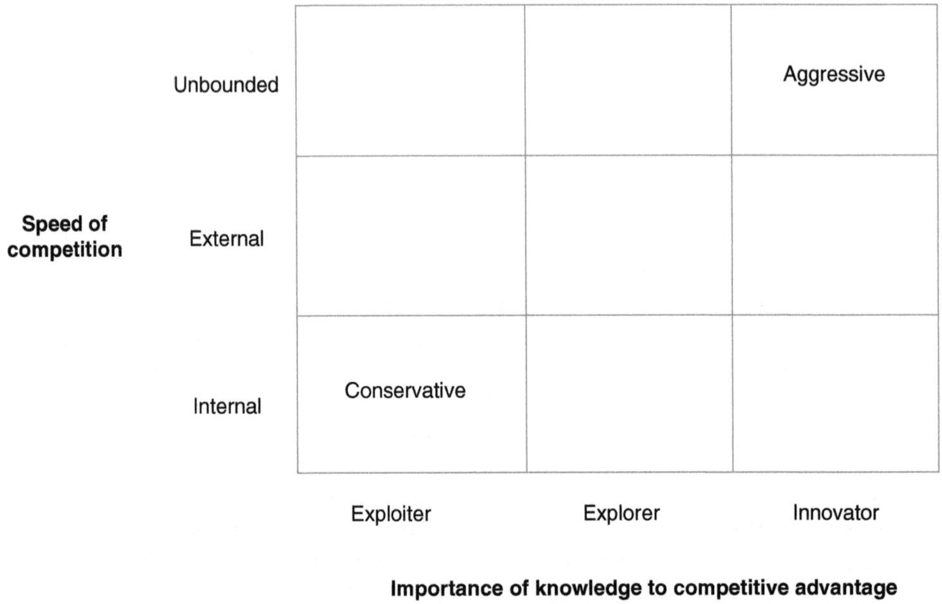

Speed of competition (vertical axis): Unbounded, External, Internal

Cells: Aggressive (top right, Unbounded/Innovator), Conservative (bottom left, Internal/Exploiter)

Horizontal axis labels: Exploiter, Explorer, Innovator

Importance of knowledge to competitive advantage

FIGURE 5.1 *Zack's (2002) aggressive versus conservative knowledge strategy.* Originallly published in the *California Management Review*

advantage (horizontal axis). When an organization lags the competition or is defending a knowledge position, an aggressive strategy is needed to survive (Zack, 2002). Alternatively, organizations which focus on exploiting internal knowledge are the most conservative because they are limited to creating value from what is already known and are not investing in significant new knowledge growth.

This chapter focuses on aggressive knowledge strategy, whereas Chapter 8 – organizational learning and the learning organization – focuses on conservative knowledge strategy. Figure 5.2 presents a framework for growing knowledge resources.

INTERNAL DEVELOPMENT: KNOWLEDGE CREATION

Grant (2013) explains that the firm may fill its knowledge gaps internally from learning by doing, knowledge acquisition, and knowledge sharing (see Figure 5.2). However, it may also fill gaps by knowledge creation.

CORE CONCEPT: Knowledge resources in surplus may be exploited, resources in deficit require exploration, and those in alignment may be maintained.

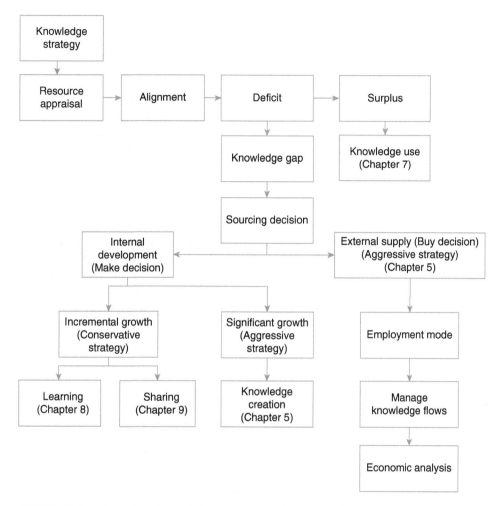

FIGURE 5.2 *Growing knowledge resources framework*

WHO CREATES KNOWLEDGE?

Knowledge creation begins with the individual. If we start with the definition of knowledge as 'justified true belief', then knowledge creation is the process of knowing. It is the individual's journey of justifying personal belief towards the truth (Nonaka and Takeuchi, 1995: 58). Knowing occurs when the individual reaches a point where they feel they can trust their belief (e.g. 'This is how I do this task') and act on it. They then 'know' how to do something. Beforehand, they did not know, but now they know: they have created new knowledge for themselves. Human capital is the source of innovation. Human capital represents the human factor in the organization: the combined intelligence, skills, and expertise that give the organization its distinctive character (Bontis, 1998).

Knowledge creation also has ontological and epistemological dimensions. Ontology is the process of having individual knowledge 'validated' by the organization so that it becomes 'justified true belief' for the organization. Otherwise, it might be just an individual's opinion. Epistemology is the interaction between tacit and explicit knowledge. Nonaka and Takeuchi (1995: 61) define knowledge creation as a process of knowledge conversion, where the epistemological dimension (tacit and explicit) occurs within the ontological dimension (social interaction). It is here that justified true belief occurs at the organizational level, and only then can we say that knowledge creation truly occurs. Knowledge creation occurs when we learn something new that is useful. It produces an increase in our stock of knowledge. But learning also selectively decreases our knowledge. Unless we are able to eliminate (forget) parts of our previous knowledge that are no longer useful, we risk information overload. We need to be willing to change our view (Boisot, 2002: 70). Experts who say they are creating new knowledge highlight the newness of their data and the differences between their findings and those of earlier investigators (Easterby-Smith and Lyles, 2003: 477). Knowledge creation, in this scientific sense, is seen as small incremental steps forward, i.e. a contribution to the existing body of knowledge or an advance. It is the idea of making progress and learning more about a topic. The key theme is building on what is already known and finding new insights, but anchored in an existing stock or body of knowledge.

THE SECI MODEL

This chapter uses Nonaka and Takeuchi's (1995) knowledge creation model as a theoretical framework to examine the internal development of knowledge (SECI: socialization, externalization, combination, internalization). Figure 5.3 presents their model, whose four quadrants are as follows:

- Quadrant 1 – *socialization* is the process of sharing experiences and creating tacit knowledge, such as shared mental models and technical skills. It can be done through observation, for example master and apprentice, but often involves getting people talking, such as brainstorming. It is effective in sharing tacit knowledge and creating new perspectives. It focuses individuals' mental models in the same direction but subtly through group harmony.

DEEP THINKING: The socialization quadrant is the social practice of sharing tacit knowledge. The process or personalization view of knowledge management looks at social practice as the best way to share knowledge (see Chapter 2). This is about providing opportunities for people to socialize for real, for instance in meetings or virtual environments (e.g. online). Knowledge is closely tied to the person who created it and is shared through person-to-person contact. The management of socialization emphasizes ways to promote, motivate, encourage, nurture, or guide the process of knowing. In the SECI model, this happens in quadrant 1, socialization, where tacit knowledge is exchanged with other tacit knowledge.

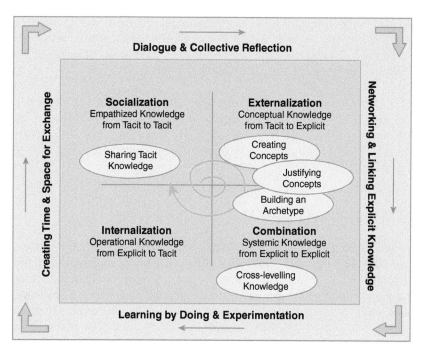

FIGURE 5.3 *Nonaka and Takeuchi's (1995) SECI model.* By permission of Oxford Univercity press, USA.

- Quadrant 2 – *externalization* is the process of articulating tacit knowledge in explicit concepts. It happens through a process of concept creation and is triggered by dialogue or collective reflection. A concept consists of metaphors, analogies, concepts, hypotheses, or theoretical models. Metaphors create novel interpretation of experience by asking the listener to see one thing in terms of something else and create new ways of experiencing reality. Metaphors try to reconcile discrepancies in meaning. Analogy harmonizes contradictions inherent in a metaphor by reducing the unknown and highlighting the common ground between two things. The method used to create a concept is to combine deduction and induction. The Mazda RX 7 car was *deduced* as a strategic car for the USA based on joyful driving pleasures. It was *induced* from concept trips to the USA and concept clinics with customers.

- Quadrant 3 – *combination* is a process of systemizing concepts in a knowledge system. It combines different bodies of explicit knowledge through documents, meetings, and telephone conversations. The knowledge is sorted, added, combined, and categorized as explicit knowledge (e.g. databases, reports). It can be used to combine mid-range concepts in an organization (e.g. product concepts) with, and integrate with, broader concepts (e.g. corporate vision).

- Quadrant 4 – *internalization* is the process of embodying explicit knowledge in tacit knowledge. It is learning by doing. When experiences through socialization, externalization, and combination are internalized in individuals' tacit knowledge bases in the form of shared mental models or technical know-how, they become valuable assets. For explicit knowledge to become tacit, it helps if the knowledge is verbalized or diagrammed in documents, manuals, or oral stories. (After Nonaka and Takeuchi, 1995)

Figure 5.3 provides guidelines on how the knowledge creation process moves through individual to group to organization levels, and on the outcomes of these interactions in terms of creating new concepts, justifying them, building arche-types, cross-levelling (embedding as organizational knowledge), and sharing tacit knowledge.

THE KNOWLEDGE-CREATING SPIRAL

Nonaka and Takeuchi (1995) combined their conversion model in a framework called the knowledge-creating spiral. This framework is the key to understanding the value of Nonaka and Takeuchi's model. It explains how organizational knowledge creation is a continuous and dynamic interaction between tacit and explicit knowledge.

Nonaka and Takeuchi (1995) conclude with five knowledge creation enablers to aid implementation of the SECI model and the knowledge-creating spiral:

1. *Intention*: a collective commitment to a certain strategy. It is often expressed as organizational vision, and directs knowledge-creating efforts in support of the goals of the business.
2. *Autonomy*: self-organizing individuals are more flexible in acquiring and relating information and producing unexpected outcomes.
3. *Fluctuation and creative chaos*: environmental fluctuation can create a sense of crisis, which can be beneficial as the organization adapts to the new context in which it finds itself, developing challenge, or introducing ambiguity – conditions advocated for innovation.
4. *Redundancy*: facilitates efficient knowledge flow and absorption, as well as empowerment of the team through participation of members on the basis of consensus and common understanding. Redundancy is knowledge overlap which helps develop competing solutions as the team looks at the problem from several perspectives and hence increases learning.
5. *Requisite variety*: encourages diversity of knowledge to ensure that employees know who owns which specific knowledge and how to access it, but they should not be exposed to it all (to avoid overload) (after Nonaka and Takeuchi, 1995).

Figure 5.4 starts on the left-hand side with the tacit and explicit knowledge dichot-omy. Explicit knowledge flows across the top of the figure, as this is where knowledge is combined and externalized (see quadrants on the right-hand side of Figure 5.3). It is the epistemological dimension of the knowledge-creating spiral. Tacit knowledge flows across the bottom of the figure, as this is where knowledge is socialized and internalized (see quadrants on the left-hand side of Figure 5.3). It is the ontological dimension of the knowledge-creating spiral. The arrows up and down show how knowledge flows, for example explicit and tacit knowledge are two sides of the same coin; they need each other. The dotted line arrows show where the four quadrants of Figure 5.3 are situated in this spiral. The bottom list shows the owners of the knowledge. The funnel shape of Figure 5.4 is designed to show how these elements interact to diffuse the knowledge being created, and as this diffusion moves from the individual to the group – and so on – it grows as others learn, and thus the figure ends with more knowledge at the right-hand side of the figure than when we started with at the left-hand side. The reverse arrows in the bottom list illustrate that this is a cycle and the process reverts back to the beginning, with the individual (e.g. with internalization – see Figure 5.3), and so it moves onwards again.

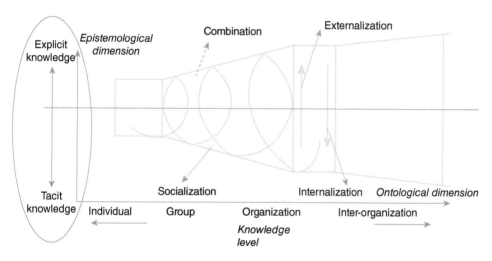

FIGURE 5.4 *Nonaka and Takeuchi's (1995) knowledge-creating spiral.* By permission of Oxford University press, USA.

MEASURING THE OUTCOMES OF KNOWLEDGE CREATION

Knowledge creation is often used interchangeably with the word 'innovation'. Innovation is defined as 'an economic or social term', as 'changing the yield of resources', and as 'changing the value and satisfaction obtained from resources by the consumer' (Drucker, 1985: 33). Innovation collaboration may be defined as 'the development and implementation of new ideas by people who engage in discussions with others' within an organizational context (Van de Van, 1986: 591). Innovation is linked to firm strategy in terms of performance improvement, profitability, and sustainability. The 'common theme among all industries involved in the knowledge-based economy is the output of the creative sector, especially for initiating discontinuous or disruptive innovation' which provides sustainable competitive advantage (Robertson, 1967, cited in White et al., 2014: 47). Howkins (2002, cited in White et al., 2014: 47) 'defines the creative economy as how people make money from ideas'. The 'core of the creative economy is individual creativity, skill, and talent' (White et al., 2014: 47).

Innovation is widely studied in relation to productivity and competitiveness. However, researchers argue that 'innovation is inherently impossible to quantify and to measure, mainly because of its various qualitative aspects' (Carayannis and Grigoroudis, 2014: 201). There has been some progress. At a broad level, innovation is considered to be one of the principal drivers of competition, influencing the cost position or the differentiation of a product (e.g. Thompson et al., 2016). More specifically, it is generally agreed that innovation may improve firm performance and competitiveness by 'influencing economies of scale, the timing of processes, and the introduction of new products, methods [and markets]' (Carayannis and Sagi, 2001: 505). Innovation efforts – such as investments in internal and external R&D, in new machines and software, in the acquisition of licences, the training of personnel, or the marketing of new products – will affect the innovation performance of firms (Ahuja et al., 2008).

National innovation performance is examined in two major ways: the first approach is based on indicators, while the second one refers to the modelling or econometric approach (Carayannis and Grigoroudis, 2014). 'Usually both public and private sources are used', from 'national statistics [and] surveys' to particular sectors and firms (2014: 200). There are various composite indexes of innovation consisting of input, process, and performance measures. For example, 'the European Innovation Scoreboard (EIS) is an aggregated innovation index that includes economy-wide measures, has a high degree of international comparability', and has three categories: enablers, firm activities, and outputs (2014: 202).

EXTERNAL DEVELOPMENT: KNOWLEDGE ACQUISITION

Firms may also choose to fill their knowledge gaps externally via knowledge acquisition. Managers may choose to acquire knowledge from external experts via three different employment modes: (a) alliance, (b) contracting, and (c) recruitment. In each case, the organization purchases external expertise in order to fill the knowledge gap.

DEEP THINKING: The acquisition of external knowledge has financial and non-financial costs. It must make economic sense to acquire the knowledge externally, i.e. the 'buy decision', otherwise the 'make decision' is best. Further, the flow of knowledge from external sources to internal users must be managed by employees with specialist roles and relationships.

Lepak and Snell (1999) propose a theory of human resource architecture based on evaluating two criteria: (1) the value of human capital and (2) the uniqueness of human capital. Figure 5.5 and Table 5.1 present and summarize the model.

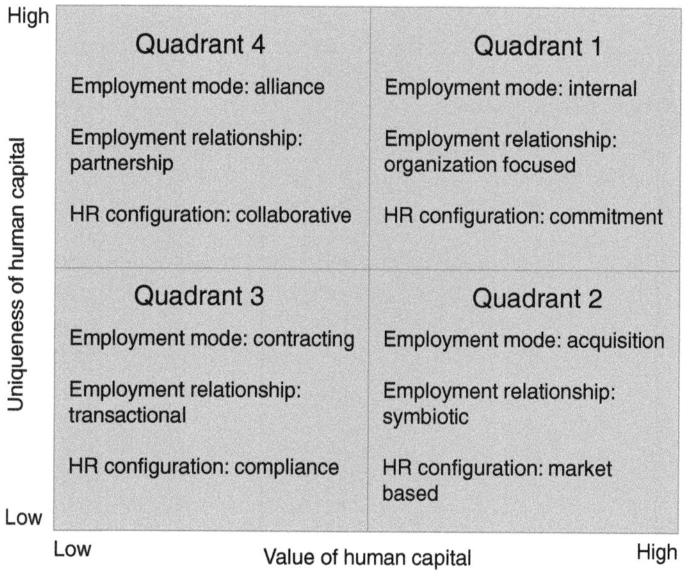

```
High
        ┌─────────────────────────┬─────────────────────────┐
        │      Quadrant 4         │      Quadrant 1         │
        │                         │                         │
        │ Employment mode: alliance│ Employment mode: internal│
        │                         │                         │
        │ Employment relationship:│ Employment relationship:│
        │ partnership             │ organization focused    │
U       │                         │                         │
n i     │ HR configuration:       │ HR configuration:       │
q t     │ collaborative           │ commitment              │
u a     ├─────────────────────────┼─────────────────────────┤
e l     │      Quadrant 3         │      Quadrant 2         │
n       │                         │                         │
e o     │ Employment mode:        │ Employment mode:        │
s f     │ contracting             │ acquisition             │
s       │                         │                         │
        │ Employment relationship:│ Employment relationship:│
        │ transactional           │ symbiotic               │
        │                         │                         │
        │ HR configuration:       │ HR configuration: market│
        │ compliance              │ based                   │
Low     └─────────────────────────┴─────────────────────────┘
        Low           Value of human capital           High
```

FIGURE 5.5 *Lepak and Snell's (1999) human resource architecture model.* By permission of the Academy of Management.

TABLE 5.1 Lepak and Snell's (1999) human resource architecture

Quadrant	Employment mode	Employment relationship	HR configuration
1: *Developing human capital* Firm-specific skills are not available in the labour market. In addition to uniqueness, skills within this quadrant are valuable. Their strategic benefit exceeds the managerial and bureaucratic costs associated with their development and deployment.	*Internal*: Since firm-specific skills are non-transferable, the value of any employee's human capital will be less with any other firm. Internal development will be less likely to result in a capital loss, due to employee turnover. These are core employees, a source of competitive advantage.	*Organization focused*: Encouraging significant mutual investment from employers and employees in developing critical firm skills. Long-term involvement and investment.	*Commitment*: Firms rely on a commitment-based HR system that nurtures employee involvement and maximizes firms' return on human capital investments.
2: *Acquiring human capital* Valuable, yet widely available throughout the labour market. The individual's value is an incentive to internalize employment.	*Acquisition*: Buying from the market does not require further investment.	*Symbiotic*: Based on the premise of mutual benefit.	*Market based*: Deploying skills for immediate contribution.

(Continued)

TABLE 5.1 (Continued)

Quadrant	Employment mode	Employment relationship	HR configuration
Since skills are not unique or specific to a firm, managers may be hesitant to invest in internal development, as they may leave and transfer the organization's investment to another firm.	Firms gain the benefits of valuable skills that have been developed elsewhere. They realize significant savings in developmental expenditures while gaining instant access to a wide variety of capabilities.	Both the employees and the organization are likely to continue the relationship as long as both continue to benefit. These types of employees are less committed to the organization than quadrant 1 employees, and are more concerned about their career (personal gain) than the organization.	These employees are not likely to receive as much training and development as quadrant 1. Managers will focus on recruiting and selecting employees who already possess the necessary skills.
3: *Contracting human capital* Generic and of limited strategic value. Public knowledge: skills that can be purchased easily on the open labour market and, therefore, can be treated essentially as a commodity.	*Contracting:* Often, this work is done off company premises (and only the product of those labours will be traded), but it is increasingly common that contractual work is performed on site. Firms are increasingly outsourcing administrative or lower-level jobs, such as clerical support, and maintenance positions, which contribute little to the competitive position of the firm. This reduces overhead costs and retains a significant degree of flexibility concerning the number of workers employed, as well as when they are employed. It may actually improve the competitiveness of firms by enabling them to strategically focus their development expenses on those skills that may contribute to the firm's competitive advantage.	*Transactional:* Focuses on short-term economic exchanges. Individuals have specific performance requirements and limited organizational involvement It is similar to the symbiotic approach of quadrant 2, but differs in the scope of involvement and the expectations underlying the exchanges. Symbiotic relationship – organizations seek some continuity and loyalty from full-time employees. Transactional relationship – firms probably do not expect (and do not obtain) organizational commitment; the relationships simply focus on the economic nature of the contract.	*Compliance:* Similar to quadrant 2, differ in the range of behaviours and expectations required of employees. Focus on securing compliance with the terms and conditions of the contract. Enforcing rules and regulations, and ensuring conformance to pre-set standards. In comparison, once hired, quadrant 2 employees are likely to be permitted a greater degree of empowerment to carry out their organizational roles.

Quadrant	Employment mode	Employment relationship	HR configuration
4: *Creating human capital alliances* Unique in some ways but not directly related to creating customer value. Given uniqueness, it suggests internal development. But some skills may take years to develop – small firms particularly may not be able to justify the expense of full-time internal employment.	*Alliance*: Some unique forms of human capital are less codified and transferable than generic skills, yet more widely available than firm-specific skills. If outright internalization is prohibitive from a cost–benefit standpoint, and complete contracting involves risks of opportunism, some form of alliance between parties may provide a hybrid employment mode that blends internalization and externalization and overcomes these problems of the creation of co-specialized assets: assets that provide value only through the combined efforts of two or more parties.	*Partnership*: Requires information sharing and trust, engendering reciprocity and collaboration. Without information sharing, partners can at best only pool their resources. Without trust, neither party is likely to give valuable information to the other, nor to act on the information they receive. This enables true partnerships that focus on mutual investment in the relationship and build trust among involved parties, while still protecting their investments and gaining access to each other's knowledge.	*Collaborative*: Encourage and reward cooperation, collaboration, and information sharing. Co-specialized rather than firm-specific assets, organizations will not be likely to expend resources for training and developing partners. Focus on process facilitation and team building. Communication mechanisms, exchange programmes, job rotations, mentoring relationships.

Table 5.1 provides knowledge strategy with a framework to choose between internal development and external development to fill knowledge gaps. The model is based on the axis of uniqueness and value. If the knowledge is both unique and valuable, internal development (knowledge creation, sharing, or learning on the job) is the best solution. Otherwise, the model provides three separate employment modes which guide the knowledge strategy decision, depending on the appraisal of the knowledge resource's uniqueness and value.

THEORY IN PRACTICE: QUADRANT 1 – DEVELOPING HUMAN CAPITAL

This knowledge is unique and high value. Jill McKeon was the group general manager of an energy company. She was in charge of commercial services, which involved a range of business support services including finance, human

(Continued)

(Continued)

resources, marketing, and customer service. One of her managers, Karina Wilson, had just resigned. Karina was in charge of the finance division. Jill was reflecting on how to replace Karina. Karina's financial skills were readily available. Jill could replace them by recruiting another senior manager externally. But there was something special about Karina. She had developed a balanced scorecard which had added significant value to the company's strategy execution. Jill considered whether she should add expertise in the balanced scorecard to the job criteria. However, it was not just the balanced scorecard that made Karina special. She had a way of communicating which enabled her to translate the measures to people at all levels. She could walk into a maintenance workshop and talk with the workers about how they could develop their own set of measures to implement the balanced scorecard. She would be difficult to replace. Jill decided to look for someone in Karina's team who had knowledge of the balanced scorecard, excellent communication and interpersonal skills, and a strong organizational commitment. She would help them grow into the role to replace Karina.

THEORY IN PRACTICE: QUADRANT 2 – ACQUIRING HUMAN CAPITAL

This knowledge is common and high value. One of Jill McKeon's managers, Anna Teslah, was sitting in her office. Anna was in charge of the marketing division. Anna was explaining her budget request for the next financial year. She was discussing how a change in the market required the company to focus more on the retail business, and that competition for major customers was increasing. Anna's request was for an increase in her workforce budget. She needed extra resources to help her tackle new competitive challenges. After discussion, Jill approved Anna's request and asked her to recruit 10 university graduates.

THEORY IN PRACTICE: QUADRANT 3 – CONTRACTING HUMAN CAPITAL

This knowledge is common with low value. Jill McKeon had been hearing complaints about her human resources division. Each of the other group general managers had their own dedicated human resources staff. While the manager in charge of the human resources division, Javier Sanchez, reported to Jill, his staff worked in the other business groups and also reported to their group general manager in a matrix structure. The complaints were about the human resources staff creating political tension in the organization. Staff in each division were working 'upwards' to keep their respective group general manager happy, but did very little for other staff. They were seen as working for management and not staff. They also created rivalry between the group general managers by encouraging competition for resources and trying to build fiefdoms (more human resources staff) in their divisions. Additionally, they were beginning to frustrate the group general managers by enforcing policy at every opportunity. The human resources staff seemed to see themselves as 'guardians' of good management practice – attending management meetings and directing both management and staff on their role and what they were allowed to do. This growing desire for power was dysfunctional. 'Human resource management is a support function, not a leadership role', thought Jill. How did these people come to assume they were the company's judge and jury? They were strangling the business. Jill made her decision: 'We will outsource the human resources function', she told Javier. 'You can stay. You will be in charge of the new contract staff. I want you to ensure they provide a service role only. They will be centralized under your leadership and not situated in the divisions. All current human resources staff will be made redundant. Draft me their letters.'

THEORY IN PRACTICE: QUADRANT 4 – HUMAN CAPITAL ALLIANCES

This knowledge is unique with low value. Jill McKeon was travelling with her manager in charge of the information technology division, Sue-Ellen Charbosky. They had met with a leading IT consultancy to discuss introducing a new IT system for the company. As the business had grown, its IT needs had also increased, particularly in terms of its customer management, including automating bills and payment. Sue-Ellen was trying to persuade Jill that she should recruit a fresh team of IT graduates to help her build the new system. Sue-Ellen felt this would be more cost-effective than using the consultancy and would also create value by building a team that could then implement and maintain the system in the long term. Jill reflected on Sue-Ellen's points. She then told Sue-Ellen that she would be hiring the IT consultants to design and implement the new system. She felt they were experts and would be a better return on investment than the company doing it themselves. She also felt that this was a one-off exercise and would not require recurring capability.

Acquisition enables knowledge strategy to explore new business models, such as hybrids (Grant, 2013), which challenge underlying assumptions about traditional hierarchical structures and organizational boundaries. The KBV offers a theoretical basis for the analysis of strategic alliances.

THEORY IN PRACTICE: STRATEGY EXECUTION

A priority in organization building necessary for strategy execution is building and strengthening valuable core competencies (knowledge resources) and organizational capabilities. There are three typical approaches:

1. *Internal development*: this incudes learning and staff development (see Chapter 8).
2. *Purchasing*: through merger or acquisition of another company with the necessary resources and capabilities
3. *Collaboration*: agreements with suppliers, competitors, or other companies with the necessary expertise.

Collaboration can occur in a joint venture, strategic alliance, or other type of partnership established for the purpose of achieving a shared strategic objective.

Saudi Arabia's research universities collaborate with overseas universities to access the knowledge necessary to make them world class. The main mechanism used is academic staff visiting Saudi universities for a period of time, such as six months, to work with local staff as a type of formal agreement. This enables Saudi staff to access the tacit knowledge of these overseas experts and also build social capital from these networks. However, problems have emerged because the Saudi government feels the local universities are not developing as quickly as hoped. The knowledge flows between the overseas experts and local Saudi staff do not seem to be working as effectively as planned: Saudi staff are not learning what the overseas experts know. This is an example of collaboration partnerships not delivering what was promised.

An alternative KBV perspective sees alliances as accessing rather than acquiring partners' knowledge (Grant, 1997). Such knowledge access permits an increased utilization of knowledge resources, an advantage which is enhanced when there are uncertainties concerning technological change and early-mover advantages in product markets. Even if collaborative alliances are less efficient than internal development, these inefficiencies may be offset by the speed of access to knowledge and its application to the production function, i.e. enabling skilful knowers. This might be a solution to the problems with collaboration partnerships outlined in the Theory in Practice example of the Saudi Arabian universities. Alliances have more commitment than partnerships. The Saudi universities could enter into a strategic alliance with overseas universities which generates mutual benefit rather than a market transaction, that is, paying for the overseas experts to visit Saudi Arabia.

MANAGING KNOWLEDGE FLOWS

Knowledge acquisition requires the management of knowledge flow from the external knowledge market to the internal user. The theoretical frameworks typically used to examine this knowledge flow include social capital and communities of practice. These are discussed further in Chapter 9. It is important to manage external networks of relationships for two reasons:

- The scope and breadth of external knowledge is much more than internal knowledge, and requires scanning and screening mechanisms to identify the best knowledge available.
- It is more difficult to manage external knowledge flows than internal knowledge flows. (Maznevski and Athanassiou, 2007: 69)

SOCIAL CAPITAL NECESSARY FOR KNOWLEDGE ACQUISITION

There are two main schools of thought about the social capital necessary to manage external to internal knowledge flows:

- *Structure*: allocate formal roles, provide training, make people accountable (Kang et al., 2007).
- *Change of managers' mindset*: people generate social capital naturally – just make them aware of the knowledge flows involved (Maznevski and Athanassiou, 2007).

Kang et al. (2007) take further steps in conceptualizing the mechanisms necessary to manage flows of knowledge, particularly in relation to unique human capital, which Lepak and Snell (2002) acknowledge their model fell short of adequately addressing. The Kang et al. (2007) model has two archetypes – entrepreneurial and cooperative – based on a configuration of three dimensions of social relations: structural, affective, and cognitive within and across firm boundaries. This extension emphasizes renewal of the firms' knowledge stocks through the use of internal and external partners. Therefore, it is a very useful model to explain knowledge growth.

The model begins with the two alternative forms of organizational learning:

- *Exploratory*: involves the pursuit of knowledge that does not exist in the firm to create new value, or that replaces existing knowledge
- *Exploitative*: involves refining and deepening existing knowledge that results in expanding or enriching value. (Kang et al., 2007)

Value is defined as the difference between 'benefits derived and costs incurred' (Kang et al., 2007: 237). Exploitative learning generates more benefits and predictable costs. It is incremental, and improves productivity, capability, and features. Exploratory learning is about radical new ideas and innovations; it involves higher potential benefits but also higher potential costs (Kang et al., 2007). They extend the HR architecture theory through a focus on knowledge flow, primarily based on the argument that knowledge requires use and this is grounded in social context. The authors introduce the relational archetypes of entrepreneurial and cooperative, derived from the unique configuration of three dimensions of social relations: structural, affective, and cognitive.

The *entrepreneurial* archetype is primarily concerned with external partners and core knowledge employees, and is characterized by a sparse network and intermittent ties (2007). Therefore, this is about knowledge acquisition. The *cooperative* archetype is concerned with internal partners (traditional employees) and core knowledge employees and is characterized by close social networks, trust, shared norms, and so forth (2007). Therefore, this is about knowledge creation.

TYPES OF SOCIAL RELATIONS

Structural social relations are defined by network density (who interacts with whom) and strength of ties (frequency of contact). This argues that organizational learning is primarily determined by the structure of relationships, that is, patterns of connections. The main benefit of having dense networks is exploitative learning, because these networks are 'efficient at sharing fine-grained and in-depth knowledge' (Kang et al., 2007: 239). Structural social relations help the firm measure the connectivity of like-minded subject matter experts who can discover new ways to apply their knowledge.

Affective social relations are defined by employees' motives, expectations, and norms, such as trust and intimacy. This argues that emotional responses to others will affect the relationships which are created and leveraged through social exchange processes. Expectations of reciprocity are required in order for employees to 'mobilize the knowledge of relational partners' (Kang et al., 2007: 239). The potential value of relationships cannot be realized if the associated parties do not trust one another and are unwilling to share knowledge. There are several types of trust: 'generalized trust, which refers to a kind of impersonal or institutional trust that is accorded to others because they are members of a social unit' (2007: 239); and 'resilient dyadic trust, which refers specifically to trust between two parties having direct experience with each other' (2007: 240). Exploitative learning is enabled by generalized trust because it does not require individuals to have personal experience with every other member of the network; instead, trust is based on the norms and expectations of the broader community or group as a whole. On the other hand, exploratory learning is enabled by resilient dyadic trust. This tends to develop through 'positive exchange experiences and encourages knowledge sharing without constraining efforts to seek other, potentially unrelated relationships' (2007: 240). This means that individuals do not need to work as hard at dyadic trust because it is already established and this makes them available to form new relationships to develop new ways to apply their knowledge.

Cognitive social relations are defined by shared representation, understanding, and systems of meaning (shared language or mental modes). It argues the importance of shared cognitive frames of reference. This cognitive aspect is similar to Cohen and Levinthal's (1990) notion of absorptive capacity, which explains how the ability to absorb new knowledge is determined by the similarity of prior knowledge bases. There are two types of knowledge that should be identified when trying to create or add value to a product or service: component and architectural (Kang et al., 2007). *Component* knowledge refers to the 'knowledge of parts rather than the whole', while *architectural* knowledge is 'related to a shared understanding of the interconnection of all parts', or of how things fit together (2007: 240–241). Exploitative learning for continuous improvement and incremental innovation is enabled by common architectural knowledge, which helps employees understand the bigger picture and also how their specialized jobs fit in. It also helps them understand and absorb deeper knowledge from their relational partners to explore exploitative learning (Kang et al., 2007). It is less likely that common component knowledge helps exploratory learning, but it is useful if employees share a common architectural understanding to 'assimilate it, interpret it, apply it, and recognize its value for commercial pursuits' (2007: 241).

Kang et al. (2007) identify two logical patterns among the structural, affective, and cognitive attributes of social relations that are aligned with either exploitative or exploratory learning: cooperative and entrepreneurial. The cooperative relational archetype is characterized by a dense social network with strong ties among its members, generalized trust based on shared norms of reciprocity, and a common architectural knowledge that provides the basis for combination and integration. The entrepreneurial relational archetype is characterized by more sparse and non-redundant network patterns with relatively weak and intermittent ties among its members.

NEW BUSINESS MODELS

The contribution of Kang et al.'s (2007) model to Lepak and Snell's (1999) human resource architecture model is to operationalize the external and internal knowledge flows within the context of social capital. In this way, it makes an important contribution to the theory of the firm, particularly the KBV's perspective on new hybrid business models with fluid organizational boundaries. From a knowledge strategy perspective, the traditional view of the firm pushes the knowledge sourcing decision towards quadrant 3 (see Figure 5.5). An economic rationalist perspective of the firm argues that everything should be outsourced because external specialists are simply more efficient due to specialization. Consider why many firms outsource logistics and transport to outside contractors. Lepak and Snell (1999) explain that the sourcing decision naturally moves from quadrant 4 (alliances) towards quadrant 3 as uniqueness decays over time, it moves from quadrant 2 (acquisition) as value decays, and it moves from quadrant 1 (internal development) through combined decay. This is a problem because, if the firm sources everything from external markets, it will not have the knowledge necessary to be a market leader or challenger, nor be able to develop innovative or advanced knowledge. Quadrant 3 dooms the firm to be a follower and to have core knowledge only. It makes the development of sustainable competitive advantage via core competencies or dynamic capabilities very difficult. Kang et al.'s (2007) model reverses this natural movement towards outsourcing. It moves the sourcing decision towards quadrant 1 (internal development).

Maznevski and Athanassiou (2007: 78) argue that a change in mindset about boundary spanner roles is necessary because managers engaged with external contacts usually focus on the immediate transaction, event, or relationship. By focusing on the immediate context, they do not see the bigger-picture opportunity for knowledge flow. By changing managers' mindset at the time of the interaction, we can focus them on creating power from the relationship with an end goal for the firm in mind. Challenges include: the individual recognizing that they represent the firm, finding the right context, and reciprocity – giving something back to the other party.

THE COST OF KNOWLEDGE FLOWS

From an economist's perspective, the primary goal of knowledge management is to bring together demand and supply (Huizing and Bouman, 2002: 189). One of the most attractive concepts driving knowledge management is connectivity. This is the idea that knowledge is the only resource which may be used without decreasing. Someone can share their knowledge with you and they do not lose that knowledge; they still have it, and you now have it too. Indeed, connectivity explains that knowledge actually increases in value the more it is used. The more people who know what you know, the better. It is the only resource that does this.

Every exchange, i.e. knowledge flow, has to be coordinated. However, coordination requires different methods because knowledge is unevenly distributed (imperfect markets). There are costs associated with transactions: (a) search, (b) communication, (c) documentation, (d) contracting, and (e) redundancy (see Huizing and Bouman, 2002). There are also agency costs. Agency exists in any relationship where one person depends on another. Agency costs are the coordination necessary to bridge the goal differences between these individuals:(a) monitoring, (b) bonding, (c) residual, (d) information representation, and (e) protection costs (see Huizing and Bouman, 2002). These knowledge exchange costs must be identified, managed, and reduced if external development is the preferred knowledge strategy.

The ways these costs are managed are explained by the KBV concept of knowledge integration, particularly coordination.

This is discussed further in Chapter 11.

DOING KNOWLEDGE STRATEGY

OVERVIEW

Definitions of knowledge strategy tend to focus on knowledge as a resource. Zack (2002: 255) suggests knowledge strategy is to 'ensure that the organization is making the best investment of its resources or that it is managing the right knowledge in the right way'. This defines knowledge strategy in terms of resource appraisal and deployment. Davenport and Probst (2002: 25) define knowledge strategy as enabling managers to plan, implement, and control actions concerning organization-relevant knowledge. This explains that knowledge strategy needs to address current and future requirements, i.e. carry out a gap analysis. Figure 5.2 summarizes this book's knowledge strategy model.

KNOWLEDGE STRATEGY PROCESS

Knowledge strategy begins with resource appraisal. Management must decide which knowledge resources are important now and in the future. Therefore, it includes future capability requirements, which adopt the framework set out below but look at future needs. This chapter presented two main frameworks to guide this decision: (1) Zack's (2002) core, advanced, and innovative typology, and (2) dynamic capabilities (Teece et al., 1997). Chapter 4 also examines this topic and recommends using the Knowledge Accounts model (Massingham, 2016). This enables managers to determine which knowledge areas are most important, and to ascertain the link between resources, capabilities (competencies), and competitive advantage (Davenport and Probst, 2002). Resource appraisal may produce three outcomes: (1) surplus, (2) deficit, and (3) alignment. Knowledge strategy explains what to do in each scenario using the exploration and exploitation dichotomy (Zack, 2002). This leads to decisions about how to use excess knowledge or access knowledge in deficit areas, i.e. knowledge gaps. Chapter 7 examines what to do with excess knowledge.

The next step in knowledge strategy is the sourcing decision. This involves decisions about whether to develop knowledge in the deficit areas internally or externally. The decision is influenced by whether the knowledge strategy is conservative or aggressive (Zack, 2002). Figure 5.2 illustrates how the conservative strategy involves incremental knowledge development via learning and sharing. This is covered in Chapters 8 and 9. The aggressive strategy involves internal development using knowledge creation, and external supply by accessing the knowledge marketplace.

The third step is the activity of knowledge creation. The organization should do this if it has time to develop its own new knowledge, and the knowledge is highly valuable and unique (see Figure 5.5). Nonaka and Takeuchi (1995)'s

SECI model is an example of the knowledge creation process. There are five knowledge creation enablers to help with implementation of the SECI model and improve the knowledge creation activity. The concept of a knowledge-creating spiral is helpful in seeing how these enablers facilitate the validation of the knowledge created and its diffusion throughout the organization.

The fourth step is the activity of external supply. The organization should do this if time is a problem, for example speed to market is important or the competitive environment is fast changing, and if the knowledge is either common or low value (see Figure 5.5). There are three main types of external supply: acquisition, alliances, and contracting. Table 5.1 and the Theory in Practice boxes provide guidelines on how to make the most appropriate decision. This activity also involves managing external knowledge flows so that the organization accesses the knowledge it needs and it is distributed to those who need it. Finally, the cost of external supply must be evaluated. There are various costs associated with the knowledge marketplace and these need to be less than the benefits generated from external supply (Huizing and Bouman, 2002). Otherwise, the organization should pursue knowledge creation, i.e. internal development. External supply introduces the importance of managing organizational boundaries, external collaboration, and new organizational structures and roles which facilitate the flow of external knowledge to internal users.

The fifth step is to design a measurement and reporting system. The most obvious goal is to evaluate whether the knowledge excess is being used (see Chapter 7) or whether the deficit has been filled. A knowledge strategy evaluation should consider whether the conservative strategy is working, i.e. whether the organization is learning and sharing in the deficit areas (see Chapters 8 and 9). The effectiveness of an aggressive strategy should examine knowledge creation and external supply in the deficit areas. Knowledge creation measures might include the inputs, for example socialization activities (e.g. how many communities of practice focus on knowledge deficit areas), as well as outputs, for example what new knowledge emerges, what proportion is validated, and how well it is diffused (see Figure 5.4).

KNOWLEDGE STRATEGY SCORECARD

Figure 5.6 summarizes the results in terms of a scorecard rating for each knowledge strategy technique tested at the case study organization (see closing case study). It represents the ratings for each tool against a set of criteria designed to cover the evaluation framework (see Massingham, 2014).

Figure 5.6 shows that, overall, the knowledge strategy tools with the most success are future capability requirements and the sourcing decision. The two least-successful tools are the acquisition barriers and the SECI model. In terms

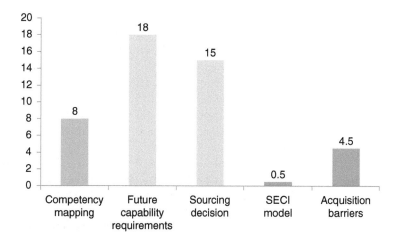

FIGURE 5.6 *Knowledge strategy scorecard*

Source: Massingham (2014)

of comparison with all KM tools implemented at the case study organization, future capability requirements was the highest-rating tool overall.

CONCLUSION

This chapter has outlined the processes involved in knowledge strategy. The chapter began with a discussion of the resource-based view (RBV). The RBV is important to knowledge management because it focuses strategic management on resources and their importance as a source of sustainable competitive advantage. The VRIN test was introduced as a criterion for evaluating knowledge's value.

An underlying theme in this chapter is knowledge gaps. This is the difference between what the firm knows and what it needs to know. A knowledge gap is a deficit in the firm's knowledge resources. The chapter explores how knowledge strategy can address this deficit. Figure 5.2 explained an approach to filling knowledge gaps including internal and external knowledge sources. Internal sources include knowledge creation (Chapter 5), learning by doing (Chapter 8), and knowledge sharing (Chapter 9). The chapter introduced knowledge creation as a method for growing knowledge resources internally, with a specific focus on a critique of Nonaka and Takeuchi's (1995) SECI model. The discussion concludes with a brief discussion of innovation and its importance in the global knowledge economy at multiple levels, including city/regional and national innovation.

The knowledge-based view (KBV) provides an important theoretical platform for knowledge management. The KBV explains how knowledge combines with other resources to create core competencies and dynamic capabilities, which are the essence of sustainable competitive advantage. However, the KBV also challenges traditional views of the organization and its management. The concept of new hybrid business models with fluid organizational boundaries has emerged from the KBV. The knowledge strategy decisions of whether to exploit or explore knowledge; whether to focus on core knowledge, advanced knowledge, or innovation knowledge; whether to be a leader, a challenger, or a follower; and whether to be aggressive or conservative – all involve defining the firm's boundaries and whether it wants to fill its knowledge gaps internally or externally or both. While the reality is that most organizations do both, to varying degrees, the increasing efficiency of external knowledge markets and the improved effectiveness of global value chains mean that firms are increasingly outsourcing.

The knowledge strategy decision to contract knowledge supply from external resources is known as knowledge acquisition. However, Grant (2013) suggests that a better perspective is to call this 'knowledge accessing' because it reflects the changing reality of strategic alliances, and that knowledge is not really transferred – rather it is shared, i.e. both parties now have the knowledge resource. For the purpose of consistency with the field, the term acquisition is used in the chapter. Lepak and Snell's (1999) model is explored to show four employment modes which may be used to fill knowledge gaps. The model explains how the fluid boundaries of the firm require management of internal and external knowledge flows involving different roles and relationships.

However, knowledge acquisition (or accessing) is difficult. Firms should develop knowledge internally – i.e. knowledge creation, learning by doing, or sharing – as their natural knowledge strategy (see Figure 5.2). But there may be circumstances where internal development is not possible because the firm lacks capability, or it is not feasible, due to changing market conditions requiring a quick response rather than longer-term development. The chapter explored how a cost–benefit analysis should be conducted to ensure that the costs of acquiring external knowledge and applying it are outweighed by the benefits. Otherwise, internal development is the correct knowledge strategy. If circumstances make external acquisition necessary, and the cost–benefit analysis is positive, then the firm needs to manage the flow of knowledge. Two methods were discussed: structural and mindset. Kang et al.'s (2007) model was used to explain how to manage the social capital flows identified by the four quadrants in the Lepak and Snell (1999) model. The essence of the Kang et al. (2007) model is the entrepreneurial archetype which brings knowledge in from alliances, and the cooperative archetype which builds density in the relationships between acquired knowledge and internally developed knowledge. Finally, the chapter concluded with a brief look at how people involved in knowledge acquisition, for instance boundary spanners, must have the correct mindset and understand their role to ensure effective knowledge flow.

CLOSING CASE STUDY: KNOWLEDGE STRATEGY AT THE CSO

The impetus for the research project, which formed the basis of these closing integrated case studies, was the threat of knowledge loss. The CSO was faced with the problem of an ageing workforce. Many of its experienced staff were moving towards retirement. The CSO risked losing a significant proportion of its knowledge resources en masse. Management were aware of the problem but they did not know how to measure its impact or how to manage it. This provided a business case for the research project.

Resource appraisal at the CSO was complicated. The evaluation of what knowledge was valuable and unique was confused by government policy. The CSO had been downsized over several decades. In the 1980s, there were hundreds of engineers and technical staff working at the CSO. These staff did ship design and maintenance. Therefore, the CSO managed the work necessary to build a ship and also administered what happened to it after it went into service. The CSO managed these costly public assets with a whole-life-cycle philosophy, i.e. from the ship's design all the way down to its decommission, once it was no longer cost-effective to maintain it in service.

In the late 1980s, the government began outsourcing the work done by the CSO to industry. It was felt that industry could do the work better than the CSO. Gradually, industry assumed control of all design work. By the time of the research study, the CSO did not do any design work and it had no design capability. Industry also took over much of the maintenance work. The government was then faced with a strategic decision of whether to outsource all of the work done by the CSO to industry.

What saved the staff at the CSO at the time of the research study was the need for government to be an intelligent customer of industry. The design, construction, and maintenance of these ships was an expensive exercise. Government needed to ensure that taxpayer funds were spent appropriately. The CSO was the government's watchdog to ensure industry did the work to specification. For example, when you go into a car dealership to buy a car, you specify what car you want by describing the model, make, colour, and so on. When you receive the car from the dealership, you may check whether it meets your specifications by examining the car and looking through the documentation provided (i.e. the technical specifications in the car manual). Some specifications, such as colour, would be simple for most people, but most would be very difficult. How would you know if the car's performance matched specifications? Would you know how much horsepower the car delivered and whether this matched the technical specification? Similarly, when you take the car to the dealership for its maintenance, do you know how to check whether the service has been done correctly? Most people are not intelligent customers of their cars. Yet we pay for their purchase and maintenance on the basis of trust. We trust industry to do the right thing.

The CSO's role was to ensure the government received the ship it paid for and that it was maintained to deliver operational capability throughout its life. It did this by regulating the technical standards necessary to design, build, and maintain the ships. These technical standards were captured in 130 documents which specified the material requirements for this. Each document was managed by an expert whose role it was to write the technical standard and maintain its

(Continued)

(Continued)

currency. The CSO staff were also responsible for advising industry on these technical standards and for ensuring they were being followed.

By the time of the research study, concerns were being raised about whether the CSO still had the capability to be an intelligent customer of industry. There were serious reservations about whether the CSO had sufficient critical mass. There were many areas where the CSO no longer had a staff member responsible for the technical standard document. This meant that the document was either immature (incomplete) or out of date. In most other areas, the CSO had only one expert left. If that staff member left the CSO, there was no one who had the expertise to replace them. It was difficult to recruit experienced staff as there were few people with this level of knowledge, and people working in industry were paid much higher salaries. Younger people did not have enough experience and would take too long to develop subject matter expertise, and there was no one to train them. Industry was aware of this problem at the CSO. They gradually began to ignore the CSO's technical standards because they did not trust them. The CSO staff spent a significant proportion of time in meetings trying to persuade industry to follow their standards, often without success. The technical regulatory framework was failing.

During the second year of the research study, the chief investigator (CI) was asked to work with the CSO's four principal engineers (PE) to help them plan for the future. The PEs needed to work out future knowledge needs by technical discipline (e.g. mechanical engineering, electrical engineering) to help workforce planning. The PEs found this task difficult for several reasons. First, they disagreed about what knowledge would be more important in the future. Each PE felt their discipline was more important and this personal bias created conflict between them and a lack of consensus. Second, technology was changing quickly and the PEs struggled to comprehend the current state of their fields and to predict what new technologies would emerge.

At a meeting of the CSO Executive, the CI gave an update on his work with the PEs. The senior partner investigator asked whether the CSO had done a similar exercise for the whole organization. Committee members acknowledged that this had never been done. The CSO had no knowledge strategy. It had not considered what knowledge it needed for the future. The senior partner investigator asked that a taskforce be formed to address the issue. The taskforce included representatives from across the whole organization.

The taskforce concluded that the main issue was to develop an objective decision-making model to decide (a) which knowledge was most important (i.e. resource appraisal) and (b) who should own the resource (sourcing decision). The committee also felt there were some areas where the make versus buy model could be improved:

1. *Dynamism*: any application of the model is an assessment at one point in time. This may be addressed by conducting analysis of knowledge resources at two time points: (a) present and (b) future (e.g. in five years' time). In this way, we can take into account changes in terms of the model's dimensions, i.e. importance, uniqueness, and risk.
2. *Movement*: knowledge naturally decays and this actually pushes everything towards quadrant 3 over time (see Figure 5.5). The most efficient way to run an organization is to outsource

everything except the stuff you can do better than an outside specialist (because they have economies of scale, economies of learning, etc). Organizations should only do things internally for very good reasons, mainly because the knowledge gains value from insiderness, which the CSO does have (i.e. CSO engineers are not the same as external engineers). It was suggested that people begin in quadrant 3 (theoretically) and progress upwards over time (like a triangle placed on top of the quadrant with the bottom facing the top right-hand corner). The CI agreed, except that the real movement is from quadrant 2 upwards to quadrant 1, and from quadrant 4 across to quadrant 1 (quadrant 3 knowledge should be monitored but not be a focus of movement). The CI felt this should be used to identify which knowledge resources may move into quadrant 1 from quadrant 4 because they will increase in importance over time, and which knowledge resources may move into quadrant 1 from quadrant 2 because they will increase in uniqueness over time (i.e. become more scarce).

3. *Validation*: the results of the knowledge strategy were important drivers in defining the role, capability requirements, and resources for the CSO into the future. Decisions about what knowledge resources need investment versus alliance versus outsourcing or contracting will come under scrutiny. Therefore, validation of the results will be necessary to give stakeholders confidence. Three options were proposed for validating the results:

   a. Executive endorsement of the decision model
   b. Inviting submissions from staff using a template which they can complete to provide information on the importance, uniqueness, and risk of their knowledge resource(s)
   c. Customer engagement.

CASE STUDY QUESTIONS

1. Describe the case study organization's knowledge strategy problem.
2. Use Figure 5.2 to examine the CSO's knowledge strategy.
3. Design a knowledge strategy process for the CSO.
4. How should the CSO fill its knowledge gaps? Why?
5. Evaluate the taskforce recommendations to improve the make versus buy model.

REVIEW AND DISCUSSION QUESTIONS

1. How does the knowledge-based view of the firm change your perspective about organizations and their management?
2. Critically evaluate the knowledge growth model presented in Figure 5.2.
3. What is the better knowledge strategy: internal development or external development? Why?
4. Discuss how to manage knowledge acquisition.

FURTHER READING

Grant, R.M. (2002) The Knowledge-based View of the Firm. Chapter 8 in Choo, C.W. and Bontis, N. (eds) *The Strategic Management of Intellectual Capital and Organizational Knowledge*, New York, Oxford University Press, pp. 133–148. This chapter provides insight into the KBV and the problem of coordination in particular.

Huizing, A. and Bouman, W. (2002) Knowledge and Learning, Markets and Organizations. Chapter 11 in Choo, C.W. and Bontis, N. (eds) *The Strategic Management of Intellectual Capital and Organizational Knowledge*, New York, Oxford University Press, pp. 185–206. This chapter provides further information on the costs of knowledge acquisition.

Kang, S.C., Morris, S.S. and Snell, S.A. (2007) Relational Archetypes, Organizational Learning, and Value Creation: Extending the human resource architecture. *Academy of Management Review*, 32 (1): 236–256. This article gives further information on the management of internal and external development.

BIBLIOGRAPHY

Ahuja, G., Lampert, C.M. and Tandon, V. (2008) Moving beyond Schumpeter: Management research on the determinants of technological innovation. *Academy of Management Annals*, *2* (1): 1–98.

Barney, J. (1991) Firm Resources and Sustained Competitive Advantage. *Journal of Management*, 17: 99–129.

Boisot, M. (2002) The Creation and Sharing of Knowledge. In Choo, C.W. and Bontis, N. (eds) *The Strategic Management of Intellectual Capital and Organizational Knowledge*, New York, Oxford University Press, pp. 65–78.

Bontis, N. (1998) Intellectual Capital: An exploratory study that develops measures and models. *Management Decision*, *36* (2): 63–76.

Carayannis, E. and Grigoroudis, E. (2014) Linking Innovation, Productivity, and Competitiveness: Implications for policy and practice. *Journal of Technology Transfer*, *39*: 199–218.

Carayannis, E.G. and Sagi, J. (2001) 'New' vs. 'Old' Economy: Insights on competitiveness in the global IT industry. *Technovation*, *21* (8): 501–514.

Carson, E., Ranzijn, R., Winefiel, A. and Marsden, H. (2004) Intellectual Capital: Mapping employee and work group attributes. *Journal of Intellectual Capital*, 5 (3): 443–461.

Cohen, W.M. and Levinthal, D.A. (1990) Absorptive Capacity: A new perspective on learning and innovation. *Administrative Science Quarterly*, *35*: 128–152.

Davenport, T.H. and Probst, G. (2002) *Knowledge Management Case Book: Siemens best practices*, 2nd edition, New York, Wiley.

Drucker, P. (1985) *Innovation and Entrepreneurship: Practice and principles*, New York, Harper & Row.

Easterby-Smith, M. and Lyles, M.A. (eds) (2003) *Handbook of Organizational Learning and Knowledge Management*, Hong Kong, Blackwell.

Easterby-Smith, M. and Prieto, I.M. (2008) Dynamic Capabilities and Knowledge Management: An integrative role for learning? *British Journal of Management*, *19* (3): 235–249.

Grant, R.M. (1996) Toward a Knowledge-based Theory of the Firm. *Strategic Management Journal*, 17: 109–122.

Grant, R.M. (1997) The Knowledge-based View of the Firm: Implications for management practice. *Long Range Planning, 30* (3): 450–454.

Grant, R.M. (2002) The Knowledge-based View of the Firm. Chapter 8 in Choo, C.W. and Bontis, N. (eds) *The Strategic Management of Intellectual Capital and Organizational Knowledge*, New York, Oxford University Press, pp. 133–148.

Grant, R.M. (2013) Reflections on Knowledge-based Approaches to the Organization of Production. *Journal of Management and Governance, 17* (3): 541–558.

Howkins, J. (2002) *The Creative Economy*, London, Penguin.

Huizing, A. and Bouman, W. (2002) Knowledge and Learning, Markets and Organizations. In Choo, C.W. and Bontis, N. (eds) *The Strategic Management of Intellectual Capital and Organizational Knowledge*, New York, Oxford University Press, pp. 185–206.

Kang, S.C., Morris, S.S. and Snell, S.A. (2007) Relational Archetypes, Organizational Learning, and Value Creation: Extending the human resource architecture. *Academy of Management Review, 32* (1): 236–256.

Lepak, D.P. and Snell, S.A. (1999) The Human Resource Architecture: Toward a theory of human capital allocation and development. *Academy of Management Review, 24*: 31–48.

Lepak, D.P. and Snell, S.A. (2002) Examining the Human Resource Architecture: The relationship among human capital, employment, and human resource configurations. *Journal of Management, 28*: 517–543.

Massingham, P. (2010) Managing Knowledge Transfer between Parent Country Nationals (Australia) and Host Country Nationals (Asia). *International Journal of Human Resource Management, 21* (9): 1414–1435.

Massingham, P. (2014) An Evaluation of Knowledge Management Tools Part 1: Managing knowledge resources. *Journal of Knowledge Management, 18* (6): 1075–1100.

Massingham, P. (2016) Knowledge Accounts. *Long Range Planning, 49* (3): 409–425.

Maznevski, M. and Athanassiou, N. (2007) Bringing the Outside in: Learning and knowledge management through external networks. In Ichijo, K. and Nonaka, I. (eds) *Knowledge Creation and Management*, New York, Oxford University Press, pp. 69–82.

Nonaka, I. and Takeuchi, H. (1995) *The Knowledge-creating Company: How Japanese companies create the dynamics of innovation*, New York, Oxford University Press.

Polanyi, M. (1962) *Personal Knowledge*, Chicago, IL, University of Chicago Press.

Porter, M. (1980) *Competitive Strategy: Techniques for analyzing industries and competitors*, New York, Free Press.

Prahalad, C.K. and Hamel, G. (1990) The Core Competence of the Corporation. *Harvard Business Review, 68* (3): 79–91.

Quinn, J.B. (1992) *Intelligent Enterprise*, New York, Free Press.

Robertson, T.S. (1967) 'The process of innovation and diffusion of innovation', Journal of Marketing, 31 (1): 14–19.

Storey, J. and Barnett, E. (2000) Knowledge Management Initiatives: Learning from failure. *Journal of Knowledge Management, 4* (2): 145–156.

Teece, D.J. (1986) Profiting from Technological Innovation. *Research Policy, 15* (6): 285–305.

Teece, D.J. (2007) Explicating Dynamic Capabilities: The nature and microfoundations of (sustainable) enterprise performance. *Strategic Management Journal, 28* (13): 1319–1350.

Teece, D.J. and Al-Aali, A. (2011) Knowledge Assets, Capabilities, and the Theory of the Firm. Chapter 23 in Easterby-Smith, M. and Lyles, M.A. (eds) *Handbook of Organizational Learning and Knowledge Management*, Hoboken, NJ, Wiley, pp. 505–534.

Teece, D.J., Pisano, G. and Shuen, A. (1997) Dynamic Capabilities and Strategic Management. *Strategic Management Journal, 18* (7): 509–533.

Thompson, A.J., Jr., Peteraf, M.A., Gamble, J.E. and Strickland, A.J. (eds) (2013) *Crafting and Executing Strategy: The quest for competitive advantage – Concepts and cases,* 19th edition, New York, McGraw-Hill Irwin.

Thompson, A.J., Jr., Peteraf, M.A., Gamble, J.E. and Strickland, A.J. (eds) (2016) *Crafting and Executing Strategy: The quest for competitive advantage – Concepts and cases,* 20th edition, New York, McGraw-Hill Irwin.

Tordoir, P.P. (1995) *The Professional Knowledge Economy*, Dordrecht, Springer Science & Business Media.

Van de Van, A.H. (1986) Central Problems in the Management of Innovation. *Management Science, 32* (5): 590–607.

Wernerfelt, B. (1984) A Resource-based View of the Firm. *Strategic Management Journal, 5*: 171–180.

White, D.S., Gunasekaran, A. and Roy, M.H. (2014) Performance Measures and Metrics for the Creative Economy. *Benchmarking: An International Journal, 21* (1): 46–61.

Winter, S.G. (1995) Four Rs of Profitability: Rents, resources, routines, and replication. In C. Montgomery (ed.) *Resource-based and Evolutionary Theories of the Firm: Towards a synthesis*, Hinham, MA, Kluwer, pp. 147–177.

Zack, M.H. (2002) Developing a Knowledge Strategy. Chapter 15 in Choo, C.W. and Bontis, N. (eds) *The Strategic Management of Intellectual Capital and Organizational Knowledge*, New York, Oxford University Press, pp. 255–276.

6

MEASURING AND MANAGING KNOWLEDGE LOSS

CHAPTER OUTLINE

LEARNING OUTCOMES

After completing this chapter, the reader should be able to:

1. Define knowledge loss
2. Discuss the impact of knowledge loss
3. Evaluate several theoretical frameworks measuring the impact of knowledge loss
4. Compare approaches to managing knowledge loss from the disciplines of knowledge management, human resource management, and operations management
5. Evaluate several theoretical frameworks managing the impact of knowledge loss, including short-term burning bridge, long-term capture, and long-term prevention

MANAGEMENT ISSUES

Knowledge loss requires managers to:

1. Understand the impact of knowledge loss on the organization's performance
2. Understand the benefits of taking action
3. Decide whether to take a short-term or long-term approach to solutions

Knowledge loss involves these challenges for management:

1. Knowing what the best impact framework(s) is to use
2. How to implement the chosen solution
3. Planning for, rather than reacting to, the problem

LINKS TO OTHER CHAPTERS

Chapter 3: on the process of managing risk

Chapter 4: concerning identifying which knowledge resources to protect

Chapter 9: regarding knowledge sharing between individuals as a solution to knowledge loss

OPENING MINI CASE STUDY

HOW NASA FORGOT HOW TO SEND A MAN TO THE MOON: HOW COULD THE WORLD'S BEST KNOWLEDGE FACTORY LOSE KNOWLEDGE?

The USA's National Aeronautics and Space Administration (NASA) was established in 1958, partially in response to the Soviet Union's launch of the first artificial satellite the previous year. NASA grew out of the National Advisory Committee on Aeronautics (NACA) which had been researching flight technology for more than 40 years.

NASA's vision: We reach for new heights and reveal the unknown for the benefit of humankind.

NASA headquarters, in Washington, DC, provides overall guidance and direction to the agency, under the leadership of the administrator. Ten field centres and a variety of installations conduct the day-to-day work, in laboratories, on air fields, in wind tunnels and in control rooms.

NASA conducts its work in four principal organizations, called mission directorates:

- *Aeronautics*: manages research focused on meeting global demand for air mobility in ways that are more environmentally friendly and sustainable, while also embracing revolutionary technology from outside aviation.
- *Human Exploration and Operations*: focuses on International Space Station operations, the development of commercial spaceflight capabilities and human exploration beyond low-Earth orbit.
- *Science: explores the Earth, solar system, and universe beyond*; charts the best route of discovery; and reaps the benefits of Earth and space exploration for society.
- *Space Technology*: rapidly develops, innovates, demonstrates, and infuses revolutionary, high-payoff technologies that enable NASA's future missions while providing economic benefit to the nation.

NASA's work today: In the early 21st century, NASA is extending our senses to see the farthest reaches of the universe, while pushing the boundaries of human spaceflight farther from Earth than ever before.

Since its inception in 1958, NASA has accomplished many great scientific and technological feats in air and space. Its technology has also been adapted for many non-aerospace uses by the private sector. NASA remains a leading force in scientific research and in stimulating public interest in aerospace exploration, as well as in science and technology in general. Perhaps more importantly, our exploration of space has taught us to view Earth, ourselves, and the universe in a new way. While the tremendous technical and scientific accomplishments of NASA demonstrate vividly that humans can achieve previously inconceivable feats, we are also humbled by the realization that Earth is just a tiny 'blue marble' in the cosmos. Check out our 'Thinking about NASA History' folder online as an introduction to how history can help you.

Source: From an article by former NASA chief historian Roger Launius on the accomplishments of the NASA History Division, www.nasa.gov

(Continued)

(Continued)

The following scenario at NASA is loosely based on an idea from DeLong (2004).

Roberta Jackson was sitting in her office at NASA Headquarters. She was a senior scientist in NASA's Science Directorate. She had just finished talking with her boss, Alison Blunt. Alison had told Roberta that the new Federal Administration had given NASA a directive to land a person on Mars by 2025. There was a perception in the public that NASA was spending too much money on space exploration. The new administration felt it was time for a public relations exercise. Growing awareness of the negative impact of our species on the planet had led to increasing interest in colonizing a new planet. While NASA was focusing on finding new planets in the universe which seemed to resemble Earth's conditions and, therefore, be suitable for life, these were too far away to colonise with existing technology. While NASA had sent spacecraft to Mars, no one had yet set foot on Mars. The new administration wanted this to happen. Alison told Roberta that she had to make it happen.

Roberta began thinking about the Apollo 11 mission which led to Mission Commander Neil Armstrong and pilot Buzz Aldrin landing the lunar module Eagle on the surface of the moon on 20 July 1969. Armstrong became the first to step onto the lunar surface six hours later on 21 July 1969. There were a total of six manned US landings between 1969 and 1972. No one had landed on the moon for 45 years.

Roberta called John Olson, director of NASA's Exploration Systems Mission Directorate Integration Office. She explained her discussion with Alison. John asked her if she knew much about Project Constellation. She said no. He told her to call Jeff Hanley, NASA's Constellation programme manager. At the end of her conversation with John, she asked him why NASA had stopped landing people on the moon. John replied: 'We no longer needed to. We had achieved the goal set by President Kennedy. It was expensive. There was no point to further missions.'

Roberta called Jeff Hanley. She explained her brief and asked Jeff to tell her about Project Constellation. He said the project was launched in 2004 and planned to return humans to the moon by 2020. Roberta asked why it will have taken 16 years to do this. The initial moon landing took half that time. Jeff explained that there were a few important differences. First, the scope of the project was bigger. 'This is much more than filming footsteps in the lunar dust', said Jeff. 'We're going for a sustained human presence in space.' Jeff explained that rather than visit the moon for hours or days at most, Constellation astronauts will embark on missions that could last months. They will need new tools and technologies for living on the moon, and must construct semi-permanent habitats on the lunar surface. Besides the challenge of designing these systems, NASA must build a spaceship that can transport all the extra supplies.

This led Jeff to the second problem: lack of rocket science. He explained that NASA's current rockets and space shuttles are not capable of surpassing low-Earth orbit to reach the moon with the amount of gear required for a manned expedition. 'The amount of rocket energy it takes to accelerate those kinds of payloads away from Earth doesn't exist anymore', said Jeff Hanley. 'It existed in the Apollo era with the Saturn V. Since that time this nation has retired that capability.' 'Do you mean we have lost the knowledge to land a human on the moon?' asked Roberta.

She was shocked. 'Yes', replied Jeff. 'But we are working on it. The Chinese say they know how and will sell it to us for a billion dollars. But we can't afford the public relations disaster. After all, we invented this. We can't buy it from someone else.' Roberta couldn't tell if he was serious or joking. 'But how could this happen?' she asked. 'How did we lose that knowledge? We have the smartest people in the world working for us. Can't they figure it out? Surely they know more than the scientists working in the 1960s?' 'Well, we can't ask those guys to help because they are all dead', replied Jeff. 'It was a long time ago. In terms of how smart our current people are – well, it is harder than it sounds – there is a particular problem with the thrusters that get us off the moon surface. It is actually harder to ensure we can get our people off the moon and back home than it is to get them there in the first place.' 'Well, I have only got half the time you had with your project to get people on Mars', replied Roberta. 'Do you have any information that can help me get started?' 'Talk to Frank Peri', replied Jeff.

Roberta was sitting in the office of Frank Peri, director of NASA's Exploration Technology Development Program at Langley Research Center in Virginia. Frank was sympathetic. He explained that Project Constellation could help her project. 'We had always planned to go farther than the moon', said Frank. 'The lunar voyages were to be a staging ground to prepare humans to journey to Mars.' 'But', he added, 'there are problems. The complexity of leaving Earth's orbit, we understand that. But getting back to the moon is not trivial, staying on the moon is not trivial, and going on to Mars is even beyond that.'

Roberta was stunned. 'Can you tell me how to land a person on Mars?' she asked. 'No', replied Frank. 'Do we have any information on NASA's intranet that can help me?' she asked. 'No', replied Frank. 'Is there anyone who still works here that knows anything about what we did with the Apollo missions?' she asked. 'No', replied Frank. 'Surely someone knows something', Roberta sighed. 'What exactly did we lose that we have to rediscover?' she asked. 'It was a set of blueprints', Frank said. 'Apparently the secrets were found in these blueprints. You have to understand that this was before NASA had personal computers, or intranets, or could scan documents like blueprints into electronic form. We lost the blueprints. We know they once existed but they are gone now. Someone probably threw them in the rubbish.' 'Can we talk to someone who saw those blueprints?' she asked. 'No', replied Frank. 'Why didn't we at least interview those staff before they retired to capture what they knew?' she asked. 'We never thought we would need that capability again', replied Frank.

Roberta walked out of Frank's office and thought to herself, 'I will have to start again from scratch'.

CASE STUDY QUESTIONS

1. What knowledge is necessary for NASA to land a person on Mars? (See Chapter 1)
2. How did NASA forget how to land a person on the moon? (See Chapter 2)
3. Why did NASA lose the capability to land a person on the moon? (See Chapter 5)
4. What should NASA do to ensure they do not lose this capability again?

INTRODUCTION

Organizational knowledge loss has emerged as one of the most important corporate risks today (Massingham, 2010). Knowledge loss occurs when an individual with valuable knowledge exits an organization. The knowledge-based view (KBV) of the firm proposes that knowledge is the most valuable organizational resource (Grant, 1996). Given the widespread acceptance of the importance of knowledge, it is surprising there has been so little research into what happens if it is lost, and how to manage this problem (Levy, 2011). Furthermore, the problem is increasing due to workforce mobility and our ageing society. This chapter explores why knowledge loss matters and how to address it.

DEFINITION: Knowledge loss occurs as a result of employee exit, lost codified knowledge, or knowledge decay.

The first part of the chapter measures the impact of knowledge loss. The chapter will provide a model which examines the likelihood and consequences of knowledge loss from multiple perspectives and adds a temporal dimension to this important organizational phenomenon. The model considers what happens after knowledge loss at the individual level, i.e. the impact on the remaining employees, and at the organizational level in terms of performance.

The second part of the chapter discusses how to manage knowledge loss. This topic has received more attention in the literature, and three previous studies will be discussed (DeLong, 2004; Levy, 2011; Martins and Meyer, 2012) to represent existing research. A new model for managing knowledge loss will be presented with short-term and long-term perspectives. The two new models presented in the chapter emerged from the research study discussed as the integrated closing case study at the end of each chapter in this book.

KNOWLEDGE LOSS

OVERVIEW

Knowledge loss occurs when an organization no longer has access to knowledge it previously had (Massingham, 2018). Loss of codified knowledge occurs when knowledge that has been captured in a document, report, database, policy, or other written format is no longer available. It may have been deleted, discarded, or still exist but cannot be located. Knowledge decay involves knowledge losing its value over time. It may have become obsolete or no longer relevant or applicable. Employee exit occurs when an individual leaves an organization, either voluntarily or involuntarily (Carnahan et al., 2012). This includes seeking work elsewhere, redundancy, and retirement. This chapter focuses on knowledge loss caused by employee exit.

DEEP THINKING: There has been limited research on knowledge loss because: (1) Knowledge loss was not considered a significant problem because there was a feeling that a quasi-equilibrium was reached through employee replacement (Starke et al., 2003). (2) There is disagreement about the nature of the knowledge lost and whether it is a knowledge subject (codified) or people (tacit) (Dalkir, 2011). (3) There is conflict over the longer-term approach of most knowledge management solutions and the short-term crisis presented by the unintended exit of valuable employees (Levy, 2011).

INCREASING RISK OF KNOWLEDGE LOSS

Population ageing is taking place in nearly all countries. Globally, the proportion of older persons (60 years or older) was 841 million in 2013, which is an increase of 400% since 1950, and this will double again by 2050, when it is expected to pass the two billion mark (United Nations, 2013). This creates problems as the workforce is ageing and the experience and wisdom gathered by older people over their careers leaves with them when they retire.

CORE CONCEPT: Knowledge loss is an increasing corporate risk for two reasons. First, there are demographic changes globally which have significant impact on the workforce. Second, there is increasing employee turnover due to changes in the emotional relationship between employers and their employees.

Workforce mobility is also a global phenomenon. In Australia, for example, 2.5 million people separated from their job in 2012, which represents almost 20% of the total workforce; 68% of these separations were voluntary and 38% were involuntary (e.g. retrenchments) and overall around 20% of people were in their first year of their job at their employer (D'Arcy et al., 2012). This data indicates high employee turnover, which is a problem as employees take valuable knowledge with them as they exit and join another organization.

PREVIOUS RESEARCH ON KNOWLEDGE LOSS

Previous research on knowledge loss may be summarized into three themes. First, there is an impact on the employees who remain, called survivors. This may be classified into psychological impact, such as anxiety, stress, job insecurity or anger; or work disruption causing increased workload or lost social networks. This impact suggests that knowledge loss affects the survivors' emotional relationship with their employer, called the psychological contract (see Argyris, 1960). The outcome may be decreased morale and productivity. Massingham and Tam (2015) recently found that psychological contract constructs, such as affective attachment, locus of control, and personal outcome expectancy, may be used to explain the effect of decreased psychological contract on human capital.

Second, there is an impact in terms of subject matter expertise. Employees who exit take with them their tacit knowledge or the knowledge in their heads (see Polanyi, 1962). This impact suggests that knowledge loss involves an object, such as know-how, which is gone. The outcome may be decreased experience.

Third, there is an impact in terms of organizational capability. This may be defined in terms of the ways knowledge creates value, for instance through innovation, problem solving, or creativity. This impact suggests that knowledge loss involves a resource. The outcome may be decreased performance and profitability. DeLong (2004) identified five ways that knowledge loss may undermine organizational strategy and, therefore, increase risk: (1) a reduced capacity to innovate, (2) a threatened ability to pursue growth, (3) a decreased capacity for low-cost strategies caused by reduced efficiency, (4) giving competitors an advantage, and (5) increased vulnerability (DeLong, 2004: 31). These impacts may be summarized as decreases in specialized knowledge, unique experience, and competitive position; and increases in mistakes, and risk of catastrophic events.

The capacity to unlearn (routines, assumptions, values, behaviours) can be an important catalyst for change (Becker, 2010). This chapter focuses on how to prevent knowledge loss, not encourage it, and therefore it looks at unintended knowledge loss. Unintentional knowledge loss is when 'people in an organization who operate at an individual, group and organizational level [who] are the carriers of knowledge' (Martins and Martins, 2011, cited in Martins and Meyer, 2012: 79) exit and take their knowledge with them.

A NEW MEASUREMENT MODEL OF KNOWLEDGE LOSS

This chapter introduces (from Massingham, 2018) a new measurement model to identify the impact of lost organizational knowledge caused by employee turnover. The model includes concepts of: (1) knowledge resources, (2) employee engagement, (3) organization performance, (4) risk management, and (5) organizational problems (Massingham, 2018: 722–723).

EMPLOYEE TURNOVER

Employee turnover (ET) is the percentage of employees leaving the organization for whatever reason (Phillips and Connell, 2003: 2). This chapter's conceptualization of ET captures the flow of knowledge over time, and includes the movement of staff exiting, as well as those entering the organization. Four ET factors influence the five knowledge loss concepts over time:

1. '*Withdrawals*: when employees exit, they take knowledge with them.
2. *Decay*: surviving employees, i.e. those who were employed by the organization at the start and the end of surveys, may lose knowledge or their knowledge may decrease in value.' (Massingham, 2018: 728)

   (These both represent decreases to what the organization knows.)

3. '*Deposits*: when employees enter, they bring knowledge with them.
4. *Growth*: surviving employees may gain knowledge or their knowledge may increase in value.' (2018: 728)

   (These both represent increases to what the organization knows.)

This conceptualization reflects the notions that ET is a 'dynamic phenomenon and that the organization's knowledge is a fluid resource' (Massingham, 2018: 728). It allows us to track this fluidity and therefore report on the impact of knowledge loss over time, while capturing 'the organizational reality that staff come and go' (2018: 728).

DEEP LEARNING: The chapter's conceptualization of employee turnover suggests that the organizational knowledge base is dynamic and will change over time to reflect how knowledge flows out of the organization when employees exit; flows into the organization when new employees join; and changes with existing employees whose knowledge may increase, such as by learning, or decrease, by obsolescence or other negative factors influencing the KA score (e.g. a decreased psychological contract).

The case study in the Theory in Practice boxes in this section is loosely based on a case by Corbitt (2005).

THEORY IN PRACTICE: SPLITTING HEWLETT-PACKARD (HP)

Hewlett-Packard (HP) decided to split its large company into two smaller companies – HP and Agilent. The company aimed to make the two new companies fully functional within a year by cloning the systems and core competencies needed to support these systems. In 1999 the company allowed about 1,000

(Continued)

(Continued)

employees in the Global Financial Services area to choose which of the two new companies they wanted to work for. Most of the staff with expertise in accounts receivable decided to stay with HP, leaving a void in this area in Agilent. Almost all of the general ledger people went to Agilent, leaving a void in this area at HP. The biggest problem was in Europe where all but a handful of employees decided to stay with HP, meaning Agilent in Europe had to hire university graduates to fill the gap.

Three distinct groups of employees emerged:

1. New employees hired to fill gaps created by exiting employees (e.g. Agilent in Europe)
2. Current employees who were to do job A but were now doing job B due to the restructure
3. Current employees who were left in a reduced skill area where only one or two people were left who had the required knowledge.

KNOWLEDGE RESOURCES

The model's conceptualization of what the organization knows adopts the Knowledge Accounts model (Massingham, 2016). This enables the impact of knowledge loss to be audited at any point in time, tracked over time (i.e. trend analysis), and analysed at multiple levels (e.g. see Figure 4.1; Chapter 4 provides more details). This measurement of knowledge loss is different from the other four constructs in the model because it focuses on resources, i.e. the individual. Therefore, it measures the impact of knowledge loss on the individual's tacit knowledge. The KA enables changes to the organization's knowledge resources to be tracked in terms of each of the four ET factors.

THEORY IN PRACTICE: HP AND AGILENT'S CORE COMPETENCIES

HP's World Wide Financial Services group and Agilent's Global Financial services group conducted an evaluation of the core competencies needed for (a) career advancement and (b) rebuilding of the company. They were classified as either corporate-specific or non-corporate, and technical or non-technical. Corporate competencies were those that were specific to the company, such as product knowledge. Non-corporate were generic competencies available to anyone doing similar work in a financial services company, such as accounts receivable processes. Technical competencies are job-related skills, such as systems design. Non-technical competencies are organizational skills, such as relationships.

The company's competencies for career advancement were as follows (% of respondents):

	Technical	Non-technical	Total
Corporate-specific	4%	10%	14%
Non-corporate	17%	69%	86%

The company's competencies for rebuilding the company were as follows (% of respondents):

	Technical	Non-technical	Total
Corporate specific	21%	18%	39%
Non-corporate	44%	17%	61%

The data shows that respondents felt that different competencies were necessary at the individual level, i.e. their own career growth, compared with the organizational level, i.e. to fill the gaps created by the restructure. The main competency for career advancement was non-corporate, non-technical knowledge. This is human capital. The KA would identify the areas of knowledge deficit at the individual level in terms of employee engagement (loyalty) and satisfaction (morale).

Example: Julius Ijanti worked in accounts receivable at Agilent (Europe). Julius was an expert in accounts receivable with many years of experience. His employee capability score was very high. But his overall KA score was low. Agilent was not getting the best out of him. His employee engagement and satisfaction scores were very low and dragged down his overall score. Close examination showed that he was unhappy because many of his colleagues had left the company. His career growth required action to improve his psychological contract with Agilent. If this was not addressed, it was likely his productivity would continue to decline and he would probably exit, taking with him his valuable knowledge.

The main competency for rebuilding the company was non-corporate, technical knowledge. This is human capital. The KA would identify the areas of knowledge deficit at the organizational level in terms of employee capability.

Example: Agilent's challenge was to recruit new graduates with accounts receivable knowledge. Kristo Dragevic was a young graduate. He scored high in his human capital scores but low in social capital, structural capital, and relational capital. While Agilent's immediate need was to fill the gap of non-corporate, technical knowledge, it needed its young graduates to quickly develop knowledge in the three other areas. Kristo found the job difficult because he did not know who to turn to for help (social capital) and he could not find information on the intranet (structural capital); 12 months after his initial KA score, his overall score had decreased by 15% because he was unhappy.

EMPLOYEE ENGAGEMENT

Employee engagement is the individual's emotional relationship with their organization. The theoretical basis for this definition is the psychological contract (PC) (Argyris, 1960). This chapter divides PC into two factors: peace and participation. PC may be understood within the motivational processes of social exchange theory and the norm of reciprocity (e.g. Homans, 1961; Blau, 1964). This means that the more employees perceive an organization gives them, the more they will give to the organization in return. Employees give, in this sense, in terms of quantity and quality of work. Therefore, high PC scores reveal employees with high job satisfaction, which is likely to translate into high productivity and work performance. On the other hand, low PC scores can lead to a lack of the creativity and sharing necessary to generate value from employees (Massingham and Tam, 2015).

Peace combines wellbeing and empowerment (Massingham, 2018). It has two constructs: (1) work–life balance and (2) flexibility. It measures 'whether employees feel they have appropriate balance between work and family life, and autonomy and control over work decisions' (Massingham, 2018: 738–739). These constructs 'combine to give a sense of calm' (2018: 739). *Participation* is a 'perception that the organization is encouraging positive work attitudes and behaviours' (2018: 739). It has nine constructs: (1) leadership, (2) recruitment and selection, (3) cross-unit cooperation, (4) learning and development, (5) involvement, (6) organizational culture, (7) rewards and recognition, (8) performance appraisal, and (9) career management. It measures employees' 'feelings about management in terms of trust, merit, being valued, recognized, and rewarded; as well as their perceptions of their workplace in terms of sharing, learning, attitude, and personal development' (2018: 739).

This measurement of knowledge loss is different from the other four constructs in the model because it focuses on enablers, i.e. a perception of organizational support for KM. Therefore, it measures the impact of knowledge loss in terms of staff perception of how well the organization is managing knowledge loss.

THEORY IN PRACTICE: HP AND AGILENT'S EMPLOYEE ENGAGEMENT

HP and Agilent suffered a decrease in employee engagement. The restructure created anxiety and stress for the surviving staff who faced working for a new company, seeing work colleagues exit, and developing new relationships with new staff. Staff perception of how well the company managed this process, and of the resulting knowledge loss, was important for each individual's emotional relationship with the company.

Example: Alice Schultz worked in HP's general ledger business. She was one of the few experienced staff left in her office in Boston (USA). In the first six months after the split, she found she was working increasingly long hours, and even on weekends, to cover her increasing workload. During business hours, she was continually asked for help from new young people who did not know what to do. She found time to do her job after hours. She had a teenage son in middle school who was struggling with his studies. She found she could not give him the time he needed. Her peace score was very low, particularly her work–life balance score. She also had concerns about the quality of the young graduates being recruited. Many seemed to lack the basic practical skills needed to do their jobs. She raised her concerns with management but they were unsympathetic. She wanted to be rewarded and recognized for her hard work outside office hours but she was told she would not be paid overtime or promoted for doing this. As a result, Alice's participation score was very low, particularly in her perception of recruitment, rewards and recognition, performance appraisal, and career management. She was suffering from low wellbeing and negative work behaviours and attitudes. Alice felt the company was not managing the impact of knowledge loss well. If the company did not address these issues, Alice may fall sick, decrease productivity, stop helping others, and leave.

ORGANIZATION PERFORMANCE

Learning organization capacity (LOC) (e.g. see Garratt, 1987; Senge, 1990) is used as a measure of organization performance. This chapter divides LOC into three concepts: 'purpose, enablers, and people' (Massingham, 2018: 740). *Purpose* has four constructs: (1) organizational direction (2), results focus, (3) mission and values, and (4) role clarity. The first examines whether the organization is focused on learning organization goals; the second examines whether the organization sets targets and conducts benchmarking; the third examines whether there are shared mental models based on an awareness of knowledge management; and the fourth identifies whether employees understand their role and how they contribute (2018: 740). An organization with strong performance in these areas is likely to be able to manage knowledge loss because it can measure the impact and it embraces the importance of knowledge management as a solution.

Enablers has three constructs: (1) resources, (2) processes, and (3) technology. The first examines whether the organization provides the physical environment and investment in systems to allow people to share their tacit and codified knowledge. The second examines whether there are procedures and standards aimed at ensuring consistency and efficient workflow. The third examines whether there are adequate information technology and information systems. An organization with strong performance in these areas is likely to be able to manage knowledge loss because it provides knowledge sharing, codified best practice, and technology to facilitate the flow of knowledge (Massingham, 2018).

People has three constructs: (1) motivation and initiative, (2) talent, and (3) teamwork. The first examines whether employees feel they will be recognized and rewarded, as well as levels of initiative; the second examines employees' perception of the quality of other employees; the third examines how well employees work in teams. An organization with strong performance in these areas is likely to be able to manage knowledge loss because employees feel they work with people they respect and can learn from (Massingham, 2018).

This measurement of knowledge loss is different from the other four constructs in the model because it focuses on systems, i.e. enablers, rather than the individual. Therefore, it measures the impact of knowledge loss in terms of the organization's response.

THEORY IN PRACTICE: HP AND AGILENT'S ORGANIZATION PERFORMANCE

HP and Agilent suffered a decrease in organization performance. The decline in learning organization capacity was illustrated by the company's staff training strategy to address the competency gaps created by the restructure. Five levels of knowledge were identified:

1. *New-hire training*: company history, company culture, business standards, behaviours
2. *Team-specific overview*: an induction including a site tour, an introduction to a mentor and colleagues, payroll, performance appraisal, and performance expectations
3. *New-hire boot camp*: overview of business processes, business controls, systems, audio conferencing, working in a global financial services organization
4. *Core competency topics*: critically important areas for a broad-based audience which extends beyond a work group or department; this may involve layers of knowledge separated into modules for training
5. *Core competency team-specific*: work group or department-specific job-related knowledge which is unique to that area; it may require mentoring or job shadowing or other tacit-to-tacit sharing.

This list illustrates how the company was trying to improve its learning organization capacity. New-hire training (level 1) is about purpose. It particularly helps new staff get a sense of the company's direction, and its mission and values. Team-specific overview (level 2) and new-hire boot camp (level 3) are about enablers, particularly resources and processes. Core competency topics (level 4) are about people, particularly talent and teamwork. Core competency team-specific is about People, particularly motivation and initiative.

This explains how the company was trying to use KM to improve its performance as a learning organization. Changes to ratings in the areas above would show that KM is working effectively and that staff training is achieving its goals.

RISK MANAGEMENT

The fourth step in the conceptualization is to measure the organization's knowledge risk management. It identifies the risk associated with losing knowledge in important activities, the level of exposure (i.e. likelihood and consequences of the risk occurring), and the organization's response (Massingham, 2010). In recent years, corporate disasters (e.g. Enron), catastrophic natural disasters (e.g. earthquakes), and man-made tragedies (e.g. terrorism) have increased the awareness of risk and its consequences (Massingham, 2010). Knowledge and knowledge management can help risk management by reducing environmental uncertainty and cognitive constraints. Risk is reduced by making risk assessment more objective and less complex.

Traditional decision tree models of risk management aim to quantify the likelihood and consequences of a risk event occurring. In our context, the risk event is the worst possible outcome associated with a work activity. The main problem with these models is personal bias. Risk is typically assessed by individuals with subject matter expertise in the work activity because it is assumed they will understand the nature of the risk better than others. Massingham (2010) found two problems with allowing these individuals, known as risk managers, to quantify risk. First, they tend to see their activity as more important than others and, therefore, to overestimate the significance of the risk event. Second, they tend to focus on the activity itself. This means that their risk assessment focuses on what will go wrong if the activity is not performed satisfactorily. Massingham (2010) found that these two problems could be addressed if the risk assessment focuses on the knowledge necessary to manage the risk event rather than the activity itself.

This chapter's knowledge loss model conceptualizes risk management by focusing on the impact of losing the knowledge necessary to manage risk events. It adopts Massingham's (2010) knowledge risk management model to measure the impact of lost knowledge about a risk event in three steps:

1. Calculate the level of risk associated with each of the organization's main activities. This follows a conventional decision tree method, i.e. the likelihood and consequences of an unwanted event occurring, with the addition of a weighting based on the relative importance of each activity.

2. Calculate the level of risk associated with the knowledge necessary to manage the risk factors for each activity.

3. Prioritize risks for action by considering the outcomes of step 1 and step 2 in isolation and then in combination.

The chapter's knowledge loss model focuses on step 2 – the knowledge risk – which is calculated as follows, involving three knowledge risk characteristics (individual, knowledge, and organizational) and their six constructs.

INDIVIDUAL CHARACTERISTICS

1. 'Recruitment effectiveness is determined by the organization's ability to attract suitably qualified staff, which is defined as Necessary Qualification Levels (NQL). NQL is measured by the levels of pre-requisite knowledge (i.e. qualifications) necessary to manage the risk factor (i.e. the unwanted event). The higher the qualification levels, the more difficult it will be to recruit, and vice versa. The higher the qualifications, the greater the risk that human capital cannot be bought' (Massingham, 2018: 743).

2. 'Training efficiency is determined by the length of time necessary to train staff, which is defined as Time To Learn (TTL). TTL is measured by the time required to develop the necessary human capital. The more time required to learn, the greater the risk that human capital cannot be developed' (2018: 743).

KNOWLEDGE CHARACTERISTICS

1. 'Tacitness is determined by the location of the knowledge necessary to manage the risk factor, which we define as Receiver Transfer Access (RTA). RTA is measured by the degree to which individuals who need knowledge can access it. If the knowledge necessary to manage the risk is only found in people's heads, i.e. tacit knowledge, then the organization is vulnerable if they are unavailable. Alternatively, if the necessary knowledge is codified and readily accessible, the risk of not knowing what to do if something goes wrong is much lower' (Massingham, 2018: 743).

2. 'Complexity is determined by the amount of new knowledge that must be created to manage the risk factor, which we define as Degree of Creativity (DoC). DoC is measured by levels of knowledge. If the knowledge necessary to manage the risk is highly complex, then the organization is vulnerable because if it is lost or otherwise unavailable it must be recreated. Alternatively, if the necessary knowledge required is simple, it is likely to be more easily replaced. Deeper levels of knowledge require more time to learn and, therefore, increase the possibility of inaction, i.e. when no one knows what to do' (2018: 743).

ORGANIZATIONAL CHARACTERISTICS

1. 'Potential capacity is determined by the organization's stock of knowledge, which is defined as Risk Management Capability (RMC). RMC is measured by the proportion of staff with the necessary knowledge to manage the risk factor (i.e. the unwanted event). If only one or a relatively few staff have sufficient knowledge, the organization has low RMC. It is vulnerable if these staff leave the organization or are unavailable for any reason' (Massingham, 2018: 743).

2. 'Realized capacity is determined by the organization's willingness to allocate staff resources, which is defined as risk management motivation (RMM).

RMM is measured by the degree to which the organization replaces staff required to manage the risk factor. Knowledge is about action and it must be put to some use in order to create value. The organization might have many staff who know what to do to manage the risk factor (i.e. high RMC) but not release them to perform this role, or the staff themselves may be unwilling to take on this role' (2018: 743).

The three knowledge risk characteristics and their six constructs combine to produce a knowledge risk score. This quantifies the impact of losing the knowledge necessary to manage risk events. It combines with the traditional decision tree method of likelihood and consequences, i.e. the risk score, to generate an overall knowledge risk score. This measurement of knowledge loss is different from the other four constructs in the model because it focuses on the work activity, rather than the individual. Therefore, it measures the impact of knowledge loss on the work itself.

THEORY IN PRACTICE: HP AND AGILENT'S RISK MANAGEMENT

HP and Agilent's knowledge risk management score worsened as a result of the knowledge loss caused by the restructure. The scores were calculated by examining the risks associated with two types of activities: functional areas and job families.

Functional areas were: vendor payables, accounts receivable, assets, tax, and general ledger, identified in a knowledge needs assessment. Strategic job families were: system developers, process engineers, SAP (software) implementers, and production systems and support personnel. The main risk categories were individual-level knowledge, particularly training efficiency (time to learn), and organization-level knowledge, particularly potential capacity (risk management capability). These risks were high in most of the functional areas and job families, but particularly so in accounts receivable for Agilent and in general ledger for HP, as well as for system developers at Agilent.

Example: Bob Costanza was meeting with his team in the general ledger department of HP in New York (USA). They were discussing a major crisis with an important customer. When the problem had emerged, the risk manager, Katy Blizzard, was on sick leave. No one else was able to solve the problem. 'We are one brick wide in some of these areas', said Beck Hall, a colleague of Katy. 'We just don't have enough experienced people. In some critical areas, we are completely vulnerable if someone leaves or is sick or just unavailable.' 'Why can't we train people, like succession planning?' asked Bob. 'Who is there to train?' replied Beck.

In this case, HP needed to improve its on-the-job training to accelerate the time to competence of young graduates so that they could improve their learning potential and be ready for people like Katy to share her knowledge.

ORGANIZATIONAL PROBLEMS

The fifth step in the conceptualization was to measure the impact of knowledge loss on the organization's knowledge management (KM). KM performance is measured by changes to significant and recurring organizational problems (Massingham and Massingham, 2014). There are seven problems:

1. Large proportions of new staff due to high employee turnover rates or an ageing workforce (e.g. retirements). The solution is better organizational learning, i.e. learning curve economies. KM performance accelerates the time to competence of new staff. The negative impact of knowledge loss is measured by longer time to competence (i.e. worse organizational learning).

2. Large proportions of young staff due to exiting older staff. The solution is better sharing of experience, i.e. experience curve economies. KM performance increases the sharing of experience of older staff with younger staff. The negative impact of knowledge loss is measured by longer time to attain subject matter expert status (i.e. less creativity, innovation, and problem solving).

3. High proportions of incompetent staff caused by poor workforce planning. The solution is objective decision models, i.e. strategic alignment. KM performance ensures the right people are in the right job. The negative impact of knowledge loss is measured by an increased proportion of incompetent staff (i.e. worse strategic alignment).

4. High proportions of staff with weak social networks. The solution is improved social network structure, i.e. connectivity. KM performance improves search cycle efficiency. The negative impact of knowledge loss is measured by longer time to access social capital (i.e. worse connectivity).

5. Poor corporate governance. The solution is providing customers with better 'why' context, i.e. risk management. KM performance increases confidence in work outputs. The negative impact of knowledge loss is measured by decreased customer satisfaction (i.e. worse risk management).

6. The organization is not able to explain how it creates value caused by poor relationships or communication with stakeholders. The solution is improving stakeholder satisfaction with organization performance, i.e. value management. KM performance improves stakeholder perception of the value of the organization. The negative impact of knowledge loss is measured by decreased stakeholder satisfaction (i.e. worse value management).

7. The job is not meeting the expectations of its staff in terms of their emotional relationship with their organization. The solution is improving human resource management, i.e. a psychological contract. KM performance reduces employee turnover and increases productivity and work quality. The negative impact of knowledge loss is measured by decreased job satisfaction, organizational commitment, and loyalty (i.e. a worse psychological contract).

Knowledge loss caused by employee turnover may be measured in terms of changes in these seven organizational problems (Massingham, 2018). Many organizations will face these challenges; for example, high proportions of new staff or low morale are common problems. This conceptualization captures the impact of knowledge loss in terms of KM ability to address these problems. This measurement of knowledge loss is different from the other four constructs in the model because it focuses on capability, i.e. KM, rather than the individual. Therefore, it measures the impact of knowledge loss on the organization's performance.

THEORY IN PRACTICE: HP AND AGILENT'S ORGANIZATIONAL PROBLEMS

HP and Agilent suffered from almost all of the seven organizational problems due to the knowledge loss caused by the restructure. The most urgent problem was large proportions of new staff due to the influx of young graduates. This caused a negative impact in terms of decreased productivity (longer learning time). The most serious problem was large proportions of young staff, which caused decreased creativity, innovation, and problem solving (fewer subject matter experts).

Example: Hannah Georgio looked around the room at the people who had been called to the meeting. She had been asked to chair a taskforce to develop a knowledge strategy for Agilent Europe. The taskforce was to include staff at middle management level from across the organization. They were supposed to contribute to the knowledge strategy by representing their area, and to evaluate current and future knowledge resource needs. Hannah asked each person to introduce themselves and provide some background on their experience. As they went around the room, Hannah considered how young they were. They did not have the experience to do this task. She wondered where the company's wisdom had gone. However, she knew she would have to treat this group carefully. Morale was already low. Many young graduates had struggled to adjust to the company's change as a result of pressures exerted by the restructure. The job was not meeting their expectations. Management had tried to address this and empower these staff by including them on this taskforce. Hannah had to find a balance between helping them feel valued and guiding them on their decisions. It would be a difficult role. 'Giving people years of experience quickly is much harder than it sounds', thought Hannah.

Now that knowledge loss has been defined and a model for measuring its impact established, we turn to the problem of how to manage to reduce its impact.

MANAGING KNOWLEDGE LOSS

The management of knowledge loss has been examined from multiple discipline perspectives including knowledge management, human resource management, and operations management.

Different disciplines have tackled knowledge loss from diverse perspectives, reflecting what was interesting to their field's researchers and practitioners (Daghfous et al., 2013). There are three disciplines exploring knowledge loss. Knowledge management (KM) has focused on measuring the impact of knowledge loss and knowledge sharing as a method to prevent knowledge loss (e.g. see Massingham and Massingham, 2014). The human resource management (HRM) literature mainly focuses on employee retention strategies such as succession planning, policies to retain older workers or engage retirees, or building a retention culture including motivation and reward systems (e.g. see DeLong, 2004). The operations management (OM) literature has focused on solutions by integrating the activities of the value chain (Closs et al., 2008), on codification strategies including investments in information technology tools and systems (such as data mining and knowledge discovery from data technology) (Rothenburger and Galarreta, 2006), and on standard operating procedures (SOPs) (Han and Park, 2009). These varying discipline approaches have created confusion about the methodology required to manage knowledge loss. There is limited empirical research on what methods work.

KNOWLEDGE MANAGEMENT SOLUTIONS TO KNOWLEDGE LOSS

Knowledge management looks at knowledge loss from a strategic perspective guided by the knowledge-based view (KBV) of the firm (Grant, 1996). This perspective has several assumptions: (a) the problem of knowledge loss must first be recognized; (b) the impact of knowledge loss must be identified and accepted; and (c) knowledge management is the solution.

Many studies refer to the challenge of convincing managers that a problem of knowledge loss exists (e.g. Levy, 2011). Some managers are aware of the phenomenon; for example, their workforce is ageing and they may be aware they will soon have a lot of employees retiring, or employee turnover rates seem to be increasing and some valuable staff are leaving, but they are not aware that it is a problem (Levy, 2011). The KBV of the firm provides the theoretical basis for this decision. The KBV adopted theories from the strategic management field such as the resource-based view (Barney, 1991), dynamic capabilities (Nelson and Winter, 1982), and their integration into the firm's routines (Cohen and Bacdayan, 1994) to help understand knowledge loss. These theories explain the value of knowledge resources and their importance to firm performance. They also suggest a solution by embedding tacit knowledge into capabilities and routines. This makes the resource more sustainable as a source of competitive advantage, and also helps minimize the impact of knowledge loss by capturing some valuable knowledge from employees before they leave, as codified organizational knowledge.

While this provides managers with an awareness that knowledge is valuable and is being lost, it is still only a perception and managers may need stronger evidence before they invest in a solution (e.g. see Massingham and Massingham, 2014). There are two approaches used. First, managers attempt to gain a sense of the significance of the risk from a workforce planning perspective. This may involve assessing probable retirees by age distribution (Beazley et al., 2002), by asking employees when they plan to retire (Massingham and Tam, 2015), or by assessing the organizational risk level (Massingham, 2008). Second, managers may adopt a knowledge strategy approach and try to identify the current and future capability gap caused by losing valuable employees. This may involve conducting skill inventories for all essential professional and management positions (DeLong, 2004) or a detailed assessment of workforce capability trends (Massingham, 2016). This defines the knowledge to be retained (Levy, 2011). It may involve identifying areas of critical knowledge that are at risk (DeLong and Davenport, 2003).

Knowledge management has focused on knowledge sharing as a method to prevent knowledge loss. Researchers have tended to look at the problems associated with capturing and transferring tacit knowledge from older employees to younger employees (Massingham, 2015). Typical retention strategies include: capturing and storing knowledge by codifying it, conducting exit interviews, and capturing lessons learned or best practice from projects that departing employees contributed to (Daghfous et al., 2013). An alternative view is that knowledge may be captured by being embedded in social relationships (Fisher and White, 2000). If one person in the network exits the organization, others may retain some of their knowledge shared with the group.

The most comprehensive frameworks in the literature are provided by DeLong (2004) and Martins and Meyer (2012). DeLong stated that organizations will vary significantly in their knowledge-sharing practices because they serve different purposes. He described five practices which are widely used: (1) interviews/video taping, (2) training, (3) storytelling, (4) mentoring, and (5) communities of practice (DeLong, 2004). Martins and Meyer (2012) developed a model that identifies the factors that need to be considered when addressing issues of knowledge loss. The model begins with knowledge loss risks in terms of whose and what type of knowledge should be retained. The next step is to demonstrate knowledge behaviour during the knowledge construction processes, and the behavioural threats/enhancers at individual, group, and organizational levels. The strategic risks caused by lost knowledge are assessed, and typically include a reduced capacity to innovate, a threatened ability to pursue growth, reduced efficiency undermining low-cost strategy, and not giving competitors an advantage (DeLong, 2004). Martins and Meyer (2012) conclude that the strategic risks of knowledge loss and identifying the knowledge loss risks (whose and what type of knowledge) can be regarded as the organizational factors that influence knowledge retention. The behaviour component of the model is illustrated in the knowledge behaviour processes (learning, knowing, creating, sharing, transferring, and applying knowledge) and the behavioural threats or enhancers. Martins and Meyer's (2012) study explored how the factors in their model impact on one another and could influence the knowledge retention strategy that should be implemented.

HUMAN RESOURCE MANAGEMENT SOLUTIONS TO KNOWLEDGE LOSS

The human resource management (HRM) literature has studied knowledge loss from an employee turnover perspective. The literature has taken three paths. The main path focuses on retention strategies such as succession planning, policies to retain older workers or engage retirees, or building a retention culture including motivation and reward systems (e.g. see DeLong, 2004). According to Sambrook (2005: 580), succession planning refers to the 'attempt to plan for the right number and quality of managers and key-skilled employees to cover retirements, death, serious illness or promotion, and any new positions which may be created in future organization plans'. Succession planning is, therefore, a long-term approach and an effective way to assist an organization's continuity (Cabrera-Suárez et al., 2001), particularly in small to medium-sized enterprises.

Human resource practices such as motivation and reward systems (Menon and Pfeffer, 2003) can motivate employees to engage in interaction, collaboration, and knowledge sharing and diffusion (Droege and Hoobler, 2003) and are proposed to reduce knowledge loss in organizations. Activities encouraging positive social relationships build loyalty (Feldman, 2000), trust (Leana and Van Buren, 1999), and reciprocity (Nahapiet and Ghoshal, 1998), which combine to enhance job satisfaction and organizational commitment (Massingham and Tam, 2015), leading to improved employee retention (Capelli, 2000) while also capturing knowledge and embedding it in social networks. The field looks too at organizational culture as a way to reduce employee turnover rates, and at initiatives such as acculturation programmes to help entry-level employees quickly align themselves with organizational goals and beliefs (Yeh, 2000) and build organizational commitment. Recruitment strategies which target people willing to contribute to a positive environment, including encouraging relationships that facilitate knowledge sharing (Droege and Hoobler, 2003), is another way of developing the type of organizational culture which minimizes knowledge loss.

The second path examines specific knowledge capture activities, which tend to be ad hoc and reactive (Daghfous et al., 2013). These activities include exit interviews for departing employees (Winkelen and McDermott, 2008). Organizations have tried to introduce longer-term strategies such as expert seminars to focus on knowledge-sharing behaviour (Slagter, 2009); phased retirement plans where future retirees work on a part-time basis before retiring (DeLong, 2004); or recruiting their retirees as consultants or even as members of their Board of Directors so that they continue to have access to their experience (Aiman-Smith et al., 2006). At a workforce planning level, organizations have introduced a range of initiatives designed to minimize risks, including the following. During economic downturns, organizations may reduce salaries instead of laying off employees so that minimal loss of skills and knowledge occurs (Lesser and Prusak, 2001). During downsizing strategy, organizations can reallocate the workforce to maintain knowledge of core competencies and still achieve the cost reductions necessary to achieve improved organizational effectiveness (Sitlington and Marshall, 2011). And job rotation programmes help share knowledge and make organizations less dependent on certain individuals (Hofer-Alfeis, 2008).

The third path adopts a strategic perspective and examines the impact of knowledge loss. Research has looked at the problem in terms of a gap analysis, i.e. systems for evaluating skills bases (DeLong, 2004). The field is also interested in the psychological impact in terms of heavier employee workloads and disrupted normal social interactions and networks that would otherwise lead to organizational learning and knowledge creation (Winkelen and McDermott, 2008). Durst and Wilhelm (2012) discuss how the exit of valuable employees can cause disruption as others must adjust their workload to cover for them.

OPERATIONS MANAGEMENT SOLUTIONS TO KNOWLEDGE LOSS

The operations management (OM) literature has focused on knowledge loss from a business process management perspective. This literature has two main paths. The first path looks at performance improvement and proposes integrating the activities of the value chain as a way to minimize knowledge loss (Closs et al., 2008). OM tends to look at decreased efficiency and effectiveness. Knowledge loss might be measured in terms of the effect on the learning curve and the experience curve (Massingham and Massingham, 2014). For example, knowledge loss increases the time required by experienced employees to train new recruits, thereby decreasing productive capacity, quality, and productivity levels, and putting the supply chain at a considerable risk (Jiang et al., 2009). This field looks at the impact of inexperience in terms of mistakes, unsatisfied customers, and inefficiencies related to the duplication of services (Jiang et al., 2009).

The second path concentrates on the technology view of knowledge management and codification strategies including investments in information technology tools and systems and in standard operating procedures (SOPs) (Clark and Fujimoto, 1991). The OM literature recommends the use of information technology tools and SOPs to document, map, and codify knowledge (Gold et al., 2001). Technology can capture information about employees to address gaps in organization knowledge (e.g. databases) (Idinopulos and Kempler, 2003), for example the use of knowledge maps and capturing business stories related to their elements (Hofer-Alfeis, 2008).

A NEW MODEL FOR MANAGING KNOWLEDGE LOSS

The research project which is explored through this book's integrated closing case studies produced several groups of findings about what works and what does not work in managing knowledge loss. The results are used to propose the model in Figure 6.1.

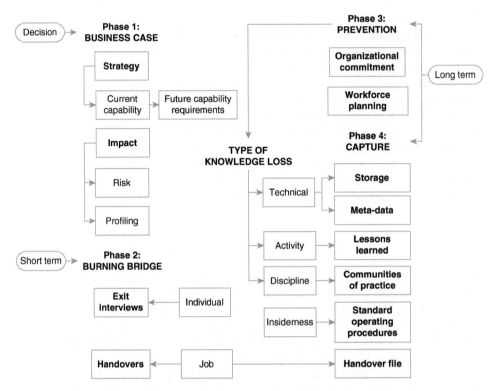

FIGURE 6.1 *Theoretical model: managing knowledge loss*

BUSINESS CASE

The business case explains the need to manage knowledge loss. It has two constructs: strategy and impact. Strategy identifies what knowledge is valuable and needs to be retained. The underlying principle is that not all knowledge is worth preserving and, therefore, it is necessary to develop a method to determine what to preserve. The strategy construct includes current and future capability dimensions. Impact demonstrates the likelihood and consequences of knowledge loss. It assumes that managers will need to be convinced that the problem is significant if they are to invest in a solution. The impact construct includes risk assessment and the profiling of high-risk employees.

SHORT-TERM SOLUTIONS: THE BURNING BRIDGE STRATEGY

Short-term solutions are required when valuable knowledge loss is imminent. This situation occurs at the individual level when an employee resigns, is transferred elsewhere in the organization, or retires; or at the group level when downsizing or restructuring leads to the loss of teams. These events can be unplanned and emerge without warning. Under these circumstances, the organization must respond and act to minimize the impact of the knowledge that will be lost. This is called the burning bridge strategy. It includes two parts: exit interviews and handovers.

Exit interviews are commonly used by human resource management to survey staff about their reasons for leaving. The aim is to identify causes of employee turnover, which is then used to reduce turnover in the remaining staff. Traditionally, exit interviews are not used to capture knowledge. The burning bridge model focused on developing correct cognitive triggers to identify the individual's most valuable tacit knowledge during the exit interview. The questions used to unlock these cognitive triggers switched the person from their focal awareness (consciousness) to their subsidiary awareness (sub-conscious), thereby discovering their tacit knowledge. Exit interviews should be conducted, transcribed, and organized into key themes, and presented to the individuals involved in the relevant job, i.e. the incumbent and the successor.

Handovers are about incumbents sharing their essential knowledge about the job, including tacit knowledge, with successors to ensure that the new employee benefits from the valuable knowledge accumulated by the exiting employee. The handover captures the experience of the exiting employee and enables the new employee to build on this experience rather than having to start from scratch.

LONG-TERM SOLUTIONS: PREVENTION

Prevention is required when management accepts that knowledge loss is a significant ongoing problem, and wants to take action to reduce or eliminate it in the future. It involves organizational commitment and workforce planning.

Organizational commitment aims to improve the employee's emotional relationship with their organization. Improving organizational commitment has two behavioural outcomes: reduced employee turnover and increased knowledge sharing. The model uses the psychological contract outlined in phase 1's profiling to measure employees' happiness at work and satisfaction with their workplace. This identifies high-risk individuals. They are classified as high risk if they have valuable knowledge and show signs of low psychological contract. The value of their knowledge is determined by their Knowledge Accounts score (Massingham, 2016). Low psychological contract is identified by low scores in peace and/or participation. Once the high-risk individuals are identified, action is taken to address the lowest rating constructs for this group of individuals (i.e. the mean scores for this group). In this way, the psychological contract method involves risk identification (profiling) and risk response (organizational commitment).

Workforce planning involves a range of human resource management ideas developed by leading knowledge management researchers (e.g. DeLong, 2004) to address knowledge loss. Examples include: career development/succession planning programmes, phased retirement programmes, knowledge recruiting processes, and mapping competencies to career continuums.

LONG-TERM SOLUTIONS: CAPTURE

Knowledge capture is required when knowledge loss is recognized as a long-term corporate risk, and the solution is to codify knowledge. The difference between knowledge capture and knowledge loss prevention is the nature of the solution. Knowledge capture adopts a technology view of knowledge management. It aims to codify valuable knowledge. The right-hand side of Figure 6.1 presents the six tools used.

Storage is grounded in theories about content management (e.g. see Koenig and Srikantaiah, 2007). Content management fits here by helping us understand how best to 'warehouse' this knowledge so it is accessible and therefore used by others. To be successful, this technique needs to address any underlying issues associated with the existing systems. Typically, large organizations will have already invested considerable funds in existing information technology, and will be reluctant to invest in a new system to store captured knowledge. The aim should be to integrate the knowledge storage system by using existing tools and systems as much as possible.

Meta-data provides participants with the context and meaning of the data represented by the knowledge repository (e.g. computer file) so it can be accurately used by the organization (Inmon et al., 2007). Meta-data is 'data about data'. This technique identifies how to make the knowledge stored accessible. The meta-data technique builds on the need for classifying knowledge resources in ways that make the repositories more searchable and the knowledge more accessible. At the case study organization, this technique had to be introduced by management at the organizational level. Individual staff did not have the skills, time, or resources to design and build meta-data fields into their knowledge capture. The first problem was that staff needed to be trained in terms of meta-data field categories and then in how to build these into documents within the constraints of their existing information technology systems. This required investment in external consultants with expertise in this area. Second, this meta-data activity is extremely time-intensive and staff felt they were too busy to properly code their documents with meta-data fields. Third, consultants tend to lack sufficient knowledge of the knowledge captured to add the meta-data fields themselves. Ideally, this activity should be done by subject-matter experts, once trained in the process by the consultants, which once again raises the barrier of being too busy.

The lessons learned database is widely used in best practice learning organizations around the world. It is grounded in learning theory and builds on the principle of sharing experience so that mistakes and duplication are avoided. It stores information from the past that can be drawn upon and brought to bear on present decisions and/or actions.

Communities of practice (CoP) are used in many organizations. They aim to establish groups of like-minded people who meet regularly to share ideas and information. The literature on CoP suggests that they are usually self-regulated and managed activities, i.e. voluntary (e.g. Gorelick et al., 2004). However, this makes them difficult to manage, and it is hard to monitor outcomes. CoPs may be used for knowledge capture by embedding valuable knowledge in social relationships (e.g. see Fisher and White, 2000).

Using standard operating procedures is a method of preserving valuable, job-related knowledge as best practice. It is helpful in a situation where considerable variance in the way the job is being performed leads to unsatisfactory performance, particularly where some employees are not doing the job the way it was intended.

The handover file is a folder containing the employee's main work outputs accumulated during their period in a job, as well as contextual information about the what, why, how, who, and where questions associated with this work. It should also contain behavioural dimensions including critical incidents, lessons learned, and social capital, as well as personal reflections relevant to the job. The employee maintains and updates the file over their time in the job. In this sense, it is a continual learning process, capturing the accumulated wisdom of the individual about their job. The aim is to build knowledge incrementally and have the file ready to hand over to the successor. The successor then builds on the file by creating their own handover file which should be an advance on the knowledge of the predecessor's. The organization's knowledge therefore builds continually as these handover files capture and grow knowledge.

EVALUATING THE MANAGING KNOWLEDGE LOSS MODEL

The graph in Figure 6.2 summarizes the results in terms of a scorecard rating for each knowledge loss technique tested at the case study organization (see closing case study). It represents the ratings for each tool against a set of criteria designed to cover the evaluation framework (see Massingham and Massingham, 2014).

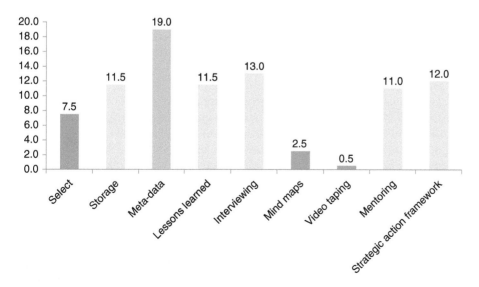

FIGURE 6.2 *Knowledge loss scorecard*

Figure 6.2 shows that, overall, the knowledge loss tool with the most success is meta-data. This supports the technology view of knowledge management and the notion that structuring data and making knowledge more accessible are seen as the most effective solution. The two least successful tools are mind maps and videotaping, which are knowledge capture techniques. In terms of comparison with all KM tools implemented at the case study organization, meta-data is the highest rating tool overall. However, it is the only 'green' technique of the knowledge loss solutions. There are five 'orange' techniques, suggesting some success, and only three 'dark red' techniques, indicating failed implementation. Overall, then, the knowledge loss tools tested from the literature were moderately successful.

The model's techniques fit into these fields as follows (see Figure 6.1):

- *Knowledge management*:
  o Phase 1 strategy: current capabilities, future capabilities;
  o Phase 1 impact: risk, profiling;
  o Phase 2 handovers;
  o Phase 4 communities of practice

- *Human resource management*:
  o Phase 1 impact: risk;
  o Phase 2 exit interviews;
  o Phase 3 organizational commitment, workforce planning

- *Operations management*:
  o Phase 1 impact: risk;
  o Phase 4 storage, meta-data, standard operating procedures, lessons learned, handover file.

While there is overlap – for example, knowledge management might claim lessons learned, exit interviews, and indeed perhaps all of these techniques – the point of the analysis is to illustrate how the nature of the techniques vary. The techniques have varying impact in terms of how well they manage knowledge loss. The knowledge capture techniques worked best, which provides support for operations management and the technology view of knowledge management. The knowledge management techniques are next most helpful, and the chapter provides a new perspective on their implementation. The human resource management techniques were least successful; however, the chapter provides guidelines on how they may be improved.

CONCLUSION

This chapter sought to examine how to measure the impact of knowledge loss and then how to manage it. A new model for measuring the impact of knowledge loss was introduced (see Massingham, 2018). It has five measurement concepts which combine to provide a new perspective on knowledge loss and enable the impact to be measured in financial and non-financial terms. It extends previous research which had discussed the topic in broad terms such as decreased productivity, morale, and performance, translating these into specific measurable constructs which may be used to properly appreciate the potentially destructive nature of knowledge loss.

The second half of the chapter introduced a new model to manage knowledge loss (see Figure 6.1). Phase 1 combines strategy and impact to develop a compelling business case that knowledge loss is a significant problem requiring investment in solutions. Phase 2 suggests exit interviews and handovers to manage knowledge loss in emergency situations, i.e. the burning bridge strategy. It captures codified and tacit knowledge. Phase 3 looks at how to prevent knowledge loss by improving employees' psychological contract with their organization (organizational commitment), and workforce planning to address the strategic alignment issues associated with employee exit. Phase 4 offers six techniques to capture knowledge before it exits the organization.

A challenge for researchers and practitioners is that the three fields most interested in knowledge loss have varying perspectives on how to manage it. Knowledge management adopts a strategic perspective focusing on identifying the impact of knowledge loss and using knowledge sharing as a solution. Human resource management focuses on retention strategies to reduce employee turnover, specific knowledge capture exercises such as exit interviews, and impact in terms of skill gap analysis. Operations management focuses on knowledge capture, specifically the use of information technology to codify knowledge, as well as on knowledge standardization or best practice (e.g. standard operating procedures). These lines between the disciplines are somewhat arbitrary, as many knowledge management researchers investigate the technology perspective of knowledge management, but this distinction is used to illustrate different perspectives.

CLOSING CASE STUDY: MANAGING KNOWLEDGE LOSS AT THE CSO

The case study organization (CSO) experienced employee turnover of 48% during the research study. This resulted in significant knowledge loss. This closing case study explores several scenarios based on the four ET factors which influence the five knowledge loss concepts over time:

1. *Withdrawals*: when employees exit, they take knowledge with them.
2. *Decay*: surviving employees, i.e. those who were employed by the organization at the start and the end of the surveys, may lose knowledge or their knowledge may decrease in value.

    (These both represent decreases to what the organization knows.)

3. *Deposits*: when employees enter, they bring knowledge with them.
4. *Growth*: surviving employees may gain knowledge or their knowledge may increase in value.

    (These both represent increases to what the organization knows.)

(Continued)

(Continued)

The closing case scenarios illustrate what happened at the CSO in each of these four ET situations and how the knowledge loss model presented in this chapter (see Figure 6.1) tried to address them.

SCENARIO 1: WITHDRAWAL

Peter Herringtin was nearing 55 years of age. He was still a relatively young man, but he decided to retire. His superannuation was designed so that he was encouraged to retire at 55. It maximized his pension. Peter was the subject matter expert in ship propulsion. He knew more about this topic than anyone else in the country. His retirement created a significant loss of knowledge for the CSO.

Three techniques were used to try to manage the knowledge loss created by Peter's retirement. The first technique was videotaping – an idea from DeLong (2004) based on work done at the World Bank. The objective was to film participants sharing their reflections about working at the Case Study Organization. This exercise enabled exiting employees to leave their legacy for the organization. This was done at a workshop involving Peter and other staff due to retire. Participants were encouraged to think about what they would like to be remembered for, and to share this on video. Those participants who participated in the filming offered interesting insights into their work history, which contributed to the stock of organizational memory. Those who watched the filming found participants' comments interesting, and there was often a lively discussion after filming. Peter fell into this category: his filming was a success. However, most of the other participants found the idea of being filmed to be intrusive and uncomfortable. Some appeared to be self-conscious about their appearance and worried that the film would be a lasting representation of them and their reputation.

The second technique was mentoring. This is a widely used form of directly transferring tacit knowledge from experienced employee to younger employees (DeLong, 2004). At the CSO, mentoring was done on an informal basis, particularly at a subject matter expertise (i.e. discipline) level. This worked for Peter. He would share his knowledge with younger staff by telling stories. However, this was done only with staff in his section who were in hearing distance when he felt like sharing. There was a struggle with mentoring when we tried to make it a formal process and to introduce structure around the activity. A young engineer from another section was assigned to work with Peter for succession planning, but Peter did not know this person and he struggled to share his stories with him. When we tried to impose structure on the mentoring process, he felt it was restrictive and unnecessary.

Peter agreed to do an exit interview in the days before he retired. He was quite happy to share and told the chief investigator (CI): 'I will tell you anything you want to know, but I don't know where to start. Tell me what you want to know.' The development of this type of questioning developed as cognitive switches worked very well. The structured approach developed specifically for this technique enabled participants to surface important organizational memories which proved very valuable. Peter found the experience to be worthwhile and often cathartic, as the interview surfaced deep emotional issues about his career based on the hard reality of lessons learned. Feedback from successors who were given the interview outcomes was also positive.

The Monday after Peter retired, the CI was surprised to see him at work. He walked over and said 'What are you doing here? I thought you retired on Friday?' 'I did', replied Peter. 'I'm now working here as a consultant. They are paying me more than when I worked here as staff.'

SCENARIO 2: DECAY

Klaus Arnberger was a young engineer. He was smart and ambitious. At the start of the research project, he achieved a high KA score. However, by the end of the project, his KA score had declined dramatically. His value to the CSO was now 25% less. His human capital score had particularly declined. A closer look at the levels in his KA score revealed that his emotional relationship with the CSO was suffering. More specifically, his ratings in reward and recognition were particularly low. His social capital scores had also decreased. It seemed that he felt unappreciated and was choosing to withdraw from social contact.

One technique was used to try to manage the knowledge decay identified by Klaus's decreasing KA score: organizational commitment. The main decreases in Klaus's scores were career management, and recruitment and selection. These were important signs of discontent. They were two of the main reasons experienced staff were leaving the CSO. Career management and recruitment and selection suggest dissatisfaction with the opportunities provided by the organization – more specifically, exiting employees' promotion applications – and they felt forced to look elsewhere to grow their career. Now that the KA changes told the CSO why Klaus's productivity was declining, management needed to take action to improve his psychological contract with the organization.

SCENARIO 3: DEPOSITS

The CI was sitting in the office of Admiral Sheldon Field. The Admiral had recently assumed the position of Head of the CSO, replacing the senior industry partner who had worked with the CI from the beginning of the research project. The CI was a little nervous. He had not met the Admiral. It was important that the project had continuity with this leadership change.

The CI began by asking the Admiral what he had heard about the project. The Admiral replied by showing him a sheet of paper. On it was written a series of bullet points. One of the bullet points began with the name of the project and the words 'Next meeting 26th April'. 'That is all I know about your project', the Admiral said. The CI was stunned. 'Surely the CSO valued the project more than this', he thought. He began by explaining the strategic objectives of the project and how it aimed to measure and manage knowledge loss. The Admiral seemed only mildly interested. The CI continued to say that the project had been signed off by the previous head on behalf of the Australian government, and that there was a contract which had been agreed to. 'Just because we committed to something years ago, does not mean we have to continue with it forever', replied the Admiral. The CI felt he was in deep trouble. He began to discuss some of the work that had been completed. Suddenly the Admiral interrupted and said 'See this page', and he waved the sheet of paper in front of him. 'This is all of the handover I got. One page. What do you think of that?' The CI seized the opportunity. He explained how one of the ideas being introduced was a handover which captured the knowledge of key people when they are leaving. 'OK', said the Admiral, 'Do one of those for me, and we'll have another meeting about your project.'

The CI contacted the previous head (the senior industry partner) and explained the situation. They agreed to meet for a handover interview. The interview explored a range of issues including

(Continued)

(Continued)

job-related knowledge, social relationships, and major challenges or difficulties. It also aimed to capture lessons learned. The CI wrote up the interview in a structured way (not a transcript) which organized the knowledge gathered into key themes. He then sent it to the previous head for checking. Once finalized, the report was sent to the Admiral; the Admiral met with the previous head to discuss the report.

The Admiral then contacted the CI and indicated he was happy to meet to discuss the future of the project.

SCENARIO 4: GROWTH

Evan Thompson was one of the CSO's most senior engineers. He had developed very strong technical knowledge over many years and was widely regarded as a subject matter expert in his area.

In the first KA survey, Evan had a low KA. Overall, his KA scores were lower than many of the junior staff who lacked his experience and technical knowledge. Something did not seem right. The KA was supposed to measure the value of an individual's knowledge for the organization. The CI was puzzled. Surely Evan had more knowledge than the KA scores revealed. The CI had a close look at Evan's results and found that his psychological contract scores were low, and he also had very low scores in social and relational capital. It seemed that Evan was very unhappy and he was socially isolated. The CSO was not getting the best out of Evan, particularly because he was one of four principal engineers and his role was to be the leader of his discipline.

The CI began observing Evan to decide how best to help him. In meetings, Evan was vocal and engaged but he was mainly critical of the organization and management. When he had the opportunity, he would tell the same stories illustrating why management were doing a bad job. It seemed Evan had formed mental scripts which he rolled out to reinforce his position at every chance. The CI organized to meet with Evan over coffee to discover more. The main source of his anger was that he was overlooked for promotion earlier in his career. The promotion had gone to Jim Clarenbold, who was now his boss and one of the project's industry partners. Evan felt that he had more experience and capability than Jim. He had never forgiven the organization, nor Jim, for being overlooked.

The CI felt for Evan. He saw Evan as a valuable knowledge resource who had been mismanaged. He wanted to help Evan so that he was happier at work and the CSO could get more value from him. First, he asked others how they felt about Evan. Most felt he was quite pleasant but they were tired of his constant complaining. They felt he wasted time in meetings going over the same old ground. He also emerged as bitter and angry and a recalcitrant. Others did not want to be associated with him because he was seen as difficult. However, the CI did not see him as difficult, rather mistreated. The CI began to show an interest in Evan. He engaged him in conversation whenever they came across one another. He listened and smiled politely while Evan got things off his chest. One day he said, 'You know Evan, the most difficult people are often the most brilliant. Creative people aren't compliant, obedient, rule followers. I reckon me and you are pretty much alike.'

Evan started volunteering for activities within the research project. He was an enthusiastic and useful contributor to discussions. He began using his experience to discuss solutions rather than problems. The CI told others about Evan and how useful he was to the project. Gradually, people changed their attitude towards Evan. While he would never be the most popular member of staff, he began to be accepted. The CI smiled to himself when he saw the results of the final KA survey. The first name he looked for was Evan. He had increased his score by 21%. He was still lower than expected in social and relational capital, but there was strong improvement; he was much happier and his human capital scores were near the top where they should be. The CSO was now getting the best out of Evan. The CI liked Evan and was happy for him. Maybe finally he could let go of the past and move on to the future.

CASE STUDY QUESTIONS

1. Consider the four scenarios presented. Which do you feel represents the most serious problem for the CSO? Why?
2. Classify each of the four scenarios to fit into the managing knowledge model presented in Figure 6.1.
3. Describe the managing knowledge loss method used in each scenario (see Figure 6.1). Would other methods have worked better?
4. Do you feel the problem in each scenario was managed well? Why or why not?

REVIEW AND DISCUSSION QUESTIONS

1. Why is knowledge loss an important topic for managers to address?
2. Consider the five concepts in the new measurement model to identify the impact of lost organizational knowledge caused by employee turnover. Which do you feel is the best measure of impact? Why?
3. Critically evaluate the managing knowledge loss model presented in Figure 6.1.

FURTHER READING

DeLong, D.W. (2004) *Lost Knowledge: Confronting the threat of an ageing workforce,* Oxford, Oxford University Press. A comprehensive knowledge loss text.

Martins, E.C. and Meyer, H.W.J. (2012) Organizational and Behavioural Factors that Influence Knowledge Retention. *Journal of Knowledge Management*, 16 (1): 77–96. This article gives information on a recent knowledge loss model.

Massingham, P. (2018) Measuring the Impact of Knowledge Loss: A longitudinal study. *Journal of Knowledge Management*, 22 (4): 721–758. This article gives further details on measuring knowledge loss.

BIBLIOGRAPHY

Aiman-Smith, L., Bergey, P., Cantwell, A. and Doran, M. (2006) The Coming Knowledge and Capability Shortage. *Research Technology Management, 49* (4): 15–23.

Argyris, C. (1960) *Understanding Organizational Behavior*, Homewood, IL, Dorsey Press.

Barney, J.B. (1991) Firm Resources and Sustained Competitive Advantage. *Journal of Management, 17* (1): 99–120.

Beazley, H., Boenisch, J. and Harden, D. (2002) *Knowledge Continuity*, Hoboken, NJ, Wiley.

Becker, K. (2010) Facilitating Unlearning during Implementation of New Technology. *Journal of Organizational Change Management, 23* (3): 251–268.

Blau, P.M. (1964) *Exchange and Power in Social Life*, New York, Wiley.

Bontis, N. (1998) Intellectual Capital: An exploratory study that develops measures and models. *Management Decision, 36* (2): 63–76.

Borgatti, S.P. and Foster, P.C. (2003) The Network Paradigm in Organizational Research: A review and typology. *Journal of Management, 29* (6): 991–1013.

Brockner, J. (1988) The Effects of Work Layoffs on Survivors: Research, theory, and practice. In B.M. Staw and L.L. Cummings (eds) *Research in Organizational Behavior 10*, Greenwich, CT, JAI Press, pp. 213–255.

Cabrera-Suárez, K., De Saá-Pérez, P. and Garcia-Almeida, D. (2001) The Succession Process from a Resource- and Knowledge-based View of the Family Firm. *Family Business Review, 14* (1): 37–47.

Capelli, P. (2000) A Market-driven Approach to Retaining Talent. *Harvard Business Review, 78* (1): 103–113.

Carnahan, S., Agarwal, R. and Campbell, B.A. (2012) Heterogeneity in Turnover: The effect of relative compensation dispersion of firms on the mobility and entrepreneurship of extreme performers. *Strategic Management Journal, 33*: 1411–1430.

Clark, K. and Fujimoto, T. (1991) *Product Development Performance*, Boston, MA, Harvard Business School Press.

Closs, D.J., Jacobs, M.A., Swink, M. and Webb, G.S. (2008) Toward a Theory of Competencies for the Management of Product Complexity: Six case studies. *Journal of Operations Management, 26* (5): 590–610.

Cohen, D. and Bacdayan, P. (1994) Organizational Routines as Stored Procedural Memory: Evidence from a laboratory study. *Organization Science, 5* (4): 554–568.

Corbitt, G. (2005) Rebuilding Core Competencies When a Company Splits: A case study of assessing and rebuilding expertise. Chapter 4 in Jennex, M.E. (ed.) *Case Studies in Knowledge Management*, Hershey, PA, Idea Group Publishing, pp. 51–64.

Daghfous, A., Belkhodja, O. and Angell, L.C. (2013) Understanding and Managing Knowledge Loss. *Journal of Knowledge Management, 17* (5): 639–660.

Dalkir, K. (2011) *Knowledge Management in Theory and Practice*, Cambridge, MA, MIT Press.

D'Arcy, P., Gustafsson, L., Lewis, C. and Wiltshire, T. (2012) *Labour Market Turnover and Mobility*, Reserve Bank of Australia, Bulletin, December Quarter.

Davenport, T.H. and Prusak, L. (1998) *Working Knowledge: How organizations manage what they know*, Cambridge, MA, Harvard Business School Press.

DeHolan, P. and Phillips, N. (2004) Remembrance of Things Past? The dynamics of organizational forgetting. *Management Science, 50* (11): 1603–1613.

DeLong, D.W. (2004) *Lost Knowledge: Confronting the threat of an ageing workforce*, Oxford, Oxford University Press.

DeLong, D.W. and Davenport, T. (2003) Better Practices for Retaining Organizational Knowledge: Lessons from the leading edge. *Employment Relations Today, 30* (3): 51–63.

Droege, S. and Hoobler, J. (2003) Employee Turnover and Tacit Knowledge Diffusion: A network perspective. *Journal of Managerial Issues, 15* (1): 50–64.

Durst, S. and Wilhelm, S. (2012) Knowledge Management and Succession Planning in SMEs. *Journal of Knowledge Management, 16* (4): 637–649.

Dychtwald, K., Erikson, T.J. and Morison, R. (2006) *Workforce Crisis: How to beat the coming shortage of skills and talent*, Boston, MA, Harvard Business School Press.

Edvinsson, L. and Malone, M.S. (1997) *Intellectual Capital: Realizing your company's true value by finding its hidden roots*, New York, Harper Business.

Eisenberger, R., Fasolo, P. and Davis-LaMastro, V. (1990) Perceived Organizational Support and Employee Diligence, Commitment, and Innovation. *Journal of Applied Psychology, 75* (1): 51–59.

Feldman, D.H. (2000) Forward. In John-Steiner, V. (ed.) *Creative Collaboration*, New York, Oxford University Press, pp. ix–xiii.

Fisher, S. and White, M. (2000) Downsizing in a Learning Organization: Are there hidden costs? *Academy of Management Review, 25* (1): 244–251.

Garratt, B. (1987) Learning is the Core of Organizational Survival: Action learning is the key integrating process. *Journal of Management Development, 6* (2): 38–44.

Goh, S.C. (2002) Managing Effective Knowledge Transfer: An integrative framework and some practice implications. *Journal of Knowledge Management, 6* (1): 23–30.

Gold, A., Malhorta, A. and Segars, A. (2001) Knowledge Management: An organizational capabilities perspective. *Journal of Management Information Systems, 18* (1): 185–214.

Gorelick, C., Milton, N. and April, K. (2004) Going Deeper: Elements of knowledge for action to produce results, Chapter 3 of *Performance through Learning: Knowledge management in practice*, Amsterdam, Elsevier Butterworth-Heinemann, pp. 41–50.

Gotthart, B. and Haghi, G. (2009) How Hewlett-Packard Minimizes Knowledge Loss. *International Journal of Human Resources Development and Management, 9* (2/3): 305–317.

Grant, R.M. (1996) Toward a Knowledge-based Theory of the Firm. *Strategic Management Journal, 17*: 109–122.

Han, K.H. and Park, J.W. (2009) Process-centred Knowledge Model and Enterprise Ontology for the Development of Knowledge Management System. *Expert Systems with Applications, 36*: 7441–7447.

Hislop, D. (2011) *Knowledge Management in Organizations: A critical introduction*, 3rd edition, Oxford, Oxford University Press.

Hofer-Alfeis, J. (2008) Knowledge Management Solutions for the Leaving Expert Issue. *Journal of Knowledge Management, 12* (4): 44–54.

Homans, G.C. (1961) *Social Behaviorism*, New York, Harcourt Brace and World.

Housel, T. and Bell, A.H. (2001) *Measuring and Managing Knowledge*, New York, McGraw-Hill.

Huizing, A. and Bouman, W. (2002) Knowledge and Learning Markets and Organizations. In Choo, C. and Bontis, N. (eds) *The Strategic Management of Intellectual Capital and Organizational Knowledge*, New York, Oxford University Press, pp. 185–204.

Idinopulos, M. and Kempler, L. (2003) Do You Know Who Your Experts Are? *The McKinsey Quarterly*, 4: 60–69.

Inmon, W.H., O'Neil, B.K. and Fryman, L. (2007) *Business Metadata: Capturing enterprise knowledge*, Burlington, MA, Morgan Kaufmann.

Israilidis, J., Siachou, E., Cooke, L. and Lock, R. (2015) Individual Variables with an Impact on Knowledge Sharing: The critical role of employees' ignorance. *Journal of Knowledge Management*, *19* (6): 1109–1123.

Jiang, B., Baker, R.C. and Frazier, G.V. (2009) An Analysis of Job Dissatisfaction and Turnover to Reduce Global Supply Chain Risk: Evidence from China. *Journal of Operations Management*, *27* (2): 169–184.

Joe, C., Yoong, P. and Patel, K. (2013) Knowledge Loss When Older Experts Leave Knowledge-intensive Organizations. *Journal of Knowledge Management*, *17* (6): 913–927.

Kluge, J., Stein, W. and Licht, T. (2001) *Knowledge Unplugged: The McKinsey Global Survey of Knowledge Management*, New York, Palgrave.

Koenig, M.E.D. and Srikantaiah, T.K. (2007) Three Stages of Knowledge Management. Chapter 1 in Koenig, M.E.D. and Srikantaiah, T.K. (eds) *Knowledge Management Lessons Learned: What works and what doesn't*, Medford, NJ, Information Today Inc., pp. 3–8.

Leana, C.R. and Van Buren, H.J., III (1999) Organizational Social Capital and Employment Practices. *Academy of Management Review*, *24* (3): 538–555.

Lee, L.L. (2005) Schemes and Tools for Social Capital Measurement as a Proxy for Intellectual Capital Measures. Chapter 6 in Rao, M. (ed.) *Knowledge Management Tools and Techniques: Practitioners and experts evaluate KM solutions*, Oxford, Elsevier, pp. 123–136.

Lepak, D. and Snell, S. (1999) The Human Resource Architecture: Toward a theory of human capital allocation and development. *Academy of Management Review*, *24* (1): 31–48.

Lesser, E. and Prusak, L. (2001) Preserving Knowledge in an Uncertain World. *MIT Sloan Management Review*, *43* (1): 101–102.

Levy, M. (2011) Knowledge Retention: Minimizing organizational business loss. *Journal of Knowledge Management*, *15* (4): 582–600.

Marsick, V. and Watkins, K. (2003) Demonstrating the Value of an Organization's Learning. *Advances in Developing Human Resources*, *5* (2): 132–151.

Martins, E.C. and Martins, N. (2011) The Role of Organizational Factors in Combating Tacit Knowledge Loss in Organizations. *South African Business Review*, *15* (1): 49–69.

Martins, E.C. and Meyer, H.W.J. (2012) Organizational and Behavioural Factors that Influence Knowledge Retention. *Journal of Knowledge Management*, *16* (1): 77–96.

Massingham, P. (2008) Measuring and Managing the Impact of Knowledge Loss: More than ripples on a pond? *Management Learning*, *39* (5): 541–560.

Massingham, P. (2010) Knowledge Risk Management: A framework. *Journal of Knowledge Management*, *14* (3): 464–485.

Massingham, P. (2015) Knowledge Sharing: What works and what doesn't work – A critical systems thinking perspective. *Systemic Practice and Action Research*, *28* (3): 197–228.

Massingham, P. (2016) Knowledge Accounts. *Long Range Planning*, *49* (3): 409–425.

Massingham, P.R. (2018) Measuring the Impact of Knowledge Loss: A longitudinal study. *Journal of Knowledge Management*, *22* (4): 721–758.

Massingham, P. and Diment, K. (2009) Organizational Commitment, Knowledge Management Interventions, and Learning Organization Capacity? *The Learning Organization, 16* (2): 122–142.

Massingham, P. and Massingham, R. (2014) Does Knowledge Management Produce Practical Outcomes? *Journal of Knowledge Management, 18* (2): 221–254.

Massingham, P. and Tam, L. (2015) The Relationship between Human Capital, Value Creation, and Employee Reward. *Journal of Intellectual Capital, 16* (2): 390–418.

Menon, T. and Pfeffer, J. (2003) Valuing Internal versus External Knowledge. *Management Science, 49* (4): 497–513.

Mertins, K., Heisig, P. and Vorbeck, J. (eds) (2003) *Knowledge Management: Concepts and practices*, New York, Springer, pp. 16–44.

Moilanen, R. (2005) Diagnosing and Measuring Learning Organizations. *The Learning Organization, 12* (1): 71–89.

Nahapiet, S. and Ghoshal, J. (1998) Social Capital, Intellectual Capital, and the Organizational Advantage. *Academy of Management Review, 23* (2): 242–266.

Nelson, R. and Winter, S. (1982) *An Evolutionary Theory of Economic Change*, Cambridge, MA, Belknap Press.

Neuman, W.L. (2006) *Social Research Methods: Qualitative and quantitative approaches*, 6th edition, Boston, MA, Pearson International.

Nunally, J.C. (1978) *Psychometric Theory*, 2nd edition, New York, McGraw-Hill.

Osterman, P. (1987) Turnover, Employment Security, and the Performance of the Organization. In M. Kleiner (ed.) *Human Resources and the Performance of the Organization*, Champaign, IL, Industrial Relations Research Association, pp. 275–317.

Perrott, B.E. (2007) A Strategic Risk Approach to Knowledge Management. *Business Horizons, 50* (6): 523–533.

Phillips, J.J. and Connell, A.O. (2003) *Managing Employee Retention: A strategic accountability approach*, New York, Elsevier Butterworth-Heinemann.

Polanyi, M. (1962) *Personal Knowledge*, Chicago, IL, University of Chicago Press.

Porter, L., Steers, R. and Mowday, R. (1973) Organizational Commitment, Job Satisfaction, and Turnover among Psychiatric Technicians. *Journal of Applied Psychology, 59* (5): 603–609.

Probst, G., Raub, S. and Romhardt, K. (2002) *Managing Knowledge: Building blocks for success*, Chichester, Wiley.

Reed, K.K., Lubatkin, M. and Srinivasan, N. (2006) Proposing and Testing an Intellectual Capital-based View of the Firm. *Journal of Management Studies, 43* (4): 867–893.

Robinson, S.L. and Rousseau, D.M. (1994) Violating the Psychological Contract: Not the exception but the norm. *Journal of Organizational Behavior, 15* (3): 245–259.

Rothenburger, B. and Galarreta, D. (2006) Facing Knowledge Evolution in Space Project: A multi-viewpoint approach. *Journal of Knowledge Management, 10* (2): 52–65.

Sambrook, S. (2005) Exploring Succession Planning in Small, Growing Firms. *Journal of Small Business and Enterprise Development, 12* (4): 579–594.

Senge, P. (1990) *The Fifth Discipline: The art and practice of the learning organization*, New York, Doubleday/Currency.

Sitlington, H. and Marshall, V. (2011) Do Downsizing Decisions Affect Organizational Knowledge and Performance? *Management Decision, 49* (1): 116–129.

Slagter, F. (2009) HR Practices as Predictors for Knowledge Sharing and Innovative Behaviour: A focus on age. *International Journal of Human Resources Development and Management*, 9 (2/3): 223–249.

Starke, F.A., Dyck, B. and Mauws, M.K. (2003) Coping with the Sudden Loss of an Indispensable Employee: An exploratory case study. *Journal of Applied Behavioral Science*, 39 (2): 208–229.

Stone, W. (2001) Measuring Social Capital: Towards a theoretically informed measurement framework for researching social capital in family and community life, Research Paper No. 24, February, Australian Institute of Family Studies.

Thompson, A.J., Jr., Peteraf, M.A., Gamble, J.E. and Strickland, A.J. (2015) *Crafting and Executing Strategy: The quest for competitive advantage – Concepts and cases*, 20th edition, New York, McGraw-Hill Irwin.

United Nations (2013) *World Population Ageing 2013*, Department of Economic and Social Affairs Population Division,United Nations, New York.

Winkelen, C. and McDermott, R. (2008) Facilitating the Handover of Knowledge. *Knowledge Management Review*, 11 (2): 24–27.

Yeh, Y. (2000) *Job and organizational determinants of employees' practices of Total Quality Management in the public sector,* The University of Wisconsin, Madison.

7

USING KNOWLEDGE

CHAPTER OUTLINE

Learning outcomes

Management issues

Links to other chapters

Opening mini case study: Winning the unwinnable consulting assignment

Introduction

The knowing–doing gap

Peer assists

After action reviews

Retrospects

The knowledge management bridge

Knowledge usage framework

Practical outcomes

Conclusion

Closing case study: Knowledge usage at the CSO

LEARNING OUTCOMES

After completing this chapter, the reader should be able to:

1. Define knowledge usage
2. Understand the importance of knowledge usage
3. List barriers to knowledge usage
4. Discuss solutions to knowledge usage barriers
5. Define action learning
6. Apply action learning
7. Define the problem of demonstrating practical outcomes from knowledge management
8. Discuss financial and non-financial measures of the knowledge management investment decision
9. Discuss and define the seven practical outcomes of knowledge management

MANAGEMENT ISSUES

Knowledge usage requires managers to:

1. Understand why there is a knowing–doing gap in organizations
2. Identify the consequences of not using knowledge
3. Understand the three main theoretical models to ensure effective knowledge usage

Effective knowledge usage involves the following challenges for management:

1. Which knowledge usage model will create most value for my organization?
2. How do I use experience?

LINKS TO OTHER CHAPTERS

Chapter 3: on getting value from knowledge management

Chapter 8: regarding learning in action

Chapter 11: concerning embedding knowledge to become skilful knowers

OPENING MINI CASE STUDY

WINNING THE UNWINNABLE CONSULTING ASSIGNMENT: HOW TO PERSUADE MANAGEMENT THAT THEY NEED TO USE KNOWLEDGE (TAKE ACTION)

Walter Mitty was under pressure to win the assignment on the large US bank. Walter worked for a leading global management consulting firm. The bank was a major client of the firm.

The bank had issued a request for proposal (RFP) to all of the major consulting firms. It required a scope of work with professional fees of about $900,000. It was a very large and important assignment. Walter had been asked to ensure the firm won the assignment.

First, he talked to the partner-in-charge of the firm who was responsible for the bank. She was in charge of the bank's accounting and taxation services. Walter asked her what the bank needed with this assignment. She explained that they wanted change and performance improvement, not diagnostics. He asked whether they would choose the consulting firm for the assignment based on price and whether he should try to compete based on cost. She said that no, price was not the issue.

Second, he contacted the executive in charge of the assignment at the bank. At their meeting, the executive gave Walter four reports from previous assignments completed by other firms. The executive said 'These didn't help us, but they might give you some useful background for your proposal.' Walter thanked the executive and left.

Third, after reading the four previous consulting reports, Walter contacted the consultant in charge of the most recent assignment for the executive at the bank. He explained to the consultant that he wanted to submit a proposal for the bank's latest project. The consultant told Walter that his firm did not intend to submit a proposal this time, but he would be happy to meet for a cup of coffee and share his experience with Walter. At their meeting, the consultant explained what happened.

'When I started that assignment, the executive at the bank you met with also gave me the three previous reports completed by other firms. I read them and I thought they were very good. I put them aside and completed the assignment. Just before I was ready to complete my report, I read the previous reports again. They had benchmarked best practice from around the world, had summarized the most successful training programmes from leading companies, and explained how to implement the recommendations. As our analysis was based on much the same information and ideas, our recommendations were basically the same as the previous studies. Although we could develop a few new ideas, our results were almost a copy of the previous consulting reports. We had done this in isolation and hadn't looked at the reports when doing our work. Yet we had come up with the same solutions. The client already had the information we were about to give them. Understandably, they weren't impressed by our report.'

Walter thanked the consultant. He was now ready to complete his proposal.

Walter sat outside the executive board room waiting his turn to present his proposal to the bank's senior executive team. As each consultant was led into the room to do their pitch, he heard the

(Continued)

(Continued)

executive assistant tell them, 'You have 30 minutes only.' The other firms had teams of people and proposal documents of 100 pages plus. He glanced at some of the presentations as the other consultants nervously flicked through their work while waiting. They were full of flashy graphs, figures, tables, and lots of colour and impact.

When Walter was asked to come into the boardroom, he walked to the front of the room and thanked the executive team for their time. He said, 'I have only one slide.' He put up his slide which listed the recommendations of the four previous consulting assignments completed in the past six years for the bank. All four assignments came to the same conclusions. Walter asked the executive team to look at the slide and asked them, 'Why do you want to pay for the same thing a fifth time?'

Walter got the job.

CASE STUDY QUESTIONS

1. Why do you think the bank had not used any of the four consulting assignment reports prior to Walter?
2. Why did Walter get the job?
3. Do you think Walter will do a good job? Will the bank need to get a sixth firm to do the assignment next year? Why do you feel that way?

INTRODUCTION

The problem of knowledge usage is non-intuitive. Knowledge seems to be everywhere. We are bombarded with information everywhere we turn: on the internet, on television, at work, school and university. Knowledge usage, like creativity (Chapter 5), learning (Chapter 8), and sharing (Chapter 9) seems to be a naturally occurring phenomenon. However, information diffusion does not equate to knowledge usage. Simply making knowledge available does not automatically assure organizational benefits. There has to be a need to do something with this knowledge. Someone has to make a conscious decision to use the knowledge resource. There are many reasons why this does not happen naturally.

CORE CONCEPT: Knowledge usage is the application of knowledge resources to create value for an organization.

In Chapter 1, knowledge was defined as skilful knowing. Chapter 4 explained that knowledge is an idle resource unless it is used to create value. Chapter 5 discussed how knowledge combines with other resources to generate capabilities for the firm. Chapter 11 will show how embedding knowledge into organizational routines and processes improves productivity. A theme of this book is that knowledge is a valuable resource. This value emerges in the act of doing: when employees use their knowledge, the knowledge of others, and their organization's knowledge to perform work for their organization.

This chapter explores why knowledge usage is a problem for organizations. While it is the role of individuals to use knowledge, it is the responsibility of the organization to help make this happen. The chapter provides guidelines for understanding the nature of the problem and possible solutions. A major focus in the chapter is how to learn from experience. Three knowledge management tools will be discussed: peer assists, after action reviews, and retrospects. These explain that knowledge usage involves learning from experience before, during, and after activities. This temporal perspective ensures that we learn from the past, improve the present, and plan for the future. Gorelick et al.'s (2004) knowledge management bridge is used to explore links between knowledge and action.

The chapter concludes with some lessons learned from Massingham and Massingham's (2014) article. If an individual, group, or organization is unsure about whether to act on knowledge, they could use the practical outcomes method to decide. First, they could determine which of the seven organizational problems might be addressed by acting on the knowledge. Second, they could identify the financial and/or non-financial performance indicators which may be affected. This approach might persuade people to use knowledge because they can see the benefits, that is, the practical outcomes, in the form of organizational problems it can solve.

The chapter, therefore, has three main themes: awareness of the problem of knowledge usage, frameworks for learning from experience, and a method for evaluating the value created from using knowledge.

THE KNOWING–DOING GAP

CORE CONCEPT: Knowledge has no value until it is applied (Dove, 1999). The knowing–doing gap is the difference between knowing what to do and not doing it. The gap represents wasted knowledge resources.

Research has estimated that organizations 'waste' between 60% and 80% of knowledge, as it is unused (Schüppel et al., 1998). Dalkir argues that knowledge usage is based on a large and unfounded assumption – that if knowledge is made accessible to knowledge workers (employees) then it will be used (Dalkir, 2011: 184). Dalkir points to Nonaka and Takeuchi's (1995) knowledge creation spiral as evidence that this does not occur. The fourth step in the spiral – internalization – is where knowledge usage fails. Unless the individual internalizes the knowledge, i.e. decides that the knowledge is good, trustworthy, and a better way of doing things, then the knowledge may be available to them but they will not use it.

A major theme in this book is how to ensure employees are skilful knowers. Chapter 5 identifies what employees need to know, now and in the future, and then how best to develop knowledge to fill capability gaps. Chapter 8 looks at how to help employees learn themselves. Chapter 9 explores how they can share their knowledge with others. These chapters focus on helping employees get access to the knowledge they need to create value for their organization via the work they do. Management can take action by understanding what knowledge is useful for which employees and then how best to make that knowledge available to them. However, making knowledge accessible is not enough. Management must ensure that employees are aware of the knowledge made available to them, that they understand how to use it, and that they believe using it will lead to an improvement in their work (Dalkir, 2011: 183).

DEEP THINKING: This chapter assumes that knowledge is available but employees either cannot or will not use it. This problem is bigger than making employees skilful knowers. Knowledge usage assumes they are skilful knowers. The bigger issue is about change: doing things differently with new knowledge.

Organizations spend substantial amounts of money on external resources or internal reviews, to write reports and suggest changes and improvements, many of which are potentially valuable for the organization; however the advice is rarely implemented (Pfeffer and Sutton, 2000). The knowledge usage gap is about doing things differently and using new knowledge to improve performance, at the individual, group, and organizational levels.

The knowing–doing gap occurs for several reasons and the following analysis is based on Pfeffer and Sutton's ideas (2000). The first is talk substituting for action (after 2000: 29–55). Pfeffer and Sutton (2000) are highly critical of higher education, particularly MBA programmes, for rewarding people who are good talkers and presenters. Students who can express an opinion are rewarded with good marks. In the competitive environment of business schools, those who speak loudest seem to be the smartest. This has developed a generation of talkers rather than doers. In the workplace, this has spillover effects. Making decisions and preparing documents and reports are seen as a substitute for action. The diagnosis of problems is rewarded, rather than the provision of solutions. Negative people are seen as smarter because they appear to understand the nature of the problem. Employees compete at meetings by seeking status through jargon (Pfeffer and Sutton, 2000). This develops a poor organizational culture where talking about something is seen as the equivalent of doing something about it.

The second is memory being a substitute for thinking (after Pfeffer and Sutton, 2000: 69–92). While organizational memory can be a very useful source of competitive advantage (see Chapter 5) because it captures 'what works around here', it can also be a major barrier to change. If employees continue doing things the way they have always been done, without reflecting, nothing will change. This assumes that solutions to problems of the past will always be right for today's problems. There is no opportunity for improvement because no one even thinks about what they are doing. Conventional wisdom exerts pressure for consistency. When people are unsure about what to do or just cannot be bothered to learn how to do it, they tend to copy what has been done by others in the past. Strong organizational cultures may also influence people to conform rather than be seen as ineffective or confused. A strong culture (a double-edged sword) can carry expectations of the past about what is or is not possible (Pfeffer and Sutton, 2000). While it is a positive factor for shared mental models (see Chapters 5 and 8), strong culture can also deny change because employees are simply programmed to behave in a somewhat mindless fashion. By not thinking about what they are doing, work becomes so routinized that employees accept norms without questioning.

The third reason is fear preventing us acting on knowledge (after Pfeffer and Sutton, 2000: 109–127). Most people recognize that fear, and its relation, distrust, are negative organizational forces. But the myth of the 'tough boss' still persists. There is a sense that 'tough love' is necessary to get the best out of employees and make the organization perform (2000: 110). Many managers use fear as a deliberate strategy to create anxiety and job insecurity in the workforce, believing this will make employees work harder and be more productive.

THEORY IN PRACTICE: DOWNSIZING

Albert 'Chainsaw' Dunlap was a famous example of creating a fear culture. Pfeffer and Sutton (2000) tell the story of Dunlap presenting to a class of 300 students at a graduate school of business in Chicago where he drew 'big laughs' from describing how much he enjoyed firing a 'morale officer' at one of his organizations. When Dunlap joined Sunbeam as CEO, the share price rose by 49% on the first day. His reputation seemed to be respected by the market. His style of management encouraged staff to avoid delivering him bad news. He only wanted positive information. However, the fear culture has many negatives. It is an incentive for falsification, and therefore breeds a culture of lies and inaccuracy. Employees disengage from change for fear of their jobs. For example, why would employees contribute to business process re-engineering to reduce the workforce when it might lose them their job (Pfeffer and Sutton, 2000)? When Dunlap left Sunbeam two years after joining, the place was 'in tatters' (2000: 110–113).

Fourth is measurement obstructing good judgement (after Pfeffer and Sutton, 2000: 139–160). Many managers focus on short-term financial performance, mainly because both their performance and employment contract depend on quick results. Many organizations have overly complex measures, measuring the wrong things (after Pfeffer and Sutton, 2000). Fifth is when internal competition turns friends into enemies (after 2000: 177–203). Organizations which develop a competitive culture often mistakenly believe that this will make employees work harder and improve performance as they fight one another for resources and opportunities. However, this culture creates several problems. It undermines organizational loyalty, creating high employee turnover due to the competitive individualistic culture; it undermines cooperative behaviours such as knowledge sharing and the spread of best practices because employees identify with their unit instead of the company; and it undermines teamwork because employees hide mistakes to protect incompetence and, therefore, do not share lessons learned (Pfeffer and Sutton, 2000).

Pfeffer and Sutton (2000) provide the following list of solutions for the knowing–doing gap:

1. Why before how: philosophy is important. Why has General Motors found it impossible to imitate Toyota's production system despite 20 years of trying? The company has focused on the how rather than the why. It has tried to copy practices, behaviours, and techniques, rather than the why of general guidance and philosophy (e.g. culture).

2. Knowing comes from doing and teaching others how. You learn as you teach. You also learn by trying yourself. The two go hand in hand. Knowing by doing creates a much deeper level of knowing, and by definition eliminates the knowing–doing gap.

3. Action counts more than elegant plans and concepts. Act, even if you haven't had time for careful planning and analysis – for instance, you don't have all the facts and figures. Use your judgement and intuition, and trust yourself. Without taking some action, learning is more difficult and less efficient as it is not grounded in real experience.

4. There is no doing without mistakes. What is the organization's response? The most important cultural element in an organization of action is: What happens when things go wrong? Will the organization provide a 'soft landing'? Are people afraid of failure? There is no learning without some 'failure'.

5. Fear fosters knowing–doing gaps, so drive out fear. A 'forgiveness framework rather than a fear framework' is necessary (Pfeffer and Sutton, 2000: 254). People need to be encouraged to take risks and be empowered to think; i.e. treating failure to act as the only failure (not unsuccessful actions) encourages leaders to discuss failures and what they have learned from them. Do not punish people for trying new things.

6. Beware of false analogies: fight the competition, not each other. Don't confuse motivation with competition. Don't measure performance against each other. Don't place staff in competition with other staff. Instead, foster

cooperation and collaboration. Get people willing to act together, i.e. hire, reward, and retain parties on their ability and willingness to work cooperatively for the benefit of the organization; focus energy on external threats (not each other).

7. Measure what matters and what can help turn knowledge into action. Keep the strategy simple and have just a few key measures that are routinely tracked. Don't think that if you measure more, more will get done. Organizations also tend to measure the past (lag indicators), such as what happened. This seldom explains why things have happened. Organizations tend to measure processes instead of outcomes. Focus instead on the why, i.e. focus on those things critical to success, and focus on measures that promote learning (process and the means to an end); measurement should close the loop (i.e. ensure the organization acts on what it knows).

8. What leaders do, how they spend their time, and how they allocate resources – these matter. Good leaders don't need to control and command. They need to listen and respond to change. Leaders change things for the better. And the best way to do this is to provide staff with the capacity to know and to do. (After Pfeffer and Sutton, 2000: 246–262)

DEEP THINKING: Pfeffer and Sutton's (2000) list of solutions to the knowing–doing gap have two main themes: (1) cultural change, and (2) action learning.

'Why before how' encourages reflection; 'Beware of false analogies' encourages cooperation; and 'What leaders do' encourages participation. These are positive cultural behaviours suggesting learning (reflection), sharing (cooperation), and empowerment (participation), and that if organizations are to overcome the knowing–doing gap, they should embrace these positive cultural behaviours.

The list also includes several solutions related to taking action. 'Teaching others' suggests a two-way learning process involving both the knower (teacher) and the receiver (student). 'Action counts' argues the need to get on with it even if you do not feel completely confident or competent. Similarly, 'No doing without mistakes' tolerates failure if it allows people to try. 'Drive out fear' similarly encourages risk taking. 'Measure what matters' ensures that people will do what is recognized and rewarded. These ideas suggest that changing people's mindset is important in addressing the knowing–doing gap and its barriers. Mindset seems akin to persuading someone to take their first bungee jump. The aim is to focus the individual on what they are doing (i.e. jumping off a cliff) rather than the negative consequences of the act (i.e. the rope might break!). Doing something even though you feel you do not fully know how to do it (action counts), or you may not do it correctly (mistakes), or you are frightened of the consequences (fear), is necessary because you will learn from the process (teaching) and you will be recognized and rewarded (measure). Figure 7.1 illustrates the knowledge usage mechanisms presented in this chapter.

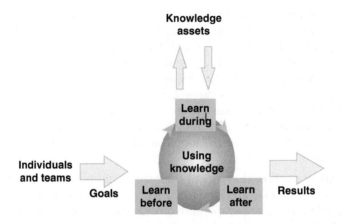

FIGURE 7.1   *Using experience*

Source: Gorelick et al. (2004). Reprinted by permission of the publisher (Taylor & Francis Ltd, www.tandfonline.com).

PEER ASSISTS

Peer assists aim to help people learn from others' experience before they begin a new task or project. The tool is used at the start of the learning cycle.

Employees who do not know what to do at work waste time in two ways:

1. They try to do the new task for themselves and cannot work it out or make mistakes.
2. They search for the necessary information or knowledge without knowing where to look.

In a work environment, it is likely that somebody has done this task before, and it is, therefore, good practice to find what knowledge is available before carrying out any piece of work. This is where peer assist can help. A peer assist is 'a meeting or workshop where other people are invited to share their experience, insights, and knowledge with an employee(s) who has requested some help early on in a piece of work' (Collison and Parcell, 2004: 98). It allows peers to share their experience, both good and bad, and the context that they gained it in, and allows the learner(s) to take what is appropriate and develop a solution. According to Milton (2004: 171), 'people [peers] with experience in similar operations ... share ... with the team to help them devise the optimum ... design'. A peer assist is best used at the initial or planning stages of a task or project (Milton, 2004).

THEORY IN PRACTICE: DOING A PEER ASSIST

Note: this section is adapted from Collison and Parcell (2004).

PLANNING A PEER ASSIST

Collison and Parcell (2004: 103–113) provide a 12-step process for planning a peer assist:

1. *Communicate a clear purpose*: the purpose must be clear and communicated to participants.
2. *Has the problem already been solved?* Search the organization's knowledge base to identify what others have already learned.
3. *Get an external facilitator*: the role of the facilitator is to manage the process to reach the desired outcome.
4. *Timing is important*: schedule a date early enough to be able to deliver the outcome.
5. *Select participants*: with a diversity of skills, competencies, and experience necessary.
6. *Be clear about the deliverables*: the desired deliverables should be options and insights rather than answers. The person who asked for assistance should decide on actions. Be prepared to have the objectives reframed.
7. *Ensure that the team socialize*: create opportunities for the team to get to know one another via a social event (dinner), or time to talk together prior to the peer assist. (After Collison and Parcell, 2004: 103–108)

CONDUCTING A PEER ASSIST

8. *Define the purpose and lay the ground rules*: explain the peer assist objectives, deliverables, and importance. Focus on the activity rather than the person.
9. *Start by sharing information and context*: the host team should present the context, history, current status, identified risks and issues, and plans for the future. Give the visiting team opportunity to present their experience and understanding of details and issues: visitors advise the host team on what they are doing well and therefore should continue doing, what the host team should start doing and why, and what the host team should stop doing and why.
10. *Encourage the visitors to ask questions and give feedback*: provide analysis and feedback. Reflect on whether further information is required, such as by talking with others outside the host team, before providing advice. The visitors do not have to solve the problem but they should offer insights and options based on their unique experience. (After Collison and Parcell, 2004: 110–111)

(Continued)

(Continued)

FOLLOWING UP A PEER ASSIST

11. *Analyse what you have heard*: reflect on the lessons learned and adapt this to the local context. Share the outcomes with a wider host team group to disseminate the findings.
12. *Present the feedback and agree on actions*: reflect on the outcomes and whether they meet the desired deliverables. Enable both the host and visiting teams to give feedback on the outcomes. Reflect on the process of the peer assist and whether it may be improved next time. Codify the outcomes in a report and share with others. (After Collison and Parcell, 2004: 112–113)

AFTER ACTION REVIEWS

After action reviews (AARs) aim to help people learn from others' experience *during* a new task or project. AARs are defined as 'a professional discussion of an event focused on performance standards that enables participants to discover for themselves what happened, why it happened, and how to sustain strengths and improve on weaknesses' (Senge et al., 2005: 473). AARs occur in the middle of the learning cycle. They create value for the organization by improving performance when it needs to occur, not afterwards. Unlike typical project reviews or post-mortems (this is the third technique – retrospects), 'you do not need to wait until the patient is dead to figure out what went wrong' (Baird et al., 2000: 187). By taking time to reflect on what is happening during a major task or project, participants can recognize problems and correct performance, perhaps adopting a different approach. This avoids continuing with ineffective methods or poor performance and taking action to change them. In this way, AAR embraces the fundamental principles of the learning organization, i.e. learning from experience (e.g. see Senge, 1990).

AAR discussion always revolves around four key questions:

1. What was supposed to happen?
2. What actually happened?
3. Why were there differences between 1 and 2?
4. What can we learn from 3? (After Collison and Parcell, 2004: 134)

The US Army's insistence that 25% of every AAR be devoted to determining the facts (questions 1 and 2) is a critical insight into the benefits of taking the time upfront to clarify goals and targets and set unambiguous standards (Garvin, 2000).

THEORY IN PRACTICE: DOING AN AFTER ACTION REVIEW

Note: this section is adapted from Collison and Parcell (2004: 135–140).

PLANNING AN AFTER ACTION REVIEW

1. *Hold the AAR immediately*: all of the participants are still available and their memories are fresh. Learning can be applied right away.
2. *Create the right climate*: a climate of openness and commitment to learning is required. AARs are events rather than critiques, and should not be treated as a personal evaluation. Everyone at the event participates and everyone is on an equal footing. Participants have earned their right to comment by being part of the action.
3. *Appoint a facilitator*: the facilitator is not there to have the answers but to help the team learn the answers. They may be required to set a climate of openness and honesty, to guide discussion, and to keep the group focused. The role of facilitator is best left to those with least at stake. (After Collison and Parcell, 2004: 135–137)

CONDUCTING AN AFTER ACTION REVIEW

4. *Ask 'What was supposed to happen?'* The facilitator should start by dividing the event into discrete activities, each of which had (or should have had) an identifiable objective and plan of action.
5. *Ask 'What actually happened?'* This means that the team must understand and agree the facts about what happened. Remember, though, that the aim is to identify a problem, not a culprit.
6. *Ask 'Why did it happen?'* Compare the plan with reality. The real learning begins as the team of teams compares the plan to what actually happened in reality and determines 'Why were there differences?' Identify and discuss successes and shortfalls. (After Collison and Parcell, 2004: 137–139)

FOLLOWING UP AN AFTER ACTION REVIEW

7. *Recording an AAR* provides the basis for broader learning in the organization. Benefits of the AAR come from applying its results to future situations. AARs generate summaries of learning points. By identifying actionable recommendations, the AAR defines steps for improvement. (After Collison and Parcell, 2004: 139)

RETROSPECTS

A retrospect is simply a meeting called immediately after the completion of a significant piece of work (Milton, 2004). It 'focuses on what has been learned', and 'uses a structured process to draw out lessons' for other teams in the future

(2004: 171). It is a way of transferring lessons immediately to the next similar activity as it is about to start. In many ways, its structure resembles that of an AAR; however a retrospect is much more in-depth (Collison and Parcell, 2004). AARs are meant to be quick reflections on what is happening. Retrospects are complete reviews about what has happened.

Retrospects aim to help people learn from others' experience *after* a new task or project is finished. The tool is used at the end of the learning cycle. It creates value for the organization by improving performance for the next time something needs to occur. Learning on task completion recognizes that most of our activities are not one-off events. By taking time to reflect on what happened after a major task or project has been completed, participants learn what needs to be done differently, so it may be done better next time.

THEORY IN PRACTICE: DOING A RETROSPECT

Note: this section is adapted from Collison and Parcell (2004: 149–164).

PLANNING A RETROSPECT

1. *Call the meeting*: hold a face-to-face meeting as soon as you can after the activity ends (within weeks rather than months). The meeting itself can take up to half a day. A general rule of thumb is to multiply the number of people on the team by 20–30 minutes depending on the complexity of the activity.
2. *Invite the right people*: the project leader and key team members should be involved. It is also useful to invite people from a new, similar project that is about to start, as the learning may be shared quickly and efficiently. (After Collison and Parcell, 2004: 150–153)

CONDUCTING A RETROSPECT

3. Ensure the retrospect report is available on the firm's intranet, with appropriate signposting to ensure employees can access it, and contact employees who do similar work to inform them that the retrospect is available.
4. Revisit the deliverables and objectives of the project. Ask: What were we trying to do? What did we achieve? Also ask the customer or sponsor whether they got what they wanted.
5. Go through the project step by step: asses the project plan; look for deviations and points in the work flow where things could be improved next time.
6. Ask, what went well? Start positively: What emerged as good practice? What will help avoid mistakes in the future?
7. Find out why these aspects went well and express the learning as advice for the future: deal with experience rather than opinions (facts rather than feelings) and look for specific, repeatable advice.

8. Ask, what could have gone better? Be reflective, use personal disclosure, be aspirational. Even success can be improved on. (After Collison and Parcell, 2004: 153–160)

FOLLOWING UP A RETROSPECT

9. Ensure that the participants leave the meeting with their feelings acknowledged. Ensure that there are no issues left unexplored, and encourage people to rate the project process and discuss any residual improvement areas.
10. Record the meeting: ensure the retrospect report is available on the firm's intranet, with appropriate signposting to ensure employees can access it, and contact employees who do similar work to inform them that the retrospect is available. (After Collison and Parcell, 2004: 160–164)

DEEP THINKING: There is a weakness in reflection in action. Too much can be akin to navel gazing. The new focus on learning from experience has meant that management is often trying to meet the needs of the past but never catching up with the future. The solution is to balance reflection with action. Balance comes from knowing what matters in terms of learning while doing. Not all tasks require a peer assist, an after action review, or a retrospect. A good rule of thumb is the Pareto principle: if the organization conducts reflection in action for 20% of its most important work activity, this may create 80% value from knowledge usage.

THE KNOWLEDGE MANAGEMENT BRIDGE

Chapter 8 examines how employees learn from doing. Learning from action is contrasted with action learning to explain how it is more effective to introduce learning into performance (train staff at the act of doing) than performance into learning (better staff training). The idea is that employees need knowledge at the moment of doing if they are to become skilful knowers and create maximum value for their organization.

Gorelick et al. (2004) developed a framework for increasing performance from learning, which they called the knowledge management (KM) bridge. The bridge is conceptualized as a link between knowledge providers (knowers) and knowledge seekers (learners). These two groups are seen as separate 'islands' within an organization. The KM bridge provides a way for easy movement across these islands. The bridge connects knowers and learners by allowing knowledge to flow between them. Problems may emerge if people see only one way of knowledge flowing from knowers to others and they cannot see the two-way flow.

The two knowledge flows may be explained as follows:

1. Utilization: flow from the knower to the learner. This is about taking action. It connects the knower and the learner and allows the knowledge to be shared in the act of doing.
2. Learning: flow from the learner to the knower. This is about feedback. It can involve feedback on both the process and the content of the knowledge flow, from the learner's perspective. This feedback may allow the knower to improve the process (how the knowledge was shared) and the content (the knowledge itself). (After Gorelick et al., 2004)

At face value, the KM bridge seems to be a knowledge sharing framework, rather than a knowledge usage framework. It seems to describe the process of sharing knowledge between a knower and a learner, with the addition of a feedback loop. However, it is more than that. Its relevance to knowledge usage is found in its relationship to organizational change to bring about improved performance. This occurs through action learning. The KM bridge facilitates the flow of knowledge directly to performance, and combines action and performance to create new learning. In this way, it generates a continuous learning cycle which brings about positive change and improved performance.

Learning from action and action learning are two sides of the same coin. They should co-exist. However, the knowing–doing gap shows that they often do not. The difference between these two frameworks is illustrated by the KM bridge. Action learning is the utilization flow. Learning from action is the learning flow. The key to understanding the difference between them and how knowledge usage should work is a theoretical lens called 'two equations for change'.

To sustain performance improvement and growth, an organization must continuously learn. Ultimately, in a learning organization, performance and learning are so closely intertwined that they are inseparable. This is not current reality in most organizations and teams. Institutionalizing learning is a goal for any change-management function. Historically, individuals and organizations have separated performance and learning.

The first equation is:

Change = Performance + Learning (Gorelick et al., 2004)

This implies that one can exist without the other. According to Gorelick et al. (2004), an example of how this happens is provided by a case of racial discrimination at work. An individual lodges a claim of discrimination. Management investigates and finds the claim to be true. In response, management arranges for a new policy to be written, including a clear statement that such behaviour will not be tolerated. The policy is distributed to all staff. There are no cases of racial discrimination lodged for the next three years. It appears successful. Staff have learned about racial discrimination and why it is inappropriate behaviour. Performance has improved because this behaviour has stopped. The example is one of positive change.

However, Gorelick et al. (2004) provide an illustration of what happens when a new case of racial discrimination suddenly emerges. Management is asked, 'Why has this happened?' It occurred because the learning was not institutionalized. The change programme only really addressed performance in the first equation. To embed learning, the organization needed to introduce a mandatory staff training programme on racial discrimination. By issuing the information via policy, the responsibility was placed on staff to read, interpret, and learn from the policy. The fact that the problem re-emerged was evidence that not all staff took this opportunity.

When learning is essential to the desired change, the equation becomes:

Change = Performance × Learning (Gorelick et al., 2004)

If either performance or learning does not take place, there is no sustainable change (Gorelick et al., 2004: 44). The problem will reoccur. As a result, organizations have tried to introduce performance in learning. This happens through improved staff training. To understand this, consider how individuals learn at work and how organizations try to train staff. Trainers try to get real issues into the learning process, use real case studies, bring organizational problems into the training room, give work-related assignments, and increasingly go online with learning (Gorelick et al., 2004). While this improves training, it has limited impact. Consider the last time you attended staff training. How much of it did you use the next day at work?

To achieve sustained performance improvement and create value from knowledge usage, learning should be taken out of the classroom and into the workplace. Rather than bringing learners to the knower (staff attend a staff training workshop), the answer is to bring the knower to the learner. This happens when the knower visits the learner in their work environment and helps them learn when they most need it, i.e. to improve their actual work activity. This achieves the second equation. The most important concept underlying the second equation is immediacy. To truly create value from knowledge usage, learners need knowledge at the moment they need to use it. The challenge for an organization's knowledge management is to stimulate performance and enable correct action by getting the right knowledge to the right people at the right time (Gorelick et al., 2004: 42).

This makes the KM bridge more than a feedback loop. It is triple-loop learning (see Torbet, 1994). Whereas double-loop learning requires the employee to challenge the underlying assumptions about the work they are doing, triple-loop learning improves the process of learning itself. The KM bridge implements triple-loop learning by closing the feedback loop. Implementing the KM bridge requires learning before, learning during, and learning after (Gorelick et al., 2004: 50).

PRACTICAL OUTCOMES

Knowledge usage will increase if management and employees perceive value in taking action to use new knowledge. While the usage mechanisms (e.g. peer assists) make experience available to employees, and the KM bridge provides a system which will encourage employees to use new knowledge, they still need to be persuaded to take action. They need to see that their existing knowledge, knowledge that has enabled them to become a skilful knower, should be replaced by other knowledge. Whether accessing codified knowledge such as a retrospect report, or tacit knowledge such as a peer assist, the employee must be convinced to then use that new knowledge to supplement or even replace what they already know. The knowing–doing gap showed us that this is a difficult challenge for many people and explains why it is estimated that 80% of knowledge in organizations is unused. The problem is bigger than management not using consultant reports (see the opening mini case study) or employees returning from staff training courses and not using what they have learned. The main knowledge usage problem is that employees will not use the knowledge their organization makes available to them. The practical outcomes framework presents a way to persuade employees to use new knowledge and for managers to take action to ensure they do so.

CORE CONCEPT: It is important to persuade people to use new knowledge. First, at a philosophical level, if employees are to see the value in using new knowledge, they need to see personal gain. Second, at a pragmatic level, if management is to take the action necessary to improve knowledge usage, they must be persuaded that there is organizational gain.

Personal gain in using new knowledge may be found in the seven organizational problems identified by Massingham and Massingham (2014):

1. New staff
2. Young staff
3. Capability gap
4. Slow task completion
5. Work outputs not used (i.e. waste)
6. Resource cuts
7. Low productivity.

PERSONAL GAIN

Having high proportions of new staff is caused by high employee turnover. The more time new staff spend on becoming fully competent, the more at risk they are of performing unsatisfactorily and of losing their job, and the more pressure is exerted on existing staff to take up the slack. It is in the interests of both new and existing staff to get these new staff using the knowledge provided by their organization.

Having high proportions of young staff is also caused by losing experienced staff. Inexperienced staff may not be trusted to do complex work even if their job requires it. Retrospects are one way experienced staff can share knowledge with inexperienced staff. Both groups should recognize that enabling inexperienced staff to do the work they were hired to do will lead to higher job satisfaction.

The capability gap is the gulf between the capability of the staff member and the organization's job requirements. It may cause significant customer dissatisfaction in terms of mistakes and other poor quality work. Both competent and incompetent staff would recognize that giving incompetent staff new knowledge to supplement or replace their existing knowledge would reduce the risk of losing customers and, ultimately, their jobs.

Slow task completion is caused by unsatisfactory connectivity. Poor connectivity creates waste points in knowledge flows across the organization (see Chapter 11). After action reviews are a way to build connectivity and increase staff social capital. Both connected and disconnected staff would recognize the benefits in removing these waste points, improving job satisfaction for the disconnected, and improving workflow for the connected.

Work outputs not being used is caused by unsatisfactory risk management. If the organization cannot explain the quality of its work outputs to its customers, i.e. the users of its knowledge-based products and services, two critical problems emerge: customer dissatisfaction and low staff morale. The KM bridge would provide systems support to improve corporate governance. All staff would recognize the importance of improved risk management, particularly as it would ultimately protect their jobs and increase job satisfaction.

Resource cuts are caused by unsatisfactory value management. This means that the organization is not able to explain how it creates value. Value management is a system issue, so the KM bridge would be helpful here. All staff would feel the effects of these cuts in terms of job security, increased work pressure to maintain work outputs with fewer staff, fewer career development opportunities, and other, indirect impacts in terms of a reduced staff training budget. Therefore, it is in the interests of all staff to improve value management.

Low productivity is caused by an unsatisfactory psychological contract. This means low morale. The knowledge usage mechanisms (e.g. peer assists) will address reciprocity, work meaning and purpose, and insiderness by giving unhappy staff a sense that their organization cares for them, sees them as valuable, and gives them opportunities to build internal and external respect and reputation. All staff would embrace these concepts.

ORGANIZATIONAL GAIN

There is a wide range of financial metrics that may be used to assess the organizational gain from using new knowledge. They include return-on-investment (ROI), cost–benefit analysis, and value appropriation (see Massingham and Massingham, 2014). These measures are commonly used in financial reports which assess performance as well as investment. They are particularly useful for evaluating the use of capital from a forward-thinking perspective (Langfield-Smith et al., 2012).

There is also a wide range of non-financial metrics that may be used to assess the organizational gain from using new knowledge. They include market share, employee turnover, and customer satisfaction (e.g. see Tiwana, 2001). These measures cannot be directly incorporated into ROI analysis. Qualitative benefits are assumed but not measured, mainly because they cannot be done reliably. For example, action to increase new knowledge usage may produce better decision making but this is difficult to measure objectively. The non-financial criteria used to assess the organizational gain from using new knowledge are:

1. Corporate governance
2. Benchmarking
3. Performance drivers
4. Problem solving.

This framework may be used to persuade managers and employees that using new knowledge creates organizational and personal gain. This should improve knowledge usage as people see the value to be gained from using knowledge to take action. (For further information, see Massingham and Massingham, 2014.)

REFLECTIVE THINKING

In this chapter, the approach to knowledge usage has three steps:

1. Raise awareness of the problem (knowing–doing gap)
2. Address the problem (action learning)
3. Commit to action (practical outcomes).

The approach is based on the definition of knowledge management adopted by this book – that knowledge only creates value through action. The central premise of the approach to knowledge usage is to increase the value of knowledge fundamentally by introducing learning into performance. The focus on the action learning tools – peer assists, after action reviews, and retrospects – is designed to bring knowledge to the user (learner) when they need it and to share relevant knowledge.

However, there are alternate views on knowledge usage. Dalkir (2011) has an excellent chapter on knowledge usage in his book, *Knowledge Management in Theory and Practice*. In this chapter, Dalkir presents three fundamental concepts:

1. *The individual*: their learning style and motivation. Dalkir uses profiling to identify how people like to work and learn. In terms of knowledge usage, the most interesting idea is that some people prefer to talk to others, while some prefer to read. This allows profiling in terms of tacit knowledge and

codified knowledge. For social individuals, access to tacit knowledge is the solution, for example communities of practice. For readers, access to codified knowledge is critical, such as semantics, or content management. On motivation, Dalkir proposes a dynamic profiling system including a behaviour model based on Bloom's taxonomy of cognitive domains. This is helpful in identifying how an individual makes decisions related to internalization: Is this knowledge good? Will it help me? Is it better than what I already know? Dalkir calls this the 'psychomotor domain' which allows for a user profile that management may use to ensure users (learners) have access to tacit or codified knowledge, depending on their preferred learning style and motivation. In this book, this approach is called psychometric analysis, and it is included in Chapter 9 as part of the knowledge sharing system.

2. *The task*: this involves modelling the work activity associated with the user's (learner's) needs. Dalkir gives examples of how to do task analysis, using shoelaces as an illustration. The distinction between beginners and experienced individuals is a good point. It highlights how users (learners) differ in terms of their knowledge of the domain they want to use, and this needs to be taken into account in respect of both the task modelling and the knowledge transfer to the user. Dalkir presents some interesting ideas on improving the accessibility of codified knowledge. These ideas focus on providing system and task support electronically via standard operating procedures or content management tools. This topic includes information system design and KM organizational architecture from an information technology perspective.

3. *The group*: this involves the concept of knowledge reuse and the social context of knowledge sharing. Dalkir presents frameworks for understanding the work context when knowledge is used in social settings. This topic is examined in this chapter in terms of action learning. (After Dalkir, 2011)

Becerra-Fernandez and Sabherwal (2010) present further textbook coverage of knowledge usage (which they call knowledge application). In their chapter, they cover the topic from an information systems perspective, including technologies for applying knowledge, types of knowledge application systems, and their implementation.

KNOWLEDGE USAGE FRAMEWORK

Figure 7.2 summarizes the knowledge usage framework presented in this chapter. It shows that creating from knowledge involves two activities: skilful knowing and applying new knowledge. On the left-hand side of the figure is skilful knowing. This begins by identifying what the learner – the employee, group, or organization – needs to know and whether they know it. Addressing the

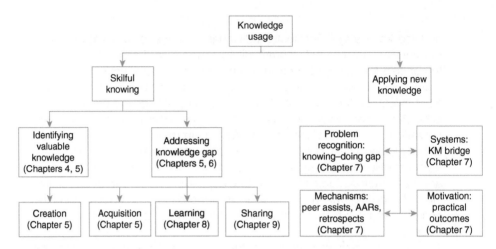

FIGURE 7.2   *Creating value from knowledge framework*

knowledge gap involves four ways to help the learner become a skilful knower. Skilful knowing ensures the employee knows what to do at the act of doing. This creates efficiency and effectiveness in the work process. The first part of knowledge usage, therefore, is ensuring people have the knowledge they need to create value for their organization when doing work.

On the right-hand side of the figure is applying new knowledge. This is the focus of Chapter 7. It involves problem recognition, usage mechanisms, enabling systems, and motivation. Problem recognition is raising awareness of the knowing–doing gap. It explains that new knowledge is available which might help the employee do their job differently. This new knowledge may be codified or tacit knowledge. Codified knowledge includes databases, policies, procedures, reports, and other organizational knowledge which employees might access via information technology systems. Tacit knowledge is experience which is available to the employee. At this point, we can distinguish between skilful knowing and applying new knowledge. Skilful knowing is the process of ensuring the employee knows what they need to in the act of doing work. Applying new knowledge encourages employees to use knowledge they do not normally use. The knowing–doing gap explains that once employees reach competence, or a sense that they are skilful knowers, they tend to reach a state of stability. Their knowledge is useful and their application of it becomes routinized. The employee becomes more efficient, meaning they can do the work quicker, and more effective, meaning they make fewer mistakes and produce more output. The work also becomes easier as there is less thinking time and the knowledge becomes increasingly subsidiary (i.e. subconscious). This is the stage employees reach after progressing through the left-hand side of Figure 7.2. However, knowledge usage also involves change. If we did work the same, all of the time, forever, there would not be any opportunity to improve performance. The right-hand side of Figure 7.2 asks employees to look beyond what they know as skilful knowers and consider what others know, and then to use that new knowledge to improve the way they do work. Skilful knowing is single-loop learning – doing things right. Applying new knowledge is double-loop learning – are we doing the right things? Triple-loop learning is feedback on the lessons learned from reflection in action so we can continue to improve.

The knowledge usage mechanisms – peer assists, after action reviews, and retrospects – provide the tools to learn from others' experience. They are different from knowledge sharing (see Chapter 9) because of the theory of learning in action. These mechanisms share experience before, during, and after the work activity, providing the opportunity to reflect on, learn from, and improve the new knowledge. The process of reflection on learning in action provides the mechanism for knowledge usage. The employee only gains access to experience in the act of doing, therefore they must use the knowledge. Hence, knowledge usage mechanisms encourage knowledge usage.

Figure 7.3 summarizes the results in terms of a scorecard rating for each knowledge usage technique tested at the case study organization (see closing case study). It represents the ratings for each tool against a set of criteria designed to cover the evaluation framework (see Massingham and Massingham, 2014).

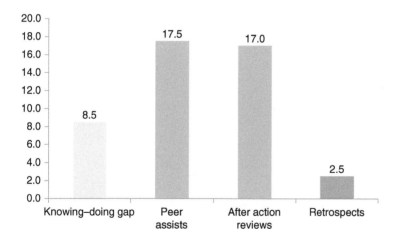

FIGURE 7.3 *Knowledge usage scorecard*

Figure 7.3 shows that, overall, the knowledge usage tools with the most success were peer assists and after action reviews. The two least successful tools were the knowing–doing gap and retrospects. In terms of comparison with all KM tools implemented at the case study organization, two of the knowledge usage tools – peer assists and after action reviews – were ranked second and third highest rating tools overall.

The enabling systems are provided by the KM bridge. The KM bridge may appear to be another learning feedback loop (e.g. see Chapter 8) but it is not. It is used in this chapter as a system supporting knowledge usage because it provides a process to address the knowing–doing gap (the four right-hand-side boxes in Figure 7.2); it provides opportunity for improving both the content (the new knowledge) and the process (sharing experience); and it addresses the accessibility of codified knowledge (structuring) and motivation (sensemaking).

Finally, the practical outcomes are used to address motivation. Massingham and Massingham's (2014) practical outcomes article was about ways that knowledge management (KM) can demonstrate practical value for organizations. It presented seven practical outcomes of KM as methods to persuade managers to invest in it. Its main focus in this book is in Chapter 3, to evaluate the performance of KM. It is also included in this chapter to help employees and managers evaluate the benefit of knowledge usage. A common theme in the knowing–doing gap is resistance to change. Employees who become skilful knowers may become satisfied with the way they do work and not want to do things differently. They require motivation, a reason for change, before they are willing to apply new knowledge. The practical outcomes framework gives them a business case for new knowledge. The first step is to evaluate whether using new knowledge will address any of the seven practical outcomes. The second step is to demonstrate personal and/or organizational gain from the financial and non-financial performance criteria.

CONCLUSION

This chapter has shown the importance of knowledge usage. Knowledge is the most valuable resource (see Chapters 4 and 5). It creates value in the act of doing. This chapter has presented a dichotomy of knowledge usage. Figure 7.4 illustrated that employees create value for their organization in two ways. First, the left-hand side of the figure examines how employees become skilful knowers. This enables them to become competent at their job, and they create value by using their knowledge to perform work expected by their organization. Until they reach competence, they have a knowledge gap, and while they still create value while doing work, it is not what is expected. Once they reach competence, they can create the expected value. Therefore, the left-hand side of Figure 7.2 covers how employees reach a level where both they and their organization feel comfortable about their knowledge and how they use it to create value. This is explained in Chapters 4, 5, 8 and 9.

This chapter explored the right-hand side of Figure 7.2 and how employees may create value from using new knowledge. The knowing–doing gap showed why an estimated 80% of knowledge is not used by many organizations (Schüppel et al., 1998). This means that much of the codified and tacit knowledge available to employees is being wasted. The experience gathered in terms of organizational memory, best practice, and lessons learned is not being used. Knowledge usage creates value through change and improved business performance. The chapter discussed mechanisms to enable employees to create, share, and access experience: peer assists, after action reviews, and retrospects. These enable employees to learn new knowledge before, during, and after an activity. The difference between these mechanisms and other frameworks in this book (e.g. learning in action in Chapter 8) is the opportunity to reflect on and change the way things are being done. This separation from existing knowledge and the current way of doing things is the difference between the left-hand side and right-hand side of Figure 7.2. The KM bridge provides a system to enable the mechanisms to become embedded organizational behaviour, with access to codified knowledge (structuring) and tacit knowledge (sensemaking). Practical outcomes were used to determine the personal and organizational gain for employees and managers, in order to persuade them of the benefits in using new knowledge.

CLOSING CASE STUDY: KNOWLEDGE USAGE AT THE CSO

Edward Rodgers was walking along a corridor to the office of Stuart Mizelli. Edward was a mechanical engineer at the case study organization (CSO). Stuart was a captain. He worked in an organization called the Ship Repair Office (SRO). The SRO was part of the federal government department which also included the CSO. Stuart was a customer of the CSO in the sense that the SRO used CSO staff for technical advice related to its work.

The CSO specified the technical standards necessary to design, build, and maintain the ships. The SRO was responsible for managing contractors who did the last part – maintenance. The CSO acted as the technical regulator. It worked with other parts of the department to ensure that ships were built, designed, and maintained according to the standards. The standards were specified in a large set of knowledge repositories which we will call the operational requirement set (ORS). The ORS represented the CSO's collective wisdom. It was the codified organizational memory. It defined the material requirements for the public assets the CSO managed on behalf of the federal government. For example, if the customer was constructing a new office block, the ORS would specify how many lights were required in each office, the type of air conditioning, the furnishings, the security for the information technology system, and so on.

The ORS involved a total of 128 documents. Together, the 128 documents specified exactly what customers should do when building an office (for example). The aim of the documents was to ensure that customers met operational requirements by designing, building, and maintaining the public assets to specification. Any deviation from the specification represented a risk. For example, a building that did not follow the specifications of the ORS might not be structurally sound. The consequences are that it might collapse and lives would be lost. The ORS represented effective risk management.

Each of the 128 documents was owned by a subject matter expert (SME). The document represented the SME's lifetime experience and knowledge of the topic area. Their job was to write and then maintain their ORS. The topic area within their ORS document(s) was their lifetime passion. The CSO had invested considerable funds in the development of the ORS. The ORS represented about eight years of development, i.e. CSO staff had been working on the documents for up to eight years to get them to the state of maturity where the CSO could tell customers they must follow them. This represented an investment of about AU$30 million in staff salaries.

(Continued)

(Continued)

Edward was nervous as he walked towards Stuart's office. He knew it would be a difficult meeting. After civilities, the men began discussing business. Edward asked why the SRO was not following the technical specification regarding structural impact. Edward was the SME in charge of several ORSs related to structural impact. Stuart explained that he was not using the ORSs at all. Instead, he had engaged external consultants to write new specifications, replacing the ORS. Edward asked why he was ignoring the CSO's technical advice. Stuart replied: 'The problem with the ORSs is the technical content itself. It lacks currency. There are unclear interrelationships, as well as usability issues such as structure and applicability.'

When Edward objected, the discussion became heated. Stuart described the ORSs as 'useless' and a 'waste of time'. Edward asked Stuart why he felt that way. He replied:

The ORSs are outdated and potentially designed to address issues that may no longer exist. The technology is moving faster than the ORS. They are very slow to be revised; while this might be due to your resourcing issues, it doesn't help us. Many ORSs just repeat other standards without adding any additional value.

Edward considered this response and then said: 'The ORSs capture our corporate memory. They provide lessons learned.' Stuart replied:

But it is no longer relevant. Some situations, for example suffering impact damage, have not occurred for decades, so we no longer need that skill. Plus, we have really lost it anyway because no one knows about it and we don't use it. Why tell us to follow a specification like that?

Edward replied: 'That is the value of the ORS. It is only because it is captured in the ORS that we retain some knowledge of those standards. Something that happened 20 years ago has not been forgotten.'

Stuart argued: 'But if we followed those old rules, people would now term a solution "over designed" and unnecessary, as well as being expensive.'

Edward countered: 'The ORS argues against the softer option; it provides the relevant history as to why it was designed that way. It is better to over-design than under-design and lose lives.'

Stuart changed tack: 'There are conflicts in the documents. We can't trust them. Some ORSs refer to the same requirement; however, the actual requirement (e.g. acceptable level of performance) is different within these documents. It is ambiguous.'

Edward realized this was a critical point in the discussion. It was criticism of product quality from a customer. As the regulator of technical risk, their product's integrity could not survive this type of attack. He tried to explain that the technical regulatory system covered these problems: 'The ORSs provide guidance in terms of system and subsystem source selection. The ORS becomes a contract and specification, and at the end we test it and make sure that is what the department got.'

Stuart went on the attack again:

The ORSs do not highlight interrelationships. There is no cross-referencing or linkages between the ORS documents, so we can't understand the linkages. We do not know which requirements rely on other requirements. As a result, when we drop a requirement, the impact on other requirements is not known.

Edward felt outmatched. He concluded by saying:

> The ORSs provide a useful starting point. They provide a baseline of where to start, so that you do not have to start at the beginning every time. I accept they may not be your end point (i.e. certification basis). Would you please consider using the structural impact ORSs?

'No', replied Stuart.

As Edward walked back to his office, he felt very depressed. These types of meetings were very unpleasant. He felt he should not have to argue with people to use his work. He did not like conflict. He felt unappreciated. He felt his knowledge wasn't valued. He felt that the years he spent on his ORSs were a waste of time. He felt his work had little purpose or meaning. As he walked into his boss's office to report on his meeting with Stuart, he wondered what to say.

CASE STUDY QUESTIONS

1. Describe the knowing–doing gap in this case.
2. Why were customers behaving this way?
3. What should Edward say to his boss?
4. What can Edward do to persuade Stuart to use his knowledge, i.e. his ORSs?

REVIEW AND DISCUSSION QUESTIONS

1. Would raising awareness of the knowing–doing gap improve knowledge usage? Why or why not? Which of the Pfeffer and Sutton knowing–doing gap barriers are most important in improving knowledge usage? Would the solutions offered by Pfeffer and Sutton work?

2. How does action learning improve knowledge usage? Explain the phrase 'learning into performance'. How is this different from 'performance into learning'? How does this involve action learning? Which is the better way to improve knowledge usage? Why?

3. Why would persuading managers to invest in knowledge management improve knowledge usage? What practical outcomes from knowledge management are related to improved knowledge usage? How might improved knowledge usage create direct and indirect benefits for the organization?

FURTHER READING

Massingham, P. and Massingham, R. (2014) Does Knowledge Management Produce Practical Outcomes? *Journal of Knowledge Management*, 18 (2): 221–254. This article explains the practical outcomes in more detail.

Pfeffer, J. and Sutton, R.I. (2000) *The Knowing–Doing Gap*, Boston, MA, Harvard Business School Press. This text explains the knowing–doing gap.

BIBLIOGRAPHY

Baird, L., Deacon, S. and Holland, P. (2000) From Action Learning to Learning from Action: Implementing the after action review. Chapter 9 in Cross, R. and Isrealit, S. (eds) *Strategic Learning in a Knowledge Economy*, Oxford, Butterworth-Heinemann, pp. 185–202.

Becerra-Fernandez, I. and Sabherwal, R. (2010) *Knowledge Management: Systems and processes*, Armonk, NY, M.E. Sharpe.

Bloom, B.S., Engelhart, M.D., Furst, E.J., Hill, W.H. and Krathwohl, D.R. (1956) *Taxonomy of educational objectives: The classification of educational goals. Handbook I: Cognitive domain*. New York: David McKay Company.

Collison, C. and Parcell, G. (2004) *Learning to Fly: Practical knowledge management from leading and learning organizations*, Chichester, Capstone Publishing.

Dalkir, K. (2011) *Knowledge Management in Theory and Practice*, 2nd edition, Cambridge, MA, MIT Press.

Day, G.S. and Montgomery, D.B. (1983) Diagnosing the Experience Curve. *Journal of Marketing*, *47* (2): 44–58.

Dove, R. (1999) Knowledge Management, Response Ability, and the Agile Enterprise. *Journal of Knowledge Management*, *3* (1): 18–35.

Garvin, D.A. (2000) *Learning in Action: A guide to putting the learning organization to work*, Boston, MA, Harvard Business School Press.

Gorelick, C., Milton, N. and April, K. (2004) *Performance through Learning: Knowledge management in practice*, Burlington, MA, Elsevier Butterworth-Heinemann.

Langfield-Smith, K., Thorne, H. and Hilton, R. (2012) *Management Accounting: Information for managing and creating value*, 6th edition, London, McGraw-Hill Education.

Massingham, P. and Massingham, R. (2014) Does Knowledge Management Produce Practical Outcomes? *Journal of Knowledge Management*, *18* (2): 221–254.

Milton, N. (2004) Knowledge Management in Business Performance at BP Well Engineering. Chapter 9 in Gorelick, C., Milton, N. and April, K. (eds), *Performance through Learning: Knowledge management in practice*, Burlington, MA, Elsevier Butterworth-Heinemann, pp. 163–180.

Nonaka, I. and Takeuchi, H. (1995) *The Knowledge-creating Company: How Japanese companies create the dynamics of innovation*, New York, Oxford University Press.

Pfeffer, J. and Sutton, R.I. (2000) *The Knowing–Doing Gap: How smart companies turn knowledge into action*, Boston, MA, Harvard Business School Press.

Schüppel, J., Müller-Stewens, G. and Gomez, P. (1998) The Knowledge Spiral. In von Krough, G., Roos, J. and Kleine, D. (eds) *Knowing in Firms: Understanding, managing and measuring knowledge*, London, Sage.

Senge, P.M. (1990) *The Fifth Discipline: The art and practice of the learning organization*, New York, Doubleday Currency.

Senge, P., Kleiner, A., Roberts, C., Ross, R., Roth, G. and Smith, B. (2005) *The Dance of Change: The challenges of sustaining momentum in learning organizations*, London, Nicholas Brealey Publishing.

Tiwana, A. (2001) *The Essential Guide to Knowledge Management: E-business and CRM applications*, Hoboken, NJ, Prentice-Hall.

Torbert, W.R. (1994) Managerial Learning, Organizational Learning: A Potentially Powerful Redundancy, *Management Learning*, 25 (1): 57–70.

8

ORGANIZATIONAL LEARNING AND THE LEARNING ORGANIZATION

CHAPTER OUTLINE

LEARNING OUTCOMES

After completing this chapter, the reader should be able to:

1. Understand the cognitive and behavioural approaches to learning
2. Explain the value of learning for the individual and the organization
3. Discuss how learning leads to skilful knowing
4. Evaluate several theoretical frameworks involving the process of organizational learning
5. Compare organizational learning with the learning organization
6. Define the learning organization and its operationalization
7. Explain the benefits of being a learning organization
8. Evaluate the implementation of the learning organization

MANAGEMENT ISSUES

Organizational learning requires managers to:

1. Identify the strategic value of learning
2. Decide when learning (make decision) is a better decision than knowledge acquisition (buy decision)
3. Get learning into the workplace rather than the training room

Becoming a learning organization involves the following challenges for management:

1. Knowing what the best learning organization model is to use
2. How to implement the learning organization model
3. Integrating the learning organization within knowledge management

LINKS TO OTHER CHAPTERS

Chapter 1: on the process of becoming a skilful knower
Chapter 5: concerning the capability gap and the make decision
Chapter 7: on the value in using knowledge
Chapter 9: regarding knowledge sharing between individuals as part of organizational learning

OPENING MINI CASE STUDY

HOW DID SHAKESPEARE, DA VINCI, AND BRONTË LEARN? WHAT OR HOW THESE GREAT PEOPLE LEARNED – IS IT DIFFERENT FROM US?

Consider the great people of history. Who pops into your head when you think of them? Who do you admire most? You might suggest Cleopatra, Aristotle, William Shakespeare, Leonardo Da Vinci, or Charlotte Brontë, and the list will go on. Let us consider the last three names in this list. How did they learn? Did how they learned differ from how you learned? There are some things you have in common with these great names: like learning to walk, talk, and make it through your teenage years. These are part of being human, and experience of them is something we share with everyone else.

What made Shakespeare, Da Vinci, and Brontë different from us? What did they learn that helped their genius? You might suggest that they had a high IQ or other natural talents. Yet they still had to learn how to think, write, discover, create, and express their talents in ways which made them very unique. Was what they learned different from what we have learned, or was it how they learned, or who they learned with? This mini case study looks briefly at these three individuals and how they may have learned in their formative years.

WILLIAM SHAKESPEARE

Shakespeare was born on 23 April 1564. Before he died in April 1616, he wrote many of the most famous works of literature in the history of humankind. He was born in Stratford-upon-Avon. It was a mediaeval country town with a population of about 1,900 people when Shakespeare was a boy.

Critics or cynics argue that Shakespeare did not write, and indeed could not have written, all his plays himself. They base their argument on the assertion that a boy from rural England could not possibly know enough to write all these plays. This was not really a criticism of his talent as a playwright, rather a reference to the content in his plays. Shakespeare's plays contain references, symbols, and descriptions that seem to require deep local knowledge of geography, history, and social context. For example, *The Merchant of Venice* and *Romeo and Juliet* are two plays that are based in Italy but Shakespeare never travelled to Italy. How could he write so well about a country and a people he never visited?

Scholars have defended Shakespeare from this criticism by arguing that there is evidence from his life which explains his rich narratives. For example, the Forest of Arden was the last remnants of the ancient forest that covered the English midlands. While it was being greatly reduced by housing's demand for timber, even in Shakespeare's teen years, he did walk through the woods, perhaps on the way to visit his future wife, Anne Hathaway, who lived on the outskirts of the forest, at a time when they still held mystery and were seen as a place of concealment and wonder. In *As You Like it* and *A Midsummer Night's Dream*, the forest becomes a symbol of folklore and ancient

(Continued)

(Continued)

memory. Scholars have always been fascinated by Shakespeare's religion at a time when there was substantial tension between Catholics and Protestants. Shakespeare's father was considered a secret Catholic and suffered for it. These conflicts surface in plays like *Hamlet*. Shakespeare's mother came from an upper-middle-class family, the Ardens, and scholars feel she had a powerful influence on his sense of society and on household management, including servants. Shakespeare's childhood street was a busy merchant marketplace with census records showing very large families living closely together. This open-life concept of town life was found in *The Two Gentleman of Verona, The Taming of the Shrew*, and even the Venice of *Othello*.

Shakespeare attended the King's New School where he received a free education as a son of a local alderman. He learned to read and write English at a local petty school, and also had to demonstrate that he was 'fit' to study the Latin tongue and that he was ready to learn the principles of grammar. The school day was strictly controlled and supervised. School began at 7.00 am and continued until 5.00 pm, six days out of seven. The curriculum was based on Latin grammar and rhetoric, through the art of reading, memorizing, and writing. Shakespeare would have spent 30–40 hours a week memorizing and repeating prose and verse in Latin. Scholars suggest that Shakespeare's Latin would rival the knowledge of any undergraduate in Classics at a modern university. He used a text by Lily called *A Short Introduction of Grammar*. Scholars have proved that the way Shakespeare quotes from classical authors is found in passages that he read and memorized from Lily. In later years, he studied the classics, Virgil, Horace, and he most loved the *Metamorphoses* of Ovid. In the final stages of his education, he moved from grammar to oratory and learned the arts of elocution, or creative writing, or what the Elizabethans called rhetoric. He learned to look at both sides of every question, immortalized in the famous line 'To be, or not to be?' He was exposed to plays being regularly performed at school. Two of his schoolmasters, Jenkins and Cottam, were educated at a school famed for teaching through drama, particularly acting. (Adapted from Ackroyd, 2006)

LEONARDO DA VINCI

Da Vinci was born in Anchiano, Italy in 1452 and died in France in 1519. He was an inventor, sculptor, painter, architect, scientist, and musician. He painted the *Mona Lisa*, he invented prototypes of the helicopter, he engineered prototypes for the armoured tank and machine gun, and as a scientist he pioneered the sciences of anatomy, botany, and physics. He has been described as the universal genius.

Da Vinci's mother was a peasant; his father (who was not married to his mother) was a prosperous accountant in Florence. At the age of five, da Vinci was taken to be raised by his grandfather, who was a notary. If the rules at the time had not denied him training because he was classified as a bastard, da Vinci might have become the greatest accountant of all time! He was sent to be an apprentice in the studio of the master sculptor and painter Andrea del Verrocchio (1435–1488). The first work known to be done by da Vinci's hand is the angel and some landscape at the lower left-hand corner of Verrocchio's *Baptism of Christ*.

Da Vinci's talent attracted the attention of Verrocchio's main patron Lorenzo de' Medici, il Magnifico. Da Vinci was introduced to an extraordinary range of intellectuals cultivated by Lorenzo, including philosophers, mathematicians, and artists. As da Vinci continued his apprenticeship, he lived in the Medici home. After six years with Verrocchio, da Vinci was admitted to the Company of St Luke, a guild of apothecaries, physicians, and artists, where he deepened his study of anatomy. His reputation in his late teens and early 20s was as a storyteller, humourist, and musician. He was highly sociable and had a large social network. Soon after, he was involved in a criminal enquiry and was banished from Florence. (Adapted from Gelb, 1998)

CHARLOTTE BRONTË

Brontë was born on 21 April 1816 and died on 31 March 1855. She was the eldest of three sisters who wrote some of the greatest novels in the English language, including *Jane Eyre* (Charlotte), *Wuthering Heights* (Emily), and *The Tenant of Wildfell Hall* (Anne). The girls grew up in a small English village in rural Yorkshire called Haworth. Their mother died when they were young. They were raised by their father, the local reverend, and their aunt who came to live with them when their mother died.

Charlotte attended the Clergy Daughter's School at Cowan Bridge for a period but was unhappy and sickly there and returned home. The school she did attend was typical of small rural schools at the time and had about eight young girls. Another student wrote of her observations of Charlotte:

> She looked like a little old woman, so short sighted that she always appeared to be seeking something … she was very shy and nervous … when a book was given her, she dropped her head over it till her nose nearly touched it … we thought her very ignorant, for she had never learned grammar at all, and very little geography. (Gaskell, 1975: 129)

However, she would later 'confound us by knowing things that were out of our range altogether … she was acquainted with most of the short pieces of poetry that we had to learn by heart, would tell us the authors, the poems they were taken from … and tell us the plot' (Gaskell, 1975: 130). She was an 'indefatigable student' who was 'constantly reading and learning' and who strongly valued education, which was considered 'very unusual in a girl of fifteen' (1975: 132). She had a 'craving for knowledge' (1975: 131).

After her brief time at school, she was largely educated at home. Her father was a graduate of Cambridge. She also took responsibility for teaching her younger sisters. She wrote a letter on 21 July 1832 describing a typical day at the parsonage where she lived with her father and sisters: 'In the morning from nine o'clock till half past twelve, I instruct my sisters, and draw, then we walk till dinner time. After dinner, I sew till tea time, and after tea I either write, read, or do a little fancy work, or draw as I please' (Gaskell, 1975: 143–144). The girls lived like recluses and were 'shy of even familiar faces' (1975: 144). When they walked on the wild moors, they usually did not see another person, and hoped that they would not. As the girls grew into young women, they began crafting

(Continued)

(Continued)

their great works of literature. They did this largely at night where they would sit at their dinner table under lamplight and one would tell the others about their story and its characters and plot, and the others would give feedback. They would take turns pacing the room, sharing their ideas with their sisters, receiving feedback, crafting their work. In this small, isolated room in the middle of nowhere in rural England in the early 1800s, some of the greatest novels ever written were produced by three sisters shut off from the rest of the world. None of them had married, none had even loved, and yet they imagined some of the greatest love stories ever told. All of them died young. (Adapted from Gaskell, 1975)

CASE STUDY QUESTIONS

1. Compare and contrast how Shakespeare, Da Vinci, and Brontë learned.
2. Describe the learning styles of Shakespeare, Da Vinci, and Brontë.
3. Compare your learning style with that of Shakespeare, Da Vinci, and Brontë. Which are you most like?
4. What makes these three great people different from us?

INTRODUCTION

Learning is a naturally occurring phenomenon. Humans are naturally curious. If we do not know how to do something, we want to know how. Know-how involves bridging the gap between what you know and what you need to know. It requires conscious awareness of the gap, willingness to fill that gap, and cognitive processes necessary to combine what you know with new knowledge. The outcome is skilful knowing (see Chapter 1). Learning seems to be part of our DNA. If learning comes naturally, why do we need to manage it?

Learning is an important part of knowledge management. Learning occurs in the process of knowledge creation, knowledge sharing, knowledge acquisition, and knowledge use. Effective knowledge management requires efficient learning. Learning occurs at the individual, group, and organizational levels. Managers may take action at each of these levels to improve organizational learning, bridge the capability gap within the organization's workforce, grow knowledge resources, and improve its knowledge management performance.

CORE CONCEPT: Organizational learning is the process of moving from unskilful knowing to skilful knowing, which may involve individuals, groups, or organizations, depending on the nature of the knowledge required.

This chapter begins by defining organizational learning at the individual, group, and organizational levels. The process of organizational learning is then explored with a focus on the cognitive and behavioural aspects of learning. The way knowledge is combined to achieve skilful knowing is discussed through the theory of absorptive capacity. Action learning is used to differentiate between classroom learning, i.e. staff training, and learning on the job. The main learning frameworks are then introduced as models for managers to consider when choosing to take action about learning gaps. The conventional learning models, such as those of Kolb (1984) and Huber (1991), are contrasted with contemporary models, such as single-, double-, and triple-loop learning (Bell and Morse, 2010).

The second part of the chapter explores the learning organization. It is presented as an aspirational business model referred to as learning organization capacity (LOC). It describes an organization that learns from experience, responds to change, and grows its knowledge resources (Massingham and Diment, 2009). It emerged as a precursor to the knowledge-based view of the firm (Grant, 1996) when the ability of an organization to learn faster than its competitors was the only sustainable source of competitive advantage (de Geus, 1988). It was popularized by Senge (1990) and Garvin (1993). While it has tended to be confused by the knowledge management literature with organizational learning (e.g. see Easterby-Smith and Lyles, 2003), it is a separate concept.

This chapter adopts the view that the LOC model is aspirational but it still has important value for knowledge management, particularly in terms of how to improve organizational learning. The value in the model begins with the influence of systems thinking. This thinking leads to a focus on behaviours designed to create synergy such as teamwork, collaboration, and cooperation. The model is a perfect fit for organizations wanting to develop effective organizational learning. However, the inherent weakness in the LOC model is its implementation. It needs to be translated from abstract concepts, such as the ability to respond to change, to actions that management may take to improve LOC performance. The chapter examines previous research on the measurement of LOC, and concludes with a new model designed to assist organizations in achieving LOC.

WHAT IS LEARNING?

The learning literature is large and multi-disciplinary and, therefore, fails to agree on a common definition of learning. A basis for understanding the diversity of views about learning is presented by the fields of behaviourism and cognitive psychology. Behaviourism is based on stimulus–response models (Gutherie, 1935). Behaviourists believe in consequences. Behaviourism focuses on motivation, particularly extrinsic rewards, involving positive and negative reinforcement. In knowledge management, it is associated with two psychological contract constructs: calculative reward and calculative approval (Massingham, 2016). Both constructs are grounded in psychology's expectancy theory, which explores the connection between work behaviour and consequences (Eisenberger et al., 1990): calculative reward is based on the logic that 'If I work hard, I will be rewarded' and is often called extrinsic rewards, while calculative approval is based on the logic that 'If I work hard, I will be recognised'. Its view of knowledge is deductive and rational. In a training environment, it is teacher-centred learning.

THEORY IN PRACTICE: CALCULATIVE REWARD AND RECOGNITION

Catherine Fryer was meeting with Suzie Ong, who was a member of her staff working in the human resource management department at United. United was a community service organization for the disadvantaged. It was moving towards a corporatization business model due to government deregulation. Catherine had become aware that Suzie was not fully cooperating with the change model introduced by external consultants. The model aimed to introduce positive work behaviours such as teamwork, cooperation, collaboration, and sharing. The consultants were holding training sessions for staff. Suzie had been reported for 'acting out' at a training session and for not attending further sessions.

When Catherine asked Suzie to explain her behaviour, Suzie replied 'I don't agree with the training. I don't believe in it.' During the discussion which followed, Suzie revealed that she was not learning anything from the training workshops. She felt that she had been a role model for positive work behaviours for many years. She was a mentor; she conducted internal seminars to share her knowledge; and she willingly helped staff who did not know what to do. She had particularly helped younger staff by sharing her experience. However, she felt she was not recognized or rewarded for her efforts. She noticed that staff who had not previously demonstrated these behaviours, were now being noticed by management, simply because they were doing what the consultants told them to do. This made Suzie feel angry. Catherine was perplexed: Suzie should be a change agent but she is a roadblock. She wondered how she could turn this situation around.

Cognitive psychology sees learning as changes in states of knowledge (Bruner et al., 1956). It considers motivation as intrinsic, where learners set their own goals and motivate themselves to learn. In knowledge management, it is associated with one psychological contract construct: personal efficacy beliefs (Riggs et al., 1994). This is people's judgements of their capacity to act to attain desired performance – in other words, an individual's confidence in their capacity to do their job. Its view of knowledge is inductive and empirical. In a training environment, it is student-centred learning.

THEORY IN PRACTICE: PERSONAL EFFICACY BELIEFS

Catherine Fryer was talking to Kristo Zeven. Kristo had embraced the training by the consultants and many people had noticed positive changes in his behaviour. Kristo was nearing retirement. Catherine smiled to herself as she walked to his office: 'Who said you can't teach an old dog new tricks?' she thought. Catherine wanted to know why Kristo was so enthusiastic about the training workshops. He explained that the ideas just made sense to him. He had always wanted to build better relationships with people at work but did not know how. He was seen by others as 'prickly' but he felt this was unfair. He wanted to be friendly but he lacked the social skills. He saw the training workshops as an opportunity to learn new skills, but they were also a license to change. While others were changing because of the workshops, he felt people would accept that he could change too, and they would accept his new behaviour. 'It has made me much better at my job', he added. 'I am now leveraging, by sharing the workload, and I get more done.'

Social constructivism sees learning as easier to do by observing and interacting with others (Bandura, 1977). It considers motivation as both intrinsic and extrinsic, in the sense that intrinsic learning goals and motives are determined by learners, and extrinsic rewards are provided by the knowledge community. In knowledge management, it is associated with two social capital constructs: collective efficacy beliefs and collective outcome expectancy (Massingham, 2016). Collective efficacy beliefs measure individuals' assessments of their group's ability to perform job-related behaviours (Reed et al., 2006), whereas collective outcome expectancy measures individuals' perception of whether the group's performance matches organizational expectations (Riggs et al., 1994). Its view of knowledge is inductive and empirical. In a training environment, it is practice-based learning. Social learning proposes that humans learn at work through interaction between behavioural, cognitive, and environmental factors.

THEORY IN PRACTICE: COLLECTIVE EFFICACY BELIEFS

Catherine Fryer was talking to Sarah Paulefont. Sarah was one of the people who reported positive changes in Kristo Zeven's behaviour. Catherine was checking in on Kristo's point about leveraging. Sarah explained that she had noticed her unit's performance had always seemed to lag behind other units. When they had meetings, Kristo often dragged the group down by complaining about management or the way things used to be done better in the 'old days'. Sarah felt her unit should

(Continued)

(Continued)

be doing much better because it contained highly qualified and experienced people, but morale was low. The training workshops had helped the unit surface some of the problems and realize they could achieve synergy from working together. Sarah was happy that she'd learned new skills from the workshops which helped her understand people like Kristo, and she also enjoyed seeing him share his experience with others. She was proud that her unit was now leading the monthly performance reports.

Social networks in the broad sense involve communication, dialogue, and individual or group interaction that enhance and encourage knowledge-related employee activities (Leonard and Sensiper, 1998). Social media is a contemporary method for building and maintaining social networks, and it may be used to facilitate 'the management and externalization of both personal and organizational knowledge' (Razmerita et al., 2016: 1226). Externalization of knowledge, i.e. quadrant 2 of Nonaka and Takeuchi's (1995) model, may occur through videos, pictures, blogs, wikis, answering questions, or ongoing online conversations (Razmerita et al., 2014). By using social media, organizations use 'new forms of interaction, collaboration, and knowledge sharing through leveraging the social, collaborative dimension of social software' (2014: 74).

Enterprise social media is defined as:

> web-based platforms that allow workers to (1) communicate messages with specific co-workers or broadcast messages to everyone in the organization; (2) explicitly indicate or implicitly reveal particular co-workers as communication partners; (3) post, edit, and sort text and files linked to themselves or others; and (4) view the messages, connections, text, and files communicated, posted, edited, and sorted by anyone else in the organization at any time of their choosing. (Leonardi et al., 2013: 2)

Using social media, staff may enhance individual and organizational learning. At an individual level, staff 'can take more time to improve their message through written communication' (Razmerita et al., 2016: 1226) which provides an opportunity to reflect and learn. Social media also allows staff more control over what is perceived because they will be more conscious of how their message represents them in the social media community. This means that they should take more care with what they say, which encourages deeper learning. At an organizational level, social media 'offers the opportunity for communal presentation of individual knowledge' (Razmerita et al., 2016: 1226) which enhances validation of learning as well as its diffusion.

Despite these different views about learning, there are several principles which are widely accepted which we can use as a platform for our definition of learning. These principles are that there are learning modes, learning types, and learning levels. Learning modes are the cognitive, behavioural, and social perspectives outlined above. Learning types are typically seen as single-loop, double-loop, and triple-loop. Learning levels are individual, group, organizational, and inter-organizational.

This produces a typology of organizational learning processes: learning through formal education and training, typically university degrees and staff training courses where learning occurs in a classroom; learning via interventions in workplaces, typically described as action learning where learning occurs during the act of doing; and learning that is embedded in and emerges from day-to-day work activities and employees' reflection on how this work is done, typically viewed as business improvement within the context of change management.

The chapter examines the process of becoming a skilful knower and the context which influences who is learning, how, and why.

SKILFUL KNOWING

Conscious learning requires awareness of the need to know. This means that we become aware that there is a gap between what we know and what we need to know. This contrasts with unconscious learning, which is knowledge we are unaware of. This might include learning to read body language, or developing empathy, or gaining emotional intelligence. While these may be taught in a training session, most people develop these naturally, with varying success, without making a conscious effort to learn them. Our focus is on conscious learning because it may be managed.

CORE CONCEPT: Conscious learning is a cognitive process where the individual becomes aware that they are unskilled at a particular work-related activity. This is called unskilful knowing. When the individual feels confident in their competency to perform the activity, and this is recognized by others, they achieve skilful knowing.

According to Polanyi (1962), knowing involves 'skilful action'. This means that knowledge emerges in the act of doing something. It is only in the act of doing that the individual becomes fully aware of the knowledge necessary to complete the activity. It is at this point that conscious learning occurs.

The process of skilful knowing varies by learning levels. Skilful knowing occurs by the individual in the act of performing tasks within the process. This knowledge is tacit and subjective; knowledge is not separated from the knower. The outcome of skilful knowing is individual know-how. It requires the individual to work out the best solution themselves. This recognizes that there are multiple best solutions and the process enables this multiplicity due to its context-sensitive nature. Skilful knowing occurs by the group in the act of performing tasks within the process. This knowledge is social and tacit and more subjective than objective. Knowledge may or may not be separated from the knower. The outcome of skilful knowing is group know-who; it requires the individual to learn from others. This recognizes that there is more than one best solution but the group is best placed to decide on these solutions. It allows for multiple contexts and multiple expert groups. Skilful knowing occurs by the organization in the act of performing tasks within the process. This knowledge is codified and objective. Knowledge is separated from the knower. The outcome of skilful knowing is organizational know-what. It requires the individual to learn from their organization. This recognizes that there is one best solution and the same process may be applied across any context.

This theory of skilful knowing may be understood by looking at Aakhus's (2007: 3–10) discussion of professional practice and reflective inquiry and his review of Schön (1983). (The discussion which follows is based on Aakhus's interpretation of reflective practice, with reference to the original source where possible. Readers may refer to Schön (1983) for further information.) Aakhus (2007: 3) argues that the nature of work involves 'a sharp divide between theory and practice'. This divide is caused by the idea that professional practice applies technical or discipline knowledge, such as nursing, but does not contribute to it. Aakhus (2007: 3) explains that Schön (1983) sees work as an adaptive process where the individual tries to 'turn given situations into preferred situations' (2007: 3). Aakhus (2007: 3) explains that Schön (1983) felt that rather than follow bureaucratic guidelines, professional practice involves a 'process of problem framing and problem solving based on the practitioner's personal theory of practice' (Schön, 1983). This interpretation by Aakhus appears based on Schön's (1983) discussion of professionals' freedom to determine who shall be allowed to practice (1983: 5), and competing views of professional practice in terms of images of the professional role, the central values of the profession, the relevant knowledge and skills (1983: 17). My view of these ideas is that they emphasize the importance of the individual using their experience to make sense of the work situation. Aakhus (2007: 3) describes how Schön (1983) sees experience as 'artful competence'. In this way, Aakhus explains that Schön (1983) is able to blend theory and practice together, overcoming the sharp divide. Aakhus (2007: 3) interprets Schön's (1983) artful competence as 'handling complexity, instability, and value-conflict when engaging people and problem situations at work'. This interpretation by Aakhus appears based on Schön's (1983) discussion of technical rationality and problem setting (1983: 40), knowing in action (1983: 54), and reflecting in action (1983: 55). My view of these ideas is that professional practice knowledge involves technical knowledge but also judgement.

This discussion of professional practice focuses on individual knowledge because it allows the individual to learn from their experience, i.e. reflect-in-practice, and to apply this to a new work situation. It recognizes that knowledge may be created within a group and produce collective know-how (e.g. Edmondson et al., 2003), and even across and between organizations, producing organizational know-how (e.g. see Reagans and McEvily, 2003). The personalization perspective of knowledge management focuses on how individuals address unskilful knowing within the business processes associated with doing their work.

The personalization view of knowledge management proposes that tacit knowledge may be gained, i.e. the act of skilful knowing, by individuals, groups, or organizations. Tacit individual knowledge (know-how) is the act of learning by doing. Tacit group knowledge (know-*who*) is the act of accessing social capital. Tacit social capital is organizational knowledge found within unique organizational context and work situations. Individuals can only access this knowledge through social interaction with those in the know, i.e. other organizational members who know the corpus of generalizations. Further, individuals will vary in their capacity to access this knowledge. Each individual has only a partial view of knowledge about a particular organizational routine or practice (Newell et al., 2006). Tacit organizational knowledge is integrated across groups and communities. It is often described as structural capital, captured in databases, policies, procedures, and reports.

This discussion presents knowledge as skilful knowing and this occurs at the individual, group, and organizational levels. How the organization manages skilful knowing at these three levels is determined by its knowledge management. This chapter looks at how learning occurs to move the individual from being an unskilful knower to a skilful knower, and then to progress to higher levels of skilful knowing.

ABSORPTIVE CAPACITY

Once the need for conscious learning is accepted, and the gap between unskilful knowing and skilful knowing established, the next cognitive step is to acquire and use new knowledge, to learn and bridge the gap. The concept of absorptive capacity helps explain how this is done. Cohen and Levinthal (1990) introduced absorptive capacity as the firm's ability to value, assimilate, and apply new knowledge. Mowery and Oxley (1995) defined it as a broad set of skills needed to deal with the tacit component of transferred knowledge, and the need to modify this imported knowledge. Kim (1998) defined it as the capacity to learn and solve problems. These definitions all involve an input and output dimension: the input is the ability to acquire and the output is the capacity to use knowledge. Zahra and George (2002) suggested that the firm may create competitive advantage from absorptive capacity by developing dynamic capabilities. They define this as the firm's ability to create and deploy the knowledge necessary to build other organizational capabilities, such as marketing and distribution (Zahra and George, 2002). This approach builds on the three earlier definitions by specifying the output: other organizational capabilities. Further studies suggest that absorptive capacity should be conceptualized as being composed of both employees' ability and motivation (Minbaeva et al., 2003) to transfer knowledge. This focuses on the individual, whereas the earlier studies focus on the organization.

The concept of absorptive capacity has evolved over time. Recent research tends to conceptualize it as a creativity technique rather than a learning framework. Easterby-Smith et al. (2008) define absorptive capacity as the ability to locate new ideas and incorporate them into the business process. The phrase 'new ideas' suggests new knowledge as the input, and the incorporation into processes is the output or how the new idea is used. It seems to be more about business process improvement than skilful knowing. Lane et al. (2006) focus on the knowledge acquisition process, and define absorptive capacity as exploratory learning, transformative learning, and exploitative learning. These descriptors simply refer to knowledge being acquired from external sources, assimilated with existing knowledge, and used to improve performance. The focus on external knowledge positions absorptive capacity within the 'buy' part of the knowledge strategy decision about what to do if there is a capability gap. Proposed outcomes of absorptive capacity such as improved problem solving and diversity are part of knowledge creation rather than organizational learning. In this chapter, learning is positioned as the solution to the 'make' part of that strategic decision, i.e. filling the gap yourself rather than going outside the organization. Absorptive capacity, therefore, is a cognitive process to identify the knowledge necessary to fill the knowledge gap and how to use it, rather than a knowledge acquisition or creation tool.

To clarify this point, I go back to early research which included absorptive capacity as a barrier to knowledge sharing. Researchers examining problems associated with the knowledge source (knower) and the recipient (learner) found motivation, absorptive capacity, and retentive capacity (Szulanski, 1996). Both the sender and the receiver must be willing and able to participate in the knowledge exchange. Absorptive capacity examines the ability to participate in knowledge sharing. If the learner knows too little or too much about a topic in comparison with the knower, they will not be able to learn, or will have nothing to learn from the knower and vice versa.

DEEP THINKING: The role of absorptive capacity, therefore, is to identify the type of knowledge necessary to learn. It explains the need for the learner to recognize what they need to know to acquire and use the new knowledge necessary to become a skilful knower. It is prerequisite knowledge and, in this sense, is subsidiary awareness.

Massingham (2010) developed a model which explains how absorptive capacity interacts with the type of knowledge, for instance focal versus subsidiary awareness, to produce four learning roles. In Massingham's (2010) model, the concept of absorptive capacity provides an ideal framework for understanding the unique dimension of the knower, particularly if we adapt Zahra and George's (2002) input–output model. Figure 8.1 presents a framework for examining the interaction between tacitness and absorptive capacity derived from Polanyi's (1962) tacit triangle.

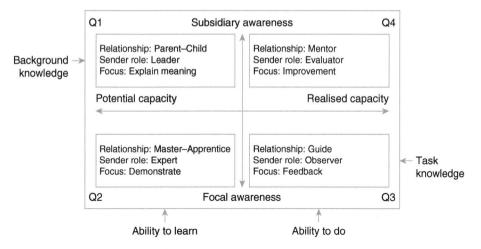

FIGURE 8.1 *The interaction between tacitness and absorptive capacity in international knowledge transfer (Massingham, 2010).* Reprinted by permission of the publisher (Taylor & Francis Ltd, www.tandfonline.com).

THEORY IN PRACTICE: SENDER AND RECEIVER ROLES IN KNOWLEDGE SHARING

The framework has four quadrants, each representing different scenarios in the knowledge transfer between Parent Country Nationals (PCNs) and Host Country Nationals (HCNs). The easiest way to interpret Figure 8.1 is to see the quadrants as progressing from being uninformed to knowledgeable. Starting at quadrant 1, recipients move through each quadrant, gaining incremental knowledge until they reach quadrant 4, the highest level. Individuals move from the left-hand side of the matrix (quadrants 1 and 2) to the right-hand side (quadrants 3 and 4) as they progress from the ability to learn to the ability to do. The left-hand side comprises individuals who must learn how to do something (that is, potential capacity). The right-hand side comprises individuals who know how to do something, but need to do it better (that is, realized capacity). In learning how to do something or do it well, individuals need both specific knowledge about the task and related background knowledge. The top half of the matrix (quadrants 1 and 4) involves background knowledge (subsidiary awareness) and the bottom half (quadrants 2 and 3) relates directly to the task (focal awareness). In this way, Figure 8.1 provides a framework for combining the nature of tacit knowledge (Polanyi) with stages of learning (Zahra and George, 2002). The model's contribution is to use these frameworks to explain the changing nature of relationships between senders and receivers as individuals cycle through the four quadrants.

Source: Massingham (2010: 1419)

ACTION LEARNING

Once the learner recognizes and accepts the need to learn and the type of knowledge they need, they need to act. Researchers have been examining conscious and unconscious reasoning processes for decades (see Dick and Dalmau, 1990), including a belief that people are designers of action (Argyris, 1987). People design action in order to achieve intended consequences and then check to learn if their actions are effective. This thinking is grounded in behaviourism, where people take responsibility for their actions, while aware of the consequences. Researchers have designed theories of action to help people plan, implement, and review their actions (Argyris and Schön, 1974). These theories aim to help people make correct decisions about their behaviour at work.

Action learning is 'a continuous process of learning and reflection, supported by colleagues, with the intention of getting things done' (McGill and Beaty, 2001: 12). Action learning is based on the relationship between reflection and action. We learn through experience by 'thinking through past events, seeking ideas that make sense of the event and help us find new ways of behaving in similar situations in the future' (2001: 12). We can learn about the world and about ourselves through reflection on past action. We can then 'construct our future action from our reflections on learning' (2001: 19). The knowledge usage mechanisms – peer assists, after action reviews, and retrospects (see Chapter 7) – are techniques which embrace action learning.

LEARNING FROM ACTION

Learning in action is the interaction between thinking and doing. The concept is similar to reflection in action, with the added need for expediency, as explained by Schön: 'reflection in action is where we may reflect in the midst of action without interrupting it. Our thinking serves to reshape what we are doing while we are doing it' (Argyris and Schön, 1978: 26). Baird et al. (2000: 186) argued that there is a need to 'get more learning into the performance process'. They proposed that learning from action was more effective than action learning, and explained how the increasing focus on organizational learning has improved the way learning is managed by organizations. Improvements include identifying the skills needed to perform, establishing a learning agenda, structuring the development experience, and developing skills. All this helps because it gets more performance into the learning process. In other words, it improves traditional staff training in the classroom (e.g. courses). But Baird et al. (2000: 187) argue that 'it does not help fast enough'.

CORE CONCEPT: Learning from action is about learning from experience. It is either the experience you gain or feedback from others with more experience.

Building learning into performance is about getting knowledge to people when they most need it, when they are doing work. The main organizational learning frameworks include those of Kolb (1984), Huber (1991), and Crossan et al. (1999). Kolb (1984) developed a cycle of experiential learning (Figure 8.2). In Kolb's theory, the impetus for the development of new knowledge is provided by new experiences: 'Learning is the process whereby knowledge is created through the transformation of experience' (Kolb, 1984: 38). The theory works on two levels: a four-stage cycle of learning and four separate learning styles.

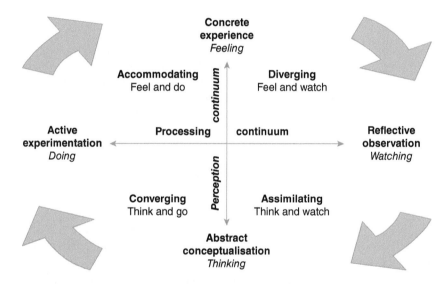

FIGURE 8.2 *Kolb's (1984) theory of experiential learning*

Like most of the popular learning models, Kolb's theory is linear in the sense that the learner moves through a series of steps, representing progress from ignorance (unskilful knowing) to competence (skilful knowing). The arrows in Figure 8.2 represent continuous learning, suggesting that the learner does not stop at any step but carries on gathering experience and improving competence levels and performance over time.

At the end of the two-dimensional matrix are four descriptors, indicating a four-stage learning cycle which the learner has to move through to progress from being an unskilful knower to becoming a skilful knower. The four stages are:

1. *Concrete experience (CE)*: a new experience or situation is encountered, or a reinterpretation of existing experience.

2. *Reflective observation (RO)*: of the new experience. Of particular importance are any inconsistencies between experience and understanding.

3. *Abstract conceptualization (AC)*: reflection gives rise to a new idea, or a modification of an existing abstract concept.
4. *Active experimentation (AE)*: the learner applies the new idea to the world around them to see what results. (After Kolb, 1984: 68–69)

DEEP THINKING: In the view of organizational learning presented in this chapter, stage 1 is conscious learning, stage 2 is absorptive capacity, stage 3 is action learning, and stage 4 is learning from action.

Much of Kolb's theory is concerned with the learner's internal cognitive processes; however, it also includes behavioural aspects, particularly with active experimentation. The descriptors at the end of the two-dimensional matrix include four action words: feeling, watching, thinking, and doing. The theory combines its elements to produce four learning styles, representing the way people prefer to learn. These are described in the middle of the four quadrants:

1. *Diverging* (feeling and watching – CE/RO): these people are able to look at things from different perspectives. They are sensitive and creative, and like brainstorming. They are interested in people and are imaginative and feeling-oriented.
2. *Assimilating* (watching and thinking – AC/RO): the preference here is for a concise, logical approach. These people excel at understanding complex information and organizing it in a clear, logical format. They are most interested in ideas and abstract concepts.
3. *Converging* (doing and thinking – AC/AE): such people use their learning to find solutions to practical issues. They prefer technical tasks, and are less concerned with people and interpersonal aspects. They solve problems and make decisions by finding answers to questions. These people like to experiment with new ideas, to simulate, and to work with practical applications.
4. *Accommodating* (doing and feeling – CE/AE): these people are hands-on and rely on intuition rather than logic. They prefer a trial-and-error approach to problem solving, i.e. experiential learning, and tend to rely on others for information rather than carry out their own analysis. These people are at 'ease with people but are sometimes seen as impatient or pushy'. (After Kolb, 1984: 77–78)

Whatever influences the choice of style, the learning style preference itself is the outcome of two separate 'choices' that we make, which Kolb presented as lines of axes, each with contrasting modes at either end. A typical presentation of Kolb's two continuums is that the east–west axis is called the processing continuum (how we approach a task) and the north–south axis is called the perception continuum (our emotional response, or how we think or feel about it). Kolb believed that we cannot perform both variables on a single axis at the same time, for example think and feel, so we must make a choice. The choice is your preferred learning style.

Huber (1991) designed an organizational learning framework, which has become popular because it tries to integrate the diverse learning literature and it attempts to connect learning to organizational outcomes. Huber adopted an information-processing perspective about organizational learning, similar to the assimilation concept within absorptive capacity, and connected this to outcomes via changes in behaviour. Huber's model has four dimensions:

1. *Knowledge acquisition*: here the focus is on how knowledge is gathered via processes of congenital learning, a type of legacy linked to organizational culture which influences shared cognition, and experiential learning, developed via challenging underlying assumptions. This appears to be how staff learn insiderness or tacit organizational knowledge. Other aspects of knowledge acquisition are experiential learning, vicarious learning, grafting, and searching (Huber, 1991: 91).

2. *Information distribution*: the focus is on the way knowledge is captured, shared, and used. This appears to be how the organization learns, by combining knowledge from its various sub-units. Huber builds on the concept that organizations do not know what they know. He argues that new knowledge is developed by 'piecing together items of information that they obtain from other organizational units' which 'leads to more broadly based organizational learning' (Huber, 1991: 100–101).

3. *Information interpretation*: here the focus is on the meaning and shared interpretation of organizational knowledge, leading to a diversity of understanding, improved creativity and innovation, and the management of problem areas such as information overload and unlearning. This appears to be how learning organization capacity is developed. Aspects of information interpretation include: '(1) the uniformity of prior cognitive maps possessed by the organizational units, (2) the uniformity of the framing of the information as it is communicated, (3) the richness of the media used to convey the information, (4) the information load on the interpreting units, and (5) the amount of unlearning that might be necessary before a new interpretation could be generated' (Huber, 1991: 102).

4. *Organizational memory*: the focus is on knowledge loss caused by employee turnover, lost tacit knowledge (e.g. white board meeting notes not recorded), and ignorance of others' knowledge elsewhere in the organization. This appears to be how learning organization capacity may be improved by accessing organizational memory. This is typically done by capturing lessons learned, sharing best practice, structuring in storage and retrieval systems, and enabling access to those who need to know. Factors 'likely to influence the ongoing effectiveness of organizational memory include (1) membership attrition, (2) information distribution and organizational interpretation of information, (3) the norms and methods for storing information, and (4) the methods for locating and retrieving stored information' (Huber, 1991: 105).

Huber's framework is heavily focused on organizational systems, rather than people, and ignores important cognitive and behavioural aspects such as motivation and social interaction. It has also been criticized for not explaining how to implement organizational learning, i.e. it is too abstract or conceptual (e.g. see Easterby-Smith, 1997).

DEEP THINKING: Organizational unlearning is the process of identifying and discarding useless or obsolete knowledge. It is letting go of the past to allow room for the future. By discarding old knowledge, organizations remove a major barrier in the acquisition and creation of new knowledge. There are two factors which make unlearning necessary. First, changes in the environment gradually make knowledge obsolete and it loses value. Second, old knowledge 'blocks the inflow of new knowledge' (Zhao et al., 2013: 903), so that the organization cannot update knowledge, or new knowledge creation is slowed (2013: 903). Unlearning creates the motivation to learn to fill the gap left by discarding old knowledge.

Crossan et al. (1999) developed a popular organizational learning framework based on six learning processes and three levels of learning, which was later extended by Zietsma et al. (2002). The characteristics of this model are explained in Table 8.1.

TABLE 8.1 Characteristics of learning process in the Crossan/Zietsma model. Reprinted by permission of Wiley.

Process name	Level	Process description
Intuition	Individual	Cognitive process involving the preconscious recognition of patterns. Intuition is subjective and grounded in individual experience
Attending	Individual	Action-based individual process of searching for and absorbing new ideas
Interpretation	Individual–group	Explaining personal insights through words or action. Individuals reflect on action, or groups discuss shared insight
Experimenting	Individual–group	Attempting to implement new learning through practice of change
Integration	Group–organization	Developing shared understanding and practices, which may occur through dialogue and coordinated action
Institutionalization	Organization	The process of ensuring that routinized action occurs through being embedded in organizational systems and processes

The characteristics in Table 8.1 illustrate how the Crossan/Zietsma learning model has similarities with Nonaka and Takeuchi's (1995) knowledge creation spiral in terms of knowledge diffusion through the levels, and with the feedback loops of action learning. Its value lies in how it has packaged these ideas into an integrated model.

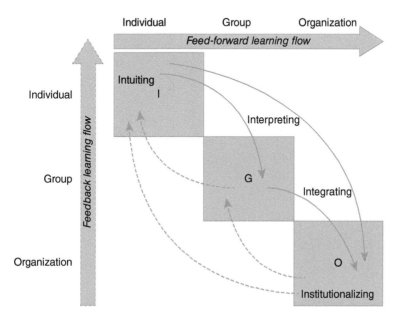

FIGURE 8.3   *The 4I model of organizational learning*

Source: Vera and Crossan (2004). By permission of the Academy of management.

The theory works on two levels: a four-stage cycle of learning and four separate learning styles. Figure 8.3 describes the combined Crossan/Zietsma model. The model has two learning flows. The feed-forward loop, described as the exploration-based learning process, involves the development and assimilation of new knowledge. It begins with the individual and cascades through the organization as the knowledge is diffused and shared. The best outcome is that the organization validates the individual's knowledge as best practice and it is then embedded as organizational knowledge for others to use. The feedback loop (or feed-backward loop), described as an exploitation-based learning process, utilizes existing knowledge. It begins with what the organization has captured and cascades down to groups and then individuals. The best outcome is that organizational knowledge is widely accessible and used. The model has two contributions. It helps explain how learning occurs across levels and how it diffuses up and down these levels. This shows how creativity at the individual level may ultimately benefit the whole organization, and also how organizational knowledge may ultimately benefit all employees. What makes it a learning model rather than a knowledge-sharing model is the concept of feedback, which occurs as a continuous sequence of sensemaking, validation, and contextualization as the knowledge flows up and down the organization. This feedback process is the second contribution as it helps us understand the cognitive and behavioural processes involved. Crossan et al. (1999) argued that the inherent tension in the model between exploration and exploitation represents a barrier to learning and to change. However, knowledge strategy theory explains that exploration is a better option than exploitation because it leads to higher rates of innovation and sustainable competitive advantage (see Chapter 5).

SINGLE-, DOUBLE-, AND TRIPLE-LOOP LEARNING

Behaviourism explains that learning is influenced by consequences, particularly the motivation to learn. When confronted with the awareness of unskilful knowing, the individual or group might ask what will happen if I/we do not learn how to do this. The implication is that unskilful knowing will result in work that is performed ineffectively (low quality) or inefficiently (slowly). In either case, unskilful knowers have a negative impact on organizational performance. Under these circumstances, learners must be reminded of the consequences of their inaction (i.e. the failure to learn), as well as the consequences of action (i.e. the benefits of learning). The concepts of single-loop learning (behavioural) and double-loop learning (cognitive), introduced by Argyris and Schön (1978), and later triple-loop learning (Easterby-Smith and Lyles, 2003) help us understand how organizational learning may become embedded as shared mental concepts.

Single-loop learning is about compliance. It is about learning to do things the right way. In this sense, it is the outcome of the feed-backward loop in the Crossan/Zietsma learning model, where individuals perform activities based on organizational best practice. Single-loop learning emerged from Argyris and Schön's (1978) definition of organizational learning as a process of correcting errors within organizational contexts. This definition sees learning as improving work performance, but it also includes the need to prevent or even eliminate mistakes. Single-loop learning is about doing work correctly. It provides management with control over work activity. It does this by capturing organizational knowledge as best practice and making it accessible to employees via policies and procedures. Employees are expected to follow this best practice as the organization's theory-in-use (Argyris and Schön, 1978). It gives management the power to control by enabling it to use single-loop learning to detect and correct errors in performance. The implication is that employees are breaking the rules if they do not follow policy. There are negative consequences for employees who do not become skilful knowers. For example, management can blame sales employees for declining sales because they were not doing customer relationship management the way the organization expected, i.e. according to the sales manual. The outcome is usually staff training to take corrective action and ensure these employees do things the right way. Lehr and Rice (2005: 55) described single-loop learning as corrective action. It is scientific management; it stifles creativity and innovation. But it ensures consistency and allows management the power to control.

When people make decisions and act in situations, they engage in situation handling (Wiig, 2003). Situation handling involves four primary tasks: (1) sensemaking, (2) decision making/problem solving, (3) implementation, and (4) monitoring (2003: 8). Wiig (2003: 11) describes sensemaking as follows:

> Any time a person encounters a situation, she observes it by receiving and accepting information about it and uses her knowledge to make sense of it from the accepted information. She normally understands the general context. During the sensemaking task, she uses her a priori situational awareness capability to understand the situation. Her situational awareness capability determines the extent to which the current situation, its context and environment are observed and perceived and the accuracy with which the resulting perception mirrors reality. Without appropriate situational awareness she does not have sufficient understanding of the situation and cannot make proper sense of it.

DEEP THINKING: Sensemaking is a cognitive process to determine what to do when faced with a new problem at work, such as a knowledge gap. In this situation, staff may seek knowledge to help them fill the gap, i.e. discover what to do. When staff are exposed to a different set of knowledge, they may attempt to make sense of this new knowledge by asking 'What's the story in my case?' This question brings intrinsic (tacit) knowledge into their context. When staff then ask 'Now what should I do?', this brings meanings into action (Weick et al., 2005). Sensemaking is connected to organizational learning by the process of a 'continued redrafting' of knowledge by reconstructing it in the individual's context and assessing its likelihood of implementation (2005: 415). It is the individual's assessment of whether they can trust the knowledge. The process of evaluation involves learning about the new knowledge and, subsequently, the individual's knowledge becomes more holistic.

Three important elements play critical roles in sensemaking:

1. *Generic understanding*: when staff notice the intrinsic value of knowledge (Weick et al., 2005: 412)

2. *A specific situation*: enables staff to discover a new, more useful meaning in their own circumstances (2005: 414)

3. *Action*: 'is always just a tiny bit ahead of cognition, meaning that we act our way into belated understanding' (2005: 419).

Sensemaking involves an evaluation of the knowledge and whether it may be trusted and used in the individual's situation. In this way, sensemaking enables knowledge quality. Only knowledge that may be used to take action passes the sensemaking test. This fits this book's view of knowledge value (see Chapter 3) as skilful knowing creating value in the act of doing work. While this benefits the individual by enabling them to solve their problem, learn, and use new knowledge, it also has organizational benefits. Actionable knowledge quality resulting from sensemaking increases the likelihood of innovation (Yoo, 2014). Sensemaking is included in this discussion of single-loop learning because it may contribute to individuals answering the question: 'How am I supposed to do this?'

Double-loop learning is about innovation. It is about learning to do the right things. In this sense, it is the outcome of the feed-forward loop in the Crossan/ Zietsma learning model, where individuals create new and better ways to perform work activities and this becomes organizational best practice. Double-loop learning emerged from change management literature, and it provided insight by a 'rethinking of existing rules according to why things are being done; [and] involves understanding reasons for current rules and then questioning these reasons' (Easterby-Smith, 1997: 1106). Double-loop learning recognizes that knowledge is not static. What an organization learns at any one time may become irrelevant or even harmful at a different time (Lehr and Rice, 2005). Single-loop learning is static; it suggests that organizational best practice applies now and in the future and across all organizational contexts. Double-loop learning recognizes that organizations change, as do their customers and their competitive environment. Employees are encouraged to challenge the underlying assumptions about the work they do. Rather than ask 'Am I doing this right?', they ask 'Am I doing the right thing?' Employees are encouraged to be entrepreneurial, to be risk takers, to play creativity games, to develop new ideas, experiment, discover, and innovate. There are positive consequences for employees who become skilful knowers. For example, rather than management blaming sales employees for declining sales, they accept that the process for customer relationship management was wrong, and they empower the sales team to find a better way to do it. The outcome is often revised business processes. Lehr and Rice (2005: 55) discuss double-loop learning as an underlying process; it may

---

DEEP THINKING: Double-loop learning may generate indirect learning by integrating the 'expansion of peripheral awareness through reflexively learning in experience' (Paton et al., 2014: 272). This encourages enquiry, challenge, and reflexivity to bring about new perceptions and understanding. Indirect learning is necessary because 'existing assumptions are challenged indirectly as they are often tacit, deeply held, and rarely articulated' (2014: 272). Reflection is a cognitive activity, whereas practical reflexivity is a dialogical and relational activity and it is about 'unsettling conventional practices' (Cunliffe and Easterby-Smith, 2004, cited in Paton et al., 2014: 272).

be considered to have taken place if improvements consequently incorporate 'the lesson into the practices and routines of the organization'. Double-loop learning is humanistic management. It encourages creativity and innovation, but it may take some time to implement and the outcomes may be uncertain and ambiguous.

DEEP THINKING: Reflexivity is a process using critical dialogue to develop new ideas and new ways of seeing the world (Paton et al., 2014). It uses a 'multiple-futures approach to challenge business-as-usual assumptions' to produce deep, insightful learning (2014: 285). The difference between reflexivity and the action learning tools (e.g. after action reviews) is reflexivity's way of thinking about experiential learning.

Reflexivity begins with finding relevance or irrelevance in an existing body of knowledge, for example a theory, a concept, a framework, or research. It does this by discovering the contribution of a theory to 'an area of managerial practice' (e.g. direct relevance) (Paton et al., 2014: 271). Paton et al. (2014: 285) describe this as relevating, which is 'raising awareness of experiences that open up new possibilities'. Relevating 'extends practical reflexivity' (Cunliffe and Easterby-Smith, 2004, cited in Paton et al., 2014: 285) by encouraging management thinking about day-to-day managerial practice. This concept privileges skilful knowing (see Chapter 1) as it proposes that the deep learning created by reflexivity can only happen in the act of dialogue between those who do the work being challenged. Practitioners are the only ones who can 'make the connection between their experiences and the limitations of their practices' due to their insiderness (Paton et al., 2014: 282). Reflexivity is included in this discussion of double-loop learning because it may contribute to individuals answering the question, 'Can I do this better?'

Triple-loop learning is about the learning itself. It is about getting learning into performance. In this sense, it is the process of learning from action, where individuals reflect on how they created new and better ways to perform work activities and how this became organizational best practice (double-loop learning), and how they might do this better next time. It is change and improvement in how the organization learns. Triple-loop learning questions not just what has been learned but the way it was learned (Easterby-Smith, 1997). There are positive consequences for employees who can reflect on how they and their organization learn and improve. These benefits are conceptualized as learning economies. The learning curve (LC) describes the 'productivity increases due to learning' (Schenkel and Teigland, 2008: 111). In simple terms, the LC follows the adage that practice makes perfect. In a work context, it argues that the more you do something, the better you get at it. The usefulness of this model is that it tries to quantify the value of learning to the organization, primarily in terms of reduced cost. From a strategic management perspective, firms that are able to achieve a dominant position on the LC have achieved superior performance. Therefore, LC dominance is seen as a source of competitive advantage. The dominant position is attained by accelerating down the LC quicker than rivals, i.e. accumulating the necessary learning faster. The measure of LC presented is the productivity gains generated by better organizational learning. The practical outcome of triple-loop learning, therefore, is whether it 'accelerates time to competence; in the sense that it reduces the amount of time necessary to become competent, by accelerating learning' (Massingham and Massingham, 2014: 229). Triple-loop learning is learning organization management. It enables the benefits of becoming a learning organization.

DEEP THINKING: Wisdom is understood as a meaningful, procedural, and justified abstraction of existence based on experience. It has a purpose and relates to procedures, but it is also based on a coherent judgement of existence justified through experience. Wisdom therefore permits sound action and use of experience. Wisdom requires a higher level of understanding than data, information, and knowledge.

Research generally considers wisdom as a cognitive process of discovering reality. Researchers agree that there is a hierarchy among the concepts of data, information, and knowledge. The knowledge hierarchy is usually seen as a pyramid ascending from data to wisdom. The idea is that data is the lowest form of knowledge and is combined with other data to form information, and so on, up the levels until wisdom is attained. The following is a typical definition of these terms:

- Data is considered to be unprocessed, raw representations of reality.
- Information is considered to be data that has been processed in some meaningful ways.
- Knowledge is considered to be information that has been processed in some meaningful ways.
- Wisdom is considered to be knowledge that has been processed in some meaningful ways. (After Faucher et al., 2008: 5)

The tacit versus explicit continuum suggests that wisdom is the highest level of tacit knowledge, whereas data is the lowest level of codified knowledge. If we accept the KBV assumption that tacit knowledge is the most valuable knowledge, then this continuum indicates that wisdom is the highest level of knowledge. The ultimate aim of organizational learning, therefore, is to attain wisdom.

Faucher et al. (2008) argue that conventional views of wisdom incorrectly adopt a linear approach by placing wisdom at the top of a knowledge hierarchy. They feel this is wrong because the components in the knowledge hierarchy comprise parts of the same basic unit. They argue that the components are all labels used to structure human understanding of the same construct: existence. Faucher et al.

(2008) also argue that there is a level of knowledge higher than wisdom which they describe as enlightenment or existence. In this book, we would describe this as reality or justified true belief (see Chapter 1).

The key to understanding Faucher et al.'s (2008) alternative view of the knowledge hierarchy is how the individual attains higher levels in the knowledge hierarchy and the result of this progression, i.e. understanding. They propose a non-linear model based on a simple mathematical notation, which argues that everything is based on 'abstractions from existence' (Faucher et al., 2008: 10). What is important, according to Faucher et al. (2008: 10), is 'the coefficient that differs among them'. The distinction among these constructs is a level of abstraction and understanding. The transformation from data to wisdom represents a different level of understanding, 'suggesting an exponential degree of thinking' (Faucher et al., 2008: 10).

Faucher et al.'s (2008) non-linear view of the knowledge hierarchy is helpful for our understanding of triple-loop learning. The non-linear model sees existence, data, information, knowledge, wisdom, and enlightenment as forming a feedback system with positive and negative feedback loops. This non-linear view is consistent with complexity theory and enables the connection of learning and feedback loops to the attainment of wisdom. Faucher et al. (2008: 12) conclude with this definition of wisdom:

> Wisdom is understood as a meaningful, procedural, and justified abstraction of existence based on experience. It has a purpose, relates to procedures, but it is also based on a coherent judgement of existence justified through experience. Wisdom therefore permits sound action and use of experience. Wisdom requires a higher level of understanding than data, information, and knowledge.

Wisdom is included in this discussion of triple-loop learning because it may contribute to individuals answering the question: 'What can I learn from doing this better?'

Argyris and Schön (1978) considered organizational learning correctly *practised* only when organizational members become learning agents who respond to changes in internal and external environments by detecting and correcting errors while sharing results. Easterby-Smith and Lyles (2003) provide a systems perspective which enables evaluation of the practice of organizational learning, distinguishing between single-, double-, and triple-loop learning. They propose that there are four *practical* stages to organizational learning: local, control, open, and deep learning (Easterby-Smith and Lyles, 2003). Figure 8.4 illustrates this concept.

Figure 8.4 illustrates that the local stage represents knowledge based on individual experience. In this stage, those who tacitly know underlying structures and assumptions make decisions, where they tend to focus on what needs to be done rather than why it is done. At the control stage, knowledge resides in silos. Work groups generate formal routines to make processes uniform and predictable. Standardization, performance feedback, and statistical measurement

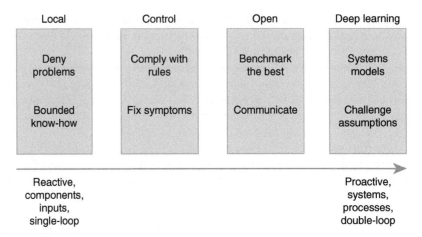

FIGURE 8.4   *The four stages of organizational learning*

Source: Easterby-Smith and Lyles (2003)

are the key at this stage. Learning is directed towards exploitation of the known rather than exploration of the unknown; it is single-loop learning. The open stage explores wide learning possibilities; it is double-loop learning. Deep learning profoundly questions the way things are done and brings reflection to all actions; it is triple-loop learning. The hierarchical relationship between single-, double-, and triple-loop learning is explored further by Massingham (2015), who developed a model of learning in action which contains four types of learning flows: strategic, tactical, operational, and activity.

THE LEARNING ORGANIZATION – AND DEFINITIONS AND POPULAR MODELS

The learning organization is an aspirational business model. It emerged as a precursor to the knowledge-based view of the firm (Grant, 1996) when the ability of an organization to learn faster than its competitors was the only sustainable source of competitive advantage (de Geus, 1988). It was popularized by Senge (1990) and Garvin (1993). In broad terms, the learning organization is one which focuses on learning; it is (as illustrated by this quote):

> a consciously managed organization with 'learning' as a vital component in its values, visions and goals, as well as in its everyday operations and their assessment. The learning organization eliminates structural obstacles of learning, creates enabling structures and takes care of assessing its learning and development. It invests

in leadership to assist individuals in finding the purpose, in eliminating personal obstacles and in facilitating structures for personal learning and getting feedback and benefits from learning outcomes. (Moilanen, 2001: 11)

Similarly, Pedler et al. (1997: 3) define it as an 'organization which facilitates the learning of all its members and consciously transforms itself and its context'.

Senge (1990: 231) defined the learning organization as a workplace 'where people continually expand their capacity to create the results they truly desire, where new and expansive thinking are nurtured, where collective aspirations are set free and where people are continually learning how to learn together'. His use of phrases like 'people ... continually expand their capacity', 'new patterns of thinking', 'collective aspiration', and 'continually learning' show that Senge's view of the ideal organization was very much humanistic management. It is an organization that genuinely cares for employees and wants to help them be the best they can.

DEEP THINKING: Critics have described Senge's learning organization model as propaganda (e.g. see Coopey, 1998) for two reasons: (a) it is too prescriptive and only valued by consultants and practitioners, and (b) it is naïve in the sense that it relies on the emancipation of employees (humanism) and their self-development (e.g. personal mastery), when the reality is that management seeks to use its power to exploit workers rather than nurture them.

This chapter adopts the view that the learning organization is aspirational but it still has important value for knowledge management, particularly in terms of how to improve organizational learning. The value in Senge's model begins with the influence of systems thinking. This led to a focus on behaviours designed to create synergy such as teamwork, collaboration, and cooperation. His model was a perfect fit for organizations wanting to develop effective organizational learning. The model has five disciplines:

1. *Personal mastery* represents staff commitment to and a passion for lifelong learning. It reflects a feeling from staff that their work matters, and the excitement of continual learning. They desire to be master craftsman or experts in their field. They may also feel that their organization invests in their continual learning, i.e. staff training or recognition of their experience. This means that staff feel they are growing as people and professionals. Senge explained how creative tension enables learning and creativity to build innovative individuals. He then argued that those innovative individuals who practise the personal mastery discipline are those who build creative organizations.

Senge asserts the importance of two underlying triggers to creativity, whether individual or collective:

a. to continually clarify what is important through double-loop learning

b. to continually learn how to clearly comprehend existing reality by being aware of ignorance and incompetence.

Senge argues that people working together while embracing these concepts create an innovative team and ultimately an innovative organization.

2. *Shared mental models* means that there is meaning, creativity, and reflection for staff in relation to their work. This is the capacity for reflective practice. Staff are encouraged to challenge underlying assumptions, i.e. why are we doing this or is there a better way? Polanyi's (1962) view of language as an internal cognitive process helps us understand how shared mental models emerge. It is the way that individuals process ideas in their mind and, in this sense, mental models emerge via meaning and interpretation found in unspoken language, i.e. the individual talking to themselves. Shared mental models are tacit organizational knowledge. They represent justified true belief about how the organization works. True belief is the individual's internal mirror. It is their reflection about what works for them; it is their mental model. *Justified* true belief means this mirror is seen by others and agreed on. It is a collective reflection and consensus about what works; it is a shared mental model.

3. *Shared vision* means staff have a common identity and a sense of destiny. Do employees have a shared vision about knowledge management that aligns with their organization's goals? Employees tend to naturally base their decisions on self-interest (Kluge et al., 2001). Instead of trying to alter or work against this behaviour, organizations should try to align it with organizational direction by designing a win-win scenario that ensures both the employee and the organization have the same goals. It means having a shared commitment about the organization's future, which in a learning organization should be that knowledge matters and needs to be managed.

4. *Team learning* means that employees have the type of relationships with colleagues that allow people to suspend assumptions and think together. Team learning is much more than working in groups or telling people what to do or running a good meeting. It means developing relationships based on mutual trust, respect, and honesty, leading to collective learning. Employees are learning together. This may be done via dialogue that empowers and encourages a diversity of thinking, i.e. divergence, and a toleration of different views.

5. *Systems thinking* is about changing the organization by seeing a new and different perspective. Systems citizenship begins with 'seeing the organizational systems we shape and which in turn shape us at work.

Being stuck in a system that is not working inevitably leads to feeling frustrated and trapped' (Senge, 1990: 343). These negative emotions can affect morale and productivity and increase employee turnover. Systems thinking encourages us to see the larger patterns of interdependency in our organizations and our own role in these relationships. Once we can see this bigger picture, it builds empathy, understanding, and new alternatives. It surfaces systemic problems, but also solutions. (After Senge, 1990)

While Senge's model has been very popular, particularly among consultants and practitioners, it has been heavily criticized by academics who argue that the five disciplines lack empirical data and that there are no guidelines on how to implement the model. Managers might ask: How do we become a learning organization? How do I develop personal mastery in my employees? Senge responded to this criticism, to some degree, with his 2005 co-authored book *The Dance of Change*, which positions the learning organization within the context of change management, rather than knowledge management. It reads as a collection of anecdotes and recipes from his work with colleagues in the 15 years since his original book. It is certainly interesting but might be seen as a collection of consulting war stories.

Another popular learning organization model was developed by Garvin (1993). This also has five dimensions: (1) problem solving, (2) experiential learning, (3) experimenting, (4) knowledge sharing, and (5) vicarious learning. It focuses more on organizational learning than Senge's model, but it is really just a simple version of a knowledge management system, concentrating on creativity, sharing, and acquisition. Garratt (1987) is similarly seen as a pioneer of the learning organization concept. His work was interesting because it focused on action learning and involved feedback loops in a three-level hierarchy of policy, strategy, and operations. Garratt is interesting too because he later wrote an article reflecting on the learning organization 15 years after he devised the concept. In this later article, he makes several interesting observations. He felt that the learning organization itself was not a new concept; that it dated back to the end of World War II, and has roots in scientific management where active learning was a process seen as the engine that drives learning organizations (Garratt, 1999). The link to scientific management was the argument that management could take control by directing their employees to learn in order to improve performance. However, Garratt accepted that the nature of business had changed and that contemporary views of the learning organization 'must assume continuous critical review of what is happening within and outside organizational boundaries, to allow for its adaptation to changing environments' (Garratt, 1999: 205). He also responded to criticism that the model ignored organizational power imbalances, which made it 'highly challenging and unnerving', by proposing organizational culture as necessary 'structural facets' that would enable learning activities to be supported and implemented in the workplace (Garratt, 1999: 205).

COMPARING ORGANIZATIONAL LEARNING WITH THE LEARNING ORGANIZATION

The terms organizational learning and the learning organization are often used interchangeably by researchers and practitioners, inferring that they mean the same thing. However, they are very different concepts. Figure 8.5 explains the differences and also compares them with organizational knowledge and knowledge management.

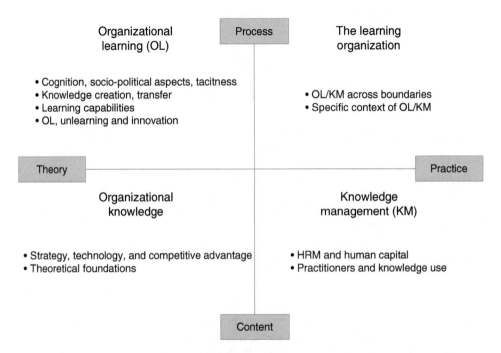

FIGURE 8.5 *Easterby-Smith and Lyles' (2003) comparison of organizational learning and the learning organization.* Reprinted by permission of Wiley.

Figure 8.5 includes a broader range of concepts in organizational learning than that adopted by this book, for example knowledge creation and transfer, which are considered separate concepts by this book (see Chapters 5 and 9). However, it is a useful framework. The two axes classify the four topics into quadrants. Organizational learning is in the top left-hand quadrant intersected by theory and process. It is informed by theory, particularly what organizational knowledge is, i.e. what is to be learned, and also by process, particularly how to become a learning organization. The learning organization is in the top right-hand quadrant intersected by process and practice. It is informed by the process of organizational learning and the practice of knowledge management.

LEARNING ORGANIZATION CAPACITY

The learning organization is a construct that has emerged in recent years, largely in response to the growing recognition that intangible assets such as knowledge, rather than tangible assets, are now an organization's most valuable strategic resource (see Grant, 1996). This has changed the way many organizations operate.

In measuring learning organization capacity, researchers typically adopt a normative perspective that 'presumes that learning is a collective activity which takes place under certain conditions' (DiBella, 1995: 287). There are numerous measurements of the necessary conditions. Senge (1990), as we have seen, lists personal mastery, mental models, shared vision, team learning, and systems thinking. Griffey (1998: 71) describes the characteristics of a wise organization as including abilities that convey wisdom such as 'questioning, problem finding, tolerating ambiguity, and valuing direct experience'. Other common themes in the literature include the capacity to constantly learn (Gorelick et al., 2004), effective leadership (Richardson, 1995), the ability to change behaviour (Sun and Scott, 2003), organizational culture (Sicilia and Lytras, 2005), organizational commitment (Ikehara, 1999), and effective knowledge sharing (Thomas and Allen, 2006).

The challenge is how to measure these constructs. There has been some progress. Organizational culture, for example, may be measured by commitment to learning, open-mindedness, and shared vision. Gorelick et al. (2004) argued that continuous learning requires structuring and sensemaking variables, where structuring variables are using information technology, roles, norms, leaderships, rewards and recognition, and education and development, whereas sensemaking variables are collective cognitive schema and behavioural actions such as value, language, scripts, and schema. Change management requires all members and levels in the organization to change behaviours (Sun and Scott, 2003). Organizational culture has been examined using Gestalt theory, arguing that learning is not solely based on cognition, rather learning is also based on 'emotional, physical, and spiritual elements' (Ikehara, 1999: 63). Knowledge sharing has been measured as the capacity to learn and create knowledge in individuals and the ability to distribute this knowledge throughout the organization; as well as 'continuous environmental reviews intended to maintain or improve performance' (Thomas and Allen, 2006: 126–127).

However, these measurements do not lend themselves to empirical investigation, such as survey research. For example, it would be pointless to ask respondents to rate their organization's open-mindedness or mental models; and questions about the organization's spiritual elements seem doomed to failure. This is necessary for academic purposes (validity) as well as for practitioners (implementation).

Researchers have tried to make the learning organization concept more operational. At the broadest level, Senge argued that organizational commitment results when people are treated with dignity and respect. He suggests measurements such as 'positive stories', 'amount of union grievances', 'support for management', 'degree of openness, honesty, and trust', and 'lay-off practices' (Senge et al., 2005: 312). However, these are still vague and abstract measurements. Massingham and Diment (2009) identified a total of 86 factors from extant literature (e.g. Kluge et al., 2001; Moilanen, 2001). These factors were then aggregated into two dimensions. First, there were measurements of learning organization attributes, aggregated into five scale items:

1. Driving forces: building the organization
2. Finding the purpose: where and why?
3. Questioning: Why not? What are the barriers?
4. Empowering: in what ways?
5. Evaluating: to know if you have succeeded (Moilanen, 2001).

Second, there were measurements of learning organization behaviours, aggregated into seven scale items:

1. Knowledge pull
2. Subjectivity
3. Transferability
4. Embeddedness
5. Self-reinforcement
6. Perishability
7. Spontaneity (Kluge et al., 2001).

Phillips (2003) identified 10 characteristics to make an ideal learning organization:

1. Will (commitment)
2. Leadership
3. Strategic thinking and vision
4. Communication
5. Learning and development
6. Innovation and decision making
7. Change management
8. Intellectual capital and knowledge management
9. Measurement and assessment
10. Reward and recognition.

The Total Learning Organization (TLO) framework is proposed as a method to benchmark organizations on learning capabilities and is based on the grounds that all members of an organization must learn, and the organization transforms continuously (Ho, 1999).

MEASURING LEARNING ORGANIZATION CAPACITY

This chapter suggests a new approach to measuring learning organization capacity based on empirical research as part of the measuring and managing knowledge loss research project, which is the integrated case study in this book. The proposed model has two dimensions:

1. Employee engagement
2. Organization performance. These dimensions are organized into five constructs:
   a. people
   b. peace
   c. purpose
   d. enablers
   e. participation.

Employee engagement measures changes in employees' emotional relationship with their employer from two perspectives:

a. employees' sense of calm created by wellbeing and empowerment
b. employees' evaluation of how well their employer encourages positive work attitudes and behaviours.

This measures employees' happiness at work and their satisfaction with their workplace. The theoretical basis for this definition is the psychological contract (PC) (Argyris, 1960). This chapter divides PC into two factors: peace and participation. PC may be understood within the motivational processes of social exchange theory and the norm of reciprocity (e.g. Homans, 1961; Blau, 1964). This means that the more that employees perceive an organization gives them, the more they will give to the organization in return. Employees give, in this sense, in terms of quantity and quality of work. Therefore, high PC scores reveal employees with high job satisfaction, which is likely to translate into high productivity and work performance. On the other hand, low PC scores can lead to a lack of the creativity and sharing necessary to generate value from employees (Massingham and Tam, 2015).

Peace combines wellbeing and empowerment (Massingham, 2018). It has two constructs:

1. Work–life balance
2. Flexibility.

It measures whether employees feel they have an appropriate balance between work and family life, and autonomy and control over work decisions. These constructs combine to give a sense of calm. Participation is a perception that the organization is encouraging positive work attitudes and behaviours. It has nine constructs:

1. Leadership
2. Recruitment and selection

3. Cross-unit cooperation
4. Learning and development
5. Involvement
6. Organizational culture
7. Rewards and recognition
8. Performance appraisal
9. Career management.

It measures employees' feelings about management in terms of trust, merit, being valued, recognized, and rewarded, as well as their perception of their workplace in terms of sharing, learning, attitude, and personal development (Massingham, 2018).

Organization performance measures changes in organizational systems affecting productivity (efficiency) and quality (effectiveness), and it has three constructs: purpose, enablers, and people (Massingham, 2018). These constructs were defined in Chapter 6. Refer to the section titled Organization Performance.

Employees are then asked to rate how they feel about themselves for the employee engagement dimension, and about their organization for the performance dimension. The next step in this model is to introduce knowledge management to improve learning organization capacity. Table 8.2 lists eight knowledge management systems (e.g. knowledge creation) and matches them to learning organization goals (e.g. learn from experience), performance measurement model constructs (see Figure 8.6), the knowledge management objective, the knowledge management tools, and lead and lag indicators.

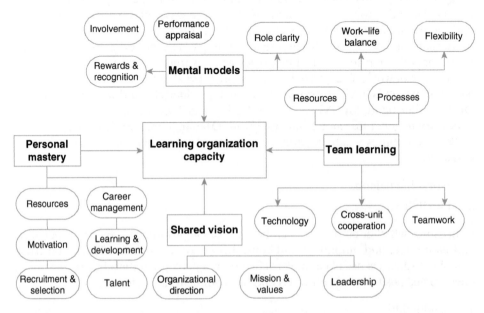

FIGURE 8.6 *Learning organization capacity model*

TABLE 8.2 Knowledge management and improved learning organization capacity

Description	Learning organization goals	Performance measurement model constructs	Knowledge management objective	Knowledge management tools Technique	Lead indicator Metric	Lag indicator
Knowledge measurement	Better grow our staff	Resources, career management, motivation, learning, and development	Auditable knowledge accounts	Knowledge Accounts software, cultural change measurement (LOC model), risk management model	Conduct survey annually and on staff entry and exit, analysis and reporting, action plan	Measured capability
Knowledge creation	Better able to respond to change	Change and innovation	Double-loop learning	Parallel thinking, expert teams (group), and improved work quality based on businees process improvement (BPI) (individual)	Challenge underlying assumptions, use parallel thinking, time in meetings to create outcome, BPI model applied to identify waste points in the system	Improved problem solving
Knowledge strategy	Better respond to change	Organizational direction, mission and values, role clarity	Objective future workforce capability decisions	Make versus buy model	Awareness of knowledge management, awareness of value of knowledge resources, what do we do? what do we know? what do we need to do in 5 years? what do we need to know to do that well? competency map, capability gap analysis, decision model to address future capability gap, consultation process, apply information to model, decisions made	Future capability is met

(Continued)

TABLE 8.2 (Continued)

Description	Learning organization goals	Performance measurement model constructs	Knowledge management objective	Knowledge management tools Technique	Lead indicator Metric	Lag indicator
Knowledge acquisition	Better respond to change	Cross-unit cooperation, teamwork, customer satisfaction	Customer relationship management	Business process improvement, knowledge brokers, KM contract specification	BPI methods conducted and waste points addressed, knowledge flow roles identified along with performance metrics and reward and recognition indicators	External knowledge flows are improved
Knowledge sharing	Better respond to change; better grow our staff	Cross-unit cooperation, teamwork, job satisfaction, organizational culture	Increased connectivity (more people know)	Psychometric model, communities of practice, communication skills, social network mapping, relationship management	Analyse and act on survey psychometric data, create communities of practice and track outcomes, communication skills training, mechanisms for sharing (e.g. seminars), SNA (Social Network Analysis) mapping and CRM (Customer Relationship Management) training	Increased internal connectivity
Knowledge retention	Learn from experience	Processes	Tacit knowledge capture	Handovers, exit interviews (reactive), psychological contract (proactive)	Handover files established, handovers conducted, quality of handover, time to full competence	Job-related continuity/productivity
Knowledge preservation	Learn from experience	Processes	Storing knowledge	Selection model (what is valuable), storage, meta-data fields	Use tacit capture model, capture, code, store, and distribute	Valuable organizational memory is accessible
Knowledge usage	Learn from experience	Processes, technology	Make knowledge/experience accessible	Expert directory, peer assists, after action reviews, combined with easy-to-use storage of lessons learned in intranet	Expert directory created and used, peer assists and AARs happen, outcomes captured and shared, meta-data fields used to enhance accessibility	Experience is shared, lessons learned used

Finally, the model connects the operationalization of learning organization capability to the five Senge disciplines to demonstrate how the model's concepts and their measurement constructs may be used at this broad level of understanding. Figure 8.6 maps these connections.

This new approach to measuring and implementing learning organization capacity extends previous models by providing measurable attributes (performance) and behaviours (employee engagement) linked to knowledge management actions. In this way, the model provides a method to track how well the organization is learning and actions to address problem areas.

CONCLUSION

This chapter has shown the importance of organizational learning. It enables the individual or group to move from unskilful knowing to skilful knowing. This is the internal response to capability gaps. The cognitive and behavioural approaches to learning were discussed. The chapter examined the process of becoming a skilful knower and the context which influences who is learning, how, and why. Skilful knowing begins with conscious learning which is an awareness of the need to know. The process of skilful knowing varies by learning levels, and this was explained for individuals, groups, and organizations. Once the need for conscious learning is accepted, and the gap between unskilful knowing and skilful knowing established, the next cognitive step is to acquire and use new knowledge, to learn and bridge the gap. The concept of absorptive capacity helps explain how this is done. Action learning was introduced to explain how unskilful knowing best emerges in the act of doing work; and learning from practice was used to show how skilful knowing is best gained from knowledge learned in the act of doing. The difference between improved performance in learning (better staff training) and improved learning in performance (learning by doing) was presented. The popular learning models of Kolb (1984), Huber (1991), Crossan (1999), Zietsma et al. (2002) were examined to show the nature of organizational learning. Single-, double-, and triple-loop learning was used to explain the integration of cognitive and behavioural approaches to learning.

The learning organization was presented as an aspirational business model designed to improve organizational learning. It describes an organization that learns from experience, responds to change, and grows its knowledge resources. The popular models of Senge (1990) and Garvin (1993) were examined. Criticism of the learning organization includes the argument that it is propaganda and unable to be measured or implemented. Learning organization capacity was proposed as a solution to these criticisms. While there has been previous empirical research in this area, it is fragmented and lacks managerial application.

Learning within organizations is diverse and complex, involving learning modes, types, and levels. Learning modes are the cognitive, behavioural, and social perspectives. Learning types are typically seen as single-loop, double-loop, and triple-loop. Learning levels are individual, group, organizational, and inter-organizational. These principles combine to help us identify who is learning (levels), how (types), and why (modes). How learning is managed is controversial, with critics suggesting that the learning organization is naïve and ignores the reality that management tends to exploit employees rather than nurture them. However, this chapter argues that organizational learning is not a naturally occurring phenomenon. It can and should be managed, not to exploit employees, but to bridge the gap between unskilful and skilful knowing. A new model of learning organization capacity was proposed. Implementation of this model will improve organizational learning and lead to sustainable competitive advantage.

CLOSING CASE STUDY: LEARNING ORGANIZATION CAPACITY AT THE CSO

When we began the research study to measure and manage organizational knowledge loss at the case study organization (CSO) in 2008, a fundamental objective was to make the CSO a learning organization. It was felt that learning organization capacity (LOC) would build an organization able to develop the systems and culture necessary to minimize the impact of knowledge loss.

Figure 8.7 presents the CSO data at the start of the project. The percentages represent the proportion of respondents who felt very positively about the CSO's performance in this area.

Passion index is a measure of psychological contract, i.e. how positive the workforce's emotional relationship with the organization is.

Progress index is a measure of organization performance, i.e. how positive the workforce feels about the organization and its future growth prospects.

The results of the project indicated several problems at the CSO:

1. *Human resource management is unsatisfactory*. This relates to recruitment, staff training, workload allocation, and workforce planning. Employees felt that the CSO does not invest in them and does not care for them. This affects the psychological contract, in turn affecting morale and job satisfaction. Employees felt the CSO was not giving them what they expected and, therefore, they were not willing to reciprocate by sharing their knowledge.
2. *There is employee resistance to change*. Employees are focused on doing things right, rather than doing the right things. Underlying assumptions are not questioned. Employees blame lack of time, lack of help, lack of relevance, and management for their refusal to engage in change. Management blames employees for being cynical and jaded.
3. *Employees suffer from an unsatisfactory organizational learning performance*. Employees felt that they could no longer see the consequences of their own actions, i.e. what happens is beyond their horizon. As a result, employees do not learn from mistakes and there is little shared learning from experience.
4. *A sense of personal mastery is missing*. Employees had lost the feeling that their work matters and the excitement of continual learning. They felt that their organization does not invest in their continual learning, i.e. there is a lack of staff training or a lack of recognition of their experience. This creates a culture of apathy and employees no longer desire to be master craftsmen or experts in their field.
5. *There is a lack of shared mental models*. There is a lack of meaning, creativity, and reflection by employees about their work. The CSO lacked the capacity for reflective practice. Employees were not encouraged to challenge underlying assumptions, e.g. why are we doing this, or is there a better way? Employees' mental models, i.e. how they make sense of their world at the CSO or 'How we do things around here', were not surfaced or challenged.

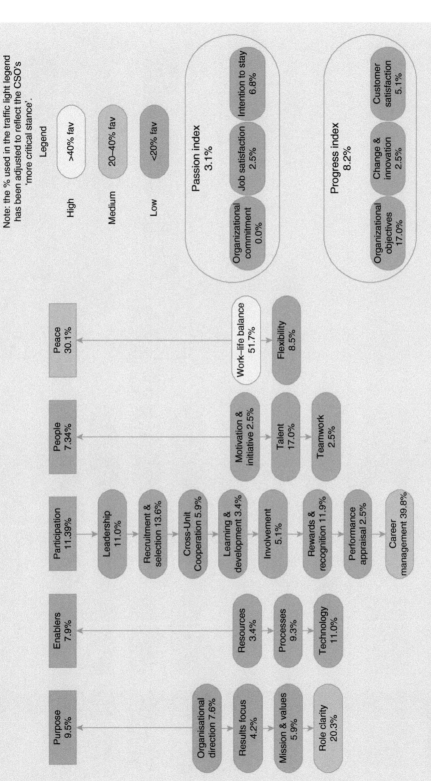

FIGURE 8.7 *CSO LOC performance measurement model, 2009*

(Continued)

(Continued)

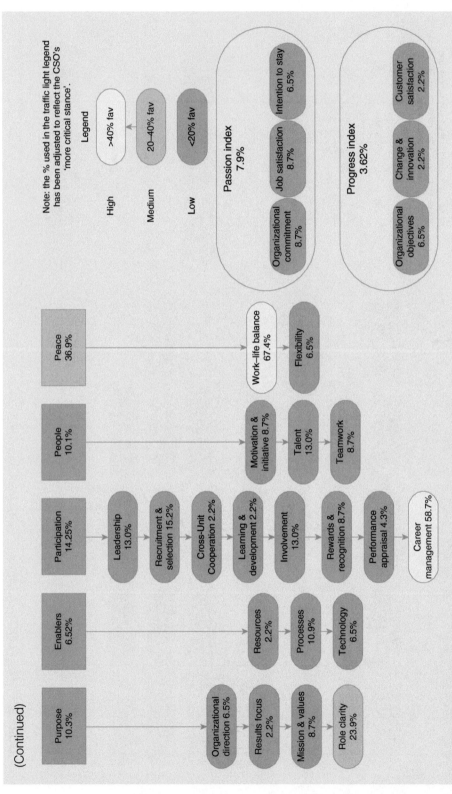

FIGURE 8.8 *CSO LOC performance measurement model, 2010*

6. *A shared vision is missing.* Employees did not have a common identity and a sense of destiny. They lacked a set of values and guiding practices that fit their collective 'picture of the future'. Employees saw little or no future for the CSO due to the threatening external environment (e.g. downsizing and budget cuts).
7. *There is a lack of team learning.* Employees did not have the types of relationships with colleagues that allow people to suspend assumptions and 'think together'. People may attend meetings to listen to others or be told what to do, but they do not learn as a group. Relationships lack the mutual trust, respect, and honesty necessary for collective learning. Work at the CSO is seen mainly as stovepipes of expertise where employees work as individuals or in small work cells, and interact for the purposes of task completion rather than learning.

Figure 8.8 presents the CSO data in the middle of the project.

The percentage in the figures refer to the proportion of respondents who felt positively about their organisation's performance in these areas by strongly agreeing or agreeing with the statements (5 and 6 on a 6-point likest scale). Figure 8.8 shows that the CSO's performance as a learning organization improved slightly in 2010. The most significant improvement was found in career management and work–life balance. Figure 8.9 presents the CSO data at the end of the project. The highest performance areas in 2011 were:

1. Work–life balance (81%)
2. Culture (64%)
3. Career management (61%)
4. Mission and values (55.3%)
5. Role clarity (54.5%).

The top three indicators reveal an organization where employees are happy because the job offers lifestyle benefits; people are treated with respect, trust, and honesty; and employees feel that the organization cares about them. These are very positive cultural impacts on employee retention and productivity. The remaining top indicators involve purpose. This means that employees have much better awareness of knowledge management and its importance, and they better understand their role and its contribution. This indicates an organization where employees find meaning in their work and feel the organization values their knowledge.

The best-performing LOC attributes are most associated with personal mastery. The next-strongest association with these top-rating attributes was with team learning, followed by shared vision and shared mental models.

The improved performance as a learning organization since 2009 occurred due to cultural change caused by an increased awareness of knowledge management principles underlying the research project and a growing momentum that these principles, such as sharing knowledge, were seen as a good thing to do. This caused some dramatic increases in performance indicators; for example teamwork increased from 2.5% in 2009 to 48.5% in 2011.

Direct impact from the research project emerged from the training workshops, where employees learned from the experience and took away ideas or techniques and used them in their workplace. For example, activities, peer assists, handovers, and communities of practice sent employees a

(Continued)

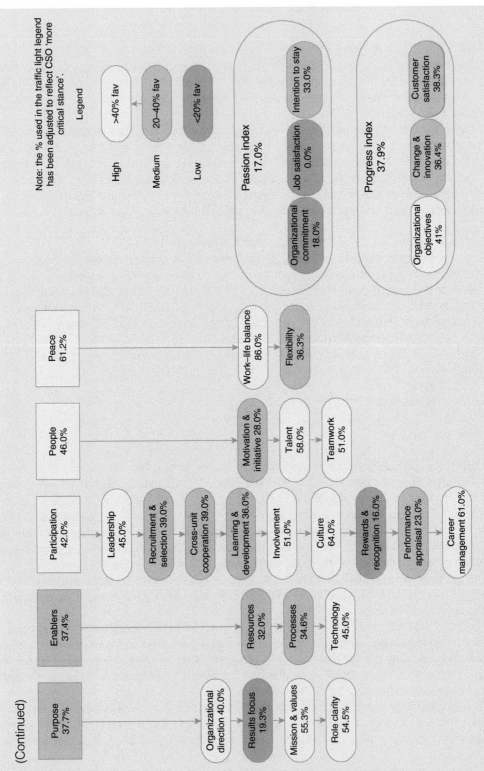

FIGURE 8.9 *CSO LOC performance measurement model, 2011*

clear message that knowledge sharing is an important cultural behaviour, and this is reflected in improved ratings; for instance respondent perception about how well the CSO encouraged knowledge sharing increased from 33% in 2009 to 66% in 2011. Indirect impact emerged in employees' exposure to project ideas at multiple levels. Employees developed shared mental models that the CSO was trying in order to manage the problem of knowledge loss. There were specific initiatives which were introduced to address problems which emerged in 2009. For example, the increase in career management from 39.8% in 2009 to 61.0% in 2011 was a result of more flexible attitudes to employee rotation and job changes, introduced by management after reflecting on the 2009 survey results.

CASE STUDY QUESTIONS

1. Explain the changes in the case study organization's learning organization capacity (LOC) performance between 2009 and 2011.
2. Would the CSO executive be satisfied with these results? Why or why not?
3. How would these changes in LOC improve organizational learning at the LOC?
4. What action would you take to improve LOC performance at the CSO in the future?

REVIEW AND DISCUSSION QUESTIONS

1. Which of the three theories of organizational learning – behavioural, cognitive, and social – do you prefer and why?
2. Critically evaluate the three organizational learning models of Kolb (1984), Huber (1991), and Crossan/Zietsma (1999, 2002). Which best explains how organizational learning occurs?
3. Critics of the learning organization argue that it is naïve and ignores the reality that management exploits workers rather than nurturing them. Discuss.
4. The new model of learning organization capacity presented in this chapter has two dimensions: performance (attributes) and employee engagement (behaviour). Which dimension do you feel would best improve organizational learning?

FURTHER READING

Kolb, D.A. (1984) *Experiential Learning: Experience as the source of learning and development*, Englewood Cliffs, NJ, Prentice-Hall. A useful book on learning models.
Moilanen, R. (2001) Diagnostic Tools for Learning Organizations. *The Learning Organization*, 8 (1): 6–20. A useful article on learning organization capacity.

BIBLIOGRAPHY

Aakhus, M. (2007) Conversations for Reflection: Augmenting transitions and transformations in expertise. Chapter 1 in McInerney, C.J. and Day, R.E. (eds) *Rethinking Knowledge Management: From knowledge objects to knowledge processes*, Berlin, Springer.

Ackroyd, P. (2006) *Shakespeare: The biography*, London, Vintage Books.

Argyris, C. (1960) *Understanding Organizational Behavior*, Homewood, IL, Dorsey Press.

Argyris, C. (1987) Reasoning, Action Strategies, and Defensive Routines: The case of OD practitioners. In Woodman, R.A. and Pasmore, A.A. (eds) *Research in Organizational Change and Development*, Vol. 1, Greenwich, JAI Press, pp. 89–128.

Argyris, C. and Schön, D. (1974) *Theory in Practice: Increasing professional effectiveness*, San Francisco, CA, Jossey Bass.

Argyris, C. and Schön, D.A. (1978) *Organizational Learning: A theory of action perspective*, Reading, MA, Addison-Wesley.

Baird, L., Deacon, S. and Holland, P. (2000) From Action Learning to Learning in Action: Implementing the after action review. In Cross, R.L. and Isrealit, S.B. (eds) *Strategic Learning in a Knowledge Economy*, Oxford, Butterworth-Heinemann, pp. 185–202.

Bandura, A. (1977) *Social Learning Theory*, London, Prentice-Hall.

Bell, S. and Morse, S. (2010) Triple Task Method: Systemic, reflective action research. *Systemic Practice and Action Research*, *23*: 443–452.

Blau, P.M. (1964) *Exchange and Power in Social Life*, New York, Wiley.

Bruner, J.S., Goodnow, J.J. and Austin, G.A. (1956) *A Study of Thinking*, New York, Wiley.

Cohen, W.M. and Levinthal, D.A. (1990) Absorptive Capacity: A new perspective on learning and innovation. *Administrative Science Quarterly*, *35*: 128–152.

Coopey, J. (1998) Learning the Trust and Trusting to Learn: A role for radical theatre. *Management Learning*, *29* (3): 365–382.

Crossan, M., Lane, H. and White, R. (1999) An Organizational Learning Framework: From intuition to institution. *Academy of Management Review*, *24* (3): 522–537.

Cunliffe, A.L. and Easterby-Smith, M. (2004) From Reflection to Practical Reflexivity: Experiential learning as lived experience. In Reynolds, M. and Vince, R. (eds) *Organizing Reflection*, London, Ashgate Publishing, pp. 30–46.

de Geus, A. (1988) Planning as Learning. *Harvard Business Review*, *66* (March/April): 70–74.

DiBella, A.J. (1995) Developing Learning Organizations: A matter of perspective. *Academy of Management Journal*, Best Papers Proceedings, pp. 287–290.

Dick, B. and Dalmau, T. (1990) *Values in Action: Applying the ideas of Argyris and Schön*, Brisbane, Interchange.

Easterby-Smith, M. (1997) Disciplines of Organizational Learning: Contributions and critique. *Human Relations*, *50* (9): 1085–1113.

Easterby-Smith, M. and Lyles, M.A. (2003) Introduction: Watersheds of organizational learning and knowledge management. Chapter 1 in Easterby-Smith, M. and Lyles, M.A. (eds) *Handbook of Organizational Learning and Knowledge Management*, Hong Kong, Blackwell, pp. 1–15.

Easterby-Smith, M., Graca, M., Antonacopoulou, E. and Ferdinand, J. (2008) Absorptive Capacity: A process perspective. *Management Learning*, *39*: 483–501.

Edmondson, A.C., Winslow, A.B., Bohmer, R.M.J. and Pisano, G.P. (2003) Learning How and Learning What: Effects of tacit and codified knowledge on performance improvement following technology adoption. *Decision Sciences*, *34* (2): 197–223.

Eisenberger, R., Fasolo, P. and Davis-LaMastro, V. (1990) Perceived Organizational Support and Employee Diligence, Commitment, and Innovation. *Journal of Applied Psychology*, *75* (1): 51–59.

Faucher, J.B., Everett, A.M. and Lawson, R. (2008) Reconstituting Knowledge Management. *Journal of Knowledge Management*, *12* (3): 3–16.

Garratt, B. (1987) *The Learning Organization*, Gower, Aldershot.

Garratt, B. (1999) The Learning Organization 15 Years On: Some personal reflections. *The Learning Organization*, *6* (5): 202–207.

Garvin, D.A. (1993) Building a Learning Organization. *Harvard Business Review*, *71* (4): 78–91.

Gaskell, E. (1975) *The Life of Charlotte Brontë*, London, Penguin.

Gelb, M. (1998) *How to Think like Leonardo Da Vinci: Seven steps to genius everyday*, London, Thorsons.

Gorelick, C., Milton, N. and April, K. (2004) *Performance through Learning: Knowledge management in practice*, Burlington, MA, Elsevier Butterworth-Heinemann.

Grant, R.M. (1996) Toward a Knowledge-based Theory of the Firm. *Strategic Management Journal*, *17*: 109–122.

Griffey, S. (1998) Conceptual Frameworks beyond the Learning Organization. *The Learning Organization*, *5* (2): 68–73.

Gutherie, E.R. (1935) *The Psychology of Learning*, New York, Harper & Row.

Ho, S.K.M. (1999) Total Learning Organization. *The Learning Organization*, *6* (3): W116–120.

Homans, G.C. (1961) *Social Behaviorism*, New York, Harcourt Brace and World.

Huber, G.P. (1991) Organizational Learning: The contributing processes and the literatures. *Organization Science*, *2* (1): 88–115.

Ikehara, H.T. (1999) Implications of Gestalt Theory and Practice for the Learning Organization. *The Learning Organization*, *6* (2): 63–69.

Kim, L. (1998) Crisis Construction and Organizational Learning: Capability building in catching up at Hyundai Motor. *Organizational Science*, *9*: 506–521.

Kluge, J., Stein, W. and Licht, T. (2001) *Knowledge Unplugged: The McKinsey Global Survey of Knowledge Management*, New York, Palgrave.

Kolb, D.A. (1984) *Experiential Learning: Experience as the source of learning and development*, Englewood Cliffs, NJ, Prentice-Hall.

Lane, P.J., Koka, B.R. and Pathak, S. (2006) The Reification of Absorptive Capacity: A critical review and rejuvenation of the construct. *Academy of Management Review*, *31*: 833–863.

Lehr, J.K. and Rice, R.E. (2005) How are Organizational Measures Really Used? *The Quality Management Journal*, *12* (3): 39–60.

Leonard, D. and Sensiper, S. (1998) The Role of Tacit Knowledge in Group Innovation. *California Management Review*, *40* (3): 112–132.

Leonardi, P.M., Huysman, M. and Steinfield, C. (2013) Enterprise Social Media: Definition, history, and prospects for the study of social technologies in organizations. *Journal of Computer-Mediated Communication*, *19* (1): 1–19.

McGill, I. and Beaty, L. (2001) *Action Learning: A practitioner's guide*, New York, Routledge.

Massingham, P. (2010) Managing Knowledge Transfer between Parent Country Nationals (Australia) and Host Country Nationals (Asia). *International Journal of Human Resource Management*, *21* (9): 1414–1435.

Massingham, P. (2015) Knowledge Sharing: What works and what doesn't work: A critical systems thinking perspective. *Systemic Practice and Action Research*, *28* (3): 197–228.

Massingham, P. (2016) Knowledge Accounts. *Long Range Planning, 49* (3): 409–425.

Massingham, P.R. (2018) Measuring the Impact of Knowledge Loss: A longitudinal study. *Journal of Knowledge Management, 22* (4): 721–758.

Massingham, P. and Diment, K. (2009) Organizational Commitment, Knowledge Management Interventions, and Learning Organization Capacity. *The Learning Organization, 16* (2): 122–142.

Massingham, P. and Massingham, R. (2014) Does Knowledge Management Produce Practical Outcomes? *Journal of Knowledge Management, 18* (2): 221–254.

Massingham, P. and Tam, L. (2015) The Relationship between Human Capital, Value Creation, and Employee Reward. *Journal of Intellectual Capital* (Special Issue), *16* (2): 390–418.

Minbaeva, D., Pedersen, T., Bjorkman, W., Fey, C.F. and Park, H.J. (2003) MNC Knowledge Transfer, Subsidiary Absorptive Capacity, and HRM. *Journal of International Business Studies, 34* (6): 586–613.

Moilanen, R. (2001) Diagnostic Tools for Learning Organizations. *The Learning Organization, 8* (1): 6–20.

Mowery, D.C. and Oxley, J.E. (1995) Inward Technology Transfer and Competitiveness: The role of national innovation systems. *Cambridge Journal of Economics, 19* (1): 67–93.

Mowery, D.C., Oxley, J.C. and Silverman, B.S. (1996) Strategic Alliances and Interfirm Knowledge Transfer. *Strategic Management Journal, 17*: 77–91.

Newell, S., Robertson, M. and Swan, J. (2006) Interactive Innovation Processes and the Problems of Managing Knowledge. Chapter 6 in Renzl, B., Matzler, K. and Hinterhuber, H. (eds) *The Future of Knowledge Management*, New York, Palgrave Macmillan.

Nonaka, I. and Takeuchi, H. (1995) *The Knowledge-creating Company: How Japanese companies create the dynamics of innovation*, New York, Oxford University Press.

Paton, S., Chia, R. and Burt, G. (2014) Relevance or 'Relevate'? How university business schools can add value through reflexively learning from strategic partnerships with business. *Management Learning, 45* (3): 267–288.

Pedler, M., Burgoyne, J. and Boydell, T. (1997) *The learning company: a strategy for sustainable development*, London, McGraw-Hill.

Phillips, B.T. (2003) A Four-level Learning Organization Benchmark Implementation Model. *The Learning Organization, 10* (2): 98–105.

Polanyi, M. (1962) *Personal Knowledge*, Chicago, IL, University of Chicago Press.

Razmerita, L., Kirchner, K. and Nabeth, T. (2014) Social Media in Organizations: Leveraging personal and collective knowledge processes. *Journal of Organizational Computing and Electronic Commerce, 24* (1): 74–93.

Razmerita, L., Kirchner, K. and Nielsen, P. (2016) What Factors Influence Knowledge Sharing in Organizations? A social dilemma perspective of social media communication. *Journal of Knowledge Management, 20* (6): 1225–1246.

Reagans, R. and McEvily, B. (2003) Network Structure and Knowledge Transfer: The effects of cohesion and range. *Administrative Science Quarterly, 48* (2): 240–267.

Reed, K.K., Lubatkin, M. and Srinivasan, N. (2006) Proposing and Testing an Intellectual Capital-based View of the Firm. *Journal of Management Studies, 43* (4): 867–893.

Revans, R. (1980) *Action Learning: New techniques for management*, London, Blond & Briggs.

Richardson, B. (1995) Learning Contexts and Roles for the Learning Organization Leader. *The Learning Organization, 2* (1): 15–33.

Riggs, M.L., Warka, J., Babasa, B., Betancourt, R. and Hooker, S. (1994) Development and Validation of Self-efficacy and Outcome Expectancy Scales for Job-related Applications. *Educational and Psychological Measurement, 54* (3): 793–802.

Schenkel, A. and Teigland, R. (2008) Improved Organizational Performance through Communities of Practice. *Journal of Knowledge Management, 12* (1): 106–118.

Schön, D. (1983) *The Reflective Practitioner*, New York, Basic Books.

Senge, P.M. (1990) *The Fifth Discipline: The art and practice of the learning organization*, New York, Doubleday Currency.

Senge, P., Kleiner, A., Roberts, C., Ross, R., Roth, G. and Smith, B. (2005) *The Dance of Change: The challenges of sustaining momentum in learning organizations*, London, Nicholas Brealey Publishing.

Sicilia, M.-A. and Lytras, M.D. (2005) The Semantic Learning Organization. *The Learning Organization, 12* (5): 402–410.

Sun, P.Y.T. and Scott, J.L. (2003) Exploring the Divide: Organizational learning and learning organization. *The Learning Organization, 10* (4): 202–215.

Szulanski, G. (1996) Exploring Internal Stickiness: Impediments to the transfer of best practices within the firm. *Strategic Management Journal, 17* (Winter Special Issue): 27–43.

Thomas, K. and Allen, K. (2006) The Learning Organization: A meta-analysis of themes in literature. *The Learning Organization, 13* (2): 123–139.

Tsoukas, H. and Vladimirou, E. (2001) What is Organizational Knowledge? *Journal of Management Studies, 38* (7): 973–993.

Vera, D. and Crossan, M. (2004) Strategic Leadership and Organizational Learning. *Academy of Management Review, 29* (2): 222–240.

Weick, K.E., Sutcliffe, K.M. and Obstfeld, D. (2005) Organizing and the Process of Sensemaking. *Organization Science, 16* (4): 409–421.

Wiig, K.M. (2003) A Knowledge Model for Situation-handling. *Journal of Knowledge Management, 7* (5): 6–24.

Yoo, D.Y. (2014) Substructures of Perceived Knowledge Quality and Interactions with Knowledge Sharing and Innovativeness: A sensemaking perspective. *Journal of Knowledge Management, 18* (3): 523–537.

Zahra, S.A. and George, G. (2002) Absorptive Capacity: A review, reconceptualization, and extension. *Academy of Management Review, 27* (2): 185–203.

Zhao, Y., Lu, Y. and Wang, X. (2013) Organizational Unlearning and Organizational Relearning: A dynamic process of knowledge management. *Journal of Knowledge Management, 17* (6): 902–912.

Zietsma, C., Winn, M., Branzei, O. and Vertinsky, I. (2002) The War of the Woods: Facilitators and impediments of organizational learning processes. *British Journal of Management, 13*: S61–74.

9

KNOWLEDGE SHARING

CHAPTER OUTLINE

LEARNING OUTCOMES

After completing this chapter, the reader should be able to:

1. Define knowledge sharing from multiple perspectives
2. Discuss how epistemology and ontology influence knowledge sharing
3. Discuss knowledge sharing from a critical systems thinking perspective
4. Discuss barriers to knowledge sharing
5. Discuss solutions to knowledge-sharing barriers
6. Explain the value of knowledge sharing for the individual and the organization
7. Evaluate how to effectively implement knowledge sharing in organizations

MANAGEMENT ISSUES

Knowledge sharing requires managers to:

1. Identify what knowledge needs to be shared
2. Decide who has the necessary knowledge (knowers/senders) and who needs that knowledge (learners/receivers)
3. Get knowledge to people when they need it

Effective knowledge sharing involves these challenges for management:

1. What are the main barriers to knowledge sharing in your organization?
2. Deciding on the best solutions to improving knowledge sharing
3. Implementing an effective knowledge sharing strategy

LINKS TO OTHER CHAPTERS

Chapter 1: on the process of becoming a skilful knower

Chapter 5: concerning the capability gap and the make decision

Chapter 8: regarding knowledge sharing between individuals as part of organizational learning

OPENING MINI CASE STUDY

TECHSTRATEGY: A TOXIC ORGANIZATIONAL CULTURE – HOW ORGANIZATIONAL CULTURE CAN INFLUENCE KNOWLEDGE SHARING

Richard Gostman worked at a management consulting company called TechStrategy. TechStrategy was a division of Hamish Inc., a Melbourne (Australia) based company with interests in innovation, entrepreneurship, and business growth.

TechStrategy was run by Angelina Aristotal. Ms Aristotal started her career as a consultant in another of Hamish Inc.'s divisions. She quickly built a strong business based on leveraging from the relationships of Hamish Inc. customers from other divisions. Her product was market intelligence. After three years, her sales grew to be large enough to persuade Hamish Inc. to establish a new division, TechStrategy, with her as the director.

Aristotal began by appointing a new graduate, Michael Jones. Michael was smart, hardworking, a quick learner, and charming. He quickly established a reputation for pleasing clients and helped Aristotal build the business. In the first 18 months, Aristotal recruited four consultants, each with a secretary, and a field support team. TechStrategy was thriving.

Aristotal's business model was simple. She employed young, ambitious staff, with no family responsibilities, and paid them low wages. She charged clients high fee rates which meant she generated high profits. A senior consultant was paid $60,000 per annum and charged to clients at a daily fee rate of $1,500. If the consultant was engaged for 48 weeks of the year (accounting for four weeks' annual leave), they would generate $360,000 in fees (240 days @ $1,500 per day). This was a profit of $300,000 per consultant. Placing this in a different context, the consultant was paid $230 a day and charged at $1,500 a day, generating $1,270 a day in profit. It was a very profitable business model. Large consulting companies use a different business model described as the 33% x 3 model. This model allocates consultants' daily fee rates into three parts: (a) 33% is the consultant's salary, (b) 33% is to cover expenses/costs, and (c) 33% is profit for the partners. At $1,500 a day, one of Aristotal's consultants would be paid $500 a day at one of the large consulting companies, twice the salary Aristotal paid, and would generate $500 a day profit, 40% of the profit demanded by Aristotal.

Aristotal was able to create this situation for several reasons. First, she recruited inexperienced consultants who saw her as an opportunity to learn and start their career. Second, she knew that most young people had to stay at their job for three years in order to demonstrate commitment. Staff who left before three years were considered undesirable by recruiters because they were likely to 'job hop'. Third, she chose people who had very little social life or social/family commitments, which meant that their work became their life.

Richard Gostman was different to the other consultants at TechStrategy. He was older (in his late 20s), he had previous experience as a consultant, he was highly qualified (including having a PhD), and he was married. Aristotal took a risk hiring Richard. However, he had a desperation to succeed, which she felt she could exploit.

As Richard settled into his new job, he recognized that TechStrategy was different from any other company he had worked for. Each consultant had their own office. There was a glass wall to allow people to see what you were doing. The glass meant staff could be easily monitored. Under constant review, consultants ensured they spent their time in their office working hard. Consultants were given roles as project leaders which enabled them to manage consulting assignments, including their own clients and team resources. Consultants would be assigned by Aristotal to work for other consultants as team members on their projects. The consultants competed fiercely with one another for clients, projects, and team resources. They also competed to complete projects satisfactorily, which meant high client satisfaction ratings, completion on time or early, and on budget or below budget. Aristotal spent most of her time encouraging this competition.

Aristotal's main strategy was to encourage rivalry based on time. Consultants were encouraged to start work early and to leave late. The number of hours worked became a badge of honour. Instead of saying good morning, consultants would greet one another by asking 'When did you start today?', followed up by 'When did you finish last night?' The ultimate recognition was allocated by doing an 'all-nighter', which was working all through the night and into the next day. Consultants had pillows and blankets next to their filing cabinets and would sleep in their offices.

One day, Aristotal announced that Hamish Inc. was introducing a knowledge management system, and the chief executive officer wanted her to implement it at TechStrategy. The knowledge management system had two parts:

1. *An intranet.* This provided portals for consultants to download their completed work assignments, and share experiences and lessons learned, and intelligence about customers. There were also portals to access organizational knowledge such as processes, how to write a proposal, product information, industry intelligence, and company policies and procedures.
2. *An online discussion forum* where consultants could seek experts, ask questions, get answers, share their knowledge, and access the knowledge of others.

Ms Aristotal declared that all staff would receive training in the new system and that participation was non-negotiable. Consultants must use the new system.

Richard sat at his desk after the staff meeting to announce the new knowledge management system. He gazed out of his window and wondered how the system would work at TechStrategy. He looked out of his glass wall at the other consultants working furiously in their offices. Would they share their knowledge with him? Everything about this company was competitive. Aristotal rewarded those who were more competitive. He considered how rewards did not equate to more money. He had just worked a 105-hour week, which included the weekend. At his daily salary of $230, this worked out to be about $9 an hour (he was not paid on weekends). He smiled to himself and considered how he earned more money as a paper boy when he was 13 years old, delivering newspapers to people on his pushbike for the newsagent. Aristotal rewarded people by playing favourites and giving project manager roles and team resources to those she liked. She gave them more work, not more money.

Richard had three university degrees and a wife he rarely saw. He felt he knew more than the other consultants, but he was not paid more. He asked himself why he should share what he knew with

(Continued)

(Continued)

others. His only competitive advantage was his knowledge. It was the only power he had. Why should he share this and dilute his advantage? Particularly at $9 an hour! He sat at his desk thinking what to do and whether he should comply with this new directive from Aristotal.

CASE STUDY QUESTIONS

1.   What are the barriers to knowledge sharing at TechStrategy?
2.   What are the solutions to knowledge sharing at TechStrategy?
3.   Would a community of practice work at TechStrategy? Why?
4.   What do you feel Richard should do? Why?

INTRODUCTION

Knowledge sharing is a naturally occurring phenomenon. Humans are social beings: we enjoy talking to other people; we ask questions; we answer questions; we share our knowledge. The internet, intranets, social media, email, and information technology have all made information widely available and easily accessible. If knowledge sharing comes naturally, why do we need to manage it? If information is so easy to find, why do we need to manage that?

CORE CONCEPT: Knowledge sharing is activities associated with knowers (senders) and learners (receivers) exchanging knowledge, and includes both codification and personalization strategies; it may be one-way and two-way, and it may involve individual, group, intra-organizational, and inter-organizational knowledge flows.

There are four reasons why knowledge sharing must be managed. First, having people talking is not enough. The chapter will explain that there are numerous barriers to knowledge sharing including individual-level factors such as fear, mistrust, and power. People vary in their sociability and their willingness to talk with others at work. Second, information is not knowledge (see Chapter 1). Information and communication technology (ICT) may make others' knowledge available, but it is only information until the employee is able to interpret it, find meaning in it, and use it at work (see Chapter 1). Third, knowledge sharing creates value through the concept of connectivity. If you tell five people what you know, and they each tell five different people, suddenly 125 people know what you know. You still have your knowledge – you have not lost it – but 125 people have gained it. Knowledge is the only resource that does not lose its value when it is used. Connectivity explains that knowledge actually gains value with use. If we accept that knowledge is the most valuable resource, then knowledge sharing is the most important capability in any organization. Fourth, knowledge sharing generates positive outcomes in terms of improved knowledge flows, increased innovation, and changes in organization performance (Rhodes et al., 2008), such as increased productivity, decreased task completion time, and increased organizational learning (Argote and Ingram, 2000).

This chapter will begin by defining knowledge sharing. There are three main approaches in the literature. The conduit model of knowledge sharing sees knowledge as an object which is passed from the knower (sender) to the learner (receiver). The process model of knowledge sharing describes it as a series of steps which must be moved through to achieve learning. The constructivist model of knowledge sharing focuses on the social interaction of people who find meaning via dialogue.

Epistemological and ontological perspectives on knowledge sharing will be discussed. Epistemology is the philosophy of knowledge. It defines knowledge and helps us understand what is being shared. From an epistemological perspective, we need to consider the definition of knowledge presented in Chapter 1, i.e. knowledge is defined as the capacity of an individual to find interpretation and meaning, leading to action that creates value for the organization. From an epistemology perspective, knowledge sharing enables a learner (seeker) to access knowledge which they can then make useful and meaningful. Ontology refers to the ownership of knowledge. From an ontology perspective, confusion emerges around the differences between individual and organizational knowledge, and also causes barriers to knowledge sharing.

The chapter will explore a systems thinking approach to knowledge sharing. Systems thinking 'advocates thinking about real social systems that it assumes exist in the world' (Flood, 2010: 269); and meaning comes from 'building up whole pictures of phenomena, not by breaking them into parts' (Flood, 2010: 270). There are multiple social systems which influence knowledge sharing in any organization. The chapter develops a paradigm that views knowledge as a 'systemic, socially constructed, context-specific representation of reality' (Parent et al., 2007: 81).

The chapter will examine knowledge-sharing barriers in terms of three constructs: individual, organization, and the knowledge itself. Some knowledge is difficult to share due to its causal ambiguity, tacitness, specificity, complexity, and language. Individual barriers include fear, mistrust, power, and capability problems, as well as low motivation caused by job dissatisfaction, low organizational commitment, and isolated social relationships. Organizational barriers include cultural problems, social connectivity, and inadequate information and communication technology. Solutions to these problems will be discussed.

WHAT IS KNOWLEDGE SHARING?

Knowledge sharing has been defined in many ways. Knowledge sharing has also been called knowledge transfer, organizational learning, and social capital (Easterby-Smith and Lyles, 2003). Tangaraja et al. (2016) suggest that the literature has been confused about knowledge sharing. This confusion has emerged because knowledge sharing and knowledge transfer are being used interchangeably (Kumar and Ganesh, 2009) which has caused misconception (Paulin and Suneson, 2012) and a lack of clarity about the concepts (Liyanage et al., 2009). Tangaraja et al. (2016) argue that the literature's confusion over this topic is problematic because it can lead to misleading findings and a lack of trust in the results. Furthermore, it threatens the validity of the measures used because 'some scholars end up using the same instruments to measure both knowledge sharing and knowledge transfer' (Tangaraja et al., 2016: 654). Given that knowledge management is often criticized (see Chapters 2 and 3), conceptual confusion is an unnecessary distraction for researchers and practitioners.

There are two main reasons for the conceptual confusion. First, epistemology has caused different perspectives about what is being shared or transferred. Paulin and Suneson (2012: 81) argue that the key element used to differentiate between knowledge sharing and knowledge transfer is the perspective used to view knowledge as a 'subjective contextual construction' or an object. This is the personalization and codification dichotomy (see Hansen et al., 1999) discussed in Chapter 2. Perspective about what is being shared or transferred defines how this is done. Codification structures explicit knowledge and stores it in repository systems, such as intranets, to enable knowledge transfer (Joia and Lemos, 2010). Personalization creates the opportunity to socialize and share tacit knowledge via direct personal contact (Joia and Lemos, 2010). This dichotomy suggests that there are two types of knowledge transfer, codification and personalization, which lead us to the second reason for conceptual confusion.

Second, researchers argue that knowledge sharing is a subset of knowledge transfer. Knowledge sharing is seen as a stage of knowledge transfer (Liyanage et al., 2009). Tangaraja et al. (2016) argue that this confuses knowledge sharing with the second form of knowledge transfer, which was explained above as personalization, because sharing is one of the processes involved. The confusion is whether knowledge sharing and knowledge transfer are different activities, one is part of the other, or they are the same. Support for the argument that they are different activities comes from the processes themselves. Knowledge sharing involves the cognitive processes of sensemaking and understanding (Paulin and Suneson, 2012), whereas knowledge transfer involves communication: both oral and via technology (Liyanage et al., 2009).

DEEP THINKING: Whereas knowledge transfer involves a one-way transmission of knowledge from knower to learner, knowledge sharing has an interactive element where 'individuals mutually exchange knowledge, i.e. it is two-way' (Liyanage et al., 2009: 122). The difference is the depth of interaction between the knower (sender) and the learner (receiver).

Liyanage et al.'s (2009) inclusion of oral communication in knowledge transfer confuses the concept because it is personalization and not codification. Tangaraja et al. (2016) conclude that knowledge transfer is more complex than knowledge sharing for two reasons. First, knowledge transfer involves both codification and personalization, which is explained by epistemology; and second, knowledge transfer involves individuals, groups, and organizations, which is explained by ontology. According to Tangaraja et al. (2016), therefore, the complexity of knowledge transfer is due to its broad scope.

Tangaraja et al.'s (2016) focus is to examine the topic from a directional perspective. Their article examines knowledge exchange in terms of the type of knowledge flow using the dichotomy of unidirectional, one-way flow from knower to learner, and bidirectional, two-way flow between knower and learner. The direction dichotomy differentiates the level of interaction. This is the point where this book's view of knowledge sharing takes a different path. The levels of interaction are more complex for personalization (a two-way flow) than with codification. The book's philosophy is that knowledge management is a socially constructed reality based on privileging individual knowledge (see Chapter 1). If we accept the book's definition of knowledge as individuals finding interpretation and meaning (see Chapter 1), then knowledge exchange is the activities associated with knowers helping learners discover this for themselves.

CORE CONCEPT: Knowledge sharing, therefore, is not a subset of knowledge transfer. In this book, knowledge sharing replaces knowledge transfer. It is the words sharing and transfer that are important in making this distinction. Transfer privileges knowledge as an object, in the sense that it is moved from one place (the knower's head) to another place (an intranet or even another person's head), which does not make sense from this book's perspective. Knowledge does not move from one person's head to another's. It stays with the knower. They do not lose it: it has been shared, not transferred.

Sharing privileges behaviour, whether the knower shares their knowledge with their organization via codification, for example by writing a report or uploading data on the intranet, or by personalization, for example by giving a seminar or acting as a mentor or just helping someone with their work. Therefore, this book examines the topic of knowledge sharing rather than knowledge transfer. Knowledge sharing is more complex, represents a more accurate perspective on the social reconstruction of work, and creates more value for organizations.

There are three models of knowledge sharing: the conduit model, the process model, and the constructivist model.

THE CONDUIT MODEL

CORE CONCEPT: The conduit model defines knowledge sharing as the movement of knowledge between entities, which includes individuals, organizational units, and organizations (Boudreau, 2003: 365).

This perspective on knowledge sharing assumes that knowledge can be separated from the knower. It sees knowledge as an object, and that knowledge can also be objective. (See also the section on skilful knowing in Chapter 8.) The conduit model privileges codified knowledge. While researchers accept that organizational knowledge contains tacit components which can be embedded in organizational routines (Szulanski, 1996), the conduit model focuses on the exchange of organizational knowledge between a knower (sender) and a learner (receiver) as a one-way transmission. It suggests that knowledge is shared by transferring codified (explicit) knowledge, such as reports, policies, procedures, emails, databases, and figures, from a knower (sender) to a learner (receiver).

The power in the conduit model is the opportunity for knowledge to be shared across distance. The sender and the receiver may be completely separated. Indeed, they may not know one another and may never meet. Yet they may share knowledge via the organization's information and communication technology, e.g. intranets. This is a particularly attractive concept in the knowledge economy as many organizations are global, some with many thousands of employees, and it is simply not possible for them to share knowledge via socialization. The lack of physical proximity of the knower (sender) to the many learners (receivers) makes the conduit model an alluring prospect, particularly in large organizations. The model explains that the knower (sender) transmits the codified knowledge to the learner (receiver). The receiver then accepts this knowledge and is able to understand it and use it without any form of personal interaction with the sender. The transfer assumes that no important knowledge is lost in the transmission process. If we conceptualize knowledge as a fluid flow of an intangible resource and see this flow being managed in a series of pipes (i.e. processes) connecting knowers and learners, then the conduit model considers that the pipes are watertight and there is no leakage. When the knowledge arrives for the receiver, both they and the sender should have the same understanding and find the same meaning.

DEEP THINKING: Consider this book you are reading. It is my knowledge. I have codified what I know about knowledge management and presented it for you in this book. You and I may never meet. Reflect on the definition of knowledge presented in Chapter 1. Can you find meaning and interpretation in this book and use it without my help? If so, my knowledge has become your knowledge. Otherwise, the book is information only. Consider if you were/are studying knowledge management at university and this book is your set text. Would students who are taught by me at my university have an advantage over you if you are being taught by another lecturer at another university? Could you find meaning and interpretation from another expert who did not write this book but may provide their own perspective on the ideas within it? How may this explain differences in student performance? If we accept the conduit model's 'no leakage' concept, then should not all students understand this book equally and, ultimately, receive the same grade? Or is there another possible explanation? Is the variance in student performance explained by not all knowledge being transferred by the author of the book to the student via the book? Or is it due to differences in student's ability to understand?

THE PROCESS MODEL

The process model helps explain some of the questions about the conduit model raised in the adjacent Deep Thinking box.

CORE CONCEPT: The process model defines knowledge sharing in a series of steps representing dyadic exchanges of knowledge between the knower (sender) and the learner (receiver).

At face value, these models seem to be another example of learning cycles with feedback loops (see Chapter 7 for the KM bridge and Chapter 8 for the KOLB learning model). However, the process model of knowledge sharing is different because it includes a cognitive process where the receiver combines the knowledge transmitted by the sender with their own knowledge to create their own new knowledge. Voelpel et al. (2005) use the term 'source recipient's knowledge' in their definition of knowledge sharing. Williams (2011) argues that knowledge sharing has two main processes: the transmission of knowledge and its integration and application by the user (receiver). The cognitive process, therefore, has three components:

1. Transmission of knowledge from the knower (sender) and the learner (receiver)
2. Reflection, where the receiver gathers feedback from the sender
3. Application, where the receiver integrates the knowledge and creates new knowledge in the act of doing. (After Williams, 2011)

These three processes involve cognitive acts where the receiver finds interpretation and meaning in the sender's knowledge and creates their own knowledge which they may use to create value for the organization (see Chapter 7).

Szulanski (1996: 28) emphasized that 'the movement of knowledge within the organization is a distinct experience, not a gradual process of dissemination.' This experience may then be managed, and the best way to manage it is to organize it into distinct processes. Szulanski (2000) developed a four-stage process model of knowledge sharing, consisting of initiation, implementation, ramp-up, and integration. Szulanski's interest has always been the barriers to knowledge sharing, for which he coined the term 'stickiness'. This is the same idea as the Cartesian split, which is simply the difficulty in separating knowledge from the knower (see Chapter 1). Therefore, Szulanski's definition of the knowledge-sharing process inherently includes stickiness at each stage. He conceptualizes stickiness as 'eventfulness'; the more eventful, the more difficult it is to separate knowledge from the knower at each stage. The four stages can be described as follows:

1. *Initiation*: an opportunity to share knowledge must exist. This is seen as recognition of a knowledge gap, which triggers a search for suitable solutions. Initiation stickiness is the difficulty in recognizing opportunities to share and in acting upon them. The knowing–doing gap (see Chapter 7) is an example of initiation stickiness because the learner (receiver) fails to accept the need for new knowledge, i.e. there is no knowledge gap. Eventfulness becomes more demanding when existing operations are inadequately understood or when relevant and timely measures of performance as well as internal or external benchmarks are missing. Eventfulness, therefore, is associated with the need for change, i.e. the motivation to seek knowledge. The problem at this stage is really about the learner (receiver) not knowing what they need to know.

2. *Initial implementation effort*: this is the exchange of information and resources between the knower (sender) and the learner (receiver). Knowledge flows typically increase and possibly peak at this stage. Management of the process aims to avoid problems experienced in previous sharing of the same knowledge, and 'to help make the introduction of new knowledge less threatening to the receiver' (Szulanski, 1996: 29). Eventfulness is determined by the communication gap between the knower (sender) and the learner (receiver) necessary to fill the latter's knowledge gap. This may be due to problems caused by language, coding schemes, and culture.

3. *The ramp-up to satisfactory performance*: once the receiver begins using the new knowledge, the main concern becomes identifying and resolving unexpected problems caused by the receiver using new knowledge ineffectively. This opportunity may be short-lived because the receiver will quickly embed the ineffective routine. Management requires ramping up gradually toward a satisfactory level of performance, often with external assistance. Eventfulness is defined by the number and seriousness of unexpected problems and the effort required to solve them (e.g. see agency costs in Chapter 5). Significant problems may emerge due to a new operating environment, if training was insufficient or incomplete, or the new practices involve significant changes in the way work is done.

4. *Subsequent follow-up/integration*: once satisfactory results are initially obtained, the use of new knowledge becomes gradually routinized. This happens quite naturally. However, if difficulties are encountered, the new practices may be abandoned and, when feasible, the receiver will usually revert to the previous practice, making the knowledge sharing a wasted effort. Eventfulness depends on the effort required to remove obstacles and to deal with challenges to the routinization of the new practice. This introduces socio-cultural problems including resistance to change, and requires a balancing of power inequities caused by external events such as the arrival of new employees, or by internal events such as individual lapses in performance, unmet expectations, unclear rationale for the practice, evidence of the dysfunctional consequences of using new knowledge, or sudden change in the scale of activities. (After Szulanski, 1996)

While the first two stages comprise all events that lead to the decision to transfer and the actual flow of knowledge from the knower (sender) to the learner (receiver), the latter two stages begin when the receiver starts using the transferred knowledge. Clearly, pure transmission of knowledge from the source to the recipient has no useful value if the recipient does not use the new knowledge. The key element in knowledge sharing is not the underlying (original) knowledge, but rather the extent to which the receiver acquires knowledge which is potentially useful and then uses this knowledge to create value in their work.

Szulanski's model is useful, particularly as an input and output framework highlighting that knowledge sharing does not end when it is transmitted, and that there are other important cognitive processes necessary to make sense of the knowledge, and to interpret it and find meaning, before it can be used to create value for the organization.

Tangaraja et al. (2016: 661) identified the core processes they consider crucial to ensure complete knowledge transfer. They differentiate between processes associated with knowledge transfer via codification and personalization. Codification involves five core processes (knowledge identifying, recognizing, acquiring/absorbing, assimilating, and applying/utilizing by the recipient), whereas personalization involves six core processes (knowledge identifying, recognizing, sharing, acquiring/absorbing, assimilating, and applying/utilizing) (Tangaraja et al., 2016: 661). These processes seem to replicate knowledge management processes and, therefore, represent a broad interpretation of knowledge sharing.

Managing the process model of knowledge sharing requires us to identify the barriers at each stage, i.e. the causes of stickiness, and address them. Whereas Tangaraja et al.'s (2016) framework provides a starting point, it needs deeper evaluation of the underlying issues causing stickiness. This is discussed later in the chapter as knowledge, individual, and organizational barriers to knowledge sharing.

THE CONSTRUCTIVIST MODEL

The constructivist model defines knowledge sharing as embedded and inseparable from the employee in the act of doing work. It suggests that knowledge sharing requires facilitating socialization, i.e. interpersonal communication and collaboration between employees.

CORE CONCEPT: The constructivist model privileges individual knowledge and sees knowledge as subjective and empiricist (see Chapter 1). Rather than knowledge being an object that is simply transferred from one person's head to another's (Easterby-Smith and Lyles, 2003), it is reconstructed by the learner (receiver) in dialogue with the knower (sender).

The constructivist model involves two or more people – the knower (sender) and the learner(s) (receiver) actively interacting and reconstructing meaning.

Von Krogh (2005) defines knowledge sharing as knowledge recreation constructed as a sequential collective action problem. This means that the learner (receiver) recreates the knowledge shared by the knower (sender) in the cognitive process of learning it. The sharing occurs in the interpretation and meaning found, making sense of it, and in the doing process of using the new knowledge. This brings knowledge sharing to the point of knowing in action. It is at the point of doing work where the knowledge is best shared. It also reflects the importance of context or situated knowledge. Rather than the knowledge being transmitted from the sender to the receiver unchanged, i.e. the conduit model, the constructivist model argues that the knowledge will, and indeed must, change to adapt to the receiver's unique operating environment. The environment is not unique because the receiver does the work differently from everyone else (although this is possible); rather, it is the reconstruction event which combines the knowledge of the individuals involved in the knowledge sharing within the action of doing the work. The reconstruction involves interaction and a combination of existing and new knowledge possessed by these individuals which makes the outcome, the new knowledge shared, unique.

THEORY IN PRACTICE: IMPLEMENTING THE BALANCED SCORECARD

Greg Collins was the general manager of Shared Services at Bega Valley Energy. Greg became passionate about the balanced scorecard after reading Kaplan and Norton's (1996) book. His implementation of the balanced scorecard at Bega Valley Energy proceeded this way. First, he discussed his ideas with people at all levels of the organization and across all its business units. These discussions were not formal meetings or interviews. Rather, Greg's management style was to get out of his office and walk around, talking to people in casual conversations. Second, he showed his executive assistant the parts of the book he really liked, and talked to her about how he thought it would work at the company. She produced a series of reports, along with figures and tables to illustrate them. Third, Greg went to each manager and worked with them to develop their own balanced scorecard based on his broad ideas. He asked the managers to work with their staff to develop their own versions to fit their operating context.

A few months later, Greg walked into the transport service depot. Its staff were mainly blue-collar workers. Greg regularly visited the staff, so they had met him before, and were not surprised to see him. One of the workers approached Greg as he walked into the depot. His name was Joe. He was a migrant from southern Europe who had arrived in Australia as a young man with little education. Joe had worked at the company for 22 years and mainly in this depot.

Joe welcomed Greg and began talking to him about the balanced scorecard. Greg was surprised at how well he grasped the concept. Joe showed Greg a chart on the depot wall which detailed the balanced scorecard. He began explaining how the depot was meeting its objectives. Greg was particularly impressed by how Joe was able to explain the connections between the work he did and his contribution to the depot's performance. His eyes shone as he described how he was helping the depot achieve its strategy. Greg asked Joe how he came to understand this chart so well. Joe explained that his manager had explained the balanced scorecard to them. He said, 'We couldn't understand it at first. We are simple men. But we know our depot best. We explained to him how we thought we could help him. He told us how to do the chart. We told him how to measure it. We worked together on how to improve our work.'

When he retired, Greg remembered that conversation as one of the proudest moments of his career.

EPISTEMOLOGY AND ONTOLOGY

Epistemology is the philosophy of knowledge. It defines knowledge and helps us understand what is being shared. From an epistemological perspective, knowledge sharing requires the learners (receivers) to interpret the knower's (sender's) knowledge by properly contextualizing it in their act of doing at work. If the seeker cannot make sense of the knower's knowledge and use it, then the knowledge remains with the knower and has not been shared. In other words, efforts at knowledge sharing can occur whenever a knower tries to share knowledge with learners, but knowledge sharing is not complete unless the learner understands and can use the knowledge.

The cognitive processes of finding interpretation and meaning can occur whether the learner is accessing the knowledge from another employee (tacit knowledge), or from knowledge made available by the organization in the form of reports, procedures, databases, and so on (i.e. codified knowledge). Epistemology presents challenges for knowledge sharing over the definition of what is being shared. This book's philosophy is that knowledge is personal. If we accept this view, then codified materials only contain information, and to create knowledge from this information, the learner needs to interpret it 'using their previous experiences and insights, and this involves thinking processes in the individual's mind' (Tangaraja et al., 2016: 657).

DEEP THINKING: Codification places responsibility on the learner to find meaning, and management needs to ensure the learner can access the codified material and can make sense of it. The view that knowledge is an object to be transferred (e.g. see Paulin and Suneson, 2012) contradicts this argument if we accept that knowledge can never be separated from the knower (e.g. Tsoukas, 2003). The personalization view argues that people must interact to share knowledge. The responsibility for this approach lies with both the knower and the learner to share knowledge, and management needs to ensure this tacit-to-tacit exchange occurs efficiently.

Ontology refers to the ownership of knowledge (e.g. see Nonaka and Takeuchi, 1995). From an ontological perspective, knowledge sharing occurs at multiple levels – between individuals, individual and groups, groups and groups, groups and organizations, and organizations and organizations. Ontology explains that the knower shares their knowledge with the organization in two ways:

- Tacit-to-tacit exchange: sharing with another individual(s) through communication
- Tacit-to-explicit exchange: writing down their knowledge, or codifying it, in the form of reports, policies, databases, and other work outcomes.

This highlights the ownership issue involved in knowledge sharing.

DEEP THINKING: The knower's knowledge is information until a learner can interpret it and find meaning in it, and use it to create value at work. Until the learner can progress through the cognitive processes necessary to do this, the knowledge has not been shared. The knower helps the learner through these cognitive processes until they understand.

Therefore, ontology helps establish the notion that knowledge sharing focuses on the tacit-to-tacit exchange, the social interaction between people (the knower and the learner), to share knowledge. Going beyond this point moves into the management of information – structural capital.

SYSTEMS THINKING

Systems thinking views organizations as a series of connected elements which interact with one another in the daily routine of performing work. Systems thinking is particularly useful for understanding knowledge sharing. It focuses on knowledge in action by looking at how organizations transform input into desired outputs. It also examines organizational boundaries (see Chapter 5) and how organizations allow inputs from and outputs to the external environment. This open systems approach introduces external knowledge flows and knowledge acquisition (see Chapter 5). The concept of a socio-technical system introduced by Trist (1959) explained the importance of the interaction between the social elements of the system – people, relationships, capability – and the technical elements – tangible assets, processes, technology. The socio-technical systems view enables the personalization and technology views of knowledge management (see Chapter 2) to be compared and contrasted in the discussion of knowledge sharing. Systems thinking encourages thinking about organizations being influenced by external and internal environments as they seek resources and strive to survive and prosper. Chapter 11 will examine systems thinking in more detail.

Critical systems thinking is used in this chapter to reconstruct the social reality of knowledge sharing in organizations by surfacing and questioning the assumptions and values inherent in any systems design (e.g. Ulrich, 1983) and by exploring the strengths and weaknesses and theoretical underpinnings of systems methodologies and the associated methods and techniques (e.g. Flood and Jackson, 1991).

CORE CONCEPT: Systems thinking provides awareness of the social rules and practices that make knowledge sharing acceptable.

Recent research has developed a knowledge-sharing paradigm that views knowledge as a systemic, socially constructed, context-specific representation of reality. In this conceptualization, knowledge dissemination describes the internal transfer of knowledge within an organization, and the disseminative capacity builds on social capital networks (Apostolou et al., 2007) and explains knowledge flow as the rotation between the sender and the receiver to enable dissemination. In this way, useful knowledge *spreads* and remains embedded within multiple social structures (Swan and Scarbrough, 2005). The management of knowledge sharing, therefore, should focus primarily on building social structures that can diffuse and embed tacit knowledge.

Critical systems thinking enables us to consider how knowledge sharing creates value for organizations. Impact may be found in comparisons between knowledge-intensive organizations and traditional organizations. The lead indicator is the increase in the movement of knowledge between entities. If organizational learning is a source of competitive advantage (DeNisi et al., 2003) then increased knowledge flow must create value. The lag indicator is the financial return via innovation measures, such as new product sales (revenue increase) or process improvement (cost reduction). The value in knowledge sharing involves filling the knowledge gap (see Figure 5.2 in Chapter 5) or maintaining capability (see phase 1 in Figure 6.1 in Chapter 6). Knowledge sharing may also lead to changes in the learner's behaviour or the development of some new idea that leads to new behaviour (Davenport and Prusak, 1998).

Connectivity explains knowledge sharing at a conceptual level. The theoretical lens for connectivity is labour productivity theory. This topic is covered at both the macro and micro levels. At the macro level, researchers claim that 'diverse, informal localized linkages and knowledge flows (e.g. spillovers) are often cited as core components of a dynamic and productive knowledge economy' (Martinus, 2010: 727). At the micro level, connectivity generates value through social relationships, which creates social capital. The value of social capital is measured by the ability to draw on social status and reputation to access remote, rare, and valuable knowledge resources. The measure of connectivity in this chapter is the productivity gains generated by social capital (Massingham and Massingham, 2014). The practical outcome of effective knowledge sharing, therefore, is whether it increases search cycle efficiency, i.e. the time taken to find the knowledge necessary to perform a new task. Existing measurement methods of connectivity consider how it 'fosters the diffusion of information and knowledge, lowers uncertainty and transaction costs', and, depending on the level of trust within networks (a key measure of social capital), can enhance performance and growth (Sabatini, 2006: 6). Researchers argue that an increase in trust-based relations, i.e. social capital, reduces the average cost of transactions, just as an increase in physical capital reduces the average cost of production (Paldam and Svendsen, 2000).

Researchers have tried to explain connectivity in terms of a knowledge production function. This is defined as the most efficient allocation of the resource inputs (human capital and ideas) to create maximum production outputs (innovation or knowledge) (Mishra, 2007). For our purposes, we defined the knowledge production function as search cycle efficiency. When people recognize a knowledge gap, i.e. a difference between what they know and what they need to know, they seek to close that gap through a knowledge search. This search cycle involves several steps: (1) learning by doing; (2) asking a work colleague for help; (3) using codified knowledge such as policies, procedures, reports, and the intranet; and (4) if all else fails, going outside the organization for help, such as using consultants. Connectivity demonstrates practical outcomes by accelerating this search cycle, i.e. reducing the time needed to access knowledge.

KNOWLEDGE CHARACTERISTICS

Knowledge itself creates barriers to sharing.

CORE CONCEPT: Some knowledge is simply difficult to explain and understand. Characteristics of this type of knowledge include complexity, tacitness, specificity, causal ambiguity, and language.

COMPLEXITY

Some knowledge is just complicated. Schulz's (2001) typology has three levels of complexity:

1. *Simple*: knowledge that is codified; examples include market research data, policies, and procedures – the role of the knower is to explain the codified knowledge
2. *Re-combined*: combining the knowledge of staff from different functional areas, or with different absorptive capacity in the knowledge domain, to create a small, incremental increase in knowledge; examples include business improvement – the role of the knower is to help the learner combine their knowledge with the sender's knowledge to learn something new.

3. *Problem solving*: involves ill-structured and unknown cause-and-effect relationships; examples might include new technical standards for new systems – the role of the knower is to work with the learner to create new knowledge.

The solution is to use a typology, such as Schulz's (2001), to classify the type of knowledge being shared so that both the knower and the learner can assess the most effective way to share. Complexity, therefore, is about awareness of the knowledge being shared, but also the capacity of the learner to find meaning. Simple knowledge may be managed by enabling the learner to access codified knowledge, whereas more complex knowledge will require more interaction between the knower and the learner.

TACITNESS

Tacit knowledge is highly personal and context dependent (Nonaka and Takeuchi, 1995). Tacitness presents significant challenges for knowledge management (see Chapters 1 and 2). For knowledge sharing, tacitness may be summarized by the concept of stickiness, which is the difficulty in separating the knowledge from its source. Tacitness generates a range of behavioural and attitudinal issues associated with knowledge sharing. If knowers have valuable knowledge in their head, they must be willing and able to share that knowledge. Motivation and capability are further discussed later in this chapter. The solution to tacitness is to make people aware of knowledge that is highly tacit, and then to create an environment for socialization, i.e. tacit-to-tacit conversion, between knowers and learners. Communities of practice are groups which enable socialization. This is also discussed further, later in this chapter.

SPECIFICITY

Specificity argues that knowledge may be valuable within one context but of little use in another. It is based on the view that the interpretation of knowledge is heavily dependent on the individual's background and the context in which it is used (Kluge et al., 2001). This suggests that knowledge is relational and truth is subjective or in the eye of the beholder (Nonaka and Toyama, 2003). The solution is to help the sender and the receiver understand how the knowledge will be applied and to assess whether it needs to be adapted to fit a different context.

CAUSAL AMBIGUITY

Causal ambiguity is the inadequate understanding of the reasons for the success or failure of a practice (Szulanski, 1996). It involves the connections between what causes an event and what happens after an event. This may be difficult to explain to others if the receiver cannot see the importance or consequences of the knowledge being shared. The solution is to map the processes involved, usually in a workflow diagram, to help the receiver see the bigger picture and where the knowledge being shared assists them in terms of personal and organizational gain.

LANGUAGE

Comprehension is defined as the internal, subjective process of understanding the *meaning* of something. In the context of knowledge sharing, the practical outcome to this construct means that seekers can accurately and efficiently comprehend what is conveyed to them by the knower. Language is more than words: it is about understanding jargon, terminology, ideas, even shared mental models (e.g. see Senge, 1990). The solution is to provide insiderness via tacit communication, i.e. exposure to socialization (e.g. see Tsoukas, 2003), and codified glossaries.

INDIVIDUAL-LEVEL BARRIERS AND SOLUTIONS

Research has identified a set of constructs that may moderate, i.e. enable or prevent, knowledge sharing in organizations (Yoo and Torrey, 2002).

CORE CONCEPT: Constructs such as trust (Nahapiet and Ghoshal, 1998), anticipated reciprocal relationships (Bock et al., 2005), identification (Kankanhalli et al., 2005), image (Wasko and Faraj, 2005), organizational rewards (Bock et al., 2005), knowledge self-efficacy (Bock et al., 2005), loss of knowledge power (Davenport and Prusak, 1998), and ignorance (Israilidis et al., 2015) have all been identified as having an impact on knowledge sharing at an individual level.

In reviewing the literature on the individual variables with an impact on knowledge sharing, Israilidis et al. (2015) identified 84 dependent variables affecting knowledge sharing in organizations. These variables, in turn, have been classified into 11 categories: employees' actions, attitudes, beliefs, emotions, expectations, motivators, needs, perceptions, traits, skills, behaviour and authority, and values. Table 9.1 provides definitions. (For further details on the literature behind these variables, see Israilidis et al., 2015.)

MOTIVATION

Motivation is defined as those 'psychological processes that cause the arousal, direction, and persistence' of voluntary actions that are goal oriented (Mitchell, 1982: 81). Motivation is an individual-level barrier to knowledge sharing because

TABLE 9.1 Individual variables that impact on knowledge sharing (KS) (Israilidis et al., 2015. © Emerald publishing Limited all rights reserved.)

Employees':	
Attitudes	Attitudes toward KS, attitudes toward organization, collectivism, espousement, intention to KS, job satisfaction, loyalty, organizational commitment, orientation to collaboration, orientation to change, and orientation to work
Beliefs	Psychological contract fulfilment, (knowledge) self-efficacy, basis of truth and rationality and self-consistency
Needs	Affiliation, identification, reputation, linking (networking), and personal needs
Perceptions	Perceived behavioural control, perceived ease of use of KS and perceived usefulness of KS, perceived enjoyment, perceived cost, personal perceptions, considerations of past experience, self-image, prospective engagements in practice, enjoyment in helping others, personal benefit from contributions, self-worth through KS behaviour and self-development, and enhanced reputation and psychological contract breach
Traits, skills, abilities, behaviours, and authority	Work experience, task-identified employees, orientation to change, orientation to work, orientation to collaboration, orientation and focus, intention to KS, internal control, individual initiative, flow experience, coordination and responsibility, level of IT usage, civic virtue, inter-employee helping, helping behaviour and Confucian dynamism, extensive social networking, job-autonomous employees, coercive power, legitimate power, reference power, and expert power
Expectations	Anticipated extrinsic rewards, anticipated reciprocal relationships, anticipated usefulness, expected associations, expected contribution, expected reciprocal benefit, personal outcome expectations, and community-related expectations
Values	Self-expression, trust/trusting relationships, altruism, sportsmanship, and ethical concerns
Emotions	Job involvement
Actions	Organizational citizenship behaviour
Motivators	Self-interest, self-development, rewards, affiliation, employees intrinsically motivated, employees' external motivations, and employees motivated by introjections

it affects the willingness of knowers to share their knowledge, and also the willingness of seekers to receive knowledge or learn from knowers.

Researchers explain that knowledge sharing is not a natural or spontaneous process; it depends on people's willingness to share their knowledge (Cabrera and Cabrera, 2005). Many employees lack the desire to transfer their knowledge to other members of the organization (Denning, 2006). Therefore, identifying 'which factors promote or impede the sharing of knowledge' (Van den Hooff and de Ridder, 2004: 114) and what organizations can do to increase their employees' willingness to share their knowledge, are important areas of research (Martin-Perez and Martin-Cruz, 2015).

The factors that prevent motivation to share knowledge are identity and psychological contract. The first factor, identity, is associated with employees' sense of ownership of their knowledge, which is influenced by trust, fear, and power. Employees' psychological ownership of knowledge is a manifestation of 'psychological territoriality that prevents' knowledge sharing 'beyond personal boundaries' (Li et al., 2015: 1150). Employees tend to realize that sharing knowledge with others does not mean they lose ownership of the knowledge; however, social interaction increases the individual's perception that conflicts of personal interest between knowers and learners will occur (von Krogh, 2011). These conflicts of personal interest emerge if employees expect infringement on their perceptions of ownership, and they may then act to protect their territory and demonstrate their ownership of the knowledge (Avey et al., 2009). Employees are more likely to conduct territorial behaviours when they hold stronger psychological ownership (Brown et al., 2005). Employees' fear of losing their territory and social identity at work, for example as a subject matter expert, may prevent 'collaboration, transparency, and sharing' (Avey et al., 2009: 176). Li et al. (2015: 1151) conclude that 'employees who care about personal knowledge', for instance, take most pride in what they know, and 'are more likely to protect their ownership of knowledge by avoiding sharing it with others'.

THEORY IN PRACTICE: SHARING IN A KNOWLEDGE FACTORY

Universities are knowledge factories. While the primary purpose is to provide students with teaching and learning, academic staff also use their knowledge for research. A colleague told me the following two contrasting stories about sharing knowledge with others in a university.

In the first story, my colleague Alan was new to academia after working in industry in the manufacturing sector. After a few years, he realized that if he wanted to get ahead, he needed to do research and produce some papers. He visited the office of his head of school. He asked the professor to explain to him the types of conferences he should attend and the journals he should try to write papers for. The professor replied 'You can find that on the internet.'

When I asked Alan why the professor acted that way he said, 'I think he wanted me to earn my own stripes, plus he didn't like me.'

In the second story, Alan was approached in his office by a colleague. Alan had just won a major research grant. The colleague asked Alan to put him on the grant, offering to co-supervise the students on the grant in return. Alan replied, 'I'm sorry, this is my grant, and I do not need a co-supervisor for my students.'

The colleague walked out, never spoke to Alan again, and Alan received a reputation for not being a team player.

When I asked Alan why he acted that way he said, 'I couldn't believe this guy. I had worked hard for six years to get that grant, and he wanted to waltz in and take a share of the glory. He hadn't earned the right to be part of that project.'

Employees with a strong sense of work identity created by their knowledge ownership perceive knowledge as a source of power and control (Chennamaneni et al., 2012). Employees may be unwilling to share their knowledge (Storey and Barnett, 2000). Critical discourse on knowledge management argues that the field has tended to ignore socio-political relationships at work. The reality of work is that employees vary in their levels of power, and this has an influence in activities such as knowledge sharing. Power is the ability of an employee to 'change or control the behaviours, attitudes, or values of other(s)' (Liao, 2008: 1882). There are various types of power at work here, including:

- *Reward power*: influence due to the ability to give others rewards
- *Coercive power*: influence due to the capacity to punish others for non-compliance
- *Legitimate power*: influence due to the right to control (e.g. position or role status)
- *Reference power*: influence due to others' admiration or need to gain your approval
- *Expert power*: influence due to having a particular expertise or skill. (After Hislop, 2013: 191)

Expert power is the most relevant for explaining psychological ownership of knowledge. Hoarding occurs when the employee uses their expert power to exert their ownership and protect their sense of work identity. Hoarding means the employee does not want others to know what they know. It provides several perceived individual benefits, including making employees less substitutable or replaceable (Chennamaneni et al., 2012); it maintains organizational influence (Willem and Scarbrough, 2006); and it avoids the fear that others may evaluate their knowledge as irrelevant, inaccurate, or unimportant (Ardichvili et al., 2003). Sharing knowledge with a community may lead to ridicule, for instance by 'losing face' or 'letting colleagues down' (Ardichvili et al., 2003: 70), so knowledge hoarding protects the individual from these risks.

The management of identity, psychological ownership of knowledge, and hoarding must address the factors explained above. Most importantly, employees must be persuaded that their sense of identity is not threatened by knowledge sharing and may actually increase due to the positive behaviours and attitudes shown by knowledge sharing.

The second factor preventing the motivation to share knowledge is psychological contract. Psychological contract is 'the emotional relationship between the employee and their organization' (Massingham, 2013: 163). This relationship is also described as affective commitment, which is defined as organizational commitment and reflects an important aspect of employees' motivation to work in an organization (Allen and Meyer, 1990). Allen and Meyer (1990: 3) conceptualize organizational commitment in terms of the following: 'employees with strong affective commitment remain because they want to, those with strong continuance commitment because they need to, and those with strong normative commitment because they feel they ought to do so.' An individual who is committed to the organization and has trust in both management and co-workers has affective commitment and is more likely to be willing to share their knowledge (Massingham and Tam, 2015). Organizational commitment is based on reciprocity theory (Blau, 1964). Reciprocity explains that employees will be willing to give to their organization, by sharing their knowledge, if the organization is willing to give them something in return.

The types of social behaviours required for effective knowledge sharing, such as cooperation, teamwork, and collaboration, are often considered 'outside those prescribed by job descriptions and are voluntary in nature' (Jarvenpaa and Staples, 2001: 156); thus, people must be motivated to share what they know. Organizations try to improve psychological contract to encourage employees to provide discretionary effort, such as knowledge sharing, for the organization (Storey and Quintas, 2001). Psychological contract may be improved by job characteristics, motivation, job involvement, and job satisfaction; work environment; participation in decision making; financial and personal rewards; a collective sense of identity; and a feeling of belongingness (Cabrera and Cabrera, 2002).

More specifically, psychological contract uses social exchange theory (Blau, 1964) to explain that positive social behaviours at work, including knowledge sharing, are a function of rewards that employees receive from their jobs. As willingness to share usually depends on reciprocity, many organizations design a reward system specifically aimed at 'encouraging their employees to share their knowledge with others' (Bartol and Srivastava, 2002: 64).

There are two types of rewards which may be used to motivate knowledge sharing. Calculative reward measures whether people are willing to work hard for their organization because they feel they will be rewarded; it is commonly referred to as extrinsic rewards (Eisenberger et al., 1990). Calculative outcomes measures whether people are willing to work hard for their organization because they feel they will be recognized; they are commonly referred to as intrinsic rewards (Eisenberger et al., 1990). Recognition creates a barrier to knowledge sharing if both seekers and knowers feel they will not be appreciated for positive knowledge-sharing behaviours, such as teamwork and cooperation. Research has found a need for the knowledge worker to make a sustained and valued contribution to the relevant body of knowledge, that is, a contribution that transcends the organization (Sharkie, 2005). An associated need is the expectation that the organization will provide the opportunity to make that contribution

(Sharkie, 2005). This suggests an ideological need, i.e. does my work matter to society, apart from the organization or its customers? It also suggests that individuals may be motivated to share knowledge if they feel their reputation will be enhanced.

Some researchers argue that the influence of psychological contract on knowledge sharing is still unproven because there has been limited empirical research in this area (Hislop, 2003). However, since Hislop's statement, there has been recent research which has tested the relationship. Martin-Perez and Martin-Cruz (2015: 1176) found that reward systems are important to motivate employees' desired behaviours regarding knowledge transfer, 'but this influence does not take place in a direct way'. Reward systems are the necessary condition to support the development of employees' affective attachment. Li et al. (2015) found that different kinds of rewards have different impacts: intrinsic rewards are the most powerful determinants of psychological contract, and, by comparison, extrinsic rewards have a smaller influence on affective commitment and are not significantly related. Organizations typically try to improve employees' psychological contract extrinsically because management possesses more control over extrinsic rewards than over intrinsic ones. However, Li et al. (2015) found that extrinsic rewards, such as pay and opportunities for advancement and training, are less effective than intrinsic rewards, related primarily to autonomy and job content, in improving employees' emotional relationship with their organization, i.e. developing psychological contract.

CAPABILITY

Capability refers to the individual's ability to send and receive knowledge within the knowledge-sharing activity. Capability differs from motivation in two ways. First, it tends to involve both the knower (sender) and the learner (receiver) whereas motivation focuses more on the willingness of the knower to share. Second, it implies a linear relationship with motivation in the sense that motivation comes first. If employees are not motivated to share, their capability is largely irrelevant.

Researchers explain that knowledge-sharing capability involves both the knower and the learner. Li et al. (2015: 1147) develop a conceptual model based on the logic that links 'how I feel' (psychological contract), 'what I should do' (psychological ownership), and 'what I do' (knowledge sharing). Knowledge sharing, i.e. 'what I do', is based on an employee's action, but it requires interactions with other employees and needs to be placed in a social context (Li et al., 2015). Therefore, knowledge-sharing capability requires social interaction skills, such as relationship management and communication skills. It also requires competence in the knowledge domain for the knower to share what they know and for the learner to know enough to begin to learn from the knower.

The factors that represent barriers to sharing knowledge are absorptive capacity, communication skills, and social capital (covered by relationships).

Absorptive capacity is an important knowledge-sharing capability for several reasons. First, the knower needs to determine how much the learner knows, so that they can then position the sharing of knowledge at an appropriate level. If the knower focuses on too low a level, the learner will not learn because they already know. If the knower starts at too high a level, the learner will not understand them, and cannot learn. Massingham (2010) (see Figure 8.1 in Chapter 8) explains how absorptive capacity affects the relationship between the knower and the learner, and how the knower can identify at what stage the learner needs to begin.

Second, absorptive capacity helps the learner recognize their awareness of the knowledge domain. Israilidis et al. (2015) develop a new variable influencing knowledge sharing which they call ignorance. Ignorance suggests incompetence. In a knowledge-sharing sense, ignorance implies not knowing enough to learn from others who are willing to help by sharing their knowledge. People often find it intrinsically difficult to get a sense of what they do not know, thus being unable to recognize their own incompetence (Kruger and Dunning, 1999). Absorptive capacity may then be used to measure ignorance. Israilidis et al. (2015) extend traditional views of absorptive capacity's ability to learn to encompass a broad range of unskilful knowing. They found that 'ignorant employees, i.e. those who lack critical organizational knowledge, may not be able to get involved in knowledge-sharing activities' (Israilidis et al., 2015: 1116). The contribution of Israilidis et al.'s research is that it adds social capital and structural capital to the human capital concept of traditional views of absorptive capacity. Learners who lack social capital 'may be ignorant of the knowledge possessed by the subject matter experts within the organization in which they are employed, and they waste time and effort in seeking similar knowledge externally' (i.e. from outside knowledge suppliers) (Israilidis et al., 2015: 1116). Equally, employees' ignorance about their organization's structural capital – i.e. the codified knowledge available via reports, policies, databases, and/or the information and communication technologies available to access this knowledge – may lead them to learn obsolete or out-of-date knowledge (Israilidis et al., 2015). Both types of ignorance create search cycle inefficiencies where the learner's ignorance creates waste in the knowledge-sharing activity. Israilidis et al. (2015: 1113) also found that 'employees who make use of imperfect information, due to ignorance, could increase the risks of making incorrect or inappropriate decisions', impacting on work quality and organizational effectiveness.

Based on the 11 categories presented in Table 9.1, employees' ignorance can be classified within the category of employees' traits, skills, abilities, behaviours, and authority. As such, employees' ignorance can be viewed as an inability that prevents employees from effectively accessing organizational knowledge. On the other hand, employees who are well informed (and thus less ignorant) can perform the activities needed for the implementation of successful organizational knowledge-sharing processes.

Communication skills are necessary for both the knower and the learner. The knower may be motivated to share but find it difficult to articulate or codify their knowledge. Alternatively, the learner needs to be able to express their needs and current level of understanding so that the knower can assess how best to help them. Communication skills for the knower include narratives (Garud et al., 2011), storytelling (Denning, 2006), and conversation (Garcia, 2006); and for the learner they include listening and appreciation (Abrashoff, 2002). The closing integrated case study provides more details.

Social capital (SC) is the value of social contacts at work. This value includes power, leadership, mobility, employment, individual performance, individual creativity, entrepreneurship, and team performance (see Borgatti and Foster, 2003). Knowledge management views SC as providing the opportunity to create, share, and combine knowledge resources (Massingham, 2014a). SC generates benefits for the individual, the group, and the organization, from having relationships with or access to resource-filled others at work. SC fits within the broader research area of network analysis. Network studies may be 'distinguished in terms of whether they are about the causes of network structures or the consequences' (Borgatti and Foster, 2003: 1000). This distinction involves the direction of causality. 'The majority of network research has been concerned with the consequences of networks' and there is a need for further empirical research on causes (Borgatti and Foster, 2003: 1000). While there is growing research on causes, much of this focuses on macro issues like inter-organizational networks, or group characteristics like homophily. Previous research on the value of SC has identified a range of concepts. SC can create value by goodwill that facilitates action (Adler and Kwon, 2002); it can reduce the amount of time and investment required to gather information (Burt, 1992); it may represent valuable conduits for knowledge diffusion and transfer (Coleman, 1988); it can facilitate knowledge combinations supporting knowledge creation (Nonaka and Takeuchi, 1995); and it can grow intellectual capital (Nahapiet and Ghoshal, 1998). In this way, SC captures the complex social processes that evolve as a result of productive employee interactions (Boxall, 1996).

ORGANIZATION-LEVEL BARRIERS AND SOLUTIONS

The effectiveness of organizational knowledge transfer is influenced by key organizational factors such as strategy, structure, culture, processes, and information technology (Ives et al., 2003).

CORE CONCEPT: Previous research has found a number of important organization-level influences on knowledge sharing, such as organizational structure (Pierce, 2012) and controls; organizational culture (Bock et al., 2005); HRM policies including training and education, processes and activities, and leadership (Wong, 2005); and structured information technology (O'Dell and Grayson, 1998) and networks (Hansen et al., 2005).

Rhodes et al. (2008) have developed a conceptual model for managing organization-level barriers to knowledge sharing. Their conceptual framework is presented in Figure 9.1.

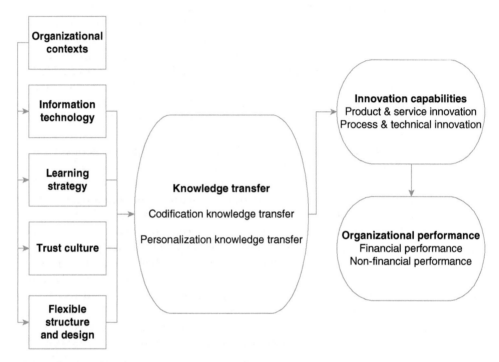

FIGURE 9.1   *Organization-level barrier solutions*

Source: (Rhodes et al., 2008 © Emerald Publishing Limited all rights reserved.)

Rhodes et al. (2008: 86) explain that 'organizational factors are contextual, resulting in varying degrees of influence on the knowledge-sharing ability of the organization'. Furthermore, a range of organizational factors can have a significant impact on the innovation capability, such as IT, and the relationship between knowledge sharing, innovation, and organizational performance can be determined.

The key organizational factors are as follows:

- *Information technology*: Davenport and Prusak (1998) concluded that information technology improves organizational performance by enabling access via search and retrieval tools, as well as supporting collaboration and communication between employees (Alavi and Leidner, 2001). The integration of IT systems via tools such as portals, data mining, workforce search, customer relation management, and e-learning also increases knowledge sharing (see Chapter 11).

- *Learning strategy*: Senge (1990) explains the importance of learning within the context of the learning organization (see Chapter 8).

- *Trust culture*: 'competence-based trust can build respect' (Levin and Cross, 2004: 1480) and relational factors such as perceived trustworthiness play important roles in knowledge sharing with others. Cultural change also helps employees to understand the desirable knowledge-sharing attitudes and behaviours and to develop shared mental models about them (McDermott and O'Dell, 2001).

- *Flexible structure and design*: organizational structure can influence how well knowledge may be efficiently integrated within the organization (Grant, 1996). When an organization faces a dynamic environment, it may need to use several structures to support knowledge management in the firm (Nonaka and Takeuchi, 1995). Cross-functional teams may facilitate the formulation of a knowledge map for employees to use to find the appropriate knowledge (Greengard, 1998). Flexible structures can encourage increased knowledge sharing. An equitable reward or incentive system motivates individuals to share knowledge readily and reinforces individuals' understanding of an organizational trust culture (Massingham and Tam, 2015).

COMMUNITIES OF PRACTICE

Communities of practice (CoP) are 'groups of people who share a concern, passion, or set of problems about a topic, and who deepen their knowledge in this area by interacting on a regular basis' (Wenger et al., 2002: 4). CoP can support and enable innovation processes in organizations (Bertels et al., 2011) and improve organizational performance (Bradley et al., 2011). CoP have traditionally been seen as informal, self-selecting, self-managing groups that operate open-ended without deadlines or deliverables (Baumard, 1999). This voluntary aspect can be both a strength and a weakness. The strengths are the democracy and participation that enable the knowledge-sharing practices that CoP strive for (Massingham, 2014a). This empowerment seems necessary for the creativity and adaptability that effective CoP require. As a result, CoP have been handled with a light touch and tend to be nurtured rather than commanded and controlled (Ward, 2000). The weaknesses are that CoP are dependent on participants' motivation and goodwill, which threaten their continuity, and they are not accountable. This means that CoP may become little more than opportunities to chat with limited personal or organizational gain or practical outcomes in terms of innovation.

Research has recognized that CoP have heterogeneous purpose and performance with different characteristics and dynamics (Amin and Roberts, 2008). Increasingly, external professional or occupational social networks are being distinguished from CoP, and are subject to more formal controls such as membership criteria and performance outcomes (Swan et al., 2002). This denies the empowerment rights of participants driving voluntary CoP in favour of a greater managerial or professional agenda. These external CoP in particular must be managed. However, this introduces problems of power, conflict, and internal dynamics in CoP (Fox, 2000). This threatens the need for the democracy and participation considered essential to knowledge sharing within CoP.

Whereas typical CoP have a shared sense of communal identity created by being employees within the same organization (Bettiol and Sedita, 2011), external CoP have a much more limited sense of common identity. Participants must play a boundary-spanning role to establish cross-community collaborations which will require intra- and inter-firm knowledge transfer processes (Easterby-Smith et al., 2008). This will involve factors such as absorptive capacity, transfer capability, and motivation for both the knower (donor) and the seeker (recipient) in the CoP knowledge exchange, as well as an understanding of the nature of the knowledge being transferred and inter-organizational dynamics such as 'power, trust and risk, structures and mechanisms, and social ties' (Easterby-Smith et al., 2008: 679). This raises attitudinal and behavioural issues for CoP, which lack the sense of identity and goodwill generated by employee membership. Professional practice CoP have diverse characteristics created by people who do not usually work together and who come from different knowledge perspectives (Hislop, 2013). This includes situations such as multi-disciplinary work (Oborn and Dawson, 2010); cross-functional collaboration (Majchrzak et al., 2012); inter-organizational supply-chain-based collaboration (Mason and Leek, 2008); cross-business collaboration within multinationals (Massingham, 2010); and the outsourcing of business services to third parties (Williams, 2011). Hislop (2013) argues that cross-community CoP require special knowledge processes to build the identity, trust, and social relations necessary for effective knowledge transfer.

An appropriate CoP model might adapt the guidelines provided by Massingham's (2014b) study of communities of action research (CAR). A CAR embeds 'change-oriented projects within a larger community of practitioners, consultants and researchers, to produce knowledge that is useful to people in their everyday lives' (Senge and Scharmer, 2001: 238). Massingham (2014b) found that the principles of participation and democracy were difficult to follow in CARs. This chapter's approach to CoP maps the system issues and the CoP learning flows, and adapts Massingham's recommendations for finding cohesion within the CoP. Figure 9.2 summarizes this CoP model.

IMPLEMENTING EFFECTIVE KNOWLEDGE SHARING

Previous research has developed some integrated models for implementing effective knowledge sharing in organizations. Easterby-Smith and Prieto (2008) developed a model of knowledge management as dynamic capabilities which they proposed as the best way to manage organizations in dynamic and discontinuous environments. As discussed in Chapter 5, operational capabilities enable the operational functioning of the organization; dynamic capabilities are the modification of operational routines to create sustainable competitive advantage; and learning capabilities facilitate the creation and modification of dynamic capabilities. Figure 9.3 presents this model.

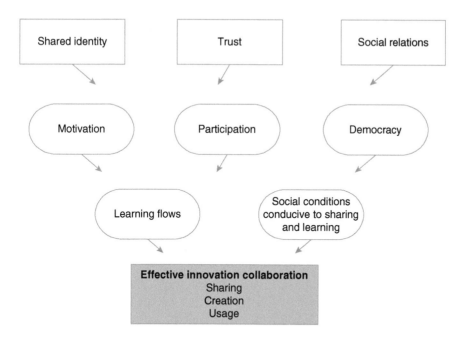

FIGURE 9.2 *Innovation collaboration: communities of practice model*

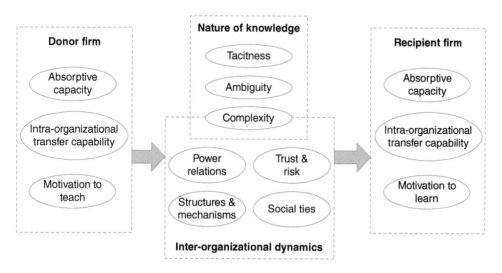

FIGURE 9.3 *Factors influencing inter-organizational knowledge sharing*

Source: Easterby-Smith et al. (2008). Reprinted by permission of Wiley.

The model focuses on inter-organizational knowledge sharing, i.e. between two organizations: a donor (knower) and a recipient (learner). It reinforces some of the elements of knowledge sharing identified in this chapter, such as absorptive capacity, motivation, the characteristics of knowledge, and socio-political and socio-technical dynamics.

Parent et al. (2007) proposed a systems-based Dynamic Knowledge Transfer Capacity (DKTC) model focusing on the capacities that must be present in organizations and social systems as a precondition for knowledge sharing to occur. The model includes pre-existing conditions for implementing knowledge sharing, need and prior knowledge, and 'four categories of capacities – generative, disseminative, absorptive and adaptive/responsive – that social systems must have for knowledge sharing to take place' (Parent et al., 2007: 81).

Armbrecht et al. (2001) proposed a knowledge flow model for research and development firms. The model has a cyclical approach to knowledge sharing and covers important ontological and epistemological elements. It also links strategy with implementation. The model has a technology view of knowledge management. Its focus is infrastructure and technology as the best way to deal with knowledge flow barriers; however, it complements this with organizational culture. It also includes individual and organizational levels.

O'Dell (2000) identified five stages in the implementation of successful knowledge sharing:

1. Getting started, which includes creating a vision, igniting a spark, and collecting success stories to be shared within the organization

2. Connecting the knowledge-sharing effort to the business need, and finding advocates for knowledge sharing who will support the identification of knowledge-sharing initiatives, explore different possibilities, and continue the effort by spreading success stories about knowledge sharing within the organization

3. Launching knowledge-sharing initiatives and supporting them through support strategies and activity and outcome measures

4. Creating a support structure for the selected pilots, building the capability to expand and support the knowledge-sharing process, bringing the knowledge-sharing initiative up to the enterprise level, and continuing with activity and outcome measures that were initiated in stage 3

5. Institutionalizing the knowledge-sharing initiative and sustaining business measures to reflect the benefits of knowledge transfer activities via the way of doing business, i.e. the routines, processes, and norms of organizational functioning. As a holistic solution model, the implementation of stages of knowledge transfer initiatives involves both gaining buy-in and creating enormous cultural change. (O'Dell, 2000)

Ringberg and Reihlen (2008) propose the socio-cognitive approach outlined in Figure 9.4. This model suggests that meaning is mediated by private and cultural models generated by the individual's own cognitive dispositions, including memory and emotions, as well as socio-cultural interaction. The model shows links between context, process, feedback, and outcome. Managing the constructivist

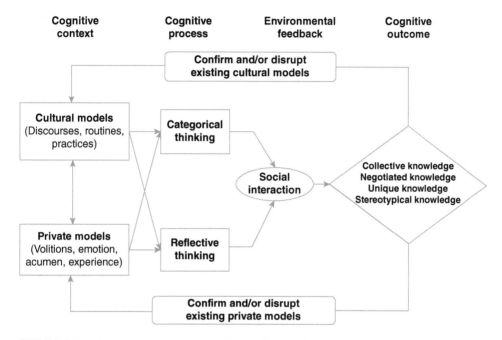

FIGURE 9.4 *Cognitive outcomes in knowledge sharing*

Source: Ringberg and Reihlen (2008). Reprinted by permission of Wiley.

model requires socialization opportunities and skills in terms of communication, language, and technology, as well as socio-cultural enablers. Ringberg and Reihlen also used a bipolar typology in Figure 9.5 along axes of high–low social interaction and reflective-categorical thinking.

The intersection of these constructs produces quadrants of knowledge transfer outcomes: negotiated knowledge, unique knowledge, collective knowledge, and stereotypical knowledge. The managerial challenge is to match knowledge transfer types with the needs of the organization. For example, the bottom left-hand quadrant combines reflective thinking with low social interaction. Employees in this quadrant might be considered socially inept, extreme idealists, or even nerds. However, they are valuable because they can produce unique knowledge. The way to manage employees in this quadrant is to encourage them to reflect on practice and share the lessons learned with others.

The discussion so far has defined knowledge sharing and has explored barriers to knowledge sharing in terms of knowledge (e.g. tacitness), the individual (e.g. motivation), and the organization (e.g. culture). The chapter has presented the literature's views on the challenges associated with knowledge sharing and some ideas on how to manage them. Figure 9.6 presents a new model of knowledge sharing based on the discussion.

When reflecting on the models above, it is necessary to consider empirical evidence of effective knowledge sharing. There have been only a few longitudinal

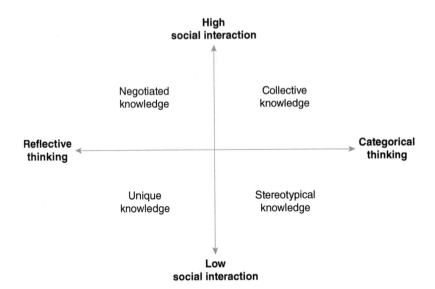

FIGURE 9.5 *Knowledge-sharing outcomes*

Source: Ringberg and Reihlen (2008). Reprinted by permission of Wiley.

studies which claim to have tested knowledge-sharing models. The findings are presented in terms of individual-level and organization-level solutions.

INDIVIDUAL-LEVEL RESULTS

Employees often share the knowledge they possess, predominantly when they are intrinsically motivated (self-motivated) or when they anticipate specific personal benefits in return, such as enhanced reputation, perceived usefulness of the acquired knowledge, self-development, association, and reciprocal relationships (Bock et al., 2005). Employees also share knowledge when they are driven by behavioural control (Ryua et al., 2003) or enjoyment in helping others (Kumar and Rose, 2012), or when they choose to be socially engaged in knowledge-exchange activities (Israilidis et al., 2015).

On the other hand, the findings about expected rewards (extrinsic rewards) are inconsistent (Israilidis et al., 2015). Burgess (2005) argues that the expected rewards positively influence the knowledge-sharing behaviour of employees. However, Gupta et al. (2012) claim that there is no consensus among researchers on the topic, and Bock et al. (2005) found that expected rewards do not affect knowledge-sharing behaviours. Orientation to work (Jones et al., 2006), anticipated reciprocal relationships (Kim and Lee, 2011), and organizational commitment (Gupta et al., 2012), as well as coercive and legitimate power, have been found to have no significant effect on knowledge sharing. Additionally, the usage of information technology on its own does not have any significant effect on the sharing of organizational knowledge (Israilidis et al., 2015).

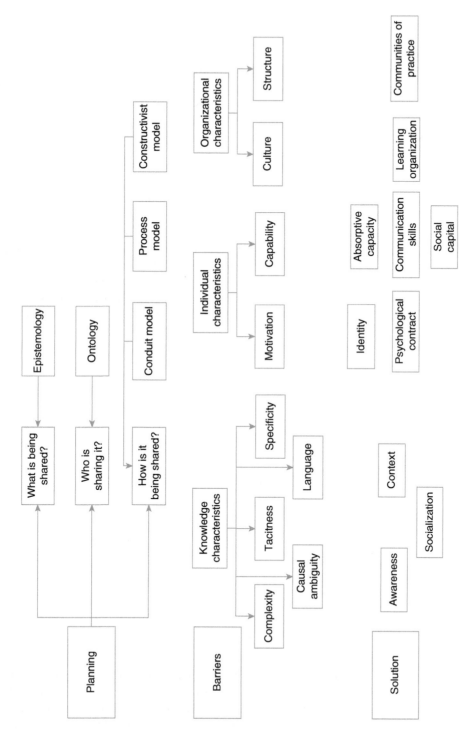

FIGURE 9.6 *A knowledge-sharing model*

ORGANIZATION-LEVEL RESULTS

Information technology has the greatest impact on knowledge sharing (Rhodes et al., 2008). It is generally accepted that an integrated IT system enhances the storage and accessibility of knowledge (Small and Sage, 2005). However, the IT system is only an enabler. Human activities such as a willingness to share knowledge, the learning capability of employees, and the perceived equity of rewards from sharing can play a significant role. Integrated control systems (Turner and Makhija, 2006) to formalize codified knowledge and improvements in multiple social networks (Hansen et al., 2005) can significantly increase the sharing of tacit knowledge.

Learning strategy is the second most important organization-level factor (Rhodes et al., 2008). Management can provide equitable reward systems to motivate individuals to share with and learn from each other (e.g. Hansen et al., 2005). Trust culture was the third most important factor. Flexible structure and design had the least impact on knowledge sharing in the Rhodes et al. (2008) study.

Figure 9.7 summarizes the results in terms of a scorecard rating for each knowledge-sharing technique tested at the case study organization (see closing case study). It represents the ratings for each tool against a set of criteria designed to cover the evaluation framework (see Massingham, 2014a).

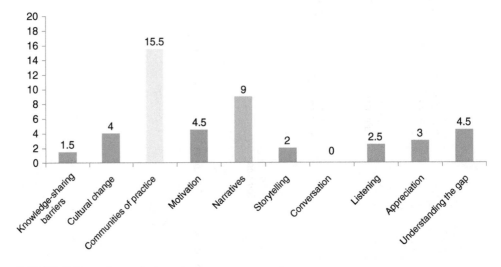

FIGURE 9.7   *A knowledge-sharing scorecard*

Figure 9.7 shows that, overall, the knowledge-sharing tool with the most success was communities of practice. The two least-successful tools were conversation and knowledge-sharing barriers. In terms of comparison with all KM tools implemented at the case study organization, communities of practice was ranked fifth-highest tool overall.

CONCLUSION

This chapter has highlighted the challenges presented by knowledge sharing. Rather than being a naturally occurring phenomenon, knowledge sharing is difficult, and managers need to be aware of the factors that represent barriers to knowledge sharing in organizations. This chapter presented a framework for understanding these barriers in terms of the knowledge itself, at the individual level, and at the organizational level. The chapter also explained how knowledge sharing occurs from three perspectives: the conduit model, the process model, and the constructivist model.

A number of models of knowledge sharing were presented, culminating in a new model (see Figure 9.6) which summarizes the chapter's discussion. Finally, the chapter highlighted the importance of implementing effective knowledge sharing by using successful tools as an integrated system. Various models were discussed. Findings from previous research suggest that individual factors influencing knowledge sharing are more closely related to perceived personal benefits than to organizational context, structures, and command. In other words, personal gain is more important than organizational gain or management actions. At the organizational level, knowledge sharing may be managed effectively by IT systems and social network structures. More specifically, Massingham's (2014a) research found that communities of practice are the most successful organization-level solution.

CLOSING CASE STUDY: KNOWLEDGE SHARING AT THE CSO

Matthew Underich was thinking about the meeting he was walking towards. It was part of the knowledge loss project that the department had started a few years ago. The meeting was with the Chief investigator (CI) of the project and the four principal engineers (PEs). The meeting had been organized to talk about how to improve knowledge sharing within the department's four main technical disciplines. The PEs were the discipline leaders in each of these areas. Matthew was wondering why they were having the meeting. Knowledge sharing was not a problem for the department. There were about 150 professional staff. Most of them were located in the same building and on the same floor. If people wanted to share knowledge, they simply got up from their desk and walked along the open office area to talk to someone. Everyone knew everyone else. Knowledge sharing was about people talking to one another. It wasn't like people worked in different cities or even countries. They were 100 metres away from your desk at worst.

As the meeting began, the CI explained that he wanted to talk to the PEs about communities of practice (CoP). The CI indicated that CoP was a technique that he wanted to test as part of the project's research. He explained that CoP consisted of groups of like-minded people who regularly

(Continued)

(Continued)

interact to share and create new knowledge. He discussed how the commodore wanted the PEs to take leadership for building CoP across their disciplines.

The CI asked the PEs to describe how their existing communities worked. The PEs explained that their communities were staff who were members due to their qualifications. For example, electrical engineers were part of the electrical engineering group. This group were all part of a business unit which did electrical engineering work. The staff interacted regularly in doing their work, similar to any organizational unit. The staff were located together in an open office layout. Knowledge sharing often meant yelling out a question for someone else without even leaving your seat. It seemed very straightforward to the PEs. They agreed that knowledge sharing was not a problem and did not need any intervention from the CI's project.

The CI asked the PEs to humour him and let him study how they ran their CoP. He explained that he might discover some ways to improve how they shared knowledge. The PEs were sceptical but they were nice people and they got along well with the CI so they agreed to participate. The CI gave them two tasks to complete before the next meeting:

1. Begin designing a knowledge strategy for your technical discipline. This would determine what the department knew in terms of their discipline and what it needed to know in the future. The outcome would be a knowledge gap analysis, i.e. the difference between what was known and what needed to be known in five years' time.
2. To reflect on how the group shared knowledge regarding the above task.

Matthew walked out of the meeting feeling quite positive. He was a naturally cynical and critical person. But he was also a deep thinker, and he could see there was value in the CI's ideas, even if it was not always clear. His technical discipline was the most fragmented of the four PEs because it was not a natural discipline. Whereas mechanical engineering and electrical engineering had common ground due to the lessons learned at university, Matthew's discipline was a combination of structural engineering, design, and architecture. He could see that he may have some problems with the tasks the CI gave him. But he approached this challenge with enthusiasm.

Two weeks later, the PEs met with the CI to discuss what had happened and how they were progressing with their tasks. Each PE had a different experience. The first PE, Sarah Fitzpatrick, reported that she had decided a formal community of practice (CoP) was unnecessary. She felt her discipline was working well and did not need any improvements. She concluded that she would be deciding on the knowledge strategy for her discipline as she was in the best position to know current and future capability requirements.

The second PE, Eric Ong, had decided to continue with his current interpretation of a CoP. It was a regular annual meeting with a network of professionals from different organizations. Eric had cultivated this network over his career. Members were friends who met to share a catch-up, as well as knowledge of common issues and challenges in their discipline. Eric felt that this network had served him and the department well over many years and that there was no need to change. When the CI reminded Eric about the knowledge strategy, Eric replied that his discipline was relatively static, i.e. that knowledge changed slowly. He was well aware of current capabilities in his discipline. His annual meeting would be enough to keep up to date with any changes. He concluded that he would be relying on his external contacts, rather than internal staff, to help him frame his ideas about the knowledge strategy.

The third PE, Evan Andreison, was enthusiastic about the idea of a formal CoP. His discipline was also relatively stable. The senior staff in Evan's discipline were, however, the most cynical and disgruntled group in the department. While they were highly experienced and capable, they preferred working alone and did not want to share their knowledge. Each person had their own niche technology area which they felt they owned. They tended to hoard knowledge so that their expertise made them indispensable, and this provided them with a sense of job security and self-esteem. Evan, and everyone else at the meeting, were well aware of these problems. Evan also suffered from a bad reputation as a disruptive influence and someone who challenged management and the underlying assumptions of what the organization was doing. The CI admired Evan because he practiced triple-loop learning. Unfortunately, no one recognized Evan for doing this. Evan surprised everyone at the meeting by embracing the concept of a formal CoP. He wanted it to give him the authority to assume a leadership role in the group. While he was the PE, it was really in title only. The others did not respect him and did not cooperate with him. But Evan knew that it would be difficult to implement the type of CoP that the CI was proposing. The group would simply not cooperate. Therefore, he announced that he wanted to introduce a CoP which represented an internal group of professionals getting together to discuss and address challenges or share stories of problems solved and innovations discovered. Evan announced that he wanted to develop the knowledge strategy with his colleagues. He knew that they liked to talk about the past and he felt that finding a forum where they could share their experiences would be the best way to build a sense of a team. From this activity, Evan hoped that he could persuade the team to contribute ideas towards the knowledge strategy.

The fourth PE, Matthew Underich, was keen to adopt the CI's recommendations on establishing a CoP. His discipline was relatively fast moving in terms of changes in knowledge. While some structural design issues still retained the core discipline knowledge used for decades, technology was continually improving the way data was gathered, analysed, and reported. Matthew was also keen to adopt a leadership role within his group. His focus was internal rather than external. He additionally had a collegial approach and wanted to build a sense of teamwork, cooperation, and collaboration within the group. He discussed the idea of a formal CoP and the knowledge strategy with the group. They agreed to set up an informal but regular session to share relevant organizational knowledge that would help professionals to better understand the bigger picture in terms of the political, economic, social, and technological issues and future directions of the CSO. Matthew was keen to meet regularly with his team and to share knowledge and learn together. He felt that the best way to develop a sense of meaning and purpose for these meetings was to focus on organizational issues and

(Continued)

(Continued)

give people access to knowledge they normally wouldn't get. He felt that sharing knowledge about specific technical domains known by individual staff wouldn't be helpful because others were not interested. He needed to focus on a higher level of knowledge rather than individual-level knowledge. Staff only wanted to know about knowledge that helped them do their job. In his discipline, the fragmented nature meant that staff were specialists and did not need to maintain core discipline knowledge. The knowledge strategy would focus on how the discipline could help the organization in the future.

The CI reflected the feedback from each of the PEs. He understood their positions. He felt it was interesting that each had found a different interpretation of CoP and what would work for them. He focused on Matthew and his group as he seemed most willing to embrace the ideas presented by the CI. He worked with Matthew in developing a formal standard operating procedure (SOP) for CoP. He hoped that the SOP would guide Matthew but that it might also become a tool for the other PEs. Perhaps if they saw how it was helping Matthew, the other PEs might also adopt the SOP. As the CoP SOP took shape, Matthew found problems with it. He didn't like how prescriptive it was. The CI was testing an idea that informal CoP were ineffective because they lacked an outcomes focus. The CI felt getting people together to have a chat was not enough. The CoP needed to be formalized and given tasks, deadlines, and expected outcomes. Matthew felt this was unnecessary and he preferred a more relaxed approach. In the end, Matthew rejected the SOP and indicated that he would follow a much more simplified version of it and adapt it as needed.

CASE STUDY QUESTIONS

1. How would the communities of practice (CoP) model presented in this case study address barriers to knowledge sharing?
2. Evaluate its implementation.
3. At the CSO, only one of four discipline leaders embraced the CoP model presented here. Why do you feel the model had this response?

REVIEW AND DISCUSSION QUESTIONS

1. Consider the three models of knowledge sharing: conduit, process, and constructivist. Would the choice of appropriate model depend on the nature of work performed at the organization? Why?

2. Evaluate the three categories of knowledge-sharing barriers summarized in Figure 9.6: knowledge, individual, and organizational. Which do you feel represents the major barrier? Why?

3. What is more important to effective knowledge sharing: motivation or capability? Why?

FURTHER READING

Bock, G.-W., Zmud, R.W., Kim, Y.-G. and Lee, J.-N. (2005) Behavioral Intention Formation in Knowledge Sharing: Examining the roles of extrinsic motivators, social-psychological forces, and organizational climate. *MIS Quarterly*, 29 (1): 87–111. This article examines factors influencing individual behaviour associated with knowledge sharing.

Rhodes, J., Hung, R., Lok, P., Lien, B. and Wu, C.M. (2008) Factors Influencing Organizational Knowledge Transfer: Implication for corporate performance. *Journal of Knowledge Management*, 12 (3): 84–100. This article explores organization-level factors influencing knowledge sharing.

BIBLIOGRAPHY

Abrashoff, D.M. (2002) *It's Your Ship: Management techniques from the best damn ship in the navy*, New York, Business Plus.

Adler, P.S. and Kwon, S.-K. (2002) Social Capital: Prospects for a new concept. *Academy of Management Review*, 27 (1): 17–40.

Alavi, M. and Leidner, D.E. (2001) Review: Knowledge management and knowledge management systems – Conceptual foundations and research issues. *MIS Quarterly*, 25 (1): 107–136.

Allen, N.J. and Meyer, J.P. (1990) The Measurement and Antecedents of Affective, Continuance and Normative Commitment to the Organization. *Journal of Occupational Psychology*, 63: 1–18.

Amin, A. and Roberts, J. (2008) *Community, Economic Creativity, and Organization*, Oxford, Oxford University Press.

Apostolou, D., Abecker, A. and Mentzas, G. (2007) Harmonising Codification and Socialisation in Knowledge Management. *Knowledge Management Research and Practice*, 5 (4): 271–285.

Ardichvili, A., Page, V. and Wentling, T. (2003) Motivation and Barriers to Participation in Virtual Knowledge-sharing Communities of Practice. *Journal of Knowledge Management*, 7 (1): 64–77.

Argote, L. and Ingram, P. (2000) Knowledge Transfer: A basis for competitive advantage in firms. *Organizational Behavior and Human Decision Processes*, 82 (1): 150–169.

Armbrecht, F.M.R., Chapas, R.B., Chappelow, C.C., Farris, G.F., Frigga, P.N., Harts, C.A., et al. (2001) Knowledge Management in Research and Development. *Research Technology Management*, 44 (4): 28–48.

Avey, J.B., Avolio, B.J., Crossley, C.D. and Luthans, F. (2009) Psychological Ownership: Theoretical extensions, measurement and relation to work outcomes. *Journal of Organizational Behavior*, 30: 173–191.

Bartol, K.M. and Srivastava, A. (2002) Encouraging Knowledge Sharing: The role of organizational reward systems. *Journal of Leadership and Organizational Studies*, 9 (1): 64–76.

Baumard, P. (1999) *Tacit Knowledge in Organizations*, London, Sage.

Bertels, H., Kleinschmidt, E. and Koen, P. (2011) Communities of Practice versus Organizational Climate: Which one matters more to dispersed collaboration in the front end of innovation? *Journal of Product Innovation Management, 28* (5): 757–772.

Bettiol, M. and Sedita, S. (2011) The Role of Community of Practice in Developing Creative Industry Projects. *International Journal of Project Management, 29*: 468–479.

Blau, P.M. (1964) *Exchange and Power in Social Life*, New York, Wiley.

Bock, G.-W., Zmud, R.W., Kim, Y.-G. and Lee, J.-N. (2005) Behavioral Intention Formation in Knowledge Sharing: Examining the roles of extrinsic motivators, social-psychological forces, and organizational climate. *MIS Quarterly, 29* (1): 87–111.

Borgatti, S.P. and Foster, P.C. (2003) The Network Paradigm in Organizational Research: A review and typology. *Journal of Management, 29* (6): 991–1013.

Boudreau, J. (2003) Strategic Knowledge Measurement and Management. In Jackson, S.E., Hitt, M.A. and Denisi, A.S. (eds) *Managing Knowledge for Sustained Competitive Advantage: Designing strategies for effective human resource management*, San Francisco, CA, Jossey-Bass, pp. 360–398.

Boxall, P.F. (1996) The Strategic HRM Debate and the Resource-based View of the Firm. *Human Resource Management Journal, 6*: 59–75.

Bradley, K., Mathieu, J., Cordery, J., Rosen, B. and Kukenberger, M. (2011) Managing a New Collaborative Entity in Business Organizations: Understanding organizational communities of practice effectiveness. *Journal of Applied Psychology, 96* (6): 1234–1245.

Brown, G., Lawrence, T.B. and Robinson, S.L. (2005) Territoriality in Organizations. *Academy of Management Review, 30*: 577–594.

Burgess, D. (2005) What Motivates Employees to Transfer Knowledge outside their Work Unit? *Journal of Business Communication, 42* (4): 324–348.

Burt, R.S. (1992) *Structural Holes: The social structure of competition*, Cambridge, MA, Harvard University Press.

Cabrera, A. and Cabrera, E.F. (2002) Knowledge-sharing Dilemmas. *Organization Studies, 23* (5): 1687–710.

Cabrera, E.F. and Cabrera, A. (2005) Fostering Knowledge Sharing through People Management Practices. *International Journal of Human Resource Management, 16* (5): 720–735.

Chennamaneni, A., Teng, J. and Raja, M.K. (2012) A Unified Model of Knowledge Sharing Behaviours: Theoretical development and empirical test. *Behavior & Information Technology, 31* (11): 1097–1115.

Cohen, W.M. and Levinthal, D.A. (1990) Absorptive Capacity: A new perspective on learning and innovation. *Administrative Science Quarterly, 35*: 128–152.

Coleman, J.S. (1988) Social Capital in the Creation of Human Capital. *American Journal of Sociology, 94*: 95–120.

Davenport, T. and Prusak, L. (1998) *Working Knowledge: How organizations manage what they know*, Cambridge, MA, Harvard Business School Press.

DeNisi, A.S., Hitt, M.A. and Jackson, S.E. (2003) The Knowledge-based Approach to Sustainable Competitive Advantage. Chapter 1 in Jackson, S.E., Hitt, M.A. and DeNisi, A.S. (eds) *Managing Knowledge for Sustained Competitive Advantage: Designing strategies for effective human resource management*, San Francisco, CA, Jossey-Bass, pp. 3–36.

Denning, S. (2006) The Steps to Get More Business Value from Knowledge Management. *Strategy and Leadership, 34* (6): 11–16.

Easterby-Smith, M. and Lyles, M.A. (2003) Introduction: Watersheds of organizational learning and knowledge management. Chapter 1 in Easterby-Smith, M. and Lyles, M.A.

(eds) *Handbook of Organizational Learning and Knowledge Management*, Hong Kong, Blackwell, pp. 1–15.

Easterby-Smith, M. and Prieto, I. (2008) Dynamic Capabilities and Knowledge Management: An integrative role for learning? *British Journal of Management*, 19 (3): 235–249.

Easterby-Smith, M., Lyles, A. and Tsang, E. (2008) Inter-organizational Knowledge Transfer: Current themes and future prospects. *Journal of Management Studies*, 45 (4): 677–690.

Eisenberger, R., Fasolo, P. and Davis-LaMastro, V. (1990) Perceived Organizational Support and Employee Diligence, Commitment, and Innovation. *Journal of Applied Psychology*, 75 (1): 51–59.

Flood, R.L. (2010) The Relationship of 'System Thinking' to Action Research. *Systemic Practice and Action Research*, 23: 269–284.

Flood, R.L. and Jackson, M.C. (1991) *Creative Problem Solving: Total systems intervention*, Chichester, Wiley.

Fox, S. (2000) Practice, Foucault, and Actor-Network Theory. *Journal of Management Studies*, 37 (6): 853–868.

Garcia, B.C. (2006) Learning Conversations: Knowledge, meanings and learning networks in Greater Manchester. *Journal of Knowledge Management*, 10 (5): 99–109.

Garud, R., Dunbar, R.L.M. and Bartel, C.A. (2011) Dealing with Unusual Experiences: A narrative perspective on organizational learning. *Organization Science*, 22 (3): 587–601.

Grant, R.M. (1996) Toward a Knowledge-based Theory of the Firm. *Strategic Management Journal*, 17: 109–122.

Greengard, S. (1998) Storing, Shaping and Sharing Collective Wisdom. *Workforce*, 77 (10): 82–88.

Gupta, B., Joshi, S. and Agarwal, M. (2012) The Effect of Expected Benefit and Perceived Cost on Employees' Knowledge Sharing Behaviour: A study of IT employees in India. *Organizations and Markets in Emerging Economies*, 3 (1): 8–19.

Hansen, M.T., Nohria, N. and Tierney, T. (1999) What's Your Strategy for Managing Knowledge? *Harvard Business Review*, March–April: 106–116.

Hansen, M., Mors, M. and Lovas, B. (2005) Knowledge Transfer in Organizations: Multiple networks, multiple phases. *Academy of Management Journal*, 48 (5): 776–793.

Hislop, D. (2003) The Complex Relationship between Communities of Practice and the Implementation of Technological Innovations. *International Journal of Innovation Management*, 7 (2): 163–188.

Hislop, D. (2013) *Knowledge Management in Organizations: A critical introduction*, 3rd edition, Oxford, Oxford University Press.

Israilidis, J., Siachou, E., Cooke, L. and Lock, R. (2015) Individual Variables with an Impact on Knowledge Sharing: The critical role of employees' ignorance. *Journal of Knowledge Management*, 19 (6): 1109–1123.

Ives, W., Torrey, B. and Gordon, C. (2003) Knowledge Transfer: Transfer is human behaviour. In Morey, C., Maybury, M. and Thuraisingham, B. (eds) *Knowledge Management: Classic and contemporary works*, Cambridge, MA, MIT Press.

Jarvenpaa, S.L. and Staples, D.S. (2001) Exploring Perceptions of Organizational Ownership of Information and Expertise. *Journal of Management Information Systems*, 18 (1): 151–183.

Joia, L.A. and Lemos, B. (2010) Relevant Factors for Tacit Knowledge Transfer within Organizations. *Journal of Knowledge Management*, 14 (3): 410–427.

Jones, M.C., Cline, M. and Ryan, S. (2006) Exploring Knowledge Sharing in ERP Implementation: An organizational culture framework. *Decision Support Systems*, 41 (2): 411–434.

Kankanhalli, A., Bernard, C. and Wei, K.-K. (2005) Contributing Knowledge to Electronic Knowledge Repositories: An empirical investigation. *MIS Quarterly, 29* (1): 113–143.

Kaplan, R.S. and Norton, D.P. (1996) *The Balanced Scorecard: Translating strategy into action*, Boston, MA, Harvard Business School Press.

Kim, L. (1998) Crisis Construction and Organizational Learning: Capability building in catching up at Hyundai Motor. *Organizational Science, 9*: 506–521.

Kim, T. and Lee, G. (2011) A Modified and Extended Triandis Model for the Enablers: Process–outcomes relationship in hotel employees' knowledge sharing. *Service Industries Journal, 32* (13): 2059–2090.

Kluge, J., Stein, W. and Licht, T. (2001) *Knowledge Unplugged: The McKinsey Global Survey of Knowledge Management*, New York, Palgrave.

Kruger, J. and Dunning, D. (1999) Unskilled and Unaware of it: How difficulties in recognizing one's own incompetence lead to inflated self-assessments. *Journal of Personality and Social Psychology, 77* (6): 1121–1134.

Kumar, J.A. and Ganesh, L.S. (2009) Research on Knowledge Transfer in Organizations: A morphology. *Journal of Knowledge Management, 13* (4): 161–174.

Kumar, N. and Rose, R. (2012) The Impact of Knowledge Sharing and Islamic Work Ethic on Innovation Capability. *Cross Cultural Management: An International Journal, 19* (2): 142–165.

Levin, D.Z. and Cross, R. (2004) The Strength of Weak Ties You Can Trust: The mediating role of trust in effective knowledge transfer. *Management Science, 50* (11): 1477–1490.

Li, J., Yuan, L., Ning, L. and Li-Ying, J. (2015) Knowledge Sharing and Affective Commitment: The mediating role of psychological ownership. *Journal of Knowledge Management, 19* (6): 1146–1166.

Liao, L.F. (2008) Knowledge Sharing in R&D Departments: A social power and social exchange theory perspective. *International Journal of Human Resource Management, 19* (10): 1881–1895.

Liyanage, C., Elhag, T., Ballal, T. and Li, Q. (2009) Knowledge Communication and Translation: A knowledge transfer model. *Journal of Knowledge Management, 13* (3): 118–131.

McDermott, R. and O'Dell, C. (2001) Overcoming Cultural Barriers to Sharing Knowledge. *Journal of Knowledge Management, 5* (1): 76–85.

Majchrzak, A., More, P. and Faraj, S. (2012) Transcending Knowledge Differences in Cross-functional Teams. *Organization Science, 23* (4): 951–970.

Martin-Perez, V. and Martin-Cruz, N. (2015) The Mediating Role of Affective Commitment in the Rewards–Knowledge Transfer Relation. *Journal of Knowledge Management, 19* (6): 1167–1185.

Martinus, K. (2010) Planning for Production Efficiency in Knowledge-based Development. *Journal of Knowledge Management, 14* (5): 726–743.

Mason, K. and Leek, S. (2008) Learning to Build a Supply Network: An exploration of dynamic business models. *Journal of Management Studies, 45* (4): 774–799.

Massingham, P. (2010) Managing Knowledge Transfer between Parent Country Nationals (Australia) and Host Country Nationals (Asia). *International Journal of Human Resource Management, 21* (9): 1414–1435.

Massingham, P. (2013) The Relationship between Contextual Factors, Psychological Contract, and Change Outcomes. *Strategic Change: Briefings in Entrepreneurial Finance*, May (Special Issue), *22*: 157–173.

Massingham, P. (2014a) An Evaluation of Knowledge Management Tools Part 2: Managing knowledge flows and enablers. *Journal of Knowledge Management, 18* (6): 1101–1126.

Massingham, P. (2014b) The Researcher as Change Agent. *Systemic Practice and Action Research, 27*: 417–448

Massingham, P. and Massingham, R. (2014) Does Knowledge Management Produce Practical Outcomes? *Journal of Knowledge Management, 18* (2): 221–254.

Massingham, P. and Tam, L. (2015) The Relationship between Human Capital, Value Creation, and Employee Reward. *Journal of Intellectual Capital* (Special Issue), *16* (2): 390–418.

Minbaeva, D., Pedersen, T., Bjorkman, I., Fey, C. and Park, H. (2003) MNC Knowledge Transfer, Subsidiary Absorptive Capacity and Knowledge Transfer. *Journal of International Business Studies, 34* (6): 586–599.

Mishra, S.K. (2007) A Brief History of Production Functions. Available at: https://mpra. ub.uni-muenchen.de/5254 (accessed 7 November 2018).

Mitchell, T.R. (1982) Motivation: New directions for theory, research, and practice. *Academy of Management Review, 7* (1): 80–88.

Mowery, D.C., Oxley, J.C. and Silverman, B.S. (1996) Strategic Alliances and Interfirm Knowledge Transfer. *Strategic Management Journal, 17*: 77–91.

Nahapiet, J. and Ghoshal, S. (1998) Social Capital, Intellectual Capital, and Organizational Advantage. *Academy of Management Review, 23* (2): 242–266.

Nonaka, I. and Takeuchi, H. (1995) *The Knowledge-creating Company: How Japanese companies create the dynamics of innovation*, New York, Oxford University Press.

Nonaka, I. and Toyama, R. (2003) The Knowledge-creating Theory Revisited: Knowledge creation as a synthesizing process. *Knowledge Management Research & Practice, 1* (1): 2–10.

Oborn, E. and Dawson, S. (2010) Knowledge and Practice in Multidisciplinary Teams: Struggle, accommodation, and privilege. *Human Relations, 63* (12): 1835–1857.

O'Dell, C. (2000) *Stages of Implementation: A guide for your journey to knowledge management best practices*, Houston, TX, American Productivity and Quality Center.

O'Dell, C. and Grayson, C.J. (1998) If Only We Knew What We Know: Identification and transfer of internal best practices. *California Management Review, 40* (3): 154–173.

Paldam, M. and Svendsen, G.T. (2000) An Essay on Social Capital: Looking for the fire behind the smoke. *European Journal of Political Economy, 16*: 339–366.

Parent, R., Roy, M. and St-Jacques, D. (2007) A Systems-based Dynamic Knowledge Transfer Capacity Model. *Journal of Knowledge Management, 11* (6): 81–93.

Paulin, D. and Suneson, K. (2012) Knowledge Transfer, Knowledge Sharing and Knowledge Barriers: Three blurry terms in KM. *Electronic Journal of Knowledge Management, 10* (1): 81–91.

Pierce, L. (2012) Organizational Structure and the Limits of Knowledge Sharing: Incentive conflict and agency in car leasing. *Management Science, 58* (6): 1106–1121.

Rhodes, J., Hung, R., Lok, P., Lien, B. and Wu, C.M. (2008) Factors Influencing Organizational Knowledge Transfer: Implications for corporate performance. *Journal of Knowledge Management, 12* (3): 84–100.

Ringberg, T. and Reihlen, M. (2008) Towards a Socio-cognitive Approach to Knowledge Transfer. *Journal of Management Studies, 45* (5): 912–935.

Ryua, S., Hob, S.H. and Hanb, I. (2003) Knowledge Sharing Behaviour of Physicians in Hospitals. *Expert Systems with Applications, 25* (1): 113–122.

Sabatini, F. (2006) The Empires of Social Capital and Economic Development: A critical perspective. In *The Fondazione Eni Enrico Mattei Note di Lavoro Series Index*. Available at: www.feem.it/Feem/Pub/Publications/WPapers/default.htm

Schulz, M. (2001) The Uncertain Relevance of Newness: Organizational learning and knowledge flows. *Academy of Management Journal, 44* (4): 661–681.

Senge, P.M. (1990) *The Fifth Discipline: The art and practice of the learning organization,* New York, Doubleday Currency.

Senge, P. and Scharmer, O. (2001) Community Action Research: Learning as a community of practitioners, consultants, and researchers. Chapter 22 in Reason, P. and Bradbury, H. (eds) *Handbook of Action Research: Participative inquiry and practice,* London, Sage, pp. 238–249.

Sharkie, R. (2005) Precariousness under the New Psychological Contract: The effect on trust and the willingness to converse and share knowledge. *Knowledge Management Research & Practice, 3*: 37–44.

Small, C. and Sage, A. (2005) Knowledge Management and Knowledge Transfer: A review. *Information Knowledge Systems Management, 23*: 153–169.

Storey, J. and Barnett, E. (2000) Knowledge Management Initiatives: Learning from failure. *Journal of Knowledge Management, 4* (2): 145–156.

Storey, J. and Quintas, P. (2001) Knowledge Management and HRM. In Storey, J. (ed.) *Human Resource Management: A critical text,* London, Thomson Learning, pp. 339–363.

Swan, J. and Scarbrough, H. (2005) The Politics of Networked Innovation. *Human Relations, 58* (7): 913–943.

Swan, J., Scarbrough, H. and Robertson, M. (2002) The Construction of Communities of Practice in the Management of Innovation. *Management Learning, 33* (4): 477–496.

Szulanski, G. (1996) Exploring Internal Stickiness: Impediments to the transfer of best practice within the firm. *Strategic Management Journal, 17* (Winter special issue): 27–43.

Szulanski, G. (2000) The Process of Knowledge Transfer: A diachronic analysis of stickiness. *Organizational Behavior and Human Decision Processes, 82* (1): 9–27.

Tangaraja, G., Rasdi, M.H., Samah, B.A. and Ismail, M. (2016) Knowledge Sharing is Knowledge Transfer: A misconception in the literature. *Journal of Knowledge Management, 20* (4): 653–670.

Trist, E.L. (1959) Socio-technical Systems. Thesis, University of Cambridge.

Tsoukas, H. (2003) Do We Really Understand Tacit Knowledge? Chapter 21 in Easterby-Smith, M. and Lyles, M.A. (eds) *Handbook of Organizational Learning and Knowledge Management,* Hong Kong, Blackwell, pp. 410–427.

Turner, K. and Makhija, M. (2006) The Role of Organizational Controls in Managing Knowledge. *Academy of Management Review, 31* (1): 197–217.

Ulrich, W. (1983) *Critical Heuristics of Social Planning,* Berne, Switzerland, Haupt.

Van den Hooff, B. and de Ridder, J.A. (2004) Knowledge Sharing in Context: The influence of organizational commitment, communication climate and CMC use on knowledge sharing. *Journal of Knowledge Management, 8* (6): 114–130.

Voelpel, S., Dous, M. and Davenport, D. (2005) Five Steps to Creating a Global Knowledge Sharing System: Siemens' Share Net. *Academy of Management Executive, 19* (2): 9–23.

von Krogh, G. (2005) Knowledge Sharing in Organizations: The role of communities. Chapter 19 in Easterby-Smith, M. and Lyles, M.A. (eds) *Handbook of Organizational Learning and Knowledge Management,* 2nd edition, Hong Kong, Blackwell, pp. 403–432.

Ward, A. (2000) Getting Strategic Value from Constellations of Communities. *Strategy and Leadership, 28* (2): 4–9.

Wasko, M.M. and Faraj, S. (2005) Why Should I Share? Examining social capital and knowledge contribution in electronic networks of practice. *MIS Quarterly, 29* (1): 35–57.

Wenger, E.C., McDermott, R. and Snyder, W.M. (2002) *Cultivating Communities of Practice: A guide to managing knowledge,* Boston, MA, Harvard Business School Press.

Willem, A. and Scarbrough, H. (2006) Social Capital and Political Bias in Knowledge Sharing: An exploratory study. *Human Relations*, *59* (10): 1343–1370.

Williams, C. (2011) Client–Vendor Knowledge Transfer in IS Offshore Outsourcing: Insights from a survey of Indian software engineers. *Information Systems Journal*, *21*: 335–356.

Wong, K.Y. (2005) Critical Success Factors for Implementing Knowledge Management in Small and Medium Enterprises. *Industrial Management & Data Systems*, *105* (1): 261–279.

Yoo, Y. and Torrey, B. (2002) National Culture and Knowledge Management in a Global Learning Organization. In Choo, C.W. and Bontis, N. (eds) *The Strategic Management of Intellectual Capital and Organizational Knowledge*, Oxford, Oxford University Press, pp. 421–434.

Zahra, S.A. and George, G. (2002) Absorptive Capacity: A review, reconceptualization, and extension. *Academy of Management Review*, *27* (2): 185–203.

PART 3
KNOWLEDGE MANAGEMENT PERSPECTIVES

10

PRODUCTIVITY

LEARNING OUTCOMES

After completing this chapter, the reader should be able to:

1. Understand how performance improvement occurs via change management
2. Define and discuss both directed and facilitated approaches to change management
3. Define process management
4. Examine the relationship between process management and knowledge management
5. Discuss how to embed knowledge management in business processes

MANAGEMENT ISSUES

Productivity improvement requires managers to:

1. Understand the forces for change and how to respond to them
2. Decide whether to use directed or facilitated change models
3. Understand how knowledge management can improve performance

Using knowledge management to increase productivity involves these challenges for management:

1. What is the best change model to use?
2. How can knowledge management help implement this model?
3. Integrating knowledge management with process management

LINKS TO OTHER CHAPTERS

Chapter 2: on the technology view of knowledge management

Chapter 3: regarding creating value from knowledge management

Chapter 5: concerning responding to change

OPENING MINI CASE STUDY

WHY SAUDI ARABIA'S EXPERTS DO NOT LEARN FROM OVERSEAS EXPERTS: HOW IMPROVING BUSINESS PROCESSES CAN INCREASE KNOWLEDGE FLOWS

Source: Massingham, P. and Al Holaibi, M. (2017) Embedding Knowledge Management into Business Processes. *Knowledge and Process Management*, *24* (1): 53–71.

Saudi Arabia is a wealthy country. Historically, its wealth has been generated by natural resources, such as oil. This case involves Saudi Arabia's three leading research institutes. It explores problems associated with knowledge flows between institute staff and external experts and users. In the past, the institutes have tried to acquire knowledge by employing external experts. These experts typically come from leading overseas universities. Their work with the institutes varies but a common method is to second them for a three- to six-month visit. During this stay, the external expert works with local staff on their research. The external experts are paid very high salaries and represent a significant cost for Saudi Arabia and its research institutes.

The need for this study emerged when the government decided that it wanted to build local capability. It was felt that the current method of using external experts to visit Saudi Arabia to train local researchers was not working. Furthermore, the government wanted the research institutes to share their knowledge with local industry to benefit the country. However, local industry was reluctant to work with local researchers. If Saudi Arabia was to develop world-class research institutes, something had to change.

The study adopted a business process improvement approach. It surveyed senior managers, external experts, and local industry to identify what was happening. The first step was to identify the research institutes' core activities. Work was classified into four capabilities: academic governance, administration, research, and teaching. This is the broad nature of work at universities and for academic staff around the world. The capabilities were given context in terms of how they contributed to knowledge flow. Three knowledge flows were identified:

1. *External-to-internal*: the flow of knowledge from external partners to the research institutes and their staff. This is System 1.
2. *Internal-to-internal*: the flow of knowledge between staff at the research institutes, with each research institute treated as a separate organization in its own right. This is System 2.
3. *Internal-to-external*: the flow of knowledge from research institutes and their staff to external partners – that is, local Saudi industry. Each research institute is again treated separately. This is System 3.

The capabilities were disaggregated into business processes common to each of the research institutes. A total of 60 processes were identified. These were mapped to explain how they were

(Continued)

(Continued)

currently done. From a process management perspective, the study was planned change involving a fundamental rethink about how things get done at the case study organizations (CSOs). A typical first step in planned change is initiation, which involves scanning for organizational problems and opportunities for improvement. This involved the senior managers reviewing their core business processes to consider whether they were operating at optimal capacity. In this review, the managers were asked to consider the nature of knowledge necessary to perform each process. Processes were rated as operating at optimal capacity if the managers perceived that the necessary knowledge was either widely known and, therefore, there was no knowledge gap, or it was easily accessible, so individuals could quickly learn what to do. Of the 60 core processes, only three (5%) were rated as performing well; 33 processes (55%) needed some improvement; and 24 processes (40%) were rated as needing to significantly improve. These priority processes were major waste points, and knowledge flow was either stuck or slowed to a level causing workflow inefficiencies. The problem processes were spread fairly evenly across the three organizational systems: nine of these processes (38%) related to the internal-to-external organizational system (OS); eight processes (33%) involved the external-to-internal OS; and seven processes (29%) involved the internal-to-internal OS.

This case study looks at three of the problem processes in detail, one from each of the OSs. The first process was from System 1: external to internal – 'national coordination' and the capability of academic governance. This was defined as work of the government to coordinate external partnerships for the CSOs. The following suggests that this was poorly managed:

> The problem is that there is no national agency responsible to coordinate for this task [external–internal knowledge sharing]. More importantly, there is no national agency qualified to do this kind of job … Saudi Arabia should have a ministry for scientific research like many other countries in the world. All national research institutions, whether governmental, private, or part of universities, would report to this ministry. If a ministry was present, then complete databases would be made available and updated, and it would be checking after research activities, controlling the progress of research on a national scale and so on.

The respondent is explaining that there is no government control of the first organizational system, external-to-internal knowledge flows, which means that priorities cannot be set at a national level, nor progress monitored.

The second process was from System 2: internal to internal – 'researcher attributes' and research capability. This was defined as the capability of research staff to share knowledge. Some respondents felt that sharing knowledge across disciplines was an essential part of being a researcher, as illustrated by the following quotes:

> As you know, if I'm a geophysicist, and if I want to build a system, then I need electrical engineers, electrical communication engineers, because this is not my field. For that reason we join with other people to help us in some steps.

> It's not only useful, it's a must. In research, there's no way you can do research on your own nowadays. You cannot find one single successful professor without global collaboration and

multi-discipline collaboration. We need nowadays a multi-disciplinary collaboration; we need something from a computer background, in mathematics, biology, chemistry. In our field, we are seven different divisions. We run several samples from different areas of collaborations. This is a must.

There are efforts that cannot be achieved on an individual level.

These comments focus on the need to collaborate, particularly if the researcher needs knowledge they do not have, such as from another discipline. Respondents also recognized that it was difficult to share knowledge across disciplines owing to its complexity as a task. The following quotes illustrate this:

Researchers find little synergy to deal with complex engineering problems due to non-availability of a multi-disciplinary team. They have difficulty finding overseas experts when they realize that a niche area expert is not available.

One of the real barriers to knowledge sharing is the multi-disciplinary nature of the knowledge to be transferred. Multiple disciplinary requirements demand involvement of teams or groups, which mean more management and logistical skills and resources. It is extremely difficult to transfer complex knowledge using only one individual.

These quotes explain that cross-disciplinary research collaboration is difficult because of the coordination costs of organizing teams and finding suitable experts. It is made even more difficult by motivational problems, i.e. whether individuals are willing to learn or share, as illustrated here:

I have people here that have been experts for around 30 years. But he is an expert in one particular subject. If you want him to open a new dimension, you will always feel he is hesitant, and he doesn't want to really go there.

These problems combined to cause waste in research collaboration across disciplines. This led to unsatisfactory performance, as illustrated by this quote:

Many opt to give up without anyone knowing. They would just pass through the project to reach an end, and get it over with.

The third process was from System 3: internal to external – 'train industry' and the capability of teaching. This was defined as industry staff working with researchers on campus. Staff felt that this process was ineffective because of confusion about the role of the research institutes, as illustrated here:

We are talking about companies. Companies need performance. Performance needs skilled professionals. If we cannot perform outside in the industry then we cannot compete as they can. I mean, if we cannot have the same resources as our competitors, then we cannot perform. We don't have the knowledge.

(Continued)

(Continued)

Although the CSOs are non-profit government bodies, respondents felt that they position themselves to local industry as profit-oriented. As a consequence, the CSOs were unwilling to share experience and knowledge with local industries unless they were paid for their knowledge. However, local industry did not value the knowledge of the local researchers, as illustrated by this quote:

> You cannot deny that. You cannot compare the outcome coming from us or other local universities with research outcomes coming from MIT or Stanford, or Cambridge or those guys. The positions of these universities is different, so naturally the results and the competencies they have are different and for those industrial firms who have the money, they can request any experienced house to do the research for them. So, it is an open market.

CASE STUDY QUESTIONS

1. Why are local researchers not learning sufficiently from external experts?
2. Why is local industry not using the knowledge of the local researchers?
3. Why are local researchers not sharing their knowledge with other local researchers?
4. What would you do to fix these problems?

INTRODUCTION

Organizations are living organisms. They strive to survive. Survival 'would be relatively easy to achieve were it not for the fact that organizations operate in dynamic environments, both externally and internally' (Myers et al., 2012: 12). This dynamism requires change. The principles of the learning organization (see Chapter 8) argue that organizations must respond to change, learn from experience, and grow their resources. This chapter explores the themes of change, learning, and growth within the context of how knowledge management may improve productivity.

Productivity presents challenges for the dichotomy of the technology and personalization views of knowledge management presented in this book. The motivation issues surrounding knowledge sharing (see Chapter 9) are an example of performance improvement at the individual level. The chapter explores how the fields of information science, computer science, and process management have a technology view of knowledge management. Business process management is organizational transformation leading to improvements in business performance and innovation (Harkness et al., 1996). Several theoretical models explaining process management will be discussed.

CORE CONCEPT: The personalization view approaches productivity in terms of individual employees. This is about improving performance via work quality (better work) and work quantity (doing more). The technology view looks at productivity from an organizational perspective. This is about codifying best practice, sharing this with employees, and ensuring compliance.

A challenge for knowledge management surrounding this topic is that traditional productivity improvement methods are based on scientific management rather than humanistic management. Tools such as business process re-engineering, total quality management, Six Sigma, and lean thinking are examples of directed change. Directed change is driven by the top of the organization, i.e. management telling employees what they need to do, whereas the personalization view of knowledge management adopted in this book requires facilitated change. Facilitated change involves employees in the shaping of what needs to be done (Myers et al., 2012).

A dilemma emerges when designing knowledge management to improve productivity. People 'tend to focus on their own roles, rather than the purposes and performance of the whole organization, and see themselves in a system in which they have limited power and no need to accept responsibility for the future of their organization' (Myers et al., 2012: 179). Employees, therefore, feel they cannot change their organization and that it is not their role. This suggests that the personalization view of knowledge management cannot effectively implement organization-wide change and productivity improvement. This is supported by systems thinking which adopts 'a stakeholder perspective' to change management, requiring a mapping of the relationships between external and internal factors influencing change, and seeing their interaction as a whole system rather than as separate issues (Senge et al., 2005: 139). This suggests that the technology view of knowledge management is the most effective way to pursue productivity gains, primarily because its method of codifying knowledge and sharing it as best practice enables system-wide improvements. However, this chapter challenges this thinking and presents an alternative view.

CORE CONCEPT: The chapter bridges the gap between the technology and personalization views of knowledge management by integrating them into a new productivity model. It does this by focusing on skilful knowing (see Chapter 1), which is an important theme throughout this book.

By focusing the individual employee on making them skilful knowers, within the context of improving the work processes they do, this will help them adopt a systems thinking perspective and allow knowledge management to be embedded in problem routines. This will improve workflow and achieve efficiencies by reducing waste via reduced search cycle time (looking for knowledge) and accelerated time to competence (becoming a skilful knower). It elevates individual-level change and performance improvement to organization-level productivity gains.

The chapter begins with a discussion of performance improvement within the context of change management. The main productivity models are then examined. Following this, the chapter develops a new model of productivity for knowledge management, before drawing conclusions.

PERFORMANCE IMPROVEMENT

Performance improvement occurs through effective change management. There are two theories of organizational change: directed change, which is driven by management, and facilitated change, which involves employees.

CORE CONCEPT: Directed change is associated with hard management, focusing on economic changes, particularly 'reducing costs', but also structural change and workforce issues such as redundancies (Myers et al., 2012: 194). It is about efficiencies. It is planned change. It interprets people as machines and adopts a scientific management approach.

CORE CONCEPT: Facilitated change is associated with soft management, focusing on employee participation, particularly cultural change, including positive work attitudes, behaviours, and values (Myers et al., 2012). It is about effectiveness. It may be either planned or emergent change, but more usually the latter. It interprets people as having value and adopts a humanistic management approach.

In reality, organizations tend to use a combination of both directed and facilitated change, even within single-change programmes which may include stages of both approaches (Myers et al., 2012: 195). Change differs in terms of scale and span – from fine tuning which may involve small incremental adjustments within a small group, to corporate transformation (also referred to as discontinuous change) affecting the whole organization in a fundamental way (2012: 196). Figure 10.1 summarizes these approaches to change; it plots four scenarios based on the scale and scope of change involved. *Developmental transitions* are incremental change requiring voluntary commitment and trust. *Task-focused transitions* are targeted directed change, for example for a department or functional area, which has more employee involvement allowed by local management but is still a formal directive. *Charismatic transformation* is an

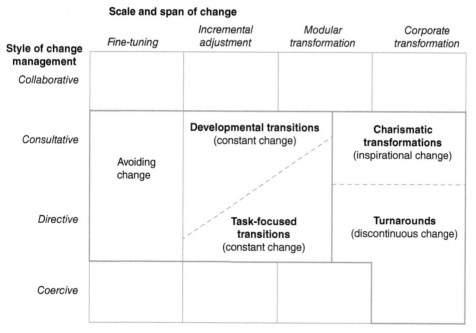

FIGURE 10.1 *Approaches to change.*

Source: Myers et al. (2012). By permission of Oxford University Press, USA.

integrated model with organization-wide change driven by emotional attachment from employees to a leader, done using top-down communication but with feedback loops to empower and involve employees. *Turnarounds* are strong, directed change with levels of coercion to ensure employees cooperate (after Myers et al., 2012: 196–197).

DIRECTED CHANGE MODELS

There are a range of directed change models that have emerged over the past 30 years to achieve business process improvement (BPI).

CORE CONCEPT: Business process improvement is a management tool which aims to fundamentally rethink and radically redesign business processes to bring about significant improvements in performance (Terwiesch and Bohn, 2001).

A business process is defined as a complete end-to-end set of activities that together create value for a customer, where the customer can be internal or external, and activities can be cross-functional or cross-organizational

(Sharp and McDermott, 2001). This definition introduces a range of relevant literatures, including lean thinking (LT), knowledge management (KM), business process re-engineering (BPR), and total quality management (TQM).

While these literatures share the objective of improving organizational output, each has a slightly different improvement objective: (a) LT on waste, (b) BPR on change, (c) TQM on compliance, and (d) KM on sharing and learning (Ricondo and Viles, 2005). KM focuses on strategic competencies, i.e. activities which may contribute the most value, while the other approaches trace inefficiencies regardless of the value the process represents. This is summarized in Figure 10.2.

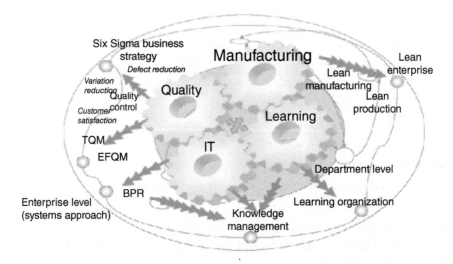

FIGURE 10.2   *The different origins of performance improvement methods*

Source: Ricondo and Viles (2005). By permission of Inderscience Publsihers.

At the enterprise level, business process re-engineering (BPR) is an approach to corporate transformation that requires 'radical redesign and dramatic improvements, achieved through a fundamental rethinking of how things get done' (Myers et al., 2012: 200). It embraces the philosophy of double-loop learning which this book promotes as best practice for today's learning organizations (see Chapter 8) and, therefore, BPR is considered a very useful form of directed change. However, its impact on productivity is limited by two factors. First, it discards the old and replaces it with the new. This all-or-nothing approach (Myers et al., 2012) neglects the cultural and political realities of organizations. The ruthless nature of the win-at-all-costs reputation gained by BPR, particularly in terms of redundancies as a cost saving, generates natural opposition from employees. Further, discarding existing processes risks losing the valuable organizational memory embedded in routines and practices.

Six Sigma and total quality management focus on eliminating mistakes by reducing variation (inconsistent work quality) or defects (poor quality work). The key to these methods is measurement. Six Sigma's advantages are: its 'clear focus on measurable and quantifiable returns', with 'finance personnel tracking projects'; its use of verifiable 'data to inform decisions, rather than observations and assumptions'; and its use of 'fully trained' experts (Myers et al., 2012: 209). Six Sigma works this way:

- Defining what the customer needs
- Counting the defects, i.e. the instances where the product or process does not meet the customer requirement
- Calculating the percentage of items without defects
- Then calculating the number of errors that would be experienced if the activity were repeated a million times: defects per million opportunities (DPMO)
- Working to reduce the incidence of defect. (Pande et al., 2000, cited in Myers et al., 2012: 208)

The main problem with Six Sigma is illustrated by the DPMO calculation. To work, it requires highly repetitive routine tasks, such as those found in manufacturing or lower-level activities. It is highly unlikely to suit the type of work that knowledge workers do. The volume of tasks simply would not allow a Six Sigma score to be calculated. It is also contrary to the creativity and innovation associated with knowledge management, as it is limited and narrow in focus and encourages uniformity rather than creativity (Myers et al., 2012: 210).

Lean thinking has become accepted by academics and practitioners as the 'dominant approach in manufacturing management' (Boyle et al., 2011: 587).

CORE CONCEPT: The goal of lean thinking is to determine waste in the value stream, to eliminate those wasteful activities, and 'to create and sustain value-added activities' (Chongwatpol and Sharda, 2013: 240). Waste may be visualized as blockages which impede the flow of work, information, or knowledge within an organization.

The issue of waste is a concern for many organizations (Hines et al., 2004). Waste usually leaves business processes functional, but not functioning at an optimal level (Harrington, 1991). Lean thinking provides a way to manage problems caused by waste points by specifying value, improving the alignment of value-creating activities, understanding the way activities may increase effectiveness, and reducing the time to perform tasks (Womack and Jones, 1996).

This chapter uses lean thinking to identify and resolve workflow inefficiencies. The philosophy of lean thinking focuses on eliminating waste within business processes (Chongwatpol and Sharda, 2013). There is a 'complex inter-action between knowledge management and workflow structure' (Raghu and Vinze, 2007: 1065). This interaction is explored by how individuals learn from the application of knowledge in a process and then share these lessons learned with their organization via problem solving and documentation.

DEEP THINKING: Whereas previous research on business improvement tends to look at knowledge management as capturing and sharing best practice about a process (Raghu and Vinze, 2007), this chapter makes knowledge management part of the process.

This approach to business improvement differs from previous research, such as Linderman et al. (2010), because it is not developing an improved knowledge management capability, that is, in knowledge sharing. Rather, the approach in this chapter looks at how knowledge sharing can be embedded in the processes necessary to improve workflow.

FACILITATED CHANGE MODELS

Facilitated change usually involves change that is incremental, such as issues about organization value or team performance, rather than transformational change issues such as restructuring or strategy which tend to involve directed change (Myer et al., 2012: 218–219).

CORE CONCEPT: Facilitated change aims to involve employees in the change man-agement process. However, there are degrees of involvement. Consultative approaches allow for limited involvement, whereas collaborative approaches enable more widespread involvement (Dunphy and Stace, 1993).

An emergent change strategy enables facilitated change in two ways: (a) lead-ership stimulating new forms of social interaction to maximize the diversity in decision making, and (b) social constructionism, i.e. where reality is constructed by what people do and say together (Lewis et al., 2008). Figure 10.3 summarizes the facilitated change purpose and methods.

Facilitated change is grounded in organizational development (OD) theory. OD is a planned approach to change which involves all parts of the organization. Change from an OD perspective is managed from the top, focuses on dealing with the human reaction, and typically takes a long-term approach (Myers et al., 2012: 223). The change programme is based on a set of key humanistic values related to openness, honesty, involvement, and the capacity to grow

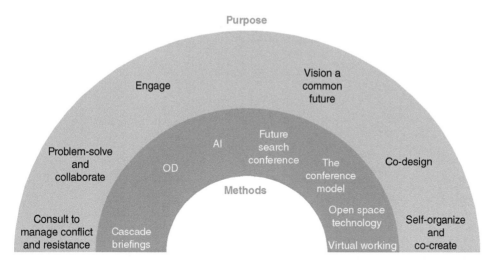

FIGURE 10.3 *Facilitated change models*

Source: Myers et al. (2012). By permission of Oxford University Press, USA.

(Myers et al., 2012: 223). This type of change embraces many of the themes proposed in this book, including humanistic management, cultural change, and the aspirational values of the learning organization. OD has a consulting approach to change management with three phases. Phase 1 is change strategy, where the problem is agreed on, solutions are accepted, and employees allow access. Phase 2 is unfreezing the current system. Phase 3 is moving through the change solution and refreezing it as the new system (2012: 224–228).

Other popular facilitated change models include appreciative inquiry and large group methods. Appreciative inquiry is planned change, led from the top, but aims for full participation of the whole organization system. All employees are invited to participate and asked to focus on the 'strengths' that exist in the organization. It is often used in facilitated workshops, i.e. groups, using dialogue. Large group methods assume that change works best when representation of the whole system is present. It also uses dialogue to enable employees to work together with high involvement and sustainable commitment to change (Lewis et al., 2008). Some examples are provided by Myers et al. (2012: 233–237): *Future Search* is run as an action-planning conference with up to 100 attendees, including employees, leaders, suppliers, and customers, and with an emphasis on growing common ground (not solving differences) and moving forward on areas of agreement. The *Conference Model* comprises a series of five conferences over 5 months, each lasting 2–3 days, with 80+ attending each time and work undertaken between each conference; customers and suppliers are invited to join the conferences, with a focus on discovering what people want. *Open Space Technology* is networking and community building to create new energy and new ideas; it may include virtual conferencing, and the aim is to facilitate brainstorming (Myers et al., 2012).

THEORY IN PRACTICE: SHATTERING A FROZEN CULTURE

Anastasia Marquez was the new chief executive officer at a government research organization. Its workforce consisted of highly qualified research scientists, many of whom had spent their whole careers at the organization.

Anastasia's first goal was to smash the organizational culture. She felt the culture was toxic and dysfunctional. Staff were recalcitrant, non-compliant, and difficult to manage. The key cultural assumption was that staff were entitled to decide how they spend their time. Anastasia wanted to introduce a new culture based on scientific management principles. She wanted staff to be accountable, to be more efficient, to follow policies: she wanted them to follow the rules. She saw staff as a cost to be reduced. In her view, staff did not create value, but were a problem to be fixed. She perceived them as naughty children who lacked discipline and she was determined to change them. Her aim was to introduce a new key cultural assumption that staff are managed by policy.

Her first task was to create a fear culture. She targeted key individuals who were seen to represent role models for the existing non-compliant culture. She made life very difficult for them and forced them to resign. While these were the staff with the most valuable knowledge, Anastasia felt the benefits outweighed the loss. No one felt safe in their jobs. She then ensured the remaining recalcitrant staff were bullied to force them to comply. They were also isolated socially to highlight that they did not fit in. She promoted those who did comply. She froze the new culture by focusing on cultural fit rather than merit.

She held a 'town hall' meeting of all staff. She presented results vindicating positive change. She allowed two questions from staff to demonstrate her efforts to involve staff in the change. The organization was never the same again.

This section has explained how performance improvement occurs through effective change management. Knowledge management can aid both directed change and facilitated change. It can improve efficiency through directed transformation change such as business process re-engineering. It can help effectiveness through facilitated incremental change such as socio-technical support.

PROCESS MANAGEMENT

Formally, a business process is an organized group of related activities that work together to create a result of value to the customer (Hammer, 2002: 26).

Process management includes a range of methods including just-in-time, Six Sigma, total quality management, and business process re-engineering (Silver, 2004). This suggests an operations management focus, a concentration on measurement, and application in manufacturing. Each method is concerned with a

---

CORE CONCEPT: Business process management is defined as a structured approach to performance improvement that centres on careful execution of a company's end-to-end business processes (Harkness et al., 1996).

---

fundamental rethinking and radical redesign of business processes to achieve significant improvements in performance, more specifically in areas such as cost, quality, service, and speed (Hammer and Champy, 1993). The outcome is planned transformational change.

Early research had an information-technology-centric position (Guha et al., 1997). This emerged through the early promise of technology to enable control and standardization of business processes, which led to assumptions that business process re-engineering, for example, was 'typically enabled by information technology' (Grover et al., 1995: 111). However, the field has evolved. Researchers recognized the need for 'a more holistic approach to process management' (Guha et al., 1997: 120). This began by broadening the discipline scope beyond information technology to include 'strategic management, organizational structure, change management', evaluation methods, and more incremental than transformational change (Guha et al., 1997: 120). This included a more socio-technical view of change which recognized the importance of people, particularly their motivation, resistance, and commitment to the change desired by the process management method (Grover et al., 1995: 113). Knowledge emerged as a critical factor for achieving performance goals from two disciplinary perspectives. Strategic management's knowledge based-view of the firm explained how knowledge was the firm's most valuable resource and that it led to sustainable competitive advantage (Grant, 1996). Information technology saw 'knowledge as facilitating timely and effective decision making' (Han and Park, 2009: 7441). Researchers developed a business process context for knowledge management based on an operational core of knowledge supported by three main knowledge management activities: knowledge synthesis, knowledge storage and retrieval, and knowledge sharing (Raghu and Vinze, 2007: 1065).

CORE CONCEPT: Methods to integrate process management and knowledge management in a single information technology architecture are called process-oriented knowledge management (Jung et al., 2007).

This focuses on the accessibility of knowledge repositories and tries to build artificial intelligence to replicate the socio-technical perspective of work. Researchers have tried to address this with 'mobility systems', which are mobile processes pervading information technology in order to capture the 'real world' and how people create community and change their work (Smith, 2003).

KNOWLEDGE PROCESS MANAGEMENT

The use of knowledge management in business process management has become widely accepted (e.g. Linderman et al., 2010). Business process change 'designs business processes to achieve significant change in terms of quality, cost, flexibility, and responsiveness – through changes in the relationships between management, information, and technology' (Guha et al., 1997: 121). Knowledge and knowledge management help achieve process change. Researchers have aimed to integrate business process management and knowledge management in process-centred knowledge models (e.g. Jung et al., 2007; Raghu and Vinze, 2007; Han and Park, 2009). The focus of this previous research is to develop capabilities leading to effective knowledge management (Raghu and Vinze, 2007, Linderman et al., 2010) (see Figure 10.4). This approach considers knowledge management as a separate organizational system and uses process management to improve it. This chapter develops an alternative approach which embeds knowledge management in business processes as an integrated system rather than as a separate one.

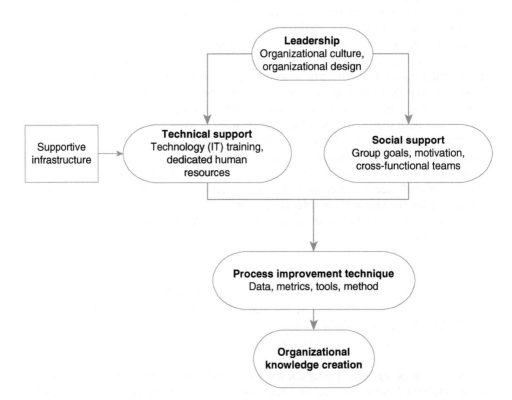

FIGURE 10.4 *Knowledge framework of process management system*

Source: Linderman et al. (2010). Reprinted by permission of Wiley.

Process management regards knowledge management as separate from the activity of work itself, for instance that it is an enabler. In this sense, 'knowledge management is a business process' in itself (Sarvary, 1999: 95) which helps organizations create and use knowledge. The way that this process is done has many interpretations. Nonaka and Takeuchi's (1995) knowledge-creating spiral is often used to explain how knowledge is created and diffused across the three levels of individual, group, and organization (e.g. see Sabherwal and Becerra-Fernandez, 2003; Jung et al., 2007).

The technology view sees knowledge management as information-seeking behaviour. If an individual does not know something, they use technology to help find the answers (e.g. see Kearns and Lederer, 2003). This is about knowledge capture and codification (e.g. see Alavi and Tiwana, 2005). The technology view dominated the early evolution of knowledge management; however, recent research has set technology as a support function rather than the main driver of connectivity (Aakhus, 2007). On the other hand, the personalization view looks at social practice as the best way to manage knowledge (Gardner, 2011). The implication is that learning comes from the cultivation of judgement rather than the acquisition of information (Aakhus, 2007). Knowledge comes from interaction and debate, where people work out the truths, commitments, perspectives, and identities central to their work (Aakhus, 2007). People find justified true belief via interaction with other people, not via interaction with technology. This is about providing opportunities for people to socialize for real, such as in meetings, or in virtual environments such as online (e.g. see von Krogh, 2005).

The aim of process management is 'organizational transformation resulting in sustained process improvement' (Harkness et al., 1996: 349). From this perspective, knowledge management contributes to process management via systems, technologies, and tools which enable knowledge to be captured, stored, and shared to benefit the organization (Becerra-Fernandez and Sabherwal, 2010).

DEEP THINKING: Process-centred knowledge management tends to focus on separating knowledge from the knower, i.e. the technology view of knowledge management (e.g. see Sabherwal and Sabherwal, 2005). This previous research focuses on knowledge as an informational product and presents a technocratic conceptualization of work. It sees work as information-seeking behaviour.

This fits with the definition of process management itself which is 'to design, control, improve, and redesign processes' (Silver, 2004: 274). This focuses on codifying and capturing knowledge by writing it down. The technology view focuses on organizational knowledge because it asks the individual to follow the organization's guidelines rather than think for themselves.

The discussion so far has looked at how individuals, groups, or organizations become skilful knowers, i.e. move from unskilful knowing to skilful knowing within a process. The technology and personalization views provide contrasting ideas about how this is done. This chapter builds a connection to process management by examining the act of skilful knowing. Researchers have accepted that knowledge is created and used during the 'execution of business processes' (Han and Park, 2009: 7441) and, therefore, value is created by the individual in the activity of doing work. This view holds that if knowledge is 'separated from the business process context, it does not lead to the ability to take the right action for target performance' (2009: 7441). This means that knowledge loses value if it is separated from its context, that is, how it is used to perform work.

CORE CONCEPT: Productivity is gained from process-centred knowledge management driven by the individual in the act of doing.

Recent research recognizes that process management and knowledge management should be unified rather than operate as separate organizational systems. This is achieved by attaching knowledge to 'executed tasks, so that individuals capture and use knowledge as part of their normal work' (Han and Park, 2009: 7441). In this way, knowledge is embedded in business processes (Han and Park, 2009). The literature has taken two paths on this topic. The first highlights the importance of knowledge about the process itself, referred to as process knowledge (Jung et al., 2007). This includes a definition of the process and its mapping, described as process template knowledge; performance measures evaluating its value, defined as process instance knowledge; and awareness of how the knowledge is created and used, discussed as process-related knowledge (Jung et al., 2007). The second path looks at knowledge management activities, such as knowledge creation, as an outcome of process management developing a set of dynamic capabilities leading to sustainable competitive advantage (Linderman et al., 2010). This view examines how process management creates knowledge which becomes embedded as organizational routines. Linderman et al. (2010) explore how process management leads to effective knowledge creation by factors associated with monitoring and changing the activity, such as leadership, culture, design, technology, and human resources.

Employees who spend 100% of their time on projects are called dedicated human resources (Flynn et al., 1999). Researchers have argued that teams with dedicated human resources can better meet project objectives (Flynn et al., 1999). They can do this by having the necessary skills, and the necessary work capacity to effectively complete project activities. Knowledge management can help by ensuring dedicated knowledge resources for business improvement projects. There are two types of knowledge required. First is the technical (subject matter) knowledge that project members bring to the task. However, cross-functional problem-solving teams can find it difficult to 'share discipline-specific knowledge' (Linderman et al., 2010: 701), and knowledge management can help here via socialization (e.g. communities of practice). Second is knowledge of the business improvement technique. Six Sigma, for example, requires dedicated human resources trained in decision-making tools and methods. Knowledge management can help by using a common language (technical support) to encourage sharing of knowledge across the Six Sigma team, and a data-driven culture to achieve improvement goals (social support) (after Linderman et al., 2010).

Raghu and Vinze (2007) developed a model of business process context for knowledge management incorporating four key aspects of the operational core of knowledge: workflow execution, information processing, decision making, and motivational structure. This model includes the technical view of knowledge management (information processing) with the need for work context (workflow execution) and the individual system of knowledge (decision making and motivation) (see Figure 10.5).

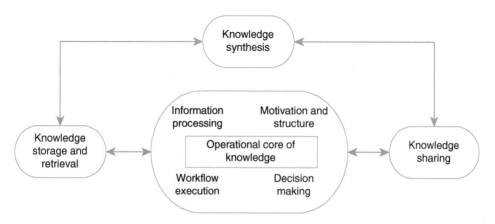

FIGURE 10.5   *The business process context for knowledge management*

Source: Raghu and Vinze (2007). With permission from Elsevier.

In this chapter, the embedded model of process-centred knowledge management is connected to process management through workflow execution. This execution addresses the fact that 'workflow concerns usually surround issues of efficiency and flexibility' (Raghu and Vinze, 2007: 1065). The technology view of knowledge management aims to increase workflow efficiency by reducing hand-offs and increasing automated tasks within the process (Han and Park, 2009). The personalization view of knowledge management aims to increase efficiency by reducing time spent accessing the necessary knowledge about tasks within the process via information systems, social capital, or learning by doing. This chapter uses lean thinking to explore time and efficiency in workflow.

AN INTEGRATED PRODUCTIVITY MODEL

The chapter's integrated productivity model differs from previous research on process-centred knowledge management which focused on how knowledge can improve process performance (Raghu and Vinze, 2007) and on how process management may improve knowledge management capability, such as knowledge creation (Linderman et al., 2010).

CORE CONCEPT: The integrated productivity model examines how to embed knowledge management in business processes to improve efficiencies in workflow.

This model focuses instead on how knowledge management can improve business processes. It does this by showing how knowledge management may become part of the process and not a separate organizational system. By embedding knowledge management in business processes, it identifies and addresses inefficiencies in the workflow. The result is improved knowledge flow within the process. This approach situates knowledge management as a socially constructed reality of work focusing on people rather than technology. It views knowledge as a process rather than a product and, therefore, its management should occur in the act of doing. At this point, the individual develops 'skilful knowing' (Tsoukas, 2003). This approach captures the elements of process-centred knowledge management's view of the operational core of knowledge: workflow execution, information processing, motivation, and decision making (Raghu and Vinze, 2007) within the context of the tasks in performing a business process. Knowledge management may improve efficiency within the process by enabling skilful knowing in minimum time. The conceptual model is presented in Figure 10.6.

Figure 10.6 compares the field's contrasting views about knowledge, knowledge management, and the act of skilful knowing. The framework is used to classify the method for embedding knowledge management in the problem processes. By determining the nature of the knowledge needed, the type of knowledge management required, and the process of becoming a skilful knower, the framework allows the design of process change which will improve the efficiency of the workflow within the process. The design is influenced by classifying the owner of the task in terms of whether it is the responsibility of the individual, the group, or the organization. This classification is determined by who should do the newly designed knowledge management task.

VALUE STREAM MAPPING

This model aims to achieve process management by improving workflow efficiency. The first aspect of the business process context for knowledge management is workflow execution (Raghu and Vinze, 2007). This usually involves coordination costs caused by the need for increased communication and information flow, such as that between supervisors and staff. The technical view of knowledge management uses information technology to automate tasks within the process (Raghu and Vinze, 2007) in order to reduce coordination costs.

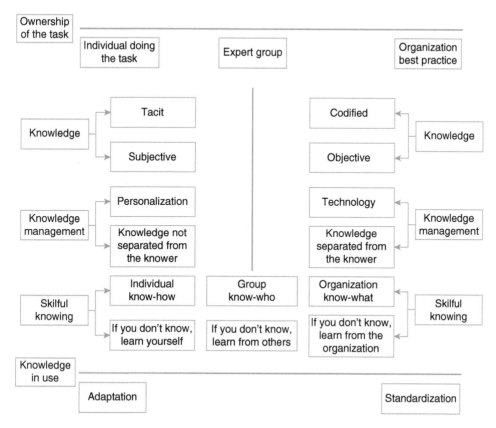

FIGURE 10.6 *An integrated productivity model*

Source: (Massingham and Al Holaibi, 2017).

The personalization view of knowledge management adopted by this model argues the need to consider the knowledge resources necessary for employees to perform these tasks. In order to identify these resources, it is necessary to conduct business process modelling to answer the question: what do employees need to know to do this task well? Having adequate knowledge resources, i.e. skilful knowing, will reduce coordination costs. Value stream mapping (VSM) (e.g. see Rother and Shook, 2003) enables effective business process modelling and will identify several layers of workflow.

IDENTIFYING THE LOCATION OF WASTE POINTS

Following the principles of process management, the model needs to address a strategic initiative where 'senior managers define their vision for change' (Guha et al., 1997: 121). The strategic initiative may be to improve the flow of knowledge from external experts to local employees. The change required may be to identify the reasons for the unsatisfactory knowledge flow and to address these problems. From a process management perspective, this is planned change involving a fundamental rethinking about how things get done (Hammer and Champy, 1993). A typical first step in planned change is initiation, which involves 'scanning for organizational problems and opportunities for improvement' (Grover et al., 1995: 112). This may involve senior managers reviewing their core business processes to consider whether they are operating at optimal capacity. In this review, the managers are asked to consider the nature of the knowledge necessary to perform each process. Processes may be rated as operating at optimal capacity if the managers perceived that the necessary knowledge was either widely known and therefore there was no knowledge gap, or that it was easily accessible, so individuals could quickly learn what to do.

DETERMINING THE NATURE OF THE WASTE USING LEAN THINKING

Massingham and Al Holaibi (2017: 60) found that 'the main type of waste is often reworking largely caused by employees having incorrect or incomplete knowledge about how to perform a task within the process.' Shingo and Dillon (1989, cited in Massingham and Al Holaibi, 2017) see reworking as a waste because it produces defective products or work below the established quality standard. This means that employees do work incorrectly, make mistakes, and produce work outputs of low quality because they lack knowledge about the process. This also causes high agency costs (e.g. see Huizing and Bouman, 2002) as supervisors or other employees are required to correct unsatisfactory work.

THEORY IN PRACTICE: INTRODUCING MENTORING AS A PROCESS

Stuart Chen was sitting in his director's office. He was in trouble. His director, Marion Broghton, was explaining that his work performance was unsatisfactory. He had delivered an incorrect risk assessment report after a sea trial on one of the Navy's vessels. Marion asked Stuart to explain how he went about this task.

As Stuart explained, Marion realized he had competency gaps. When she probed about why he did not know how to do some aspects of the task, it became clear that Stuart had been unable to identify procedures to help him or identify other staff that could advise him.

When the meeting finished, she called Paul Adams and asked him to see her. Paul was an experienced senior, engineer who had conducted many sea trials. He was widely acknowledged as the country's leading expert on hull stability. Marion explained the problem with Stuart and asked Paul whether he had helped him. Paul explained that Stuart had approached him but he was very busy and did not have time to help him. Marion asked Paul to mentor Stuart so that he could learn from Paul's experience and the problem could be avoided in the future. Paul said he was still too busy to mentor Stuart. When Marion pushed the point, Paul responded by saying that it was not part of his job description and he would not do it.

Several months later, Paul returned from a visit to sea. As he sat at his desk, those staff nearby asked him how his trip went. He launched into a summary of what he found in the sea trial, then went back to work. By chance, Marion was walking past and overheard this exchange. Later that week, she called Paul into her office and explained that when he returned from sea trials, he was to write a brief report on what he found and ensure it was distributed to all relevant staff, including Stuart. When Paul objected, she explained that this was now a process step in a new standard operating procedure regarding conducting sea trials. Paul had no choice. He had to comply as following standard operating procedures was part of his job description. Marion called Stuart to explain to him that he could now expect regular reports from Paul, and to ensure he learned from them.

Massingham and Al Holaibi (2017: 60) found that 'the next main type of waste is usually related to time, that is, waiting for approvals.' Shingo and Dillon (1989, cited in Massingham and Al Holaibi, 2017) see waiting as a waste because it is lost productivity in the time interval in which no task or operation is executed. Loss from waiting occurs when the employee needs to remain within the work process in order to complete the task. Lost productivity occurs when the employee is unable to perform other work while being delayed within the process. Examples are when employees are forced to repeat requests for clarification or other help, or to seek multiple alternatives.

DEEP THINKING: Other significant types of waste include underutilized people and transportation. Instances of under-utilized people occur owing to, for example, experienced researchers being unable or unwilling to share their knowledge with less experienced researchers. Waste occurs because these less experienced researchers spend time seeking help which is not given and then have to learn something that is already known, that is, reinvent the wheel. Transportation is akin to waiting in a queue. Waste points are created due to attitudinal factors. Decision makers see the knowledge surrounding the process as difficult and, therefore, defer making decisions, or they do not see the benefit to be gained from resolving the issue. Shingo and Dillon (1989) see transportation as a waste because it does not add value and only adds cost. It is a measure of non-productive time, including inefficiencies in learning, organizing others, encouraging cooperation, and communicating value.

Source: Massingham and Al Holaibi (2017: 60)

APPLYING THE CONCEPTUAL FRAMEWORK

Process management aims to improve performance by designing or redesigning processes (e.g. see Silver, 2004).

CORE CONCEPT: The integrated productivity model uses lean thinking to identify inefficiencies in workflow. These are tasks within processes which have waste caused by unskilful knowing.

The conceptual framework (see Figure 10.6) enables examination of the nature of this waste. The following analysis classifies the priority processes, i.e. those in the most need of improvement, in terms of who has main ownership of the problem task: the individual, group, or organization. Ownership is determined by the nature of the knowledge necessary to achieve skilful knowing. The process-centred knowledge management model involves designing or redesigning tasks within these priority processes to enable skilful knowing. Knowledge management is embedded in processes as the new or redesigned task. Performance improvement occurs via increased workflow execution (e.g. see Raghu and Vinze, 2007).

INDIVIDUAL

These processes are owned by the individual (see the left-hand side of Figure 10.6). This means that skilful knowing is experienced by the individual in the act of performing tasks within the process. This knowledge is tacit and subjective. Knowledge is not separated from the knower. The outcome of skilful knowing is individual know-how. It requires the individual to work out the best solution for themselves. This recognizes that there are multiple best solutions, and the process enables this multiplicity due to its context-sensitive nature. The waste exists because the individual is unable to work out the solution by themselves or this is done inefficiently, i.e. slowly. Knowledge management may be embedded in the process by enabling the individual to adapt the task to fit their context.

GROUP

These processes are owned by the group (see the middle of Figure 10.6). This means that skilful knowing is experienced by the group in the act of performing tasks within the process. This knowledge is social, tacit, and more subjective than objective. Knowledge may or may not be separated from the knower. The outcome of skilful knowing is group know-how. It requires the individual to learn from others. This recognizes that there is more than one best solution but the group is best placed to decide on these solutions. It allows for multiple contexts and multiple expert groups. The waste exists because the individual is unable to access the group's knowledge, or the group is unable to find a solution. Knowledge management may be embedded in the process by enabling the individual to access the group's solution or to help the group find a solution.

ORGANIZATION

These processes are owned by the organization (see the right-hand side of Figure 10.6). This means that skilful knowing is experienced by the organization in the act of performing tasks within the process. This knowledge is codified and objective. Knowledge is separated from the knower. The outcome of skilful knowing is organizational know-what. It requires the individual to learn from their organization. This recognizes that there is one best solution and the same process may be applied across any context. The waste exists because the individual is unable to access the organizational knowledge or it does not yet exist. Knowledge management may be embedded in the process by enabling the individual to access the standardized knowledge, such as best practice.

CONCLUSION

Performance improvement occurs through effective change management. There are two theories of organizational change: directed change, which is driven by management, and facilitated change, which involves employees. The chapter examined a range of directed change methods, including business process re-engineering, and how these relate to knowledge management. It then looked at facilitated change methods, which aim to involve employees in the design and conduct of the change programme. While this book argues for the personalization view of knowledge management rather than the technology view and, therefore, prefers a humanistic to a scientific management approach, it recognizes that large-scale transformational change must be managed if it is to be successful. Process management provides the theoretical platform for understanding how knowledge management can improve productivity.

The chapter discussed how knowledge management is now used in business process management to achieve improvements in terms of quality, cost, flexibility, and responsiveness. Knowledge and knowledge management help achieve process change. Researchers have aimed to integrate business process management and knowledge management in process-centred knowledge models that consider knowledge management as a separate organizational system and use process management to improve it. This chapter develops an alternative approach which embeds knowledge management in business processes as an integrated system rather than as a separate one.

The chapter's integrated productivity model examines how to embed knowledge management in business processes to improve efficiencies in workflow (see Figure 10.6), and provides guidelines on how to use the model to improve productivity at the individual, group, and organizational levels.

CLOSING CASE STUDY: KNOWLEDGE PRODUCTIVITY AT THE CSO

Commodore Pablo Pubnix sat in his office waiting for the arrival of the university researcher (referred to as the chief investigator, CI). He had been working with the CI on this project for five years. It was now completed. He was taking the CI out to lunch.

As the CI walked through the familiar corridors of the high security building towards the commodore's office, he felt a sense of nostalgia. He first came here 11 years earlier when he was still new to academia. He had met the commodore who was then in charge of the organization he was now studying. He was interviewing that commodore as part of another project he was doing for another commodore in Sydney. After that interview, the commodore had asked him if he knew anything about knowledge loss. From that encounter, a pilot study was begun, followed by two applications to the Australian Research Council for funding. Six years after that interview, the project began with high hopes. The CI had worked with six different commodores since the project idea began at that interview. He wondered what each would think now.

As he walked through the corridors, the CI was greeted with smiles, waves, and hellos. He had worked extremely hard to build trust among the management and staff. He had spent an average of one day a week in Canberra at this high security building for the past five years. He felt he was part of the team. But it was now coming to an end.

The commodore greeted him like an old friend. Instead of going to the on-site cafeteria, the commodore drove them to a suburban mall where they sat in a quiet little restaurant. The CI thought to himself that this was not an official lunch and the commodore would be paying for this out of his own pocket. It was also surprising that the commodore had chosen a place where no one would know them. It was a friendly discussion. They reflected on the project a little, but they mainly talked about personal issues, like family and health, and the future. It was strange that they were really getting to know each other at the end when they would probably not see each other again: two men sharing.

The commodore seemed a little anxious on the drive back to the office. He told the CI that he was retiring. However, he was most concerned about the CI's final report to the Australian Research Council. The CI assured him that it was never his intent to embarrass the department or harm it in any way. He had only ever intended to help. While the final report had to be truthful, the CI assured the commodore that it would be positive. While the project might be considered a failure by some, the CI felt it had been a great success.

As they arrived back at the office, the commodore presented the CI with a plaque in appreciation of his service to the department. They shook hands and promised to keep in touch. As the CI walked out of the office for the last time, the commodore reflected on the CI. He felt sorry for him. He knew how hard he had worked on the project. The department had made him so many promises. There were promises about goals, resources, participation, commitment, cooperation, outcomes. Every promise had been broken. He considered why this had happened. Was it something about him?

Had he failed the project? He felt the answer was no. He had tried to persuade his management and staff to cooperate. He genuinely believed in the project and felt it could help the department. He had tried to make it work. He turned to think about the CI. Was this his fault? He certainly was naïve. He kept trying to complete the project despite the many barriers. He seemed to continually adjust and adapt to whatever the department asked of him. The commodore wondered why. It was not ambition. The CI had not been promoted as a result of the project. It seemed that he was working in the wrong place and wasn't liked. It was not financial gain. Some staff felt the project was a vehicle for the CI to build a reputation and become rich as a consultant. But the commodore knew that the CI's conduct had always been honourable. The commodore's assessment of the CI was that he simply wanted to help. The commodore sensed a deep sense of obligation from the CI to the department for giving him the chance to do this project. Irrespective of how difficult the project became, the CI was determined to make it work, and to achieve the project goals. Why? The commodore wondered. Nobody except the CI seemed to care. As far as the commodore was aware, the CI's university had little or no involvement or interest in the project. The department had given up on it long ago and just wanted it to end. The commodore had placed no pressure on the CI. If it wasn't his fault or the CI's fault, who was to blame? The department broke promises every day. It was a complex organization driven by government. Decisions were made by politicians. The commodore was no politician.

The CI walked away from the office reflecting on lunch. He would miss the commodore. On the ground floor, he went to the security office and handed in his security pass. He could no longer come and go unescorted. He was no longer one of them. As he drove the 2½ hours home, he reflected on the project and why the department had not used his knowledge. He felt a bit sorry for himself. He felt he had done his best. Sure, he had made mistakes, but he had learned from them. When the training workshops had not worked, he switched to workplace engagements. He moved the learning out of the classroom into the workplace. He was doing best practice action research where he adapted and adjusted to the industry partner. As he learned, the project learned and the department learned. It seemed to be an exemplar research project from a methodology perspective. He focused on significant organizational problems. He tried to introduce positive social change by improving the workplace. His project was designed to sustain a capability that maintained national security. Everybody talks about doing research with impact. This project was significant. But nobody cared. He blamed himself. He knew that he was not a leader. He was no change agent. People would not follow him. He inspired no one. He lacked the personal charm, charisma, and likeability to persuade others to do what he asked. It seemed that his personality had failed the project. His knowledge was useful, but no one wanted to use it. He reflected on his failed promotions. If he had changed the name on the application, that other person would have been promoted. Maybe if someone else, someone more senior, or someone better with people had led this project, it may have worked. But he realized he was being self-indulgent. There were many reasons why this project had failed. He was just one of them.

Commodore Pubnix reflected on a meeting with his senior uniform staff early in the project. 'This won't work, Sir', said a senior staff member. The commodore looked at him. He knew him well. He was 56 years old. The grey hair symbolized a lifetime of service for the department. This man had

(Continued)

(Continued)

served around the world in difficult situations. He understood their business and the organization. He knew his men. The commodore respected his opinion. 'Why?' The commodore replied: 'I know what he (the CI) is trying to do. But it just won't work here.' So he understands the project and its goals, the commodore reflected to himself. The problem is not due to the project being too abstract or academic. The senior officer continued: 'The problem is the posting cycle. The staff just don't care enough to make this happen.' The commodore thought about what he had said. The posting cycle meant that staff were in his organization for a short period only, often two to three years, before being posted elsewhere, never to return to that organization again. 'But surely the staff can see that this will help the department overall. If we can share our knowledge and sustain our capability, that will help protect Australia. Isn't that what they signed up for?', asked the commodore. 'Yes, Sir', replied the senior officer, 'but they are not paid to sustain the organization. That is someone else's problem. That is your problem. Their job is to do what is on their desk today. This problem is too big for them. When they post out, the problem will still be here, and life goes on. The organization will still open for business tomorrow whether we fix this or not. The project was never going to work'.

Commodore Pubnix was reflecting on a meeting with the senior colleague towards the end of the project. 'Sir', he asked, 'I would like to request that we carry on with this research project as a programme of work once the university team have finished'. The colleague looked at the commodore. He knew that the commodore knew that he didn't like receiving bad news. He wondered why the commodore was bringing this project to him and forcing him to make this decision. 'We can't do this', replied the colleague. 'The staff don't want to do it'. 'Sir' – continued the commodore – 'the CI has produced six final reports for us. The reports are based on five years of study. I believe there are useful practical outcomes for the department. This will help us sustain our capability. Would you reconsider?' 'See if you can find some money from Project Demoza'.

Commodore Pubnix was reflecting on a meeting with the new commodore in charge of Project Demoza. Project Demoza was a special initiative funded to introduce significant organizational improvements across the department. The previous commodore in charge of Project Demoza had rejected including the CI's project as part of Demoza. However, the new commodore was a supporter of the CI's project. The CI received an email indicating that Project Demoza would find funding to support the transition of the project to an ongoing programme of work. The CI was elated. Three weeks later, the federal government announced there would be an election. Project Demoza's budget was cut by 75% to fund new election promises by the government. The CI received an email explaining that there was no longer funding for the project from Project Demoza. The project was now officially dead.

A year later, the CI contacted commodore Pubnix to ask him to act as a referee for another promotion application. A few months later, the commodore contacted the CI to check how the application went. When the CI explained that his application was unsuccessful, the commodore became angry and said 'Didn't they trust what I said in my reference for you? Why wouldn't they believe me?' The CI smiled as he considered the irony of the situation.

CASE STUDY QUESTIONS

1. Describe the change the CI was trying to introduce in this case study in terms of how he was trying to improve performance at the case study organization.

2. Would directed or facilitated change have been effective in implementing the change necessary? What method should the CI have used and why? What method should commodore Pubnix have used and why?
3. Use the integrated productivity model (Figure 10.6) to design a solution to the problems faced by the CI and commodore Pubnix in the case study.

REVIEW AND DISCUSSION QUESTIONS

1. Consider the directed and facilitated change dichotomy. Which approach best suits knowledge management? Why?
2. Evaluate the integrated productivity model in Figure 10.6. Would it improve productivity? Why, or why not?
3. Would embedding knowledge management in problem processes improve productivity? Why, or why not?

FURTHER READING

Massingham, P. and Al Holaibi, M. (2017) 'Embedding Kowledge Management into Business Processes,' *Knowledge and Process Management*, 24(1): 53–71.
Myers, P., Hulks, S. and Wiggins, L. (2012) *Organizational Change: Perspectives on theory and practice*, Oxford, Oxford University Press. This book explains change, particularly directed and facilitated change. It also examines factors influencing individual behaviour associated with knowledge sharing.
Raghu, T.S. and Vinze, A. (2007) A Business Process Context for Knowledge Management. *Decision Support Systems*, 43: 1062–1079. This article explains process management and how it relates to knowledge management.

BIBLIOGRAPHY

Aakhus, M. (2007) Conversations for Reflection: Augmenting transitions and transformations in expertise. Chapter 1 in McInerney, C.J. and Day, R.E. (eds) *Rethinking Knowledge Management: From knowledge objects to knowledge processes*, Berlin, Springer.
Alavi, M. and Tiwana, A. (2005) Knowledge Management: The information technology dimension. Chapter 6 in Easterby-Smith, M. and Lyles, M.A. (eds) *Handbook of Organizational Learning and Knowledge Management*, Hong Kong, Blackwell, pp. 104–121.
Becerra-Fernandez, I. and Sabherwal, R. (2010) *Knowledge Management: Systems and processes*, Armonk, NY, ME Sharpe.

Boyle, T.A., Scherrer-Rathje, M. and Stuart, I. (2011) Learning to Be Lean: The influence of external information sources in lean improvements. *Journal of Manufacturing Technology Management, 22* (5): 587–603.

Chongwatpol, J. and Sharda, R. (2013) Achieving Lean Objectives through RFID: A simulation-based assessment. *Decision Sciences, 44* (2): 239–266.

Choo, A.S., Linderman, K. and Schroeder, R.G. (2007) Method and Psychological Effects on Learning Behaviours and Knowledge Creation in Quality Improvement Projects. *Management Science, 53* (2): 437–450.

Dunphy, D. and Stace, D. (1993) The Strategic Management of Corporate Change. *Human Relations, 46* (8): 905–920.

Edmondson, A.C., Winslow, A.B., Bohmer, R.M.J. and Pisano, G.P. (2003) Learning How and Learning What: Effects of tacit and codified knowledge on performance improvement following technology adoption. *Decision Sciences, 34* (2): 197–223.

Flynn, B., Flynn, E., Amundson, S. and Schroeder, R. (1999) Product Development Speed and Quality: A new set of synergies. In Stahl, M. (ed.) *Perspectives in Total Quality*, Oxford, Blackwell, pp. 245–271.

Gardner, A. (2011) *Personalisation in social work*, Exeter, Learning Matters.

Grant, R.M. (1996) Toward a Knowledge-based Theory of the Firm. *Strategic Management Journal* (Special Issue), 17, Winter: 109–122.

Grover, V., Jeong, S.R., Kettinger, W.J. and Teng, J.T.C. (1995) The Implementation of Business Process Reengineering. *Journal of Management Information Systems, 12* (1): 109–144.

Guha, S., Grover, V., Kettinger, W.J. and Teng, J.T.C. (1997) Business Process Change and Organizational Performance: Exploring an antecedent model. *Journal of Management Information Systems, 14* (1): 119–154.

Hammer, M. (2002) Process Management and the Future of Six Sigma. *MIT Sloan Management Review, 43* (2): 26–32.

Hammer, M. and Champy, J. (1993) Reengineering the Corporation: A manifesto for business revolution. *Canadian Business Review, 20* (3): 37–38.

Han, K.H. and Park, J.W. (2009) Process-centred Knowledge Model and Enterprise Ontology for the Development of Knowledge Management Systems. *Expert Systems with Applications, 36*: 7441–7447.

Harkness, W.L., Kettinger, L. and Segars, A.H. (1996) Sustaining Business Process Improvement in the Information Services Function: Lessons learned at the Bose Corporation. *MIS Quarterly, 20* (3): 349–368.

Harrington, H. (1991) *Business Process Improvement: The breakthrough strategy for total quality, productivity, and competitiveness*, New York, McGraw-Hill.

Hines, P., Holweg, M. and Rich, N. (2004) Learning to Evolve: A review of contemporary lean thinking. *International Journal of Operations & Production Management, 24* (10): 994–1011.

Huizing, A. and Bouman, W. (2002) Knowledge and Learning, Markets and Organizations. In Choo, C.W. and Bontis, N. (eds) *The Strategic Management of Intellectual Capital and Organizational Knowledge*, New York, Oxford University Press, pp. 185–206.

Jung, J., Choi, I. and Song, M. (2007) An Integration Architecture for Knowledge Management Systems and Business Process Management Systems. *Computers in Industry, 58*: 21–34.

Kearns, G.S. and Lederer, A.L. (2003) A Resource-based View of Strategic IT Alignment: How knowledge sharing creates competitive advantage. *Decision Sciences, 34* (2): 1–29.

Lewis, S., Passmore, J. and Cantore, S. (2008) Using Appreciative Inquiry in Sales Team Development. *Industrial and Commercial Training, 40* (4): 175–180.

Linderman, K. Schroeder, R.G. and Sanders, J. (2010) A Knowledge Management Framework Underlying Process Management. *Decision Sciences, 41* (4): 689–719.

Locher, D. (2007) In the Office: Where lean and six sigma converge. *Quality Progress, 40* (10): 54–55.

Massingham, P. and Al Holaibi, M. (2017) Embedding Knowledge Management into Business Processes. *Knowledge and Process Management, 24* (1): 53–71.

Myers, P., Hulks, S. and Wiggins, L. (2012) *Organizational Change: Perspectives on theory and practice*, Oxford, Oxford University Press.

Nonaka, I. and Takeuchi, H. (1995) *The Knowledge-creating Company: How Japanese companies create the dynamics of innovation*, New York, Oxford Univer-sity Press.

Pande, P., Neuman, R., and Cavenagh, R. (2000) *The Six Sigma Way: How GE, Motorola and other top companies are honing their performance*, New York, McGraw-Hill.

Raghu, T.S. and Vinze, A. (2007) A Business Process Context for Knowledge Management. *Decision Support Systems, 43*: 1062–1079.

Reagans, R. and McEvily, B. (2003) Network Structure and Knowledge Transfer: The effects of cohesion and range. *Administrative Science Quarterly, 48* (2): 240–267.

Ricondo, I. and Viles, E. (2005) Six Sigma and its Link to TQM, BPR, Lean and the Learning Organization. *International Journal of Six Sigma and Competitive Advantage, 1* (3): 323–354.

Rother, M. and Shook, J. (2003) *Learning to See: Value stream mapping to create value and eliminate muda*, Cambridge, Lean Enterprise Institute.

Sabherwal, R. and Becerra-Fernandez, I. (2003) An Empirical Study of the Effect of Knowledge Management Processes at Individual, Group, and Organizational Levels. *Decision Sciences, 34* (2): 225–260.

Sabherwal, R. and Sabherwal, S. (2005) Knowledge Management Using Information Technology: Determinants of short-term impact. *Decision Sciences, 36* (4): 531–567.

Sarvary, M. (1999) Knowledge Management and Competition in the Consulting Industry. *California Management Review, 41* (2): 95–107.

Schön, D. (1983) *The Reflective Practitioner*, New York, Basic Books.

Senge, P., Kleiner, A., Roberts, C., Ross, R., Roth, G. and Smith, B. (2005) *The Dance of Change: The challenges of sustaining momentum in learning organizations*, London, Nicholas Brealey Publishing.

Sharp, A. and McDermott, P. (2001) *Workflow Modelling: Tools for process improvement and application development*, Norwood, NJ, Artech House.

Shingo, S. and Dillon, A. (1989) *A Study of the Toyota Production System from an Industrial Engineering Viewpoint*, Portland, OR, Productivity Press.

Silver, E.A. (2004) Process Management Instead of Operations Management. *Manufacturing & Service Operations Management, 6* (4): 273–279.

Smith, H. (2003) Business Process Management – The Third Wave: Business process modelling language (bpml) and its pi-calculus foundations. *Information and Software Technology, 45*: 1065–1069.

Terwiesch, C. and Bohn, R. (2001) Learning and Process Improvement during Production Ramp-up. *International Journal of Production Economics, 70* (1): 1–19.

Tsoukas, H. (2003) Do We Really Understand Tacit Knowledge? Chapter 21 in Easterby-Smith, M. and Lyles, M.A. (eds) *Handbook of Organizational Learning and Knowledge Management*, Hong Kong, Blackwell, pp. 410–427.

von Krogh, G. (2005) Knowledge Sharing and the Communal Resource. Chapter 19 in Easterby-Smith, M. and Lyles, M.A. (eds) *Handbook of Organizational Learning and Knowledge Management*, Hong Kong, Blackwell, pp. 372–392.

Womack, J.P. and Jones, D.T. (1996) Beyond Toyota: How to root out waste and pursue perfection. *Harvard Business Review, 74* (5): 140–158.

11

ORGANIZATIONAL SYSTEMS

CHAPTER OUTLINE

LEARNING OUTCOMES

After completing this chapter, the reader should be able to:

1. Discuss systems thinking and how it contributes to knowledge management
2. Discuss the role of information technology in knowledge management
3. Discuss the role of human resource management in knowledge management
4. Discuss the role of accounting in knowledge management
5. Discuss the role of organizational structure in knowledge management
6. Examine how knowledge creation fills knowledge gaps internally
7. Examine how knowledge acquisition fills knowledge gaps externally

MANAGEMENT ISSUES

Organizational systems require managers to:

1. Consider how knowledge management fits with other organizational systems
2. Determine the role of information technology in terms of socio-cultural context, accessibility, and facilitated collaboration
3. Decide on how human resource management can play a role in building strategic capability
4. Consider how accounting can measure the value of people
5. Determine the organizational structure and control necessary to facilitate knowledge sharing and improved productivity

Effective organizational systems involve the following challenges for management:

1. How to use IT to enable knowledge management rather than information management
2. How to achieve strategic alignment of the workforce
3. Seeing employees as value creating rather than as a cost
4. Choosing an organizational structure based on two drivers: effectiveness and efficiency

LINKS TO OTHER CHAPTERS

Chapters 2 and 9: on knowledge management and systems thinking

Chapters 4 and 5: regarding strategic alignment of the workforce

Chapter 10: concerning change management

OPENING MINI CASE STUDY

THE INTRANET: HOW STORING WORK IN ONLINE KNOWLEDGE REPOSITORIES IS NOT ENOUGH

John McDonald was walking back from a meeting. As he walked through the open plan office, he saw a small group of his staff sitting at a table having a meeting. As he walked past them on his way to his office, he overheard something that sparked his interest. The staff were talking about something that stirred deep in his memory. He turned back and walked up to the group:

'Are you talking about the smythsonian stabilizer?'

When the group confirmed they were, he sat down and asked them about their problem. After 10 minutes, he told the group that he had written a report on this topic and it would solve their problem. He promised the group he would find the report and send it to them.

As he walked back to his office, he muttered to himself how lucky the group was that he had overheard their discussion. The report would save them weeks of time.

When he returned to his office, he sat down at his computer and opened the intranet and started looking for the report. He looked at his work calendar and realized he had many other things to do. His priority was to write a report briefing the senior executive on the issue they had discussed at the meeting he had just returned from. But this report on the smythsonian stabilizer was now on his mind. He wanted to help the group. He felt proud that he already knew the answer to their problem. As their boss, he felt it was his role to help solve their problems. He was the man they turned to for help. He knew more than them. That was why he was the boss. So he began searching the intranet for the report.

Two hours later, he was still sitting at his computer looking for the report. It was now 12.30pm. One of his senior managers, Bill Thompson, knocked on his door and asked John if he wanted to have lunch. John said no, he was looking for something. Bill asked what it was. When John described the report, Bill suggested searching for the words smythsonian stabilizer. John explained that this was the first thing he had done. He scratched his head and explained: 'The words are not there for some reason. I just can't find it.' Bill suggested giving up. 'Don't waste any more time on this. Just tell the guys you can't find it. They can just do it themselves.' John told him to go ahead to lunch without him. He was frustrated. He could not understand why he could not find the report. He knew he had filed it on the intranet. All staff were required to file all of their work on the intranet once completed. He was determined to find the report.

Bill returned at 13.30 and asked John how he was going. They sat down together and searched the intranet. After 20 minutes, Bill stood up and said he would ask for help. Bill returned with Chris Jakemen and Ewan Ball, two of the other senior managers. The four sat around John's computer looking at the screen while John tapped at the keyboard searching without success. Everyone offered their opinion on where to find the report and how to search the intranet. After a further 40 minutes, Ewan left and returned with Paul Thomas. Paul was the division's computer geek. He was 20 years younger than the youngest of the senior managers sitting around John's computer. They briefed Paul and he sat down at John's desk. The four senior managers stood watching Paul. They felt a sense of obligation to stay and see this to its end. It was their problem now. If they left, it would seem like they were passing the problem onto someone else and avoiding their responsibilities in some way. Bill, Chris, and Ewan felt a sense of loyalty to John and felt it was their role to help make John's job easier. They could see this distressed him in some way and felt they had to help him. But Paul couldn't find the report either.

It was now 16.30. John had been trying to find the report for six hours. He had done no other work since returning from his first meeting of the day. He had not eaten lunch. He did not write the report for his boss that he had promised he would finish by the end of the day. The four other staff left his office in defeat. John sat at his desk and considered what to do. He was angry. He felt inadequate. He rose and walked out of his office to tell the group that he could not find the report and that they had to start work on their own report. As he walked back to his office, he reflected on what a bad day it had been. It started well. He wondered what had gone wrong. He felt incompetent. He felt old. He felt he had let his staff down.

CASE STUDY QUESTIONS

1. Should John have got involved in this task? Why, or why not?
2. Why could John not find his report?
3. Is there anything John should have done differently on this day?
4. Why did John feel the way he did?

INTRODUCTION

This chapter explores the organizational systems supporting knowledge management. It adopts a systems thinking perspective. This approach recognizes that knowledge management is part of a bigger picture which includes other organizational systems. These systems can be enablers and barriers to effective knowledge management and, therefore, the relationship between these systems and knowledge management must be managed.

CORE CONCEPT: Knowledge management often suffers from lack of ownership. This means that knowledge management activities fail to find a sponsor or a champion to take responsibility for implementation.

While organizations are increasingly appointing chief knowledge officers and establishing knowledge management departments, the reality is that knowledge management must compete with other functional areas for resources and priority. While these other areas are important enablers for effective knowledge management, they also represent barriers due to the socio-political realities of modern organizations.

This chapter will explore these issues and look at the role of information technology, accounting, human resources, and structure in enabling knowledge management. Each of these areas plays a crucial role in effective knowledge management. The chapter provides an introduction to each topic. There is also the opportunity to examine knowledge management from these subject matter perspectives. As discussed in Chapter 2, knowledge management is multi-disciplinary and the various disciplines look at it from quite different perspectives.

The chapter provides a further perspective on the social reconstruction of the reality of knowledge management. Knowledge management faces challenges to demonstrate its value and to justify its return on investment (see Chapter 3). In organizational systems where competition for resources is often fierce, knowledge management needs to work with, rather than against, competing forces. The chapter discusses how this may be done.

SYSTEMS THINKING

Systems thinking provides a perspective on how knowledge management fits in with other organizational systems. As discussed in Chapter 9, systems thinking explains that organizations have multiple social systems, including people, technology, culture, leadership, structure, as well as internal and external systems. In organizational terms, the theory of autopoiesis explains that 'the system is closed and generates its own boundary' (Mingers, 2006: 84). Systems may be 'self-bounding' in the sense that organizational culture defines the boundaries, i.e. those who accept the norms and values feel they belong (Mingers, 2006: 94). It is similar to Tsoukas's (2003) concept of insiderness. Organizational social systems are typically defined by employment, i.e. membership status ascribed by the employer. Mingers (2006: 165) concludes that our role in social systems is defined by our embodied self or our identity, our individual cognition which is similar to the individual concept in Polanyi's (1962) tacit triangle, and communication which connects us with others. Mingers states that 'people do come to understand one another and act coherently', which is similar to Senge's (1990) concept of shared mental models, but Mingers adds that this empathy is developed by 'structural coupling within a linguistic domain rather than the transmission of information' (Mingers, 2006: 165). This emphasizes the importance of social relations in developing membership of organizational systems. Knowledge management can suffer from being an outsider, i.e. 'the new kid on the block', and facing exclusion from other systems. In the experience of working with the case study organization (see closing integrated case study), there was often strong resistance from other systems, such as human resource management, mainly due to the 'not invented here' syndrome.

Systems thinking about knowledge management has two main paths. First is the technological view of knowledge management, influenced by information science, which focuses on document management systems, decision support systems, group support systems, workflow management systems, and customer relationship management systems. Second are the integrated models of knowledge management, which attempt to provide blueprints for implementing knowledge management. A third perspective is to recognize how knowledge management fits with other organizational systems, which is the main focus of this chapter. Knowledge management is a system within a broader organizational system bounded by employee membership and defined by multiple other systems.

INFORMATION TECHNOLOGY

Information technology (IT) is an important part of knowledge management (KM).

CORE CONCEPT: Information technology enables many of the functions of KM, including evaluating, capturing, storing, sharing, and using (enabling access).

The importance of IT is a legacy of KM's evolution. In 2004, four phases of KM were identified:

1. Information to support decision makers
2. Tacit and explicit knowledge
3. The use of narrative in organizations
4. An integrated KM framework. (After Gorelick et al., 2004: 11–18)

KM began from the need to get information to decision makers and, therefore, from an information science perspective. Koenig and Srikantaiah (after 2007: 3–4) identified three stages:

1. Begun with the internet and grown by the field of intellectual capital
2. Human and cultural dimensions
3. Content management and taxonomies.

This shows how the explosion of information created by the internet led the KM boom as organizations struggled to manage this new resource, how the field turned to focus on the people side (i.e. the personalization view) when technology seemed to be failing, and then rebounded towards IT as an integrated solution.

The early dominance of IT is illustrated by the work of both practitioners and researchers. Ruggles (1998) reported that at the time of the field's early evolution (the late 1990s) the four most popular KM projects were intranets, data warehouses, decision support tools, and groupware (technologies that support collaboration and communication). Ponzi (2007) reported, in an analysis of KM publications by discipline, that the early stages (1995–2001) were completely dominated by computer science and information science journals and trade magazines.

The focus on IT was largely due to the view that knowledge could be managed by technology, i.e. it could be codified, stored, and distributed. However, over time this view has changed as the underlying assumptions about IT have been challenged. Markus Raebsamen, director of corporate development at Zurich Financial Services, observed that 'pure technology-led knowledge facilitation initiatives have a high failure rate' (Beerli, 2003: 10). Despite the criticisms of IT, it has continued to grow and evolve.

CORE CONCEPT: Improvements to information technology's role in knowledge management has taken three paths: (1) socio-cultural context, (2) accessibility, and (3) facilitated collaboration.

SOCIO-CULTURAL CONTEXT

The socio-cultural context is explained by the importance of organizational politics, culture, and social networks. Chapter 10 examined the role of change management in KM. The introduction of a new IT system or tools is like any new initiative which introduces change in the organization. Employees must be willing and able to use IT if it is to be effective. The solution is to embrace the principles of effective change management. This includes employees' collective norms and values, as well as their relationships with and trust in the management introducing the IT. Tiwana (2002: 78) argues that IT's most valuable role in knowledge management is to broaden the reach and enhance the speed of knowledge transfer. He argues that technology has three main purposes in KM:

1. To facilitate communication
2. To provide the infrastructure for storing codified knowledge
3. To map the interrelationships between tacit and codified knowledge. (Tiwana, 2002: 78)

Tiwana suggests that organizations can leverage their IT infrastructure with these guidelines:

- Collaborative synergy
- Real knowledge, not artificial knowledge
- Conversation as a medium for thought
- Sources and originators, not just information

- Decision support
- Pragmatism, not perfection
- The user is king. (Tiwana, 2002: 78–79)

These guidelines may address common change barriers to the introduction of IT and assist the success of its implementation.

ACCESSIBILITY

Accessibility is about ensuring the knowledge stored in IT systems, i.e. within knowledge repositories, is searchable. Accessibility is typically done by structuring. This involves knowledge taxonomies which code knowledge into different topics and then generate hierarchical classifications to show the relationships between the topics. Jashapara (2011: 190) provides this example of knowledge taxonomies:

- *Structured*: financial data, sales data, customer data, demographic data
- *Semi-structured*: cases, policies, procedures, action plans
- *Unstructured*: documents, emails, presentations, videos.

One of the failures of knowledge repositories is that employees dump all of their work into intranets as unstructured documents. The result may be that much of this work cannot be found, even by the authors.

There are many IT systems that try to address the need for accessibility. This chapter will present two. The first IT framework is that of Becerra-Fernandez and Sabherwal (2010) and can be broken down as follows:

1. *Knowledge application systems*: these are systems that utilize knowledge. These enable employees to use knowledge possessed by other employees without actually acquiring or learning that knowledge. The role of IT is to facilitate processes of routines and direction. Mechanisms which facilitate routines include organizational policies, work practices, and standards. Mechanisms which facilitate direction include hierarchical relationships, help desks, and support centres. The main technology is artificial intelligence (AI). AI includes rule-based expert systems, case-based reasoning, and traditional management information systems. There are different types of knowledge application systems: expert systems, help desk systems, and fault diagnosis systems. (Adapted from Becerra-Fernandez and Sabherwal, 2010: Chapter 6.)

2. *Knowledge capture systems*: these are systems that preserve and formalize knowledge. They are designed to help elicit and store knowledge, both tacit and codified. The role of IT is to capture knowledge which can then be shared and used by others. Knowledge capture mechanisms that facilitate externalization (the conversion of tacit knowledge into explicit form)

include the development of models and prototypes and the articulation of stories. Knowledge capture mechanisms that facilitate internalization (the conversion of explicit knowledge into tacit form) include learning by observation and face-to-face meetings. The main techniques used to support externalization are concept maps and context-based reasoning. Technology has been used to replicate internalization including behavioural cloning and radio frequency identification (known as RFID). (Adapted from Becerra-Fernandez and Sabherwal, 2010: Chapter 7)

3. *Knowledge-sharing systems*: these are systems that organize and distribute knowledge. They are designed to help users share their knowledge. The role of IT is to provide knowledge repositories for employees to store their knowledge. The two main types of sharing mechanisms are lessons learned systems and expertise locator systems. They are supplemented by virtual communities of practice, which are concerned to protect organizational memory and prevent knowledge loss. Technology focuses on collaborative computing illustrated by workflow management systems. Specific knowledge-sharing techniques include incident report databases, alert systems, best practice databases, lessons learned systems, and expertise locator systems. The sharing of tacit knowledge focuses on communities of practice. (Adapted from Becerra-Fernandez and Sabherwal, 2010: Chapter 8)

4. *Knowledge discovery systems*: these are systems that create knowledge. They support the development of new tacit or explicit knowledge from data and information, or from the synthesis of prior knowledge. The role of IT is to support the combination and socialization processes. Combination mechanisms enable the integration of multiple streams of knowledge, usually through joint activities rather than codified instructions. Socialization mechanisms include conferences, brainstorming camps, and facilitated workshops. The main technology in use for discovering new knowledge is data mining. Web mining is also becoming increasingly popular. (Adapted from Becerra-Fernandez and Sabherwal, 2010: Chapter 9)

The second IT framework presented in this chapter is from Tiwana (2002). Figure 11.1 illustrates the variety of typical IT tools used to support knowledge management. The following systems are discussed briefly: document management systems, decision support systems, group support systems, workflow management systems, and customer relationship management systems.

Organizations increasingly produce a huge volume of codified knowledge in the form of reports, policies, procedures, presentations, databases, and so on. *Document management systems (DMS)* tend to replicate the role of organizational libraries by focusing on enhanced access to organizational knowledge for employees. The difference is that libraries used to focus on printed material, whereas DMS stores information in electronic form, usually accessed via intranets. A main theme in DMS research is to improve accessibility by structuring. This is a process of indexing or adding meaning to documents to help users find the

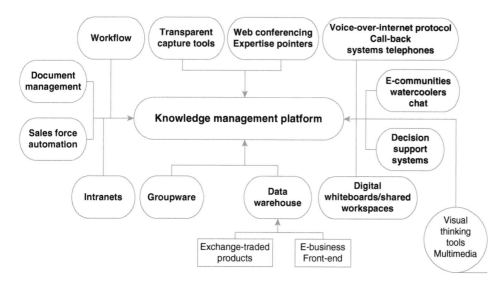

FIGURE 11.1 *Key components of a KM platform*

Source: Tiwana (2002: 83). Reprinted by permission of Pearson Education, Inc, New York.

knowledge they need. However, DMS does much more than provide access to organizational knowledge. It enables document control, including audit trails and security access, to ensure material is up to date and valid; it organizes material using folders and indexing; it enables effective searching using meta-data and web-based tools; and it enables the quick combination of materials using scanning and file conversion (Raynes, 2002).

Decision support systems (DSS) combine data with analytical models to support non-routine decision making. DSS is software that provides users with an interactive interface which combines analytical frameworks with models to use complex data to make decisions. A main theme in DSS is to reduce the environmental complexity and risk associated with important decisions. DSS includes artificial intelligence and data-mining tools. It provides users with support to make sequential and interdependent decisions; it is adaptable, flexible, and supports different stages in decision making and different decision-making styles; and it creates value by improving confidence and trust in decisions, as well as their accuracy and timeliness (Turban and Aronson, 2001).

Group support systems (GSS) are technologies to facilitate collaboration and cooperation in teams. Products such as Lotus Notes and Microsoft NetMeeting were popular GSS tools. GSS was designed to support simultaneous idea generation, the facilitating of priorities, and the finding of consensus on agendas. It has evolved to include tools supporting virtual collaboration, including online communities of practice. It provides users with communication tools such as email, Skype, and video conferencing; the capacity to store group codified knowledge such as Dropbox; and cooperation tools to enable brainstorming and the tracking of document changes (e.g. see Andriessen, 2003).

Workflow management systems (WMS) are process maps designed to capture best practice and improve efficiency. They are codified organizational knowledge about work activity. They map tasks, i.e. processes or routines, into logical, sequential units of work associated with an activity. WMS is used in business process re-engineering and is part of enterprise resource planning (ERP) (see Chapter 10). WMS is most effective in work that is routine and standardized. Therefore, it suits work that benefits from the specialization of tasks in the sense that repetition leads to improvement and refinement and, eventually, a single best practice. It fits with scientific management's view of knowledge management (see Chapter 2). WMS is a tool for back-office integration processes (van der Aalst and van Hee, 2002).

Customer relationship management systems (CRMS) contrast with the back-office focus of WMS and instead look at the front office, particularly marketing. The aim of CRMS is close interface with the market to ensure organizations can respond quickly to customer needs. The type of response differentiates CRMS from normal marketing. CRMS requires knowledge about how to integrate technology and business processes to adjust and adapt to changing customer needs. CRMS includes tools such as data warehousing (e.g. market intelligence), data-mining techniques, and search tools via the intranet and the internet. The challenge with CRMS is that to be effective they need to be cross-functional, in the sense that they integrate multiple activities such as research and development, operations, human resources, and finance. The workflow processes are not simply about capturing market data. CRMS needs to capture stakeholder involvement with the customer at multiple levels (e.g. planning); the operating context including structure, culture, information technology systems, and suppliers (e.g. research); systems thinking including employee information needs and fit with existing systems (e.g. IT); and implementation including training and monitoring (after Jashapara, 2011).

FACILITATED COLLABORATION

IT has moved towards facilitated collaboration. Recent research explained that 'the main role of new information and communication technologies (ICTs), such as Web 2.0/3.0, collaborative technologies 2.0, social networking tools, wikis, [and] internal blogging, is to help people share knowledge through common platforms and electronic storage' (Soto-Acosta and Cegarra-Navarro, 2016: 417). These new ICTs represent the social web encompassing 'the design of websites and software to support and foster social interaction' (2016: 418). The social web can be defined as the 'second generation of community-driven web services ... where everyone can communicate, participate, collaborate and refine the information space' (Colomo-Palacios, 2010). The term KM 2.0 has been coined to summarize these new trends in KM; it describes the acquisition, creation, and sharing of collective intelligence through 'social networks and communities of knowledge' (Sigala and Chalkiti, 2014: 802).

Bhatt (2001) pioneered an integrated view of knowledge management. He felt that defining knowledge management through technological or social systems alone overemphasized one aspect at the expense of the other, and that both are equally important in knowledge management. The 'conversion between data and information is efficiently handled through information technologies', but IT does not convert information into knowledge. The conversion between information and knowledge 'is achieved through social actors, but social actors are slow in converting data to information'. That is one of the reasons that knowledge management is 'carried out through the optimization of technological and social subsystems'. 'The roots of this view can be found in the socio-technological perspective of the organization.' (Bhatt, 2001: 68–69)

An example of facilitated collaboration is virtual communities of practice. Diemers (2003) explains that there are three types of communities: communities of blood (e.g. families), communities of place (e.g. neighbourhoods), and communities of mind (e.g. common interests). A virtual community is a community that 'constitutes itself … in virtualized interaction spaces' (Diemers, 2003: 164). Virtual communities, therefore, do not usually meet the criteria of blood or place, but do meet the criteria of mind. Virtual communities of practice are common in large consulting firms and are used to share best practice and lessons learned. They are particularly useful in organizations where employees are separated by distance, such as global firms. Diemers (2003: 164) identifies seven factors of cohesion for communities of practice: shared interests, shared norms and values, common interaction platform, emotional bonds, continuity, reciprocity, and identity construction. However, the only one of these factors that would be relatively easy to achieve with virtual communities of practice is the common interaction platform (i.e. IT systems).

Tapscott and Williams (2006: 18) argue that the ability to 'integrate the talents of dispersed individuals and organizations is becoming the defining competency for managers and firms'. This integration is done within broad horizontal networks called mass collaboration. It is the idea of people volunteering opinions, ideas, information, and knowledge online for free. As this collective collaboration builds, it develops a life of its own, regenerating and improving on what was collected before. Tapscott and Williams (2006) argue that it replaces the previous model of collaboration where people sit together in a room discussing ideas. Implementing 'mass collaboration requires four concepts: openness, peering, sharing, and acting globally' (2006: 20). This takes the concept of virtual communities of practice to another level.

Mass collaboration promises to develop new rules for global business. An internet that manages knowledge rather than information would transform business, making knowledge markets accessible and low cost. It would also make

(Continued)

(Continued)

access to the knowledge resource difficult to sustain as a competitive advantage, making knowledge management capability, i.e. the ability to combine resources, the main source of advantage in the 21st century.

HUMAN RESOURCE MANAGEMENT

Human resource management (HRM) is an important enabling system for knowledge management. However, HRM sometimes struggles to integrate with other organizational systems. Lengnick-Hall and Lengnick-Hall (2003: 1) argue that HRM's traditional focus on 'simple operational' practices, such as attracting, selecting, developing, retaining, and using employees to accomplish specified tasks and jobs, is limiting organizations' capacity to create value from their human resources. Many organizations claim that their employees are their most valuable resource, but the knowledge-based view of the firm (Grant, 1996) argues that knowledge is the most valuable resource. Knowledge has become even more important in the global knowledge economy where knowledge is the main driver of economic value (Drucker, 1999). The personalization view of knowledge management proposes that tacit knowledge, i.e. the knowledge in employees' heads, is the most valuable knowledge. Therefore, the management of human resources and their human capital should be a critical part of organizational strategy. However, HRM has been criticized for failing to evolve into a strategic role and remaining stuck in operational support. Before looking at the strategic role, we will examine HRM's traditional role.

TACTICAL HRM

For knowledge management to be successful, one essential element is the use of training and development to provide the necessary education, facilitation, and support for staff. Dalkir (2011) listed types of KM roles and responsibilities within organizations, and the only HRM-related role on the list was training. However, Dalkir does define training in broad terms as involving 'coaching, mentoring, communities of practice, life-cycle training support, and incorporating feedback from lessons learned and best practice' (Dalkir, 2011: 410). Training is 'a planned process to help modify the attitudes, knowledge or skill of an individual through a learning process, whereas development is more long term and can be associated with an individual's maturity or career growth' (Jashapara, 2011: 308). HRM has traditionally played an important role in a systematic training cycle involving identifying training needs, designing training solutions, implementing training solutions, and evaluating their effectiveness (Stewart, 1999). While staff training still provides an important benefit in addressing competency gaps (see Chapter 5), it has been discredited as an ineffective way of organizational learning (see Chapter 8).

HRM can create value by designing effective reward and recognition systems to encourage positive knowledge management behaviours and attitudes such as knowledge sharing. Chapters 8 and 9 discussed the concept of the psychological contract and theories such as calculative reward as a means for improving the emotional relationship between employees and their organization. Tactical HRM tends to use more straightforward incentives such as bonus point schemes and overseas holidays (Newell et al., 2002). The idea is that these rewards will create more job satisfaction and, therefore, more commitment to support initiatives such as knowledge management.

Motivation is 'a controversial issue in theory and practice' (North and Kumta, 2014: 133). Hislop (2013: 221) argues that HRM's main role in motivation is to address the knowledge hoarding/sharing dilemma (see Chapter 9). This dilemma involves an individual assessing the benefits of sharing knowledge against the costs. It involves a trade-off decision regarding organizational gain versus personal gain. Research has proposed that this trade-off decision involves feelings of belonging and trust (Massingham and Tam, 2015). HRM may help employees resolve this trade-off decision by improving intrinsic and extrinsic motivation. Intrinsic motivation is direct needs fulfilment and is 'related to the joy of doing the work itself or perceived commitment, whereas extrinsic rewards are indirect and linked to factors such as money and power' (North and Kumta, 2014: 133). Research suggests that the most effective motivator 'is the work itself', and that this is linked to personal goal setting which may be driven at the individual level as well as by commitment to others (i.e. the group), the organization, or even society (2014: 134). However, this is challenging for the following reasons:

1. 'Intrinsic and extrinsic motivation cannot be generated and changed to the same degree for each employee.
2. Intrinsic and extrinsic rewards are not separated from one another, i.e. you cannot do one without considering the other.
3. Intrinsic motivation may not be aligned with the goals of the organization and is very difficult to change.' (North and Kumta, 2014: 134)
4. Intrinsic motivation may be related to the job rather than the organization; for example the individual may love being a nurse but hate the hospital where they are working.

Knowledge workers provide further unique challenges for HRM in trying to address these issues. Research has found that three key factors drive motivation: the quest for autonomy, the desire for mastery, and the need for purpose (Pink, 2009, cited in Norgh and Kumta, 2014: 134). This provides an opportunity for HRM to elevate itself from the traditional role of providing incentives, such as performance bonuses and career progression. Research is asking HRM to seek innovative solutions to the challenges listed above by giving knowledge workers 'attention, challenging work, support, recognizing their contribution' (Carleton, 2011, cited in North and Kumta, 2014: 134), and the opportunity to work with people they respect and trust (Massingham and Tam, 2015). This latter point is particularly important as knowledge workers become more specialized and valuable. Motivating well-trained professionals may be achieved by giving them task variety which challenges their knowledge and gives them the opportunity to learn and grow (North and Kumta, 2014). Enabling advanced learning by providing knowledge workers with the opportunity to attend seminars or conferences or to work with external experts is much more likely to increase their motivation than a pay increase (North and Kumta, 2014). Massingham and Tam (2015) add that providing opportunities for knowledge workers to be recognized for their knowledge externally, i.e. by other subject matter experts, is a particularly effective motivator.

THEORY IN PRACTICE: THE IMPACT OF DIFFERENT APPROACHES TO STAFF TRAINING

Dora Mostard was reading the annual career development reports for two of her staff. She was surprised. The two staff members, Agnetha Stenson and Rory McDonald, had very similar career trajectories. They graduated with the same degree, from the same university, in the same year. They joined the company at the same time. They had then followed one another in their career development and had reached the same level after 24 years with the company. They were both equally regarded and widely respected.

Dora's surprise was that the reports differed so much. While Agnetha showed expected performance, Rory had a truly outstanding year. She called their supervisor, Terry Wotherspoon, to discuss it. Terry did not know why they had performed so differently this year. It was not because they had been paid differently, or received different performance bonuses, or that Terry had praised one more than the other. Dora asked whether there had been any change in behaviour. Terry thought Rory seemed a bit happier this year but could not explain why.

After the meeting, Dora called human resource management and asked for a report on the staff training Agnetha and Rory had completed that year. The report showed that Agnetha had completed four courses on a range of policy areas such as advanced occupational health and safety, and advanced equal employment opportunity (EEO). Rory had not completed any training courses, but had applied for and been granted small funding to attend two international conferences where he presented papers before global experts in his field.

Dora called Agnetha and asked her if she wanted to attend some international conferences next year. She replied that she would be very happy to do this. Five minutes later, Terry called Dora to say that she saw Agnetha walk by her office with a big smile on her face. Terry said she did not know why, but Agnetha seemed happier today. Dora smiled to herself.

Trust is a crucial element of psychological contract (Massingham and Tam, 2015) and an important driver of intrinsic motivation. Knowledge management activities, such as knowledge sharing, involve more than knowledge as a thing, and are more a social process that 'evolves from the ongoing iteration of conversation, reflection, questioning, and absorbing new knowledge, all filtered through a base of individual experience' (McInerney and Mohr, 2007: 65). Trust is 'a mutual confidence that no party involved in a social exchange will exploit another' (Barney and Hansen, 1994: 176). Knowledge management requires goodwill. Sharing knowledge, for example, is 'an act of generosity' because it requires the knower to be willing to offer what they know (McInerney and Mohr, 2007: 70). The goodwill required to motivate this generosity is driven by two factors: competition and consequences. Knowledge workers operate in a competitive socio-political environment, and this creates rivalry with others and doubt about whether to help others. It raises concerns about what the rival will do with your special knowledge and whether they may benefit at your expense, such a through promotion (2007: 70). There is also an expectation that the act of engaging in knowledge management, such as sharing knowledge, 'will be seen as helpful and used only for good' (2007: 70). There are two challenges for organizations seeking a culture based on trust. First, the changing nature of organizations means that employees are increasingly separated from managers who must trust them by focusing on the work they produce rather than monitoring how they do it (2007: 71). Second, the fast-paced nature of work, including high employee turnover rates, means that it is increasingly difficult to build trusting relationships (2007: 71). HRM might help address these challenges by developing a culture which values being responsive, timely, and fair in decision making and communication, as well as allowing employees to take risks and make mistakes (2007: 72).

STRATEGIC HRM

Lengnick-Hall and Lengnick-Hall (2003: 1) argue that 'unless HRM is able to reinvent itself to embrace the challenges of the knowledge economy, it will become a constraining factor that undermines a firm's competitiveness rather than a crucial source of competitive advantage.' This means that if HRM is to become a dynamic capability (Easterby-Smith and Prieto, 2008), it must embrace its strategic role. Dynamic capabilities are 'the capacity (1) to sense and shape opportunities and threats, (2) to seize opportunities, and (3) to maintain competitiveness through enhancing, combining, protecting, and, when necessary, reconfiguring the business enterprise's intangible and tangible assets' (Teece, 2007: 1319).

HRM tries to play a strategic role in two ways: through workforce planning and cultural change. 'Workforce planning balances supply and demand; it ensures the supply of skills and talent that the organization needs to achieve its business strategy and goals', now and in the future (Dychtwald et al., 2006: 28). Workforce planning is traditionally driven by financial resources. Managers negotiate a budget to cover staff costs. A typical model used is salary plus on-costs, where the latter includes indirect costs associated with employing the staff member such as office space, information and communication technology, staff services, and so on. At this level, human resources and their knowledge are seen as a cost to the organization. Workforce planning becomes a numbers game which is reduced to measuring and negotiating staff numbers. However, workforce planning is much more complex than that. The first issue is that the labour market is constantly moving; globalization, technology, and outsourcing are changing the shape of employment (Dychtwald et al., 2006). Some current jobs may not exist in five years' time. HRM must respond to these challenges by 'anticipating necessary labour and skills' and 'preventing talent shortages by retaining key employees' and accessing new sources of knowledge resources (Dychtwald et al., 2006: 29). HRM faces further challenges in planning its workforce:

- *Productivity and business growth*: what is the impact if resources cannot be accessed or are lost, e.g. through employee turnover?
- *Work processes*: how can an increasingly diverse workforce be encouraged to collaborate within the context of the changing nature of work?
- *Learning processes*: how do you replace experience, particularly organizational memory, and adjust to the changing learning styles of your demographics – both older and younger workers?
- *Leadership and management styles*: how do you adjust to depleting leadership talent due to the ageing demographic and increasing retirement, and develop new leadership competencies to address the needs of the new knowledge workers?
- *Culture and continuity*: how can strong positive organizational cultures be maintained within the context of increasing employee turnover, retirements, and changing business models, e.g. mergers, acquisitions, and outsourcing?
- *Competitiveness in global markets*: how can you retain top talent with increasing competition for knowledge resources globally, and how can you achieve your strategy and goals within the context of increasing forces fragmenting your workforce? (After Dychtwald et al., 2006: 24–25)

These challenges illustrate how HRM has an opportunity to play a key role in building strategic capability, which is defined as 'the capacity to create value based on the intangible assets of the firm' (Lengnick-Hall and Lengnick-Hall, 2003: 2). This value emerges from developing human resources which fit the criteria of the resource-based view of the firm, i.e. valuable, rare, unimitable, and non-substitutable (see Chapter 5). In this way, HRM can become strategic by helping build a workforce whose knowledge fits the VRIN model for sustainable competitive advantage. This may be done with human capital flexibility which is defined by process and outcome (Lengnick-Hall and Lengnick-Hall, 2003). The process is an organization's ability to sense and respond quickly to changing strategic and environmental needs, while the outcome reflects workforce diversity and its ability to capitalize on having the right resources for the opportunities which emerge (Lengnick-Hall and Lengnick-Hall, 2003).

Massingham (2016: 422) developed a framework of decisions which would enable HRM to play a strategic role in supporting knowledge:

1. 'Do I have enough staff?
2. Do I have the right staff?
3. Do I have the right staff in the right jobs?
4. What staff will I need in the future?
5. How well is the organization learning?
6. Are we growing our strategic knowledge resources?
7. Are the organization's non-financial resources being managed wisely?'

These are important questions for organizations seeking to maximize their workforce capability. Massingham (2016) explained how HRM could use knowledge management tools, such as the Knowledge Accounts (KA) at the strategic and tactical levels. He distinguished between tactical HRM, tactical HCM, strategic HRM, and strategic HCM as follows:

1. *Tactical human resource management* (HRM) identifies workforce gaps. This answers the question: do I have enough staff? This is about the *quantity* of knowledge resources, i.e. staff. Organizations typically answer this question in terms of staff numbers or budget. Capability deficits are typically addressed by recruiting new staff. However, this is a short-term solution because it makes the organization bigger, not better. A solution is to increase the mean knowledge score (see Chapter 4) by addressing the competency gaps identified by the KA, which would increase the organizational knowledge base and make the organization better. (After Massingham, 2016: 418)

2. *Tactical* HCM identifies job-related competencies. This answers the question: do I have the right staff? Organizations typically answer this question in terms of seniority levels or job families. This is about the *quality* of knowledge resources, i.e. staff. The KA compares the mean knowledge score with the mean baseline score, to measure the quality of its staff. If the mean KA is above the baseline, then knowledge is in surplus, and the organization may exploit this by leveraging this excess capacity. However, if the mean KA is below the baseline, then knowledge is in deficit, and the quality of its staff is less than required to meet the organization's capability (see Chapter 4). (After Massingham, 2016: 418)

3. *Strategic HRM* can provide a broader perspective regarding job inputs and outputs. This answers the question: do I have the right staff in the right jobs? Organizations typically answer this question in terms of recruitment or internal transfers that let people 'grow into the job'. The KA is used here to measure strategic alignment (SA). SA measures the match between an individual and the job requirements. The KA provides a more accurate measure of SA by looking at technical and cognitive tacit knowledge

(e.g. see Nonaka and Takeuchi, 1998). The primary technical knowledge is human capital (HC) as it measures traditional views on job competency, for example experience, skills, and qualifications. These may be seen as job inputs because they are required competencies. The cognitive knowledge may be called 'soft' capabilities in the sense that they measure work attitudes and behaviours. In this sense, they may be seen as job outputs because they surface in the act of doing and in the use of technical knowledge (see Chapter 4). (After Massingham, 2016: 419)

4. *Strategic HCM* identifies where and how to grow the organizational knowledge base (OKB). This answers the question: what staff will I need in the future? Organizations typically answer this question in irregular strategic reviews, often driven by external consultants. The KA is used here to measure future value-creating competencies from both a technical (hard) and cognitive (soft) perspective. The KA identifies future value by measuring system families in the four KA dimensions (e.g. HS, SC). By system, we mean classifying knowledge resources at multiple levels: job-related, activity-related, technical domains (i.e. subject matter expertise), and network-related. It is particularly applicable when we look at the system families: job-related (for new jobs), activity-related (new types of work), technical domains (new types of subject matter expertise), and network-related (new types of social interaction at work). (After Massingham, 2016: 420)

Questions 5,6 and 7 from the list above are discussed in Chapter 9, Organizational Learning and the Learning Organization.

CULTURAL CHANGE AND HRM

Cultural change is the opportunity for human resource management to facilitate humanistic management rather than scientific management. Human systems management is 'primarily about living beings, their learning and action, their networks, orders and systems, and interaction and communication' (Zeleny, 2005: 48). Zeleny argues that telecommunications, globalization, and socio-economic turbulence mean management must address the 'basics of human systems' communication, conversation, and attitudes towards change' (2005: 48). Zeleny (2005: 48–55) explains the social reconstruction of work within the context of these challenges:

1. *The notion of change*: people and organizations live in the continuing present. We can describe the past and plan for the future, but we can only act now. Organizations are living systems, and although people leave, the organization remains. There is organizational memory embodied in its structure, culture, and policies. This is the conservation of the organization and the true contents of its history. It is the organization's identity. Information describes the past and the future; knowledge guides

the action of the present but what is conserved is the organization's wisdom. HRM's role can be conservation. In knowledge management terms, it is preservation of organizational memory.

2. *The impact of communication*: the true purpose of language in organizations is to coordinate action. Exchange of information is not communication. Knowledge is a purposeful coordination of action, and human communication produces human knowledge. The coordination of action puts the 'management' into human systems management and enables us to coordinate human action. HRM's role can be to enable social communication. In knowledge management terms, it is knowledge sharing.

3. *The nature of love and respect*: this creates a form of coordinated action which results in a desired pattern of coexistence with others. It is a form of relationships with others which helps negate the many negative aspects of organizations such as rivalry, jealousy, hate, and aggression. HRM's role can be to build organizational culture based on reciprocity. In knowledge management terms, it is the emotional relationship, i.e. psychological contract.

4. *Purpose and identity*: organizational systems are defined by their identity and their sense of meaning. There is a difference between the employee's identity and the identity of their organization. However, they may be related. People with strong emotional relationships with their organization create loyalty and commitment. The success of the organization becomes their success. The challenge is to differentiate between employees' sense of the job identity and organizational identity. A person may like being an engineer and have strong individual identity associated with this role but not like where they work as an engineer. In this case, they have strong vocational meaning but weak organizational meaning. HRM's role can be to build shared mental models about the organization's identity and connect that with employees' identity of themselves. In knowledge management terms, it is knowledge retention.

Zeleny (2005) concludes that human systems management explains how to coordinate the actions of people without managing them. Management suggests power and control, commands, and orders. This is scientific management, which this book argues is ineffective in the 21st century knowledge economy. It is about obedience and compliance. Knowledge workers need humanistic management. It requires giving people responsibility and a willingness to accept the consequences of their actions. This requires freedom to make choices.

This discussion is about how HRM might develop learning capabilities or a learning culture (see Chapter 8). The learning organization's adaptation and flexibility require capabilities with a focus on enhancing new ideas, intellectual capital, and innovation incentives (McMillan, 2016). This raises questions distinguishing between the roles of HRM and KM in developing these learning capabilities. KM enables decision-making processes through social interactions that enable knowledge creation, sharing, and usage to address role expectations and organizational uncertainties (Nonaka and Konno, 1998). Tichy (2008) described this as becoming teachable organizations. HRM's role is to provide programmes to improve decision making such as 'internships, formal courses, apprenticeships, on-the-job training, self-learning programs, Six Sigma or quality circles' (McMillan, 2016: 1356). This manages risk by ensuring employees with incomplete knowledge, experience, and understanding receive the necessary training to make them competent. KM's role, therefore, seems to be to establish the environment to learn, and HRM's role is to ensure learning takes place. Further confusion emerges when the concept of social capital is introduced. Social capital is the knowledge generated from access to social networks at work (see Chapter 4). Researchers have used social exchange theory as a theoretical background to discuss how HRM can provide supportive social networks to facilitate 'knowledge exchange and build efficient relationship exchanges and interactions between various entities in the organization' (Oparaocha, 2016: 535). This seems to be the domain of KM rather than HRM.

KNOWLEDGE MANAGEMENT'S INFLUENCE ON HRM

Saint-Onge (2000: 275) argued that human resource management must 'change to adapt to the knowledge-driven enterprise'. Knowledge management requires 'both conventional and novel human resource strategies to mobilize intellectual capital and social learning' (McMillan, 2016: 1355). This involves a range of activities that might be considered traditional HRM, such as investment in training to develop knowledge, organizational culture providing 'employment security, and rewards contingent on individual, group, and organizational performance' (Pfeffer, 2007: 119). These activities address competency, organizational commitment, and motivation. However, there are also a range of activities considered novel for HRM because they cross into areas not normally considered HRM, such as organizational design and KM. Pfeffer (2007: 119) adds that 'decision-making structures, such as decentralization and self-management teams', enable the outcomes of the traditional HR, i.e. 'trained and motivated employees, to create value by influencing decisions'. Pfeffer (2007: 119) concludes that information must be shared so that employees 'can understand the business and know what to do and how to do it'. This latter point reveals a grey area blurring the boundaries between HRM and KM: is this information staff training or something else?

This blurring of role boundaries is further illustrated by Saint-Onge (2000), who argues that human capital may be managed by combining technology infrastructure with knowledge architecture and organizational culture. Technology infrastructure's main role is 'to convey information in a way that allows individuals and teams to translate it into knowledge' (Saint-Onge, 2000: 285). Human resource management might contribute by helping shape the intranet, preparing templates for effective knowledge sharing across communities of practice, and integrating these activities cost-effectively (Saint-Onge, 2000). Knowledge architecture is how to 'harvest and disseminate knowledge' within the organization, i.e. the processes of knowledge management (2000: 286). Human resource management may help in managing knowledge resources by designing platforms for storing explicit knowledge; and in knowledge as practice by allowing access to the tacit knowledge of lessons learned through experience (Saint-Onge, 2000). Culture establishes the knowledge strategy (see Chapter 5) and enables the behaviours and attitudes necessary to do effective knowledge management including agility, collaboration, speed of decision making, learning, coherence, and innovation (Saint-Onge, 2000). The challenge for HRM professionals is to see this as their role and to contribute to their organization's activities in these areas. The outcome will be increased human capital which should be a goal for HRM.

SUMMARY OF HRM'S ROLE IN KM

Previous research argues that HRM plays three key roles in knowledge management: motivation, organizational commitment, and socio-cultural change (Hislop, 2013: 221). Lengnick-Hall and Lengnick-Hall (2003) went further to suggest that HRM should be involved in organizational design and in knowledge management itself. They state that HRM should contribute to strategic capability (see Chapter 5) by 'designing an appropriate mix of core, associate, and peripheral groups of employees, supplemented by external suppliers such as temporary staff and contractors who are willing and able to contribute to the organization's productivity' (Lengnick-Hall and Lengnick-Hall, 2003: 172). This elevates HRM's role to one of designing organizational boundaries and providing innovative and flexible solutions to the balance of internal and external knowledge resources. The authors also propose that HRM should be expert knowledge facilitators. This role involves a range of activities typically associated with KM including 'expanding the data, intelligence, and information that is available; facilitating access, sorting, and interpretation so that information is useful for action; and maintaining a rich diversity of ideas while seeking agreement on purpose' (2003: 173). While it is commendable that HRM researchers should want HRM to expand into the area of KM and see that as their role, this indicates how HRM has been left behind by the emergence of KM as a new discipline. The management of human capital has always been the domain of HRM. However, its tendency to stay stuck in its tactical role has constrained its growth as a discipline. This section has discussed how HRM should realistically consider its role in KM to be to provide rewards, motivation, and trust (tactical), and workforce planning and cultural change (strategic). The discussion has highlighted the blurred boundaries between HRM and KM, and how KM has influenced HRM to become more strategic. The future of HRM requires practitioners to work with KM rather than against it in competition for organizational space such as resources and priorities. This book has argued that KM and HRM are two sides of the same coin, but HRM's role has been described implicitly rather than explicitly. The challenge for HRM is to make its role in KM more explicit in a complementary rather than competitive way.

Chapter 6 (Figure 6.2) presented the results in terms of a scorecard rating for each human resource management technique tested at the case study organization (see closing case study).

ACCOUNTING

The accounting discipline has been interested in knowledge management for many years. Research in this field has three main paths:

1. What causes firms to be worth so much more than their book value?
2. What specifically is this intangible asset?
3. What is the value of intangible assets and how may this be reported?

The interest in accounting may be traced to 50 years ago (Hermanson, 1964) with the emergence of human resources accounting (HRA). The purpose of HRA is to 'quantify the economic value of people to the organization' (Sackman et al., 1989: 235). Bozbura (2004) provided empirical evidence that there is a positive relationship between the human capital and the book/market value of the firm. This research found that increases in employee capabilities are seen to directly influence financial results, leading to a direct relationship between human capital and organizational performance (Bozbura, 2004). HRA models may also be calculated as assets in financial terms, and organizations can assess the value of employees through tools such as the Hay methodology, which is commonly used to compare and determine salary scales, and as a way to identify high performance and appropriate rewards.

However, the HRA method has three fundamental weaknesses. First, it is subjective and, therefore, a value assessment, rather than valuation measurement. Thus, even though HRA can yield a solid numerical figure of value of intellectual capital, the necessary estimations made while using HRA can bring about inaccuracies that will lead to false value measures (Bontis, 1999: 443). Second, human capital is very difficult to define in a single framework, because it consists of a range of qualitative measures, including 'employees' knowledge accumulation, leadership abilities, and risk-taking and problem-solving capabilities' (Bozbura, 2004: 358). For example, the large number of assumptions, such as the projected company size in the future, the tenure per employee, turnover, and salary increases that the HRA models are based on, are seen as a disadvantage (Bontis, 1999). Third, HRA values human capital despite the fact that the firm does not explicitly own it (Johnson, 2002). Organizations do not own people, and employees may leave at any time and take their knowledge with them.

CORE CONCEPT: While there is now widespread acceptance that knowledge has economic value for the firm, there is little consensus on how to measure this.

As a result, a wide range of knowledge measurement methods have been developed. Andriesson (2004) identified over 30 methods for valuing or measuring intangible assets. However, many of these methods simply label things differently and are much the same (Bontis, 1998). More importantly, the methods cover such a broad range of different problem categories that it is difficult to determine their effectiveness as solutions, and impossible to accept that they can do all that the authors claim. For example, three of the better-known methods – the Skandia Navigator (Edvinsson and Malone, 1997), the intangible asset monitor (Sveiby, 1997), and the intellectual capital index (Roos et al., 1997) – do not measure value at all, despite their intentions (see Andriesson, 2004). They are measurement methods only. Indeed, in his extensive review of the field, Andriesson (2004) found that none of the ten major methods had a value assessment component, and only Kaplan and Norton's (1996) balanced scorecard had a value measurement component, but this was designed for improving internal management (not external reporting), which does not help investors. Ideally, a method is needed that measures value and also addresses the need for improved internal management, improved external reporting, and regulatory reporting requirements.

A review of the literature found several themes which summarize the different approaches to the problem of measuring the value of knowledge resources. These are presented in Table 11.1. It is interesting as it shows how researchers interpreted the pioneering attempts of others to measure value. The table summarizes each method along three dimensions: first, the problem the method aims to solve (problems are aggregated into three categories: improving internal management, improving external reporting, and transactional and statutory motives); second, the type of measurement or valuation involved; and third, a summary of the method used.

The theory of intellectual capital emerged in the early 1990s in response to a growing interest in intangible assets. Chapter 4 discussed the field's evolution and its current position.

DEEP THINKING: An important challenge for intellectual capital research is the inability of the field to identify a set of measures which are widely accepted and adopted. The field's focus on measurement appears to suggest that it must get 'accurate' intellectual capital measures before progressing to managing intellectual capital. As no consensus on the measures has been reached, intellectual capital research risks becoming stagnant or being dismissed, and intellectual capital is seen as an abstract idea that cannot be acted upon. This risk is generated because action, rather than measurement, is the way to create organizational value.

The third wave of intellectual capital research aims to persuade managers to use intellectual capital (Marr, 2003). Massingham and Tam (2015) examined the use of intellectual capital as a basis for employee compensation with a secondary focus on assessing strategy execution. Massingham and Tam (2015) explained how intellectual capital may be used to achieve strategic alignment. Strategic alignment occurs when the organization aligns its people, systems, and culture to execute its strategy (Kaplan and Norton, 2006).

TABLE 11.1 Classification of existing methods of measuring intellectual capital

Method	Why dimension	How dimension	Description
Process methods:			
Innovation capital	Improved external reporting	Financial valuation	Tangible end result of innovation such as commercial rights (Ordóñez de Pablos, 2003).
Process capital		Value measurement	Value from intellectual capital is only created when raw materials are transformed into an end product through process, and the benefit from this exceeds the cost (Robinson and Kleiner, 1996).
			The combined value of value-creating and non-value-creating processes (Ordóñez de Pablos, 2003).
Knowledge value added (KVA)			'KVA analysis produces a return-on-knowledge (ROK) ratio to estimate the value added by given knowledge assets, regardless of where they are located' (Housel and Bell, 2001: 91). KVA measures the revenue change that results from a process improvement against the cost of knowledge acquisition which enabled the improvement.
Financial methods:			
Economic value added	Improved external reporting	Measurement	The objective of EVA is to calculate the net present value of an item – whether it yields more value than it consumes. It links capital budgeting, financial planning, goal setting, performance measurement, stakeholder communication, and incentive compensation.
Financial method of intangible assets measurement (FiMIAM)	Improved external reporting	Financial valuation	The FiMIAM provides a 'link between a firm's customer, process, and innovation capital and financial capital as well as showing their interactions and interdependencies' (Rodov and Leliaert, 2002: 335). It can assess the 'monetary value of the three intellectual capital (human, structural, and customer) components and add them to balance sheets' (2002: 330). It has the ability to 'link intellectual capital value to market valuation, extending beyond book value' (2002: 330).
Human asset accounting systems			Human resources accounting (HRA) has evolved from earlier attempts to measure employees as assets. Roslender (2000) explains that the field began in the mid-1960s with Hermanson's finance-oriented human asset accounting. In the late 1960s, Flamholtz introduced the first management-oriented human resource accounting system. This was concerned with human resource cost and revenue information for the management processes of control, planning, and decision making. It was followed by the sociology-oriented human worth accounting, which is based on a range of subjective employee worth assessments, and on softer measurement metrics such as retention rates. The current view is referred to as human competence accounting.

Method	Why dimension	How dimension	Description
Intellectual capital reports:			
The balanced scorecard		Value measurement	Within the BSC, the term 'balanced' reflects the balance between financial and non-financial measures, short- and long-term goals, reflective and predictive indicators (i.e. lag and lead), and so on (Hepworth, 1998: 559). This balance is achieved through four different perspectives: financial, customer, internal business, and, of course, learning and growth (Kaplan and Norton, 2001: 77).
Skandia value scheme			Values 'components that result in intellectual capital' (Ordóñez de Pablos, 2003: 66).
The Skandia Navigator			Provides a balanced view of both financial and intellectual capital with its advantage being labelled as 'the balanced total picture it provides of the operations' (Ordóñez de Pablos, 2003: 66). This means that a description of intellectual capital development is 'matched with financial results, capital, and monetary flows, and level and change indictors of both terms of capital are emphasized' (Ordóñez de Pablos, 2003: 66).
Tango			The Tango method studies intangible assets in comparison to financial assets (Ordóñez de Pablos, 2003). It identifies, measures, and manages intangible assets on three bases including 'growth and renewal, efficiency, and stability of the firm's parameter' (Ordóñez de Pablos, 2003: 67).
Intellectual capital accounts (ICAP)	Improving internal management	Value assessment	The ICAP methodology emphasizes the 'strong link between intellectual capital and business performance by focusing on the value chain' (Engström et al., 2003: 290).
Action research		Measurement	The process of measuring intellectual capital is beneficial because it creates new knowledge and, therefore, makes an important contribution itself (Mouritsen, 2004).
Tobin's Q	Improved external reporting	Financial valuation	Developed by the Nobel Prize winner James Tobin, it 'measures the ratio between market value and reposition value of organizational physical assets' (Ordóñez de Pablos, 2003: 66).

(Continued)

TABLE 11.1 (Continued)

Method	Why dimension	How dimension	Description
People methods:			
Human resource accounting (HRA)	Improving internal management	Value assessment	HRA's main aim is to 'quantify the economic value of people to the organization in order to provide input for managerial and financial decisions' (Bontis, 1999: 443). 'There are three types of HRA measuring models, which are: 1. Cost models which consider the historical, acquisition, replacement or opportunity cost of human assets; 2. HR value models which combine non-monetary behavioural with monetary economic value models; and 3. Monetary emphasis models which calculate discounted estimates of future earnings or wages.' (Bontis, 1999: 443)
Hay Skills Audit		Value assessment	This measures human capital based on using an 'indicator' of the human skills used to create value. The rationale behind this method is to retain the human capital that yields competitive advantage within the organization (Robinson and Kleiner, 1996: 37), thus retaining the intellectual capital that produces value. It measures the potential capability and actual impact of employees through evaluating job categories using the three 'Hay factors': know-how, problem solving, and accountability (1996: 37). This measures the intellectual capital brought by each employee to the organization and allows the level of skill of individual employees to be tracked, determining where skills are needed for new positions and human resources development (Robinson and Kleiner, 1996).
Learning organization capability		Measurement	Learning in organizations is based on the mental models of decision makers that aid routine decision making and also make new learning possible (Robinson and Kleiner, 1996). By identifying the organization's learning ability through evaluating these mental models, intellectual capital can be measured as the ability to respond to the need for change and learn from experience (Robinson and Kleiner, 1996).
Learning efficiencies		Measurement	Turner and Jackson-Cox (2002) argue that knowledge can be valued in quantified terms. Their model quantifies the value of knowledge derived from cost, investment return, and the time taken to obtain knowledge. It is similar to the KVA method, except this approach focuses on the time taken to acquire or learn the necessary knowledge, and therefore includes the trade-off or opportunity cost involved in learning.

ORGANIZATIONAL STRUCTURE

The knowledge strategy (see Chapter 5) should be aligned with an organizational structure which enables its implementation. A firm's organizational structure comprises the formal and informal arrangement of tasks, responsibilities, lines of authority, and reporting relationships by which the firm is administered (Thompson et al., 2016). Organizational structures can be classified into a limited number of standard types:

1. *Simple structure*: a central executive (often the owner-manager) handles all major decisions and oversees the operations of the organization with the help of a small staff.
2. *Functional structure*: is organized along functional lines, where a function represents a major step in the firm's value chain, such as R&D, engineering and design, manufacturing, sales and marketing, logistics, and customer service.
3. *Multidivisional structure*: a decentralized structure consisting of a set of operating divisions (organized along market, customer, product, or geographic lines) and a central corporate headquarters, which monitors divisional activities, allocates resources, performs assorted support functions, and exercises overall control.
4. *Matrix structure*: a combination structure in which the organization is organized along two or more dimensions at once (e.g. business, geographic area, value-chain function) for the purpose of enhancing cross-unit communication, collaboration, and coordination. (Thompson et al., 2016)

CORE CONCEPT: The type of organizational structure that is most suitable for the organization will depend on its size and complexity as well as its strategy. The main influence on this decision is the organization's control systems.

The main issue with control systems is how much to delegate. This decision is captured by the centralization versus decentralization dichotomy. These represent the two extremes of the location of organizational power: whether to centralize decision making at the top (the CEO and a few close lieutenants) or to decentralize decision making by giving managers and employees considerable decision-making latitude in their areas of responsibility. The adjacent box contains an extract from Thompson et al. (2016) which summarizes the two approaches to organizational control.

Early knowledge-based view (KBV) research suggested that managing knowledge workers would represent a significant challenge and this would change the way organizations were managed. Grant (1997: 452) introduced the importance of knowledge sharing when he summarized management challenges as 'establishing the mechanisms by which cooperating individuals can coordinate their activities in order to integrate their knowledge into productive activity'. Grant suggested that knowledge management would require a reformulation of some of the principles of organization design: 'displacement of scientific management by various forms of participative, employee-empowering management approaches partly reflects the motivational benefits of these systems, but is also a result of the greater efficiency of these systems in accessing and integrating the relevant knowledge' (Grant, 1997: 453). This explains that traditional hierarchies are deficient as an organizing device for knowledge-intensive organizations. It introduces the new business models with flatter structures and fluid control systems to empower employees and enable the flow of knowledge vertically and horizontally.

EXTRACT ON ADVANTAGES AND DISADVANTAGES OF CENTRALIZATION AND DECENTRALIZATION (THOMPSON ET AL., 2016)

Centralized decision making:

1. Key advantages:
   a. Fixes accountability through tight control from the top
   b. Eliminates potential for conflicting goals and actions on the part of lower-level managers
   c. Facilitates quick decision making and strong leadership under crisis situations
2. Key disadvantages:
   a. Lengthens response times by those closest to the market conditions because they must seek approval for their actions
   b. Does not encourage responsibility among lower-level managers and rank-and-file employees
   c. Discourages lower-level managers and rank-and-file employees from exercising any initiative

Decentralized decision making:

1. Key advantages:
   a. Encourages company employees to exercise initiative and act responsibly
   b. Promotes greater motivation and involvement in the business on the part of more company personnel
   c. Spurs new ideas and creative thinking
   d. Allows for fast response to market change
   e. Entails fewer layers of management

2. Key disadvantages:

   a. Higher-level managers may be unaware of actions taken by empowered personnel under their supervision

   b. Puts the organization at risk if empowered employees happen to make 'bad' decisions

   c. Can impair cross-unit collaboration. (Thompson et al., 2016, after Table 10.1, p. 308)

The Thompson et al. (2016) extract provides criteria which help align knowledge strategy with organizational structure. The simple structure and the functional structure allow strong central control and generate efficiencies such as cost control and process improvement. However, they also restrict creativity, innovation, and collaboration. They suit scientific management and a compliance culture. On the other hand, the multidivisional structure and the matrix structure allow for decentralized control and generate effectiveness in terms of initiative, creativity, and market responsiveness. But they also result in higher costs and duplication. They suit humanistic management and a learning organization culture.

Grant too supported decentralized decision-making authority: the KBV emphasizes the 'importance of co-locating decision making and knowledge; whether this involves decentralization or centralization of decision-making depends very much upon the characteristics of the knowledge required' (Grant, 1997: 453). Tacit knowledge should be decentralized to the subject matter experts with decisions depending on local context, whereas codified knowledge may be centralized and managed as best practice. This introduces the importance of matrix structures.

Grant argues that in the 20 years since the emergence of the KBV, organizational theory has still not resolved the problem of coordination. The difficulty with coordination is to 'devise mechanisms through which the knowledge resources of many different individuals can be deployed in the production of a particular product' (Grant, 2013: 543). It is a challenge because it requires integrating mechanisms (see above discussion) while preserving the efficiencies of specialization. This means that the scale economies of being an expert must be traded off against the time it takes to engage with others. In organizational structure terms, specialization is vertical knowledge flows, and integration is horizontal knowledge flows (Massingham, 2010). Grant concludes that 'any system of production that requires that each individual learns what every other individual knows is inherently inefficient' (Grant, 2013: 543). This statement raises many questions about knowledge management. The most obvious is that codifying individual knowledge, storing it, sharing it, and making it accessible for others is inefficient. This argues against the technology view of knowledge management. It also tends to privilege individual knowledge, particularly tacit knowledge, and suggests that the individual creates most value working alone or with small groups of other, similar experts to increase their knowledge, rather than by learning others' knowledge.

Acquisition enables knowledge strategy to explore new business models, such as hybrids (Grant, 2013), which challenge underlying assumptions about traditional hierarchical structures and organizational boundaries. The KBV offers a theoretical basis for the analysis of strategic alliances. An alternative KBV perspective sees alliances as accessing rather than acquiring partners' knowledge (Grant, 1997). Such accessing of knowledge permits an increased utilization of knowledge resources, an advantage which is enhanced when there are uncertainties concerning technological change and early-mover advantages in product markets. Even if collaborative alliances are less efficient than full internalization in supporting the knowledge integration mechanisms that form the basis of productive activity, these inefficiencies in integration may be offset by the advantages of knowledge utilization and the speed of knowledge access (Grant and Baden-Fuller, 2004).

In examining this issue, Grant criticizes the view of knowledge as an object, particularly the literature's focus on organizational knowledge. He clearly does not see information technology as the solution to the problem of coordination. His perspective requires a fundamental change in mindset. Rather than seeing knowledge as a resource to be captured and shared (which is the cooperation problem), he focuses instead on the process of work itself and how knowledge is used to create value (which is the problem of coordination). He does this by focusing attention on capability rather than the resource:

> The concept of organizational capability comes closest to capturing and operationalizing the notion of organizational knowledge. The concept of organizational capability allows us to specify organizational knowledge in terms of the productivity activities that an organization can perform and provides a basis for measuring these productive capacities. (Grant, 2013: 545)

He repeats the claims in his earlier work that the key to efficiency in knowledge integration is to create mechanisms that economize on learning. He concludes that whether you accept the knowledge-based rationale for the firm (coordination) or transaction cost economics (cooperation), the problem of defining the firm will emerge. This introduces the need for new business models which make organizational boundaries more fluid and allow knowledge strategy to access rather than acquire knowledge resources from external knowledge markets. Grant's 2013 update on the KBV concludes with ideas about the design of new organizational structures which better coordinate knowledge in the act of production.

The decentralized structure seems an ideal model for knowledge management. This claim may be made owing to the control systems that decentralization creates. Decentralization provides autonomy and empowerment and this enables creativity, innovation, and performance improvement.

CORE CONCEPT: Decentralization can help knowledge management in organizations of any size, but it is particularly helpful in large organizations. In the global knowledge economy, large multinational corporations are increasingly designing new organizational structures to cope with the complexity of international business and manage knowledge flows globally.

Bartlett and Ghoshal's (1992) transnational strategy explains that there are two competing forces driving international structure and decisions about organizational design and control: pressures for market responsiveness and pressures for cost reduction. The transnational strategy employs a network matrix structure which enables both coordination and integration; it enables specialization via vertical knowledge flows and integration via horizontal knowledge flows. Chapter 12 provides further details on the transnational strategy. The network matrix structure is helpful for diversified companies who want to capture cross-business strategic fits (Thompson et al., 2016). Diversified companies striving to capture cross-business strategic fits have to give business unit leaders the power to operate independently when cross-business collaboration is also essential in order to gain strategic fit benefits (2016: 310).

Figure 11.2 presents a model for choosing organizational structure based on two drivers: effectiveness and efficiency.

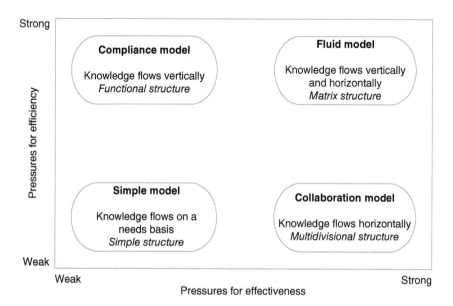

FIGURE 11.2 *An organizational structure model for knowledge management*

There are four structural models described in Figure 11.2:

1. *Simple model*: a strategy for small businesses, start-ups, or where knowledge resources are not a source of competitive advantage.
2. *Compliance model*: a strategy for bureaucracies, where capabilities are standardized and there is little change internally or externally. It coordinates action with strong, centralized HQ control and ensures compliance with codified knowledge by requiring employees to follow policies and procedures.
3. *Collaboration model*: a strategy for innovators, where creativity drives the pursuit of new or improved capabilities, and change is constant. It empowers action with decentralized control and enables collaboration using tacit knowledge, requiring employees to socialize and learn in the act of doing.
4. *Fluid model*: a strategy for mature knowledge organizations, where tacit and codified knowledge combine to create capabilities, and change is incremental rather than transformational. It balances central and local control and focuses on multidirectional knowledge flows to involve the whole organization in leveraging learning economies.

Figure 11.3 provides criteria for evaluating the most appropriate organizational structure to fit the strategy. On the left-hand side, there is a list of factors describing pressures for efficiency. The more of these factors, the stronger the pressures for efficiency, and the structure decision moves up the left-hand side (see Figure 11.2) from the simple model to the compliance model. On the right-hand side are the factors describing pressures for effectiveness. The more of these factors, the stronger the pressures for effectiveness, and the structure decision moves up the right-hand side (see Figure 11.2) from the collaboration model to the fluid model.

The model outlined in Figures 11.2 and 11.3 developed guidelines for designing appropriate organizational designs in the knowledge economy. As Grant (2013) explained, decisions about structure and control seem to be the most under-developed area of knowledge management research, and the evolution of the knowledge-based view of the firm has not kept up with the changing demands of the knowledge economy on this topic. The guidelines presented in this chapter suggest a way forward. Efficiency is about cost reduction and performance improvement via reducing mistakes and duplication. It is about capturing best practice and standardizing this across the organization. Effectiveness is about value creation and performance improvement via innovation and creativity. It is about enabling multiple best practices which recognize different operating contexts across the organization. The key to understanding the movement in the model, e.g. moving from the bottom left-hand quadrant to the top left-hand side, is the importance of cooperation versus coordination. If the organization's integrating mechanisms are designed to focus on getting employees to cooperate with one another and, most importantly, management, then its structure should be in the

FIGURE 11.3 *The efficiency and effectiveness framework: competing pressures on knowledge management*

two left-hand-side quadrants (see Figure 11.2). The more need for cooperation, the more it moves up the left-hand side. On the other hand, if the organization's integrating mechanisms are designed to focus on coordinating employees to work collaboratively, particularly horizontally, then its structure should be in the two right-hand-side quadrants. The more need for coordination, the more it moves up the right-hand side.

CONCLUSION

This chapter has examined the organizational systems necessary to implement knowledge management. It began by discussing systems thinking and how knowledge management fits with other organizational systems. The chapter then examined the role of information technology (IT) by exploring its dominance in knowledge management's evolution, and the current themes of socio-cultural context, accessibility, and facilitated collaboration. It discussed Becerra-Fernandez and Sabherwal's (2010) four IT platforms: knowledge application systems, knowledge capture systems, knowledge-sharing systems, and knowledge discovery systems. It looked at how human resource management has an opportunity to reinvent itself as a tactical or operational back-office function (e.g. recruitment) to play a key role in building strategic capability. Massingham's (2016) guidelines for using the Knowledge Accounts illustrated how this may be done, for instance by strategic alignment of the workforce. Zeleny's (2005) theory of human systems management explained how to coordinate the actions of people without managing them, which provided an interesting contrast to the command and control of scientific management, which this book argues is ineffective in the 21st century knowledge economy.

The chapter continued by looking at the long history of accounting's interest in valuing knowledge, more specifically human resources accounting (HRA). It explored why HRA has never really caught on. This has led to much interest in measuring the value of intellectual capital. Many methods have been developed but most do not measure value and there has been no consensus. The Knowledge Accounts (see Chapter 4) (Massingham, 2016) may provide a way forward. The third wave of intellectual capital research looks at having a more managerial perspective, particularly in terms of how intellectual capital is or can be applied. Organizational structure was defined in terms of the main types of control systems. Grant (1997, 2013) argued that the knowledge-based view (KBV) would change the way organizations were managed. The management challenges were the mechanisms by which cooperating individuals can coordinate their activities in order to integrate their knowledge with productive activity. The chapter explored the role of structure and control in facilitating knowledge sharing, leading to positive organizational outcomes, i.e. a productivity function. A new model for choosing organizational structure was proposed based on two drivers: effectiveness and efficiency (Figure 11.2). A range of factors influencing this decision were developed (Figure 11.3).

In the 20th century, scientific management has always placed power with top management. However, in the 21st century knowledge economy, the most successful organizations are implementing radical changes in their governance systems. Different business models, such as network matrix structures, are emerging. The complexity of modern business, caused by accelerating technological and geopolitical changes, is driving organizations towards decentralization. Competitive advantage will be created by enabling systems which focus on technology that facilitates knowledge sharing and usage, accounting which values people, human systems which build strategic capability, and tolerance for independent self-governance with structures which are hierarchical and flat, with matrixed control systems.

CLOSING CASE STUDY: HUMAN RESOURCE MANAGEMENT AT THE CSO

The final closing case study looks at the CSO's human resource management within the context of workforce planning. The CSO considered its workforce in terms of budget and staff numbers. In other words, staff members were a cost. Managers were allocated a staff budget annually, and this determined how many staff they could employ. The manager's first task was to assess the annual budget necessary to pay existing staff their salaries for the year. Any money left over could be used to employ new staff. If there was not enough money, staff numbers would need to be reduced via natural attrition, redundancies, or lay-offs. Workforce planning was usually limited to asking for a percentage increase on last year's staff budget and determining where to allocate new staff.

I attended a meeting of senior federal government executives from across the public sector, including senior executives from the CSO. I gave a presentation to the meeting on managing knowledge loss. During the discussion which followed, the executives debated the investment necessary to deliver the workforce capability required by the government. The debate focused on the budget and not staff numbers. While capability was discussed, it was only considered in the context of types of positions. The CSO was a very hierarchical organization. Its middle managers would be classified as lieutenants or Australian Public Service 6 (APS6). These middle managers might have a team of up to five staff. The workforce planning discussion at my presentation focused on questions like 'How many lieutenants do we have?' and 'How many do we need?' The questions had logic because they helped determine how many staff were needed above and below them. For example, 100 lieutenants would equate to 500 lower-level staff reporting to them. On the other hand, a senior manager, such as a captain, might have five lieutenants reporting to him/her; 100 lieutenants would mean 20 captains. An executive such as a commodore might have three captains reporting to them, meaning seven commodores. A senior executive like an admiral might have two commodores reporting to them, leading to three or four admirals. The salaries for each of these job types was the same, e.g. all lieutenants would receive the same pay. The staff budget could then be calculated by multiplying the number of lieutenants needed, by their average annual salary plus on-costs (at 30%).

The remainder of the case study looks at some of Massingham's (2016) framework for using the Knowledge Accounts data. It considers how the CSO responded to some of the frameworks for human resource management for use in workforce planning (see Chapters 4 and 11).

Tactical human capital management (THCM) identifies job-related competencies. This answers the question: do I have the right staff? In 2009, the CSO's mean knowledge score was already in deficit by 25.6%. While the CSO knew that it had lost experience as high proportions of senior staff had retired in the years preceding the project (i.e. prior to 2009), it did not know what the impact was, other than it had fewer senior staff. It tried to fix the problem by promoting staff to fill the seniority gaps. However, it could not quantify whether its capability had been affected. The KA provided this information. It provided better information than traditional methods, e.g. job family analysis by seniority levels, by specifying capability gaps against management expectations (i.e. the baseline). Rather than saying 'We have only 200 lieutenants, and we need 250', the latter figure, based on abstract modelling (the KA providing hard data) stated that, for example, 'We have 200 lieutenants and they know 30% less than the job requires.' Even if they had promoted 50 staff to lieutenants to fill the gap from a seniority perspective, these new staff would not know what the baseline expected. The CSO would still be in deficit even though it had the required number of senior staff. The KA would reveal this capability gap, whereas the existing method, i.e. seniority analysis, would mask the problem.

Strategic human resource management (SHRM) can provide a broader perspective regarding job inputs and outputs. This answers the question: do I have the right staff in the right jobs? Social capital (SC) is a measure of cognitive knowledge. Between 2009 and 2011,

(Continued)

(Continued)

the CSO's mean SC score decreased by 6.3%. The value generated from social networks (network quality, NQ) was the main cause of this decrease – down by 8.2%. Looking further into this problem, we found that NQ's action factors had decreased significantly. By action, we mean how individuals act within their social networks. Two factors in particular were significant: mentoring and tie importance. Mentoring is about whether an individual is willing to help others and share their experience. Mentoring decline was probably due to having fewer experienced staff as well as some attitudinal changes. Tie importance is about knowing the right people. It has a seniority dimension, i.e. whether contacts are superiors, peers, or staff. The result shows that the social networks at the CSO became 'more horizontal' in the sense that there was less interaction with senior people. NQ action is a job output. The decreased performance in this area means that staff were creating less value from their networks. From a strategic alignment perspective, this highlights how the CSO did not have the right staff in the right jobs, and that addressing social capital would help address this problem, particularly in terms of cognitive knowledge gaps.

Strategic human capital management (SHCM) identifies where and how to grow the organizational knowledge base (OKB). This answers the question: what staff will I need in the future? The KA may be used to inform the 'make versus buy decision' for future capability growth. The 'make' decision is to identify capability requirements, i.e. future staff in terms of their KA scores, and to fill the gap between existing and future OKB internally. This may be done by either promoting or developing existing staff to fill the KA scores required in the future. At the CSO, significant future capability gaps were identified in both technical (hard) and cognitive (soft) competencies. Examples included new technology areas where existing staff had some prerequisite knowledge but would need considerable training to reach full competency. There were also substantial cognitive competency gaps in terms of relational capital, where existing staff required training to meet the strategic goal of improved customer relationships. The 'buy' decision is to fill the gap externally. This may be done by recruitment to find new staff with the required KA scores. The KA can be particularly helpful in the recruitment process because it provides a more holistic and accurate assessment of a candidate's knowledge. Job interviews typically cover activities, qualifications, and experience. Increasingly, recruiters are using techniques such as psychological and personality profiles to assess work attitudes and behaviours difficult to unearth at a job interview. The KA can assess both types of competencies, i.e. technical and cognitive knowledge. While some aspects of the KA might score quite low prior to employment (e.g. social capital), because work relationships have not yet been established, others will still be very relevant. HC2 (employee satisfaction) and HC3 (employee sustainability) scores would bring to the surface important information about the candidate's mindset and work attitudes and behaviours. HC2, for example, can tell as much about a person's feelings about their job, as their employer (i.e. where they do their job). Relational capital may also be important, as a candidate may bring stronger relationships with customers and suppliers, for example, than existing staff, particularly if their previous employment was in the same industry. These issues could be accounted for in scoring candidates against management expectations (i.e. the baseline) – for example, social capital is simply taken out of the equation when recruiting new staff.

CASE STUDY QUESTIONS

1. Critically evaluate the case study organization's approach to workforce planning.
2. Compare the typical approach to tactical human capital management (THCM) with the approach recommended in the case study.
3. Compare the typical approach to strategic human resource management (SHRM) with the approach recommended in the case study.
4. Compare the typical approach to strategic human capital management (SHCM) with the approach recommended in the case study.

REVIEW AND DISCUSSION QUESTIONS

1. Evaluate how information technology may support knowledge management.
2. Is human resource management reluctant to embrace knowledge management? Why, or why not?
3. Is accounting for intellectual capital dead? Why, or why not?
4. Critically evaluate the organizational structure model presented in Figures 11.2 and 11.3.

FURTHER READING

Becerra-Fernandez, I. and Sabherwal, R. (2010) *Knowledge Management: Systems and processes*, Armonk, NY, ME Sharpe. This text examines the role of information technology from a systems perspective.

Dumay, J. (2014) 15 Years of the Journal of Intellectual Capital and Counting: A manifesto for transformational IC research. *Journal of Intellectual Capital*, 15 (1): 2–37. This article examines the role of accounting in measuring the value of intellectual capital.

Lengnick-Hall, M.L. and Lengnick-Hall, C.A. (2003) *Human Resource Management in the Knowledge Economy*, San Francisco, CA, Berrett-Koehler. This book examines the role of human resource management from a strategic perspective.

BIBLIOGRAPHY

Abeysekera, I. (2013) A Template for Integrated Reporting. *Journal of Intellectual Capital*, 14 (2): 227–245.

Andriesson, D. (2004) *Making Sense of Intellectual Capital*, Burlington, MA, Elsevier Butterworth-Heinemann.

Andriessen, J.H.E. (2003) *Working with Groupware: Understanding and evaluating collaboration technology*, London, Springer.

Barney, J.B. and Hansen, M.B. (1994) Trustworthiness as a Source of Competitive Advantage. *Strategic Management Journal, 53* (15): 175–190.

Bartlett, C.A. and Ghoshal, S. (1992) *Transnational Management: Text, cases and readings in cross-border management*, Burr Ridge, IL, Irwin.

Becerra-Fernandez, I. and Sabherwal, R. (2010) *Knowledge Management: Systems and processes*, Armonk, NY, ME Sharpe.

Beerli, A. (2003) Why Knowledge Management Strategies Fail. Chapter 1 in Beerli, A., Falk, S., and Diemers, D. (eds) *Knowledge Management and Networked Environments: Leveraging intellectual capital in virtual business communities*, New York, AMACOM, pp. 3–15.

Bhatt, G.D. (2001) Knowledge Management in Organizations: Examining the interaction between technologies, techniques, and people. *Journal of Knowledge Management, 5* (1): 68–75.

Bontis, N. (1998) Intellectual Capital: An exploratory study that develops measures and models. *Management Decision, 36* (2): 63–76.

Bontis, N. (1999) Managing Organizational Knowledge by Diagnosing Intellectual Capital: Framing and advancing the state of the field. *International Journal of Technology Management, 18* (5–8): 433–463.

Bozbura, F.T. (2004) Measurement and Application of Intellectual Capital in Turkey. *The Learning Organization, 11* (4/5): 357–370.

Carleton, K. (2011) How to Motivate and Retain Knowledge Workers in Organizations: A review of the literature. *International Journal of Management, 28* (2): 459–469.

Colomo-Palacios, R. (2010) Web 2.0: New and challenging practical issues. *The Learning Organization, 17* (6): 476–477.

Dalkir, K. (2011) *Knowledge Management in Theory and Practice*, 2nd edition, Cambridge, MA, MIT Press.

Diemers, D. (2003) Virtual Knowledge Communities and the Issue of Information Quality. Chapter 8 in Beerli, A., Falk, S. and Diemers, D. (eds) *Knowledge Management and Networked Environments: Leveraging intellectual capital in virtual business communities*, New York, AMACOM, pp. 157–177.

Drucker, P.F. (1954) *The Practice of Management*, New York, HarperCollins.

Drucker, P. (1999) Knowledge-worker Productivity: The biggest challenge. *California Management Review, 41* (2): 79–94.

Dumay, J. (2014) 15 Years of the Journal of Intellectual Capital and Counting: A manifesto for transformational IC research. *Journal of Intellectual Capital, 15* (1): 2–37.

Dumay, J. and Rooney, J. (2011) Measuring for Managing? An IC practice research project. *Journal of Intellectual Capital, 12* (3): 344–355.

Dumay, J. and Tull, J.A. (2011) Intellectual Capital Disclosure and Price-sensitive Australian Stock Exchange Announcements. *Journal of Intellectual Capital, 8* (2), 2007: 236–255.

Dychtwald, K., Erikson, T.J. and Morison, R. (2006) *Workforce Crisis: How to beat the coming shortage of skills and talent*, Boston, MA, Harvard Business School Press.

Easterby-Smith, M. and Prieto, I. (2008) Dynamic Capabilities and Knowledge Management: An integrative role for learning? *British Journal of Management, 19* (3): 235–249.

Edvinsson, L. and Malone, M.S. (1997) *Intellectual Capital: Realizing your company's true value by finding its hidden brainpower*, New York, Harper Business.

Engström, T.E.J., Westnes, P. and Westnes, S.F. (2003) Evaluating Intellectual Capital in the Hotel Industry. *Journal of Intellectual Capital, 4* (3): 287–303.

Flood, R.L. (2010) The Relationship of 'System Thinking' to Action Research. *Systemic Practice and Action Research, 23*: 269–284.

Goh, P.C. (2005) Intellectual Capital Performance of Commercial Banks in Malaysia. *Journal of Intellectual Capital*, 6 (3): 385–396.

Gorelick, C., Milton, N. and April, K. (2004) *Performance through Learning: Knowledge management in practice*, Burlington, MA, Elsevier Butterworth-Heinemann.

Grant, R.M. (1996) Toward a Knowledge-based Theory of the Firm. *Strategic Management Journal*, 17 (Winter Special Issue): 109–122.

Grant, R.M. (1997) The Knowledge-based View of the Firm: Implications for management practice. *Long Range Planning*, 30 (3): 450–454.

Grant, R.M. (2013) Reflections on Knowledge-based Approaches to the Organization of Production. *Journal of Management and Governance*, 17 (3): 541–558.

Grant, R.M. and Baden-Fuller, C. (2004) A Knowledge Accessing Theory of Strategic Alliances. *Journal of Management Studies*, 41 (1): 61–84.

Guthrie, J. and Petty, R. (2000) Intellectual Capital: Australian annual reporting practices. *Journal of Intellectual Capital*, 1 (3): 241–251.

Guthrie, J., Petty, R. and Ricceri, F. (2006) The Voluntary Reporting of Intellectual Capital: Comparing evidence from Hong Kong and Australia. *Journal of Intellectual Capital*, 7 (2): 254–271.

Guthrie, J., Ricceri, F. and Dumay, J. (2012) Reflections and Projections: A decade of intellectual capital accounting research. *British Accounting Review*, 44 (2): 68–92.

Hepworth, P. (1998) Weighing It Up: A literature review for the balanced scorecard. *Journal of Management Development*, 17 (8): 559–563.

Hermanson, R.H. (1964) Accounting for Human Assets. Occasional Paper No. 14. Bureau of Business and Economic Research, Michigan State University, East Lansing, MI. [Reprint Georgia State University, 1986.]

Hislop, D. (2013) *Knowledge Management in Organizations: A critical introduction*, 3rd edition, Oxford, Oxford University Press.

Housel, T. and Bell, A.H. (2001) *Measuring and Managing Knowledge*, New York, McGraw-Hill.

Jashapara, A. (2011) *Knowledge Management: An integrated approach*, Harlow, Pearson Education/Prentice Hall.

Johnson, W.H.A. (2002) Leveraging Intellectual Capital through Product and Process Management of Human Capital. *Journal of Intellectual Capital*, 3 (4): 415–429.

Kaplan, R.S. and Norton, D.P. (1992) The Balanced Scorecard: Measures that drive performance. *Harvard Business Review*, 70 (1): 71–79.

Kaplan, R.S. and Norton, D.P. (1996) *The Balanced Scorecard: Translating strategy into action*, Boston, MA, Harvard Business School Press.

Kaplan, R.S. and Norton, D.P. (2001) *The Strategy Focused Organization*, Boston, MA, Harvard Business School Press.

Kaplan, R.S. and Norton, D.P. (2006) *Alignment: Using the balanced scorecard to create corporate strategies*, Cambridge, MA, Harvard Business School Press.

Koenig, M.E.D. and Srikantaiah, T.K. (2007) Three Stages of Knowledge Management. Chapter 1 in Koenig, M.E.D. and Srikantaiah, T.K. (eds) *Knowledge Management Lessons Learned: What works and what doesn't*, Medford, NJ, Information Today, pp. 3–8.

Lengnick-Hall, M.L. and Lengnick-Hall, C.A. (2003) *Human Resource Management in the Knowledge Economy*, San Francisco, CA, Berrett-Koehler.

Marr, B. (2003) Why Do Firms Measure their Intellectual Capital? *Journal of Intellectual Capital*, 4 (4): 441–464.

McInerney, C.J. and Mohr, S. (2007) Trust and Knowledge Sharing in Organizations Theory and Practice. Chapter 3 in McInerney, C.J. and Day, R.E. (eds) *Rethinking Knowledge*

Management: From knowledge objects to knowledge processes, Berlin, Springer, pp. 65–86.

McMillan, C.J. (2016) Old Wine in New Bottles: Docility, attention scarcity and knowledge management. *Journal of Knowledge Management, 20* (6): 1353–1372.

Massingham, P. (2010) Managing Knowledge Transfer between Parent Country Nationals (Australia) and Host Country Nationals (Asia). *International Journal of Human Resource Management, 21* (9): 1414–1435.

Massingham, P. (2016) Knowledge Accounts. *Long Range Planning, 49* (3): 409–425.

Massingham, P. and Tam, L. (2015) The Relationship between Human Capital, Value Creation, and Employee Reward. *Journal of Intellectual Capital* (Special Issue), *16* (2): 390–418.

Mingers, J. (2006) *Realising System Thinking: Knowledge and action in management science*, New York, Springer Science.

Mouritsen, J. (2004) Measuring and Intervening: How do we theorise intellectual capital management? *Journal of Intellectual Capital, 5* (2): 257–267.

Newell, S., Robertson, M., Scarbrough, H. and Swan, J. (2002) *Managing Knowledge Work*, Basingstoke, Palgrave.

Nonaka, I. and Konno, N. (1998) The Concept of 'Ba': Building a foundation for knowledge creation. *California Management Review, 40* (3): 40–54.

North, K. and Kumta, G. (2014) *Knowledge Management: Value creation through organizational learning*, Cham, Switzerland, Springer International.

Oparaocha, G.O. (2016) Towards Building Internal Social Network Architecture that Drives Innovation: A social exchange theory perspective. *Journal of Knowledge Management, 20* (3): 534–556.

Ordóñez de Pablos, P. (2002) Knowledge Management and Organizational Learning: Typologies of knowledge strategies in the Spanish manufacturing industry from 1995 to 1999. *Journal of Knowledge Management, 6* (1): 52–62.

Ordóñez de Pablos, P. (2003) Intellectual Capital Reporting in Spain: A comparative view. *Journal of Intellectual Capital, 4* (1): 61–81.

Pfeffer, J. (2007) Human Resources from an Organizational Behaviour Perspective: Some paradoxes explained. *Journal of Economic Perspectives, 21* (4): 115–134.

Pink, D. (2009) *Drive: The surprising truth about what motivates*, New York, Riverhead.

Polanyi, M. (1962) *Personal Knowledge*, Chicago, IL, University of Chicago Press.

Ponzi, L.J. (2007) Knowledge Management: Birth of a discipline. Chapter 2 in Koenig, M.E.D. and Srikantaiah, T.K. (eds) *Knowledge Management Lessons Learned: What works and what doesn't*, Medford, NJ, Information Today, pp. 9–26.

Raynes, M. (2002) Document Management: Is the time right now? *Work Study, 51* (6): 303–308.

Robinson, G. and Kleiner, B.H. (1996) How to Measure an Organization's Intellectual Capital. *Managerial Auditing Journal, 11* (8): 36–39.

Rodov, I. and Leliaert, P. (2002) FiMIAM: Financial method of intangible assets measurement. *Journal of Intellectual Capital, 3* (3): 323–336.

Roos, J., Roos, G., Dragonetti, N.C. and Edvinsson, L. (1997) *Intellectual Capital: Navigating the new business landscape*, London, Macmillan Press.

Roslender, R. (2000) A Contemporary Management Accounting Perspective. *Management Accounting: Magazine for Chartered Management Accountants, 78* (3): 34–7.

Ruggles, R. (1998) The State of the Notion: Knowledge management in practice. *California Management Review, 40* (3): 80–89.

Sackman, S.A., Flamholtz, E.G. and Bullen, M.L. (1989) Human Resource Accounting: A state of the art review. *Journal of Accounting Literature, 8*: 235–264.

Saint-Onge, H. (2000) Shaping Human Resource Management within the Knowledge-driven Enterprise. Chapter in Part 7 in Phillips, J.J. and Bonner, D. (eds) *Leading Knowledge Management and Learning: 17 case studies from the real world of training*, Alexandria, VA, American Society for Training and Development, pp. 275–299.

Senge, P.M. (1990) *The Fifth Discipline: The art and practice of the learning organization*, New York, Doubleday Currency.

Sigala, M. and Chalkiti, K. (2014) Investigating the Exploitation of Web 2.0 for Knowledge Management in the Greek Tourism Industry: A utilisation-importance analysis. *Computers in Human Behavior, 30* (1): 800–812.

Soto-Acosta, P. and Cegarra-Navarro, J.G. (2016) New ICTs for Knowledge Management in Organizations. *Journal of Knowledge Management, 20* (3): 417–422.

Stewart, J. (1999) *Employee Development Practice*, London, Pitman.

Stewart, T.A. (1997) *Intellectual Capital: The new wealth of organizations*, New York, Doubleday.

Sveiby, K.E. (1997) The Intangible Assets Monitor. *Journal of Human Resource Costing & Accounting, 2* (1): 73–97.

Tapscott, D. and Williams, A.D. (2006) *Wikinomics: How mass collaboration changes everything*, London, Penguin Books.

Teece, D.J. (2007) Explicating Dynamic Capabilities: The nature and microfoundations of (sustainable) enterprise performance. *Strategic Management Journal, 28* (13): 1319–1350.

Thompson, A.J., Jr., Peteraf, M.A., Gamble, J.E. and Strickland, A.J. (eds) (2016) *Crafting and Executing Strategy: The quest for competitive advantage – Concepts and cases*, 19th edition, New York, McGraw-Hill Irwin.

Tichy, N. (2008) *The Cycle of Leadership: How great leaders teach their companies to win*, New York, HarperCollins.

Tiwana, A. (2002) *The Knowledge Management Toolkit: Orchestrating IT, strategy, and knowledge platforms*, 2nd edition, Upper Saddle River, NJ, Prentice-Hall.

Tsoukas, H. (2003) Do We Really Understand Tacit Knowledge? Chapter 21 in Easterby-Smith, M. and Lyles, M.A. (eds) *Handbook of Organizational Learning and Knowledge Management*, Hong Kong, Blackwell, pp. 410–427.

Turban, E. and Aronson, J.E. (2001) *Decision Support Systems and Intelligent Systems*, Upper Saddle River, NJ, Prentice-Hall.

Turner, G. and Jackson-Cox, J. (2002) If Management Requires Measurement How May We Cope with Knowledge? *Singapore Management Review, 24* (3): 101–112.

Van der Aalst, W. and Van Hee, K. (2002) *Workflow Management: Models, methods, and systems*, Cambridge, MA, MIT Press.

Whyte, M. and Zyngier, S. (2014) Applied Intellectual Capital Management: Experiences from an Australian public sector trial of the Danish Intellectual Capital Statement. *Journal of Intellectual Capital, 15* (2): 227–248.

Zeleny, M. (2005) *Human Systems Management: Integrating knowledge, management, and systems*, Hackensack, NJ, World Scientific Publishing.

12

INTERNATIONAL BUSINESS MANAGEMENT

CHAPTER OUTLINE

LEARNING OUTCOMES

After completing this chapter, the reader should be able to:

1. Discuss the role of knowledge management in international business
2. Explain the three generic international business strategies and the role of knowledge management in these strategies
3. Examine the organizational structures used by multinational enterprises and how knowledge flows in these structures
4. Evaluate how knowledge management influences international human resource management
5. Consider the influence of national culture on knowledge management

MANAGEMENT ISSUES

International business management requires managers to:

1. Understand why knowledge management is important for multinational enterprises
2. Use knowledge management to implement the transnational strategy
3. Understand how knowledge flows differently according to the organizational structure used
4. Use knowledge management to improve the performance of global managers
5. Understand how differences in national culture affect knowledge management

International business management involves the following challenges for management:

1. What role will knowledge management play in our organization's strategy, structure, and people management?
2. Should we standardize or adapt our knowledge management activities globally?
3. How can knowledge management help us create sustainable competitive advantage in the global knowledge economy?

LINKS TO OTHER CHAPTERS

Chapter 3: regarding the value of knowledge management

Chapter 5: on the role of knowledge and knowledge management in competitive advantage

Chapter 11: regarding new business designs and structures

OPENING MINI CASE STUDY

ACER: THE SMILING ASIAN TIGER – HOW ORGANIZATIONAL STRUCTURE MAY HELP IMPLEMENT TRANSNATIONAL STRATEGY AND ACHIEVE LEARNING CURVE ECONOMIES

Founded in 1976 in Taiwan, Acer is one of the world's top ICT companies and has a presence in over 160 countries, with more than 7,000 employees. Acer's focus is on 'enabling a world where hardware, software and services will infuse with one another to open up new possibilities for consumers and businesses alike' (www.acer-group.com). From service-oriented technologies to the Internet of Things, to gaming and virtual reality, Acer creates value with the research, design, marketing, sale, and support of products and solutions that break barriers between people and technology (www.acer-group.com).

In the 1990s, inspired by leadership from its chairman and CEO Stan Shih, Acer had grown to be the number five computer company in the world, Taiwan's leading brand-name exporter, and the largest PC-compatible manufacturer in South-East Asia. Mr Shih introduced an international business strategy designed to address the complexities of competing in the global computer industry. At the start of the 1990s, Mr Shih realized that Acer needed to change. Profitability had begun to decline due to the company's heavy dependence on personal computers (PCs). PCs had become a commodity product which was very difficult to differentiate, meaning cost leadership seemed the only strategy. Mr Shih, however, realized that this was a short-lived strategy, as PC prices would be driven down by intense competition, eroding profitability. In response, he decided to broaden the product range by moving into more sophisticated segments of the computer industry.

To succeed in the increasingly competitive global computer industry, Acer had to enhance efficiency, cut costs, and scale down the organization to strengthen its competitiveness. This was achieved by establishing independent business units, planning a new global business model, downsizing, and the development of an innovative fast-food-style logistics and assembly structure. Acer also faced problems in terms of its human capital. It lacked managers with international experience. Its top management were technically focused and unable to exploit these capabilities to help Acer's global expansion. Mr Shih recognized that it was very difficult to develop people who combined technical skills and global perspective. The company also suffered a brain drain as numerous top people had left when Acer went public, attracted by cashing in their shares.

Mr Shih could see the way the global computer industry was changing. This Shih referred to as the disintegrated mode, which contrasted with the traditional integrated mode. The disintegrated mode recognized that each standard component represented an industry segment. These segments represented an industry infrastructure created by third parties and included hardware, software, and component suppliers. The alternative – integrated mode – was to manufacture all of these components internally. Mr Shih felt Acer could succeed using the integrated mode if it could add value in each of its business segments. He did this with what he called his smiling curve business model. The smiling curve model has components such as software, monitors, and motherboards on the left-hand side. It is driven by technology innovation, global competition, and volume, i.e. economies of scale. On the right-hand side is distribution, including brand, channel, and logistics. It is driven by competition within a country. Acer felt that there was no longer any value added in assembling computers, which could be done by anyone, and that to succeed in the new IT age, it was necessary to gain a top position in component segments and as a distribution leader in a country or region.

To implement the smiling curve business model, Mr Shih re-engineered Acer as a fast-food model of computer supply, based on McDonald's. The aim was to assemble Acer products locally while still maintaining consistency. The assembly process was spread to 35 sites around the world but tightly controlled for consistency. Components were prepared in large mass-manufacturing facilities to achieve economies of scale and then shipped to assembly sites close to local customers. Acer guaranteed customers' computers with the freshest ingredients which meant the latest technology. Motherboards were flown in directly, while CPUs, hard drives, and memory were purchased locally to meet individual user requirements. This created economies of scale, plus the ability to tailor individual products to suit the needs of individual customers.

To implement the fast-food model, Mr Shih designed a client–server business model. It tried to achieve independence simultaneously with cooperation among Acer group members. The model was driven by a network matrix structure. On one side of the matrix were strategic business units (SBUs) which did research and development, manufacturing, product management, and original equipment manufacturer (OEM) sales. On the other side were regional business units (RBUs) which led distribution, customer service, and marketing. This structure allowed for faster decision making based on changing conditions in each region, while local autonomy improved motivation and incentive. Yet Mr Shih's objective was not to recreate a multi-domestic structure comprising largely independent country operations. Following the computer network analogy, Acer wanted each business unit to act as both a client and a server within the global network. In addition to acting as clients for the SBUs' products, the RBUs act as servers, providing local market intelligence and best practice to SBUs and other RBUs. The quasi-independent SBUs, meanwhile, also act as both clients and servers to each other through the joint purchasing, design, and manufacturing of common components and shared R&D.

Source: Adapted from a case study by Clyde-Smith (2003)

CASE STUDY QUESTIONS

1. Describe Acer's approach to competing in the global computer industry.
2. What are Acer's knowledge management challenges?
3. How would Acer's smiling curve model benefit from knowledge management?
4. How would Acer's fast-food model benefit knowledge management?
5. How could the client–server model help Acer's knowledge management?

INTRODUCTION

The objective of this chapter is to examine the role of knowledge management in international business. International business refers to cross-border trade and investment activities by firms (Cavusgil et al., 2017). The primary reason why multinational enterprises (MNEs) exist is because of 'their ability to transfer and exploit knowledge more effectively and efficiently in the intra-corporate context than through external market mechanisms' (Gupta and Govindarajan, 2000: 473). This thinking is grounded in research into the motivation of firms to seek business opportunities abroad – known as the internationalization process theories. One of these theories is internalization theory, which argues that firms pursue foreign direct investment due to the need to internalize intangible assets (Hymer, 1960). Knowledge management is a source of competitive advantage for multinational enterprises (MNEs) (Bartlett et al., 2004). Internalization theory argues that this advantage lies in a superior ability (vis-à-vis markets) to engage in internal knowledge transfer (Gupta and Govindarajan, 2000: 474). This chapter's primary focus is on how knowledge flows in international business.

CORE CONCEPT: The value of knowledge management in international business is MNE capacity to manage internal knowledge flows across the borders of international operations.

The chapter begins with a brief introduction to international business. This provides context for how knowledge resources are used and why they need to be managed by MNEs. It includes discussion of how knowledge management may contribute to MNEs' strategy, particularly when implementing the transnational strategy. Global knowledge flows are examined in terms of the process of knowledge sharing, the influence of organizational structure, and new business models for MNEs. The chapter then moves to international human resource management (IHRM). The question of how to globally develop and integrate strategic human capital is of practical and theoretical significance (Morris et al., 2016). The role of IHRM is assessed in terms of traditional (e.g. training) and new (e.g. socialization) perspectives. Global managers are a crucial knowledge resource for MNEs. The chapter examines global managers' competencies and criteria for selection and development. The global mindset is the global manager's most valuable knowledge resource. Finally, the chapter explores the influence of differences in national culture on whether the MNE uses a standard approach to knowledge management globally or adapts to suit local conditions.

INTERNATIONAL BUSINESS MANAGEMENT

Multinational enterprises (MNEs) conduct value-adding activities on a global scale, i.e. they organize, source, manufacture, market, sell, and employ market-entry strategies such as exporting, strategic alliances, and direct investment (Cavusgil et al., 2017). International business is more complex than domestic business. It involves complex decisions, such as entry mode, which are not required in domestic markets, as well as different economic, cultural, political, legal, and competitive environments. MNEs face having different customers, competitors, and suppliers.

CORE CONCEPT: Management decisions are more complex for international business than for domestic business, with greater uncertainty and increased risk.

Knowledge can 'reduce managerial uncertainty and the related anxiety, as well as the financial and opportunity cost of incorrect decisions' (Massingham, 2010: 1414).

RESOURCES

Knowledge resources are necessary to make decisions associated with international business including strategy, organizational structure, market assessment, location, and entry mode, as well as the functional areas of marketing, human resource management, and operations, supply chain management, and finance. Research has classified the knowledge resources required to build MNEs' international competitiveness into the following:

1. Individual and institutional customer knowledge
2. Branch (subsidiary) knowledge
3. Knowledge of current and prospective customers, suppliers, partners, and other stakeholders
4. Knowledge of the economic, social, and cultural environment and the political and legal conditions in the region
5. Knowledge of technology and science development
6. Knowledge of advisory and training centres, scientific and research institutions
7. Product knowledge
8. Knowledge of employees, management methods, and the social environment of the organization. (After Karaszewski, 2008: 66–67)

This list explains what MNEs need to know to succeed in international business. Morris et al. (2016) develop a model of human capital in the global context, based on two dimensions: general and specific human capital. Firm-specific (or general) human capital is developed and maintained internally by the MNE itself.

It is 'contextually embedded within the firm, reflecting structural capital about the MNE's culture, routines, and systems' (Morris et al., 2016: 724). The second dimension is 'the degree of location specificity' (2016: 725). 'Location-specific human capital' is knowledge that is 'relevant [to] or applicable in a particular country' (2016: 725).

THEORY IN PRACTICE: FOREIGN MARKET ASSESSMENT IS THE PROCESS USED BY MNEs TO MAKE THE LOCATION DECISION

It involves these steps:

1. *Analysing organizational readiness to internationalize*: Is senior management committed? If products and processes have to be adapted to market needs, is the firm willing to do so?
2. *Assessing the suitability of products and services for foreign markets*: Who buys the product? Who uses it? Why do people buy it? What local factors might limit sales?
3. *Screening countries to identify target markets*: gradual elimination to focus in-depth investigation as potential target markets, and eliminating unattractive markets quickly; and then indexing and ranking the more attractive markets by assigning scores to countries for their overall market attractiveness based on various criteria, and weights to each market-potential indicator to establish its relative importance.
4. *Assessing industry market potential*: for those markets who pass screening, conducting an in-depth analysis of the industry structure. Methods include trend analysis (typically over three years) observing key industry-specific indicators, key competitors, key customers, and supplier networks. The assessment has now transitioned from a macro level to a micro level, i.e. industry. Industry market potential requiring an estimate of the likely sales for all firms in a particular industry over a particular period.
5. *Choosing foreign business partners*: once the firm has selected a target market, identifying the types of partners it needs, negotiating terms with chosen partners, and supporting and monitoring their practices. Partners may include distribution-channel intermediaries, suppliers, and collaborative venture partners such as joint venture partners, licensees, and franchisees, depending upon the entry mode chosen.
6. *Estimating company sales potential*: estimating the share of annual industry sales the firm expects to generate in a particular target market. This requires detailed information, as well as [the] judgment and creativity necessary to make some fundamental assumptions to project the firm's revenues and expenses into the future.

CAPABILITY

Knowledge management is a source of sustainable competitive advantage in international business. One survey of world business leaders provided 'clear evidence that knowledge management does influence MNEs' international competitiveness' (Karaszewski, 2008: 69). Research into connections between knowledge management and international business competitiveness has taken two main paths. First, how does KM help implement strategy and achieve the organization's goals? Second, what KM activities contribute to competitiveness by adding value to performance?

There are four types of international business strategies:

1. *International strategy*: expanding abroad is viewed as an opportunity to generate additional sales for domestic product lines, e.g. via export.

2. *Global standardization strategy*: universal products or services, with a focus on cost reduction, central coordination, and control of international operations.

3. *Localization strategy*: allows subsidiaries abroad to operate independently and pursue local responsiveness.

4. *Transnational strategy*: seeks to be both more responsive to local needs and to retain sufficient central control of operations to ensure efficiency and learning. It aims to maximize the major advantages of the multi-domestic and global strategies, while minimizing their disadvantages. The strategy is flexible and tries to standardize where feasible and adapt where appropriate. (After Hill and Hult, 2019: 383–385)

The main way knowledge management can help international business strategy is in implementation of the transnational strategy. Bartlett et al. (2004) proposed the transnational strategy as the solution for firms who felt they were being driven simultaneously by forces for regional integration and responsiveness. The transnational strategy is complex and costly. It tries to exploit scale economies by organizing production, marketing, and other value-chain activities on a global scale, while also optimizing local responsiveness and flexibility (Cavusgil et al., 2017). Pressures for integration may be addressed by sourcing from a reduced set of global suppliers and concentrating manufacturing in relatively few locations where competitive advantages can be maximized (Cavusgil et al., 2017). Pressures for local responsiveness may be addressed by allocating decision-making authority (i.e. autonomy) to host country managers in activities requiring adaptation.

Morris et al. (2016) have developed a framework aligning levels of human capital with international business strategy. They list three strategies: multi-domestic, mega-national, and transnational; and three levels: firm, unit, and individual. In regards to the transnational, Morris et al. (2016: 741) explain that alignment may be achieved as follows:

- *'Firm level*: has a governance structure that encourages coordination and resource flexibility, pushing decentralized centralization; HQ plays a role in integrating ideas from local units.
- *Unit level*: practices are governed by principles, with a great deal of freedom allowed and enough overlap in practices to ensure a common language.
- *Individual level*: employees are expected to become flexible and to build the requisite variety in employee base.'

DEEP THINKING: Developing global, sustainable, competitive advantage depends on three strategic objectives (Bartlett and Ghoshal, 1992: 242–246):

1. *Efficiency*: lowering the cost of the firm's operations and activities on a global scale. This may be done by building efficient international value chains. For example, automotive companies seek scale economies by concentrating manufacturing and sourcing activities in a limited number of locations.
2. *Flexibility*: developing worldwide flexibility to accommodate diverse, country-specific risks and opportunities. This may be done by accessing local resources and exploiting local opportunities – for example, by adapting marketing and human resource practices to suit unique country conditions.
3. *Learning*: creating the ability to learn from operating in international environments and exploiting this learning on a worldwide basis. The diversity of the international environment presents the internationalizing firm with unique learning opportunities – for example, new technical and managerial know-how, new product ideas, and improved R&D capabilities, partnering skills, and survival capabilities in unfamiliar environments.

International success is determined by the degree to which the firm develops capabilities in all three areas: efficiency, flexibility, and learning. However, these capabilities vary in importance within the context of the firm's competitive environment.

Each country has distinctive resources such as raw materials and skilled knowledge workers that provide foreign firms with competitive advantages (Hill, 2014). MNEs are becoming increasingly aware of country differences in suppliers of factors of production. This requires a knowledge of global value-chain management. The value-chain model was introduced by Porter (1985) and comprised nine value-adding activities: five primary and four secondary. These activities create value by connecting competitive strategy formulation and implementation. The value chain is a particularly interesting concept for knowledge management because Porter and Miller (1985) identified the importance of knowledge well before the emergence of the knowledge-based view of the firm and KM as a discipline in the mid-1990s. They highlighted that information permeates the value chain, supporting the performance of every value activity and the linkages among them, concluding that information may therefore provide an organizational competitive advantage (Porter and Miller, 1985).

Holsapple and Singh (2001) developed a KM framework analogous to Porter's value-chain model. Their knowledge chain model is a tool for diagnosing competitive advantage and enhancing it (Holsapple and Singh, 2001). It identifies technologically and economically distinct activities called 'value activities', which involve primary activities: acquisition, selection, generation, internalization, and externalization; and secondary activities: leadership, coordination, control, and measurement (2001: 80). The model is useful because the nine activities are common across many organizations. Thus, rather than simply saying that KM can yield a competitive advantage, the knowledge chain model provides structure to researchers and practitioners for considering specific KM activities that can be sources of competitiveness (2001: 97).

When these two research paths are combined, it may be concluded that international business success is determined by KM activities which develop capabilities in efficiency, flexibility, and learning. The transnational strategy provides a business model to develop these capabilities. Worldwide learning economies offset the high costs of the coordination and cooperation necessary to implement this strategy. The KM activity which creates learning economies is knowledge flow. While internalization theory argues that MNEs' capacity to share knowledge is the main reason for their existence, this does not mean that knowledge transfers actually take place effectively and efficiently on a routine basis (Gupta and Govindarajan, 2000: 473). Knowledge flow is problematic, and there are many barriers to knowledge sharing (see Chapter 9). MNEs try to address these problems via organizational structure design. This most closely fits with the knowledge chain's secondary activities: coordination and control. Knowledge transfers within MNEs take place within the context of an inter-organizational network of differentiated units, commonly known as subsidiaries (Bartlett et al., 2004).

The transnational strategy requires high degrees of coordination and cooperation across the MNE's global network. It can place demands on the organization to pursue conflicting objectives, i.e. headquarters' desire for integration against locals' need for autonomy. The way to reconcile these conflicts and effectively implement the transnational strategy is to offset the high costs of coordination and cooperation via worldwide learning economies. Bartlett et al. (2004) conclude that the way to balance unidimensional control and differentiated coordination is by focusing on the various flows between organization units that are involved in the execution of each of the MNEs' value-creating tasks:

> The first is the flow of goods: the complex interconnections through which companies source their raw materials and other supplies, link flows of components and subassemblies, and distribute finished goods throughout an integrated network of specialized purchasing units, focused sourcing plants, broad-line assembly operations, and localized sales subsidiaries. The second is the flow of resources, which encompasses not only the allocation of capital and repatriation of

dividends, but also the transfer of technology and the movement of personnel throughout the system. The third is the flow of information: raw data, analysed information, and accumulated knowledge, which companies must diffuse throughout the worldwide network of national units. (Bartlett et al., 2004: 464)

Bartlett et al. (2004: 465) conclude that the most difficult task is to coordinate the 'huge flow of strategic information and proprietary knowledge required to operate a transnational organization'. We now turn to look at how this may be done.

GLOBAL KNOWLEDGE FLOWS

Global knowledge flows involve sharing knowledge across MNEs' global network of operations. MNE success depends on a firm-specific advantage – typically knowledge, innovation, or practice – which must be transferred across units and borders to leverage global presence and accumulate rents (Lücke et al., 2014). The importance of sharing firm-specific advantages globally has led researchers to argue that it is the most critical task in MNEs. However, managing cross-border knowledge transfer and integration across fragmented and dispersed operations (Tippmann et al., 2012) to leverage the distributed capabilities of the MNE globally (Lücke et al., 2014) is complex. This section examines how the knowledge-sharing process, organization structure, and new business models may facilitate the flow of knowledge globally for MNEs.

KNOWLEDGE-SHARING PROCESS

Chapter 9 explained how knowledge sharing can be difficult. Researchers have argued that the scope and complexity of MNEs require theoretical work about human capital at a more macro or strategic level (Morris et al., 2016). This may be achieved by adopting a systems thinking perspective. For MNEs, knowledge is shared between headquarters (the parent company) and subsidiaries (in the host country), and among subsidiaries (Gupta and Govindarajan, 2000). Therefore, knowledge can flow laterally (horizontally) and hierarchically (vertically) between geographically distant subunits (Schleimer and Pedersen, 2014).

CORE CONCEPT: Global knowledge flows ensure that strategy is implemented, market opportunities are created and captured, and performance is controlled. It also offers an opportunity to learn from experience and share this learning among the multinational's global network. Barriers to knowledge transfer between parent company nationals (PCNs) and host country nationals (HCNs) exist, and companies need ways to manage them.

Bartlett et al. (2004) present three models which correlate with the three international business strategies: centre-for-global innovation, local-for-local innovation, and transnational innovation.

Centre-for-global innovation involves: (1) gaining the input of subsidiaries (host countries) into centralized activities, (2) ensuring that all functional tasks are linked to market needs, and (3) integrating value-chain functions such as development, production, and marketing by managing the transfer of responsibilities among them. *Local-for-local* innovation involves: (1) the ability to empower local management in the different national organizations, (2) establishing effective mechanisms for linking the local managers to corporate decision-making processes, and (3) forcing tight, cross-functional integration within each subsidiary. *Transnational* innovation involves systematically differentiated tasks and responsibilities across subsidiaries, rather than treating them as the same. This is done by replacing traditional relationships based on dependence or independence (i.e. control) with interdependence among the different units of the firm. Rather than considering control their key task, headquarters' managers search for complex mechanisms to coordinate and co-opt the differentiated and interdependent organizational units into sharing a vision of the company's strategic task (Bartlett et al., 2004).

CORE CONCEPT: The best way to implement the transnational strategy is by using a global network matrix organizational structure to balance the needs for coordination and cooperation. This will provide the structure and culture necessary to facilitate knowledge management and achieve learning economies.

The key to understanding the transition from symmetry to differentiation and from dependence (global) through independence (multi-domestic) to interdependence (transnational) is based on two concepts: willingness to vary the management of value-creating activities globally, and effective integrating mechanisms. The first concept recognizes that firms manage a broad range of activities across diverse geographic operations (Bartlett et al., 2004). The transnational strategy requires firms to differentiate their structure and control by product, or function, or geography in order to find the right balance between integration and responsiveness. The second concept involves value-chain management and people management. The transnational strategy sees the value chain as 'a configuration of resources that is neither centralized nor decentralized, but is both dispersed and specialized' (2004: 463). People management requires integration mechanisms to ensure that task interdependencies lead to the benefits of synergy rather than barriers of conflict (Bartlett et al., 2004).

Gupta and Govindarajan (2000) adapt communication theory to conceptualize knowledge flows into or out of a subsidiary in global business. They found global knowledge flows to be a function of the following five factors:

1. *The value of the source unit's knowledge stock*: knowledge flows have cost and different resources have different levels of value; therefore the greater the value of a subsidiary's knowledge for the rest of the MNE, the greater would be its attractiveness to other units.

2. *The motivational disposition of the source unit*: organizational units with uniquely valuable knowledge will enjoy an information monopoly. This combines with normal power struggles in any organization, implying that some units will use knowledge to acquire and retain relative power within the MNE.

3. *The existence and richness of transmission channels*: knowledge flows cannot occur without the existence of transmission channels (see centre-for-global innovation in Bartlett et al., 2004).

4. *The motivational disposition of the target unit*: this includes not-invented-here syndrome driven by ego-defence mechanisms (reject information that suggests others are more competent than they are) and power struggles (pretending that the knowledge possessed by others is not unique and valuable).

5. *The absorptive capacity of the target unit*: individuals and organizations may differ in their 'absorptive capacity', i.e. in their 'ability to recognize the value of new information, assimilate it, and apply it to commercial ends' (Gupta and Govindarajan, 2000: 475–476).

These five factors influence the capacity of knowledge to flow efficiently (quickly) and effectively (when needed) in the MNE's global network.

ORGANIZATIONAL STRUCTURE

MNEs' strategy, structure, and control mechanisms influence the nature of knowledge flows in international business (Gupta and Govindarajan, 2000). Massingham (2010) developed four integrating mechanisms designed to improve relationships and knowledge flows between PCNs and HCNs, leading to more effective PCNs:

1. *Relationship management*: the relationship between PCNs and HCNs is dynamic in the sense that the PCN needs to adjust roles as the HCN learns, the knowledge gap reduces, and the HCN moves through four levels of knowledge (see Figure 8.1 in Chapter 8).

2. *Talent development*: Bartlett and Ghoshal (1992) identified three transnational roles – operating level entrepreneur, senior management developer, and top-level leader. The global coach role (senior management developer) is the most important one for PCNs, particularly if we accept the view that the main value created by PCNs is the sharing of their experience (Defillippi and Michael, 1994).

3. *Organizational culture*: this is important for managing relationships and knowledge flows between PCNs and HCNs. PCNs tend to hoard their knowledge and are reluctant to share it with HCNs. The tacit nature of the diversity of experience resembles 'insiderness' (Ray and Clegg, 2005) which excludes outsiders. Managers need to be aware of PCNs' tendency to see themselves as part of an exclusive social network, and to persuade them to grant 'membership' or insider status to HCNs.

4. *Strategic consensus*: multinationals faced with the problem of unsatisfactory HCN performance should assess this against the firm's strategy. The four quadrants in Figure 8.1 (see Chapter 8) provide guidelines to evaluate what the MNE expects from their HCNs. If the firm has a global strategy, quadrant 2 knowledge (an understanding of how to perform basic tasks) may be sufficient. If the firm has a multi-domestic strategy, quadrant 3 knowledge (how to perform functional tasks at a country level) may be sufficient. Quadrant 4 knowledge requires HCNs to become 'masters' and, consequently, to develop subsidiary awareness of the task. This is deep personal knowledge: diversity of experience. If PCNs disagree over the firm's international business strategy, this leads to confusion over the roles expected of PCNs and HCNs.

These integrating mechanisms explain how relationships, roles, organizational culture, and alignment with international business strategy may lead to more efficient knowledge flows and more effective interaction between PCNs and HCNs.

Recent research has confirmed that the way in which a firm is structured and organized is an important influence on creating knowledge synergies (Claver-Cortés et al., 2007: 54). This is changing the way MNEs structure their global networks. Increasingly MNEs are adopting horizontal, flexible structures with fewer hierarchical levels and widespread communication at all organizational levels (2007: 54). Decentralization of the decision-making process and staff empowerment, particularly of subsidiary staff, is typical of MNEs seeking global synergies from their knowledge flows (2007: 54).

NEW BUSINESS MODELS

The growing importance of managing value chains globally has made organizational boundaries increasingly permeable. This was predicted by the knowledge-based view of the firm and introduces the problems of coordination and cooperation on a global scale (see Chapter 5). The complexity of blurred organizational boundaries creates different job requirements and job design. Internally, MNEs are replacing conventional 'vertical forms of organizing dependent on centralized decision-making and large-scale coordination between functions' with 'more flexible, decentralized arrangements, conducive to faster decisions and flows of communication, products, and services' (Yagi and Kleinberg, 2011: 629). Externally, MNEs are increasingly engaging in cooperative business models, such as strategic alliances, which combine with 'more rapid and accessible communication technologies' to 'necessitate dense and interactive processes' (2011: 629). Boundary spanners are employees who process information, represent the MNE externally, acquire resources, and act as agents of influence for the MNE (Yagi and Kleinberg, 2011). Yagi and Kleinberg found that much boundary spanner work is voluntary and largely invisible as employees engage in this role in order to get the job done. They concluded that more research is required on how to formalize this role, and how cultural identity relates to boundary-spanning behaviour and effectiveness.

There has been an increase in global knowledge sourcing. This is where MNEs outsource certain knowledge-intensive activities rather than carrying out all their activities internally. This has led to the rapid growth of 'new specialist organizations providing offshored knowledge-intensive services such as Infosys, as well as new markets for existing service organizations such as IBM, Accenture and Capgemini' (Chen and Lin, 2016: 1065). There has been limited research into these offshore service providers. They are also MNEs and face the same problems as other MNEs, 'particularly scarcity of skilled knowledge workers and coordinating global, virtual teams' (2016: 1065). New business models are looking at integrated organizational boundaries. Rather than simply outsourcing – where the activity moves from the internal to the external (i.e. done by someone else) – 'there is a move towards knowledge co-creation with customers and increasingly integrated information technology (IT) and production processes in knowledge-intensive services' (2016: 1070).

INTERNATIONAL HUMAN RESOURCE MANAGEMENT

Researchers have explained the importance of human resource management (HRM) practices for enhancing employees' ability and motivation within MNEs which results in effective knowledge transfer within subsidiaries (Minbaeva et al., 2003). This has developed into a new field called strategic international human resource management (SIHRM). SIHRM adds another dimension from normal HRM because it 'has to address the complexity of the differentiation and integration of organizational capabilities in a multinational context' (Lengnick-Hall and Lengnick-Hall, 2003: 75). Operating across different cultural, institutional, and social boundaries requires HRM to play a different role. Some researchers have argued that this new role for SIHRM is to build and encourage 'internal social networking' (Oparaocha, 2016: 548). This raises the issue of blurred boundaries between HRM and KM discussed in Chapter 11. The new research proposes that SIHRM can 'influence organizational culture and employees' cognition regarding collaboration' across MNE global networks, thereby influencing their motivation to innovate and share knowledge (2016: 548).

Traditionally, HRM researchers interested in MNE knowledge transfer have tended to focus on absorptive capacity, which is the capability to create, transfer, assimilate, transform, and exploit knowledge (Zahra and George, 2002). This positioned HRM within its normal role of developing capability, for instance staff training and learning. Employees contribute to MNEs' absorptive capacity by engaging in knowledge sharing across global operations. Researchers have examined those HRM practices designed to improve absorptive capacity: 'training, performance management, merit-based promotion, performance-based compensation and internal communication', and how these influence subsidiary employees' overall ability and motivation (Caligiuri, 2014: 64). However, finding empirical evidence for how HRM practices improve knowledge sharing in MNEs has been difficult.

Minbaeva et al. (2014) recently asked that future studies consider broader cultural, comparative, and strategic factors when examining the relationship between HRM practice and knowledge transfer. Research in this area tends to focus on relationship-building practices between parent company nationals (PCNs) and host country nationals (HCNs), such as socialization, equity-sensitive compensation schemes, and collaborative working conditions which encourage knowledge transfer (Bonache and Zárraga-Oberty, 2008).

In a review of literature on this topic, Caligiuri (2014) highlighted the following HRM practices designed to improve MNE knowledge transfer:

1. *Mentoring*: 'when inpatriates are boundary spanners for knowledge transfer, the presence of a headquarters-based mentor to support them while in the MNC headquarters' country increases their perceived effectiveness in the knowledge transfer process' (Caligiuri, 2014: 65).

2. *Training and development*: 'MNCs with a greater need for knowledge sharing across borders actively develop their managers' cross-cultural competencies through developmental opportunities, such as international assignments' (2014: 66).

3. *Performance management and rewards*: 'encourage knowledge transfer when they reinforce more cooperative and open group functioning, and reward effective knowledge sharing, including financial rewards' (2014: 66).

4. *Job design*: 'design global teams and international assignments to foster the maximum amount of cross-border knowledge transfer by increasing their social integration' (2014: 66).

Caligiuri (2014: 70) concludes that future research should examine 'how bundling HRM practices into a system may address some of the multilevel contingencies and drivers of knowledge transfer in MNEs'. This might involve sharing social capital across all levels of the MNE and enhancing internal networking, 'through traditional HRM practices such as formal incentives, international assignments, and cross-functional project teams, as well as new SIHRM practices such as providing intra-organizational social interaction platforms' (Oparaocha, 2016: 548).

GLOBAL MANAGERS

Strategic international human resource management (SIHRM) defines two key actors operating in international knowledge transfer: parent company nationals (PCNs) and host country nationals (HCNs) (Massingham, 2010). These two groups interact to facilitate knowledge flow between the MNE's headquarters (parent country or home country) and subsidiaries (host country). Global managers are expensive because their international business experience develops a range of skills and capabilities which help them progress quickly up the career ladder, leading to 'great man' or 'great woman' status (Bartlett et al., 2004). They also use these special capabilities to perform important work.

CORE CONCEPT: Global managers are multinational enterprise (MNE) managers who perform a variety of critical MNE tasks. They may be from headquarters (PCNs) or from subsidiaries (HCNs) or from a third country. Some MNEs also draw upon a pool of global managers who form a cadre of experienced international business managers, employed in the MNEs' global operations for varying time periods depending on need.

Research has developed a list of attributes which define global manager capabilities. These represent important human capital for MNEs. Morris et al. (2016) combine the dimensions of firm specificity and location specificity to identify four critical types of human capital within the MNE: local, subsidiary, corporate, and international, which are then mapped onto four quadrants explaining how to manage a global talent portfolio. Global manager attributes include:

1. *The ability to develop and use strategic skills*: being both a specialist and a generalist – for example, skills as diverse as understanding global financial markets and exchange rates, government relations, global supply chain management, and international marketing, and the capacity to balance local responsiveness with a need for global integration.

2. *The ability to manage change and transition*: working with HCNs to transition from dependence (global) through independence (multi-domestic) to interdependence (transnational) with careful control.

3. *The ability to manage cultural diversity*: dealing with the management challenges of diverse workforce cultures, developing cultural awareness, and transitioning from ethnocentrism (home country knows best) to geocentrism (a worldview where good ideas can come from any country).

4. *The ability to design and to function in flexible organizations*: these are borderless organizations or network matrix structures where ambiguity, creativity, innovation, coordination, cooperation, and adaptability are the key drivers.

5. *The ability to work with others and in teams*: integration in an environment where specialization and differentiation are valued requires transnational teamwork, particularly encouraging mindsets transitioning 'from not invented here syndrome to a now improved here' mentality.

6. *The ability to learn and to transfer knowledge in an organization*: being deeply curious and able to facilitate the flow of knowledge across multiple organizational and country contexts, as well as to grow learning.

(After Beamish et al., 1997: 182–192).

Over time, the global manager attributes have evolved into criteria used for selection, training, and performance 'appraisal for expatriates' (Hill and Hult, 2019: 563).

Further research has focused on leadership competency, described as global literacy with four competencies:

1. Seeing the world's challenges and opportunities expands the individual's horizons and illuminates their perception of the world.

2. Thinking with an international mindset helps develop beliefs and attitudes that enable the individual to think internationally.

3. Acting with global-centric leadership behaviours teaches new relationship skills that help navigate the global marketplace.

4. Mobilizing a world-class company inspires and motivates people across national cultures. (Rosen et al., 2000: 58)

The global mindset (the second competency listed above) is the most important knowledge resource because it develops the cognitive structures necessary for managing the complexity and risk associated with international business management.

GLOBAL MINDSET

Global mindset is 'a highly complex cognitive structure characterized by an openness to and articulation of multiple cultural and strategic realities on both global and local levels, and by the cognitive ability to mediate and integrate across this multiplicity' (Levy et al., 2007: 244). Researchers and practitioners agree that managers who have developed a global mindset are better able to deal with the complexity created by international business management (Massingham, 2013). Indeed, 'as global competition continues to intensify, global mindset has emerged as a key source of long-term competitive advantage in the marketplace' (Levy et al., 2007: 231).

According to Levy et al. (2007: 232), 'the majority of studies conceptualize global mindset in relation to two salient dimensions of the global environment, most notably in relation to (1) cultural and national diversity and/or (2) strategic complexity associated with globalization.' Research on the first dimension has argued that international business management involves significant cultural interpretive work and meaning construction, which require an understanding of multiple cultural systems (Brannen, 2004). Research has also found that cultural ability helps intercultural negotiations, ethics and leadership, and cross-border alliances and acquisitions; team effectiveness; and enhanced creativity (Venaik and Midgley, 2015). Global managers with this capability have been called multiculturals. These are individuals who have an understanding of more than one national culture, which 'allows them to make informed cultural interpretations in multiple contexts' (Lücke et al., 2014: 170). Lücke et al. (2014) developed a cognition-based explanation of how multiculturals think. These individuals have internalized 'mental representations of interconnected cultural schemas' (2014: 172), allowing them interpretations within multiple cultures. Venaik and Midgley (2015) develop a new model of national culture which they call mindscapes across landscapes. They argue against the conventional use of averages to summarize cultural dimensions. Instead, they focus on cultural values using mindscapes. Mindscapes refer to 'the way a person organizes his/her thinking and behaviour' and include ways of perceiving, reasoning, and decision making (Maruyama, 1992: 92). Venaik and Midgley (2015) develop the concept of transnational archetypes, that is, cultural archetypes or mental models that span more than one country.

The second dimension, strategic complexity, captures cognitive complexity (Levy et al., 2007). The complexity of a mindset reflects the breadth and variety of knowledge embedded in it. It is represented in the form of the total number of strategic concepts (attributes, variables, or categories) and links between concepts in the mindset: the greater the number of concepts and links between concepts, the greater the complexity of the mindset (Levy et al., 2007). 'While cognitive complexity usually represents the structural dimension of a cognitive structure (i.e. the internal organization of information units), when considering cognitive complexity in relation to a specific information domain, the structure and content (i.e., specific information units or knowledge)' are combined (2007: 243). Levy et al. (2007: 243) further explain that 'without adequate knowledge, an individual cannot form a complex representation of the information domain.'

DEEP THINKING: Research has generally found that cognitively complex individuals have superior information-processing capabilities. Such people search for more wide-ranging and novel information (e.g. see Streufert and Swezey, 1986), spend more time interpreting it (Dollinger, 1984), perceive a larger number of dimensions, and simultaneously hold and apply several competing and complementary interpretations (Bartunek et al., 1983). Levy et al. (2007: 245) developed a model proposing that global mindset has significant effects on 'information-processing patterns' that may translate into the superior managerial capabilities of MNEs.

Massingham (2013) developed a model for measuring cognitive capability in global managers in terms of information processing associated with the foreign direct investment (FDI) decision. The research introduced a new construct – cognitive clarity – to describe individuals with a global mindset that aligns knowledge structure and content. Cognitive clarity provides the global manager with a clear understanding of their firm's strategy and their own knowledge gaps associated with the decisions necessary to implement the strategy.

ADAPTATION VERSUS STANDARDIZATION

International business strategy influences everything the MNE does. This emerges in the standardization versus adaptation decision. Standardization involves performing the activity the same way in the MNE's global operations. It fits the global strategy. Adaptation requires adjusting the activity to meet the demands of the host country. It fits the multi-domestic strategy. While the trade-off decision of standardization versus adaptation is typically discussed within the context of the marketing mix, it is equally relevant for all other functions and value-creating activities.

Whenever possible, MNEs prefer to standardize their products to achieve scale economies and minimize complexity (Cavusgil et al., 2017). Standardization is easier and less costly than adaptation. As a result, MNEs tend to adapt activities only when necessary, for example to respond to local customer preferences and mandated regulations (e.g. industrial relations laws). However, as discussion of the transnational strategy has shown, there are strategic reasons why adaptation is sometimes essential. In these circumstances, management must decide not only what elements to adapt, but also how much to adapt them.

Knowledge management also involves the decision of whether to standardize or adapt. Research tends to suggest a one-size-fits-all or a standardized approach to international knowledge management. Researchers have questioned whether a standardized approach to international knowledge management is always appropriate, and to suggest that there may be conditions that lead to an adaptation decision (see Pauleen and Murphy, 2005). National culture may influence the standardization versus adaptation decision for knowledge management. Previous research has found that national culture has an effect on a range of multinational corporation operations, such as human resources or marketing (Levitt, 1983). A few studies have identified that culture has an effect on activities related to knowledge management, such as innovation (Shane, 1995) or research and development (Kedia et al., 1992).

Ang and Massingham (2007) proposed that the standardization versus adaptation decision in international knowledge management may be influenced by two dimensions: differences in national culture across the firm's global network, and economies of scope. They provide a framework for explaining

how the two opposing tensions – pressures for scope economies and pressures for cultural responsiveness – may be used to guide the standardization versus adaptation decision in international knowledge

> management. ... When the pressures for scope economies are high and pressures for cultural responsiveness are low, a standardization decision is most appropriate. ... On the other hand, when pressures for cultural responsiveness are high and pressures for scope economies are low, the most appropriate decision is adaptation. (Ang and Massingham, 2007: 16)

Research identified four types of possible outcomes from a firm's decision to standardize or adapt its knowledge management practices. These four outcomes are standardization and success, standardization and failure, adaptation and success, and adaptation and failure (Jensen and Szulanski, 2004). Jensen and Szulanski's (2004) argument is that inappropriate or insufficient adaptation may increase the stickiness of knowledge transfer. Ang and Massingham (2007: 17) argue that insufficient adaptation might be a possibility since their findings suggest 'that the greater the difference between cultures, the greater the difficulty in knowledge transfer across cultures'. They further explain (2007: 17) that 'what may be sufficient adaptation between low psychic distance cultures may be insufficient adaptation for high psychic distance cultures.'

Ang and Massingham found that a decision to standardize knowledge management practices, despite cultural differences, may still achieve a positive outcome. They found situations (2007: 17) where a 'company standardized their knowledge management practices and the decision led to failure or less effective outcomes'.

CONCLUSION

The chapter set out to examine the role of knowledge management (KM) in international business. The importance of KM was established by explaining how knowledge resources are necessary to manage risk and make complex decisions in international business management, and that KM is a source of competitive advantage for multinational enterprises (MNEs). Types of knowledge resources and capabilities were discussed within the context of MNEs' pursuit of global, sustainable, competitive advantage. There are three main drivers of MNE competitive advantage: efficiency, flexibility, and learning. These drivers were discussed in terms of the global knowledge chain (Holsapple and Singh, 2001) and the transnational strategy.

The main focus of the chapter was on global knowledge flows. This involves sharing knowledge across MNEs' global network of operations. MNE success depends on a firm-specific advantage – typically knowledge, innovation, or practice – which must be transferred across units and borders to leverage global presence and accumulate rents. The chapter adopted a systems thinking perspective of global knowledge sharing which looked at the process, the structures, and the business models which enable knowledge flow. Strategic international human resource management (SIHRM) adds another dimension from normal HRM because it has to address the complexity of the differentiation and integration of organizational capabilities in a multinational context.

Global managers have valuable skills and represent important human capital for MNEs. The unique capabilities of global managers were discussed in terms of competencies and literacies. The global mindset is the most important knowledge resource for MNEs because it develops the cognitive structures necessary for managing the complexity and risk associated with international business management. Knowledge management also involves the decision of whether to standardize or adapt. Ang and Massingham (2007) argued that the decision may be influenced by two dimensions: differences in national culture across the firm's global network, and economies of scope. Overall, the research tends to recommend a standardized approach to international knowledge management.

CLOSING CASE STUDY: CAP GEMINI AND ERNST & YOUNG – A TALE OF MERGING TWO KNOWLEDGE MANAGEMENT SYSTEMS

At the time of the merger between these two companies in the early 2000s, Cap Gemini (CG) offered IT services through its 39,626 employees in 20 countries. These services were organized in the following three core business areas: (a) management and strategy consulting, through Gemini Consulting, (b) IT consulting and systems integration, and (c) application management through infrastructure management and business process outsourcing. Ernst & Young (E&Y) was one of the big accounting firms working in (a) auditing, (b) legal and tax advice, (c) consulting, and (d) corporate finance. On 23 May 2000, CG acquired the E&Y consulting unit in order to become a global IT and management consultancy player.

The global consultancy industry is highly knowledge-intensive. Technological advances have transformed the way business is done. Information and knowledge are a key source of competitive advantage. Information technology creates a large amount of information but the simple accumulation of information does not have any special advantage, since all companies have access to it. Putting value into this information is seen as a key issue in gaining competitive advantage. The nature of the business requires distributing the knowledge across the whole organization. Knowledge tends to be specific to an industry, a client, and a geographical area, i.e. region or country. Clients seek the help of consultancy firms because their knowledge, although dispersed, is greater and more complete than they could acquire themselves. Clients expect all relevant knowledge to be used in their projects. This means that they are not paying only for the knowledge of the individuals assigned to their project, but also for access to the full range of knowledge possessed by the firm globally, including best practices and others' project experiences with other clients. As a result, global consulting firms need to ensure they capture and store information and knowledge from different parts of the organization, but also to make these resources available for consultants to use irrespective of their location globally.

Both CG and E&Y had established knowledge management (KM) systems prior to the merger. E&Y created four centres to support KM: the Centre for Business Innovation, the Centre for Business

(Continued)

(Continued)

Transformation, the Centre for Business Knowledge, and the Centre for Technology Enablement. The Innovation Centre was in charge of generating new knowledge, which usually came from multi-client research, coordinating theory and applications, identifying and investigating new business concepts, and collaborating with other organizations including universities. This centre led the research and development of new, innovative solutions related to business processes, strategies, people, and technology. The Transformation Centre's role was to structure knowledge into methodologies, techniques, and automated tools that would improve the speed and value of the services that consultants provided. The work concentrated on re-engineering processes, knowledge management, information technologies, and organizational changes. The Centre for Technology Enablement complemented the consultancy practice. This division was devoted to the research and development of high technology, and offered a wide variety of services ranging from technology architecture to networking and technology management. The Centre for Business Knowledge (CBK) was a resource with approximately 650 workers worldwide in 2000, whose purpose was to serve the consultancy and corporate finance units. It had knowledge managers, who were in charge of all KM in one region, not only for consultancy, but for all E&Y divisions. The knowledge managers were the people who managed, revised, and maintained knowledge to satisfy the consultants' local needs. The CBK offered a wide range of services to ensure that professionals had access to relevant information from any source, at any time, and for any given situation. E&Y had KnowledgeWeb, also known as KWeb, which was the link between consultants and the organization's knowledge base. KWeb was an intranet, providing immediate access to the collective knowledge globally.

Knowledge management at CG was more decentralized than at E&Y. CG recognized the importance of KM, having designed an internal university on the outskirts of Paris for staff to learn and share experiences, as well as Galaxy, a web-based intranet designed to publish, share, and manage knowledge. The intranet contained a similar range of portals as E&Y's KWeb, for example industry knowledge, products, and methodology. The difference between E&Y and CG was that CG had a more bottom-up approach. Contribution to Galaxy knowledge resources and their use was voluntary and inconsistent.

The merger made an integrated KM system necessary. At the time of the merger, CG purchased the E&Y Consulting Unit, the Centre for Innovation, and all the CBK's contents related to the consultancy practice. The companies had reached a service level agreement regarding the CBK's service (which belonged to E&Y LLP) that expired within two years. For the newly merged company, CGE&Y, the outsourcing of this service for KM maintenance was costly as well as critical for the business. Management had to decide on whether to keep CBK. The Innovation Centre was included in the merger, as it had no equivalent in CG and its role in creating knowledge, doing research, and having a long-term vision was valuable in the consultancy industry. CG believed it could easily replicate the Centre for Transformation and the Technology Centre because of its strong IT expertise, so it did not continue with those aspects of E&Y's KM. The CBK case was more complex. The CBK's knowledge resources were extensive and could not be easily replicated. On the face of it, this justified its purchase. However, its knowledge was developed for a different organization and context, with a specific culture and a given architecture, through different processes, and under a different strategy. It was also very expensive. The CBK and KWeb took around 35% of the

KM budget while Galaxy cost around 7%. The decision would be driven by the right KM approach for the new organization. The co-existence of the two systems with their corresponding procedures and roles created unnecessary complexity for CGE&Y. Complexity could interfere with business performance.

Source: Adapted from a case study by Segal-Horn and Faulkner (2010)

CASE STUDY QUESTIONS

1. What is CGE&Y's international business strategy?
2. Compare the KM approaches of E&Y and CG. Which do you prefer and why?
3. Should CGE&Y continue with CBK? Why, or why not?
4. Design a KM strategy for CGE&Y based on its international business strategy.

REVIEW AND DISCUSSION QUESTIONS

1. Describe the three international business strategies.
2. Discuss how global managers help knowledge flow in international business.
3. Discuss whether knowledge management should be standardized or adapted in international business.

FURTHER READING

Bartlett, C., Ghoshal, S. and Birkinshaw, J. (2004) *Transnational Management: Text, cases, and readings in cross-border management*, 4th edition, New York, McGraw-Hill Irwin. This text examines transnational strategy.

Levy, O., Beechler, S., Taylor, S. and Boyacigiller, N.A. (2007) What We Talk about When We Talk about 'Global Mindset': Managerial cognition in multinational corporations. *Journal of International Business Studies*, 38: 231–258. This article explains further the global manager and the global mindset.

Morris, S., Snell, S. and Björkman, I. (2016) An Architectural Framework for Global Talent Management. *Journal of International Business Studies*, 47: 723–747. This article examines international human resource management and the transnational strategy.

Schleimer, S.C. and Pedersen, T. (2014) The Effects of MNC Parent Effort and Social Structure on Subsidiary Absorptive Capacity. *Journal of International Business Studies*, 45: 303–320. This article examines social capital and absorptive capacity.

BIBLIOGRAPHY

Ang, Z. and Massingham, P. (2007) National Culture and the Standardization versus Adaptation of Knowledge Management. *Journal of Knowledge Management, 11* (2): 5–21.

Bartlett, C. and Ghoshal, S. (1992) *Transnational Management: Text, cases, and readings in cross-border management*, Burr Ridge, IL, Irwin.

Bartlett, C., Ghoshal, S. and Birkinshaw, J. (2004) *Transnational Management: Text, cases, and readings in cross-border management*, 4th edition, New York, McGraw-Hill Irwin.

Bartunek, J.M., Gordon, J.R. and Weathersby, R.P. (1983) Developing 'Complicated' Understanding in Administrators. *Academy of Management Review, 8* (2): 273–284.

Beamish, P.W., Morrison, A. and Rozenzweig, P.M. (1997) *International Management: Text and cases*, New York, McGraw-Hill Irwin.

Bonache, J. and Zárraga-Oberty, C. (2008) Determinants of the Success of International Assignees as Knowledge Transferors: A2 theoretical framework. *International Journal of Human Resource Management, 19* (1): 1–18.

Brannen, M.Y. (2004) When Mickey Loses Face: Recontextualization, semantic fit, and the semiotics of foreignness. *Academy of Management Review, 29* (4): 593–616.

Caligiuri, P. (2014) Many Moving Parts: Factors influencing the effectiveness of HRM practices designed to improve knowledge transfer within MNCs. *Journal of International Business Studies, 45*: 63–72.

Cavusgil, S.T., Knight, G. and Reisenberger, J. (2017) *International Business: The new realities*, 4th edition, Harlow, Pearson.

Chen, S. and Lin, N. (2016) The Diversity of Knowledge Management Practices: Global dispersion of offshore service providers – An information processing perspective. *Journal of Knowledge Management, 20* (5): 1065–1082.

Claver-Cortés, E., Zaragoza-Sáez, P. and Pertusa-Ortega, E. (2007) Organizational Structure Features Supporting Knowledge Management Processes. *Journal of Knowledge Management, 11* (4): 45–57.

Clyde-Smith, D. (2003) Case 21: The Acer Group – Building an Asian multinational. In Mintzberg, H., Lampel, J., Quinn, J.B. and Ghoshal, S. (eds) *The Strategy Process: Concepts, contexts, cases*, 4th edition, Upper Saddle River, NJ, Prentice Hall, pp. 217–228.

Defillippi, R.J. and Michael, B.A. (1994) The Boundaryless Career: A competency-based perspective. *Journal of Organizational Behavior, 15* (4): 307–324.

Dollinger, M.J. (1984) Environmental Boundary Spanning and Information Processing Effects on Organizational Performance. *Academy of Management Journal, 27* (2): 351–368.

Downes, M. and Thomas, A.S. (2000) Knowledge Transfer through Expatriates: The U-curve approach to overseas staffing, *Journal of Managerial Issues, 12* (2): 131–150.

Gupta, A.K. and Govindarajan, V. (2000) Knowledge Flows within Multinational Corporations. *Strategic Management Journal, 21* (4): 473–500.

Harzing, A. (2002) Acquisitions versus Greenfield Investments: International strategy and management of entry modes. *Strategic Management Journal, 23* (3): 211–225.

Hill, C.W.L. (2014) *Global Business Today* (8th edition), New York, McGraw-Hill.

Hill, C.W.L. and Hult, G.T.M. (2019) *International Business: Competing in the global marketplace*, 12th edition, New York, McGraw-Hill Education.

Holsapple, C.W. and Singh, M. (2001) The Knowledge Chain Model: Activities for competitiveness. *Expert Systems with Applications, 20*: 77–98.

Hymer, S.H. (1960) The international operations of national firms: A study of direct foreign investment. PhD dissertation, Massachusetts Institute of Technology.

Jensen, R. and Szulanski, G. (2004) Stickiness and the Adaptation of Organizational Practices in Cross-border Knowledge Transfers. *Journal of International Business Studies*, *35* (6): 508–523.

Karaszewski, R. (2008) The Influence of KM on Global Corporations' Competitiveness. *Journal of Knowledge Management*, *12* (3): 63–70.

Kedia, B.L., Keller, R.T. and Julian, S.D. (1992) Dimensions of National Culture and the Productivity of R&D Units. *Journal of High Technology Management Research*, *3* (1): 1–18.

Lengnick-Hall, M.L. and Lengnick-Hall, C.A. (2003) *Human Resource Management in the Knowledge Economy*, San Francisco, CA, Berrett-Koehler.

Levitt, T. (1983) Globalization of Markets. *Harvard Business Review*, May–June: 2–11.

Levy, O., Beechler, S., Taylor, S. and Boyacigiller, N.A. (2007) What We Talk about When We Talk about 'Global Mindset': Managerial cognition in multinational corporations. *Journal of International Business Studies*, *38*: 231–258.

Lücke, G., Kostova, T. and Roth, K. (2014) Multiculturalism from a Cognitive Perspective: Patterns and implications. *Journal of International Business Studies*, *45*: 169–190.

Maruyama, M. (1992) Changing Dimensions in International Business. *The Executive*, *6* (3): 88–96.

Massingham, P. (2010) Managing Knowledge Transfer between Parent Country Nationals (Australia) and Host Country Nationals (Asia). *International Journal of Human Resource Management*, *21* (9): 1414–1435.

Massingham, P. (2013) Cognitive Complexity in Global Mindsets. *Journal of International Management*, *30* (1) Part 2: 232–248.

Massingham, P. (2016) Knowledge Accounts. *Long Range Planning*, *49* (3): 409–425.

Minbaeva, D., Pedersen, T., Bjorkman, I., Fey, C. and Park, H. (2003) MNC Knowledge Transfer, Subsidiary Absorptive Capacity and Knowledge Transfer. *Journal of International Business Studies*, *34* (6): 586–599.

Minbaeva, D., Pedersen, T., Bjorkman, I., Fey, C.F. and Park, H.J. (2014) Retrospective: MNC knowledge transfer, subsidiary absorptive capacity, and HRM. *Journal of International Business Studies*, *45* (1): 52–62.

Morris, S., Snell, S. and Björkman, I. (2016) An Architectural Framework for Global Talent Management. *Journal of International Business Studies*, *47*: 723–747.

Oparaocha, G.O. (2016) Towards Building Internal Social Network Architecture that Drives Innovation: A social exchange theory perspective. *Journal of Knowledge Management*, *20* (3): 534–556.

Pauleen, D.J. and Murphy, P. (2005) In Praise of Cultural Bias. *MIT Sloan Management Review*, *46* (2): 21–22.

Porter, M.E. (1980) *Competitive Strategy: Techniques for analyzing industries and competitors*, New York, Free Press.

Porter, M. (1985) *Competitive Advantage*, New York, Free Press.

Porter, M. and Miller, V.E. (1985) How Information Gives You Competitive Advantage. *Harvard Business Review*, *63* (4): 149–160.

Ray, T.E. and Clegg, S. (2005) Tacit Knowing, Communication, and Power: Lessons from Japan? In Little, S. and Ray, T. (eds) *Managing Knowledge: An essential reader*, London, Sage, pp. 319–349.

Rosen, R., Digh, P., Singer, M. and Phillips, C. (2000) *Global Literacies: Lessons on business leadership and national cultures*, New York, Simon and Schuster.

Schleimer, S.C. and Pedersen, T. (2014) The Effects of MNC Parent Effort and Social Structure on Subsidiary Absorptive Capacity. *Journal of International Business Studies*, *45*: 303–320.

Segal-Horn, S. and Faulkner, D. (2010) Case Study 7: Knowledge management at Cap Gemini Ernst & Young. In *Understanding Global Strategy*, Andover, Cengage Learning, pp. 422–444.

Shane, S. (1995) Uncertainty Avoidance and the Preference for Innovation Championing Roles. *Journal of International Business Studies*, *26* (1): 47–68.

Streufert, S. and Swezey, R.W. (1986) *Complexity, Managers, and Organizations*, Orlando, FL, Academic Press.

Thompson, A.J., Jr., Peteraf, M.A., Gamble, J.E. and Strickland, A.J. (2015) *Crafting and Executing Strategy: The quest for competitive advantage – Concepts and cases*, 20th edition, New York, McGraw-Hill Irwin.

Tippmann, E., Scott, P. and Mangematin, V. (2012) Problem Solving in MNCs: How local and global solutions are (and are not) created. *Journal of International Business Studies*, *43* (8): 746–771.

Venaik, S. and Midgley, D.F. (2015) Mindscapes across Landscapes: Archetypes of transnational and subnational culture. *Journal of International Business Studies*, *46*: 1051–1079.

Yagi, N. and Kleinberg, J. (2011) Boundary Work: An interpretive ethnographic perspective on negotiating and leveraging cross-cultural identity. *Journal of International Business Studies*, *42*: 629–653.

Zahra, S.A. and George, G. (2002) Absorptive Capacity: A review, reconceptualization, and extension. *Academy of Management Review*, *27* (2): 185–203.

13

WHAT NEXT FOR KNOWLEDGE MANAGEMENT?

CHAPTER OUTLINE

Learning outcomes
Management issues
Links to other chapters
Introduction
The technology versus personalization view
Gaining respect
Theoretical development
Societal change
Conclusion

LEARNING OUTCOMES

After completing this chapter, the reader should be able to:

1. Discuss the technology versus personalization view within the context of the future of knowledge management
2. Reflect on academia's respect for knowledge management

3. Reflect on practitioners' respect for knowledge management
4. Discuss the relevance of the knowledge-based view of the firm
5. Consider the impact of our ageing population on the future of knowledge management

MANAGEMENT ISSUES

The future of knowledge management requires managers to:

1. Understand the role of technology within the context of humanistic management
2. Consider how academics may help improve knowledge management in our organization
3. Examine how knowledge resources and knowledge management capability contribute to sustainable competitive advantage
4. Understand the changing nature of organizational boundaries and the need for new business models

The future of knowledge management involves the following challenges for management:

1. What role will knowledge management play in our organization's strategy now and in the future?
2. Should we work with academics? If so, how and why?
3. Will the ageing demographic create risks for us, and if so, can knowledge management help?

LINKS TO OTHER CHAPTERS

Chapters 1–2: on the technology versus personalization view

Chapter 3: regarding the value of knowledge management

Chapter 5: on the role of knowledge and knowledge management in competitive advantage

Chapter 6: concerning the risks posed by the ageing demographic

Chapter 11: regarding new business designs and structures

INTRODUCTION

The objective of this chapter is to reflect on the lessons learned from this book and consider the future of knowledge management. First, the chapter explores the technology versus personalization view of management. As global business becomes increasingly digitized, what will this mean for knowledge management? Second, the issue of respect will be examined from the perspective of the academic literature and practitioners. If knowledge management is to continue to grow, it must be recognized as a mainstream organizational activity by the top journals and by business leaders. The leading mainstream journals publish relatively few knowledge management articles and seem to view it as a niche topic. Practitioners must see value in knowledge management if they are to invest in it because its value proposition is intangible and difficult to measure. These issues are important regarding whether knowledge management is a fad or whether it will survive in the long term. Third, the chapter will revisit the knowledge-based view (KBV) of the firm. Grant (2002) suggested that the KBV was a theory for all time. However, we must ask whether the KBV has survived, only 15 years after this prophecy, and whether it will be relevant in the future. Finally, the chapter discusses the biggest threat to business globally – the ageing demographic – and how knowledge management may help knowledge organizations survive this threat.

THE TECHNOLOGY VERSUS PERSONALIZATION VIEW

This book has aimed to present both sides of the technology versus personalization views on knowledge management. Chapter 2 explained that the technology view of knowledge management looks at information systems and information technology as the way to increase connectivity between knowers and seekers, and also provide seekers with access to organizational knowledge, such as policy, procedures, reports, and data. It is about knowledge capture and codification (e.g. see Alavi and Tiwana, 2005). The personalization view of knowledge management looks at social practice as the best way to share knowledge. This is about providing opportunities for people to socialize for real, for example in meetings or virtual environments such as online (e.g. see von Krogh, 2005).

The technology view dominated the early evolution of knowledge management, but more recent research has seen technology as a support function rather than the main driver of connectivity. It raises important questions about the relationship between knowledge, technology, and social interaction. The technology view tends to see knowledge management as information-seeking behaviour. If an individual does not know something, they use technology to help find the answers. However, researchers have argued that meaning comes from engagement practices with other people, rather than a computer. What then is the role of technology? As discussed in Chapter 2, technology is an important enabler but is idle resource unless people use it to connect with other people and their knowledge.

The book has emphasized the importance of skilful knowing (see Chapters 1 and 8). Skilful knowing ensures employees are fully competent to do their job, and this knowing is realized in the act of doing. A major objective of knowledge management is to ensure employees are skilful knowers. If they are not, competency gaps will emerge (see Chapter 4) and the organization's knowledge base will be in deficit. The technology and personalization views present contrasting ideas about how to ensure skilful knowing.

The increasing complexity of business in the global knowledge economy means that the personalization view will not be enough to manage knowledge in the 21st century. Technology must play a key role in connecting people who may never meet in person. The physical distance of global business and the sheer number of employees in large organizations mean they cannot socialize in the traditional sense of the word. Technology's role, therefore, is to establish virtual communities capable of replicating the personalization view. It must provide employees with knowledge in the act of doing. The main agenda will be to use technology to provide knowledge as well as information.

As discussed in Chapter 1, the technology view of knowledge as an objective to be captured, stored, and distributed must be challenged. The work often stored on intranets is information only until the employee can access it, understand it, and use it. Only then does it become the employee's knowledge. It is in this translation from information – other people's knowledge – to employee knowledge that technology can create most value. The major challenge is for technology to create virtual environments where knowers may interact with learners in the act of doing, and to do this efficiently so that the benefits outweigh the costs.

GAINING RESPECT

Knowledge management has been criticized as a fad which will not last (Ray and Clegg, 2005). While knowledge management has grown rapidly since the 1990s, it is still not considered a mainstream activity by either academia or practitioners. If knowledge management is to survive, it must earn respect as a discipline such as accounting, finance, marketing, human resources, supply chain, and operations. Until then, it will remain a niche area with uncertain value and limited application. Chapter 11 explained how the early period of knowledge management was dominated by computer science and information science articles. While this has changed over time, research from the technology view still dominates. This research sees knowledge as an object which may be codified, stored, and distributed. Research in these areas represents a significant proportion of published academic work. The personalization view offers an alternative perspective which sees knowledge as socially constructed (see

Chapter 1). This book has argued that the personalization view provides a more accurate reconstruction of the reality of knowledge and its management in the workplace. While constructivist research has grown in popularity, it is still marginalized in the academic literature. The evidence for this claim comes from two sources: (1) the nature of the top knowledge management journals; and (2) the reluctance of 'mainstream' leading journals to publish articles about knowledge management. The Australian federal government has introduced a system called Excellence in Research for Australia (ERA), which is designed to monitor and improve research performance in universities. ERA regularly undertakes a review of journals, and issues journal rankings by discipline. Other ranking systems such as Scimago follow the same logic and may be used to substitute for the ERA rankings. Table 13.1 lists the journals in the business and management field ranked A* or A by ERA.

TABLE 13.1 ERA journal rankings in business and management – A* or A ranked

Rank	Journal title
A*	Academy of Management Journal
A*	Academy of Management Learning and Education
A*	Academy of Management Review
A*	Administrative Science Quarterly
A*	Decision Sciences
A*	Industrial Relations: A Journal of Economy and Society
A*	Information and Management
A*	Journal of Business Venturing
A*	Journal of International Business Studies
A*	Journal of Management
A*	Journal of Management Studies
A*	Journal of Operations Management
A*	Journal of Organizational Behavior
A*	Journal of Vocational Behavior
A*	Leadership Quarterly
A*	Organization Science
A*	Organization Studies
A*	Research in Organizational Behavior
A*	Strategic Management Journal
A*	Journal of Business (Chicago)
A	Australian Journal of Management

(Continued)

TABLE 13.1 (Continued)

Rank	Journal title
A	British Journal of Industrial Relations
A	British Journal of Management
A	Business Ethics Quarterly
A	Business History Review
A	California Management Review
A	Corporate Governance (Oxford)
A	Entrepreneurship and Regional Development
A	Entrepreneurship: Theory and Practice
A	European Journal of Industrial Relations
A	Family Business Review
A	Group and Organization Management
A	Harvard Business Review
A	Human Relations
A	Human Resource Management
A	Human Resource Management Journal
A	Human Resource Management Review
A	Industrial and Corporate Change
A	Industrial Relations Journal
A	International Journal of Human Resource Management
A	International Journal of Management Reviews
A	International Journal of Operations and Production Management
A	International Journal of Project Management
A	International Journal of Selection and Assessment
A	International Small Business Journal
A	Journal of Business Ethics
A	Journal of Engineering and Technology Management
A	Journal of Industrial Relations
A	Journal of Small Business Management
A	Journal of World Business
A	Long Range Planning
A	Management International Review
A	MIT Sloan Management Review
A	OMEGA – International Journal of Management Science

Rank	Journal title
A	Organizational Behavior and Human Decision Processes
A	Organizational Research Methods
A	R&D Management
A	Small Business Economics
A	Strategic Organization
A	Supply Chain Management
A	System Dynamics Review
A	Technovation
A	Academy of Management Perspectives
A	Work and Occupations

Source: http://lamp.infosys.deakin.edu.au/era/?page=jmain

Knowledge management's top journal, *Journal of Knowledge Management* (Serenko and Bontis, 2013), is not even listed in the business and management field. Instead, it is found in the information systems field, where it is classified as coming from library and information studies, and is only ranked B. This despite the fact that the journal's website describes its subject area as 'HR, Learning & Organization Studies, Information & Knowledge Management' (www.emerald insight.com/journal/jkm). The field's other top journal, *Journal of Management Information Systems*, is the only A journal publishing knowledge management articles. However, it is a technology view journal and is also listed in the information systems field and not in business and management.

An analysis of the A journals listed in Table 13.1 looked at whether the words 'knowledge management' were found in abstracts of papers published since 2000. This search looked for the words separately, so not all of these articles would be about knowledge management; however, they look at knowledge at least. Table 13.2 presents the results.

TABLE 13.2 Journals publishing knowledge management articles since 2000

Rank	Journal title	No. of KM papers	Percentage of KM papers
A*	Academy of Management Journal	19	1.3
A*	Academy of Management Learning and Education	33	8.6
A*	Academy of Management Review	13	1.7
A*	Administrative Science Quarterly	9	2.3

(Continued)

TABLE 13.2   (Continued)

Rank	Journal title	No. of KM papers	Percentage of KM papers
A	Decision Sciences	22	3.8
A	Industrial Relations	0	0.0
A	Information and Management	55	6.1
A	Journal of Business Venturing	4	0.6
A	Journal of International Business Studies	22	3.1
A	Journal of Management	31	2.8
A	Journal of Management Studies	60	11.7
A	Journal of Operations Management	33	3.1
A	Journal of Organizational Behavior	17	1.0
A	Journal of Vocational Behavior	2	0.2
A	Leadership Quarterly	6	0.6
A	Organization Science	29	3.4
A	Organization Studies	41	3.6
A	Research in Organizational Behavior	0	0.0
A	Strategic Management Journal	28	1.7
A	Journal of Business (Chicago)	0	0.0
	TOTAL	424	2.3

Of these 20 top journals, 424 articles including the words 'knowledge' and 'management' in their abstract were published since 2000, which represents 2.3% of the articles published by these journals. The field of business and management is broad, and journals will of course publish on a wide range of topics. Therefore, knowledge management must share space with many other important topics in these leading journals. However, 2.3% is a very low figure and suggests that knowledge management is not considered by these journals to be a popular topic.

This analysis is not a criticism of these journals. They are highly respected with rigorous review processes and high impact factors. They only publish the best research. The challenge for knowledge management researchers is to understand why these top journals publish relatively small numbers of articles about KM. As with any customer–supplier relationship, it is the responsibility of the supplier (researcher) to adapt and respond to the needs of the customer (journals). However, this begs the question: why is knowledge management of limited interest to these leading journals and their reviewers?

KM researchers should consider what these journals expect from them. Mingers (2006) argues that there are philosophical problems with management science. He explains that as management science developed, it was 'dominated by empiricist philosophy that led it to see quantitative modelling and statistical analysis as the main legitimate type of research method' (Mingers, 2006: 12). This is not good news for qualitative researchers. This has led to divisive debates about 'hard' and 'soft' research (2006: 12). The debate focuses on conflict over positivist research versus interpretive or constructivist research. Researchers can, of course, have a pluralist approach and employ multiple methods, but academics tend to find a research philosophy that suits them and then to defend that against all others. The conflict is about the pursuit of knowledge from academic research, and finding justified true belief. Positivist researchers tend to feel that quality research and findings that may be trusted and generalized can only come from large quantitative data sets, i.e. surveys. If the reviewers for top journals are positivists, they simply do not see any value in qualitative research. Therefore, the research philosophy of the leading journals is important for knowledge management and whether it may become a mainstream topic. This problem is also important in attracting and retaining high quality researchers to the field of knowledge management. A colleague recently told me how she had been rejected for a job at a leading Australian university (she was not even interviewed despite having considerably more research outputs, e.g. publications, than would be expected for the position). When she sought feedback, she was told that she did not publish in the type of journals expected, that is, the positivist journals listed in Table 13.2.

There are three problems for KM researchers in responding to the problem of positivism. First, there is a lack of consensus about the concepts and measurements' meaning that it is difficult to design survey instruments. Much KM research is about theory development rather than theory testing. This reflects the fact that the field is still growing and has not reached maturity, and also denotes its multi-disciplinary nature. A challenge for knowledge management is to develop consensus about key concepts and constructs and how they should be measured. Only then can surveys be designed where the field can agree on the findings. Second, the nature of KM research does not fit with positivism's 'one best way' approach. KM is contextual and requires deep analysis, exploring feelings, attitudes, and perceptions: the stuff of qualitative research. It produces findings about the situation within the organization(s) being studied which are not always generalizable. This is confronting for positivists who prefer statistical analysis to prove that their ideas work and may be applied elsewhere. A challenge for KM researchers is to design longitudinal empirical studies which provide a sense of trust in the findings, as well as the richness of qualitative research. Third, surveys do not reconstruct the social reality of the complexity of knowledge management. Likert scale questions asking respondents to rate how well their organization creates knowledge, or how willing they are to share knowledge, may be useful for a regression analysis but tell us nothing about the reasons why. KM research may address this by developing more 'multimethodology' which is the combination or plurality of research interventions or research methods (see Mingers, 2006: 12).

Mingers (2006) explains that the main justification for a pluralist approach is to address the weaknesses in the opposing methods. Interpretive researchers tend to be highly critical of positivism because 'the social world is inherently different to the material world and is in essence a human social construction not able to be quantified and captured in statistical models' (Mingers, 2006: 13). This argues that the complexity of human social and political interaction cannot be summarized in a mathematical model. On the other hand, positivists attack the 'weak empiricist position' of constructivist research which leads to an 'impoverished view of ontology and causality' (2006: 14). In other words, qualitative research is rubbish and not real science.

Within the context of this debate, knowledge management must address the concerns of positivists if it is to gain respect. The reality of this situation is not black or white. The top journals certainly publish qualitative research, and not all reviewers are positivist. Further, there is some quantitative KM research. However, the figure of 2.3% of publications since 2000 demands an explanation. The solution for KM researchers is to adapt and change and find a way forward to multimethodology.

Practitioners are interested in knowledge management. There is no doubt that organizations 'do' knowledge management. The Most Admired Knowledge Enterprise (MAKE) Awards are evidence of the substantial investment made by many companies globally. However, are these investments managing information or knowledge? Organizations spend substantial funds on intranets, information technology (IT) tools, and IT consultancy. But is this knowledge management?

Chapter 3 presented a framework for measuring the value of knowledge management. For researchers, the seven practical outcomes address the important topic of measuring the value of KM. The seven methods were evaluated against measurement criteria and against KM's claims. Overall, common themes were time and cost, as well as capability growth and performance improvements. Financial impact was mainly found in cost savings. Non-financial impact was found across the seven practical outcomes. For practitioners, the research findings provide management with a checklist to make investment decisions regarding KM. This method should allow managers to make sensible decisions about KM's ROI. The importance of this agenda is illustrated in Table 13.3.

TABLE 13.3 Global market for knowledge management (2013 estimated)

Segments	Year	US$ billions	Year	Estimated growth
Enterprise software	2013	304	2012	6.40%
Enterprise software (SaaS)	2013	13.5	n/a	n/a
Enterprise software (SaaS)	2016	32.8	n/a	n/a
Talent management software	2012	4	2012	20%
Learning management software	2013	1.9	n/a	10%

Segments	Year	US$ billions	Year	Estimated growth
Employee engagement	2012	1.5	n/a	n/a
Business improvement platform, analytic apps, and performance management software	2011	12.2	2011	16.40%
Business improvement platform, analytic apps, and performance management software	2010	10.5	n/a	n/a
Business consultancy	2013	415	n/a	n/a
Business consultancy	2012	391	n/a	n/a

Sources: Bersin-Deloitte (2012a, b, c); Forrester (2013); Gartner (2012); Plunkett Research (2012)

Business consultancy includes human resources, finance, IT, strategy, operations management, and business advisory services. Table 13.3 illustrates the amount of funds being invested in the type of consultancy services where knowledge management can help. Large companies, with $2 billion-plus annual revenues, use more management tools than SMEs (<$2 billion annual revenues) (Bain & Company, 2013). The top five most used tools are:

1. Strategic planning
2. Customer relationship management – to increase customer value by capturing more growth opportunity
3. Employee engagement surveys – to improve employee morale and (by extension) productivity, retention, and customer loyalty
4. Benchmarking
5. Balanced scorecards – a tool to help measure and improve. (Bain & Company, 2013)

Figure 13.1 and Table 13.4 illustrate why practitioners and consultants are so interested in knowledge and its management. The world's leading knowledge management companies usually have high price-to-book ratios (see Table 13.4).

Knowledge management research cannot yet explain why Microsoft and other leading companies have such a high difference between their book value and their market value. This difference is a measure of their competitive advantage. It is their intelligible assets. But we do not yet know how to explain why and how their intangible assets create such a strong competitive advantage. There are two challenges for KM researchers: (1) which knowledge resources create most value and why; and (2) how the way these resources are managed creates heterogeneity in performance. The former examines knowledge as a resource, while the latter looks at knowledge management as a capability. Is it what Microsoft knows or how it manages what it knows that creates its competitive advantage, or is it both? This introduces the need to measure and manage the performance of knowledge management (see Chapter 3).

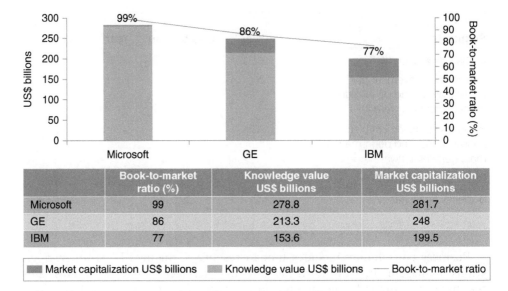

FIGURE 13.1 *Estimating the value of intangible assets (2013)*

TABLE 13.4 Indicators of the value of intangible assets (2013)

	Leading KM companies	Market capitalization (US$ billions)	Share price (US$)	Price-to-book ratios
World-leading KM companies	IBM	199.50	184.77	11.4
	Microsoft	281.70	33.76	3.6
	Siemens	105.00	123.46	2.9
	GE	248.00	24.25	2.0
	Royal Dutch Shell	205.80	64.20	1.1
Top Australian companies (not KM)	BHP Billiton	176.65	66.45	2.5
	Westfield Group	23.80	10.98	1.6
	Harvey Norman	3.30	3.10	1.4
	News Corp	9.39	16.22	0.7

Note: Price to book = the share price divided by the book value per share

Source: Current company data found on investor websites

THEORETICAL DEVELOPMENT

First, there is opportunity to revisit the fundamental principles of the knowledge-based view (KBV) of the firm. The KBV argued that knowledge is valuable and, indeed, is the most valuable resource (e.g. see Grant, 1996). Chapter 11 looked at the role of accounting and in this discussion explained how the measurement of intellectual capital seems to have run out of steam. Bontis (1998) predicted 20 years ago that we may never find a way to measure the value of knowledge. Chapter 4 explored this topic and included a new method called the Knowledge Accounts (Massingham, 2016). There is opportunity for knowledge management to continue to pursue research in this area. To claim that knowledge is the most valuable resource but that we do not know how to measure its value is a disappointing result for KM. The challenge is to develop consensus about method(s) and persuade practitioners to use it as best practice (e.g. the technology standard).

Second, the KBV explained how knowledge is a source of sustainable competitive advantage. Barney (1991) developed a list from the resource-based view of the firm which was used as a checklist for competitive advantage. This is still used today in strategic management and is known as the VRIN test (e.g. see Thompson et al., 2016). There is the opportunity to develop more empirical evidence about knowledge as a source of competitive advantage.

Third, the KBV was announced as a theory for the ages (Grant, 2002). It was supposed to challenge underlying assumptions about organizations and their management. When it emerged 20 years ago, the KBV 'promised to have one of the most profound changes in management thinking since the scientific management revolution' in the 1920s (Grant, 1997: 454). But the KBV seems to have lost its way. A recent review of some of the top journals (see Table 13.1) found few articles with the knowledge-based view in their abstract. These few articles tended to look at knowledge flows, particularly external to internal flows, and international business contexts (e.g. acquisitions and mergers). Reflecting on the KBV 20 years after its emergence, Grant (2013) feels that the main challenges are cooperation and coordination. These require innovative new business models, with fluid organizational boundaries, enabling knowledge to flow from external knowledge sources and for internal development.

There are several opportunities to revisit the knowledge-based view as theory for the 21st century, including:

1. Designing new organizational structures which implement humanistic management and learning organization
2. Changing organization boundaries and using alliances, mergers, joint ventures, and other collaborative models to outsource knowledge supply
3. The concept of mass collaboration (e.g. Tapscott and Williams, 2006) and the use of the internet to create value from knowledge rather than information

4. Using knowledge management to facilitate change
5. Whether organizations sufficiently care about employees to introduce democracy and participation into knowledge management (e.g. see Massingham, 2014c).

SOCIETAL CHANGE

The knowledge economy explains how knowledge is the main driver of economic value. In the 21st century, the knowledge economy has replaced the industrial age and, therefore, the management of knowledge has become the main focus of organizations striving to be successful in this new era (see Chapter 3). The biggest societal change within the knowledge economy is the ageing demographic, and managing the corporate risks this generates. Knowledge loss occurs when an organization no longer has access to knowledge it previously had. Knowledge loss is an increasing corporate risk for two reasons. First, there are demographic changes globally which have significant impact on the workforce. Second, there is increasing employee turnover due to changes in the emotional relationship between employers and their employees (see Chapter 6).

The ageing of society is a global phenomenon. The global share of older people (aged 60 years or over) increased from 9.2% in 1990 to 11.7% in 2013 and will continue to grow as a proportion of the world population, reaching 21.1% by 2050 (United Nations, 2013). Globally, the number of older people is expected to more than double, from 841 million people in 2013 to more than 2 billion in 2050; and older persons are projected to exceed the number of children for the first time in 2047 (United Nations, 2013). Population ageing will substantially affect social, political, and economic conditions in the developed world (e.g. see Zweifel et al., 1999; Szinovacz, 2011). The United Nations has emphasized the need for all societies to address the significant consequences of population ageing in the coming decades (United Nations, 2013).

A significant impact of population ageing is on labour force participation and productivity. The post-Second World War baby boom generation (born from 1946 to 1964) is now retiring en masse (Schlosser et al., 2012). The workforce at all levels is expected to shrink substantially, driven by the retirements of an ageing population (Rusaw, 2004) and the declining availability of younger people to replace them. Research has suggested that 'the numbers could be staggering, with up to half of senior civil servants retiring' (Kochanowski, 2011: 87). The challenges for societies concern issues of labour supply and demand (Szinovacz, 2011). 'Once the largest baby boom cohort [aged 52 to 56 in 2016] reaches retirement age, the labour supply it provides cannot be fully replenished by the succeeding cohort' (Szinovacz, 2011: 95). Older workers have valuable experience, gathered over a lifetime, and this is lost when they retire because organizations often fail to capture and retain the retirees' knowledge before they leave (Hu, 2010). Younger workers cannot fill the capability gap because of a lack in both quantity (there are fewer of them) and quality (they are relatively inexperienced). This has created significant corporate risk (Massingham, 2010). The outcomes of population ageing will be 'global shortages of human resources' and declining productivity (Schlosser et al., 2012: 149).

The problem has been recognized by governments and by the public and private sectors. At a government level, many have 'changed their retirement policies to ensure continuing work productivity levels' (Schlosser et al., 2012: 149). Research has argued that employers need to be aware of the labour drain that will occur as older workers leave the workforce, taking their human capital and skills with them (Rappaport and Stevenson, 2004). Progressive employers are starting to realize that an ageing population means they will have to 'adapt in order to remain competitive' (Timmons et al., 2011: 120). The public sector has introduced a range of activities designed to transfer retiring workers' experience to younger staff, such as mentoring, succession planning, job rotation, and one-on-one training (Liebowitz, 2004). The private sector has introduced a range of knowledge management initiatives designed to capture and preserve the invaluable knowledge of retiring workers before they leave, including career development/succession planning programmes, phased retirement programmes, knowledge recruiting processes, and mapping competencies to career continuums (e.g. see DeLong, 2004; Hu, 2010). Researchers and practitioners continue to look for innovative solutions to the capability gap created by population ageing. One solution is to have retirees work with younger staff to share their knowledge after they have left the organization. Methods include employing the retiree as a consultant, part-time employee, or mentor.

The success of having retirees return to the workforce requires younger people to want their knowledge. If we accept that the most valuable knowledge is tacit, i.e. in the individual's mind (e.g. see Polanyi, 1962), then it is locked in their mind unless they are willing to part with it on a voluntary basis. Researchers have examined how fear inhibits knowledge sharing (Newell et al., 2006). If retirees are to share their knowledge with younger people when returning to the workforce, they will need to feel that their knowledge is valued and recognized, that they are respected, that they have nothing to fear from sharing their knowledge, and that they can trust the younger staff. These issues surface generational attitudes which are important to understand if retirees are to successfully return to the workforce and share their knowledge with younger people.

Concerns about labour supply shortages have led governments in the USA and many other Western nations to shift from policies that encouraged early retirement in the 1970s and 1980s to policies that promote later-life employment (Taylor, 2007). In the USA, these policies feature a mix of sticks and carrots: among the sticks are greater benefit penalties for early retirement combined with rises in benefit eligibility; carrots include anti-age discrimination laws and elimination of the earnings test for social security beneficiaries over 65 (Hudson and Gonyea, 2007). The participation level of older workers has been one of the key objectives of policy makers in most Western countries for almost two decades (e.g. see OECD, 2001). However, research questions whether organizational policies regarding older workers have been changing in response (e.g. see Conen et al., 2011). An early policy response was to make retirement less attractive. Policy adjustments such as 'blocking unemployment schemes, reducing the maximum period of unemployment benefit entitlement, and tightening rules on eligibility criteria' were designed to make it financially more attractive for older workers to prolong their working life (Conen et al., 2011: 143).

The next approach was to develop creative ways to extend older workers' working life, such as more interesting work or phased retirement (see DeLong, 2004). Several retention strategies emerged, including: (a) job flexibility, (b) comprehensive benefits packages, (c) professional growth and development, and (d) other workplace accommodations (after Timmons et al., 2011: 126). Research suggests that workers in stressful occupations retire early, whereas those in occupations that allow for greater flexibility retire later (Hurd and McGarry, 1993, cited in Johnson et al., 2011). Many older workers transition into less demanding post-career jobs before completely withdrawing from the labour force (Johnson et al., 2011). There are non-economic factors which make work appealing and keep older people working longer. In addition, some people improve their wellbeing and self-confidence by showing commitment to organizational goals and loyalty to their employers (Noonan, 2005). Organizations have responded by developing supportive work cultures designed to help retain older workers. The values of a company can provide a framework for establishing practices that support older workers. These include a 'feeling of partnership, respect, and caring' between older people and their employer (Timmons et al., 2011: 124). Older workers tend to 'value independence and autonomy', and organizations that provide them with this develop a 'sense of reciprocal trust' between employers and their employees (2011: 125). Research has found that this level of trust is highly valued by older workers and 'strongly connected to high job satisfaction, pointing again to the fit between older workers and their work cultures' (2011: 125). Leppel et al. (2012: 64) found that 'increasing older employees' job satisfaction through job-related training can help to develop an efficient and productive workplace'.

Research has found that financial insecurity created by economic pressures, such as the global financial crisis, has led many older workers to continue working longer or, if they had recently retired, to consider a return to work (Kendig et al., 2013). Previous research has found that the concerns and uncertainty of older Americans are the same as those of older Australians regarding 'whether they would have enough money to live on in retirement and whether savings would keep up with inflation' (2013: 267). Financial insecurity may be an incentive for retirees to return to the workforce, in some capacity, and to share their knowledge.

The emergence of the knowledge management discipline has changed perspectives about the value of knowledge. Human capital theory explains that employees have values which are generated from how they use knowledge in the activity of doing work (Massingham, 2015). Organizational theory explains that organizations are goal-oriented systems that strive for profit maximization, continuity, and a positive market position (e.g. see Thompson et al., 2016). It follows that employees who can help organizations achieve these goals would be valued and this would be reflected in employers' behaviour via recruitment and retention strategies (e.g. see Phillips and Connell, 2003) and through teamwork and participative cultures. 'Employers' attitudes and behaviour toward older workers, therefore, is assumed to be dependent on older workers' contributions to achieving goals', such as profit maximization, continuity, and a healthy market position (Conen et al., 2011: 145). Employers' perception of this contribution will be influenced by their evaluation of the skill level required to do a job properly and of the skills and competencies of older workers. Researchers have proposed that knowledge-intensive organizations are more likely to value the experience of older workers. Conen et al. (2011: 146) hypothesized that 'organizations that rely more heavily on highly skilled workers are more likely to recruit and retain older employees than organizations relying more on low-skilled workers.' They found support for this human capital hypothesis, and also for a business-cycle hypothesis that labour shortages will increase the likelihood of recruitment or retention of older workers. This provides evidence that employers may turn towards retirees as a solution to the increasing capability gap being caused by population ageing.

CONCLUSION

Knowledge management is a discipline that deserves to become mainstream. Its underlying concepts that everyone has value and their knowledge is useful; that sharing and using knowledge increases its value rather than depletes it and that it is the main source of competitive advantage in the 21st century knowledge economy – make it relevant and useful. The knowledge-based view's claim that it challenges us to reconsider what management is and how we manage organizations makes its theories undeniably important. Why then does knowledge management represent less than 3% of the articles in the top business and management journals? Why are executives reluctant to invest in knowledge management other than information technology?

The challenges for knowledge management may be summarized as follows:

- The technology view of knowledge as an objective to be captured, stored, and distributed must be challenged.
- The major challenge for technology is to create virtual environments where knowers may interact with learners in the act of doing, and to do this efficiently so that the benefits outweigh the costs.
- The challenge for knowledge management researchers is to understand why top journals publish relatively small numbers of articles about KM. As with any customer–supplier relationship, it is the responsibility of the supplier (researcher) to adapt and respond to the needs of the customer (journals).
- The multi-disciplines interested in knowledge management need to develop a consensus about key concepts and constructs and how they should be measured.

- A challenge for KM researchers is to design longitudinal empirical studies which provide a sense of trust in the findings, as well as the richness, of qualitative research.

- Business presents two challenges for KM researchers: (1) which knowledge resources create most value and why; and (2) how the way these resources are managed creates heterogeneity in performance. The first examines knowledge as a resource, while the second looks at knowledge management as a capability.

- There are several opportunities to revisit the knowledge-based view (KBV) as theory for the 21st century.

- There is evidence that employers may turn towards retirees as a solution to the increasing capability gap being caused by population ageing. The challenge is to address the underlying barriers (e.g. age stereotypes) to reintroducing retirees into the workforce.

Knowledge management is at a crossroads. It may be argued that it has failed to deliver on its potential. This book has aimed to inspire the next generation of managers to think deeply about knowledge management and to consider it as an essential part of their organizations. The future for knowledge management must recognize its stakeholders. While students and researchers must be inspired to study knowledge management, its future lies with industry. Practitioners and consultants are the most important stakeholders for knowledge management. We need them to allow us to enter their organizations, study what they do, and work in partnership with them. This will produce the type of research which will advance the field, making it relevant and up to date. We need to better understand the value of knowledge and its management and how this contributes to sustainable competitive advantage. This will lead to increased investment in knowledge management, including jobs for our graduates.

Finally, the field's multi-disciplinary nature is both its strength and its Achilles heel. If we accept the constructivist theme of this book, we must agree that there is room for divergent views about knowledge management, and welcome the contributions of multi-disciplines. There is no best way to do knowledge management; there are multiple ways, depending on the context. However, this does not help gain respect from positivists or managers keen for a solution. There is evidence about what knowledge management works and what does not and why (Massingham, 2014a, 2014b). The challenge for knowledge management is to ask industry what works for them and to work together to advance the field.

BIBLIOGRAPHY

Aakhus, M. (2007) Conversations for Reflection: Augmenting transitions and transformations in expertise. Chapter 1 in McInerney, C.J. and Day, R.E. (eds) *Rethinking Knowledge Management: From knowledge objects to knowledge processes*, Berlin, Springer.

Alavi, M. and Tiwana, A. (2005) Knowledge Management: The information technology dimension. Chapter 6 in Easterby-Smith, M. and Lyles, M.A. (eds) *Handbook of Organizational Learning and Knowledge Management*, Hong Kong, Blackwell, pp. 104–121.

Bain & Company (2013) Management Tools and Trends Survey. Available at: www.bain.com/publications/business-insights/management-tools-and-trends.aspx (accessed 7 November 2018).

Barney, J. (1991) Firm Resources and Sustained Competitive Advantage. *Journal of Management, 17*: 99–129.

Bersin-Deloitte (2012a) Understanding the Employee Engagement Market. Available at: https://blog.bersin.com/new-research-understanding-the-employee-engagement-market (accessed 7 November 2018).

Bersin-Deloitte (2012b) Garr, S.S., *The State of Employee Recognition in 2012*. Available at: http://go.achievers.com/rs/iloverewards/images/analytstinsights-the-state-of-employee-recognition.pdf (accessed 7 November 2018).

Bersin-Deloitte (2012c) LMS 2013: The $1.9 billion market for learning management systems. Available at: https://blog.bersin.com/lms-2013-the-1-9-billion-market-for-learning-management-systems (accessed 7 November 2018).

Bontis, N. (1998) Intellectual Capital: An exploratory study that develops measures and models. *Management Decision, 36* (2): 63–76.

Computerworld (2013) Forrester Dispels 'Myths' about Software Industry Trends in 2013. Available at: www.computerworld.com/s/article/9241447/Forrester_dispels_39_myths_39_about_software_industry_trends_in_2013 (accessed 7 November 2018).

Conen, W.S., Henkens, K. and Schippers, J.J. (2011) Are Employers Changing their Behaviour Toward Older Workers? An analysis of employers' surveys 2000–2009. *Journal of Aging & Social Policy, 23* (2): 141–158.

DeLong, D. (2004) *Lost Knowledge: Confronting the threat of an aging workforce*, New York, Oxford University Press.

Forrester (2013) Harness Employee Engagement to Improve Customer Experience. Available at: www.forrester.com/Harness+Employee+Engagement+To+Improve+Customer+Experience/-/E-PRE5944 (accessed 7 November 2018).

Gartner (2012) Gartner Says Worldwide Business Intelligence, Analytics and Performance Management Software Market Surpassed the $12 Billion Mark in 2011. Available at: www.gartner.com/newsroom/id/1971516 (accessed 7 November 2018).

Grant, R.M. (1996) Towards a Knowledge-based Theory of the Firm. *Strategic Management Journal, 17*: 109–122.

Grant, R.M. (1997) The Knowledge-based View of the Firm: Implications for management practice. *Long Range Planning, 30* (3): 450–454.

Grant, R.M. (2002) The Knowledge-based View of the Firm. Chapter 8 in Choo, C.W. and Bontis, N. (eds) *The Strategic Management of Intellectual Capital and Organizational Knowledge*, New York, Oxford University Press, pp. 133–148.

Grant, R.M. (2013) *Contemporary Strategy Analysis*, 8th edition, Chichester, Wiley.

Hu, L.T. (2010) Same Bed, but Different Dreams? Comparing retired and incumbent police officers' perceptions of lost knowledge and transfer mechanisms. *Crime Law Society Change, 53*: 413–435.

Hudson, R.B. and Gonyea, J.G. (2007) The Evolving Role of Public Policy in Promoting Work and Retirement. *Generations, 31* (1): 68–75.

Hurd, M., and McGarry, K. (1993) The relationship between job characteristics and retirement, Working Paper No. 4558, National Bureau of Economic Research, 1050 Massachusetts Avenue Cambridge, MA 02138.

Johnson, R.W., Mermin, G.B.T. and Resseger, M. (2011) Job Demands and Work Ability at Older Ages. *Journal of Aging & Social Policy*, *23* (2): 101–118.

Kendig, H., Wells Y., O'Loughlin, K. and Heese, K. (2013) Australian Baby Boomers Face Retirement during the Global Financial Crisis. *Journal of Aging & Social Policy*, *25* (3): 264–280.

Kochanowski, Y.J. (2011) Human Capital Management in Government: Replacing government retirees. *Journal of Health and Human Services Administration*, Summer: 85–108.

Leppel, K., Brucker, E. and Cochran, J. (2012) The Importance of Job Training to Job Satisfaction of Older Workers. *Journal of Aging & Social Policy*, *24* (1): 62–76.

Liebowitz, J. (2004) Bridging the Knowledge and Skills Gap: Tapping federal retirees. *Public Personnel Management*, Winter, *33* (4): 421–448.

Massingham, P. (2010) Knowledge Risk Management: A framework. *Journal of Knowledge Management*, *14* (3): 464–485.

Massingham, P. (2014a) An Evaluation of Knowledge Management Tools, Part 1: Managing knowledge resources. *Journal of Knowledge Management*, *18* (6): 1075–1100.

Massingham, P. (2014b) An Evaluation of Knowledge Management Tools, Part 2: Managing knowledge flows and enablers. *Journal of Knowledge Management*, *18* (6): 1101–1126.

Massingham, P. (2014c) The Researcher as Change Agent. *Systemic Practice and Action Research*, *27*: 417–448.

Massingham, P. (2015) Knowledge Sharing: What works, what doesn't and why? A critical systems thinking perspective. *Systemic Practice and Action Research*, *28* (3): 197–228.

Massingham, P. (2016) Knowledge Accounts. *Long Range Planning*, *49* (3): 409–425.

Mingers, J. (2006) *Realising Systems Thinking: Knowledge and action in management science*, New York, Springer Science.

Newell, S., Robertson, M. and Swan, J. (2006) Interactive Innovation Processes and the Problems of Managing Knowledge. Chapter 6 in Renzl, B., Matzler, K. and Hinterhuber, H. (eds) *The Future of Knowledge Management*, New York, Palgrave Macmillan.

Noonan, A. (2005) 'At this Point Now': Older workers' reflections on their current employment experiences. *International Journal for Aging and Human Development*, *62*: 211–241.

Organisation for Economic Co-operation and Development (OECD) (2001) *Ageing and Income: Financial resources and retirement in 9 OECD countries*, Paris, OECD.

Phillips, J.J. and Connell, A.O. (2003) *Managing Employee Retention: A strategic accountability approach*, New York, Elsevier Butterworth-Heinemann.

Plunkett Research (2012) Consulting Industry Market Research. Available at: www.plunkettresearch.com/consulting-market-research/industry-and-business-data (accessed 7 November 2018).

Polanyi, M. (1962) *Personal Knowledge*, Chicago, IL, University of Chicago Press.

Rappaport, A. and Stevenson, M. (2004) Staying Ahead of the Curve 2004: Employer best practices for mature workers. *Mercer Human Resource Consulting*, AARP, 1–88.

Ray, T. and Clegg, S. (2005) Tacit Knowing, Communication and Power: Lessons from Japan? In Little, S. and Ray, T. (eds) *Managing Knowledge: An essential reader*, 2nd edition, London, Sage, pp. 319–348.

Rusaw, A.C. (2004) How Downsizing Affects Organizational Memory in Government: Some implications for professional and organizational development. *Public Administration Quarterly*, *28* (4): 482–500.

Schlosser, F., Zinni, D. and Armstrong-Stassen, M. (2012) Intention to Unretire: HR and the Boomerang Effect. *Career Development International*, *17* (2): 149–167.

Serenko, A. and Bontis, N. (2013) Global Ranking of Knowledge Management and Intellectual Capital Academic Journals: 2013 update. *Journal of Knowledge Management*, *17* (2): 307–326.

Szinovacz, M.E. (2011) Introduction: The aging workforce – Challenges for societies, employers, and older workers. *Journal of Aging & Social Policy*, *23* (2): 95–100.

Tapscott, D. and Williams, A.D. (2006) *Wikinomics: How mass collaboration changes everything*, London, Penguin Books.

Taylor, P. (2007) Older Workers and the Labour Market: Lessons from abroad. *Generations*, *31* (1): 96–101.

Thompson, A.J., Jr., Peteraf, M.A., Gamble, J.E. and Strickland, A.J. (2016) *Crafting and Executing Strategy: The quest for competitive advantage – Concepts and cases*, 20th edition, New York, McGraw-Hill Irwin.

Timmons, J.C., Cohen Hall, A., Lynch Fesko, S. and Migliore, A. (2011) Retaining the Older Workforce: Social policy considerations for the universally designed workplace. *Journal of Aging & Social Policy*, *23* (2): 119–140.

United Nations (2013) *World Population Ageing 2013*, Department of Economic and Social Affairs Population Division, New York, United Nations.

von Krogh, G. (2005) Knowledge Sharing and the Communal Resource. Chapter 19 in Easterby-Smith, M. and Lyles, M.A. (eds) *Handbook of Organizational Learning and Knowledge Management*, Hong Kong, Blackwell, pp. 372–392.

Zweifel, P., Felder, S. and Meirs, M. (1999) Ageing of Population and Health Care Expenditure: A red herring? *Health Economics*, 8: 485–496.

INDEX